Hunting and Hunting Reserves
in Medieval Scotland

Hunting and Hunting Reserves in Medieval Scotland

John M. Gilbert

JOHN DONALD PUBLISHERS LTD
EDINBURGH

ISBN 0 85976 030 8

Phototypesetting by Burns & Harris Limited, Dundee
Printed in Great Britain by Bell & Bain Ltd., Glasgow

Acknowledgements

THE author wishes to thank the following for permission to reproduce illustrations:

The Department of the Environment for figs. 1, 2, 3 and 5 which are Crown Copyright; the Controller of H.M. Stationery Office for fig. 18 which is Crown Copyright; Edinburgh University Library for figs. 4, 9, 11 and 12; the National Library of Scotland for fig. 10; the Royal Commission on Ancient Monuments for Scotland for fig. 6; the National Museum of Antiquities of Scotland for figs. 7 and 8; Lt. Colonel William Stirling of Keir for fig. 13; and the Public Record Office for fig. 19 which is preserved there in the class Duchy of Lancaster, Deeds Series L (DL 25/78).

Contents

Tables

Maps

Plates

Introduction

IN medieval Scotland barons probably spent more time, effort and thought on hunting than on any other activity. Although an examination of hunting and hunting organisation in medieval Scotland should contribute towards a fuller picture of medieval Scottish life, this is a little studied aspect of Scottish medieval history. Hunting reserves in medieval Scotland have already been examined by M. L. Anderson, late Professor of Forestry in Edinburgh University, and by W. C. Dickinson, late Professor of Scottish History also in Edinburgh. Professor Dickinson's study regrettably fills only two pages in Volume XX of the *Stair Society* and Professor Anderson's two-volume study, a *History of Scottish Forestry*, leaves much unsaid. From the studies of Frankish hunting reserves or forests, as they were called, and of the English forest system carried out by C. Petit Dutaillis, it was evident that there was scope for a fuller historical assessment of hunting reserves in medieval Scotland. In his presidential address to the Scottish History Society in 1975 Professor Barrow pointed the way. The purpose of this book is to provide such an assessment.

Basically such an assessment requires a full description of hunting reserves in Scotland and consideration of several problems relating to that description: firstly, how effectively did hunting reserves fulfil the purpose for which they were created; and secondly, what effect did they have on the lives of the people? The former problem necessitates an examination of the rights which the owner of a hunting reserve claimed within that reserve and the means by which these rights were enforced, and the latter necessitates an examination of economic activity within and around hunting reserves.

The plan of this book has been adapted to its purpose. It is divided into two sections: an introductory chronological narrative followed by an institutional analysis of hunting reserves. The main developments of hunting reserves in medieval Scotland have been placed in the introductory narrative, while the evidence and arguments from which these developments have emerged are given in the institutional analysis. The introductory narrative also contains material not examined elsewhere, such as the origins of hunting reserves in Scotland, comparisons of Scottish and English practices, hunting methods and the remains of hunting parks and lodges.

The institutional analysis is conducted by examining the different types of hunting reserves and their organisation and aims to describe these reserves and assess their effectiveness and the efficiency of their administration. In order to assess the effect of hunting reserves on the people, the position outside reserves is examined in detail in Chapter 12 and the evidence relating to economic activity within and around reserves is assembled in Chapter 14. As the work proceeded, it became clear that it would be necessary to edit the Forest Laws and the resulting edition is placed in Appendix A. Appendix B contains a detailed account of the tenants and tenancy of Ettrick forest and of the feuing of that forest in the early sixteenth century. Most of the maps and tables have been placed after the chapter to which they belong, but those which are relevant to the book as a whole have been placed in Appendix C. A short glossary of terms with which some readers may be less familiar has also been provided.

Throughout this work when quoting the sources I have adopted modern conventions with regard to punctuation and the use of capital letters. Fuller details of the policy adopted in transcription and quotation are given in Appendix A. The names of people and of places, if not rendered in their modern form, have been placed in quotation marks, with one or two exceptions such as the family name Steward. The use of the word 'forest' is discussed fully in Chapter 2.

In dating, allowance has been made for the start of the medieval year on 25 March. For instance, the medieval date 3 February 1248 would be given as 3 February 1248/9. The form of date 1228 x 1248 means not earlier than 1 January 1228 and not later than 31 December 1248. The dating of entries in the exchequer rolls has been treated in the following manner. Where an event occurred within a certain year of an account, for instance between June 1454 and June 1455, the date of that event has been given as 1454 x 1455. Where a procedure or process carried on continuously throughout the year of an account, the date has been given in the form 1454-1455, and where reference is made to the presentation of an account or to the act of recording an account the terminal date of the account has been given. If, for example, the account between June 1454 and June 1455 had been the first account to mention a currour, this fact would be stated in the form, 'The currour is first recorded in 1455.'

I should like to express my gratitude to Professor G. Donaldson and to Dr J. Bannerman of the Scottish History Department of Edinburgh University who supervised my PhD thesis on which this book is based. Without their help and guidance on points too numerous to mention, my thesis would never have been completed and this book, consequently, never published. Wherever I have received help from other individuals it is specifically acknowledged in the notes to the text. The assistance which I have received from the staffs of the Scottish Record Office, of Edinburgh University Library and of the National Library of Scotland has been invaluable. I am also indebted to the co-operation which I received in St Andrews University Library, Cambridge University Library, the British Museum Reading Rooms and Lambeth Palace Library. Finally I must thank my parents for their constant encouragement and for reading through this work at its various stages of development. What inaccuracies remain are nonetheless my responsibility alone.

John M. Gilbert, Galashiels.

SECTION A

INTRODUCTORY NARRATIVE

1

The Introduction of Hunting Reserves to Scotland

ALTHOUGH man from his origins has lived by hunting, it was probably not till the Upper Palaeolithic age that hunting rights became an element of man's social organisation.[1] Since then hunting has been the subject, at least in Western Europe, of rules or rights. Not till the seventh century A.D. is there clear evidence of the existence of hunting reserves in Europe, and in Scotland not till the twelfth century. The hunting reserves of the Frankish Empire, which were the first to be recorded, provide certain criteria which can be used to detect the presence of such reserves when examining early Scottish sources.

The first of such criteria must be the limitation of the principle of Roman law that game as *res nullius*[2] belonged to the person who killed it regardless of where or on whose land it was killed. Should hunting on a certain area of land be restricted to the owner or should all or part of the kill belong to the owner, then the idea of game as *res nullius* would be limited. Secondly, there must be a specific penalty other than a fine for trespass which the owner of the reserve could impose on anyone hunting within it illegally. Thirdly, while hunting reserves could be owned by the king or ruler or by his subjects, there must be evidence that the king tried to control the hunting reserves of his subjects: the subject was entitled to have a hunting reserve only with the king's permission and it was not possible for him to establish a hunting reserve purely on the basis of rights of property or ownership of land. Fourthly, in a hunting reserve the habitat of the game should be preserved along with game itself, resulting in the close association of the preservation of trees and the reservation of game within one area of land.

These criteria must not be confused with certain social phenomena which can be regarded as essential to the ultimate appearance of the concept of a hunting reserve. There is the idea, first of all, of limiting the right to hunt to certain people and secondly of possessing the right to hunt on one's own land. The former does not imply a reserve unless the right to hunt on an area of land is limited solely to the owner of that area of land, nor does the latter unless the hunting is controlled by the owner. Thirdly, the private ownership of wood, which like the previous two phenomena occurs only in a moderately advanced society, does not by itself prove the existence of a hunting reserve.

Two aspects of hunting reserves, the importance of the ownership of land

5

and the exercising of rights on that land, reflect the feudal organisation of medieval society. Consequently, although feudalism is an imprecise concept, countries with a feudal or similar system of land holding were more likely to provide conditions amenable to the establishment of hunting reserves.

When searching for evidence of hunting reserves in Scotland before the twelfth century, one has to rely, apart from the occasional reference, on the possibility of English, Irish, Welsh and Scandinavian sources representing the Scottish situation. These influences on Scotland can be conveniently grouped into Celtic, i.e., Irish and Welsh, and Germanic, i.e., Scandinavian and English.

The Germanic and in particular the Scandinavian influence on Scotland can be seen in two pieces of Scottish evidence. In 1158 x 1159 it is recorded in the *Orkneyinga Saga* that the earls of Orkney used to hunt regularly in Caithness;[3] and Aelred, to illustrate Malcolm III's generosity, relates in his *Genealogia Regum Anglorum*, written in the twelfth century, a story which, he says, he heard from David I telling how Malcolm pardoned a traitor while hunting 'secundum legem venandi quam vulgus tristam vocat'.[4] The tryst or *trista* mentioned by Aelred was the spot where the hunters awaited the drive,[5] and it occurs in several twelfth-century charters.[6] The word *trista* derived from the Old Norse *treysta*, to trust, probably passed to the Danelaw where it came to mean a hunting station and was used as such in Old English.[7] From England it had passed to north-west France by 1180 and probably to Scotland, although it is just conceivable that Scotland may have received the word direct from Scandinavia. While the existence in Scotland of this hunting custom which Aelred describes as a 'legem venandi' does not imply the existence of hunting reserves, it is clear that Scandinavian influences did reach Scotland, thus rendering Scandinavian hunting practices a guide to Scottish practice.

In Norway the idea of game as *res nullius* was limited: landowners could hunt on their own land but if their hunt passed to another man's land the kill went to the owner of the land where the hunt ended. While game, therefore, was not entirely *res nullius* since it did not belong to the hunter, there was no system of hunting reserves involved since the landowner could not prevent others hunting on his land.[8] These hunting rights depended on ownership of land, not on a royal grant, and any control Norwegians had over timber-cutting was not connected in any way with their hunting rights.[9] On common land hunting was free to all.[10] In Sweden and in Denmark similar arrangements seem to have applied.[11]

Continuing with the Germanic group, evidence can be found of Anglo-Saxon customs reaching Scotland. A *notitia* of grants by Macbeth and Gruoch of Kirkness to the church of St. Serf in 1040 x 1057 [12] includes a later addition which Lawrie suggests comes from David I's reign and which states that the land was to be held 'sine refectione pontis et sine exercitu et venatione'. Lawrie takes this to mean that the king would not hunt on that land, which might suggest a grant of something approaching a hunting reserve. He puts a similar interpretation on David I's grant of Pennick to Dunfermline 'in aquis et pratis et pascuis et in plano et nemore absque omni venatu'.[13] Lawrie's interpretation is unsatisfactory because in the Kirkness grant the grantee is being excused various duties which the grantee and not the grantor had to perform. Since it was an Anglo-Saxon practice to make service in the king's hunt a condition of land tenure,[14] it is more likely that the grantee of Kirkness was being excused the duty of helping in the king's hunt, presumably by the provision of beaters for a drive. 'Absque omni venatu' in the Pennick grant, although it occurs in the pertinents, would also fit this interpretation. Strength is given to this argument by Professor Barrow's work on shires and thanes in Scotland,[15] which examines the evidence for estates or shires as parts of the royal demesne inhabited by a class of ministerial freemen, sometimes called thegns, who gave goods and services to a royal centre. Evidence for this type of organisation is found, he states, in Scotland, England and Wales.[16] He suggests that the words 'shire' and 'thane' were borrowed from England sometime between the sixth and the tenth century to describe an already existing system in Scotland.[17] Consequently, the duty to assist in the king's hunt which was commonly found in English shires must have occurred in Scotland before the twelfth century, although it was in no way connected with the existence of hunting reserves.

In this context the same 'Swinewood' which occurs in the shire of Coldingham in a charter of King Edgar in 1095[18] suggests that the English practice of collecting pannage from pigs grazing on mast in woods, a practice which can be traced to the reign of Ine in the early seventh century,[19] was current in Scotland before the twelfth century. These instances suggest that other Anglo-Saxon customs relating to woods and hunting might also have been current in Scotland.

In Anglo-Saxon England game was in some ways considered as *res nullius* but to a lesser extent than in Norway. Cnut in his Secular Ordinance, issued between 1020 and 1023, enacted that all men be entitled to hunt in the woods and fields on their own property but that no one was to hunt on his reserves under pain of incurring the full royal forfeiture.[20] Cnut had, therefore, established royal hunting reserves where no one else could hunt, thus limiting the idea of game as *res nullius*. There is, however, no evidence that any one other than the king might possess a hunting reserve. Cnut does not state whether or not landowners could prevent other people hunting on their land or confiscate the kill of hunters who came on to their land. That he does not indicate that men were entitled to hunt outside their own lands could, however, imply that there were limitations placed on them if they did so. Free men also had rights of hunting game and taking timber in woodland, rights sometimes mentioned with grants of land, as in a charter of the king of Mercia in 822.[21] The close link of land ownership and hunting rights was obviously amenable to the establishment of hunting reserves but only the king did create reserves and only the king could enforce a special penalty for offenders in his reserves.

While Cnut's Ordinance shows that woods could be held privately and while the laws of Ine show that woods were protected,[22] there was no link between hunting rights and the preservation of woods.

Turning to the Celtic group, the evidence reveals that Irish hunting customs were practised in Scotland before the twelfth century. The Gaelic *notitiae* of the Book of Deer dating from the eleventh century record the grant of 'elerc' by Mal Coluim son of Mal Brigte to the monastery of Deer.[23] The Old Irish 'erelc' meant an ambush[24] and was connected with a drive, either as a wall or glen to assist the drive or as the spot where the hunters awaited the drive. The use in Scotland before the twelfth century of the drive, an Irish or Gaelic hunting method, is also illustrated in Gaelic literature.[25] In the ancient laws of Ireland, the idea of game as *res nullius* was restricted if it existed at all. Firstly, there is evidence to suggest that hunting on a certain area of land could be restricted to the owner. In the Book of Aicill a lengthy discussion in the commentary on 'What is lawful in deer judgements' mentions lawful and unlawful pit falls and lawful and unlawful hunters.[26] While the commentaries on these laws are written in middle Irish and, therefore, are post-thirteenth century in date,[27] the impression that in certain areas only certain people could hunt is supported by an Irish legal poem dating from the eighth to the ninth centuries edited by D. A. Binchy which mentions unauthorised stalkings.[28] In certain areas, therefore, only certain people could hunt. Binchy thinks there may have been a separate tract on stalking, hunting, trapping and netting and gives what may be a quotation from it: 'a net which is placed [on another man's land] without asking permission'.[29] The inferred mention of another man's land introduces the possibility that a land holder could hunt on his own land and prevent others from doing so, in which case game would not be considered entirely as *res nullius*. Secondly, in many cases landowners, if they did permit others to hunt on their land, were entitled to a share of the kill. On the other hand a second quotation from this lost tract gives what Binchy considers to be one of the few examples in Irish law of *occupatio*, a concept in effect the same as *res nullius*: 'there are three birds for which the owner of the land is not entitled to a share wherever they be acquired, a snipe, a hawk and and a heron'. Binchy adds that there may have been other, more important examples of *occupatio*. This second quotation introduces the concept of the owner of the land receiving part of the kill thus admitting that some game could be considered as *res nullius* to a certain extent. In Ireland, therefore, a variable picture emerges, from the landowner who could prevent others hunting on his land and so create a reserve in all but name, to the landowner who let others hunt on his land but claimed part of the kill of most animals. In this context the poem 'The Pursuit of Diarmuid and Grainne', which dates from the tenth century but which survives in a twelfth-century edition, describes how Diarmuid received permission to hunt in a certain giant's lands where otherwise hunting was forbidden by agreement between the giant and the Fian.[30] If a landholder could exclude other hunters from his land, this was a right dependent on his owner-ship of land and not on a grant from the king and he could not enforce a special penalty for illegal hunting. Nonetheless the tuath had common land for grazing, common waste and wood,[31] which suggests that there might also have been allowance for common hunting. Although woods could be owned privately and 'man trespass' was committed if certain trees were cut,[32] there was no special connection between the protection of timber and the possible reservation of game.

By contrast with Irish customs those of Wales, which throw light on the history of south-west Scotland before the twelfth century, are considerably clearer on the application of the idea of *res nullius* to game. In the Welsh laws, perhaps as a result of Roman influence,[33] the idea of game as *res nullius* is stronger than in any of the societies so far examined. Landholders could hunt on their own lands but definitely could not prevent other people hunting on their land.[34] The principle of *res nullius* was limited to the extent that if a hunter killed an animal on another's land, the owner of the land received a fourth of the kill, not the complete animal as in Norway. Nor was there any possibility of hunting on another man's land being forbidden as in Ireland: one Welsh law, which states that if a person while travelling on a road in the king's 'fforest' should wound a deer he may chase it as long as he can see it, is in accord with the treatment of game as *res nullius*.[35] The use of 'fforest' in the Welsh text cannot, however, be taken as proof of the existence of forests as hunting reserves in early Welsh society, since the codes in which it occurs, the twelfth-century Dimetian and the fourteenth-century Gwentian, were both open to Anglo-Norman influence.[36] Moreover, the earliest Latin manuscript of the late twelfth century does not mention this clause nor does it use the Latin 'foresta'. Similarly, the Venedotian Code which survives in the oldest Welsh Manuscript, the Black Book of Chirk of *c* 1200, does not use 'fforest' or mention this clause.[37]

In Welsh society the position of the king was stronger than in Ireland or in Norway, perhaps as a result of both Roman and Anglo-Saxon influence. It was clearly stated that the king was free to hunt anywhere and that his hunting parties took priority over all others.[38] The king also took an interest in protecting the hunting rights of his subjects: anyone who laid a snare on another man's land without the latter's permission had to pay a fine both to the landholder and to the king. This does not, however, amount to control of hunting rights from the centre and despite the definition of the royal rights there is no trace of royal hunting reserves being established on the Anglo-Saxon pattern. All freemen were entitled to hunt on their tribal lands,[39] and the protection of timber was unconnected with reservation of game.[40]

While one can be certain that part of the totality of Scandinavian, Anglo-Saxon, Irish and Welsh customs applied to Scotland before the twelfth century, it is more difficult to be so when examining a specific set of customs such as those concerning hunting. For that reason and also because of the differences in Celtic and Germanic hunting customs it is not possible to transpose these customs *in toto* to Scotland, but there is sufficient similarity to enable an approximate picture of hunting rights in Scotland prior to the twelfth century to be constructed. Those who had the right to hunt, which probably depended on an individual's status or degree of freedom,[41] would be able to take part in some form of common hunting either on waste ground or ground belonging to the tribe or kin. Any limitation of game as *res nullius* would stem from the right of a landholder to prevent other people hunting on his land or to take part of a stranger's kill for himself, rights based simply on the possession of land and not on a royal grant. It is conceivable that Scottish kings may have had hunting reserves of the late Anglo-Saxon pattern but it is more likely that they simply had certain favoured hunting areas, into which category may fall the 'cursus apri' granted by Alexander I to St Andrews.[42] It is most likely that there were certain established ways of hunting such as the drive and coursing, depicted on several ninth-century Pictish symbol stones,[43] which to Aelred had the character of *leges venandi* and to which certain tenants of royal lands had to render assistance. There was no general system of hunting reserves established and controlled by the king, and whatever preservation of timber there may have been would not have been directly connected with the reservation of game.

Consequently, the concept of forests as hunting reserves must have been introduced to Scotland in the twelfth century from an external source. The Frankish kings in many ways were the formulators of ideas and institutions throughout medieval Europe. The forest system was no exception. The present view of the origins of *forestae* or hunting reserves is that Roman concepts of game and the private ownership of lands and wood survived in France as *silva propria* and *silva dominica*[44] and probably also in Western Germany. They became known to the Carolingian mayors of the palace in Austrasia in the seventh century,[45] where a charter issued by Sigbert, King of the Franks, from 634-656, recorded the first known example of a forest as a hunting reserve,[46] the forest of the Ardennes. A possible earlier reference to a forest in the 'Lex Ribuaria' is in fact a mistranscription of 'sortem' in a ninth- or tenth-century manuscript.[47] Both Petit Dutaillis and Latouche agree with the etymology of forest as coming from Old High German *forst*. Latinisation as *forestis* led to contamination with *foris*, thus introducing the concept of the forest being outside common use.[48] Petit Dutaillis firmly established that a forest in early medieval Europe was a hunting reserve, not necessarily wooded. The Capitulary *de Villis* issued either by Charlemagne between 771 and 800 or by his son Louis, King of Aquitaine between 798 and 813,[49] clearly states that royal game was to be reserved in royal forests, that no one was to cut down the woods in the forest, and that grazing pigs in woods within a forest was subject to a toll.[50] Anyone stealing game from royal forests was subject to the imperial ban.[51] There is evidence that Charlemagne tried to control hunting outside his forests,[52] although landowners besides the king were allowed to hunt and create forests. They could not, however, create a forest without the king's permission.[53]

The Frankish kings thus limited the idea of game as *res nullius* by the establishment of their reserves, had a penalty for offenders in these reserves, linked timber and game reservation within their forests, and attempted to control all non-royal forests which could only be created on the basis of a royal grant. Outside these forests the customary hunting rights of the medieval Germanic laws continued to operate.[54]

The *Lex Ribuaria* and the *Lex Salica* both implied that it was illegal to hunt in certain areas. It has been argued that Frankish hunting rights closely resembled the position of Roman law where in theory everyone, in accordance with the idea of *res nullius,* owned the animal he killed no matter where he killed it, but in practice hunting rights were limited by the rights of the land-owner who, although he could not lay claim to the game, could demand damages from the intruder. By agreement, however, one could acquire freedom to hunt on another man's land.[55]

Paradoxically, Frankish society, which was to perpetuate and transmit the idea of forests as hunting reserves, was also to perpetuate and transmit the Roman Law principle of game as *res nullius,*[55] an idea which was to reach Scotland in the form in which Justinian originally stated it.

The first area to which the institution of forests was transmitted was Neustria,[56] where a fully developed forest system, presumably controlled by the Carolingian count, existed by the end of the seventh century.[57] This system, which disintegrated in the tenth century,[58] was revived by the Norman dukes by the early eleventh century, thus illustrating the Frankish as opposed to the Scandinavian inheritance of the Norman dukes. From 1017 x 1025 evidence shows that Norman dukes had hunting reserves called *silva* or *foresta,*[59] and that they exercised a system of forest jurisdiction with special pleas within these reserves.[60] The Carolingian system was not restored in its entirety, since *foresta* could be used to describe a wood and not a hunting reserve[61] and there is no recorded attempt of the dukes to control the hunting reserves of their subjects.[62] By 1066 hunting reserves, both royal and baronial, were well established throughout Normandy,[63] and it was there that many families whose descendants were to settle in Scotland first became acquainted with forests as hunting reserves. The Bruces from Brix and the Morvilles from Morville held their lands in or near the ducal reserve in the Cotentin, while the Sinclairs of St Clair sur L'Elle were close to the reserve of Cerisy, as were the Soules family from Soulles to the south of St Lô. The Avenels were probably associated with the Avranchin, where the Count of Mortain had several hunting reserves. (For the location of and evidence for Normandy's hunting reserves, see Map 1 and its Key, pp. 14, 15).

The Norman invasion and occupation of England brought the Carolingian forest system to England in the late eleventh century. By the end of Henry I's reign these features of the Carolingian system, absent in Normandy before 1066, had been restored and surpassed. The meaning of *foresta* was once more limited to hunting reserves and the king controlled hunting outside his forests both by an attempt, ultimately unsuccessful, to reserve royal game, that is deer and boar, inside and outside his forests, and by forbidding the formation of hunting reserves by his subjects unless they had received royal permission. Henry usually limited such permission to the right to reserve the lesser animals of the warren or of the chase, although on occasion he did grant part of a royal forest to a subject.[64] A more complicated organisation developed in England than in the Frankish Empire: rights of usage in the forest were defined as estovers and easements, and assart or clearing was carefully supervised. In Henry I's reign it was probably regarders who prepared for forest eyres which were held to punish offenders, and Henry himself may have taken part in hearing forest pleas. The pleas of the forest were clearly recorded in the *Leges Henrici Primi* and a code of forest law was established.[65] To the workings of this system David, brother of the king of Scotland, was introduced as earl of Huntingdon. A large part of the lands of the earldom of Huntingdon lay within royal forests of Henry I. Rutland, Northampton, Whittlewood and Salcey had all been afforested by this time, although only part of Huntingdon was afforested before the reign of Henry II. (See Map 2 and its Key, pp. 17, 18.)[66] Thus many of the lands which David's Norman associates held within his earldom of Huntingdon also lay within English royal forests: the Morvilles held Whissendine, Whitwell, Bozeat and Offord; the Soules Doddington; the Quincys Eynesbury and Long Buckby; the Riddels Wittering and the Olifards Lifford.[67] David and his tenants could not hunt on these lands without Henry I's permission, which was no doubt more forthcoming for David than for his tenants who often held lands in other parts of England. The general forest privileges received by the earls of Huntingdon and confirmed to John le Scot covered only the pasture and timber-cutting of the earl and his vassals and did not extend to hunting, thus making it unlikely that any of these barons received general exemption from the forest system in respect of hunting.[68]

Since, as has been shown, there was no native forest system, it was the Norman or Frankish system which was established in Scotland, although the exact date of its introduction cannot now be determined. It is possible that Scottish kings were acquainted with the idea of a forest system for some time before it was established in Scotland. If Malcolm III did not hear of the English forest system, his sons, Duncan and Edgar, had the opportunity of experiencing the English forest system at first hand. There is no evidence, however, to suggest that they established forests of their own in Scotland. Indeed the political climate in Scotland at the turn of the century was not conducive to the introduction and acceptance of Anglo-Norman institutions.[69] The shadow of forthcoming changes can be detected in the reign of Alexander I. David, who held most of southern Scotland from his brother, probably settled a certain 'Willelmus venator' in Cumbria in 1122, for he was a witness to the *Inquisitio* of the lands of Glasgow Cathedral.[70] If David was hunting in southern Scotland, the possibility of his establishing forests there has to be considered. David's charter to the abbey of Selkirk, probably issued towards the end of the period 1114 x 1124,[71] shows that he had fewterers or greyhound keepers, and controlled the use of timber in his woods, 'boscos meos', presumably in and around Selkirk. He also granted Selkirk a tithe of the hides of hinds and stags killed by his fewterers. The combination of a hunting establishment and the control of timber in the area which was soon to appear as the first recorded royal forest in Scotland certainly suggests that a hunting reserve was established by David before 1124, but had David created a forest there it is hardly conceivable that such a novel introduction would have escaped mention in his charter to Selkirk, especially when hunting and wood-cutting were concerned. One has to accept that while David may have established a forest in this area before 1124, as Ritchie suggests,[72] it is much more likely that he was exercising the right of a landholder to hunt on his land and protect his woods on a pattern found elsewhere in Scotland and Europe. David may well, as a result of his English experience, have formalised such arrangements to a greater extent than previously known in Scotland. Alexander I does not appear to have copied David in this, since both his grant to Scone[73] and his grant to Dunfermline[74] contain no references to hunting or to timber. David, *c* 1128, still did not refer to forests in his extant charters when one might expect him to have done so as in his grant of a tithe of brushwood and of the fat of his beasts killed in Teviotdale to the church of St John of Roxburgh,[75] or when giving Dunfermline a tithe of his beasts killed in the hunt and the right to timber from his woods.[76] The first extant references to royal forests in Scotland occur between 1136 and 1144. David's charter to Melrose Abbey in 1143 x 1144, which probably dates from 1136, grants the monks timber and pannage in 'forestis meis scilicet de Seleschirche et de Trauequair'.[77] The forests of Pentland and Moorfoot appear in *c* 1142,[78] Stirling and Clackmannan in 1143,[79] and Gala and Leader in 1150 x 1152.[80] (See Map 9 p. 360.) By 1153 David had introduced into Scotland all the main features of a forest system.

The absence of any reference to forests in appropriate contexts in the 1120s and the lapse of time between the creation of royal forests in Scotland and their appearance in the extant charters point to the 1130s as the date when David established forests as hunting reserves in Scotland.

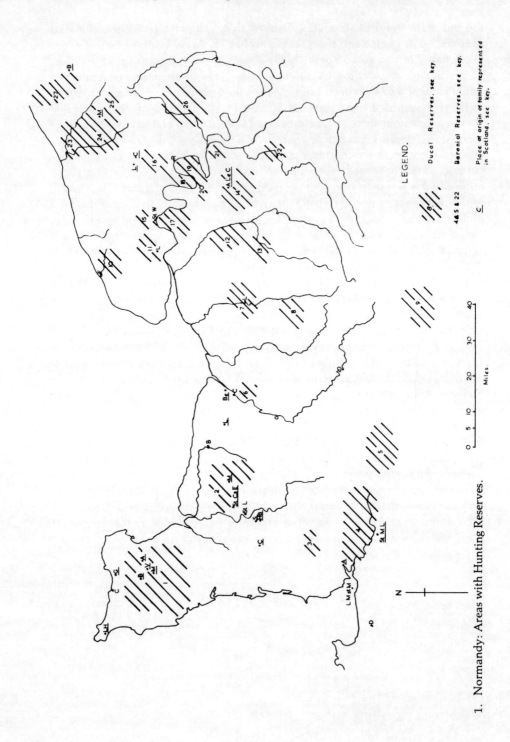

1.   Normandy: Areas with Hunting Reserves.

Map 1 shows the areas where there were hunting reserves in Normandy and not the exact extent of these reserves. The sources for this map are M. Fauroux, *Recueil des Actes des Ducs de Normandie* (F) and L. Delisle, *La Class Agricole en Normandie*, 334-417 (Delisle).

Key 1. Reserves.

No. on Map	Type[1]	Name	Source and Comment
1	D	Cotentin	F 99. 1042. Ducal *silvae* of Montebourg, Brix, Rabey, Cherbourg, Valdecie, Lutumiere.
2	D	Cerisy	F 64. 1032. *Silvae* and *nemus* of Maupertuis, Le Molay and around Cerisy.
3	D	Saultcherreuil	F 140. 1049 x 1058. *Silvae.*
4	B	Mortain	F 214. 1056 x 1066. *Silvae* of Mortain.
5	B	Domfront	F 214. 1056 x 1066. *Silvae* of Domfront castle.
6	B	Cinglais	F 234. 1082 x 1087. Forest of Robert son of Erneys.
7	B	Lisieux	F 140. 1049 x 1058. *Silva* of Assement belonging to Countess Eceline. Forester mentioned.
8	D	Vimoutiers	F 36. 1025. *Silva.* No mention of hunting.
9	B	Bellême	Delisle. Count of Perche.
10	D	Fécamp	Delisle.
11	D	Etelan	F 197. 1050 x 1066 — tithe of *nemus* of Etelan.
12	D	Vievre & Brionne	F 229. 1066, 16. Forests.
13	D	Bernay	F 35. 1025, with *silva.* Foresters as witnesses.
14	D	Haye de Theil	F 90. 1035. *Haia* in a reserve.
15	B	Vatteville	F 234. 1082 x 1087. *Silva.*
16	D	Forêt Verte	Delisle, F 94. 1035 x 1040. *Silva.*
17	B	Brotonne	F 234. 1082 x 1087. *Silva.*
18	D	Roumare	Delisle. F 27. 1042. Forest.
19	D	Rouvrai	Delisle.
20	D	Bourg Achard	F 197. 1050 x 1066. *Nemus.*
		Forêt de la Lande	Delisle.
21	D	Bord	F 15. 1014. *Silva.*
22	B	Evreux	F 208. 1055 x 1066. *Forest.*
23		Forêt d'Alihermont	Delisle.
24		Forêt d'Eawy	Delisle.
25	D	Esclavelles	F 27. Late 11th cent. Forest.
26		Forêt de Lyons	Delisle. F 64. 1032.
27		Eu	Delisle.
28	B	Bémecourt	F 120. 1050. *Silva.*
29	B?	Conches	Delisle. Forest.

1. D—Ducal. B—Baronial.

Key 2. Homes of Scots/Norman Families.

For the sources of the information given in this key see above, Chapter 1, p. 11, n. 63. For clarity, the number of the nearest reserve has been attached to certain places.

Map Letter	Place	Family Name	Source
LH	La Hague	Haig	NF 324[1]
G	Gonneville	Gundeville	NF 324
B	Brix	Bruce	NF 322
A	Amfreville	Umfraville (see A le C)	Ritchie, *Normans*, 144
V	Valognes	Valognes	NF 335
M	Morville	Morville	NF 323
C	Carantilly	Quarantilly	NF 335
S	Soulles	Soules	NF 325
HB	Haye Bellefonds	Hay	NF 325
A (4)	Avranche	Avenel	NF 325
St ML	St Martin de Landelles	Landelles	NF 327
M (2)	Montfiquet	Montfiquet (Mushet)	NF 332
St CsE	St Clair sur l'Elle	St Clair (Sinclair)	NF 317-8
L	Loucelles	Lascelles	NF 332
Be	Benouville	Burneville	NF 324
L (16)	Lanquetot	Langetoft	NF 331
C (16)	Clerès	Clerès	NF 330
AleC	Amfreville la Campagne	Umfraville	
M (24)	Mesnières	Mesnières (Menzies)	NF 332
B (27)	Bailleul en Vimeu	Balliol	NF 328

Other places

C	Cherbourg	L	Lisieux
D	Dol	F	Fécamp
Le M st M	Le Mont St Michel	L (11)	Lillebonne
St L	St Lô	St W	St Wandrille
C (6)	Caen	R	Rouen

1. NF—Barrow, 'Scotland's Norman Families', in *The Kingdom of the Scots*.

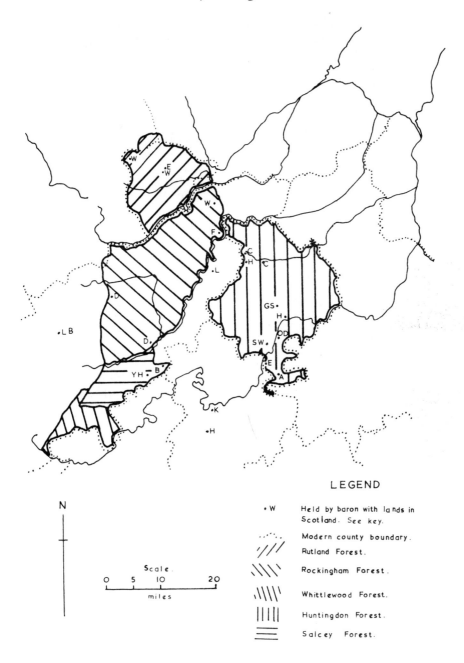

LEGEND

• W	Held by baron with lands in Scotland. See key.
·.·˙·..	Modern county boundary.
⁄⁄⁄	Rutland Forest.
\\\\	Rockingham Forest.
,\\\\\\	Whittlewood Forest.
‖‖‖	Huntingdon Forest.
≡	Salcey Forest.

N

Scale.

0   5   10   20

miles

2. English Royal Forests in the Earldoms of Huntingdon and Northampton.

Map 2 shows English royal forests in the earldoms of Northampton and Huntingdon. This key lists lands held by barons with lands in Scotland. In the time of Henry I the forest of Huntingdon covered only the north, west and east of the county.

Forest	Map Letter	Name	Family	Source[1]
Rutland	W	Whissendine	Morville	LS 31 13th c.
	E	Exton	Bruce	LS 31 13th c.
	W	Whitwell	Morville	LS 31 12th c.
Rockingham	W	Wittering	Riddel	NS 55 12th c.
	F	Fotheringay	Balliol	KF 396 13th c.
	D	Draughton (Drayton)	Corbet	KF 386 12th c.
	D	Great Doddington	Soulles	KF 325 12th c.
Salcey	B	Bozeat	Morville	LS 31 12th c.
	YH	Yardley Hastings		
Huntingdon	C	Caldecote	Bruce	KF 374 13th c.
	H	Hamerton	St Clair	NF 318 13th c.
	C	Connington	Bruce	KF 374 13th c.
	GS	Great Stukely	Kernelle	KF 360 12th c.
	H	Huntingdon		
	SW	Southoe Weston	Quincy	LS 31 12th c.
	OD	Offord Darcy	Morville	LS 31 12th c.
	E	Eynesbury	Quincy	LS 31; KF 370 12th c.
	A	Abbotsley	Balliol	LS 35 13th c.
Others	L	Lifford	Olifard	KF 354 12th c.
	LB	Long Buckby	Quincy	NF 318 12th c.
	K	Kempston	Bruce/ Balliol	KF 374 13th c; 396 13th c.
	H	Houghton	Morville	LS 31 12th c.

1. NF—Barrow, 'Scotland's Norman Families', in *The Kingdom of the Scots*;
   LS—Moore, *Lands of Scots Kings in England*;
   KF—Farrer, *Knights' Fees*, ii;
   NS—Ritchie, *Normans in Scotland*;
   c. —century.

2

Hunting Reserves in Scotland, 1124-1286

THROUGHOUT this book the word 'forest' is most frequently used to mean a hunting reserve and not an area of woodland. Where 'forest' is used to signify an area of woodland, it is clear from the context that it is so used. The use of the Scots 'forest' and the Latin 'foresta' has been and still is a source of confusion and must be clarified. They are actually both used to mean a hunting reserve.

'Forest' was employed in this sense in a proper name[1] but was also used more in the sense of a wild and rugged area than just a hunting reserve. When Douglas travelled in 'the forest', Barbour included not only Ettrick but an area west to the Lyne Water in this forest.[2] The earliest examples of 'forest' in the vernacular occur in Barbour's works and therefore belong to the second half of the fourteenth century.[3] 'Forest' could also mean woodland. The *Book of Alexander* belonging either to the late fourteenth century or to the mid-fifteenth century contains several examples of this use of 'forest'.[4] On the continent, the vernacular French 'le forest' had meant woodland since the tenth century.[5] It can, therefore, be assumed that in Scotland in the twelfth and thirteenth centuries the French-speaking aristocracy used 'le forest' to mean an area of wood as well as a hunting reserve. So it is likely that the Scots 'forest' had acquired this meaning much earlier than the first extant examples given above as the use of forest in Middle English before 1300 would suggest.[6]

The Latin 'foresta' might also be used to describe woodlands as well as a hunting reserve but the latter use is by far the more common. A charter of Robert II in 1371 refers to 'forestarum nostrarum de bosco de le Tor et de Clacmanane'.[7] 'Foresta' here, according to the context, clearly refers to a hunting reserve but when the area of a reserve as at Torwood is described as a 'boscus', a word of purely vegetational significance, it is not surprising to find that 'foresta' could mean woodland. In this sense the earliest use of 'foresta' occurs perhaps in 1234 when the bounds of Arbroath's lands of Dunnichen included 'proximam arborem foreste de Ochtirlony',[8] although in this instance the forest of Ochtirlony might be a hunting reserve. Similarly, the reference c 1250 to the lands 'que vocatur foresta de Dalkarn'[9] might refer either to woodland or to a hunting reserve. Yet another dubious example occurs in the passage in Fordun's *Chronicle*, where Edward III was ambushed in 'foresta prope Melrose'.[10] There is no evidence for a forest or hunting reserve in that area in the fourteenth century apart from the more distant Ettrick forest which

Fordun would presumably have referred to by name had he wished to convey that the ambush took place there. This meaning of 'foresta' may also occur in 1478 x 1479 when timber-cutting was mentioned 'in forestis et nemoribus de Alway et Clakmanane'.[11] The context of wood-cutting and the use of 'forestae' in the plural suggests that 'forestae' is used to mean woods. Another example occurs in James IV's charter to John Haldane of Gleneagles granting him 'silvas . . . nemora et forestas in libera foresta ubicunque infra predictas terras'.[12] The wording implies that the forests existed before the free forest grant was made and, since there are no previous hunting reserves recorded in the area, 'forestae' must refer to woods.

One less common use of 'foresta' is found in the feu charters of Ettrick, where a stead or holding in the forest is called a 'foresta'.[13]

It can now be understood how it arose that Skene defined 'foresta' as 'ane large wood without dike or closure quhilk hes na water',[14] whereas Stair wrote that the meaning of forests 'can not be extended generally to woods but only to such where deer are kept'.[15]

David I, a regular if not devoted hunter throughout his life,[16] hunted more frequently in central and southern than in northern Scotland, to judge by the location of his hunting reserves, the earliest of which — Selkirk, Pentland and Moorfoot, Stirling and Clackmannan and Gala and Leader — lay in that part of Scotland into which he had introduced many Normans (see Table 25, p. 338). David may also have claimed forest rights on the Moray coast, since a grant made in 1174 to Kinloss Abbey,[17] founded *c* 1150,[18] confirms that Kinloss held certain rights in a forest. Had David made such claims, their practical value seems dubious. Although lands alienated by royal charter were not included in hunting reserves, the forests cannot have been uninhabited since there is no indication that the native population was removed from, for example, Selkirk or Stirling or Clackmannan. Within his reserves David established all the main elements of a forest system. Hunting was controlled,[19] probably by the imposition of a £10 fine on unauthorised hunters, wood was reserved[20] and pasture was limited: the first reference to pannage in a forest probably dates to 1136.[21] The problems of introducing and maintaining this system, which were the responsibility of sheriffs and foresters,[22] may be reflected in the fact that Clackmannan, only once described as a forest in David's reign,[23] is usually referred to as a *nemus* and is not again entitled a forest till 1291.[24] The description and explanation which this system must have required upon its introduction could have been provided by the Norman settlers and also by royal assise. Such an assise may be recorded in two clauses of the surviving forest law which concern the basic topics of hunting, timber and pasture control and which may date to David's reign. (See pp. 314, 315.)

David established his control of all hunting reserves on the Carolingian pattern by instituting the forest grant which gave a subject the right to create a forest.[25] The frequency of forest grants in twelfth-century Scotland, compared with their extreme rarity in England, argues that David's Norman barons put pressure on him to ensure that their lands were never again subjected to a royal forest system as they had been in Huntingdon. Such pressure might explain why David limited his forests to royal lands or to his waste[26] and granted barons forests of their own. Whether or not David's forest grants merely recognised rights which the barons had taken for themselves, they would not only have been appreciated by his barons but would also have maintained his theoretical control of baronial hunting reserves. While only two such charters, one of which was made to Robert de Bruce in Annandale,[27] have survived from David's reign a forest was probably held at this time by Hugh de Morville in Lauderdale.[28] The reason why Eskdale where Robert Avenel had full control over hunting[29] is not described as a forest in any extant record may be that he had created a reserve on his own initiative and not on the basis of a royal grant. Similarly Ranulf de Soules' grant to Jedburgh in 1147 x 1151[30] of a tithe of his hunting in Liddesdale, which was the subject of a royal forest grant in 1315 x 1321,[31] is suggestive of though not conclusive proof of a hunting reserve, since such grants were usually but not always made from forests. (See pp. 13, 177.)

David's generosity to the church extended to his forests in the form of grants of permission to use the forest or of tithes of the produce of his forests[32] but not, so far as the extant evidence tells, to the granting of forest charters.

Malcolm IV, on account no doubt of his age and his health,[33] does not appear to have had the same interest in hunting as his grandfather, although he did continue the latter's practice of granting tithes of his kills to the church.[34] While there is no evidence to suggest that Malcolm developed the administration of royal forests, he may well have created additional forests. Clunie, visited by David,[35] first appears as a forest in 1161,[36] while the forest of Mauldslie, though not recorded till 1214,[37] might have been established at the time of Malcolm's settlement of Clydesdale.[38] Malcolm's grant to Walter the Steward in 1161 x 1162 suggests that he probably continued David's policy of accepting but trying to control baronial reserves, although in fact no forest grant has survived from this reign. The most interesting development of this reign is the appearance between 1153 and 1162 of a warren grant, the form of which was based on its English counterpart. (See Table 30, p. 354.) The king, therefore, had a choice of two types of reserves which he could grant to his subjects, a forest to reserve all game or a warren to reserve lesser game.

William I, when in Scotland, probably hunted regularly, favouring Selkirk, Jedburgh, Traquair and St. Mary's Loch to the south of the Forth and Clunie, Alyth, Kincardine and Clackmannan to the north of the Forth.[39] Of the witnesses to charters given at these places the most interesting is Countess Ada, William's mother, at St. Mary's Loch in 1166 x 1171,[40] evidence perhaps that hunting was a female as well as male pastime. A consequence of the northward extension of royal power by William was the establishment of royal forests farther north than those of his predecessors. The forest of Banchory,

c

for instance, which appears in 1171 x 1174,[41] was no doubt associated with other reserves in the Dee valley, and the forest around Elgin, Forres and Inverness, first recorded in 1189 x 1195,[42] might have been established after William's northern expedition in 1179 and during his pacification of Moray in the following years.[43] The only losses from the royal forest were Outh to an illegitimate son in 1195 x 1210[44] and Birse to the bishop of Aberdeen.[45] To assist the administration and maintenance of his reserves there is evidence that William enacted several forest laws or assises dealing with the limitation of pasture in his forests and perhaps with rights of way. (See pp. 244, 315.) The administrative difficulty of protecting a forest may have led to the construction of royal parks, the first of which was recorded at Stirling in 1165 x 1174. (See Table 31, p. 356.)

In William's reign forest and warren grants, probably because of the emergence of a full-time chancery,[46] adopted distinctively Scottish, as opposed to their previously English-based, forms. The final form of forest grant, which may be attributed to the chancellorship of Hugh de Roxburgh from 1189 to 1199,[47] appears to have copied the style of the warren grant which had by 1173 x 1178[48] significantly altered from Malcolm's original.

While the church continued to receive concessions in hunting reserves, especially from the barons in the earlier part of the reign,[49] from the 1180s onwards disputes arose between the church and the laity over the use of royal and baronial forests. The church argued the case for economic exploitation while the king and his barons tried to hold such exploitation in check.[50] (See Table 23, p. 266.) The arguments of Melrose Abbey with the de Morvilles and with the men of Wedale over Gala and Leader and Ettrick forests were settled in 1180 and 1184 respectively. Walter the third Steward also seems to have had trouble with Paisley Abbey in his forest of Renfrew and with Melrose Abbey in his forest of Ayr. The settlement of these and similar disputes reflects the conflicting claims of lay and ecclesiastical justice, since major cases might be decided either in the king's court or in a church court, perhaps through papal judges delegate. (See Table 14, p. 169.) For minor matters local arrangements were made whereby monks' servants were usually tried in the monks' court and the baron's servants in his court. William's reign was a turning point between the twelfth-century position where the barons appear to have maintained their reserves unchallenged and that of the thirteenth century where they were faced with continual economic pressure on their forests. This transformation also presented the foresters, both royal and baronial, with an increasingly difficult administrative task.[51]

Alexander II was a regular huntsman to judge by the number of charters issued at Clunie and Kincardine north of the Forth and Traquair and Cadzow to the south.[52] The only new forests to be recorded in his reign were all subdivisions of already existing reserves, namely Invercullen, Maryculter, Pluscarden and Auchtertyre, with the exceptions of Alyth which lay beside Clunie and which was probably co-eval with Clunie and of Banff where

Alexander may have created a forest at the same time as he established a sheriff.[53] In respect of royal forests, however, Alexander was a far 'sairer sanct' to the crown than David I: Pluscarden, Gala and Leader, Gladhouse and Moorfoot, South-West Ettrick and Dollar were all granted to the church, and the forest of Dundaff and Strathcarron was granted first to Patrick, Earl of Dunbar, and then to David de Graham. (See Tables 8 and 28, pp. 119, 345.)

On the other hand Alexander may have extended the reservation of his game to a purlieu (see p. 102), that is to an area around but not inside the forest. From the late twelfth century, offenders in a royal forest could be tried in a court of forestry where probably a royal justice would hear the case, assisted by the forester or the sheriff.[54] There were as yet no justiciars of the forest but during the thirteenth century foresters, like sheriffs, may have acquired the authority to hear cases on their own.

The forest grant was altered to become the free forest grant and to include the royal plural, probably on the advice of the chancellor, William de Bondington,[55] and with the help perhaps of Robert of Dunfermline, chancellor, the warren grant assumed the same form as the forest grant.

The opposition of the owners of hunting reserves to the economic activities of the monks continued with the dispute of Roger Avenel and Melrose Abbey, eventually settled in 1236.[56] Gerard de Lyndesay and Walter the third Steward, however, surrendered to the pressure of the church and alienated part of their reserves as did Alexander in Gala and Leader and in the Leithen valley. Combined with the king's numerous free forest grants to the church which would enable monks to eliminate hunters from their pastoral farms, it is evident that the economic pursuits of the abbeys in forests could not be held in check by the owners of these reserves. The firm opposition of William's reign was replaced by the acceptance of Alexander's.

Alexander III's reign opened with a minority in which the Scottish forest system was to play an interesting part. In 1251 Alexander III married Henry III's daughter, Margaret.[57] Robert de Ros, an Anglo-Scots baron sent north by Henry as one of Margaret's guardians, had probably been justiciar of the forest north of the Trent in England in 1247 and 1248.[58] Geoffrey de Langley, who was also sent north as an adviser on 29 October 1252,[59] had been justiciar of the forest on both sides of the Trent since 1250.[60] The efficient performance of his duties in England inevitably rendered him unpopular with Matthew Paris.[61] Ros and especially Langley must have been interested in the Scots forest system, and free forest grants, non-existent in England, must have seemed to Langley wanton dissipation of the royal prerogatives. It is conceivable that attempts by Langley to remedy this situation and to organise the Scots forest system on English lines may have been some of his actions which, according to Matthew Paris, the Scots magnates refused to tolerate any longer.[62] Langley left Scotland and had resumed his duties in England by July 1253.[63] In 1255, when the Durward party replaced the Comyn's faction, they claimed the right to remove and appoint not only councillors but also sheriffs, foresters and other lesser officials.[64] While this agreement illustrates the relative importance of sheriffs and foresters to the government, it may also reflect the above suggested events of 1252-1253. While the attempt of Langley to introduce English practices to the Scottish forest system can be no more than surmise, it is clear that during Alexander's minority English ideas on hunting reserves were more prevalent amongst the king's advisers than in the preceding reign.

During Alexander's majority the place dates of his charters do not point to any favoured hunting areas other than Kintore, Durris and Traquair.[65] No significant additions were made to the royal forest whereas Tillicoultry, probably part of Clackmannan forest, was granted to William, Earl of Mar, and part of Pentland forest to Henry Sinclair.[66] In keeping with the increasing economic exploitation of the royal forests several forest laws, which concern outsiders' permission to hunt in forests, tolls to be collected for pasture, and offenders in baronial forests, and which appear to have been issued as a single group, probably date to Alexander III's reign although they could be attributed to the reign of his father. (See p. 316.) Alexander may have preferred hunting in parks, for he built a new park at Stirling around 1263 and extended Kincardine park in 1266. (See p. 215.)

Apart from his forest grant of Tillicoultry to the earl of Mar, Alexander made another important forest grant of part of Lennox to the earl of Lennox in 1272. He also combined the free forest and free warren grants in a charter given to Coldingham Priory in 1276, thus illustrating the complementary nature of these grants. Baronial forests and warrens were fully formalised institutions, for not only does the phrase 'right of free forest' appear in this reign but also the form of the warren grant which, as stated, was identical to the forest grant, was incorporated in a late thirteenth-century copy of the register of writs.[67] The grant of forest rights by the king to the monks of Melrose on the Steward's lands of Mauchline in 1264/5[68] marked the end of a clash of economic and hunting interests which had started early in the century and shows that the monks were still agitating for and receiving concessions in forests, with decreasing opposition from the king and his magnates. That this is the only extant record of such a concession in this reign argues that the monks, with many of their demands satisfied, had eased their pressure on the reserves.

Although it was the Normans who introduced the forest system to Scotland, the native population both accepted and influenced it. Since the idea of some control of hunting on one's land was already known in Scotland before the twelfth century, forests (hunting reserves) would not have presented a totally unfamiliar concept to the Scots. Although the possible loss of evidence, in this context of forest grants, renders accurate conclusions impossible, it is arguable that the native population adopted varying attitudes to the forest system, or rather, to forest grants. In some cases native hunting rights may have become recognised as a forest without the receipt of a forest grant. In 1153 x 1165

Uchtred of Galloway's grant to Holyrood of a tithe of his hunting[69] and the charter to Holm Cultram which shows that he collected pannage in his demesne woods[70] suggest hunting rights of the type which would have existed in Scotland in the eleventh century. Yet in 1214 x 1249 Alan, grandson of Uchtred, was referring to his 'nemoribus et forestis',[71] although there is no extant evidence of a forest grant. On the other hand, Morgrund, Earl of Mar, never refers to a *foresta* on his lands even although he could, as in 1163 x 1172, grant a tithe of his hunting to St Andrews and control the use of timber in his *nemora*,[72] again reminiscent of native rights. In these cases it is only because Morgrund and Uchtred are native and not Norman that the rights mentioned in their charters can be considered as a possible reflection of native customs. Ranulf de Soules in Liddesdale and Earl David, brother of William I, could also grant tithes of hunting from their lands,[73] but they did so presumably on the basis of the receipt of a royal charter as any other Norman baron might have done who had received lands by royal charter. What distinction there may have been between Norman rights and residual native rights was blurred by formal charter language, since Morgrund and Uchtred were expressing what may have been their native rights in a Norman form.

In some cases a Norman may have taken over lands and rights from native landholders. Professor Barrow has suggested that twelfth-century infeftments such as Renfrew, Cunninghame, Strathgryfe and Annandale are to be compared with Welsh cantreds and commotes.[74] In Renfrew, Malcolm's confirmation of David's grants to Walter the Steward[75] included in the pertinents '. . . in foresto in tristris . . .'. While such pertinents might simply represent the confirmation of an earlier forest grant, as in William I's confirmation in 1185 x 1173 of Bruce's lands 'in forestis et tristriis',[76] the conjunction of forests and trysts, whether or not there had been a previous forest grant, shows a clear link between native and Norman hunting practices and suggests that the Bruces and the Stewards adopted native hunting arrangements on their lands. In 1172 x 1173 the only other mention of such pertinents occurs in William I's confirmation of Malise's tenure of certain lands from Gilbert, Earl of Strathearn.[77] Whether or not the earl had received a royal forest grant, he could control hawking and timber-cutting on his lands,[78] in this case illustrating perhaps the adoption of Norman customs by a native. Malise, Earl of Strathearn in c 1244 x 1258, also included hunting pertinents in one of his grants,[79] as did the earl of Lennox in 1217[80] before Alexander III's charter of 1238[81] to Maldoven, son of the earl of Lennox, and before the forest grant of 1272.[82] Although the earls of Strathearn and Lennox may have included these pertinents in their grants in consequence of the receipt of a royal charter for their lands, such pertinents could also be an expression of native hunting customs in Norman charter terms.

A picture emerges of native landholders learning of and then copying the Normans' idea of a forest as a hunting reserve and of Normans adopting some native customs. Some Scots such as Morgrund may have established their own reserve and felt no need of a forest grant nor even called their reserve a forest. Some, such as Uchtred of Galloway, may have applied the title *foresta* to their reserves whether or not they had received a forest grant and some, such as Malcolm (1), Earl of Lennox, and possibly the earls of Strathearn, received a royal forest grant which would ensure the continuance and recognition of their reserves in a Norman context.

Traces of native practices are, therefore, found in twelfth- and thirteenth-century sources. Malcolm, Earl of Lennox, made his 'toschederach' the forester of his woods of Lennox.[83] The combination of these two offices suggests that the 'toschederach' before 1200 may have performed the duties of a forester. Moreover, Professor Dickinson considered that the 'toschederach' may have been responsible for strangers in his jurisdiction, thus occasioning his association with woods and reserves.[84] The common hunting of Blarkerroch mentioned in 1224 x 1240,[85] which probably lay within the forest of Strachan, may also be a survival of the native customs of the area, and the grant in 1200 by Gilbert, Earl of Strathearn, to Inchaffray of freedom to hawk and fish anywhere on his lands almost certainly is.[86]

Earlier customs not only survived in, but also influenced the hunting arrangements of, twelfth- and thirteenth-century Scotland. As has been suggested, the treatment of game as *res nullius* in Scotland before 1100 did exist, although on private land it was probably limited. Outside private land it was not, indeed could not be, limited. To this one may attribute firstly the fact that in Scotland the principle of *res nullius* is stated far more clearly than in England and more strongly than in Roman law,[87] and secondly that a Scots law, probably of Alexander III's reign, allowed outsiders to hunt from their own lands into another's forest[88] in a manner reminiscent of Welsh custom after the introduction of forests to Wales. Finally, the methods of hunting in medieval Scotland also show the influence of the native population, since the most popular method of hunting was the drive which had been current in Scotland before 1100, and not *par force*, the classic method of hunting in England and Europe. (See p. 60.)

Throughout the twelfth and thirteenth centuries Scottish magnates and the kings were constantly in touch with the English forest system as a result both of visits to England and their tenure of lands there. Although one charter of David's son Henry in 1139 x 1142 refers to his forests and huntings, 'fugatis', in Northumberland,[89] the acts of David, Malcolm and William contain no references to English forests. They do mention grants on their English lands of pannage and dead wood, a phrase not used in any extant charter relating to Scotland till 1208 x 1214.[90] Part of the royal forest of Northumberland[91] was included in Henry II's grant of the honour of Tynedale to William I in 1157,[92] the renewal of which grant in 1237[93] permitted Alexander to try certain cases but not, it would appear, forest cases although his bailies could supervise the activities of the English foresters. Since the time of William I this forest had been run by the Bellinghams who were hereditary foresters. Direct experience of English forests was probably received by Alexander III and certain Scots barons including Alan Durward, Alexander the Steward and John Comyn, who between 1251 and 1261 received permission to hunt in English royal forests.[94]

In view of the origins of the Scots forest system, of the continuing links of Scots kings and their barons with England, of their knowledge of the English forest system and of the postulated events concerning Geoffrey de Langley in 1252-1253, the differences between the Scots and English systems are remarkable. The Scots system was less harsh both in the comparative abundance of forest grants and in the administration of the royal forests. The severity of the English forest system, which lay mainly in the numerous extortions and abuses of the law perpetrated by English forest officials in the twelfth and thirteenth centuries,[95] can best be seen by comparing Scots and English forest laws, even although the difficulty in dating the Scots laws renders a year by year comparison impossible.[96] In the reign of David I pasture, except in time of pannage and time of fence, was probably free in royal forests, whereas in England at this time tenants had such freedom only within their own woods within the forest. By the end of William I's reign the Scots law was probably becoming less lenient but still not so severe as the English on the eve of Magna Carta: the fine for poaching in Scotland was £10, whereas in England the corresponding penalty of compensation and imprisonment for one year[97] was altered by Richard I to blinding and castration,[98] but offences against the vert were perhaps more severely punished in Scotland where a £10 fine applied while in England amercement of the offender's money and stock was the maximum penalty.[99] In Scotland pasture was probably forbidden without the forester's permission or the payment of pannage for pigs. The maximum fines, 8 cows, the death of a goat or the confiscation of all pigs and horses, were not exacted till the fourth offence. In England in the late twelfth century tenants could pasture animals in the woods which they held within royal forests, but elsewhere such pasture was forbidden.[100] An offender had to provide sure pledges on the first and second offence while the maximum penalty, forfeiture of the offender's person, imprisonment, was applied on the third offence. By the end of the thirteenth century the right of holders of forests and of free landholders living beside a forest to hunt in a neighbouring forest, which was a special privilege in England, was the subject of two Scots forest laws.[101] The lawing of dogs, removing a claw, common in England, was never enforced in Scotland — 'mutulatus' of the English version of law 21 became 'vinculatus' in Scotland — nor was the complete ban on bows, arrows and dogs.[102] Although English hunting penalties had been relaxed by the Charter of the Forest in 1217,[103] imprisonment for a year and a day or banishment was still harsher than a £10 fine. No change, however, had been made in English pasture restrictions, while the foggage levy in Scotland permitted the pasture of all animals. Restrictions on travel through forests appear at first to have been more lenient in England, but there the levy of 2d per half-year applied to tenants travelling to their own woods within the forest,[104] whereas in Scotland the fine of 30d applied to anyone in the forest without permission or off the correct route.

Throughout the twelfth and thirteenth centuries not only was Scots forest law more humane than the English but it also had a more pastoral flavour than the English law which provided a more complex specification of offences against the vert and a greater amount of administrative detail. These differences may be attributed to the pastoral nature of the Scots economy, the existence of agisters in England to regulate forest grazing, thus removing pasture regulations from the sphere of royal assises, and the frequent possession of private woods within English royal forests which necessitated careful control of wood-cutting.

While comparison with England illustrates the moderate nature of the Scots forest law, it is the advanced position of royal rights in twelfth-century Scotland which emerges from comparison with France. Since royal power in France had not, by the twelfth century, recovered from the collapse of the Frankish Empire, the rights of Louis VI (1108-1137) in respect of hunting reserves could not in practice be distinguished from those of the barons,[105] nor did the king have any control over the creation of baronial hunting reserves which were entitled warrens.[106] The improvement in the royal position which began with the appointment of a *maître des eaux et forêts*[107] and with the creation of royal parks[108] by Phillip Augustus (1180-1223) was continued by Louis IX (1235-1270), who was the first king not only to claim that the king's rights were superior to those of the barons[109] but also to attempt to control the hunting reserves of the barons.[110] Although in some parts of thirteenth-century France the idea of game as *res nullius* was accepted,[111] offenders in both royal and baronial reserves were punished even more severely than in England.[112] The Capetians' reserves, however, were of small extent by comparison with those of England and Scotland.

In Scotland, opposition to hunting reserves as witnessed in the disputes between the abbeys and the owners of reserves does not appear to have attained the intensity or bitterness which it reached in England and France, for complaints against the malpractice of the foresters who enforced royal and baronial rights, frequent in England and France,[113] were absent in Scotland, although this absence could be attributed to lax administration. One reason for the comparative leniency of the Scots forest system must lie in the influence, already examined, of native custom on the imported system. Not only was the idea of game as *res nullius* clearly stated in Scotland, but a neat compromise was worked out between the existence of both hunting reserves and the concept of game as *res nullius*.[114] It is also possible that medieval Scots kings, as a result of the traditions of their predecessors, felt more concern for the people than either English or French kings, resulting partly in a moderation of the Norman forest system.

3

Hunting Reserves in Scotland, 1286-1513

DESPITE the varying fortunes of the forest system between 1286 and 1424, it survived with its main features intact to be developed and expanded in the fifteenth century. In the troubled years from 1286 to 1306 not only were there periods when there was no Scots monarch to use the royal forests but the administration of the forests was subjected to military and political interests. The guardians of Scotland probably ran the forests with no outside interference till the first interregnum, when signs of English control of the royal forests appeared. In August 1291 Edward ordered grants of deer from the forests of Spey, i.e. Enzie, and Ettrick and timber from Clackmannan to be made to three of the guardians, James Steward, Robert Wishart, bishop of Glasgow, and William Fraser, bishop of St. Andrews, and to various nobles including Reginald le Chen, father and son, Patrick, Earl of Dunbar, William and John Soules, Patrick Graham, Alexander Balliol and Simon Fraser.[1] (See Table 2, p. 50.) In June and July 1292 a further series of grants of deer from Scots royal forests was made by Edward. Deer from Durris, Cowie, Buchan in the north-east, Spey and Selkirk were to be given to the bishop of St. Andrews and John Comyn who were guardians, to Alexander Comyn, Thomas Randolph and Master Adam de Botindon, vice-chancellor of Scotland.[2] (See Map 10, p. 364.) Edward, therefore, by 1292 exercised or claimed to exercise control over the Scots forests, a control which depended primarily on the appointment of suitable head foresters in each forest, that is, men who favoured Balliol or himself, as in Ettrick in 1292 where William Comyn was appointed for life (see Table 1, p. 49) to replace the late Simon Fraser.[3] The standing of the officers appointed suggests that the keepership of a Scottish forest was a valued post.[4] That Edward felt competent to use Scots royal forests as his own at this time argues that he was acting as king or guardian, whether or not he was accepted as such. Moreover the timing of Edward's grants to the barons to coincide with the sessions of the 'Great Cause' held at Berwick in August 1291 and at Norham in June 1292[5] suggests that Edward may have used such grants to win acceptance for his claims.

Little can be said about Balliol's dealings with the forest system since the only surviving evidence is two free warren grants in the thirteenth-century form which he made in 1294 and 1295. That no free forest grant survives from this reign may reflect English influence, since there was no such grant in England, but there are not sufficient acts of John extant to be sure of this.

In September 1296, following Balliol's resignation, Edward is once more granting deer from the royal forests, on this occasion to James Steward and John of Stirling.[6] These and other grants allowed the grantee to hunt for a certain number of deer in the forest specified or in the nearest forest and instructed the keeper to let the grantee have the stated number of deer. The success of such grants in maintaining support may be witnessed in their continued use by Edward till 1306, although after 1300 they concerned timber more frequently than deer.[7]

During the second interregnum, when Edward had more control over Scots forests than had the representatives of the Scots government, the forests of Ettrick and Jedburgh were administered by pro-English officials. From 1299, when Edward I replaced Simon Fraser who was the son of a previous keeper and who had switched to the Scots side,[8] till 1306, when the last pro-English forester, Aymer de Valence, held both the forest and sheriffdom of Selkirk[9] the English were in control of Ettrick forest. They also appear to have appointed subordinate foresters, or currours as they were called in the fifteenth century, for along with John Moffat and Roger Aylmer a certain Walter le Corour is mentioned in connection with the three wards of Ettrick in 1304 x 1305.[10] Both the officials and the inhabitants of Ettrick were described as foresters although there is no evidence that the inhabitants performed any forest duties as they did in the fifteenth century.[11]

In accordance with previous custom the offices of sheriff and forester of Selkirk might be held by one man as by Aymer de Valence or they might be separated.[12] The sheriff of Roxburgh sometimes had an interest in part of Ettrick forest, as in 1302.[13] Edward I, therefore, infiltrated the forest adminis- tration with his own nominees and did not attempt any radical re-organisation of that administration.

The English did not, however, have complete control of Ettrick since it was used as a centre of resistance and they had to conduct expeditions there in 1298.[14] In 1299, at a meeting in the forest, the guardians appointed Robert Keith as a rival keeper of the forest with instructions to raid along the English border.[15] As a result, the keeper of Ettrick forest always had a small force of soldiers with which to guard the forest[16] and fulfil other military duties. Although some of the tenants or foresters did fight for the English in 1301,[17] not till 1304 x 1305 is there evidence that Edward was able to exploit the forest financially or that the keeper was able to consider anything other than defence and offence. An extent of 1304 x 1305 in which the forest was valued at £49[18] must have anticipated revenue collection, and in 1306 Aymer de Valence, who had to pay £130 *per annum* to Edward for his knight's fee of the castle of Selkirk, the manors and demesne lands of Selkirk and Traquair and the burgh and mills of Peebles,[19] was entitled to disafforest or impark the forest as he pleased and could lease it to tenants.

Other forests, such as Durris, Cowie and Aberdeen in 1292[20] and Buchan in 1304,[21] also had pro-English keepers while some, such as Darnaway and

Langmorn, also had subordinate foresters.[22] Perhaps the most interesting appointment was that of Robert Bruce to Darnaway and Langmorn by 1304 x 1305[23] and to Kintore by 1305[24] before he definitely committed himself to the assumption of the Scottish crown. In Jedburgh from 1296 to 1306[25] the English had keepers including perhaps the abbot of Jedburgh and Sir Ivo de Aideburgh.[26] Like Ettrick, Jedburgh was occupied by 'foresters'[27] but there is no record of any revenue being collected from the forest. The administration of these forests as of other lands was in the overall control of the chancellor or chamberlain of Scotland as well as Edward himself.[28] The most important royal forests not mentioned in the English records are Stirling, Clunie and Pentland.

The number of grants of deer and timber certainly suggests that the English control of the forests was fairly firm, but in some cases there was obvious difficulty in delivering the goods: in 1304 x 1305 the foresters of Darnaway and Langmorn would not, without the order of Robert Bruce, the keeper, give Rauf de Chen the timber which Edward had granted to him, and accordingly a writ was sent to Bruce;[29] there were also signs of trouble in 1298 when the constable of Jedburgh may have challenged the abbot of Jedburgh and Sir Ivo de Aldeburgh for the keepership of Jedburgh forest.[30]

The extent to which English methods were introduced into the Scottish system must have depended largely on whether or not the keeper of the forest held most of his lands in, or had been mainly brought up in, England or Scotland. It is unlikely that Robert Bruce or John Comyn would have introduced any peculiarly English practices into the forests which they controlled. On the other hand, Thomas de Burnham, Aymer de Valence and Sir Hugh de Audeley may well have done so. In effect the administration of Ettrick was little changed, and what was true of Ettrick was probably true of the whole of Scotland. It was the personnel and not the offices or the method of administration which changed. The main English innovation may well have been Edward's grants of specific numbers of deer and timber to certain individuals. Previously, Scottish kings had made such grants to religious houses in a much more general way as freedom to take wood. Specific grants had been peculiar to England[31] and were the subject of one of the six laws copied into the Scots forest law from the English law[32] which allowed any earl, bishop or baron freedom to take one or two beasts when passing through a forest whilst obeying a royal command. It seems likely, therefore, that this law was introduced to Scotland during Edward's reign along with the five laws from the Customs and Assise of the Forest as part of Edward's settlement of Scotland.

To a lesser extent baronial reserves also came under Edward's rule. In 1305 Edward granted warren rights to Sweetheart and Dundrennan Abbeys and confirmed Alexander III's free forest and warren grant to Coldingham in response to their petitions.[33] The administration of some baronial forests must have suffered in this period, but in 1294 James Steward was untroubled in his administration of Renfrew forest in which he had created a special reserve.[34]

During this period forests and parks were of considerable strategic importance since forests such as Ettrick with its game, wood and hilly country were ideal areas in which to organise military resistance. In parks not only was there game for food and wood for weapons and wagons, but the park pale formed an excellent rampart to protect a camp. Duns park[35] and Stanhope park in Weardale[36] were used to shelter Scottish armies, but the best-known example of a park and its pale being used in this manner is the New Park of Stirling before and during the battle of Bannockburn.[37] Throughout the fourteenth and fifteenth centuries a wild and unruly image continued to adhere to several forests such as Birse, which in the late fourteenth century was a resort for thieves and caterans,[38] while the records of the justice ayres in the late fifteenth century show that Ettrick forest had more than its fair share of outlaws, rebels and thieves.[39]

Forests were once again administered primarily as hunting reserves during the reign of Robert I who, especially in the latter years of his reign, took an interest in hunting and hawking. Robert had parks at Cardross and Tarbert, housed his hawks at Cardross[40] and kept his own falconers,[41] and his charters suggest that on 5 and 6 August 1326 he was hunting in Strathardle, Clunie and Alyth.[42] In 1329 he may have hunted at Gairloch.[43] No doubt he now hunted for pleasure, whereas in the past he had so often been forced to hunt from necessity.

Most of these forests which had been in royal hands before 1286 returned to the crown, although the forests in the south of Scotland were not recovered till well after 1314. In addition to the well-known Act of Disinheritance[44] Robert appears to have made a revocation, the exact terms of which are unknown, at Cambuskenneth some time after Bannockburn. If it concerned grants of lands by the king before Bannockburn,[45] it could not have been rigorously enforced, for the earldom of Moray which Randolph had first received c 1312[46] was confirmed to him in 1324 and included the forests of Lenoch, Langmorn, Darnaway, Drumine and whatever else was left of the royal forest around Elgin, Forres and Inverness. Robert granted out the lands of, but not the control of hunting in, other forests, the most important being Ettrick to Douglas, and Kintore and the New Forest of Buchan to Robert Keith. (See Table 8, p. 119.) In addition he pursued a policy of reducing several of his forests in size by granting out most of the forest, usually in free forest, and retaining only an enclosed park or reserved area as in Drum, Cowie, Boyne and Enzie, Kintore and Stocket.[47]

Under Robert the free forest grant was not only used generously but was subject to certain developments with which the chancellor, Bernard de Linton, may reasonably be associated. The grant became more flexible since it might vary from charter to charter by the inclusion or omission of forest pertinents and of the sanction clause. By contrast, all Robert's free warren grants included the sanction clause. The free forest grant and the free warren grant could be combined with the free barony grant which first appeared in Robert's reign, while at a later date the free forest grant was combined with the regality grant, although the regality grant on its own must have given the grantee forest rights if not the royal protection for his monopoly. Robert was generous to his barons with royal forests, and by the end of his reign the main royal forests must have been Clackmannan, Stirling, Plater and Alyth. The reduction in size of the royal forest during this reign can be attributed to the necessity of rewarding supporters and to economic pressure on the royal forests especially for pasture.

Probably the most significant development of this reign was the possible separation of all the lands of a forest from the forest rights. Robert on several occasions granted out the lands of the forest but retained the forest rights, a practice which led to the situation where the holder of the lands of the forest came to regard the forest as his own even though he did not hold forest rights. Previously when the king or a baron made a grant to the church of lands without hunting rights in a forest only part of the forest's lands had been alienated and never the whole forest. Robert also employed the inefficient practice of granting the keeper of the forest the lands or the use of the lands of the forest of which he was the keeper, as in Ettrick, Kilgarie and Stocket.[48] Beside this must be set the probable establishment of justiciars of the forest, a development of thirteenth-century practice whereby ordinary justiciars may have handled forest matters. Forest justiciars who travelled on two ayres north and south of the Forth may have been introduced by Robert.

Both by reducing the size of his forests and by using forest justiciars, Robert was probably able to administer fairly efficiently those forests which he still held.

The history of the royal forests in David II's reign was dominated till 1357 by the king's absences from Scotland, the penetration of the English and the government of guardians, and thereafter by a policy towards royal lands, often neglected, which strove to enable the king to live of his own.

During David's absence in France till 1341 the forests were presumably administered by a succession of guardians or governors, although from 1332 the forests in southern Scotland were in English hands. English keepers were appointed in 1334 to Jedburgh and Ettrick forests which Edward Balliol had ceded to Edward III,[49] who placed them under the chamberlain and chancellor appointed for Scotland.[50] During this occupation, the English attempted to collect more revenue from the forests which they held and from their inhabitants than had Edward I. Herbage was collected from Pentland in 1335, although by 1337 nothing could be collected from the area because of the ravages of war.[51] In 1335 William de Montague held the forest and sheriffdom of Selkirk for a ferme of £30[52] and in 1356 Henry Percy held the town and forest of Jedburgh valued at 50 merks.[53] Whatever revenues were collected from these forests were accounted for in 1349 x 1350 by the chamberlain of Berwick.[54] Ettrick forest, which was still associated with the sheriffdoms of

Roxburgh and Selkirk,[55] could have been maintained as a game reserve during the occupation, since Montague was granted the right to try all offences there except the four pleas of the Scottish crown.

The English control of the forests during this period was neither continuous nor secure, especially in the 1340s when David returned to Scotland. For example, since 1324 the Douglases could claim to be the keepers of Ettrick and the owners of Jedburgh forest[56] and in the early 1340s David II granted timber from the forests of Ettrick and Jedburgh to Kelso Abbey and deer from Ettrick to Coldingham.[57] The Percies and the Douglases, however, continued to dispute the possession of Selkirk and Jedburgh forests throughout the fourteenth century till 1374 when commissioners were appointed by Edward III to deal with their dispute over Jedburgh forest.[58] Nevertheless, in 1402, Henry IV granted Henry Percy lands in Scotland including the lordship and forest of Selkirk.[59] Although the English did maintain a foothold in the south of Scotland at Roxburgh Castle till 1460, the evidence shows that despite the Percies' claims it was the Douglases who controlled these forests.[60]

From the English occupation only one warren grant has survived, namely Edward's grant to Sir John de Molynes in Ayrshire, which in accordance with English practice granted him permission to enclose a park.[61] David, during his brief return to Scotland between 1341 and 1346, confirmed the alienation of the lands of certain forests which had first been granted out by Robert I and appointed keepers of several forests including Alyth and Glenken. (See Table 9, p. 153.) The forest system was probably unaffected by his presence since at this time he did not try to recover the forests lost by Robert I, and only one free warren grant and no free forest grants survive from this period.

From 1346 to 1357, while David was in England, the government of Scotland largely rested in the hands of Robert the Steward who was a keen hunter. Like David, he does not appear to have tried to recover any of the crown's lands. It was during this governorship that Scotland was hit by the Black Death: the continued economic exploitation of forests in the later fourteenth century suggests that its effects in some areas were less harmful to the economy than was once supposed. (See p. 257.)

Not till David's return from England in 1357 can the history of the royal forests in Scotland be held to reflect the actions and intentions of this king. David had probably learnt more about hunting in France and England than in Scotland and there is evidence of his hawking in England.[62] He also hawked in Scotland after 1357, three of his falconers from this time being recorded.[63] His charters show that he visited places in Scotland, such as Kildrummy and Drummelzier, where he could have hunted.[64]

David in 1357 was faced with the council's strong advocacy of the policy that the king should live of his own. Yet despite the council's enactment of a revocation at Scone,[65] despite the renewal of the coronation oath whereby David would not alienate his demesne possessions without sound advice[66] and despite the enquiry into royal rents, David as far as hunting reserves were concerned revoked only Clackmannan park[67] and the forest of Drum,[68] exempting that forest in the following year.[69] Moreover the sheriffs' accounts of 1359 which list numerous royal reserves for which there should have been a return but which were in fact in someone else's hands[70] show that no action was taken on the revocation.[71] Kincardine park, Boyne and Enzie, 'Galchill' park, Torwood, Cowie and Clackmannan were thus exempted. Similarly Glasgoforest in the thanedom of Kintore which should have been resumed was not.

Nor, where hunting reserves were concerned, did David pay too much attention to his renewed coronation oath. In 1363, he granted various lands to Sir Robert Erskine including the park of Clackmannan, the herbage of the forest, and the new park at Stirling in exchange for the old park at Stirling and Strathgartney which included Glenfinglas.[72] In 1362 the park of 'Dursclune' and the west park of Kincardine,[73] and in 1366 the New Forest of Glenken[74] were alienated.

The history of the royal forests illustrates the ineffectiveness of the 1357 revocation as well as the slightly more effective 1367 revocation, which hoped to restore to the crown all lands which had belonged to Alexander III and Robert I.[75] The hunting reserves concerned in 1367 included the park and forest of Clackmannan, the park of Drum, the west park of Kincardine, the park of 'Dursclune', the main park of Kincardine and possibly the forests of Cowie, Durris and Glasgoforest.[76] Unfortunately no record of the council in February 1367/8, which was to take the decisions on these revocations,[77] has survived. In July 1368, however, David restored the park of Clackmannan and the herbage of the forest to Erskine,[78] and Drum park was restored to the Moignes before 1388.[79] Although the list of lands to be revoked was large, there were omissions including the forests of Boyne and Enzie, Glenken, Torwood and Kintore.

In the last years of his reign David continued to alienate royal lands and forests,[80] although he must have benefited from the return of the earldom of Moray to the crown in 1369.

Although the administration of the royal forests may well have been hampered by the fact that keepers held rights in the forest, some effort was made to reserve the venison, for there was a fourteenth-century writ, perhaps later than the reign of Robert I, which ordered the local royal officer to hold an inquest into offences against the venison in the forest.[81] When possible David may have tried to prevent his officers becoming local magnates. For example, instead of appointing to the keepership of Darnaway the Grants who had held the office under the earls of Moray,[82] he chose Richard Comyn, thus breaking the Grants' hold on the office.[83]

Although Boyne and Enzie, Torwood and Clackmannan were still in name royal forests, the lands of these forests were in the hands of others. Thus by the end of this reign the main royal forests must have been Darnaway, Plater, Clunie, once again in royal hands, and perhaps Glenfinglas. The alienations of

Robert's reign were now unchallengeable. If David failed to resume royal forests in accord with the revocations, it is conceivable that he may not have felt the need to do so simply because he had been able to increase the financial resources of the crown, more than adequately, by other means.[84]

Robert II, on his accession to the throne, although fifty-four, was a keen hunter, as the chronicler of Pluscarden recorded.[85] The place dates of his charters show that he regularly visited areas where he was probably involved in hunting, including Loch Freuchie, Glenfinglas,[86] Methven, where he kept his greyhounds in 1384, Old Wark in Ettrick, Kincardine, Logierait, and his favourite hunting area, Kindrochit to which, between 1379 and 1385, he made annual visits. Robert's summer hunting trips were interrupted neither by invasions of the English nor by the governing of the country and in 1377 and 1384 he found time to visit both Glenfinglas and Kindrochit.[87] John Barclay, one of Robert's falconers, is also recorded.[88] Robert's constant trips to remote parts of the country in pursuit of this pastime must have rendered the government more dependent than usual on messengers, for his chancery, as his charters show, travelled with him to his various hunting seats.

It is notable that Robert hunted in areas where there is no record, at this date, of royal forests. Glenfinglas was first called a forest in the mid-fifteenth century. Loch Freuchie was part of Strathbraan, which was a forest in the earldom of Fife, and there is no reference to a forest in Mar at Kindrochit at any time. These areas may have been turned into hunting reserves or Robert may simply have been exercising his right to hunt anywhere in the absence of a royal reserve.

As far as known forests are concerned, Robert regranted the earldom of Moray to John Dunbar in 1372 but retained Lochaber, Badenoch and Urquhart, the last of which in the fifteenth century included the forest of Cluanie. In 1389, the countess of Fife resigned to the crown her earldom which contained not only Fife and Strathbraan but also Disher and Toyer which at a later date included the forests of Mamlorne and Ben More. Robert granted the earldom to his third son and so, while not in royal hands, it was obviously available for royal hunting.

Robert's extant free forest grants are unremarkable. What is of interest is that neither he nor any subsequent monarch appears to have granted free warren rights separately from free forest rights. The last surviving separate free warren grant is that of David II in 1367. The significance of this is twofold. Firstly the rabbit warrens or cunningars which were becoming increasingly common probably gave people sufficient control over lesser game. Secondly, the king's right to warren over the whole country to which he was entitled by his monopoly of the free warren grant contrasted sharply with the position that lesser game could be hunted freely outside reserves.[89] In practice the king had never enforced this theoretical right to reserve all lesser game to himself and the demise of the warren grant would have removed the above conflict.

Robert continued to use forest justiciars, but instead of giving them a large ayre over the whole country he appears to have appointed them to just one or two forests, such as Clunie and Alyth or Torwood and Clackmannan, presumably because there were fewer royal forests to cover. This probably placed less strain on the justiciars but must have encouraged the development of local ties to the detriment of justice, as would his reinstatement of the Grants as foresters of Darnaway before that forest left royal hands.[90] Robert did, however, prevent any deterioration of the forest of Plater as a result of economic activity and, like his predecessors, appointed foresters in Plater and Clackmannan, allowing them to hold the lands or the right to use the lands of the forest.[91] In 1386/7 his grant of Clackmannan in free forest to Thomas Erskine while William Menteith was still the royal forester shows that there was some confusion over the status of Clackmannan forest.[92]

At the end of Robert's reign Plater and Torwood were still royal forests in name. Clunie and Alyth were in royal hands but had seldom been used by Robert. Methven park had been granted to a son and his most frequented hunting areas, Mar, Strathgartney and Strathbraan, were probably not royal forests.

Robert III, who was in his early fifties when he succeeded to the throne, was probably not so keen a hunter as his father, though he may well have hunted while at Dundonald in 1391, Logierait in 1390 and 1405[93] and Strathyre in 1398.[94] His father's passion for the hunt had no doubt enabled him to learn about hunting and hunting methods.

There were no significant changes in royal lands and forests during Robert's reign and little can be said of his administration of the forest. In 1398, William More, the forester of Torwood, granted his office to David Fleming and Robert approved the grant.[95] Robert made two free forest and warren grants, one of which to Alexander Cockburn in 1392 contained a unique version of the sanction clause which was becoming increasingly rare and of which this is the last surviving example.[96] His other grant in 1395 was made to William Inglis for killing an Englishman in a duel.[97]

It is an example of the fortuitousness of the survival of evidence that the first extant act of parliament relating to hunting matters dates from this reign. In 1401, parliament at Scone enacted that no one should hunt hares when there was snow on the ground.[98]

During the minority of James I the royal forests and the government of the country were in the hands of the governors, Robert and then Murdoch, Dukes of Albany. The evidence, as one would expect, suggests that they did not pay much attention to the royal lands, although Robert did confirm that the Menteiths were still the keepers of Clackmannan with certain other lands in free forest.[99] It is significant not only that Robert was the only governor as far as one can tell from the surviving evidence to make a free forest grant, but also that one of only two extant baronial free forest grants which was made by Henry Sinclair, earl of Orkney, and confirmed by Robert in 1410[100] should date to this time. Apart from the other such grant of 1279 only the king

D

granted lands in free forest, thus implying that he had forest rights over the whole country. By allowing a baron to make such a grant, this theory, never enforced over the whole country but on which the formation and existence of royal forests depended, was threatened. One wonders, therefore, if in the absence of the king, any attempt whatsoever was made to preserve game in royal forests.

There was a staggering reduction in the size of the royal forest in the fourteenth century despite the efforts of David II's reign to reverse the trend. By the early fifteenth century, even the existence of royal forest rights was threatened. More promisingly, during the fourteenth century the early forest laws dating from the twelfth and thirteenth centuries were copied into legal treatises along with certain English forest laws and additional non-forest material. The forest law, if not well enforced, was not forgotten. The earliest extant copy of the forest laws dates from the mid-fourteenth century and the second from the late fourteenth century,[101] while the fifteenth century, as a result of a growing interest in formulating a definite body of Scots laws, had many more copies of the forest laws, to judge by the number of copies which have survived.

In England also the royal forest system suffered in the fourteenth century. The severity of English forest law was modified both by Edward I and by Edward III.[102] In France, on the other hand, where the crown was still establishing its hunting rights[103] and its right to control the creation of hunting reserves, it was established in the first half of the fourteenth century that the existence of a warren which applied to all animals in France was only justifiable by long possession.[104] In one respect, the constant efforts to prevent poaching on royal reserves,[105] the forests in France and England were better administered than those in Scotland.

When comparing these three countries, it is interesting to consider the attempts which were made to define those who had the right to hunt. In France, Charles IV (1322-1328) enacted that everyone, including non-nobles, could hunt everywhere outside warrens for hares and rabbits.[106] This principle lasted throughout the fourteenth century, but in 1396 Charles VI enacted that no non-noble could hunt or try to capture greater or lesser game unless he had been granted permission to do so, with the exception of clerics with the right to hunt by inheritance and of burghers living off their possessions and rents.[107] When an attempt to return to Charles IV's principle in 1414 was defeated by the nobles, hunting had become a nobles' pastime. In England similar developments occurred. Throughout the earlier Middle Ages hunting in England had probably been free outside forests and warrens, though this is disputed.[108] In 1390, however, Richard II issued a statute which ordered that no one who did not possess landed property worth 40s per year nor any clerk with an annual income of less than £10 could keep hunting dogs or use ferrets or snares to catch deer, hares or rabbits since that was gentlemen's game.[109] In both England and France, therefore, by the end of the fourteenth century, hunting was restricted to the nobility or those with a certain income.

In Scotland the principle of free hunting or the right of everyone to hunt for lesser game was not rejected till 1621.[110] The barons were probably gradually acquiring the right to keep other hunters off their lands, but as a matter of practice and not of law. That the right to hunt was not restricted only to landowners[111] can be attributed to various factors. Firstly, as in France but not in England, the theoretical position probably was that only lesser game could be hunted freely. Such a right was likely to withstand baronial pressure more successfully than a free right to hunt greater game. Secondly, the barons probably had what hunting rights they wished as a result of the free forest grant, which existed in neither France nor in England, and as a result of the alienation of the royal forests. Thirdly, there was no central authority capable of enforcing such a restriction in Scotland, and the barons in the late fourteenth century were probably able to take what rights they wished. Finally, in Scotland the right of free hunting for lesser game in a feudal context had been established more certainly than in England and earlier than in France, with the result that it was more deeply rooted and more durable in medieval Scottish society. As with the treatment of game as *res nullius* in medieval Scotland, it is possible to ascribe the early and certain declaration of the right of everyone to hunt lesser game to the influence of native hunting customs.[112]

James I, like David II, must have learnt much about hunting while a prisoner in England hawking and hunting with the English king and nobility. In England 'par force' hunting, described at this time by Edward, Duke of York in his hunting treatise, 'The Master of Game', was the method favoured by the court[113] and James may have continued to use this method on his return to Scotland, although the drive was the more common method of hunting in Scotland. James' itinerary does not obviously reveal any favoured hunting areas and it is difficult to say whether or not hunting was the main purpose for his visiting any of the places on his known itinerary[114] such as Darnaway and Auchterhouse near the Sidlaw Hills.

James started to build up the crown lands and consequently the royal forest as a result of forfeitures and escheats of lands such as the earldoms of Fife, Menteith, Strathearn, Lennox, March and Mar. These earldoms included areas which, if not already hunting reserves, became such later in the fifteenth century: that part of the earldom of Menteith retained by the crown lay next to Strathgartney and Glenfinglas and included Doune park; in Fife, there was Falkland forest (see Table 29, p. 352) and in Strathearn Glen Artney, Glen Shee, Glen Almond, Corriemuckloch and Glen Shervie, all of which were forests later in the fifteenth century; there had been a free forest in Lennox but it was not revived by the crown; the forest of Dye and Handaxwood lay in the lands of March; and Kildrummy with its forest was part of the earldom of Mar. James by contrast with his predecessors made no grants of the lands of forests and although few acts have survived from his reign it seems clear that he was very sparing with free forest grants. The one act of revocation passed in his reign applied in the forest context to only one grant made by the governor.[115]

James reorganised the administration of the crown lands by exonerating the sheriffs of many of their duties and dividing his lands into groups, each of which was placed under a *ballivus ad extra.* Although James may have appointed commissioners for crown lands who had authority to hold courts, discipline officials and let royal lands,[116] he still appointed foresters. When, in 1430, he appointed John of Airth forester of Alyth and constable of Clunie Castle[117] the lands which accompanied these offices were in Carrick not in Clunie. James did not grant rights in forests nor the lands of forests in an effort no doubt to avoid the alienation of the forest which might result as well as to maintain the extent of royal lands.

James was also concerned with his rights outside forests and in 1424/5 an act was passed, although it was most likely never obeyed, which may still have been aimed at enforcing his right to control all greater game outside as well as inside his reserves.[118]

James tried to profit not only from royal but also from baronial forests. For instance, he persuaded Archibald, Earl of Douglas, to allow him to keep sheep in Ettrick forest which the Douglases held in free warren and free regality and had probably divided into 'stedes' and wards with currours and a master currour in each ward.[119] Possibly no free forest grant of Ettrick was ever made to the Douglases and so, in theory, the king could still claim forest rights there. While James may have had neither the time nor the inclination to create new forests, he had greatly enlarged the number of potential hunting reserves in crown hands and had also reversed the trend of alienation of royal lands by grants. These actions and the act of 1424/5 ensured that the royal forest rights did not fall into disuse.

James II was able to realise the potential for hunting reserves created by his father. If Pitscottie's story that chancellor Crichton in 1439 seized the king while on his way to hunt in Stirling park is true — and it seems to be — then James, at the age of nine, was already being taught or had learned how to hunt.[120] James grew up to be a keen huntsman and after his assumption of power was frequently at Falkland[121] and Menteith,[122] at both of which places he kept dogs,[123] and in Menteith he also kept a stalker. He also hunted in Ettrick after 1455[123] and in 1460 had planned to hunt in Kildrummy and the north.[125] He had a hunting lodge at 'Down' in Glen Artney[126] and the lodges at Glenfinglas, Loch Freuchie and Newark were built or rather rebuilt by him.[127] It was probably not till after 1455 that he had time to pay much attention to the royal forests, although certain forests were acquired before that date.

During the period of Crichton's and Livingston's dominance the forfeiture of the earldom of Atholl and the lordship of Brechin in 1437 brought the forest of Corscarie to the crown,[128] while the forest of Dalton including Cocklawpark, Pyhill and Woodcockair was escheated in 1440 as part of Annandale. The earldom of Mar, which included several forests, returned to royal hands and the accounts of Mar start to appear in the exchequer rolls in 1449 x 1450.[129] Although James' dower grant to Queen Mary in 1449 included many royal forests with the pertinents, hawkings, huntings and fishings, the administration of most of these lands remained with the king.[130] Those forests alienated by James had mostly, in accordance with the act of 1445,[131] been acquired since James I's death: in 1451 he confirmed that the forest of Glengarry in Atholl was held by Robert Duncanson;[132] in 1452 he granted out lands in the forest of Dalton;[133] and in 1451 x 1453 the fermes of the forest of Dye were held by Patrick Cockburn.[134] The major additions to royal forests were made after the Douglas forfeiture of 1455. As a result, Ettrick forest, forests in the earldom of Moray, Ormond forest and possibly Kintore forest all came into royal hands. Of these, Ettrick and Ormond were annexed to the crown by act of parliament. Such lands could only be alienated with the consent of parliament and any other alienations were to be summarily resumed by the king without process of law. The earldoms of Fife and Strathearn which also included forests and hunting areas, were also annexed.[135] James' subsequent grants of forests in royal hands which included the fermes of Clunie[136] in 1459, the earldoms of Mar and Atholl, show that where forests were concerned he abided by the act of annexation. Thus, in a remarkable thirty years between 1425 and 1455, the damage of the fourteenth century to royal lands and forests had been repaired.

In the 1450s, especially after 1455, James had time to turn his attention to the forests in his hands, to create new reserves and to expand existing ones, by declaring lands waste for forest: he extended the forest of Glenfinglas in 1453 x 1454 (see Tables 5 and 6, pp. 113, 117); in the same year he created either a forest or a park at Cockburnspath; in 1455 and 1456 James probably created rather than extended the forest of Duchinloch;[137] and in 1456 x 1457 he restored the forest of Mamlorne to its original state since part of it had been let out and he probably extended the forest of Knock and Lochindorb. At roughly the same time he must have extended the forest of Strathdee.[138] As a keen huntsman James was obviously interested in the condition of his forests, making every effort to keep them waste and in some cases probably removing people who had encroached on a forest. Ettrick, Clunie and Dalton, however, he did not attempt to keep or make waste since fermes were collected from them. James, therefore, accepted that he could reserve some forests more adequately than others and adjusted his actions accordingly.

In the 1450s James II made four free forest grants, one of which was combined with a regality grant and none of which included a sanction clause. This clause had not been used since 1392, probably because the king seldom received his £10 forfeiture for an offence in a free forest and because barons tried their own forest cases in their own courts.[139]

James' forests were administered by his *ballivi* and commissioners of crown lands but in Ettrick forest, which was placed under a bailie whose sole responsibility was the forest, the administrative system of the Douglases which was based on that of the late twelfth and early thirteenth century was continued.[140] James appointed sub-foresters or men of lesser importance to keep some of his forests, thus removing the risk of his officials coming to regard themselves as the owners of their jurisdiction. For example, Mamlorne was kept by Patrick McGilcallum[141] and the foresters of Strathdee and Corriemuckloch received only 13s 4d per year as their fee.[142]

James' parliament in 1457/8 passed acts repeating Robert III's act on hares and James I's close season for certain wild fowl,[143] encouraging the killing of fowls of 'reif' and of wolves[144] and trying to protect rabbit warrens from thieves.[145]

Unlike James I, James II had the time and the inclination to turn his attention to the royal forest and to hunting matters. His reign is as important as that of James I since, if he had not been able to overthrow the Livingstons and the Douglases, the pattern of the fourteenth century might have been repeated.

Since there is more information available for James III's reign than for his predecessors', James might appear to have been as keen a hunter as Robert III or James II, but allowing for this extra information, it is most likely that he enjoyed hunting but was not an addict of the sport. James' mother, who hunted,[146] no doubt imparted both to James and his brother, who was to receive Mar and Garioch in free forest, considerable interest in the sport. Hunting trips would appear to have been more than usually exciting for young kings: James III like his father was abducted while with a hunting party in 1466.[147] Balquhidder and Glenfinglas were favourite hunting areas of James between the ages of thirteen and sixteen.[148] In 1467 he made the Port of Menteith a burgh of barony to improve the supply situation during the hunting seasons. He hunted in Mamlorne in 1467,[149] in Strathearn in 1466 x 1469[150] and in Duchray in Menteith where he had hunting lodges in 1467 x 1468.[151] After 1469 there are fewer references to James' hunting but he continued to keep dogs and falcons,[152] and his repairs to Newark in 1472 x 1473 and in 1488 suggest that he may have hunted there.[153]

During James' minority there was an attempt by the exchequer to relet the lands whose rents had been lost when James II had declared them waste for forest. The exchequer, which was always sensitive about lands which on account of their being waste paid no rent since anyone might plead waste in order to be excused from paying his rent,[154] was probably opposed to James II's positive creation of waste for his forests. In 1460 x 1461 the *ballivi* appear to have been ordered by the exchequer to relet Mamlorne,[155] Glenfinglas,[156] Duchinloch[157] and probably then or subsequently Strathdee.[158] After this attempt to relet part of these royal forests there was a considerable degree of confusion as some areas were relet and others were declared waste. This confusion can be most clearly seen in Glenfinglas, Mamlorne and Darnaway, where one finds the king, the queen mother or the lords of council trying to maintain the reserves against the inroads of the exchequer and certain officials of royal lands. Since lords of council were often auditors of the exchequer, there may well have been a difference of opinion among the lords on this matter in the 1460s.[159] In Glenfinglas, although the queen mother had declared the lands of the forest waste, some of these lands were let in 1461 x 1462, 1463 x 1464 and 1464 x 1465.[160] In 1467 x 1468 the king and lords of council declared that some but not all of the lands let were once again waste for forest.[161] The king also declared waste lands in Mamlorne forest which had been let by the bailie in 1466 x 1467.[162] The lords of council had acted earlier in Darnaway in 1464 x 1465 by closing off the forest although in 1476 the lands of the forest were recorded as unlet.[163] By 1470 the situation had settled down, for the lands waste in Glenfinglas no longer varied,[164] and in 1470 x 1471 Ben More, if it had not been made waste for a forest by James II, was embodied in a royal forest.[165] The mention of unlet lands in Corscarie in 1477 may be a late example of this process, to relet royal forests, which had failed.[166] This conflict over the fate of royal reserves illustrates the view that the king should make greater financial exploitation of his reserves by leasing them rather than leaving them waste and as such was a new form of the struggle of hunting reserves to withstand economic pressure.

In this reign there were several changes in the composition of the royal forest despite several acts passed in James' reign to ensure that the royal patrimony was not seriously diminished.[167] James' free forest grant of Plater to Alexander Lyndesay in 1474 was unaffected by the revocation of 1476,[168] and Ormond and Corscarie which had been annexed, Rannoch which had come into royal hands with the forfeiture of Ross in 1475,[169] and Garvock all went to James' second son in 1481. Of those forests alienated by James III, Plater and Clunie[170] were the most important, since the alienation of Alyth which had left royal hands by 1463 cannot be definitely attributed to James III.[171]

The lands and forests included in James' dower grants to his queen in 1473 and 1478 resembled those which James II had included in his dower grants, although only the 1473 grant mentioned huntings, hawkings and fishings in the pertinents and as in the previous reign most of the dower lands were administered by the king.[172] James' free forest grants, which included forest pertinents for the first time since David II's reign, make it quite clear that barons had their own courts to hear forest offences.[173]

The administration of royal forests and lands set up by James I and James II was continued, but it becomes apparent that the commissioners of crown lands were largely composed of lords of council and lords of the articles, thus enabling parliament and the council to keep an eye on that administration.[174] Another interesting administrative development which occurred at the start of the reign was that the accounts of Ettrick were returned by individual wards and not jointly as they had been in the previous reign. The commissioners of crown lands along with justices on ayre could also try forest offenders.[175] James, nonetheless, continued to grant remission for offences against the vert and venison in Ettrick, despite the acts made against remission of fines in the 1480s.[176] This generosity may have paid off because in 1488 most of the tenants of that forest probably supported him.[177] He continued to allow foresters to have rights in, or to hold the lands of, a forest: the Foresters of Garden who were keepers of Torwood also held the lands of Torwood.[178] James also appointed foresters to Drumine, Strathearn and Glenfinglas.[179]

In 1474 parliament passed acts to protect hawks and hounds from theft and more importantly to stop the hunting of deer in a storm or when there was snow on the ground.[180] Parliament repeated the protection for rabbit warrens but also extended it to parks[181] and made the justice ayres responsible for applying these laws.

This evidence encourages the view that James III was not really interested in his hunting reserves unless their attention was forced on him as in his early years. Otherwise, he carried on with the administration of his predecessors, made free forests grants as before and did not try to develop his forests in any particular way or to improve the efficiency of his forest administration.

James IV's hunting activities emerge more fully than those of preceding kings as a result of the survival of the treasurer's accounts. From the summer of 1488 to the end of his reign James made at least twelve hunting trips to the Menteith-Strathearn-Balquhidder area.[182] He also made hawking expeditions and took his falcons on his frequent pilgrimages to Whithorn and to Tain.[183] James was quite obviously a keen hunter and Pedro de Ayala records that when he was not at war he was hunting in the Highlands.[184] During such trips to the Highlands the business of government did not cease and messengers were constantly riding to and from the king.[185] James' hawking establishment was well known outside Scotland, and in an age when a court might be judged by its facilities for hawking and hunting this was to his advantage. One hunting expedition to Balquhidder reveals both the nature of and the organisation required for these trips.[186] The tents for the expedition were prepared by the pavilion man or tent keeper and hounds were sent to Menteith. James left Stirling on 25 August 1506 and on the 26th was hunting in Strathearn, probably in Glen Artney. Dogs were brought to him by James Murray and while he waited for the drive a local woman brought him butter and cheese. On the 27th he moved into Balquhidder where he stayed with the vicar, and while hunting in Glenfinglas he may well have received a further gift of butter. By 29 August the royal party had moved into Strathfillan, where James received news from Lewis,[187] probably concerning the siege of Torquil Macleod which started in Stornoway at this time. He stayed there till the 31st and then proceeded to Auchinnis Chalain,[188] where his evening's entertainment included cards and a clarsach player. While he was there Argyll, the king's lieutenant in the west, sent the Macleans of Lochbuie and Duart to join the king. Maclean's clarsach player was at Auchinnis Chalain on 3 September and a dog collar and arrow heads were brought to replenish the king's equipment. James then stayed with the earl of Argyll, hawked, hunted with Argyll's stalker, who was sent to Falkland with two quarters of deer for the queen, and listened to his clarsach player. On 6 September, James received hounds from

Neil Stewart and the laird of Wemyss. Further replenishments of supplies including dog collars were required and they were obtained from Robert Moncreiff. By the 8th of the month the party was moving north again and the head dogger or kennelman, Jacob Edmonstone, was sent ahead with the dogs to Darnaway. On the 9th a halt was called at Ruthven in Badenoch and more hounds were received from John Grant and the earl of Sutherland. James then visited St Duthac's in Tain and by the 14th was back in Inverness where 'aqua vite' was obtained for him. He then moved on to Darnaway on the 17th, where he no doubt met Janet Kennedy and Edmonstone with his dogs. They may well have hunted in Darnaway forest. James moved on after five days or so and on his way south received further gifts of hounds, bought leashes and collars and on 28 September at Coupar Angus met the earl of Argyll's stalker once more. On the 29th James was again at Stirling. This trip, longer than usual, may have been extended on account of events in the west. During this trip, anyone who performed even the smallest service for the king received a small gift from him, and it is from the record of such gifts in the treasurer's accounts that this journey can be reconstructed.

James was fifteen when he was crowned and appears to have taken part in the government immediately. In October 1488 parliament's revocation of all grants made by James III since 2 February of that year[189] would have included both free forest charters of Kilgarie.[190] In consequence, perhaps, of parliament's wish that James should not squander the royal lands,[191] James' grants concerning forests were only of lands which had previously passed out of royal hands, such as Clackmannan, Enzie and Bothwell. He also sought parliament's consent to grant Bothwell in free barony with the woods in free forest to Patrick, Lord Hailes,[192] although before he was twenty-one, James did grant lands in the forest of Dye in free barony to the earl of Angus.[193]

Throughout his reign James made numerous free forest grants and granted out lands of forests. In view of the number of grants which have survived, James appears to have been fairly conservative when it came to the alienation of royal forests. In 1498 he let the forest of Abernethy on a nine-year lease,[194] and in 1500 Janet Kennedy received for the same term the forest of Buchan in Galloway[195] which had been let before and was not, therefore, a new alienation. Lochaber forest, which may have been in royal hands since the fourteenth century, was granted to Alexander, Lord Gordon. In 1501 James' grant of Darnaway in free forest and warren to his illegitimate son by Janet Kennedy, James Stewart,[196] was not to hinder Janet Kennedy's liferent of Darnaway Castle and forest which was to cease only if she married.[197] In 1505 x 1506, however, the forest was being administered by the king and by the end of his reign was back in royal hands, presumably because Janet was dead and her son was still a minor.[198] The forest of Birnam or Brenan in Strathbraan was let to the bishop of Dunkeld in 1499 for 40s, and following the act of parliament of 1503/4 which allowed James to feu both annexed and unannexed lands provided it led to no loss of revenue,[199] it was granted to him in feu ferme in 1507 for the same *reddendo*.²⁰⁰ James also started feuing Ettrick forest and in 1510 he feued the forests of Glen Shervie and Corriemuckloch.²⁰¹

When James let lands of forests he retained his superiority over as well as a return from these forests and did not greatly reduce the size of the royal forest. The most important grants as far as forests were concerned were those of Birnam and Darnaway. The Strathearn-Menteith-Balquhidder hunting area was intact and the forest of Glenfinglas had been expanded since in 1502 x 1503 lands described in 1499²⁰² as let beside the forest were laid waste for forest.²⁰³ James also used the Torwood for hunting and revived Stirling old park. When he tried to exercise his right over forests of which the lands only had been granted out he failed in Stocket in 1494²⁰⁴ but probably succeeded in Torwood,²⁰⁵ which in 1499 he claimed belonged to him by common law.

James' dower grant to his wife Margaret included several forests, but although the pertinents of the grant mentioned hawkings, huntings, fishings, forests, warrens, vert and venison, the administration of the forests stayed in the king's hands.²⁰⁶ The most important developments of the free forest grant to appear in this reign were the application of free forest rights only to woods and the mention of the forest laws in such grants.²⁰⁷ The former development illustrates the growing shortage of timber, as does the protection of wood outside forests. Since the beginning of the fifteenth century the justice ayres had been made responsible for punishing thefts or destruction of wood anywhere in the country with a fine which James had raised to £5.²⁰⁸ The free forest grant must, therefore, have been as important for the control over timber it conveyed as for the control of hunting.

James continued to administer his forests through *ballivi*, commissioners and foresters. In 1499 a list of the points of inquest for the commissioners' courts which probably applied to the whole country was written into the royal rental book and it shows quite clearly that the commissioners, who were still chosen from the council and 'the Articles', were responsible for keeping the forests 'forest like' and in some places waste.²⁰⁹ Changes in the administration of Ettrick included Lord Home's appointment in 1488 as the bailie of the forest, currour and master currour of Yarrow, and in 1499 the statutes of Ettrick issued in a commissioners' court in Edinburgh abolished the currours and substituted financial and judicial officials appointed by the comptroller.²¹⁰ Thereafter the accounts were returned complete for the forest by Lord Home and not for each ward.²¹¹ These statutes which tried to ensure that the tenants of the forest performed their duties as foresters to protect the deer and the timber also forbade ploughing and sowing. The bailie of Ettrick had to hold four courts per year to ensure good neighbourhood and to check on the military service due from each 'stede', which had to provide two bows, a spear and a horse with gear. One of the miscellaneous forest laws dating from the early fifteenth century or earlier²¹² which defined the weapons to be provided by various ranks of people explains the absence of arrows from the Ettrick provisions: the poorest category had to provide a bow and arrows or a bow and a spear if they lived in a forest. The tenant of a forest would, therefore, have no excuse to possess a bow and arrows with which to poach game and it may have been for this reason that an act of Robert I required that poorer men have either bow and arrows or a spear.[213] The requirements in Ettrick were altered when a 'stede' was granted in feu ferme: for every ten librates the tenant had to provide two horsemen, one with a lance and one with a pack horse,[214] a condition which applied to many of James' feu charters.

When James appointed a forester he usually conveyed the lands of or rights in the forest to the keeper, but when he appointed John Grant of Freuchy as forester of Cluanie in Inverness with the shiels of the forest, James specifically reserved his *proprietas* of the forest.[215] That James exhorted his foresters to perform their duties more efficiently is evidenced by a Privy Seal letter to Edmonstone, the forester of Glenfinglas, ordering him to fulfil his duties, to stop people entering the forest for any reason and to publicise a proclamation establishing a *purlieu*.[216]

In 1503/4 parliament placed parks and rabbit warrens on the same footing as forests with a £10 penalty for offences committed in them, and encouraged lords and lairds to create parks and warrens.[217] James, therefore, took an interest in his forests and tried to improve them either by altering the administration, as in Ettrick, or by sending orders to his officials. It is in accordance with this attitude that he may have tried to reserve all deer to himself.[218]

In the fifteenth century the development of hunting in Scotland and the rest of Europe was similar in that there were signs that hunting was becoming a spectacle as well as a sport. In Germany by 1500, where hunting had become a nobles' sport and the peasants could only hunt vermin,[219] the nobles organised large drives where the success of the hunt was judged by the number of animals killed and not by the effort or skill involved. In France also this attitude to hunting appeared in the sixteenth century.[220] In Scotland the position where the king no longer waited on his own on horseback for the drive but in a tent and with refreshments developed into the well-known sixteenth-century drives held by James V and Mary.[221]

The fifteenth century in Scotland also saw an improvement in the royal forest system with James I's expansion of the royal lands and James II's and James IV's development of the forests and their administration. In Ettrick and similar forests there was no real social inconvenience resulting from the forest administration, but in or near any of the forests which were well run and kept waste such as the Menteith-Strathearn-Balquhidder area in the early sixteenth century the effect of the reserve could be quite severe, especially since the acts of James IV increased the penalties.[222] This contrasts sharply with developments in England where, as a result first of the policy of the Lancastrian kings and then of the Wars of the Roses, the forest system became weaker than it had been in the fourteenth century.[223] In France, where the king was strengthening his hunting reserves and hunting rights, Louis XI tried to restrict the right to hunt game solely to himself.[224] His successor, Charles VIII, again allowed the nobles to hunt but the common people were still deprived of the right to hunt.[225] In the reign of Francis I, there were numerous complaints against the harshness of the hunting laws such as the ordinance of 1515 which forbade hunting in royal reserves without permission, banned hunting weapons in and around forests and defined the penalties which included death on the fourth offence.[226] The French laws in the early sixteenth century were as severe as the English in the twelfth century and more severe than the Scots before 1513, though one must remember that in Scotland in 1535 the death penalty was introduced for a third wood-cutting offence[227] and in 1551 for shooting deer, roe and other wild animals and wild fowl.[228] In James IV's reign, while there were signs of growing severity, the laws were not so harsh as in France and commoners still had the right to hunt, although it was probably increasingly difficult for them to do so since people could most likely hunt only on their own lands.[229]

Table 1. ENGLISH FORESTERS

Forest	Forester	Date	Source
Aberdeen Cowie Durris	John Comyn	12 July 1292	*Rot. Scot.*, i, 10 a
Darnaway Langmorn Kintore	Robert Bruce	1304-5 26 Oct. 1305 26 Oct. 1305	*CDS*, ii, 1736 *CDS*, ii, 1708 *CDS*, ii, 1708
Buchan	Duncan de Ferendragh	12 April 1304	*CDS*, ii, 1708

Ettrick:
  Selkirk &
    Traquair
	Simon Fraser	18 Aug. 1291	*Rot. Scot.*, i, 4 b

,,	William Comyn	15 Jan. 1291/2	*Rot. Scot.*, i, 7 a
,,	William Comyn	6 July 1292	*Rot. Scot.*, i, 7 a
Selkirk	Thomas de Burnham	16 May 1296	*CDS*, ii, 853
,,	Robert Keith	20 Aug. 1299	*CDS*, ii, 1978
,,	Simon Fraser	20 Aug. 1299	*CDS*, ii, 1978
,,	Simon Fraser	30 Oct. 1300	*CDS*, ii, 1165
,,	Hugh de Audely	23 Sept. 1301	*CDS*, ii, 1226, 1227, 1230
,,	Hugh de Audely	13 Aug. 1302	*CDS*, ii, 1317
Selkirk, part of	Robert de Hastings	13 Aug. 1302	*CDS*, ii, 1317
Selkirk	Alexander de Balliol	Aug.-Sept. 1302	*CDS*, ii, 1321, 1324
,,	Alexander de Balliol	Sept. 1305	*CDS*, ii, 1693
Tweed Ward	John de Moffat		
Traquair Ward	Roger de Aylmer	1304-1305	*CDS*, ii, 1646
Selkirk Ward	Walter le Corour		
Selkirk	Aymer de Valence	4 Oct. 1306	*CDS*, ii, 1839
Selkirk & Ettrick	Robert de Menars	15 June 1334	*Rot. Scot.*, i, 271 b
,,	Geoffrey de Mowbray (claimant)	15 Sept. 1334	*Rot. Scot.*, i, 278 b
,,	William de Montague (holder of lands)	10 Oct. 1335	*Rot. Scot.*, i, 380 a
,,	William de Montague	*ante* 1343	*CDS*, iii, 1425
Ettrick	Henry Percy (holder of lands)	2 March 1402	*Rot. Scot.*, ii, 163 b
Jedburgh	Thomas de Burnham	*ante* 5 Oct. 1296	*Rot. Scot.*, i, 36 a
,,	Hugh de Eyland	5 Oct. 1296	*Rot. Scot.*, i, 36 a *CDS*, ii, 853
,,	Constable of Jedburgh	*ante* 1298	Stevenson, *Documents*, ii, 264
,,	Ivo de Aldeburge Abbot of Jedburgh	1298	Stevenson, *Documents*, ii, 265
,,	William of Presfen	15 July 1334	*Rot. Scot.*, i, 271 b
,,	Henry Percy	23 Feb. 1341/42	*CDS*, iii, 1377

Table 2. EDWARD I's GRANTS OF DEER AND TIMBER

Date	Grantee	Gift	Forest	Source
10 Aug. 1291	Walter Routbury	2 bucks, 4 does	Tynedale	*CDS*, ii, 510
15 Aug. 1291	Brian Jay, Preceptor of Knights Templar	4 oaks	Clackmannan	*Rot. Scot.*, i, 4 a
18 Aug. 1291	William, Bishop of St Andrews	30 deer	Ettrick[1]	*Rot. Scot.*, i, 4 b
18 Aug. 1291	Robert, Bishop of Glasgow	20 deer, 60 oaks		*Rot. Scot.*, i, 4 b
18 Aug. 1291	Bishop of Caithness	10 deer		*Rot. Scot.*, i, 4 b
18 Aug. 1291	James Steward	20 deer	[Jedburgh?][2]	*Rot. Scot.*, i, 4 b
18 Aug. 1291	Patrick Dunbar, earl of March	10 deer		*Rot. Scot.*, i, 4 b
18 Aug. 1291	William St Clair	6 deer		*Rot. Scot.*, i, 4 b
18 Aug. 1291	Brian, Preceptor of Knights Templar	2 deer, 4 oaks	[Clackmannan][2]	*Rot. Scot.*, i, 4 b
18 Aug. 1291	William Soules	10 deer		*Rot. Scot.*, i, 4 b
18 Aug. 1291	John Soules	6 deer		*Rot. Scot.*, i, 4 b
18 Aug. 1291	William Hay	4 deer		*Rot. Scot.*, i, 4 b
18 Aug. 1291	Patrick Graham	6 deer		*Rot. Scot.*, i, 4 b
18 Aug. 1291	Alexander Balliol	10 deer		*Rot. Scot.*, i, 4 b
18 Aug. 1291	Simon Fraser	10 deer	Ettrick	*Rot. Scot.*, i, 4 b
18 Aug. 1291	Thomas Clenhull	4 deer	Ettrick	*Rot. Scot.*, i, 4 b
23 Aug. 1291	Reginald Chene Jr	6 deer	Spey (Boyne & Enzie?)	*Rot. Scot.*, i, 5 a
23 Aug. 1291	Reginald Chene Sr	10 deer	Spey (Boyne & Enzie?)	*Rot. Scot.*, i, 5 a
16 June 1292	William Comyn, 'prepositus' of St Andrews	6 deer	Plater	*Rot. Scot.*, i, 8 a
6 July 1292	Alexander Comyn	6 deer	Cowie & Buchan	*Rot. Scot.*, i, 9 a
6 July 1292	John Comyn	10 deer	Spey	*Rot. Scot.*, i, 9 a
6 July 1292	Abbot of Jedburgh	6 deer	Ettrick	*Rot. Scot.*, i, 9 a
6 July 1292	Thomas Randolph	6 deer	Ettrick	*Rot. Scot.*, i, 9a
6 July 1292	Adam Botindon, vice-chancellor	4 deer	Ettrick	*Rot. Scot.*, i, 9 a
12 July 1292	William, Bishop of St Andrews	30 deer	Durris, Cowie & Aberdeen	*Rot. Scot.*, i, 10a

1. The forest in many of these grants in 1291 is not clearly stated but could have been Ettrick.
2. This is probably the forest concerned, since another grant was made by Edward from this forest to the same grantee.

Date	Grantee	Gift	Forest	Source
30 Aug. 1296	Abbot of Arbroath	50 oaks	Plater	*Rot. Scot.*, i, 24a
3 Sept. 1296	Master of Torphichen	3 oaks	Coulter	Stevenson, *Documents* ii, 98, no. 386
14 Sept. 1296	James Steward	10 deer	Jedburgh	*Rot. Scot.*, i, 33 b
20 Sept. 1296	John Stirling	10 deer	Alyth	*Rot. Scot.*, i, 33 b
1303	Abbot of Jedburgh	20 oaks	Plater	*CDS*, ii, 1428
1303	Dean of Elgin	20 oaks	Langmorn	Stevenson, *Documents* ii, 450, no. 625
5 April 1304	Bishop of Brechin	12 oaks	Plater	*CDS*, ii, 1496
12 April 1304	Bishop of Aberdeen	40 oaks	Drum	*CDS*, ii, 1506
12 April 1304	Bishop of Aberdeen	30 oaks	Kintore	*CDS*, ii, 1506
12 April 1304	Bishop of Aberdeen	30 oaks	Buchan	*CDS*, ii, 1506
1304	Bishop of Glasgow	50 oaks	Ettrick & Mauldslie	*CDS*, ii, 1626
1304 x 5	Ralph Chene	200 oaks	Darnawav & Langmorn	*CDS*, ii, 1736
18 Oct. 1305	Prior of St Andrews	20 oaks	Clackmannan	*CDS*, ii, 1704
19 Oct. 1305	Abbot of Jedburgh	20 oaks	Plater	*CDS*, ii, 1704
26 Oct. 1305	John Comyn, earl of Buchan	6 hinds, 25 oaks	Buchan	*CDS*, ii, 1708
26 Oct. 1305	John Comyn, earl of Buchan	6 hinds, 25 oaks	Kintore	*CDS*, ii, 1708
26 Oct. 1305	John Spalding, canon of Elgin	20 oaks	Langmorn	*CDS*, ii, 1708
1300 x 1307	Abbot of Melrose	40 oaks	Ettrick	*CDS*, ii, 1982.

4

Hunting and Hawking

IN medieval Europe there were basically two ways of hunting game: the huntsman might either wait for the game to be driven towards him; or he might chase after the game. In Scotland the drive was probably more important than the chase.

The drive, as a method of hunting, must have been current in Scotland long before the arrival of the Normans, since drives are described in several Gaelic poems. Of the many poems of the Finn cycle which describe hunts one mid-twelfth-century poem, 'The Magic Pig', is especially interesting since it describes a hunt round Cruachan.[1] The hunt involved large numbers of men, all of whom seem to have driven deer towards the standing Fian. Although the numbers given in these poems are exaggerated, it is clear that a large number of animals might be killed. An early twelfth-century poem, 'The Enchanted Stag',[2] which states that 120 of the Fian with 1,000 hounds, 100 women and 1,000 men in attendance killed 100 deer and 100 stags, must be describing a drive.

The use of Gaelic words to describe aspects of the drive also points to its existence in pre-Norman Scotland. The drive could be assisted by a barrier or elrick, a word which has survived as 'elerc' in the *Book of Deer*.[3] The beaters would, no doubt, drive the game along this wall or into a glen at the other end of which the hunters awaited. The elrick which was current in Scotland till the eighteenth century could also mean the spot where the hunters awaited the game.[4] In Gaelic, also, the beaters were called the 'timchioll', a word which was adopted into Scots as 'tinchell' and used in the sixteenth century by Pitscottie.[5]

The drive was current among the magnates in the late eleventh and early twelfth century because Aelred records a story which he heard from David I about a drive held by Malcolm III.[6] Malcolm and his nobles were ready with their dogs at dawn and they proceeded to a broad clearing in the middle of a thick wood. The king and nobles then took up their individual trysts or hunting positions with their dogs so that the game when driven to them could not escape. This, writes Aelred, was done, 'secundum legem venandi quam vulgus tristam vocat'. At this time the king and his magnates were not in sight of each other because a traitor, so the story goes, planned to kill Malcolm at this stage of the hunt. At this time also there is evidence that common people and landholders had to provide beaters for a royal drive.[7]

The best description of a drive, however, is found in the foundation story of Holyrood Abbey which is recorded in the early fifteenth-century *Ritual Book* of that abbey and which associates a drive with the twelfth-century foundation of the abbey. The author of the foundation story was no doubt describing a method of hunting which he had seen in use in the fourteenth and fifteenth centuries.[8] The hunt was described as a 'cursum ferarum cum canibus'. After the hunters, 'venatores', had entered the forest with their dogs they drove the game from the shelter of the woods with the assistance of the 'exploratores' and the barking of the dogs. The barking of the dogs and the cries of the trackers, 'indagantes', according to the author, seemed to fill the air with a certain melody. The king, on horseback, waited for the hunt under the shade of a leafy tree, while his nobles were hidden round about with the dogs according to the custom of hunters, 'more venatorum'. The hunters must have been out of sight of each other, since the story gives no reason as to why no one came to the king's assistance when he was attacked by a stag. In the sixteenth century Bellenden repeated the story in Scots.[9] The hunters driving through the wood were called the stable, 'staill', and the noise and din of their scenting hounds, 'raches', and horns, 'bugillis', stirred the game from their lairs. At the foot of Salisbury Crags the nobles separated from the king at different places to await the hunt.

From these accounts of a drive it is clear that the stable, which was on occasions called a 'course',[10] with as much noise as possible drove the game towards the king and the nobles who waited hidden and on horseback with their dogs. As the game approached them they would no doubt unleash their hounds, fire arrows or throw spears. It is possible that the nobles may have tried to drive some of the game to the king, since in neither version of the Holyrood drive does he appear to have dogs. This secondary drive by the waiting hunters is in accord with continental practice[11] but one must beware of reading too much into these descriptions of the Holyrood drive. It may simply have been inconvenient to the story to let the king have dogs with him, regardless of whether or not a king in practice would be accompanied by his hounds. According to Aelred, Malcolm III had dogs with him and Wyntoun, writing in the fifteenth century, states that King Duncan went to take part in a drive with a bow and a brachet.[12] The predominant features of this type of drive were that a large number of hunters were involved and that the object was to kill more than one animal.

In England and the Continent the drive was described in the hunting treatises of Twici, Gaston Phoebus and Edward, Duke of York whose descriptions have been summarised by Gunnar Tilander.[13] One group of hunters was set round a wood in a semi-circle at regular intervals within sight of each other. They were known in French as the 'défenses' or 'éstablie'.[14] They had two functions: to prevent game leaving the wood; and to drive it to the places where there were hunters with greyhounds. The hunters who held the greyhounds hid behind trees and bushes. They unleashed the hounds as soon

E

as the beast had passed and forced the game towards the archers or towards nets in the openings of a hay or fence. Although this type of hunt and that described in the Holyrood *Ritual Book* are obviously drives, there are variations in the two accounts. In the continental drive, known as 'chasse royale' or 'chasse à la haie', the hunters with their greyhounds drove the game towards archers or nets, whereas in Scotland it is uncertain whether waiters were to drive the game further or not. Both in Scotland and in England hunters awaited the drive at a 'tryst'[15] but in Scotland the spot where the hunters waited was known as a 'set'. Wyntoun's *Chronicle* records events which occurred during hunts after 'the stable and the setis' had been 'set'.[16] When describing Malcolm Canmore's adventure, already referred to, he writes that the king took the traitor 'by hym to syt at that huntynge'.[17] In the fifteenth century Wyntoun was, therefore, quite familiar with the idea of the king and his companions sitting and waiting at their sets or trysts for the stable or course to appear. The hunting station may also have been called a 'wenelacia' for the 'wenelacia Ricardi Cumin' was used to define the bounds of Ashkirk pasture beside Ettrick forest in 1179.[18] Wanlace, however, also applied to the action of dogs driving game towards a hunter.[19]

The drive might be assisted by the use of a hay or artificial barrier similar to the elrick: the hay had been common in both Normandy and Anglo-Saxon England;[20] and it continued to be used in the fourteenth and fifteenth centuries on the Continent.[21] In parks also nets and barriers were used but a park drive could be executed by only a few men, as in Falkland park in the sixteenth century.[22] At Lintrathen and Kincardine parks there were extensions which probably facilitated the capture of deer and may have enabled deer to be driven through a narrow gap in the pale of the main park into the extension while the huntsmen waited at the gap to kill the deer. Just such a gap is shown on the fifteenth-century seal of the fourth earl of Angus where the park pale of wattle fencing is turned back on itself at this opening.[23] In Kincardine the exit is at the foot of a small steep-sided valley in an ideal position for shooting arrows and throwing spears down on the driven game.[24]

In James IV's reign the sedentary aspect of the waiting hunters assumed greater importance. Where the king waited was no longer a 'set' in the sense of a trap but it was his 'seat' where he sat and waited: James had a hunting 'sete' on Ben More north of Balquhidder in 1501.[25] In 1506 when the king 'lay at the sete' probably in Glen Artney a woman brought him butter and cheese[26] and in accordance with later practice[27] there may have been a tent nearby for rest and refreshment. In 1508 in Glen Artney 306 men were at the hunting, presumably as part of the stable,[28] while further west the Macgregors may have provided the stable.[29] This type of hunt required some preparation, since the stable had to be set out over a wide area and in 1504 a boy was sent to the forester of the Torwood telling him 'to set the hunting' in the Torwood for the queen.[30]

The drive as a type of hunt popular amongst king and nobility from the twelfth century onwards is referred to in literature other than chronicles. The

Book of Alexander, perhaps written by Barbour in the late fourteenth century, includes a reference to 'settis' which its French antecedent 'Le Roman de Alexandre' does not.[31] The most numerous references, however, to this type of hunting occur in Gaelic poems, some of which have already been mentioned. Since James IV hunted in the west, he would obviously have been in touch with Gaelic traditions and it is interesting to note that a hunt of the Fian described in an early sixteenth-century Gaelic poem resembled the Scots drive more closely than descriptions in twelfth-century Gaelic poems.[32] 3,000 men of the Fian, each with two hounds, were involved. Finn arranged the hounds on east and west and the dogs' barking raised boar and deer from the hill. Finn and his dog Bran waited seated on the mountain, and every man was in his hunting position waiting for the deer. 3,000 hounds were unleashed and 6,000 deer were killed. A late fifteenth-century version of this poem is given in the book of the Dean of Lismore,[33] compiled in the mid-sixteenth century. It is quite clear in this poem that the hunters sit and wait for the drive and are not chasing the deer. The best description of this method of hunting in the sixteenth century is given by Bishop Lesley in his history of Scotland,[34] where he states that the stable might include 500 to 1,000 men and would drive the deer in from a radius of from 10 to 20 miles to a narrow valley where the lords and noblemen waited.

The drive was suited only for the king and the more important nobility since only they could muster the necessary manpower, even though in the four-teenth and fifteenth centuries it was probably not pursued on the scale described by Lesley, assuming that the numbers in the Gaelic poems are somewhat mythical. It was, for instance, possible for Iain Keir, fourth chief of Dunvegan, to take part in a drive on Harris in the late fourteenth century.[35] On the Continent, with the development of absolutism in the sixteenth century, this type of hunting became more popular,[36] and in Scotland the size of the drive which the king could raise may have been seen in the sixteenth century as a measure of his power. While this attitude may have existed in James IV's reign, his drives did not reach the opulence of those of James V and Mary.[37]

That Gaelic hunting customs were continued and adopted by the Normans can be clearly seen from the history of the drive, its currency before and after 1125, and the continuing use of elrick and tinchell throughout the medieval period. The importance or popularity of the drive cannot, however, be assessed till other methods of hunting in Scotland have been examined.

The methods of hunting by chasing deer included coursing, stalking and *par force* hunting. Not only did they require fewer people than the drive, but they were all based on hunting a single animal. Coursing and stalking were practised by commoners as well as nobles. In a Scottish connection, coursing is first mentioned in 1261/2 when John Comyn received permission to hunt in English royal forests north of the Trent.[38] Coursing, the most straightforward of all methods of hunting, usually occurred in open country where the deer had been chased or where it was found. Greyhounds were sent after the game in a straight chase with the huntsman following on horseback. On the Continent this was known as hunting by force of greyhounds as opposed to hunting by force of running or scenting hounds.[39] The greyhounds present at the raising of the game were the only hounds involved in a course.

It is into this category that many Gaelic descriptions of hunts dating to the eighth and ninth centuries belong, although in these tales the hunters often followed their hounds on foot and not on horseback.[40] The hunting scenes depicted on Pictish stones also suggest coursing, since the hounds in these portrayals are unleashed and biting at the stag and the hunter following on horseback often holds a spear to throw at the game.[41] (Figs. 1, 4.) Several of the fifteenth- and sixteenth-century Highland carved stones depict hunts very similar to those of the Pictish stones, with one, two or three unleashed hounds attacking deer.[42] (Fig. 5.) These greyhounds could supposedly pull down a stag by running close to its flank and shooting up at its throat, keeping close to avoid a blow from the antlers.[43] The duke of York in the early fifteenth century advocated that greyhounds attack all animals 'bifore or by the side' for the sake of their own safety.[44] The description of a course on Jura in 1835 explains that two greyhounds pulled down a deer with one dog jumping at the deer's hock and other at its neck. The dogs then hung on and were dragged along by the deer. As a result solely of the dogs' attack, the deer's forelegs were dislocated, its throat was perforated and its sides lacerated.[45] In 1503, when Princess Margaret was travelling between Dalkeith and Edinburgh, a deer course was arranged for her since an unnamed gentleman sent a great tame hart to her for a course. Half a mile from Edinburgh the hart was released and a greyhound set after it, 'bot the said hert wanne the towne and went to hys repayre'.[46] Coursing hares also was a popular pastime in which James IV indulged in 1502 and 1504.[47] Boece and Bellenden both stressed that certain criteria of fair play had to be observed: no one was to chase hares unless by coursing, and if the hare ran clean away it was not to be attacked thereafter.[48] Although they are both here describing the mythical past, one suspects that they were talking of customs with which they were familiar or which they may have wished to see in use.

Stalking, like coursing and *par force* hunting, was concerned with chasing one animal but unlike them was a silent pursuit with a scenting hound, not a greyhound, and would most often be carried out by only one hunter. Undoubtedly the earliest depiction of stalking in Scotland is on the Pictish stones, which portray a man disguised, crouching, waiting to kill the game with what resembles a crossbow rather than a short bow.[49] (Fig. 2 and see p. 62.) A hunter could stalk either by following game silently with a scenting hound and then shooting it with a bow or at a later date with a gun, or else by waiting silently with dog and bow beside a known deer path, say between a lair and water. In the thirteenth century stalking is mentioned in clauses 14 and 15 of the forest laws when they discuss one man following one animal with a dog,[50] and in the fourteenth century Barbour described how Bruce in Galloway went to hunt and sat alone beside a wood with two hounds, presumably stalking.[51] Because this method of hunting was ideally suited to poaching James I banned it in 1424.[52] Nevertheless, both types of stalking were practised by the king's subjects in Menteith in 1508.[53] James II and III had a stalker in the Menteith area,[54] and at the end of this period there is the first recorded use of a gun in a stalk when James IV stalked in Falkland park.[55] A third method of stalking was to employ some sort of disguise or mobile cover. Bellenden describes hunters disguising themselves with branches and leaves of trees like stalkers.[56]

While considering those methods of hunting which could be employed by the common people, the use of snares must not be forgotten. Although hunting by snares was a fairly frequent occurrence, it was regarded as an inferior method of hunting not suitable for the king and the nobility. It was very much the common man's method[57] or else a means of hunting solely to fill the larder. One can detect this attitude in Boece's and Bellenden's comparisons of the hunting methods of the Picts and the Scots. The Picts hunted by stretching nets across meadows and drove harts onto the nets and when they escaped the Picts dressed with branches and leaves of trees like stalkers slew the deer with arrows when they were lying weary. The Scots, however, who hunted with hounds alone, despised this means of hunting. Boece and so Bellenden, although describing a mythical past, are probably reflecting an attitude towards the use of nets and artificial aids common in the fourteenth and fifteenth centuries.[58] This attitude is also reflected in Bellenden's statements that hares were not to be killed by nets or traps and were only to be hunted by chase of hounds.[59] In such sentiments Boece and Bellenden were expressing a preference first recorded by Arrian in his *Kunegetikos* where he compared the use of nets and snares with thievish depredation, while the use of greyhounds was like a battle fought with main strength.[60] Nets were used in parks[61] and as in the examples from Boece they were also used in the open. Henryson, in his fable 'The Lion and the Mouse', describes a net trap, presumably of a type with which he was familiar.[62] In all these cases the game was driven into the nets but traps and snares onto which the game passed of its own volition must have been used throughout the Middle Ages, especially against wolves.[63]

The final method of chasing deer to be examined is hunting *par force* of running or scenting hounds. In view of the European importance of *par force* hunting — the classic of medieval hunting — it must be examined and an attempt made to discern some trace of its existence in Scotland. Hunting by force of hounds was described by Gaston Phoebus, Comte de Foix, in the mid-fourteenth century. His work was translated by Edward, second Duke of York, in the early fifteenth century with some additional material and alterations in accord with English hunting practice. His book, *The Master of Game*, describes *par force* hunting as follows.[64] Early in the morning before the hunt started, a huntsman, known as the harbourer, set off with a scenting hound, trained not to bark, to locate a suitable deer to hunt. He then returned to the main body of hunters and explained why he thought the deer he had harboured was not a hind or a young hart but a good deer. The master huntsman, after separating the hounds into three or four relays with perhaps two to three couples in each relay, told the men in each relay where to take their stand. This required good knowledge of the countryside since an attempt was made to foresee the path the deer was likely to follow. One relay was kept back to be uncoupled whenever the deer was unharboured. The harbourer then raised the stag from its lair and blew three notes on his horn. The first relay was uncoupled and the hunt commenced with the huntsmen following usually on horseback. Henceforth the same stag had to be followed regardless of its companions or whatever tricks it might adopt to confuse the trail. When the hunt reached the various relays of hounds the relay was supposed to be slipped after the stag and the hounds already chasing it had passed. If the hounds were slipped too soon this was called a 'vauntlay'. 'Vauntlay' was only permissible by the last relay or when the stag was nearly finished, since a 'vauntlay' could cause the stag to be driven from the line on which the other relays were stationed.

Since *par force* hunting, which came to Britain from the Continent,[65] was practised in England by the Normans in the Middle Ages, it is likely that it was practised in Scotland after 1124. That it was current in Scotland is suggested firstly by the possibility that James VI and I tried to re-establish *par force* hunting in England after his accession to the English throne. In 1603 he wrote to Henry IV of France asking for a huntsman to teach his English huntsmen how to hunt *par force*.[66] Henry replied at the end of August 1603 and sent James one of his best hunters, Seigneur de Vitry. He was ordered to demonstrate the French method of hunting and to learn the method in which James hunted.[67] De Vitry probably, therefore, had to explain the *par force* method of hunting which was common in France at this time,[68] and learn about the drive. Such conclusions, however, are fraught with difficulties since Seigneur de Vitry is not explicitly ordered to demonstrate *par force* hunting but simply the French method of hunting, which most probably was *par force*, and secondly, if James had practised this type of hunting in Scotland, he could surely have sent for a Scots hunter to train the English in this method. It is also conceivable that if *par force* hunting had died out in England it had also died out in Scotland and that James knew of it only by memory or from the visit of the Duc de Sully, as E. Jullien has suggested.[69] Secondly, James may refer to this hunting method in the *Basilikon Doron*, in the third part of which he advises the Prince to hunt 'with running hounds' since that is the most honourable and noble sort of hunting and is more martial than greyhound hunting.[70] Since running hounds were all hounds which hunted by scent and in packs,[71] since greyhounds were used for coursing and since James stresses the nobility of the former method, he seems to be advocating *par force* hunting, which was accepted throughout Europe as the most noble form of hunting.

Confusion follows when James, so that he 'would not be thought a partial praiser of this sport', recommends a study of Xenophon. Xenophon recommended coursing and stalking hares, coursing young deer,[72] laying traps for deer, and driving hares into nets, but nothing similar to *par force* hunting with relays of dogs. The striking feature of Xenophon's *Kunegetikos* is that it does not mention greyhounds but concentrates on scenting hounds, the type of dogs on which a *par force* hunt depended. Xenophon's instructions for handling scenting hounds during a hare course and for keeping them on the right track despite the hare's attempts to throw them off are similar to the instructions given in the *Master of Game* to control hounds during a *par force* hunt.[73] A knowledge of Xenophon, therefore, would not be amiss when hunting *par force*, even though his *Kunegetikos* contained no description of a *par force* hunt. Thirdly, it is possible that James VI was hunting *par force* in Falkland park in August 1600 before riding to Perth and the Gowrie 'conspiracy'. While James was standing at the stables at Falkland talking to Master Alexander Ruthven, the court objected to the delay:

The game already found, and the huntsmen so long staying in the fields on his Maiestie . . . . But his Maiestie . . . . leaping on horse backe, and riding to the dogs, where they were beginning to hunt, the said Master Alexander stayed still in that place . . . . But his Maiestie was no sooner ridden uppe to a little hill above the little woodde, where the dogges were layde on in hunting, but that not withstanding the pleasant beginning of the chase, he could not stay from musing . . . .[74]

This cannot have been a drive, since the court and the king were on horseback riding with the dogs. Nor can it have been a course within a tinchell, since the hunt was held within Falkland park and there was no danger of the deer escaping. The only remaining possibilities are, therefore, a straightforward course or a *par force* hunt. The phrase 'the game already found' strongly resembles the location of the game by a harbourer at the start of a *par force* hunt, but a similar procedure would not have been out of place at the start of a course. The key lies in the statement 'the huntsmen so long staying in the fields on his Maiestie'. The hunters were divided into two groups, the huntsmen with the hounds and the courtiers.[75] At the start of the story they had all been together on the green beside the stables, but while James talked to Alexander Ruthven, the courtiers mounted and the huntsmen apparently moved to the 'fields'. This could mean that the huntsmen were set out as the relays for a *par force* hunt while the court waited for James. There is nothing in the description of this hunt which precludes a *par force* hunt and several points which suggest it.

Returning to the period before 1513, there is no unequivocal reference to this method of hunting. In 1494 x 1495 James IV may have hunted *par force* in Ettrick, since Thomas Thomson was paid 40s 'laboranti circa invencionem ferarum in foresta de mandato domini regis',[76] which suggests that Thomson may have been a harbourer. On the other hand it was customary before a drive to find out what animals were in the area,[77] but since most of Ettrick was inhabited or grazed, it is unlikely that a drive could have been held there. Nevertheless, this does not rule out the possibility of stalking or merely filling the larder with venison.

The only definite conclusion which can be reached about *par force* hunting in Scotland is that there is no explicit reference to it in medieval Scottish sources. Consequently, coursing and stalking must have been more frequently practised than *par force* hunting, but the most important of all types of hunting was the drive, which is referred to more frequently and described more fully than any of the other forms of hunting. This raises an important problem, for elsewhere in medieval Europe *par force* hunting was the most important method of hunting. Indeed, as has been said, if the Normans hunted *par force* in England, it is logical to argue that they hunted *par force* in Scotland. The reason why *par force* hunting never became so popular in Scotland is, therefore, of the greatest importance. The history of hunting methods in Scotland before 1124 and the popularity of the drive point to the influence of Gaelic custom in hunting methods as the reason for this phenomenon. It has already been shown that Gaelic hunting customs continued throughout the medieval period, and it follows that they were adopted by the Normans. The adoption of the drive was a two-way process, for the drive, to judge by references in Gaelic literature of the sixteenth century and by the change in the nature of the drive in the sixteenth century — both of which have already been discussed — did alter in form and character throughout the medieval period.

The prominence of the drive over the *par force* hunt may also reflect native influence in another way. In the Middle Ages each type of hunting was not always practised in isolation. A stable could be set around a *par force* hunt to prevent deer escaping and if they did they might be coursed by a greyhound. The preliminary stages of a drive or a *par force* hunt were fairly similar to stalking with a scenting hound.[78] Whether or not such combinations occurred in Scotland is a matter for conjecture, but it is reasonable to suppose that an animal might first be hunted by stalking and instead of killing it, it could then be coursed or hunted *par force*. Consequently, it would have been a relatively simple development for *par force* hunting to have been replaced by coursing. Both types of hunting were very similar. The main differences lay in the exclusion of scenting hounds and of relays in a course, but scenting hounds could still be used to raise the game for a course. Coursing also had been common in pre-Norman Scotland, and if coursing did influence the decline of the more complex and sophisticated *par force* hunt, then this also could be a sign of the influence of native custom on hunting methods in Scotland.

Finally, it is noticeable that the drive and the course both depended heavily, if not entirely, on the greyhound, whereas *par force* hunting required the constant use of scenting hounds. Since Scotland, as will be shown, was renowned throughout Europe for its greyhounds — or Scots deerhounds as they are now called — it would have been natural for the Normans and their successors to favour hunting methods which exploited those hounds to the full, to favour, in other words, the drive and the course.

To organise a successful royal hunting expedition, provisions and accommodation were frequently provided for the huntsmen. Huntsmen usually provided their own gear, including weapons, horns, hounds and horses. Several officials could be concerned with the collection of equipment and with the hunt itself, and afterwards the kill or quarry might be formally conducted. Hunting, of course, was limited by the hunting seasons. Each of these aspects will be examined in turn.

Once the king had notified local officials of his intention to hunt in their jurisdiction[79] the main requisite was a supply of good food for the king and his hunting companions. James II on a six-day hunting visit to Strathbraan was supplied with bread, wine, marts, mutton, capons and fish.[80] In 1467 James III made the port of Menteith a burgh of barony in order to improve the supply of victuals during the hunting season,[81] and in 1501 victuals were carried to James IV while he was hunting in Strathfillan.[82] The expenses thus incurred were paid by local officials and an allowance was made to them thereafter. Robert II's numerous visits to Kindrochit were paid for by the sheriff of Aberdeen,[83] the bailies of Aberdeen,[84] the custumars of Perth,[85] and most frequently the custumars of Aberdeen.[86] On several occasions these local officials paid the clerk of livery, who no doubt arranged the supply of provender. In the fifteenth century the *ballivus ad extra,* who on occasion was the forester of the area,[87] bore the expense.[88] Such expenses were usually recorded in the 'libri domicilii'[89] or the 'libri dietarum'.[90] The people of Menteith often presented James IV with gifts of food, of which the most common were butter and cheese,[91] but nobles also donated delicacies: Lord Drummond sent James IV cherries when he was hunting in Glen Artney in 1508.[92]

Not only did food have to be supplied, but the accommodation for the royal party had to be prepared. This might involve the building or repair of hunting lodges, such as the Hunthall in Glenfinglas and the hunting seats in Strathbraan at Loch Freuchie and at 'Halymill'.[93] There were also lodges at Duchray in Menteith,[94] and the castles of Kindrochit in the fourteenth century and Newark in the fifteenth century must frequently have sheltered hunting parties. Other buildings might shelter the king: when hunting in Balquhidder and Strathfillan James IV stayed at the local church or found a bed where he could.[95] During a royal hunting expedition tents were used no doubt to increase accommodation at lodges or to give the king shelter while he waited for a drive or to provide accommodation where there was no lodge.[96] This type of tent, made of canvas, buckram and iron, was called either a canopy or a pavilion.[97] In James IV's reign John Hertished, the tailor and pavilion man, was responsible for their maintenance and transportation.[98]

While little is known about huntsmen's clothing, more information has survived about their weapons and horns. James IV had special hunting coats, one of which was white lined in black.[99] The hunting coat, like the hawking and riding coat, was longer and fuller than the doublet and was about the length of a modern jacket. It required 3 to 3½ ells of velvet or other narrow cloth and was lined in broad cloth or fur.[100] It is probably this sort of coat that is being worn by the two gillies portrayed on the early sixteenth-century tomb of Alexander MacLeod of Dunvegan at Rodel in Harris. (Fig. 6.) On the late fifteenth-century MacMillan cross at Kilmory in Knapdale, the huntsman wears a longer knee-length tunic.[101] (Fig. 5.)

Although not specifically recorded in Scottish sources, most hunters must have been equipped with a hunting knife and with a broad hunting sword tapered to a point.[102] Turning again to the west Highlands, on both the Rodel and MacMillan monuments the hunters are shown wielding axes which must have been used instead of swords to despatch the game. The bows most commonly used for hunting were the short bow and the crossbow, since both could be fired from horseback, unlike the long bow.[103] Broad arrows, frequently mentioned in Scotland as a blanche ferme,[104] were fired from the short bow and had a swallow tail or broad head with two large barbs sloping backwards towards the shaft.[105] Examples of these arrows have been discovered at both Kindrochit and Urquhart Castles, both closely associated with hunting. (Fig. 7.) The crossbow, which was a useful hunting weapon since it had a longer effective range than the longbow and yet required less strength and less space to fire, is portrayed on three Pictish stones, St Vigeans no. 1, Glenferness and Shandwick.[106] A fourth stone at Meigle also portrayed a crossbow but it has been lost since it was drawn last century.[107] Of the three extant stones, the Drostan stone, St Vigeans no. 1, shows the crossbow most clearly. (Fig. 2.) The hunter in a crouched position holds both hands close to his body and the bow rests vertically on the ground. One hand holds the string and the other the end of the stock. The bow would then be fired by releasing the string. In effect the stock was used simply to enable both hands to be kept close to the body. This could not possibly be a short bow because if fired by releasing the 'arrow', the hunter would still be holding the string. The St Vigeans' portrayal is also readily distinguishable from the depiction of short bows on the tenth-century Sueno's stone and the seventh- or eighth-century Ruthwell Cross.[108] The portrayals of the crossbow on the Glenferness and Shandwick stones are less informative and may be copies of the Drostan stone. They both clearly show that the hunter does not have one hand stretched forward to hold the bow itself.

The crossbow, which is first recorded in China, perhaps as early as 1500 BC,[109] had been in use in Europe from the time of the Roman Empire.[110] Crossbows are depicted on Gallo-Roman stone reliefs, and in a tenth-century manuscript two crossbowmen are shown crouched with the stock of the bow held like a rifle ready to fire.[111] The same firing position is illustrated in a sixth- or seventh-century Chinese handscroll of Ku K'aichih, *Admonitions of the Instructress to the Court Ladies*, now in the British Museum. The Pictish method of firing the bow, by releasing the string by hand, is not shown in any European representation but is shown in the above Chinese handscroll. The European style of release was a trigger or revolving nut set in the stock. That the Pictish carvings do not show a revolving nut release is surprising since that type of release had been employed in crossbows in northern Europe from an early date.[112] One such nut has been found at Buston Crannog (Fig. 8) and may belong to the sixth or seventh centuries, and another in a late Roman grave in Wiltshire.[113] When one adds to this evidence the heads of crossbow bolts found at Buston Crannog and at Dunadd fort (Fig. 8) it is clear that an elementary type of crossbow was in use in Scotland from the post-Roman period onwards.[114] The Pictish carvings are sufficiently distinctive in the dress of the crossbowman, the position in which the bow is held, the grip of the stock at the end not the middle, the hunting context and the style of representation for it to be clear that they are not merely copies of drawings of Chinese or European origin. The advantages of a crossbow as a hunting weapon lay in the ease and speed with which it could be fired once drawn, and in the absence of movement required to fire it. The crossbow continued to be used throughout the medieval period in Scotland, as the Rodel monument (Fig. 6) and the purchase of bolts and crossbows by James III and IV before setting out on hunting expeditions show.[115]

Spears and clubs were also used when hunting,[116] and the sword or spear used when hunting boar had a cross piece placed 30 cms from the point to prevent the weapon sinking too far into the boar and endangering the hunts-man.[117] The first firearms appeared only at the start of the sixteenth century,[118] and it was not till 1551 that their use for hunting was forbidden in Scotland[119] because game was, according to parliament, becoming scarce.

Most huntsmen required a horn, for it could be used in a drive to scare the game or it could be used to signal the hunter's position or the stage which the hunt had reached, since certain notes were used at certain stages in the hunt.[120] The use of the horn as a signal in the Middle Ages was universal, and no doubt slight individual differences let the hearer identify the blower: according to Barbour, Bruce's call was instantly recognisable to his men.[121] The blow and cry of the hunt, on occasion described as 'melodia', was not always thought to be so and according to Froissart, the sound produced at Otterburn by the Scots blowing on their horns terrified their enemies![122] While this type of maximum noise would be of value in a drive, the horn could be used more subtly. In Scotland individual blasts on the horn probably heralded the start of the hunt,[123] and the second clause of the forest laws mentions the signal known as the 'menée', which was originally the signal given when the game in a *par force* hunt was in full flight. Consequently, it came to mean any signal on the horn used in hunting and on other occasions generally a single long blast.[124] There are no other references to notes used when hunting, but notes common in England and Europe may have been known or have had equivalents in Scotland. The huntsman on the MacMillan cross wears a horn, and horns were frequently used as heraldic devices on seals.[125] Horns were often decorated or carved, but it is unlikely that the more ornate examples would be used as everyday hunting horns.[126]

Nearly all hunts centred on the hounds, which were of two main types, those which hunted by sight and those which hunted by scent. Hounds which hunted by sight are described by the generic term, greyhound, and those which hunted by scent were called running hounds, and the word 'hound' on its own often signified a scenting hound.[127] The use of 'running' in association with scenting hounds can be seen in the mention of running rauchs in Menteith in 1508.[128] The best description of the hounds used in Scottish hunting is given by Lesley in the introduction to his *History of Scotland*.[129] Boece also describes the types of hunting dogs used in Scotland,[130] and when in 1560 C. Gesner came to print the illustrations for his *History of Quadrupeds*, he included drawings of the dogs described by Boece. These drawings were obtained by Henry Sinclair, dean of Glasgow from 1550 to 1561, and passed to Gesner via John Ferrer of Piedmont, Boece's continuator.[131]

The first type of dog mentioned by Lesley was larger than a year-old calf and was used to hunt hart and wolf. The second was smaller but more courageous, more noble and very fast and would attack both men and wild animals. Both these dogs were greyhounds hunting by sight and not by scent. Boece describes the second dog, and Gesner's illustration of it shows an animal closely resembling the modern greyhound. (Fig. 9.) According to Barbour, Bruce went stalking with hounds which were probably greyhounds of this type, since he sat and waited for the game and since when strangers sent to kill Bruce approached, he released his hounds and they attacked the strangers.[132] J. Caius, who sent a description of English dogs to Gesner, wrote about the greyhound that

some are of a greater sorte, and some of a lesser, some are smooth skynned and some are curled, the bigger therefore are appointed to hunt the bigger beasts and the smaller to hunt the smaller accordingly.[133]

Lesley's first dog was obviously one of these bigger greyhounds and if of the rough-coated variety would have closely resembled the modern Scots deerhound. This rough-coated dog was illustrated in a mid-fifteenth-century French manuscript of the hunting treatise of the Comte de Foix and by the Italian Aldovrandus in 1637.[134] (Fig. 10.) This large hairy greyhound was not called a deerhound till the nineteenth century,[135] the nearest medieval equivalent probably being the 'deir doggis' mentioned in 1541.[136]

These types of greyhounds with rough or smooth coats had been common since the time of Arrian.[137] It is the larger greyhound which is depicted on the Pictish stones (Fig. 1), although one cannot tell whether of the rough or smooth-coated variety. In the sixteenth-century wall-paintings of Kinneil House, however, it is clearly one of the larger smooth-coated variety which is portrayed.[138] (Fig. 3.) In the documentary record all greyhounds are known simply as 'leporarii'. Scottish greyhounds were renowned in the Roman Empire[139] and throughout medieval Europe. In the fourteenth century Froissart took a white greyhound, probably a large deerhound, from Scotland to France[140] and in the seventeenth chapter of the *Master of Game* Edward, Duke of York, wrote that the best greyhounds came from Scotland. It was also presumably this type of hunting dog which James offered to Ferdinand of Aragon about 1510.[141] Greyhounds, often made the *reddendo* of a grant of land,[142] were highly valued animals, and made suitable royal gifts. The theft of a greyhound might be tried before the lords of council.[143]

Lesley begins his discussion of scenting hounds by describing hairy dogs from Germany, probably a German boarhound or perhaps a type of alaunt similar to the great dane or the German boarhound.[144] Secondly, there was a smaller scenting hound similar to the first, which hunted both on land and in water, no doubt the same type of dog as the water dog obtained for James IV in 1505.[145] This is the hound which Gesner calls a Scottish waterhound and which he says was known in Scotland as a rauch. (Fig. 11.)[146] It could also be known as a brachet.[147] The hound shown on the sixteenth-century wall-painting in the room which is now the museum in Traquair House corresponds more closely to this type of scenting hound than to the sleuthhound or bloodhound.[148] In Scotland hounds which were on a leash and hunting silently were known simply as stalking rauchs, not limers.[149] The rauch, when stalking,[150] would be kept on a leash and trained not to bark. The third type of scenting hound, which was different from the preceding two, was red with black spots or vice versa. Clever and cruel, it could follow thieves and reivers but lost the scent in water. Since it was difficult to train, the best were dear to buy. This was the sleuthhound, the best known of the scenting hounds. (Fig. 12.) The fourteenth-century stories of Bruce and Wallace being hunted by sleuthhounds, or 'strecours' as they were sometimes called,[151] which lost the trail in burns, are well known.[152] The final variety of scenting hound mentioned by Lesley was low, broad and able to enter rabbit burrows and drive foxes, badgers, martens and wild cats from their lairs. If necessary it could widen a burrow and was obviously some sort of ferreting hound like a terrier. This may have been some sort of kennet, which was a small scenting hound often used like the harrier to harry game.[153] Two other types of dogs, not mentioned by Lesley, were current in medieval Scotland, spaniels kept by James IV[154] and the type of dog carved on the west Highland monuments at Rodel and Kilmory. The latter dog does not have the body of a greyhound nor the ears of a sleuthhound or a rauch and yet was big enough to attack deer, as depicted on the MacMillan cross. (Fig. 5.) Since it has a thicker body than a greyhound, short ears and a short head, it is most probably a mastiff,[155] rather than the alaunt to which Lesley referred. Mastiffs are mentioned in those English clauses included in the Scots forest laws and were capable of attacking and pulling down deer. Wearing spiked collars, they were often used to attack wolves.

Since the king hunted in various **parts of the kingdom**, he **kept** dogs at various royal palaces and castles[156] and settled hounds on his subjects in those areas where they would be most needed. In the Balquhidder area in 1471 and 1477 James III had greyhounds at Aberlednoch near Comrie[157] and in 1488 Lord Drummond kept 40 scenting hounds at the Mill of Millnab in Strathearn and William Stewart six at the Mill of Ardbeth in Balquhidder.[158] Sir William Murray of Tullibardine may also have kept royal hounds,[159] while the bailie of Menteith was responsible for collecting these dogs when the king wished to hunt.[160] In Ettrick John Murray of Hangingshaw kept dogs for the king and usually someone was sent to collect them.[161] The maintenance, training and provision of hunting dogs of the right type in the right place at the right time was, therefore, a fairly complex matter and involved not only the king's own hunting establishment but also, at least in James IV's reign, the services of several of his subjects.

The king, of course, had his own kennelmen responsible for keeping and training his hounds. In 1373 and throughout Robert II's reign the clerk of livery paid the wages of the greyhound keepers and other dogs and paid for their food.[162] In 1379 he had stone kennels built in Edinburgh Castle[163] and in 1384 he also had greyhounds in keeping at Methven.[164] In the latter part of James IV's reign Jacob Edmonstone appears to have been the head kennelman, since he was responsible for the king's dogs on the royal pilgrimages and expeditions. The dogs did not always travel with the king and might go on ahead or wait or stay behind till the king returned.[165] In that reign Beg, Black Harry and John Kinloch were also concerned with dogs, but they were not full-time kennelmen or 'doggers'.[166] James also had an English 'dogger' who kept rauchs and who travelled to England presumably to collect or exchange dogs.[167] Although all dogs had to be trained to hunt properly, little is said of this training process, but a certain Robert Douglas was paid 14s to this end and there are references to iron dog collars, leashes, and chains.[168] It was common in medieval Europe for the leash to be attached to the dog's collar by a swivel.[169] Interestingly, the Rodel monument shows the leashes attached to the gillie's arm by a swivel which prevented the leashes becoming entangled.[170] On both the Rodel and MacMillan monuments the dogs were collared, and there is a suggestion on the Rodel tomb that the collars were studded to protect the dog's neck. The dogs were fed mainly on oatmeal and meat.[171]

In the medieval hunt, since horses were never so important as the dogs, they are mentioned less frequently in the sources. What was called an ambling horse, 'gradarius', was deemed suitable for coursing, 'cursus', and hunting, 'venatu',[172] and this was probably the same type of horse as the courser on which James IV had ridden when he met Princess Margaret near Dalkeith. James was also keen to acquire French and Spanish horses.[173] There were of course royal studs throughout Scotland, and in James II's reign the most important hill runs were in Mar, where wild unbroken horses were collected and bred. They were broken in in Strathavon and horses were sent from Mar to Dundee and Edinburgh and from Strathavon to Invernochty.[174] There were stables at all the more important royal residences, including Doune and Newark, and James IV deputed Raploch near Stirling waste for the pasture of the horses of his household.[175] Such arrangements were essential in the Middle Ages for transport, let alone for hunting.

The earliest records of officials concerned with hunting in Scotland are the mentions of 'Willelmus venator' in 1122 in Cumbria and of David I's fewterers or greyhound keepers, 'veltrarii', in southern Scotland in 1114 x 1124.[176] The king continued to employ trained hunters throughout the medieval period, as in Cardross park in 1329 x 1330 and at Gairloch in 1330.[177] Stalkers were also used to assist royal hunts[178] and, as already mentioned, 'exploratores' and 'indagatores' were used in drives. The chief hunting official, however, was the 'magister venacionum', the master of the hunts, a post held by Archibald Buchan in 1489 x 1490. Although he is the only holder of the office to be recorded, this office could well have existed long before this date.[179]

At the end of a well organised hunt there could be a curée, the ceremonial cutting up of the stag. The curée was held only when a single animal was being chased and the huntsman thereby paid his last respects to the game as well as personally rewarding the hounds. There was no need to follow any set ceremony, although the game would usually be gutted before being transported. Salt was used to preserve the venison,[180] and the haunch was the most popular portion.[181] On occasion a formal curée may have been held, for Boece, when describing a curée which he attributes to the Scots, states that the man whose dog bit the deer first received the hide of the animal while the head and antlers went to the owner of the second dog. The carcass, as Bellenden says, was to be 'curit' at the master of the hunt's pleasure and the remainder was to be left to the hounds.[182] Whether or not this form of curée was current in the fifteenth century, this account suggests that some form of ceremony could be held. It is perhaps a reflection of this ceremony which appears in the ballad of 'Johnnie Cock' when he cuts 'the liver, bot and the tongue' from a deer which he has killed.[183]

Hunting seasons, though seldom mentioned, were kept in medieval Scotland. The close season for stags, 'formeisun', was mentioned by Walter Steward in the twelfth century but, as Professor Barrow has pointed out, it was subsequently mistranscribed and gave rise to the place name Fereneze.[184] The hind and the doe could be hunted in the close season during the winter and the hart and buck in the summer in the open season, which was also called the time of grease.[185] The open season for stags appears to have begun as early as March and to have continued till the end of September,[186] but the most popular months were July, August and September.[187] An early fifteenth-century Gaelic poem from the *Book of the Dean of Lismore* implies that the hunting season stretched from May to October.[188] The close season started, therefore, around October and continued till the spring and so James IV, when hunting in Glen Artney and Glenfinglas in December 1494, cannot have been hunting stags.[189] These seasons were supplemented by a general prohibition of hunting in snow or storms: in 1474 parliament enacted that no one was to kill any deer, whether doe, roe or red deer, in such weather.[190] Their kids were similarly protected by justice ayres under pain of a £10 fine.[191] That this virtually amounted to an enactment of a close season is illustrated by Boece, who has an early Scots king enact that there be no hunting in winter and spring because at that time the ground was covered with snow which forced the deer to come down from the mountains.[192] There can be little doubt that Boece had fifteenth-century practice in mind, as one suspects he had on numerous other occasions. It was likewise forbidden to hunt hares when there was snow on the ground.[193] Although these are the only hunting seasons mentioned in Scotland, seasons for other animals common elsewhere in Europe may also have applied in Scotland,[194] since the purpose of the season was to kill the animal when it was in the best condition and to give it freedom when breeding.

Hawking, as well as hunting, was a popular royal sport in the Middle Ages. The two most common types of birds used in this sport were firstly the long-winged hawks, which were the true falcons such as the peregrine falcon, the falcon gentle, the kestrel and the merlin, and secondly the short-winged hawks such as the goshawk, the sparrowhawk and the buzzard. The female of any hawk is called a falcon[195] and the male a tercel since it is one third of the size of the female. Most of these hawks and falcons were known in Scotland, since the sources contain references to goshawks,[196] sparrowhawks,[197] falcons,[198] goshawk tercel[199] and a tercel of a falcon,[200] while James IV carries a peregine falcon in his portrait by Mytens.[201] (Fig. 13.) Hawks and falcons had quite different styles of flying, hunting and killing. Long-winged falcons flew in open spaces and often flew down their quarry by endurance. They could fly at a great height and their 'stoop' from well above the quarry was a dramatic sight. Short-winged hawks were flown in wooded country since they hunted by stealth, overtaking their quarry in a short sprint. They killed not by a glancing blow as with the falcon's stoop, but by driving their talons into their victim's body.

In the medieval period there appears to have been a reasonable supply of hawks and falcons to be found in Scotland. In 1165 x 1169 the Avenels reserved hawks and sparrow hawks nesting in their woods in Eskdale, presumably because these birds could be caught and trained. To maintain this supply of hawks, they had to prevent the men of Melrose Abbey scaring the hawks away from the trees in which they were nesting so that they might fell them.[202] The first signs of a royal hawking establishment occur in the Mearns where in 1209 x 1211 lands were granted by William I to Ranulf, the falconer.[203] By 1264 William Hamilton was in charge of the king's hawks in Angus and royal mews had also been established in the north at Forres and Elgin.[204] In the fourteenth century Adam, a royal falconer, probably operated in Angus, since he was paid by the sheriff of Forfar.[205]

In the late Middle Ages Scots kings continued to obtain hawks and falcons from various parts of Scotland. Firstly, in the reigns of James III and James IV the royal falconers conducted an annual trip to Orkney and Shetland to collect hawks and falcons,[206] and the fact that in 1342 'a certain' royal falconer was called John 'de insulis' may be an earlier reflection of this practice.[207] Secondly, hawks were also obtained at various places throughout north, east, south and south-west mainland of Scotland, namely, Caithness, Atholl, Angus, Abbot's Craig near Stirling, Fife, Craigalloway, Whithorn and Carrick.[208] Thirdly, James IV received numerous gifts of hawks from his barons,[209] while in 1488 he paid the earl of Angus 100 rose nobles for a hawk.[210] James was renowned for his hawks as a result of the time and trouble which he spent on them. He obtained hawks from Norway and England[211] and sent hawks to Henry VII of England and to France,[212] while in 1499 and 1490/91 the earl of Oxford sent to Scotland for hawks.[213]

A hawk could be taken from the nest before it had learned to fly, in which case it was known as an eyass or a 'ramysset' hawk,[214] or it might be captured by nets[215] after it had learned how to kill, when it was called a passage hawk. Hawks were kept in special quarters or mews such as the hawk house at Cardross surrounded by a fence in 1329,[216] or the gallery built for his hawks by James IV in 1507, probably in Edinburgh.[217] James also maintained falconries with warders where hawks were kept and bred: Craigforth near Stirling was kept firstly by William Adamson and then by a 'certane wif';[218] Inchkeith, which was kept by Dougal Hannay,[219] one of the king's falconers, was visited by James in 1502;[220] while Earncraig, a falconry in the Pentlands, was visited in 1505.[221] Hawks were also kept at Blabo near Stirling, Kembuck Craig in Fife and at Linlithgow.[222] Consequently, James was never far from fresh supplies of hawks.

After capture a hawk not only required special quarters. It had to be hooded in order to keep it calm. When not being flown, hawks were often set on outdoor perches or blocks. In his portrait by Mytens, James IV is shown holding a bow perch in his right hand. (Fig. 13.) This type of perch could be set upright on the ground. Later the hood[223] prevented the bird flying at prey against the wishes of the hawker. The jesses which were attached to the hawk's legs were never taken off except for renewal and were attached to the leash with which the falconer held the hawk.[224] The hawk in European fashion was, as in James IV's portrait, held on the left hand which had to be gloved, unlike James' hand in that portrait.[225] In accordance with standard European practice, James, in that portrait, holds the swivel which connected the jesses to the leash between his first and second finger and has the leash wound round three of his fingers, presumably grasping the end in the little finger, the hand being held in a lightly clenched position. The bells which were attached to the hawk's legs were probably a semi-tone apart so that the discordant note enabled the hawk to be located while some distance away.[226] The lure to recover a hawk was a mock-up of a bird with a piece of meat attached. It could be swung on the end of a

F

lure line one metre or so long or simply left on the ground.[227] If a hawk broke a feather it could be mended or imped. In 1507 the stalks or piths of colewort or cabbage were used to imp broken feathers.[228] Many live fowl were taken alive and sent to the king since ducks,[229] herons,[230] geese,[231] hens[232] and cranes[233] were all employed in training or 'making' a hawk.[234] The training period may have taken from one to two years, since a two-year old or sore hawk, 'rubeus nisus', was a fairly common *reddendo*. The recipient of the *reddendo* would obviously wish to receive a trained hawk so that he could fly it immediately.[235] Since training hawks was difficult and slow, a trained hawk was very valuable, so much so that in 1474 parliament made the theft of hawks and their eggs from another man's land a point of dittay[236] and in 1504 James IV had to hide a hawk from 'men who would have her'.[237]

Since James IV was a keen hawker, he not only was accompanied by his hawks on his journeys but he also went on special hawking expeditions. In 1497, travelling from Fife to Coupar via Scone and Kinclavin, he hawked by the Tay and the Isla[238] and in a part of Angus which had been a popular hawking area since the thirteenth century. In 1507 James went on a hawking trip through East Lothian, passing Whitekirk, Hailes, Dunbar and Cranshaws.[239] Biggar,[240] Bathgate[241] and Lauder[242] were also favoured hawking areas. Since any marshy area beside a river or loch was suitable for this sport, Falkland, Linlithgow and Edinburgh were also ideal areas for hawking.[243] On a hawking trip, after a scout called the 'Master Spyour' had spotted the fowl,[244] the birds might be raised by a dog,[245] or by beaters,[246] and a boat would often be necessary.[247] Hawk clubs were used either by the beaters to raise the game or else to stun the fowls caught by the hawk, since hawks were seldom allowed to kill their game.[248] When hawking, there was always the danger that these valuable birds would be lost and hawks were regularly returned to James IV from various parts of the country.[249]

To capture, train and look after his hawks the king required his own falconers, several of whom are recorded in the reigns of Robert I, David II and Robert II. (See Table 3, p. 77.) In the fifteenth century two of James II's falconers are mentioned and at any one time James IV probably employed more than ten falconers, and in 1500 he retained at least sixteen. Falconers were well looked after: they had their livery provided; in 1329 Mathew, a falconer, received a robe;[250] James IV provided their hose, gowns and doublets;[251] and the king met all their expenses[252] including travelling expenses.[253] At the start of James IV's reign some falconers were of higher standing than others. Certain falconers including Dande Doule, John Man, John Baty and Donald Falconer[254] always held lands near Falkland, receiving remission of all or part of their rent by way of payment. In 1498 Walter, Fynne, Dougal Hannay, Alexander Law and John Loudon also rented lands in Fife.[255] These falconers were better off or more favoured than those who held no recorded lands. Although there was a moderate turnover of falconers — fifty men in all were falconers during this reign — thirteen of James IV's falconers served for ten years or more, which also suggests that some falconers would be of higher or more senior standing than others. It is not surprising that towards the end of this reign three falconers received half-yearly pensions: Hannay in 1505 and 1507 and David Dronar in 1512 received £10.[256] The head falconer was called the master falconer and in 1511 this office was held by Sir Alexander Mackulloch of Merton, who may well have held this post since 1500.[257] For his services as master falconer he received a pension of £50 half yearly in 1507[258] and £100 annually in 1511.[259] Hannay may have been replaced as his second-in-command by David Dronar. The master falconer would probably organise the king's hawking establishment as well as carrying out the same duties as other falconers, travelling to collect hawks and seeing to their keeping. James IV, therefore, built up a large, well-equipped hawking establishment, based on a nucleus of experienced, loyal and favoured officials, which was renowned outwith Scotland.

The king's subjects also kept hawks, but not of course on the same scale as the king, although they might gift birds to the king.[260] Barons had their own hawkers and fowlers,[261] but of their status little is known. In 1508 Walter Stewart was the falconer of the bishop of Dunkeld and was paid 4d per day when the bishop was hawking.[262] Since their hawks were every bit as valuable to them as the royal hawks were to the king, theft appears to have been a fairly common occurrence: Dundrennan Abbey had hawks stolen and their keepers tied up in 1494;[263] and Oliver Sinclair of Roslin had hawks stolen from Earncraig in 1506.[264] Fowling with nets, for the common people, was a more practical since less expensive means of killing birds. Henryson's fable, 'The Swallow', concerns a fowler who set his nets and placed chaff to lure birds into them and then, when the birds were in the trap, drew his nets over them.[265] Crossbows with blunt-ended bolts were also used for fowling.[266] Although this was a less noble sport than hawking, James IV did indulge in it. He used firearms for fowling in 1508 when he was ferried round the Isle of May with his culverin to shoot at the fowls.[267] James IV had in his service fowlers[268] of whom the master was probably Witherspoon, who was also a fisher and a fiddler,[269] and in 1505 the royal fowler went to Fife to take fowl with his nets.[270]

Certain wild fowls were protected by seasons established in the fifteenth century by parliament: in 1427/8 partridges, plovers, blackcocks, grey hens and moorcocks and other such wild fowls were not to be hunted between the beginning of Lent and August under pain of 40s enforceable by the justice ayre;[271] and in 1457/8 no one was to slay any edible fowls at moulting time since they could not fly at that time.[272] This latter act offered protection to partridges, plovers and wild duck as well as pheasants, cranes, herons and quails, but did not apply to fowls of 'reif'.[273] In 1474 parliament tried further to protect wild duck and partridges by making the theft of their eggs a point of dittay with a penalty of 40s.[274] The heron was fully protected at least from 1493 onwards,[275] since it was reserved to the king. One other seasonal limitation may have been that certain hawks flew better at some times of the year than others since a season of goshawks is mentioned in 1296 x 1297.[276] Since the close season was fairly short, hawking was virtually a year-round sport, which increased its popularity.

In medieval Scotland, as in the rest of Europe, hawking and hunting were regarded as noble sports: Pitscottie, when discussing the activities of James III's brother, Alexander, Duke of Albany, called them gentlemen's pastimes or knightly games;[277] while in 1498 Andrea Trevisiano believed that most Scots nobles had great forests for hunting game on their estates.[278] Hunting was a recommended activity when training kings[279] and knights: Gilbert Hay in his translation of 'Le Livre de L'Ordre de Chevalerie' in the mid-fifteenth century advocated that knights be good riders both on war horses and on coursers and that they hawk and hunt for hart, hind, doe, roe, boar, bear, wolf and lion and practise all such honourable pleasures.[280] One reason why hunting was a noble sport was the association of hunting and fighting. Not only was hunting, whether a drive or a course or a *par force* hunt, seen as an excellent training for war since it gave practice in riding and the use of weapons, but there was also in hunting the danger of death.[281] Pitscottie draws a direct parallel when describing an ambush in 1445 by saying that one side lay in wait for the other 'as they had been settand tinchellis for the murther of wyld beistes'.[282] As in hunting, there was a warlike element in hawking, where the hawk was the predator and the fowl the prey. This is a comparison drawn explicitly in the *Book of Alexander*, where attackers are compared with sparrowhawks and defenders with quails or larks.[283]

Apart from the similarity of the techniques utilised in hunting and in fighting, both were thought of as types of play. Just as hunting and hawking were sports with certain rules and procedures to follow so, at times, fighting took on the appearance of a sport as jousts or personal combat where there were rules to be obeyed and forms to be observed. While this was not always true of war, so people did not always hunt for sport.

The popularity of hunting as a sport in the Middle Ages is well nigh self-evident, but the very existence of hunting reserves and free forest grants gives expression to its popularity. Moreover, the stories about kings, such as David I, stopping to hear petitions before setting out on a hunting expedition would lose their significance were not hunting a popular pursuit.[284] Consequently, training in hunting was received at an early age, as was the case with James II and James III.[285]

Although hunting was considered a warlike pastime, women did take part both in chases and drives throughout the medieval period.[286] More dubious, however, was the suitability of hunting as a pastime for churchmen. In the early thirteenth century Walter the third Steward did not regard hunting as a fitting activity for monks,[287] and yet in 1261 the abbot of Lindores possessed hounds.[288] There seems to have been an opinion in the thirteenth century that if monks did hunt, as their receipt of forest grants in part argues, they had to pursue such not altogether becoming activities circumspectly, since they were not countenanced by the church.[289] The cartulary of Dunfermline, for instance, includes a decree from a Lateran Council that deans on visitations are to travel without dogs, hunters and birds.[290]

Hunting was a noble sport not only because nobles among others practised it but also because a sense of fair play was required. It was not the killing but the sport which mattered. In the *par force* hunt the attempt to keep the dogs on the right line, the efforts of the stag to escape and the hunters' attempts to foil such escapes were all as important as the kill. The same was true of coursing and certain types of drive where the hunters waited hidden from the game and from each other on horseback ready to chase the game. Those Gaelic poems, common in medieval Scotland, which stressed the feats of valour performed when hunting also argue that hunting was a sport.[291] The purpose of hunting seasons embodies a sense of fair play, as did the existence of the fence month when hinds were not to be disturbed. In 1503, when a hart was coursed by a greyhound outside Edinburgh, Yonge considered the greyhound made a 'fayr course' even although the hart was not caught.[292]

The clearest statement of the desirability of fair play in the hunt can be found in Boece who, when describing the society of the early Scots, creates a semi-mythical hunter's paradise.[293] His account of the hunting laws and hunting practices which he attributes to the Scots conveys the impression that he was looking back to a golden hunting age whose customs he would like to have seen current throughout fifteenth-century Scotland. As the expression of the ideal hunting arrangements which one man would like to have seen in use, Boece's account of the Scots' hunting practices is of considerable interest.

The Scots, said Boece, had no wars or troubles and therefore they concentrated on hunting, which kept them healthy and lively. The Scots found the hunting methods of the Picts alien to them on account of the use of nets, missiles and clubs. Instead the Scots concentrated on their dogs, which were fast, keen, courageous and beautiful. Clergymen, however, should not keep horses or dogs 'voluptatis causa'. According to Boece one king stressed the importance of slaying hares only by chase of hounds and of allowing the hare to go free if it escaped for a certain length of time. He also had another Scots king enact that no one kill fawns or a hind with fawns or hunt deer when there was snow on the ground. Such laws, Boece states, were passed so that hunting, a sport for nobles, be not destroyed by sharp practice. Since fair play and love of sport were inherent in the chivalric ideal, it is not surprising to find that they were present in the medieval Scottish attitude towards hunting.

Hunting and hawking never became so formalised in Scotland in the Middle Ages as they did in Western Europe: there was a master of the hunts; there was a master falconer; and there was a master 'spyour'; but the men who kept the dogs were simply doggers; the dogs were most often known straightforwardly as greyhounds or rauchs; hawks were usually referred to as hawks or falcons;

the seasons were not the subject of precise legislation; and the official responsible for the tents was simply the pavilion man. There was not that pro-
liferation of technical vocabulary so characteristic of the hunting treatises of
England and Europe. There was perhaps a larger amount of specialised
language introduced in connection with hawking than with hunting, but
generally the terminology of huntsmen and falconers appears to have been
decided by practical considerations and was not cultivated artificially as it was
in England and France.[294]

Nevertheless, a certain amount of social distinction entered into hawking
and hunting. Scottish kings did not stint their provision for the chase or for
hawking, since facilities for the chase and falconry were the mark of a rich and
hospitable court. Georg Von Ehingen records that much honour was shown
him in hunting, dancing and feasting at the court of James II,[295] while James IV
was well known for his hawking establishment.

That this social distinction never was so pronounced in Scotland as in
England and France can be attributed to the less formal nature of hunting
methods in Scotland. The *par force* hunt in England and France was governed
by numerous rules on blowing of horns, on slipping of hounds and on killing
the quarry. In Scotland this formal type of hunt never was so important as the
drive, in which a far larger number of common people were involved than in a
par force hunt, where no one outside the hunter's household need have
participated. While there was obviously a distinction in a drive between the
king and his nobles who waited for the hunt and the stable who merely had to
drive the game towards them, the fact that commoners shared in the hunt may
have prevented the excessive degree of social distinction which appeared in
medieval French hunting.[296] Towards the end of the medieval period, however, the distinction of stable and hunters may have begun to harden, for the
king at his seat was no longer alone or with just one companion: James IV
probably had a tent in which to take refreshments while he waited for the
drive. One can see here the beginning of the process common throughout
sixteenth-century Europe by which the drive became a spectacle and ceased to
be a sport, where the success of the drive was measured not by the quality of
the hunt but by the number of kills.

Hawking, which was probably introduced to Scotland by the Normans,
developed a more detailed social hierarchy. In most countries hawks and
falcons were placed in a variety of social scales[297] which, although seldom
adhered to, are of interest in that they were drawn up in the first place. That
the idea of such a classification was current in Scotland is shown by the
fifteenth-century poem, 'The Book of the Howlett'.[298] In this poem certain
birds are personified as different people: the eagle is personified as the
emperor; the erne as the king; gerfalcons as dukes; falcons as earl marischall to
the emperor; goshawks as chieftains of war; and sparrowhawks as knights. In
practice the peregrine falcon was the most highly valued bird, and it is this bird
which James IV holds on his hand in Mytens' painting. (Fig. 13.) The goshawk

was the most efficient bird for filling the larder and was used by the lower classes as well as by the nobility.[299] In Scotland, the king hawked with all types of hawks and falcons, but one can perhaps see some reflection of the classification of birds not only in James IV's portrait but also in the fact that ballads mention the goshawk more frequently than any other hawk, since the ballads, which embodied folk tradition, probably reflect the customs of the common folk.[300]

As pursuits of lords and ladies at court, hunting and hawking entered into the courtly literature of Gavin Douglas and William Dunbar,[301] but only 'King Hart' by Gavin Douglas contains more than a passing reference to these sports. In an extended allegory of life 'Dame Pleasance' goes out hunting and captures 'King Hart', which points to an obvious allegory in 'King Hart's' name.[302] The only other extended reference to hunting so far encountered is in 'Sir Eger, Sir Grym and Sir Graysteel', where the hunt is used as an accepted literary convention for removing one of the heroes from the scene.[303] The scarcity of references to hunting in the considerable amount of Scots literature which has survived from this period is not matched in the Gaelic literature, which provides numerous poems celebrating the hunt. It is noticeable that when James IV was hunting in Glenfinglas, Balquhidder or Strathfillan, his evening's entertainment usually included a clarsach player.[304] Many of the Gaelic poems including the tales of Finn which were known in Scotland could be sung to the clarsach, and it was no doubt Gaelic hunting tales to which James IV listened.[305]

It is not surprising to find traces of such an all-pervading pursuit as hunting in matters spiritual as well as temporal. Hunting scenes are depicted on several fourteenth-, fifteenth- and sixteenth-century west Highland tombstones in a manner strikingly similar to the hunting scenes on the Pictish stones. The reason why hunting scenes should have been so regularly depicted on these monuments is by no means certain. While the west Highland scenes closely resemble the Pictish stones and while classical parallels can be found for the Pictish scenes,[306] it is unsatisfactory to say that the scenes are random copyings one from the other with neither rhyme nor reason. Firstly, there is an obvious realism about the Pictish scenes which has been remarked on by both Cruden and Anderson,[307] as there also is in the west Highland monuments.[308] Moreover, there are differences between the Pictish and west Highland stones, not only in dress, but in the type of dogs being used.[309] In a pagan context, the portrayal of hunting scenes might in some ways be associated with a deer-god like Cernunnos,[310] but this seems unlikely since no 'man/deer' is shown on the stones and since the deer have no apparent divine attributes. In an early Christian context, deer hunts could be associated with miraculous conversions resulting from the appearance of a cross between the antlers of a stag, as was the case with St Eustace and St Hubert.[311] The parallel here is with the conversion of St Paul and the voice which said to him 'Why persecutest thou me?' Such an interpretation is also unsatisfactory since the cults of St Eustace and St

Hubert did not develop till the twelfth and fifteenth centuries respectively. Indeed, it may be wrong to assume that the hunting scenes on Pictish monuments have any religious overtones and perhaps the only conclusion which can be reached is that it is pointless to search for the reason why these scenes were carved until the purpose of the stones themselves is understood. While the west Highland hunting scenes undoubtedly occur in a sepulchral context, they show no signs of stylisation which one might expect if they had served a symbolic function. The contrast of the MacLeod and the MacMillan scenes points to the hunt being carved for its own sake. If one accepts that the west Highland monuments were constructed to serve as a memorial and even an eulogy to the deceased, then it would be reasonable to find hunts portrayed on the sepulchral monuments of a society whose literature so obviously celebrated the hunt.

The best-known link of hunting and religion in Scotland is the foundation story of Holyrood abbey, where David I was saved by the appearance of a cross between a stag's antlers. It is already known that this legend, which appeared in the early fifteenth century, must be based on the cult of St Eustace and not of St Hubert.[312] In similar vein, the legend of St Gilles, the hermit accidentally wounded by the arrow from a hunting party of the Visigothic king, Wamba, led to the foundation of the Benedictine monastery at St Gilles in Provence.[313] It is notable that not only Holyrood Abbey, but also the parish church of Edinburgh, St Giles, should be associated with a saint whose legend centres on a hunting incident.

Hunting and hawking in Scotland, while clearly a part of general European developments, contained features which were peculiarly Scottish. Two such features, the prominence of the drive and literary references to hunting, can be attributed to Gaelic influence while a third, the lesser degree of formalisation of hunting and the resultant social balance, may also be attributable to Gaelic influence through the drive. In other words, the native culture of Scotland in the twelfth and thirteenth centuries had managed to influence the Norman incomers at least as far as hunting was concerned to the extent that in the fourteenth, fifteenth and sixteenth centuries Scottish hunting and hawking practices can be distinguished from their European counterparts.

Table 3. ROYAL FALCONERS

Dates	Name	Source
1209 x 1211	Ranulf	*RRS*, ii, 497
1264	William Hamilton	*ER*, i, 7, 8
1329	Matthew	*Ibid.*, i, 216
1329	Adam	*Ibid.*, i, 210
1329-1330	Simon 'de Cathania'	*Ibid.*, i, 239, 294
1342	John 'de Insulis'[1]	*Ibid.*, i, 499
1359	Adam	*Ibid.*, i, 591
1362 x 1364	{ John Fauconer { William Lely	*Ibid.*, ii, 132
1385-1388	John Barclay	*Ibid.*, iii, 672, 677, 683, 686
1449 x 1450	'Farnle'	*Ibid.*, v, (Strathearn), 419
1473-1475	John 'Cultis'	*Ibid.*, viii, 231, 291
1476 x 1477	Thomas Cramond	*Ibid.*, viii, 441
1488	David	*TA*, i, 92
1488-1503	John Callendar	*Ibid.*, i, 89; ii, 375
1488-1513	Donald (Old)	*ER*, x, 203; xiii, 503
1489-1502	John the Man	*TA*, i, 106; *ER*, xii, 9
1491-1504	Downy (Old)	*TA*, i, 194; ii, 462
1491-1492	Lang Tom Reid, Downy's man	*TA*, i, 194; *ER*, x, 321
1490-1507	Dande (Andrew) Doule	*ER*, x, 257; *TA*, iii, 414
1491-1500 (1501)	John Lyndesay	*ER*, x, 342; xi, 189, 333
1491	Pringle	*TA*, i, 194
1491	Caryk	*Ibid.*
1491	Domynico	*Ibid.*
1491	Rob Kyttock	*Ibid.*
1491-1513	John Baty (Old)	*ER*, x, 316; xiii, 503
1491-1513	John Knox	*TA*, i, 177; iv, 414
1495	Alexander Falconer	*ER*, x, 510
1495-1508	Hannay[2]	*TA*, i, 235; iv, 115
1495-1499	Fynne	*Ibid.*, i, 235; *ER*, xi, 155
1496-1505	Alexander Law	*TA*, i, 306; ii, 474
1496-1497	Maltsone	*Ibid.*, i, 306, 366
1497	Robert Liale	*Ibid.*, i, 363
1497	Cowtree	*Ibid.*, i, 352
1497	Nely	*Ibid.*, i, 375
1497-1503	John Loudon	*ER*, xi, 78
1498-1506	Walter Falconer (Old)	*Ibid.*, xi, 155; *TA*, iii, 333
1491-1501	John Lyndesay	*ER*, x, 342; xi, 333
1500-1513	Sir Alexander MacKulloch of Myreton	*Ibid.*, xi, 348; *TA*, iv, 443
1501-1512	Dougal Hannay (Young)[2]	*TA*, ii, 51; iv, 342
1501-1505	William Strang	*Ibid.*, ii, 60; iii, 137
1501-1504	Robert Merton	*Ibid.*, ii, 106, 327
1501-1503	(Hugh) Wallace	*Ibid.*, ii, 51, 368, 409
1501-1504	Ramsay	*Ibid.*, ii, 117, 451

1. Described as 'cuidam falconario'.
2. There were two falconers called Hannay and it is very difficult to distinguish them. One appears to have been called simply Hannay and the other Young Hannay or Dougal Hannay.

Table 3. Royal Falconers (continued)

Dates	Name	Source
1501-1506	Witherspoon	*Ibid.*, ii, 127; iii, 206
1502	Dick Lowdoun	*Ibid.*, ii, 157
1502-1508	Ersh Downy	*Ibid.*, ii, 301; iv, 66
1503	'Makwillin'	*Ibid.*, ii, 411
1503	Alexander Wardlaw	*Ibid.*, ii, 395
1505-1512	David Dronar[3] alias Lyndsay	*ER*, xii, 441; xiii, 503; *TA*, iv, 342, 441
1503-1513	David Falconer[3]	*ER*, xii, 189; *TA*, iv, 410
1505-1506	John MacKulloch	*ER*, xii, 419
1506-1507	Simon MacKulloch	*Ibid.*, 546
1505-1507	Adam Cockburn	*TA*, iii, 107, 385
1505-1507	Robert	*Ibid.*, iii, 136, 387
1505	Hobbe	*Ibid.*, iii, 130
1506	Wille	*Ibid.*, iii, 180
1507	John Law	*Ibid.*, iii, 377
1508	Simson	*Ibid.*, iv, 138
1508	John Makcowlik[4]	*Ibid.*, iv, 139
1508	Alexander MacKulloch, son[5]	*Ibid.*, iv, 126
(1507-1513)		(*Ibid.*, iv, 51, 416)
1512-1513	Hector Stewart	*Ibid.*, iv, 431, 418
1513	Simon Fraser	*Ibid.*, iv, 407

3. David Dronar and David Falconer may be the same person.
4. Perhaps the same as John MacKulloch 1505-6.
5. It is hard to separate Sir Alexander from Alexander. They may be identical but Alexander and Sir Alexander are both mentioned in 1508.

Table 4. JAMES IV's HUNTING AND HAWKING TRIPS[1]

Date	Month	Place	Source
1488	August	Glenfinglas? Bathgate?[2]	*TA*, i, 83, 92
1489 x 1490		Glenfinglas	*ER*, x, 187
1489-90	January	Lauder[2]	*TA*, i, 127
1492	July	Glenfinglas	*Ibid*., i, 198, 200
1493	December	Glen Artney & Glenfinglas	*RMS*, ii, 2185; *ER*, x, 429
1496	April/May	Glenfinglas	*TA*, i, 274
1496	October/November	Coupar Angus[2]	*Ibid*., i, 304
1497	September	Biggar[2]	*ER*, xi, 16; *TA*, i, 359, 360
1498 x 1499		Glenfinglas	*ER*, xi, 164
1501	September	Balquhidder & Strathfillan	*ER*, xii, 27; *TA*, ii, 119
1505	August	Strathearn & Glenfinglas	*TA*, iii, 156, 157
1505	September	Biggar[2]	*Ibid*., iii, 158, 159
1506	August/September	Strathearn, Balquhidder, Glenfinglas & North	*Ibid*., iii, 334-344
1507	August	Biggar[2]	*Ibid*., iii, 409
1507	September	Restalrig[2]	*Ibid*., iv, 72
1507	September	Glenfinglas	*Ibid*., iv, 75; *ER*, xiii, 59
1507	October	East Lothian[2]	*TA*, iv, 78-80
1507/8	January	Inchaffray Loch[2]	*Ibid*., 96
1508	June	Isle of May[2]	*Ibid*., 130
1508	July	Glen Artney & Glenfinglas	*Ibid*., 137; *ER*, xii, 192

1. This table excludes most pilgrimages to Tain and Whithorn.
2. A hawking trip.

5

Fieldwork

SINCE hunting in the Middle Ages was a widespread activity, it is not surprising to find that it has left its mark on the landscape. Such archaeological features as survive are associated not with free forests and warrens, which were juridical rights imposed on a geographical area and not in themselves physical entities, but with hunting lodges and parks. Hunting lodges used by the king fell into two categories: those which were permanent stone castles serving purposes other than the provision of accommodation during a royal hunt; and those which were less permanent structures built primarily to provide shelter for hunting parties. Newark, Kindrochit and Kincardine castles, which fall into the former category, illustrate the type of castles which might be used as hunting lodges. Kincardine Castle, probably built beside the royal park in the reign of Alexander II, was, like Kinclevin Castle which may also have lodged hunting parties, a rectangular enclosure castle of a relatively simple type with buildings ranged round a courtyard surrounded by a wall which had no projecting towers.[1] Kindrochit Castle, frequented by Robert II, was based on a hall or 'palatium' and not on a tower, a plan obviously suited to a hunting seat.[2] Newark, on the other hand, built in the early fifteenth century, was a straightforward tower-house.[3] Of these three types of castle, that which could most suitably have been adapted to the less permanent hunting lodges was the simple rectangular plan with buildings ranged round a courtyard.

Temporary hunting lodges are recorded in Glenfinglas and Strathbraan. Robert II is the most likely originator of the hunting seat in Glenfinglas which he visited in 1382.[4] It seems to have fallen into disrepair, since in 1458 x 1459 James Balfour was paid £5 6s to build one hall and two chambers there.[5] At this cost the building was probably of wood. A similar structure may have existed at Newark, for at the same time James II had one hall and two chambers built and repaired there along with the repair of some other rooms to provide shelter for himself, the chancellor and the comptroller who were no doubt attending a forest court.[6] To complete his building programme in that year James II ordered the construction of a more substantial lodge at Loch Freuchie in Strathbraan at a cost of £24.[7] It comprised a hall, a chamber, a kitchen and four other offices or outbuildings. Since these lodges were probably built of wood and only occupied for short spells, they frequently fell into disrepair. The lodge at Loch Freuchie fell into disuse after James II's reign but chairs, doors and locks were replaced in the Hunthall of Glenfinglas in 1459 x 1460 and further repairs were made in 1488.[8] This Hunthall remained in use throughout James IV's reign.[9]

From documentary evidence it is impossible to determine the plan of these lodges. It is clear from the name 'Hunthall' given to the Glenfinglas lodge and from the construction of halls at Newark and Loch Freuchie that the hall was the basic element of the lodge, a fact which recalls the 'palatium' of Kindrochit. In early medieval England royal hunting lodges were similar in size to the 'Hunthall' of Glenfinglas, and one of John's lodges included a hall and other buildings laid out around a courtyard.[10] Whether these less permanent lodges were built around a courtyard, as the plan of Kincardine and English practice would argue, or whether the hall was a central feature on the model of Kindrochit Castle could now be determined only by excavation.

The sites of the lodges in Strathbraan cannot be located from fieldwork alone. The lodge at Halymill[11] may be connected either with Millton marked on General Roy's map of *c* 1750[12] on the left bank of the Braan below Amulree or with the castle at Trochrie held by William Stewart in 1606.[13] There are three possible sites for the lodge situated near Loch Freuchie. The first site, at Easter Garra, at the head of Strathbraan, which was marked on the first edition of the Ordnance Survey 6" map of 1862 as the site of a castle,[14] today resembles a farm settlement with a sheep fank rather than a hunting lodge and it also lies some distance from Loch Freuchie. The second possible site is that of the modern hunting lodge on the south side of the loch which has recently been demolished.[15] This, however, is a low site and Roy's map places the road and, therefore, the most common route along the valley on the north side of the loch.[16] The third and most likely site for this lodge is at Wester Shian,[17] where Stobie's map of Perthshire made in 1783 marks a castle in ruins.[18] The Ordnance Survey name book, compiled in 1864, states that, according to local tradition these ruins were removed for building purposes in 1820.[19] The site of this castle, possibly the successor of James II's lodge, is a flat-topped projection from the hillside which overlooks the valley and is sufficiently near to Loch Freuchie to have been named after it. This site is in many ways similar to the possible site of the Hunthall in Glenfinglas.

In Glenfinglas the modern farms all occupy sites inhabited in the fifteenth century when they were recorded in the Exchequer Rolls as ordinary settlements and not as lodges.[20] It follows, therefore, that the Hunthall must have been on another site and has not been built over by a later farm settlement. Air photographs,[21] taken before the flooding of the glen in 1956, revealed a possible site on the west side of the valley above the settlement of Grodich. This site, accessible on foot when the reservoir is low, is an island when the reservoir is full and is marked as such on the Ordnance Survey map.[22] (Fig. 14.) This mound, which is less than 20 metres above the valley floor, stands on a flattish terrace on the west side of the valley. When viewed from the south, as in Figure 15, the mound stands between two to three metres in height. A bank and ditch run round the west and south sides of the mound but whether they are associated with the mound as a Hunthall or with later field banks and dykes of stone is uncertain. Viewed from the west, as in Figure 14, it can be seen that any approach to this mound would have been made from the north-west and that the lodge itself would have been on the higher, more southerly part of the mound. This site, like that at Loch Freuchie, was strategically placed on the side of a valley and would have served as an ideal base for hunting. Only archaeological excavation, however, could determine whether or not this mound is the site of the 'Hunthall' of Glenfinglas. If this were the site of the 'Hunthall', excavation would also reveal what plan was followed in these temporary lodges. whether a plan based on a hall or on a courtyard or on a combination of these two.

A park, as a hunting reserve, differed from a forest or a warren in that the deer were kept captive within it. A park was enclosed by an earthen bank and ditch usually surmounted by a fence or palisade or by a wall, structures often called a park pale. The ditch and bank round a park differ from defensive earthworks, since the ditch was placed on the inside of the bank,[23] thus presenting a greater obstacle to the deer within the park, and from field banks and dykes which seldom have a pronounced ditch associated with them at all. Parks can be located both by the remains of park pales and by documentary evidence.

It is documentary evidence which reveals that Stirling old park which lay to the west of the castle was built by William I,[24] but archaeological evidence must also be used to locate the bounds of the park. (See Map 3.) This old park fell out of use but was renovated by James IV in the late fifteenth and early sixteenth centuries. James IV's park, however, had extended to 3 librates and 4 merklands returning £3 13s 4d[25] to the crown, whereas the earlier park had returned £6 13s 4d.[26] The park of James IV, therefore, was probably smaller than that of William I and scme trace of this can perhaps be detected on the ground. The bounds of William I's park may have followed the line of the parish boundary marked today by a fence and a ditch, since it forms a much more natural line for the park pale to the north of the present park. The bounds of the present park would then belong to James IV's renovation and it is probably traces of this pale which were once visible on the north-east boundary of the King's Park and which are still visible to the south-east of the King's Knot.[27] The boundaries of the new park of Stirling, built by Alexander III[28] and repaired in 1288 x 1290[29] have been traced as part of the study of the site of the Battle of Bannockburn,[30] although no remains of this pale survive.

Undoubtedly the most outstanding remains of a park pale to be found in Scotland are those of Kincardine park, which may also have been constructed by William I.[31] The boundary of this park falls into two parts, the main pale and a northerly extension not previously mapped. (See Map 4.) The traces of the main pale are clearly visible to the south of Clatterin' Brig, where a dyke

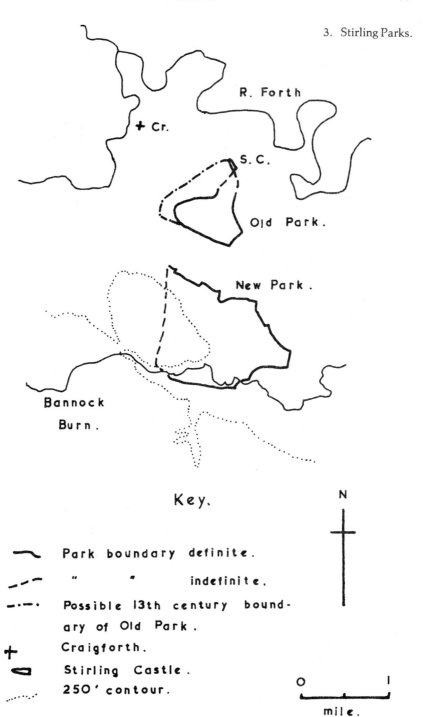

3. Stirling Parks.

R. Forth

+ Cr.

S.C.

Old Park.

New Park.

Bannock
Burn.

Key.

N

Park boundary definite.

"   "   indefinite.

Possible 13th century boundary of Old Park.

Craigforth.

Stirling Castle.

250' contour.

O   I

mile.

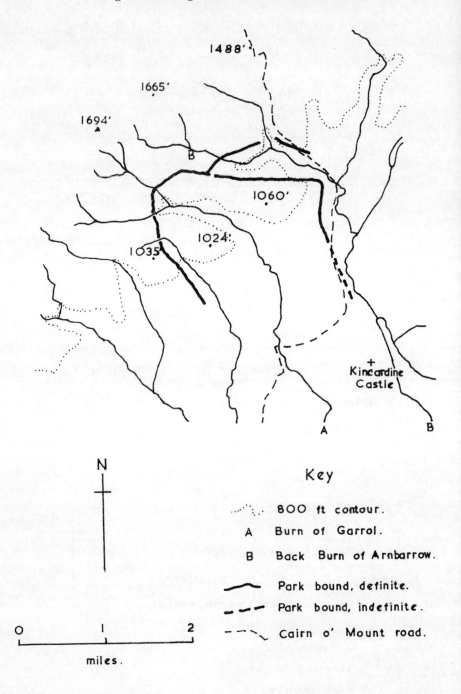

4. Kincardine Park.

has recently been built on top of the pale bank.[32] To the west of Clatterin' Brig the distance from the bottom of the internal ditch to the top of the bank varies from 1.2 to 1.5 metres and the whole earthwork is approximately 5 metres wide.[33] Moving westwards, a gap has been left where the main pale crosses a narrow steep-sided valley or cleft in the ridge which the pale follows.[34] Where the pale crosses the north tributary of the Garrol Burn,[35] it changes direction to run straight across the valley floor with a break only at the burn, which may have been closed off by a wooden fence. On the west side of the park the pale turns southwards and runs into Mon Duff wood where it is crossed by several field dykes.[36] No surface traces survive of the southern boundary of the park, but the road between Clatterin' Brig and Fettercairn does provide a convenient east and south boundary. Although there are traces of early roads within the park, a medieval predecessor of the Clatterin' Brig road may have gone round the outside of the park. Alternatively the pale may have adjoined Kincardine Castle in a manner common in the twelfth and thirteenth centuries, a possibility supported by the survival of the name King's Park immediately to the north of the castle.[37] The northern extension to this park, which may represent the work of Alexander III, leaves the main pale close to the break in the north side of the park.[38] This additional pale runs north-west across one tributary of the Back Burn of Arnbarrow, but at another tributary of that burn a gap has been left in the pale.[39] The ends of the pale have been neatly rounded off, leaving a break several hundred metres wide across a steep-sided valley. After turning south the pale appears to have been used as a field dyke before crossing the Cairn o' Mount road. The park pale then continues southwards between the present road and the old road, probably rejoining the main pale near Clatterin' Brig.

The leasing of the park[40] in the fourteenth century is reflected in the various field banks, plough marks and ruined settlements to be seen within the park on the east bank of the Garrol Burn. The park appears to have been split in two, an east and a west park,[41] in the fourteenth century, and while no traces of such a division can be seen on the ground, the Garrol Burn splits the park into a smaller west and a larger east section.

Lintrathen park, unlike the preceding examples, is known only from archaeological evidence. (See Map 5.) The park, whose pale is now partly submerged in Lintrathen reservoir, is believed to have belonged to Alan Durward in the thirteenth century, as a stone set up in 1881 records, but this is as yet unverified.[42] The clearest section of the pale with its internal ditch lies on the eastern slope of the Knock of Formal. The northern boundary of the park is of interest because the main pale is broken by a northerly addition which has been used as the boundary of a young plantation, which at present prohibits examination of the more southerly and earlier pale. These banks have obviously been repaired since the thirteenth century, if that is when they were first constructed, but what remains was probably used for a drive or for the capture of deer as at Kincardine.[43]

G

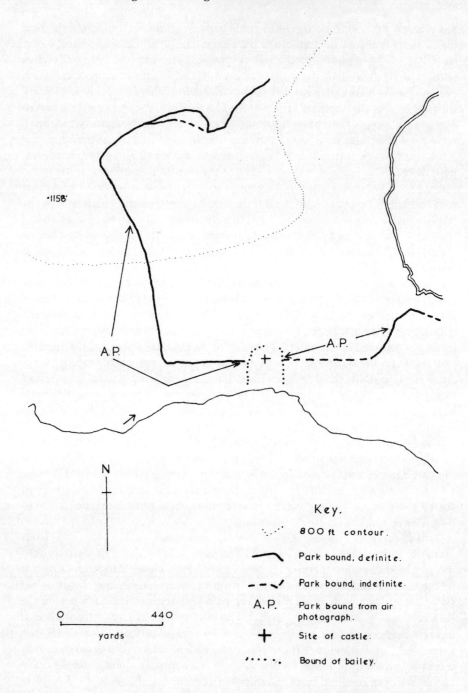

·1158'

A.P.

A.P.

N

Key.

⋰⋰⋰   800 ft contour.

——   Park bound, definite.

– – ⌐   Park bound, indefinite.

A.P.   Park bound from air
        photograph.

✝   Site of castle.

•••••   Bound of bailey.

0 ————— 440
      yards

5. Park at Lintrathen.

Although deer were supposed to be able to enter and leave a park of their own free will,[44] park owners do appear to have driven deer into their parks and constructed special extensions to facilitate this method of restocking their parks. Moreover, the purpose of the internal ditch was to present a major obstacle to the deer inside the park and so prevent them leaving freely. If the park pale was employed to aid a drive, the deer could be driven towards a break in the pale where the hunters could wait for them as at an elrick.

These three examples show that parks were usually situated close to, if not actually adjoining, the castle or residence of the owner and that the bounds of a park might be altered or extended to assist restocking or hunting. Fieldwork can tell no more about the nature of park pales, and only archaeology could reveal the methods used in constructing these pales and the precise nature of the palisade, if any, placed on top of the pale bank.

SECTION B

INSTITUTIONAL ANALYSIS

6
The Creation of Royal Forests

IT is essential to determine the social and economic impact of hunting reserves on medieval Scottish society. Since forests or hunting reserves contained resources of value, not only to their owners but also to other inhabitants of the land, they did not, indeed could not, exist in an economic and social vacuum. They included both wooded and open land. The woods provided timber for fuel, building, tanning, charcoal-burning and the manufacture of weapons and implements and sheltered animals such as deer and boar which provided meat, fat, oil, sinews and leather. Both woods and open ground provided pasture for domestic animals. Cattle, sheep, goats and horses fed on green leaves in summer and in winter on leaves gathered dry. In oak and beech woods acorns and beech mast were the diet of pigs. Finally bees' nests often found in woods provided honey which was the only form of sweetening. While woods were large enough, there was little need to regulate the exploitation of these resources, but as the population grew and as the clearing of woods for agriculture increased, these resources came under pressure. If flocks were grazed in a wood they ate leaves, broke branches, cleared the undergrowth, altered the drainage and so could destroy a wooded area which would no longer be able to harbour wild animals. Over-cropping of timber produced similar results. Because of these basic ecological facts, some form of control of grazing, felling and hunting was required. That hunting was a sport as well as a source of food complicated the situation, because the creation of reserves whose primary purpose was to provide sport occasioned control of woods and open land for only one of the many activities for which that land was valued. Consequently, hunting reserves were opposed to the use of a certain area of land for certain essential economic uses. The rights which the lord of a forest exercised within his reserve limited economic activity in order to provide the best possible conditions for the maintenance of the game.

In face of the needs of outsiders and inhabitants for wood, pasture and game these rights could never be enforced absolutely. The holder of forest rights could only impose his wishes by means of his forest administration and of his court. In many instances economic activity was permitted within a reserve, since various exemptions were granted by the lord of a forest. Usually he would profit from such exemptions by charging tolls or rents for the exploitation of the forest's resources. When granting such exemptions, the lord of a forest would wish to keep economic activity within limits consistent with the maintenance of a hunting reserve, and his success in so doing can not only be related to the efficiency of his administration but also to the amount of economic pressure which he had to face and so to the health of the economy.

Thus, by examining the rights imposed, the administration, the judicial system and the exemptions granted from forest rights, it should be possible to determine the extent to which economic activity was limited within reserves, the extent to which the owner's wishes controlled the exploitation of any reserve, and the extent to which exemptions were made and concessions granted in response to demands from outsiders; in other words, to determine the social and economic impact of hunting reserves on medieval Scottish society. This picture can be most easily assembled by examining each institution in turn.

There is evidence to support the view that royal forests were created by a royal order or proclamation, although no example of a proclamation creating an entirely new forest has survived and although the verb 'to create a forest' occurs only once, namely in 1457, as 'foristabatur'.[1] The fourteenth-century writ 'Contra transgredientes forestam' orders the local royal officer to enquire into offenders in the forest as follows:

Rex omnibus etc Quatenus A de B militibus ac omnibus aliis infra balliam vestram quos per inquisicionem quam per probos homines et fideles patrie diligenter et fideliter fieri facietis culpabiles inveneritis qui probacionem [*rectius,* prohibitionem] nostram publice proclamatam sunt transgressi forestam nostram cum canibus superfluis et sagittariis ingrediendo et venaciones nostras asportando forisfacturam nostram dicte [*rectius,* decem] librarum ad opus nostrum singillatim visis litteris capiatis Et hoc in fide et fidelitate.[2]

I am indebted to Professor Duncan for pointing out that 'militibus', 'probos homines et fideles patrie' and 'sagittariis' would be out of place in the fifteenth century and, therefore, that this is a fourteenth-century writ. It is perhaps later than the reign of Robert I, since it is found in a formulary which contains material additional to the formulary of the Ayr Ms. of Robert I's reign.[3] In what must be a rather inaccurate copy of this writ, 'probacionem' could well be a mistranscription of an abbreviated form of 'prohibitionem', in which case this writ would assume a prior royal statement prohibiting bows and arrows, dogs and hunting in the forest. More direct evidence for a royal proclamation is to be found in James IV's letter to William Edmonstone, keeper of Glenfinglas forest, in 1507/8 in which he says

forsamekle as we ar informit that divers oure liegis duelling neir about our saidis forestis daly pasturis and etis the gers thairof with thair catall and destroys and frays oure dier with stalking rachis and utherwaiis, incontrar oure command and ordinance maid thairapoun: Oure will is herefor . . . ye pas in oure name and autorite command and charge, be oppyn proclamatioun at all the paroche kirkis on the four halffis about our saidis forestis, all and sindry our liegis, that nane of thaim tak apon hand to stalk with bowis or rachis in ony place within the boundis of our saidis forestis . . . under the hiest pane of escheting of the catall and gudis that beis apprehendit within oure

saidis forestis and punysing of thair personys that stalkis haldis rachis or makis gaitis
. . ., according to our lawis and statutis maid thairapon . . .: And that ye diligently
serche and seik quhar ony personys doys in the contrar; and gif ony catall, hors, nolt,
scheip, gait . . . beis apprehendit within our saidis forestis, or ony personys usis
halking, hunting, stalking, rynnand rachis or commone gaitis in the sammyn efter our
said proclamatioun, that ye eschet the saidis catall and gudis, bowis, hundis and rachis
. . . to our use, and send to us the namys of the personis that usis the sammyn, that we
may mak thaim be callit and punist thairfor according to our lawis and as ye will
answer to us thairapoun: And for your lawbouris and deligence to be done in the
keping of the saidis forestis and deyr thairof, we giff to yow all our eschet of all catall
and gudis that beyis apprehendit thairin attour this oure inhibitioun.[4]

James IV, therefore, issued an ordinance on the subject of poachers who lived
around the forest. Beside these examples must be set the numerous cases in the
exchequer rolls in the 1450s and the 1460s where lands were declared waste for
forest 'de mandato domini regis' or 'ex ordinacione domini regis' or 'de speciali
mandato ejusdem [regis]'. (See Table 5, p. 113.) One such entry specifically
records that James III, while hunting in Mamlorne, 'proclamavit eas [terras]
vastas'. (See Table 5, p. 115.) If an area which was farmed out by the crown
was declared waste for forest, then the rent was lost and this had to be
recorded in the exchequer rolls with reference to the associated royal order.
These entries, nearly all of which occur yearly with only minor changes, bear
out that a mandate or order or precept declaring that a certain area was to be
incorporated in a forest was made, presumably publicly, and that the area
thereafter was waste for the forest. While there is no mention of the seal used
on the proclamation, the king appears to have been able to ordain an area
waste for forest on his own authority without the approval of parliament or
council. It was, therefore, an action based on the royal prerogative. In practice
the king may have sought council's advice, but the only occasions when
council was mentioned in this connection occurred in James III's minority.[5]

On a cautionary note it must be remembered that when an area was
declared waste for hunting rather than for forest the lands concerned, as at
Cockburnspath, could have been made into a park rather than a forest but
Knock, although only declared waste for hunting, was almost certainly part of
the forest of Lochindorb. The interpretation of these references to waste must
also allow for the possibility that they were simply entries of administrative
convenience. In some instances it does seem that when an area was ravaged
and could not be let it was simply declared waste for wild animals for the short
time until it was let. In Cockburnspath, for instance, the first entry recording
waste for hunting was mentioned in 1454, and yet in 1457 the lands were all
let,[6] although they may still have been devastated or burnt[7] as a result of the
ravages of the English.[8] Lands declared waste for forest must nonetheless be
considered in a different category from Cockburnspath, since there is no
evidence that they were ravaged prior to the declaration of waste and they
were not automatically relet at the earliest possible opportunity, as the events
of James III's minority illustrate.[9] Nor could the declaration of lands waste for

forest be used by a tenant as an excuse for non-payment of rent in the manner which a plea of waste pure and simple might have been.

Firstly, there was in most cases a royal order available for consultation by the exchequer. Secondly, the tenant was not merely being excused rent but he was also losing his land. Thirdly, the exchequer rolls state not only that no rents were collected from such an area but on one occasion that no rents *could* be collected.[10] Therefore, when an area was declared waste for forest to harbour wild animals, any tenants would be moved off the land, crops would be lost and stock would also have to be taken away. In some cases the rents lost may in fact have been paid by outsiders for pasture rights rather than by tenants of the land.[11] In either circumstance a previously productive area was rendered unproductive if not actually devastated. In Menteith in 1502 x 1503, when sown grain was lost in an area thus declared waste, compensation was paid by remission of rent.[12] It was perhaps rather optimistic to regard such a remission as compensation.

There is no reason to suspect that in principle this process of extending reserves by royal order or proclamation could not have been applied to the creation of reserves not only in the fifteenth century but also at an earlier date. The one possible reference to the extension of a royal forest prior to the fifteenth century does not contradict this conclusion. When William I granted Cally to Coupar Angus Abbey in 1195 x 1206, he excluded that part of Cally to the south of the river Ardle towards Clunie 'quam ad opus meum reservavi'.[13] Since Clunie, by this date, was a royal forest, it is conceivable that the use for which William reserved this piece of land was hunting.

From the twelfth century there was a close connection between waste and the lands included in royal forests. In feudal theory all land including waste belonged to the king and the king could claim property rights on land not alienated by charter, that is demesne, and superiority over other lands. The waste was, therefore, part of the royal demesne, but the area of waste practically controlled by the king depended no doubt on the extent of the king's authority. Edgar's grant of 'Ednaham desertam'[14] in 1097 x 1107 may be an early example of the king controlling waste land. Several forests were created on the royal waste. In 1193 William I called the forest of Selkirk 'wasti mei de Selechirche',[15] while Alexander II in 1236 described part of that forest as 'totum vastum nostrum'.[16] Alexander also referred to 'vasto nostro de Pentland'[17] in 1236, 'toto vasto de Dundaf et de Strathcarun quod fuit forestum nostrum'[18] in 1237 and 'vasto foresti nostri de Banf'[19] in 1242. While waste and forest have different meanings, they could obviously exist in the same area of land, pointing to the conclusion that the king could designate as forest any part of his waste over which he could in practice exercise authority. The association of forest with waste illumines William I's statement that in 1189 x 1195 he had a forest, 'circa Elgyn Foris et Invernis'.[20] The impracticality of reserving game on such a vast tract of land argues that David, or more probably William, after his expedition to Moray simply stated that his waste in the area was to become a forest perhaps with a view to increasing his hold on the area. The contention that all waste land was forest does not bear scrutiny, since forest and waste would thus have been coterminous and, therefore, in the twelfth century synonymous, thus obviating the need for two words and rendering pointless the above descriptions of waste as forest.

In this context the royal waste would not necessarily be uninhabited, but a forest described as waste was obviously not one of the more accessible and fertile parts of the kingdom. In the fifteenth century forests still lay in the remoter parts of the kingdom, although areas remote in the twelfth century were not always remote in the fifteenth. In the fifteenth century waste still occurred in connection with forests, as the examples of extension to forests mentioned above illustrated, but it was not used in the institutional sense of the royal waste, for it meant that lands had been made waste and tenants and crops removed. Nonetheless some parts of the reserves in Menteith, Mamlorne and Ben More may have comprised areas of what was the royal waste. Menteith, first described as a forest in 1454 (See Table 5, p. 114; *sub* Glenfinglas) and visited by a hunting expedition of Robert II in 1382,[21] may have been a baronial forest before it came into royal hands or it may have been erected into a forest from the royal waste sometime in the second half of the fourteenth century or the early fifteenth century. While tenants' holdings and fields in Menteith were at times included in the forest, the settlement pattern in the Menteith area suggests that only the more remote farms were included in the forest. It is very noticeable that settlements there lay below the 1000' contour, which suggests that when, as with Auchinhard and 'Westerbrigend', only part of a holding was forested, it was the upland part of the holding which was included in the forests. (See Table 6, p. 117 and Map 6, p. 123).

Not all forests were created from royal waste or from lands laid waste, as the forests of Stirling, Clackmannan, and Gala and Leader show. Such forests might include settlements of varying size and all types of vegetation. In the later Middle Ages, however, the timber aspect of forests assumed increasing importance, leading to the use of *foresta* as a wooded area.[22]

The only category into which the lands of all new royal forests fell was that of the royal demesne: all royal forests were created on lands in the king's hands. No lands granted to a subject in fee and heredity were ever incorporated in a forest without some form of forfeiture or resignation first returning the lands to the crown, unlike the practice of the Anglo-Norman kings of England. One possible exception may have been the creation of William I's forest round Elgin, Forres and Inverness in which the bishop of Moray held woods[23] and in which Dunfermline's lands of Pennick possibly lay.

When discussing demesne, a distinction must be made between 'dominica regis', lands held and worked by the king, e.g., a particular royal estate or farm, and all the lands which the king held but had not granted in fee and heredity, known as the royal demesne. R. S. Hoyt has named the former the specific demesne and the latter the general demesne,[24] terminology which could be applied to royal lands in Scotland. In Scotland the general demesne is described as 'terrae domini nostri regis'[25] and, 'omnium et singularum terrarum domini regis ubilibet infra regnum Scocie',[26] while the 1357 revocation referred to all lands, rents and possessions 'que ab antiquo pertinere solebant ad dominicum [sic] et coronam Regiam'.[27]

Examples of specific demesne are to be found in David I's reign at Roxburgh and Dunfermline[28] and in William I's reign at Liberton.[29] The distinction of specific and general demesne is not so clear-cut in the twelfth and thirteenth centuries as in the fifteenth century, but Malcolm IV in 1161 x 1162 may refer to the general demesne of David I when he granted Walter Steward Birkenside and Legerwood

ita plenarie et integre sicut rex David avus meus predictas terras in dominico tenuit[30]

and William I probably is referring to his general demesne in a charter of 1173 x 1177 which forbade anyone to detain the fugitive neyfs of Dunfermline 'si extra dominia mea inventi fuerint'.[31] While forests were part of the general demesne, they could on occasion contain areas of specific demesne such as the 'dominica terra' in Mauldslie forest in 1288-1290.[32]

This general demesne in the second half of the fifteenth century was scattered all over Scotland in groups of various sizes which were either known simply by a local name or were called 'dominium', in this case to be translated as 'lordship',[33] or 'comitatus' or 'baronia'. In any one of these lordships there would be areas of specific demesne: within the 'dominium de Strathurd' there were in 1451 'terre dominice de Strathurd'.[34] The forest of Clunie was also part of the 'dominium' of Strathurd but was not part of the 'terre dominice' of Strathurd. Ettrick forest, when in royal hands after 1455, was a 'dominium' or lordship,[35] but it contained no specific demesne lands, the closest approximation to which were lands let in stelebow. While forests, therefore, might include areas of specific demesne, they were usually regarded as part of the general demesne, that is, like all other royal lands.

It was nevertheless possible for a forest or part of a forest after its creation to leave the general demesne, since the lands of a forest and the forest rights were separable.

The distinction made between the lands of a forest and forest rights from the twelfth century onwards can be paralleled from other royal lands where the king might alienate the land yet retain, for instance, judicial rights. In the case of forests this distinction is remarkable because the very nature of a hunting reserve could be expected to render the lands and the forest rights claimed on these lands inseparable. Although in the twelfth and thirteenth centuries forest rights might be reserved over alienated forest lands, such alienated lands were only small parts of the forest and it was more usual for forest rights to lapse on alienated forest lands. (See Table 8, p. 119; sub Gala and Leader, Birse, Ettrick, Banff and Pentland.) From the fourteenth century onwards all the lands of a forest could be alienated while the king reserved his forest rights: in *c* 1320 James, Lord Douglas, received the forests of Selkirk, Ettrick and Traquair in free barony,[36] while in 1327 Ettrick was still a royal forest;[37] and in 1490 James IV granted George, Earl of Huntly 'terras domini foreste de Anze',[38] while in 1498 Huntly was referred to as the forester of Boyne and Enzie.[39] This distinction, which is most explicitly stated in 1509 when James IV made John Grant of Freuchy forester of Cluanie in Inverness-shire, granting him 46 librates of land in the forest but reserving his *proprietas* of the forest,[40] could, and did, lead to confusion as in the case of Stocket where the king reserved his vert and venison but granted the forest to Aberdeen in free burgage.[41] In 1493 Aberdeen regarded James IV's grant of 'Blairtoun', Castlehill and Stocket wood to Andrew Wood[42] as an infringement of their rights and the ensuing case came before the lords of council in 1494. The king claimed that the forest belonged to him but the bailies of the burgh produced Robert's charter and were allowed to continue in their enjoyment of the lands.[43] In a similar case which came before the lords of council in January 1498/9,[44] relating perhaps to Torwood forest, the claimant to the forest, presumably also the pursuer, sought the forestry and foggage of the forest. This claimant could have been Lord Fleming since, later in January, he was claiming the forestry of Torwood.[45] Whereas one might have expected the king to have claimed that the forest was his by right since it had been created by royal prerogative, he claimed it in fact by common law and won the case because the claimant could produce no grant of the forest from the king. That James claimed the forest by common law does not signify that forests were not created by royal prerogative but that he was basing his title to the forest on the fact that it had been his for some time past. As the editors point out in the introduction to the second volume of the *Acta Dominorum Concilii,* the common law meant simply the laws and customs of Scotland.[46] The royal right of ownership of forests was expressed in the 1499 points of inquest of the royal commissioners for crown lands who were to enquire into any encroachment of cultivation in 'ony wooddis forestis pertening to the king in properte'.[47]

As already mentioned, the king might allow his forest rights to lapse. He could also take action to deforest a reserve as Alexander II did in 1236 in Gala and Leader. (See Table 8, p. 119.) Generally an area would cease to be a royal forest or part of a royal forest either when it was granted to a baron in free forest[48] or when it was let.[49] In the former case if the king reserved the vert and venison the forest may not have been completely free of royal control. Rather, the grantee was given an exclusive right to hunt in and use the forest.[50] In the latter instance in the fifteenth century, when rents ceased to be recorded as waste for forest but were still charged by the exchequer, one can assume that the lands had been let,[51] although it is often difficult to decide whether or not lands ceased to be part of a forest when they were let. Ettrick, for instance, was still maintained as a forest even though all its lands were let. The situation is also confused by the fact that the exchequer clerks had the habit of repeating entries long after they were out of date: Clunie forest was granted in free forest to the earl of Atholl in 1481,[52] but the fermes of Clunie were included in the charge and discharge of the bailie's accounts till 1513.[53]

It should now be clear that the view[54] that the king in the twelfth and thirteenth centuries *de iure* possessed the right to all forests is mistaken. This is an error which originated with the view that Scots forests were a geographical feature which could belong to the king as of right. A royal forest did not exist unless the king created it.

Royal rights in the forest were summarised in the phrase 'viride et venatio' or vert and venison. Both words were in use in Scotland by the thirteenth century[55] but they are not found together until 1313 and thereafter.[56] Since this phrase had been current in England in the thirteenth century,[57] it is possible that it was introduced to Scotland during the first or second interregnum by Edward I. Despite the difficulty of dating the forest laws, they must be considered in any examination of royal rights, but to maintain the flow of this examination the detailed discussion of dating has been given later.[58]

The king, who could hunt anywhere, created forests as reserves where he alone could hunt. Therefore, the most important right enforced by the king in his forests was the reservation of hunting, *venatio*, to himself. It was the custom to divide game into different categories: in England there were beasts of the forest, beasts of the warren and even beasts of the chase.[59] Such categories were never so clear-cut in Scotland but it is possible to make a distinction of greater and lesser game, though it is often hard to tell which category of game is being described. The definition of greater game presents little difficulty since Alexander II specified 'cervum et cervam, caprosum et caprosam, aprum et apram' as the animals which he reserved in Pluscarden in 1230,[60] and William Bruce in 1194 x 1214 defined his *venatio* in his baronial forest of Annandale as 'cervo et bissa, porco et capreola'.[61] Fallow deer may have been added to the greater game because in 1424/5 an act of parliament defined deer as hart, hind, doe and roe.[62] In the fifteenth century boar, since they were seldom mentioned in connection with forests, may have become fairly scarce, though they were still given as a blenche ferme.[63] The wolf, usually regarded as a pest to be hunted by everyone,[64] was, according to Bishop Lesley in the late sixteenth century, a greater beast,[65] though he may not have used that phrase in a technical sense. The greater game, which were not always specified in full, could be described as 'ferae', for Alexander II referred to his game in Pluscarden, listed above, as 'feras nostras', a practice he adopted more than once.[66] Similarly, when the king in the fifteenth century declared lands waste for forest, it was waste 'pro feris' (see Table 5, p. 113) and the exchequer rolls always refer to the animals in the forests as 'cervi' or 'ferae'. Lesser game, the most important of which must have been fox, rabbit, hare, marten and wild cat, could also be reserved in royal forests. No extant evidence, however, defines the lesser game, nor is it clear when they are being referred to but the most likely occasion is in *Quoniam Attachiamenta* which refers to hunting 'ad lepores et ad alia animalia silvestria'.[67] It is also possible that 'animalia silvestria' and 'bestia silvestria' could refer to the lesser game reserved in warrens.[68] While the lesser game could be reserved in forests, they were not always so reserved, as the above charters of William Bruce and Alexander II bear witness. In 1507/8 James IV's prohibition of any sort of hunting in Glenfinglas (see p. 92) would have included lesser game, but it is clear from his stress on 'oure deir' in that prohibition that the reservation of the greater beasts was of more importance than that of the lesser animals.

Birds were also included in the game reserved in forests, for the compiler of a late thirteenth-century forgery of a charter of William I wrote that the king reserved to himself in his forest 'meis feris et avibus et venacione'.[69] This forgery was made to fit the facts of a dispute between Melrose and Wedale in 1184 and there is no reason to suppose that the compiler falsified the king's forest rights. Moreover, in the 1507/8 Glenfinglas prohibition James IV included hawking as well as hunting.

An offence against the venison was punishable by the full royal forfeiture of £10 throughout the Middle Ages. One forest law probably written in the thirteenth century but which could well date to the early twelfth century lays down a penalty of £10. (See p. 315.) It is known from forest grants that £10 was the full royal forfeiture and a charter of Alexander II granting Gladhouse to Newbattle Abbey, preparatory to a forest grant, shows that the king exacted the full royal forfeiture on hunting offenders. (See Table 8, *sub* Pentland and Moorfoot). This penalty, repeated in the fourteenth-century writ, 'Contra transgredientes forestam' (see p. 92), was not invariably applied, since a charter of Robert I in 1319 recorded that an offender against the vert or the venison

> penam hujusmodi criminis supportet in propria persona.[70]

This suggestion of corporal punishment runs counter to thirteenth- and fourteenth-century Scottish developments and one wonders if the purpose behind such a penalty was to raise money by way of remissions. In the fourteenth century one of the three laws from the English 'Customs and Assise of the Forest' which were adapted to Scottish use implied that the royal forfeiture might vary, depending on whether the culprit was a freeman or a bondman. (See pp. 296, 297, Laws 21, 23 and 24.) In the fifteenth century, while the £10 forfeiture was imposed for the death of a hart,[71] further variations in the fines occurred. The fine for killing a hind was raised from £5 to £10 in the 1470s,[72] while the fine for hind calves was half that amount.[73] The illegal hunter may have had to face more than a fine, as the Glenfinglas prohibition of 1507/8 ordered the escheat of an offender's dogs and weapons followed by trial and the penalty of the law, which was still presumably a £10 fine.

The king in practice usually did not attempt to reserve his game over the whole country for, as has been shown, reserves were established only in certain parts of the royal demesne, but in theory he may have had the right to do so even if he did not go to the length of establishing a nationwide reserve to protect it. It was, for instance, possible for the king to reserve other species of game over the whole country, for in June 1493 parliament enacted that herons were reserved as sport for the king,[74] and in November of that year Peter Hall appeared before the justice ayre at Jedburgh for killing a heron in Jedforest, which at that time belonged to the Douglases.[75] The idea of reserving one form of game throughout the country was not, therefore, alien to Scotland.

Furthermore, Petit Dutaillis, when discussing this problem in medieval England where English barons received free warren grants from the king, writes, 'From the beginning of the Norman period . . ., private warrens had existed only by the royal grant. It may safely be inferred from this that the king could claim right of warren over the whole realm.'[76] Consequently in Scotland, where not only free forests but also free warrens existed only as a result of a royal grant, the king could claim forest and warren rights over the whole country. It is important to stress that this argument shows that the king *could* claim these rights and not that he *did*.

In medieval Scotland, as will be shown, the king did not claim the right of warren, i.e., the right to reserve lesser game, over the whole country, but the position with regard to the right of forest was less certain.[77] In 1424/5, James I enacted that the justice clerk should enquire into stalkers and the masters of stalkers who slew deer, with the power to impose a fine of 40s on such a stalker and £10 on his master.[78] While this act is aimed primarily at stalkers and their masters, it is not simply an attack on the method of hunting known as stalking. It may be understood that stalkers were hunting the deer illegally, and since no geographical limitation is set on the application of this act the import is that it was illegal to hunt deer anywhere in the country. James, on his return to Scotland, faced with the virtual extinction of royal forest rights and perhaps out of touch with the Scottish forest system, may have tried to impose his theoretical title to reserve game over the whole country by forbidding anyone to kill deer without his permission. This act could also have been used by holders of free forests against people who stalked deer within their forests. No other act of this type survives, for in 1474 and 1503/4, when parliament banned deer hunting, the act applied only to parks[79] as did the point of dittay listed in 1508 in the justice ayre journal books.[80] It is interesting to note that in the draft of the 1503/4 act 'deir' was scored out and 'parkit deir' was substituted. There is, therefore, a remote possibility that the act of 1424/5 was meant to apply only to parks, but it is more likely that James I's act was modified subsequently to apply only to parks.

James IV may also have thought of enforcing this general right over the whole country. Apart from the first draft of the 1503/4 act, point 16 of the 1499 points of inquest which concerned the slayers of the king's deer supports this view.[81] These points of inquest were written at the start of the volume of crown rentals covering the years 1499 to 1507[82] and were immediately followed by the statutes and rental of Ettrick. The 20 points were written in three different hands in the following groups, clauses 1-15, clauses 16-18, and clauses 19-20, and they all presumably date from within the period in which the volume was written. The first two hands wrote other material dated to 1499, namely the rental of Ettrick for the first hand and the statutes of Ettrick for the second hand. The third hand, which should be earlier than 1507, is probably the hand of the scribe who wrote the 1504 rental of Ross and Ormond. Since they occur at the start of the volume and were added to by different clerks, these points were probably of general application and not restricted only to Ettrick. Their content also suggests that they applied to all royal lands, for points 2, 4, and 7 concern encroachment on the 'kingis landis' in general and point 9 mentions an enquiry into unlawful beasts such as goat and swine which could apply to all forests. Point 20 concerns keeping the forests 'forestlike' and the prevention of their occupation by any persons. While the use of 'forestlike' is appropriate to Ettrick, the prevention of occupation is not, since Ettrick was fully let. These points, therefore, applied to all royal lands, while some points dealt with specifically forest matters. Since commissioners of crown lands at the start of James IV's reign were appointed to deal with all royal lands and not only with individual groups of lands, they would apply the same points of inquest to all royal lands.

Returning to clause 16, which concerned an inquest on slayers of the king's deer, construction of yards and shielings, subletting and various tradesmen who used wood, the construction of yards and shielings suggests a forest context, but an act of 1457/8[83] had ordered that only living wood be used in yards and hedges whether within a forest or not. The prevention of subletting need not be restricted to forests, and the limitation on users of wood could apply both inside and outside forests. It is possible, therefore, that the reservation of the king's deer applied to all royal lands, in which case this reservation could have affected the whole country. The records of the justice ayres from James IV's reign, however, record no cases of the illegal killing of deer.[84]

In the late seventeenth century, according to Stair, the hunting or killing of deer was *inter regalia* in Scotland[85] because the king's forests were unenclosed and the animals might easily wander outside and be killed. It was not a matter beyond dispute, since he wrote that it *seemed* to be the case. Anyone could hunt or chase deer off his ground but he could not kill them. He added that deer were not *inter regalia* if they were enclosed in a park. In Stair's opinion, therefore, deer were reserved to the king if they were not in another man's reserve.

The position in England is even more uncertain than in Scotland because of the absence of the forest grant. Returning to Petit Dutaillis: he states, 'in short, the king apparently claimed the right of the chase in every part of the realm', but this only entitled the king to hunt lesser game. English sixteenth- and seventeenth-century lawyers had differing views on royal rights to game but Blackstone, taking a view reminiscent of Stair's, asserted that all game, greater and lesser, belonged to the king. Petit Dutaillis concluded that 'contemporaries had rather vague notions as to the rights of the king over game which had strayed from forests and parks'.[86] It will probably never be absolutely certain whether or not all deer were reserved as royal game in Scotland. While the king never claimed a general right of warren by reserving lesser game throughout the kingdom, he could, if he wished, claim a right of forest over the country as a whole by reserving the greater game, especially the deer, to himself, although such a claim was seldom if ever made.

It was probably as part of this right that the king established round some of his forests a purlieu, which was an area immediately outside a forest where the king's game was protected, i.e., an area on which the king exercised some forest rights although he did not hold the land.[87] Indirect evidence for the existence of purlieus can be found in the twelfth and thirteenth centuries. When William I in 1189 x 1199 restricted William de Montfort's hunting in Kinneff to the use of four greyhounds and forbade hunting in Fiddes, he may have been allowing for a purlieu around the forests of Cowie and the Mounth.[88] A much surer reference occurs in Alexander II's reign when in 1230 he gave Pluscarden Priory the forests of Pluscarden and Auchtertyre which had been part of the reserve round Elgin, Forres and Inverness.[89] He gave the priory free use of his forest apart from the hunting of his game which they, and not his foresters, had to reserve. While this area did not lie on the edge of a forest as a purlieu would usually have done, it was clearly not a case of the king alienating the lands of the forest while retaining the forest rights, since he retained only his right to game and not his control of the vert, pasture, ploughing and building, and since he asked the monks to reserve his game. The lands granted to Pluscarden were in essence a purlieu. A similar grant by Alexander in 1235 to Scone Priory of the lands of Blair[90] is less clear-cut, but the essentials are there, the withdrawal of the royal forester, the reservation only of 'feras nostras' and the proximity of a royal forest, in this case Clunie and Alyth. The fact that the king reserved his game on these lands meant that Scone in 1235 x 1249 could only receive free warren and not free forest rights there.[91]

The importance of the hunting rights of a forest's neighbours is reflected in two forest laws probably of thirteenth-century date, which define these rights and state that someone may hunt from his own land beside the forest into the forest. (See p. 294, Laws 14 and 15.) Law 14, by stating that certain people have free power to hunt on their land beside a forest, perhaps by virtue of a forest charter, implies that others had not, which would agree with the existence of purlieus.

The later Middle Ages provide further evidence of the purlieu. In 1319, Robert I granted Arbroath Abbey specific permission to build a deer leap[92] in the park of Dumbarrow and Conan and to impark all 'feris et animalibus' which entered willingly. The king, therefore, controlled 'ferae et animalia' in this area which was four to five miles from the royal forest of Plater. In February 1507/8 there is a more explicit reference to the reservation of game outside a forest, when James IV feued certain lands mostly within a mile of Glenfinglas forest to Henry Shaw,

proviso quod dictus Henricus et heredes ejus nullum faciant dampnum prejudicium nec destructionem forestis nostris ob venationes nostras per nos prius ordinatis et deputatis, et quod custodiant easdem tam quam forestas pro posse suo; ac etiam quod neque canes odoriferi neque ferarum cum arcubus insidiatores videlicet le stalkaris, super prefatas terras circa forestas nostras antedictas teneatur sub pena forisfacture hujus nostre feodifirme.[93]

Not only was Shaw instructed not to harm the forests or the king's hunting, but he had to actively protect them. Since he was allowed to keep neither scenting hounds nor stalkers on his lands, it is clear that he was to be allowed to hunt no animals from the forest which strayed on to his land and probably he was unable to hunt any other animals. The omission of greyhounds from this charter can be attributed either to the fact that he may have been free to course hares and other lesser game or to the charter's concentration on methods ideal for illegal hunting. There is reason to suppose that this ban applied to all subjects living round this forest, since in the Glenfinglas letter of March 1507/8 the king took certain action after hearing that his subjects living round about the forest of Glenfinglas grazed cattle in the forest daily and poached his deer against his command and ordinance. (See p. 92.) Not only had James issued an ordinance establishing his rights in this forest by limiting pasture and hunting, but the charter to Shaw suggests that this limitation on hunting may have applied to his lieges' lands as well as to the forest. James, therefore, had some sort of purlieu round Glenfinglas forest.

To control the use of the vert or the vegetation growing in his forests for the protection and nourishment of his game, the king regulated timber-cutting, grazing, agriculture, building and any other form of economic activity within the forest. In the twelfth century it is obvious from the fact that the king specifically granted out material from his forests to abbeys and sent writs to his foresters permitting the monks to take wood that wood-cutting was controlled.[94] Throughout the Middle Ages groups and individuals continued to receive specific grants of timber from royal forests, implying that they could not take it without permission.[95] The wood which was protected might be defined as 'grossae arbores',[96] underwood, either 'subboscum' or 'silvicidum',[97] and bark, 'cortex',[98] all of which were green wood, or living wood as opposed to dead wood, 'mortuus boscus', whose use, to judge by the practice in the Steward's forest of Renfrew in 1208 x 1214,[99] might also be controlled in forests though perhaps less rigidly than green wood. By the fifteenth century not all greenwood was equally strictly controlled, for the statutes of Ettrick in 1499 permitted tenants to take willow or thorn to make fences.[100]

The penalty for taking wood illegally from a forest was 8 cows or £10. The first part of Forest Law 13, which may belong to the twelfth century, states simply that the offence for vert was 8 cows. (See p. 293, Law 13.) Since the Laws of Malcolm MacKenneth equate the penalty of 8 cows north of the Forth with £10 to the south,[101] it is interesting that the second and probably later part of Law 13 states that 8 cows were to be paid on the first three offences and £10 on the fourth. In accordance with practice in baronial forests, £10 was probably the usual penalty. In the thirteenth century a bondman was subject to the lesser penalty of 1 cow, 5s or 40 days' imprisonment. (See p. 294, Law 16.) In the 1319 Stocket grant, offences against the vert, like those against the venison, were regarded as a crime subject to corporal punishment or imprisonment.[102] In the later fifteenth century, while the accounts for Ettrick show the penalty for cutting an oak was still £10 (see Table 13, p. 165), they also show further variations in the fines for offences against the vert:

Date	Tree	Fine
1479	ash	6s 8d[103]
1487	birch ('lentiscus')	6s 8d[104]
1496	birch	6s 6d[105]

In the fifteenth century the reservation of the vert in forests, no doubt in response to the growing scarcity of timber in certain parts of the country, was affected by acts of parliament which applied to the whole country.[106] The act of 1424/5[107] made the cutting of green wood a point of dittay subject to a penalty of 40s, while the act of 1503/4[108] made the penalty £5. Unlike the killing of deer, the fact that wood-cutting was a point of dittay does not mean that the king reserved wood to himself over the whole country, the reason being that wood, unlike game, was not *res nullius*. As a result of these acts the justice ayres heard wood-cutting offences both from inside and outside forests, which would explain the absence of any restrictions on wood-cutting in James IV's Glenfinglas letter of 1507/8.

In accordance with the act of 1424/5, the justice ayres in the 1490s imposed a fine of 40s on wood-cutting offences,[109] and in 1508 a fine of £3 was introduced for those who pleaded innocent but were convicted, perhaps in response to the 1503/4 act.[110] The 40s fine, which was only used on those who pleaded guilty 'in voluntate' was increased to 50s in 1510.[111] In 1477 x 1478 an ayre at Peebles had also enforced a 50s penalty for an offence against 'viridi ligno' in Ettrick. The justiciars, therefore, had a fair degree of independence in the size of the penalties which they imposed.

The reservation of the vert required not only the control of timber-cutting within the forest but also of pasture. The control of pasture is witnessed throughout the medieval period by charters which grant pasture rights and payments to be free of pasture restrictions and exemptions from tolls.[112] It is the forest laws, however, which provide the details of pasture control.

The first forest law,[113] which may be an assise of David I, dates to a time when pasture in forests was fairly free. This law, which is examined in more detail in Appendix A,[114] states that while no beasts were allowed to enter a forest in time of pannage or without the forester's permission in time of fence, grazing was free during the rest of the year provided the animals were not scattered when there was a keeper present who had a fire, a horn, or a dog and provided they did not sleep in the forest overnight. The time of pannage or the time of 'pessun', which lasted a month[115] from 29 September to 30 November,[116] was the time when pigs were grazed on the mast. According to this law, the time of fence when the deer were fawning lasted from 9 June to 9 July, dates confirmed in a charter of Alexander II in 1236[117] which forbade the bishop of Moray to pasture oxen or cattle in the forest at this time. An offence against the time of fence led to a forfeiture of 8 cows. The arrangements which applied to the rest of the year are more difficult to interpret, since they involve the custom of 'wardefet'.[118] The law states that 8 cows would be forfeit if animals were found scattered with a keeper who had a fire, a horn or a dog which is called 'warset'. Warset can be interpreted in two ways. It could be derived from the Old Anglian 'weardseta' and could mean a watchdog which sits on guard,[119] in which case the keeper had to avoid four separate offences, letting his animals scatter or having a fire, or a horn or a 'warset' dog. Alternatively, as Professor Barrow has suggested,[120] the 's' of 'warset' could be a mistranscription of 'f' and so the word would be derived from 'wardefet'[121] or 'cum warda facta', meaning with watch set. In this case the herd would be allowed to graze in the forest provided that a watch was set around it to prevent the animals straying and so damaging the vert elsewhere in the forest. If the forester found that the beasts were being allowed to scatter, then the 8 cows would be forfeit because of the herdsman's negligence. Since this law mentions that the animals should not be found scattered with a keeper, it seems fairly certain that this law concerns the custom of 'wardefet' which is also recorded, as Professor Barrow has noted, in Renfrew forest in 1294/5 as 'cum facta custodia'.[122]

In Scottish sources, however, there is also evidence that a fine might ensue if a keeper were present when beasts were found trespassing in a forest, regardless of whether or not a watch had been set, since the keeper's presence showed that the offence was intentional. In Strathearn in 1278 in the wood of 'Rosmadirdy', John Comyn fined the men of Inchaffray Abbey no more than 1d if their animals were found trespassing unless the beasts were found 'in nostra pastura predicta de nocte vel de die pastore tenente vel pascente'.[123] This custom is seen in Forest Laws 2 and 4.[124] In Law 2 a pasture offence is committed even if no keeper was present, and in Law 4 the presence or absence of a keeper was a matter which had to be ascertained by witnesses. In Trolhope in 1216 x 1232 the monks of Melrose would not be fined if their beasts wandered into the forest 'per incuriam vel errorem',[125] which implies that if they entered intentionally with a keeper a fine would follow. Shortly after this, Robert

Muschamp permitted the monks of Melrose to have in their pasture at Trolhope 'canes mastivos ad custodiam averiorum suorum . . . et cornua ad se invicem coortandos'.[126] That the use of mastiffs and horns was the result of a special concession is interesting, since it implies that they might otherwise have been forbidden. A mastiff was a large dog capable of attacking not only wolves but also deer and men,[127] while a smaller dog would be adequate for controlling herds, and horns could of course be used when hunting, although only in remote areas would they be used when hunting illegally. Finally, the provisions of the third part of clause 1 are repeated in Law 16, which states that a bondman would be fined if his animals were found in a forest sleeping at night or grazing by day 'cum pastore ignem et cornu habente'. Since reference to scattered animals, to the dog and to 'warset' have gone, this cannot refer to 'wardefet' but probably means that the herdsman was not allowed to have a fire or a horn, since the horn could be used for hunting and fire would be essential for staying in the forest at night and would damage the vert. While the third part of clause 1 refers to 'wardefet', it is clear that the culpability of the herdsman in medieval Scotland would be increased either if he was negligent in the watch that he set or if he intentionally trespassed in the forest with his animals.

Animals would be banned in the forest overnight probably because it was feared that the byres built to shelter the animals might damage the vert. It was customary at this date for animals to be sheltered at night to protect them from attack by wolves.[128] In 1161 x 1162 Malcolm IV stressed that Coupar Abbey must not leave their herds in Clunie and Drimmie forests overnight.[129]

Thus, the first forest law provides regulations for pasture throughout the year: no beasts in time of pannage, grazing in fence only with permission and free pasturage during the rest of the year on condition that the custom of 'wardefet' was observed and that beasts were not left in the forest overnight. By contrast, the next eight laws relate to a situation where pasture was not free during the year and where all animals must have required permission to enter the forests. It is likely that these laws date to the reign of William I when the first recorded major disputes between hunting and economic pursuits in the forest occurred.[130] If the beasts of neighbours of the forest and of burgesses were found in the forest, their owners were liable to a maximum penalty of 8 cows, whereas one of the king's *nativi* might be imprisoned for 40 days if his cattle were found in the forest. As can be seen from the following table, the maximum penalty for the intrusion of most animals was not reached till the fourth offence.

Fines for Illegal Grazing

Law	Offender	Type of Animal	1st 3 offences	4th Offence	Other penalty
2	neighbour	'animalia'	4d	8 cows	8 cows if the forester was alone.
3	burgess	"	4d	8 cows	

Fines for Illegal Grazing (continued)

Law	Offender	Type of animal	1st 3 offences	4th offence	Other penalty
3	king's *nativi*	'animalia'	1d	40 days in prison	
4		sheep			1 sheep
4	king's bondman	sheep			1d
5		goats	hang one goat on a tree	kill one goat	
6		pigs	one pig	whole herd	
9		horses	1st. one-year old horse	whole stud	
			2nd. two-year old horse		
			3rd. three-year old horse		

Sheep, goats, horses and pigs could not, therefore, be grazed without permission. Pasture in forests never again assumed the freedom of Forest Law 1, though the principles of that law were current in the thirteenth century. One of a group of laws which probably dates to the thirteenth century (see p. 294, Law 16) altered the penalties imposed on a bondman whose animals were found sleeping in the forest at night or pasturing by day with a herdsman who had a fire and a horn to one cow or 5s or 40 days in prison. Another of this group of laws provided that if a single animal was found wandering in the forest it would be escheated to the king unless its ownership could be proved. (See p. 294, Law 17.)

A relaxation of the firm prohibition of pasture just examined can be detected in the appearance in the thirteenth century of foggage and possibly of herbage as tolls payable for permission to graze animals in the forest. By far the most common toll was pannage, which had been collected throughout the twelfth century. Pannage could mean either the right to graze pigs in the forest in time of pannage — David I granted Melrose Abbey pannage in Selkirk forest[131] — or the toll which was collected when pigs were admitted — David stated that Holyrood Abbey was quit of pannage in Stirling and Clackmannan.[132] (See Table 7, p. 118.) Both uses of pannage occur in William I's charter to the bishop of Moray in 1189 x 1194[133] granting the bishop free pannage in his wood within the forest of Elgin, Forres and Inverness and at the same time allowing the bishop to collect pannage in that wood from his men. In the twelfth century the king limited the number of people who were allowed to graze pigs in time of pannage through his control of grants of pannage in forests, but in the thirteenth century pannage, except in confirmations of twelfth-century grants, was seldom used to mean the right to graze pigs and was increasingly used to mean the toll collected.[134] This would suggest that the emphasis had switched from keeping people out in time of pannage to bringing in as many as possible to maximise the pannage collected. Forest Laws 7 and 8 reflect just such a change and may well belong to the late twelfth or early thirteenth century. (See pp. 292, 293.) Far from keeping people out, whenever there was plenty of mast, the foresters had to summon burgesses and country-men to bring in their pigs that the king might collect pannage from them, as in the following table:

	Pannage[135]	
A Mixed Herds		
Rate	Forester	King
For every 10	one hog	best pig
For under 10	one hog and 1d for each old pig	
B Hogs only		
For every 10	one hog	
For under 10	½d for each hog	

When herds of several hundred swine were involved, it is apparent that the king through the sheriff and the forester[136] might collect a considerable levy, although he did not always do so. In 1288 the sheriff of Selkirk, Alexander de Synton, accounted for 13 pigs collected as pannage from Ettrick,[137] presumably the king's share of the pannage. In view of the fact that a live pig in 1288 was worth 1s[138] it is evident that pannage could be a fairly costly business for the farmer.

After 1288 x 1290[139] references to pannage survive only in the confirmation of charters or rights first granted in the twelfth or thirteenth centuries,[140] indicating that pannage as a toll was no longer collected, a view supported by the mistakes made in some fifteenth-century versions of the forest law which ascribe the time of pannage to the time of fence in June and July.[141] It is not clear why pannage fell into disuse, but thereafter pigs were presumably treated like all other animals. Alternatively large herds of pigs may simply have become less common. In the Steward's forest of Renfrew, when the pasture arrangements of 1208 x 1214 which specifically mentioned pigs were revised in 1294/5 only 'animalia' were mentioned.[142] If the owners of pigs no longer paid pannage they probably paid herbage or foggage, although possibly they were still only admitted in the autumn. This transition can be seen in southern Annandale when in *c* 1218 Robert de Bruce granted the holder of lands near Cummertrees[143] common pasture in Dalton and stipulated that his tenants had to pay pannage probably also in Dalton though the holder did not.[144] This particular instance of pannage appears to have continued and been trans-formed into the herbage or foggage which the king collected from Cocklicks, Woodcockair and Phyllis Park in 1452,[145] all within the forest of Dalton.[146]

Although herbage and foggage were ultimately indistinguishable, when first recorded in the thirteenth and fourteenth centuries they probably had different meanings. According to a forest law which probably dates to the thirteenth century, the king might set herbage in time of foggage from 1 November to 17 March and collect foggage at the rate of 1d for an animal and 2d for a mare.

(See p. 293, Law 12.) Foggage clearly was a toll collected from pasture on the winter grass,[147] while herbage is used rather loosely, and perhaps inaccurately, as pasture. The earliest references to foggage and herbage in 1264 and 1265[148] respectively do not clarify matters, since both describe a toll, but in the fourteenth century a distinction of time becomes more apparent. In 1369 in Moray the summer grass was described as 'herbas' and the winter grass as 'foragium',[149] suggesting that forage was used in the same sense as foggage. In the fourteenth century both inside and outside forests herbage and forage or foggage probably applied to summer and winter grazing[150] respectively, although there were exceptions; for example, herbage was to be collected in Pentland in 1335 in the Martinmas term.[151] (The term followed the date after which it was named.[152]) In the fifteenth century foggage and herbage were interchangeable as far as time was concerned: 40s was charged for the foggage and herbage of Woodcockair, whereas in previous accounts it had always been referred to simply as foggage.[153] Today foggage still means winter grass.

Herbage and foggage from the fourteenth century onwards were used to mean the toll levied for pasture or the right of pasture or the area on which that pasture right was exercised. The herbage for two cows which was collected in Mauldslie in 1290[154] and amounted to 20d was a considerably heavier toll than the levy of 1d or 2d mentioned in the forest laws. In 1369, when David II exchanged certain lands and the herbage of Clackmannan for other lands,[155] herbage probably signified the right to pasture as well as a pasture levy, and in 1371 in Darnaway herbage clearly meant the right to pasture when Robert appointed Thomas Grant forester with 'herbagio sive pastura pro 4 vaccis et 6 iumentis'.[156]

It is apparent that the two aspects of a forest, the land and the forest rights, were equated with herbage or grazing rights and the hunting or office of forester respectively, when on two occasions Robert II granted the herbage of a forest along with the forestership of that forest. (See Table 9, p. 153.) By the mid-fifteenth century this had developed to the stage where the fermes of the herbage of a forest were the fermes of the lands of the forest. For instance, at Dye in 1451 x 1453[157] and thereafter the fermes of the herbage, £15, appear in the charge side of the bailie's accounts, while for the same period the fermes of the lands of the forest of Dye, worth £15, were discharged because they were held by Patrick Cockburn.[158] In this and similar cases the fermes of herbage were almost certainly a payment made to the crown for the right of herbage or pasture. As such the holder of this right was regarded as the tenant of the forest and so the sum of money which he paid for the right of herbage became known as the ferme of the lands of the forest, in other words, the rent of the forest. In 1288 x 1290 the herbage of Philiphaugh may conceivably represent a very early example of lands having their rent equated with their herbage.[159]

Outside forests herbage could be used to mean the process of pasturing or the meadow on which the pasture was taken as in 1475 x 1476 when the herbage of Linlithgow Palace was eaten by the horses of the king and queen[160] or in 1504 x 1505 when the lands of Raploch near Stirling were 'deputed waste' for the herbage of the horses of the king and the household.[161]

Foggage in the fourteenth and fifteenth centuries underwent similar developments in meaning. It could be used to mean a pasture toll[162] or a meadow[163] and like herbage, foggage could accompany the keepership of a forest, as in Drum in 1323[164] and in Torwood in 1398 and possibly in 1359.[165] The process by which foggage became linked to the tenancy of the forest is more clearly seen than with herbage. In 1462, £5 per year was charged for the foggage of the 'nemus' of Bute,[166] while in 1477, £5 was charged for 'firmis fogagii nemoris de Bute'.[167] In 1498 the forest of Bute, which must be the 'nemus' of Bute, was let to Ninian Bannatyne for £5.[168] Although the accounts of the bailie still continue to charge £5 for the fermes of the foggage of the 'nemus' of Bute, it is not till 1506 x 1507 that this is changed to £5 for 'terrarum foreste de Bute'.[169] In other words the fermes of the foggage became the lease for the lands, but not of course for the hunting rights of the forest which in this case were under the keepership of William and John Reid.[170]

From this examination of herbage and foggage one can see that when a tenant held either of these rights in a forest as well as the office of forester, he was well on the way to regarding the forest as his own. In 1474, the Lyndesays, who had held the office, herbage and forage of Plater since 1375[171] eventually received the forest of Plater in free forest.[172] In 1371 Sir Robert Erskine, who had received the herbage of the forest of Clackmannan in 1364,[173] was appointed justiciar of the forest,[174] and in 1386/7 Sir Thomas Erskine, his son, received Clackmannan in free forest.[175] A claim on the forestry, i.e., the office of forester,[176] and on the foggage of a forest was a claim to the possession of that forest: as already mentioned James IV had to defend the possession of one of his forests against just such a claim.[177]

This fascinating development of herbage and foggage throws light on many aspects of the forest system, but it serves mainly to stress the fundamental importance of pasture rights and restrictions in medieval hunting reserves. The equation of foggage and herbage with the lands of the forest, though not fully developed till the fifteenth century, had its roots in Robert I's reign since it was then that foggage first accompanied a grant of the office of forester. The reason behind this equation must have been that in a pastoral society pasture would be the most highly valued of all forest rights.

Although pasture was permitted on payment of a toll, grazing was by no means possible everywhere, for in 1499 the points of inquest for the commissioners of crown lands regarded swine, goats and other unnamed animals as illegal in forests.[178] In Ettrick, where animals did graze, the time of fence was still enforced in 1499, though the penalty, forfeiture of the tenant's holding and goods, was no longer the same as in the twelfth century.[179] Similarly, the penalty for illegally grazing sheep had been altered to a heavy fine,[180] but in Glenfinglas the penalties for illegal grazing, escheat of the animals followed by trial and the enforcement of the law, still resembled twelfth-century arrangements.[181]

The prohibitition of assart or clearing, which was as important as the control of pasture for preserving the vert, is first recorded in 1189 x 1190 when William I confirmed that Melrose abbey held Blainslie in Gala and Leader forest 'sine sarto faciendo'.[182] (See Table 7, p. 118.) The control of assart can also be seen in the freedoms granted by Alexander II in 1236 to the Knights Templar of Maryculter on their lands between the Dee to the north and the royal forests of Banchory and Durris to the south:

Per omnes quoque terras suas essarta sua et hominum suorum iam facta et que in posterum fient eis in perpetuum quieta clamamus de visu forestariorum et de omnibus aliis consuetudinibus. Concedimus insuper eisdem fratribus et hominibus suis quod de omnibus boscis quos habent in presenti infra metas foreste possint essartare et colere sine licencia nostra vel hominum nostrorum vel ballivorum nostrorum.[183]

From this extract it emerges not only that the king controlled assarts but also that the forester supervised any assarts which were permitted and probably collected a rent, 'consuetudo', from assarts which were permitted. Some idea of the charge or rent placed on an assart can be seen in Cowie forest where a 'nova terra' beside the forest paid 40s per year.[184] The church also used to place a tithe on assarts and Newbattle Abbey had to pay 'novalia' for cultivation at Gladhouse within the royal forest of Pentland and Moorfoot.[185] Whether the grant of permission to assart was a frequent enough occurrence for the royal administration to have developed a system of licences is doubtful, since comparatively few references to assart are extant. One reason for this may lie in the offence of purpresture which was any action detrimental to a royal holding or high road, a specific example being when someone illegally occupied part of the royal demesne.[186] In England forest purprestures or encroachments on the royal forest were regularly being punished,[187] and so in Scotland purpresture may have replaced assart to a certain extent. In the absence of any charter reference to purpresture and of the roll of purpresture kept by the Scottish royal clerks,[188] this possibility cannot be verified.

The reason why the term assart went out of use in fourteenth-century Europe — its last extant Scottish occurrence was in 1312[189] — is generally taken to be that no new lands were broken in,[190] but this explanation is unsuitable for fourteenth-century Scotland, where agricultural activities in forests continued to expand.[191] It is possible that assarts made in the fourteenth century simply were unrecorded and also that specific restrictions on ploughing, building and ditching replaced the general restriction on assart. Whatever the explanation, the points of inquest of 1499 refer to purpresture as a general and not a forest offence[192] and order an enquiry not into assarts but into whether or not forests were occupied by any persons.[193]

Assart, though not specifically mentioned, was in substance still controlled in forests. In Ettrick illegal ploughing and sowing might lead to the forfeiture of a tenant's holding or to the escheat of his corn and goods[194] or to an equivalent composition. Building, which had been controlled in royal reserves since the twelfth century,[195] continued to be limited in the fourteenth century[196] and in the fifteenth century when two buildings in Ettrick paid a fine of £6,[197] enclosures 6s 8d[198] and 'schelis and underseddilis' or shielings and subleases £8.[199] These sums may have been collected as levies to permit building rather than as fines. Various other forms of economic activity, loosely classifiable as industrial, were also controlled in forests because they would destroy the vert or hamper the game's freedom of movement. Into this category fall mining,[200] ditching,[201] digging mill lades,[202] cutting peat and turves,[203] arrow-making, turning, tanning, charcoal-burning, bark-peeling and carpentry.[204]

By establishing certain rights of way through a forest, the king facilitated the detection of offenders against the vert and the venison, as in Alyth in 1234[205] and Drum in 1247.[206] A forester, according to one forest law which can tentatively be dated to William I's reign, had to lead a *bona fide* lost traveller to the correct route but an intentional trespasser would lose his apparel and some of his goods and might be imprisoned. (See p. 293, Law 11.) A wagon found illegally in the forest could be fined 30d, but the law recognised that once outside the forest, carts were immune from the forester. (See p. 293, Law 10.) The considerate attitude of these laws is in harmony with the collection of a toll, 'passagium', levied on travel in Clackmannan in 1359[207] but not with the complete ban on access to Glenfinglas in 1508 where a trespasser's goods were to be escheated before his trial and punishment.[208]

In theory, therefore, the king controlled everything in, on and above the ground in his forest. The theoretical control was complete. The practical control was not. The greatest attention, to judge by the content of the forest laws, was given to pasture control, a reflection of the pastoral nature of the Scots economy. From this examination of the royal rights it is easily seen how, if these rights were strictly enforced, hunting reserves were opposed to and could severely limit or prevent development and how on the other hand the king by granting exemptions from these rights could hope to profit financially.

Table 5. LANDS WASTE FOR FOREST OR HUNTING

Name	Date	Fermes lost	Wording	Source ER
Benmore	1470 x 1471	40s	'propter vastitatem terrarum de Bymore . . . deputatarum vastarum pro feris'	viii, 60
	1472 x 1473	40s	'deputato vasto pro feris nutriendis'	viii, 168
	1479 x 1480	40s	'deputatarum vastarum pro foresta'	viii, 338
	Continued till 1513			viii–xiii
Cambuskist/Strathdee	1461 x 1462	£3 15s	'deputate pro foresta de mandato domini regis et adhuc non assedate'	vii, 86
	Continued till 1469			vii
Cockburnspath	1453 x 1454	£8 13s 4d	'quia vaste pro venacione regis'	v, 646
	1454 x 1455	£25 6s 8d	'allocate pro vasta'	vi, 60
	1455 x 1456	£25 6s 8d	'non assedatarum sed relictarum ex ordinacione domini regis pro feris nutriendis'	vi, 261
	1456 x 1457	£25 7s 8d	'non assedatarum . . . sed relictarum feris nutriendis'	vi, 338
	1457 x 1458	£8 13s 4d	'propter vastitatem earundem eo quod assedabantur'	vi, 432
Corrymuckloch and Glen Shervie	1510		'que prius deputate fuerint vaste pro foresta et feris pascendis nunc assedantur in feodifirma'	xiii, 647
Corscarie	1476 x 1477		no charge for fermes of forest because it was not let and the Chamberlain had no orders to let ('super quo consulendus est rex')	viii, 441
Darnaway	1464 x 1465	53s 4d	'ex eo quod domini de consilio fecerunt claudere dictam forestam'	vii, 358
	1467 x 1468	53s 4d	'ex eo quod dominus rex mandavit vastam'	vii, 540
	1475 x 1476	53s 4d	'per vastitatem foreste de Dernway quia deputabatur vasta et adhuc non assedatur'	viii, 367

Table 5. Lands Waste for Forest or Hunting (continued)

Name	Date	Fermes lost	Wording	Source ER
Darnaway (continued)	1506 x 1507	53s 4d	'et nunc deputatur vasta de precepto domini regis'	xii, 490
Duchinloch	1455 x 1456	4s 4d	'deputatarum per dominum regem pro foresta ad feras eiusdem'	vi, 242
	1456 x 1457	26s 8d	'deputatarum per dominum regem pro foresta ad feras pascenda'	vi, 366
	Continued till 1462			vi and vii
Glenfinglas	For the lands involved see Table 6			
	1453 x 1454	£11 13s 4d	'que in forestam per dominum regem rediguntur'	v, 676
	1454 x 1456	£17 10s (2 terms only)	'assignatarum per dominum regem pro foreste de Glenfyngask'	vi, 282
	Repeated till 1460			vi
	1461 x 1462	£18	'de foresta de Glenfynglask deputata per dominum regem bone memorie pro foresta . . . sed nunc assedantur tresdecim marcate dicte foreste . . .'	vii, 68
	1461 x 1462	£4 13s 4d	'deputatarum per dominum regem pro foresta de Glenfynglask'	vii, 62
	1462 x 1463	£7 10s	'deputatarum per dominum regem pro foresta de Glenfynglask'	vii, 188
	1463 x 1464	£3 15s (1 term only)	'deputatarum ad forestam per dominum regem . . . et post ejus obitum per dominam reginam quia vaste erant nec aliqua inde poterat percipere ut asserit computans in suo juramento . . . sed nunc assedantur per abbatem Sancte Crucis'	vii, 252

Table 5. Lands Waste for Forest or Hunting (continued)

Name	Date	Fermes lost	Wording	Source ER
Glenfinglas (continued)	1464 x 1467	£26 5s (7 terms)	'deputatarum vastarum pro foresta domini regis'	vii, 487
	1467 x 1468	£12	'deputatarum vastarum pro foresta domini regis de speciali mandato ejusdem et dominorum de concilio'	vii, 574
	1470 x 1471	£12	'deputatarum vastarum ex speciali mandato ejusdem pro foresta'	viii, 70
	Continued till 1479 For lands waste after this date see Table 6			viii
Knock/Lochindorb	1456 x 1457	£10	'que de mandato domini regis proclamate vaste pro venacionibus'	vi, 480
	1458 x 1459	£7 6s 8d	'quia proclamate erant vaste pro feris de mandato domini regis, exceptis quatuor marcatis . . . assedatis ad firmam'	vi, 518
	1459 x 1460	£8 13s 4d	'deputatarum vastarum per dominum regem pro feris pascendis exceptis duabus marcatis, que . . . assedantur'	vi, 653
	1460 x 1460/61	£4 6s 8d (1 term only)	'deputatarum . . . vastarum per dominum regem pro feris pascendis exceptis duabus marcatis, que . . . assedantur . . . sed nunc mandatur assedare dictas terras'	vii, 18
Mamlorne	1456 x 1457	13s 4d (1 term only)	'deputatis per dominum regem ad feras pascendas'	vi, 366
	1457 x 1458	26s 8d	'deputatis per dominum regem ad feras pascendas'	vi, 410
	1461 x 1462	40s	'alias deputatarum pro foresta per dominum regem clare memorie et postea non assedatorum, licet mandabatur compotanti assedare easdem quas assedare nescivit easdem'	vii, 113

Table 5. Lands Waste for Forest or Hunting (continued)

Name	Date	Fermes lost	Wording	Source ER
Mamlorne (continued)	1464 × 1465	53s 4d	'vastarum pro foresta et non assedatorum'	vii, 342
	1466 × 1467	26s 8d	'deputatis vastis pro feris pascendis . . . sed nunc dicte terre assedantur'	vii, 474
	1467 × 1468	26s 8d	'deputatis vastis per regem in suis venacionibus . . . licet contineatur in rotulis . . . quod dicte terre . . . assedabantur quia proclamavit eas esse vastas'	vii, 533
	1478 × 1479	53s 4d (Disher & Glenlyon)	both Disher and Glenlyon, 'similiter deputatarum vastarum'	viii, 608
	Continued till 1513			viii-xiii

Table 6. LANDS WASTE IN GLENFINGLAS AREA

Dates when recorded waste in ER

Lands[1]	1453-4	1464-7	1467-8	1470-1	1475-6	1487-8	1499	1501-2	1502-3	1503-4
	v, 676	vii, 487	vii, 574	viii, 70	viii, 349	x, 43	xi, 417	xii, 24	xii, 144	xii, 214
Auchinhard	X									
Doune			1m[2]	1m	1m	1m		1m	6m	6m
Dowart	X								3½m	3½m
E and W 'Dowe'	X									
'Dowy'										
'Downtagarty' } 'Drumhagartane' }			X	X						
'Hagartane'	X									
Duchray					X	X		X		X
'Duchty'					X					
'Duffois'			X	X	X	X[3]		X[3]		X
Dunssyre							X			
Glenfinglas	X									
Glengyle							X			
Glen Meann	X	X	X	X	X	X	X	X		X
Grodich							X		2m	2m
Lagan							X			
Letter		X	X				X			
'Mergyngerach'	X									
'Strononych'		X	X	X	X	X	X	X		X
'Westirbrigend'			2m	X	X	X	X	X		X
'Stronewnef'	X									

1. For those lands which have been located see Map 6 and Key.
2. m — merkland.
3. 'Dowis'.

J

Table 7. PANNAGE AND ASSARTS

A *Pannage*[1]

Royal Forests

Date	Forest	Source
c 1136	Ettrick	*ESC*, 141
c 1142	Pentland	*ESC*, 146
c 1143	Stirling and Clackmannan	*ESC*, 153
c 1150	Stirling	*ESC*, 182
1161 x 1162	Drimmie and Clunie	*RRS*, i, 226
1165 x 1170	Stirling ?/Airth demesne woods	*RRS*, ii, 39
1189 x 1195	Elgin, Forres and Inverness	*RRS*, ii, 362
1264 x 1266	Ettrick	*ER*, i, 30

Baronial Forests

1161 x 1174	Dalbeattie	*Holm Cultram Chrs.*, 120, 133
1185 x 1186	Dalbeattie	*Ibid.*, 121
1214 x 1249	Dalbeattie	*Holy. Lib.*, 73
c 1218	Annandale	Fraser, *Johnstones*, i, 5, no. 7

B *Assarts*

Royal Forests

c 1155	Gala and Leader	*Dryb. Lib.*, 110
1174 x 1189	Gala and Leader	*Melr. Lib.*, 94
1189 x 1190	Gala and Leader	*RRS*, ii, 301
1215/16	Pentland and Moorfoot	*Newb. Reg.*, 223, p. 184
1235/6	Banchory/Durris	*Abdn. Reg.*, 269

Non-Royal Forests

1180 x 1203	Lesmahagow	*Kelso Lib.*, 110
1194 x 1214	Annandale	Fraser, *Johnstones*, i, 1, no. 2
1206 x 1208	Lesmahagow	*Kelso Lib.*, 113
1208 x 1214	Renfrew	*Pais. Reg.*, 17, 23
c 1218	Annandale	Fraser, *Johnstones*, i, 5, no. 7

---

1. Confirmations of grants which mention pannage are not listed.

Table 8. ROYAL GRANTS OF FOREST LANDS

Forest	Grantee	Details	Date	Source
Gala and Leader	Dryburgh Abbey	Kedslie[1]	1150 x 1152	ESC., 237 Dryb. Lib., 109
Gala and Leader	Melrose Abbey	Whitelee	1174 x 1189	Melr. Lib., 106
Gala and Leader	Melrose Abbey	Buckholm	1174 x 1189	Melr. Lib., 107
Birse	Cathedral Church of Aberdeen		1180 x 1184	RRS., ii, 251
Gala and Leader	Melrose Abbey	Blainslie	1180 x 1193	RRS., ii, 265
Gala and Leader	Melrose Abbey	Blainslie	{1174 x 1189 {1189 x 1190	Melr. Lib., 94 RRS., ii, 301
Gala and Leader	Melrose Abbey	Milsieside	1189 x 1196	RRS., ii, 307
Pluscarden/Auchtertyre	Pluscarden Priory		1230	Pluscarden, 69, 199
Pentland and Moorfoot	Newbattle Abbey	Gladhouse	1236[2]	Newb. Lib., 23, 26
Ettrick	Melrose Abbey	Tima	1235/6[2]	Melr. Lib., 264
Clackmannan	Dunfermline Abbey	Dollar	1236[3]	Dunf. Reg., 75
Gala and Leader	Melrose Abbey		1236[2]	Melr. Lib., 257
Leithen?	Newbattle Abbey	various lands	1241	Newb. Reg., 120
Banff	Walram de Normanville	Forest of Stocket	1242	A.B. Antiqs., ii, 109
Stocket	Burgh of Aberdeen	except the wood	1319[4]	RMS., i, app. 1, 4
'Glenaheuckin'	Richard Edgar	1d land	c 1319 x 1321	RMS., i, app. 2, 299
Moray	Thomas Randolph	'cum silvis et forestis'	1311 x 1324	Moray Reg., 264
			c 1312	
Cordyce	James Garrioch		1316	Abdn. Reg., i, 45
Kintore	Robert Keith	the forest except the park	1316 x 1321	RMS., i, app. 1, 46
Ettrick	James, Lord Douglas		c 1320	RMS., i, app. 2, 232
Drum	Alex Burnett	'Kellienachclerach'	1323	Burnett of Levs. 154

1. Lands in Gala and Leader may have been deforested when alienated.
2. Followed by a free forest grant.
3. Followed by a free forest grant in 1237.
4. The burgh of Aberdeen was made keeper in 1313. See Table 9.

Table 8. Royal Grants of Forest Lands (continued)

Forest	Grantee	Details	Date	Source
Kintore & 'Cardenauche'	Robert Keith } Edward Keith }		1324	RMS. i, app. 1, 47
			c 1346	RMS. i, app. 2, 1020
Enzie	Philip Meldrum		c 1342	RMS. i, app. 2, 851
Boyne	Andrew Buttirgask		c 1342	RMS. i, app. 2, 791
			repeated c 1345	RMS. i, app. 2, 987
Glasgoforest	Robert Glen		c 1345	RMS. i, app 2, 960
Kintore & 'Cardenauche'	Edward Keith		c 1346	RMS. i, app. 2, 1020
Glenken	William Gordon		ante 1358	SHS. Misc., v. 23, no. 14
Torwood	William More	foggage perhaps with lands	possibly ante 1359	ER. i, 576
Glasgoforest	Robert Glen		c 1358 x 1359	RMS. i, app. 2, 1320
Glenken	Walter Lesley and wife		1366	RMS. i, 258
Clackmannan	Robert Erskine and wife	herbage perhaps with lands	1368	APS. i, 531
Glenken	James Lyndesay		1373	RMS. i, 446
Cabrauch	William, Earl of Douglas		1373/4	RMS. i, 474
Glenken	John Maxwell		1376	RMS. i, 576
Torwood	William More		1382	RMS. i, 697
Clackmannan	Thomas Erskine		1398[1]	SRO, Mar and Kellie Papers, GD 124/1/525
Boyne and Enzie	Alexander Seton of Gordon and Egidia Hay		1426/7	RMS. ii, 73
Clackmannan	Thomas Erskine		1448[1]	SRO, Mar and Kellie Papers, GD 124/1/1

1. Erskine already held Clackmannan in free forest. See Table 28.

Table 8. Royal Grants of Forest Lands (continued)

Forest	Grantee	Details	Date	Source
Dower lands	Queen Mary	Lands which included Clunie (Perth), Glenfinglas, Mamlorne, Strathbraan, Strathearn	1449	APS, ii, 61 a
Ettrick	William, Earl of Douglas		1449/50	RMS, ii, 308
Glengarry	Robert Duncanson of Stravan		1451	RMS, ii, 491
Garvock	William, Lord Keith		1451	ER, ix, 661
Dye	Patrick Cockburn	fermes of the lands of the forest	1451 x 1453	ER, v, 581
Clunie (Perth)	John Stewart of Cardeny	fermes of the lands of the forest	1458 x 1459	ER, vi, 561
Boyne and Enzie	George, Lord Gordon		1470	RMS, ii, 991
Dower lands	Queen Margaret	lands including forests of Ettrick, Torwood, Strathearn, Glenfinglas	1473	APS, ii, 188 b
			repeated 1478	APS, ii, 117 b
Cumbernauld	David Fleming		1480	RMS, ii, 1453
Buchan	Quinton & William Shaw[1]		1480/1	ER, ix, 586
Clackmannan	Alexander Erskine		1489	RMS, ii, 1890
Enzie	George, Lord Gordon		1490	RMS, ii, 1976
Dye	Archibald, Earl of Angus	'Kettilschele'	1492	RMS, ii, 2106
Bothwell	Beatrice Drummond		1496	RMS, ii, 2311
Abernethy	John Grant of Freuchy[2]		1498	RSS, i, 268

1. Tenant paying a ferme.
2. Held on a 9 year lease.

Table 8. Royal Grants of Forest Lands (continued)

Forest	Grantee	Details	Date	Source
Cordyce	Alexander Johnston of that ilk and wife		1498/9	RMS, ii, 2475
Alyth	Patrick Gray and Janet. Lady Lyndesay		1498/9	RSS, i, 334
Birnam	George, Bishop of Dunkeld[1]		1499	RMS, ii, 2502
Buchan	Janet Kennedy[2]		1500	ER, xi, 454
Lochaber	Alexander, Lord Gordon		1500	RMS, ii, 2599
Boyne	Alexander, Lord Gordon		1501	SRO, Gordon Castle Muniments, GD 44, 106
Clackmannan	Alexander, Lord Erskine		1502	RMS, ii, 2643
'Kynnavel'	George Meldrum		1502/2	RMS, ii, 2690
Dower grant	Queen Margaret	lands including forests of Ettrick, Torwood, Glenfinglas	1503/4	APS, ii, 271
'Glentich'	Colin Campbell		1506/7	RMS, ii, 3075
Birnam	George, Bishop of Dunkeld[3]		1507	ER, xiii, 53
Cluanie	John Grant of Freuchy		1509	RMS, ii, 3390
'Glenhaitnyth'	William Scot of Balwery		1510	RMS, ii, 3472
Corriemuckloch	William Murray[3]		1510	RMS, ii, 3464

1. Tenant paying a ferme.
2. Held on a 9 year lease.
3. Held in feu ferme.

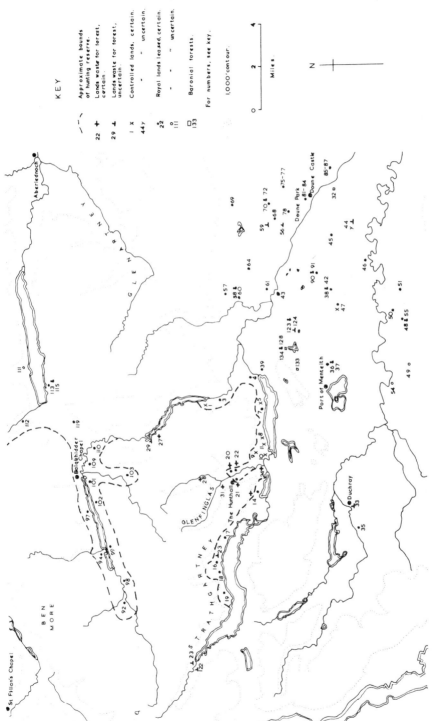

6. Royal Hunting Reserves in the Balquhidder Area in the Reign of James IV.

Settlements with Hunting Restrictions

Map 6 shows lands recorded in the royal rentals of this area. By discovering which lands were waste for forest and which were controlled because they were close to the forest in a purlieu it was possible to mark approximately the boundary of the hunting reserves in this area.

Map No.[1]	Settlement[2]	Hunting Details[3]	Source
	Strathgartney		
1	Stank	controlled	*RMS*, ii, 3193
2 u	Kernach	,,	*Ibid.*
3	Corquhromy		
4	Colyedoglen		
5	Miltoun	,,	*Ibid.*
6 u	Mill of Milton		
7	Blairgarry		
8	Estir Lanerky	,,	*Ibid.*
9	Caschdrapane	,,	*Ibid.*
	(Kathdrapane)		
10	Coschcammy	,,	*Ibid.*
	(Coschambeis)		
11	Offerens de Lanerky	,,	*Ibid.*
12 u	Hidderbrigende		
13 u	Drumquharagan	,,	*Ibid.*
14	Arcanknokenes	waste till 1499	*ER*, xi, 417
	(Ardycharknokkan)		
15 u	Larg with Island		
16	Eddirallekack		
17	Branoquhalye		
18	Strongarvald		
19	Ardmacmonan		
20	Auchinhard	waste	See Table 6
21	Grodich	,,	*Ibid.*
22	Dowart	,,	*Ibid.*
23 d	Glengalye of Lettir	,,	*Ibid.*
	(Glengyle)		
24	Westirbrigend	,,	*Ibid.*
25 u	Dountehagarty	,,	*Ibid.*
	(Downtagarty)		
26 u	Dousse	,,	*Ibid.*
	(Duffois)		
27	Lagane	,,	*Ibid.*
28	Glenmane	,,	*Ibid.*
29 d	Strononich	,,	*Ibid.*
	(Stronewnef)		
30 u	Auchandnoquhane[4]	controlled	*RMS*, ii, 3193
31	Glenfinglas[4]	waste	See Table 6

1. u if location unknown, d if location doubtful
2. From Rental of 1480, *ER*, ix, 562 ff. The names have not been modernised.
3. The information is collected from sources for period 1453-1513. Waste — waste for forest; controlled — controlled as part of a purlieu.
4. Not given in rental.

Map No.	Settlement	Hunting Details	Source
	Menteith Lordship		
32	Drummond & Mill	Free forest	*RMS*, ii, 2299
33 d	Easter Duchra	waste (Duchray)	See Table 6
34	Blairvaich		
35	Westir Duchra		
36	Rednach		
37	Mill of Rednach		
38	Buchquhoppill		
39	Dullatir		
40 u	Portbank		
41 u	Monastell		
42	Bochople		
43	Torre Estir		
44 d	Collach	controlled (Coldoch Wester)	*RMS*, ii, 3193
45	Garngabir		
46	Le Frew		
47	Warda de Gudy	waste for kings' horses	*ER*, viii, 70
48	Ernbeg		
49 d	Schirgartane		
50	Drummys		
51	Kippane		
52 u	Ernynlaw		
53 u	Le Kip		
54 d	Offerens de Kippane		
55	Ernbeg and mill		
56 d	Doune, barony of	waste	See Table 6
57	Brokclen		
58	Achlesse		
59 d	Cammisbarcle	controlled	*RMS*, ii, 3193
60	Mill of Achlessy		
61	Cammisbeg		
62 u	Ballermorik		
63 u	Eglisdisdane		
64	Balnegregane		
65 u	Estir Cammis		
66 u	Camislittil		
67 u	Cammisedward Mill		
68	Bra de Cammis		
69	Cailyebuchquhailye		
70	Lundy Skeach		
71[1]	Lundy Arthur		
72	Lundy M'Cane		
73 u	Uvirgady		
74 u	Lundylug		
75	Westir Argady		
76	Argady Corntoun		
77	Estir Argady		

1. Off the map.

Map No.	*Settlement*	*Hunting Details*	*Source*
78	Kers de Cammis		
79 u	Drumcampsy		
80 u	Balkeroch		
81	Brasina of Doune		
82	Newtoun of Doune		
83	Mill of Doune		
84	Parkland of Doun		
85	Westir Row		
86	Estir Row		
87	Bankis de Row		
88 u	Cobilland de Doune		
89 u	Fishing of Doune		
90	Sessintuly		
91	Mill of Sessintuly		
	Balquhidder		
92	Innerlochlain		
93 u	Innereoch		
94	Monnochilmar		
95	Monocheldischarroch		
96 u	Cragaw		
97	Laidereich		
98	Invernenty		
99	Monochilltarock		
100 u	Moriligain		
101	Stronvair		
102	Dalnalagane		
103	Leanach		
104 u	Innertewin		
105	Dalquhappagach	waste — perhaps not for forest	*ER*, viii, 70
106 u	Craggintulye	waste — perhaps not for forest	*Ibid.*
107 u	Cragintoar	waste — perhaps not for forest	*Ibid.*
108 u	Garochre		
109	Gartnafoir		
110	Stronislnay		
111 d	Ardbeith		
112	Glenogle and Achra		
113	Inneramble		
114 u	Fasflair		
115	Videnamble		
116 u	Gersplace		
117 u	Daliamble		
118 u	Quarterton		
119	Latir		
120 u	Auchany and Mills		
121 u	Kernage and Ardbeith		

Map No.	Settlement	Hunting Details	Source
	Additional		
122 d	Dowy	waste	See Table 6
123 d	Estir Dow	,,	*Ibid.*
124 d	Westir Dow	,,	*Ibid.*
125 d	Mergyngerach	,,	*Ibid.*
126 u	Drumhagarty	,,	*Ibid.*
127 u	Dunsyre	,,	*Ibid.*
128	Rusky	Free forest of Haldane	*RMS,* ii, 3288
129 u	Lanerkynnis	,,	*Ibid.*
130 u	Cowloch	,,	*Ibid.*
131 u	Lanuck	,,	*Ibid.*
132 u	Pond of Goody	,,	*Ibid.*
133	Over and Nethir Auchrig	,,	*Ibid.*
134	Lake of Rusky	,,	*Ibid.*

7

The Administration of Royal Forests

THE enforcement of forest rights and the maintenance of the royal forests depended on the forest administration which had to solve the central problems of preventing offences against the forest rights, capturing offenders and delivering them for trial, and at the same time accommodating those people with a right to exploit the forest. Throughout the medieval period there was a continuing link between the administration of royal lands in general and the administration of forests in particular.

In the twelfth and thirteenth centuries the offices of sheriff and forester were often combined, suggesting that in the period when a forest administration was still being developed the sheriff, as the local administrative officer for the royal demesne, had been given responsibility for the royal forests.[1] The earliest signs of such a connection can be found in 1147 x 1153, when the sheriff was in charge of Clackmannan 'nemus'[2] and not foresters as in 1143.[3]

The first clear example dates to 1165 x 1178, when John de Hastings was sheriff and forester of the Mearns, responsible not for a specific forest as a forester would have been but for all the forests in the Mearns, the jurisdiction of the sheriff.[4] The office of forester of part of Selkirk forest was possibly combined with the office of sheriff of Roxburgh in 1264[5] and possibly with the office of sheriff of Selkirk between 1265[6] and 1288 x 1290.[7] This link of the sheriff and forester, while it did not die out in the fourteenth century, was far rarer, occurring in Ettrick in 1334,[8] Clackmannan in 1382 and 1411,[9] Garvock in 1451 and Darnaway in 1501.[10] On the following five occasions sheriffdoms and forests in the twelfth and thirteenth centuries appeared in roughly the same areas at the same time:

Area	Date of Sheriff's Appearance[11]	Date of Forest's Appearance[12]
Stirling	1128 x 1147	c 1143
Clackmannan	1147 x 1153	c 1143
Perth	1147 x 1153	1161 (Clunie)
Elgin, Forres & Inverness	Possibly David I but definitely by 1173 x 1190[13]	Possibly David I but definitely by 1189 x 1195
Banff	1264	1243

Since forests were created from the royal demesne, it would be natural for forests to appear at approximately the same time as the demesne came under the control of a sheriff.

For administrative purposes a forest might be divided into several parts or conversely several forests might be grouped together. The wards of Ettrick forest or, as it was known in the twelfth and thirteenth centuries, Selkirk forest which are the best known examples of internal divisions within a forest are also the earliest. Professor Duncan has reasonably suggested that these divisions may have arisen because different areas of the forest in the twelfth century supplied different royal castles.[14] The forest of Traquair is mentioned in 1143 (probably 1136)[15] and the forest of Tima is recorded in 1165 x 1169[16] and on the occasion of its alienation to Melrose Abbey in 1235/6, when it was described as part of Ettrick.[17] The description of Hugh of Abernethy, sheriff of Roxburgh, as forester of Selkirk north of the Tweed in 1264 implies that there was a forester south of the Tweed who may be equated with Andrew of Synton, sheriff of Selkirk.[18] The portion of Ettrick forest north of the Tweed which stretched to the Gala Water could sensibly have been attached to the sheriffdom of Roxburgh, which also stretched to the Gala Water. Assuming that there was an association of the forest south of the Tweed with the sheriff of Selkirk, this division may have originated in the twelfth century, for an Andrew of Synton had received the sheriffdom of Selkirk heritably from William I.[19] It is also tempting to argue that Simon Fraser, the sheriff of Traquair in William's reign, was also the forester of Traquair, thus contending that in the twelfth century Ettrick forest was divided into four divisions, north of the Tweed, south of the Tweed, Traquair and Tima, subsequently reduced to three with the alienation of Tima. This analysis differs from that of Professor Duncan, who suggested that the forest in the twelfth century was split initially between the sheriffdoms of Edinburgh and Roxburgh and later between the sheriffdoms of Selkirk and Traquair. It is logical to argue that the sheriff of Edinburgh was responsible for part of this forest before the creation of a sheriffdom of Traquair.

During the English occupation this system of wards continued, for in 1302 there were at least two and perhaps three wardens of Selkirk forest.[20] In an extent of Edward's lands in Scotland in 1304 x 1305 three wards were mentioned in the forest: a ward on the east side of the Tweed, that is north of the Tweed; the ward of Selkirk, that is presumably south of the Tweed; and Traquair ward.[21] By *c* 1320 the ward of Selkirk may have referred to the area north of the Tweed, since Douglas received the forests of Selkirk, Ettrick and Traquair in free barony.[22] The transposition of Selkirk to the smaller part of the forest would account for the change of name of the whole forest from Selkirk in the thirteenth century to Ettrick in the fourteenth. By 1334 Traquair had been detached from the forest,[23] and by 1354 when the forest was in the hands of the Douglases the ward south of the Tweed had been split into three, Ettrick, Yarrow and Tweed.[24] By 1455 the wards had finally been established as Tweed, which included lands to the north and south of that river, Ettrick and Yarrow.[25] Apart from minor changes, the only alterations to this tripartite division were the short-lived smaller wards of 'Schotynle' in Yarrow in 1426[26] and Meigle in Tweed in 1467-1468.[27] Elsewhere internal divisions in forests were less complex than Ettrick's wards: in the fifteenth century Alyth was divided into five wards[28] which may have originated when the forest was in royal hands; and in the second half of that century Mamlorne was administered in two areas.[29]

Into the category of internal administrative divisions falls the creation by Robert I of specially reserved areas within royal forests. In 1319, when Robert I gave Aberdeen freedom to use the forest of Stocket outside the 'boscum del Stokete',[30] he was reserving that wood, and the burgh then had to protect the vert and venison in the forest both inside and outside the wood. Often Robert's reservation concentrated on an enclosed area: in 1316 x 1321 he gave Robert Keith the forest of Kintore excluding the park;[31] in Drum, Robert kept much tighter control over the park than the rest of the lands of the forest over which he appears to have reserved some rights at least till 1321, when he granted the unenclosed area in free forest;[32] on 4 April 1327 he granted Gilbert Hay of 'Loucherwarde' (Borthwick) all the lands of the forests of Boyne and Enzie outside the enclosure in free forest, though he did reserve his vert and venison;[33] and two days later he granted Alexander Fraser all the lands of the forest of Cowie in free forest outside an enclosure or park which Alexander was to have built and of which Alexander was to be the keeper.[34] These grants illustrate a policy of reserving a small part of a forest while yielding the larger area to exploitation, though Robert often granted it in free forest, thus ensuring that the game which might have escaped from his inner reserve would not be hunted indiscriminately.

Within the forest of Elgin, Forres and Inverness the appearance of the forests of Darnaway, Pluscarden and Auchtertyre[35] in the thirteenth century could represent internal divisions, but it is more likely that they illustrate the break-up of a larger reserve. Similarly the forests of Drumine, Sanquhar, Tulloch and Sluipool, which were closely connected to Darnaway,[36] probably represent the break-up of a larger reserve rather than several forests grouped together for administrative purposes. In Menteith in 1498 x 1499, when Archibald Edmonstone was keeper of all the forests in that lordship,[37] the forests of Glenfinglas, Strathgartney and Glenmain may have been subdivisions of one larger reserve or alternatively they may have been separate reserves grouped together under one forester. There is no doubt, however, that just as royal lands might be grouped together under one bailie, so forests might be placed under one official, for instance, Boyne and Enzie;[38] Corriemuckloch, Glen Shervie and Glen Artney;[39] Clackmannan and Torwood;[40] and Clunie and Alyth,[41] although the last two pairs were only combined under justiciars.

The groups or subdivisions of forests provided the framework in which the forest administrators operated. After the initial links with sheriffs and sheriffdoms, a special system of forest administration existed independently till the fifteenth century, when royal forests were once again affected by the general administration of royal lands.

Where the general royal administration did not intervene, the administrative personnel in any particular forest were usually divided into a head forester and a varying number of subordinate foresters or deputies or bailies. Foresters were usually chosen by the king, though in 1255 they could have been appointed by a council of regency. In the twelfth and thirteenth centuries the more important forests must have had their own chief forester who may usually have been a sheriff. On the occasions when foresters were mentioned separately from sheriffs in the twelfth century, they were obviously not men of standing and may well have been subordinate foresters.[42] Before 1286 there is only one possible reference to an independent head forester. Nigel de Heriz, forester, who took part in the perambulations of Leithanhope[43] in 1219 held a large tract of land to the north-west of Ettrick forest and may have been a forester of part of Ettrick or possibly in the Leithen valley.[44] Richard Comyn may also have been a forester in Ettrick but the evidence for such an appointment, the possession of a hunting station, is rather vague, as is the evidence for Norman the Hunter's role as a forester in Ettrick.[45] That head foresters were appointed before 1286 may be assumed from Edward I's appointments of head foresters, since he appears to have copied Scottish practice in this context. (See Table 1, p. 49.) The more ample evidence of the fourteenth and fifteenth centuries shows that head foresters chosen by the king were mostly appointed by Great Seal charter (see Table 9, p. 153), and that the Privy Seal was not so used till *c* 1479.[46] Such grants in the fourteenth and fifteenth centuries usually conveyed 'officium forestarie', 'officium foreste', or 'custodia foreste'. 'Forestarie', sometimes given as 'forestarii', is best translated simply as forester rather than forestry which could denote the rights of the forest. In 1504 a Privy Seal grant employed the less common wording, 'office of forestarschip' of the wood of Woodcockair.[47] The first explicit references to head foresters occur in 1327 in Boyne and Enzie[48] and in 1343 when there was a chief forester, 'capitalis forestarius', in Ettrick.[49] The justiciar of certain forests may have been the equivalent of a head forester but their duties were complementary, since Clackmannan and Torwood were under the justiciarship of Sir Robert Erskine in 1371[50] when William More was probably the forester of Torwood.[51]

The close connection of sheriffs and foresters suggests that the office of forester may have been held heritably as early as the twelfth century, as in the case of Andrew of Synton whose descendant, another Andrew, was sheriff and probably forester of Selkirk in 1264.[52] Similarly the sheriffdom of Traquair was held heritably by the Frasers and they, as has been shown, may have been foresters of Traquair. Not all foresters were, however, hereditary because Hugh of Abernethy, sheriff of Roxburgh, rendered his account to the exchequer 'de toto tempore quo fuit forestarius',[53] thus showing that he was alive but no longer forester there.

While in the twelfth and thirteenth centuries it is fairly clear that foresters held lands — Nigel de Heriz held land north-west of Ettrick, the Syntons held

Whitslaid in Ashkirk,[54] and John de Hastings, the sheriff and forester of the Mearns, held Dun — there is no evidence that these lands were within the forest or that their lands were tied to the office of forester. The Great Seal charters of the fourteenth and fifteenth centuries usually included grants of lands of which some might be attached specifically to the office,[55] as well as rights such as herbage and foggage which, as explained, came to be interpreted as a general right to use the forest. The forester might also enjoy the profits of the forest, judicial or otherwise.[56] The most commonly stated tenure on which the office was held was blenche ferme. There were also cases in the fourteenth and fifteenth centuries where the forester was given a direct grant of the lands of the forest as well as the office of forester over the same lands. (See Table 9, p. 153.) The association of the lands of a forest with the keeping of that forest leads one to suspect that in some cases when a grantee received the lands of a forest he was in fact being given the equivalent of the office of forester, although no mention was made of the forestership. In Torwood William More, who in 1359 held the foggage of the forest, which suggests he may also have held the lands of or the right to use the forest, definitely held the lands of that forest in 1382,[57] and by 1398 he or his son was the forester, thus suggesting that in 1359 More may have been the forester.[58]

This type of possession-forestership was not, however, universal, for William Edmonstone in the late fifteenth century was in no way the possessor or user of the forest of Glenfinglas which was carefully maintained as a royal hunting reserve. Some foresters who had the right to use the forest which they kept held the office for only a limited period of time and most of the Privy Seal grants were leases and did not convey the office heritably. (See Table 9, p. 155.)

Foresters by way of remuneration received certain privileges or allowances. In the twelfth and thirteenth centuries the forest laws record that foresters — and this could relate to head or subordinate foresters — were entitled to a share of the various exactions on cattle, sheep, pigs, horses and trespassers. (See pp. 291-3, Laws 2-6, 8, 9, 11.) In the later Middle Ages foresters could be paid for their services by remission of fermes, though this applied mostly to the less important foresters. In Darnaway forest the fermes of the forest amounted to 53s 4d[59] and the fee of the forester also to 53s 4d.[60] Since the former appears in the charge of the exchequer account and the latter in the discharge, the inference is that the fermes of the forest, whether for rights or lands, were remitted to the forester as payment for his services, a common way of paying officials. Allowances of various sorts were also made to foresters: Archibald Edmonstone, forester of Glenfinglas, in 1499 received an allowance of 9 chalders 8 bolls of barley and 131 sheep, which had formed the 'rests' of a previous exchequer account, in order to reduce the arrears.[61] A more tangible payment to Edmonstone was the 20s worth of lands which he held in Balquhidder and for which he may have paid no ferme.[62] It should be pointed out that when a relatively small sum appears in the discharge side of an exchequer account as an allowance to a forester and when the charge side of

the account is not given in detail, it is difficult to tell whether or not the allowance was actually a payment or only the remission of a ferme.

Whether a forester was allowed to hunt for himself in the forest of which he
was keeper is doubtful, but there is little doubt that the forester could hunt on
the king's behalf in his forest: for example, the Edmonstones had to supply and
did supply game to the king.[63] In Boyne and Enzie, where the officer received
the lands of the forest in free forest and the king still reserved his vert and
venison, the forester undoubtedly could hunt in the forest,[64] but in this case
only the king's reservation of the vert and venison prevented it becoming a
baronial forest. At the end of the seventeenth century Stair said that if a forest
was held in free barony with privilege and office of forestry, the baron had the
right to hunt deer but he was to be considered as keeper or forester,[65] which
seems to suggest that the forester could hunt deer in his own right. Although
the use of 'forestry' is confusing, since it could mean both forest rights and the
office of forester, in this case the grantee had obviously received not only the
keepership but also a separate grant of forest rights, the right to hunt in the
forest. Therefore, the right to hunt game in the forest, like other rights such as
timber-cutting in the twelfth century,[66] must have been forbidden to the
forester unless specifically granted to him. Nevertheless the value of the office
was sufficient to lead to disputes over the tenure of the offices of Darnaway,
Strathearn and Torwood.[67]

The status of head foresters in the twelfth and thirteenth centuries must be
linked to the status of sheriffs. While they often held moderately extensive
lands, they were not the first magnates of the realm. That sheriffs and foresters
were lesser officials was stated in 1255 when the letter of Alexander III and the
Durward party ousted supporters of the Comyn party from the government
and claimed:

Si vero vicecomites, forestarii, et caeteri minores ballivi delinquerint per nostrum, alias
loco eorum substitui faciemus.[68]

Foresters and sheriffs, although lesser officials, were still of some importance
to the government. Since most head foresters would appear to have been
sheriffs and since few names of foresters who were not sheriffs have survived,
it is difficult to define the status of independent foresters and to distinguish
between head and subordinate foresters who were not sheriffs.

From the English appointments of the 1290s onwards, however, the
increasing separation of head foresters and sheriffs shows that many foresters
were chosen from the most important magnates such as Robert Bruce and John
Comyn. (See Table 1, p. 49.) Although the tie of sheriff and foresters declined
in the fourteenth and fifteenth centuries, foresters could still hold other royal
offices: Lord Home, who was the forester of Strathearn from 1491-1495,[69] was
also bailie of Ettrick and of March and great chamberlain;[70] in 1498 the
chancellor, George, Earl of Huntly, was forester of Boyne and Enzie;[71] and the
foresters of Strathearn and Garioch were stewards and coroners as well.[72]

K

Most of these officials who were barons and members of important families may not have considered themselves primarily as royal foresters, but on the other hand the Reids, who held the keepership of Bute forest, do not appear to have been members of an important family[73] and may only have been small lairds. The office of forester was obviously important to men such as the Edmonstones in Glenfinglas who did hold other offices[74] at various times, but the importance of Glenfinglas as a hunting reserve was such and the resulting duties were of sufficient number that even allowing for the use of deputies much of their time must have been allotted to forest matters.

Subordinate or sub-foresters assisted the chief forester, and it would be to these foresters that the day-to-day running of a forest was entrusted. They must have been included in David's order to his foresters of Stirling and Clackmannan[75] and in the foresters of Alexander II in Selkirk,[76] and possibly in Blair and Pluscarden.[77] A reference to several foresters within one forest suggests that there were subordinate foresters in that reserve, though internal administrative divisions must be taken into account.[78]

These officials, though working for the king, were probably appointed by the head forester, for a writ proclaiming Coupar Angus Abbey's right to build a mill lade through part of Clunie forest was addressed:

Hugoni de Erth, militi ac ceteris forestariis suis de Clony qui pro tempore fuerint salutem[79]

and in 1327 the foresters of Boyne and Enzie were 'sub' Gilbert Hay.[80] Most officials of royal lands in the fifteenth century had the right to appoint deputies and servants, for example, the forester of Strathearn in 1483[81] and Simon Carruthers of Mouswald, the keeper of the wood and forest of Woodcockair, in 1503.[82] The number of sub-foresters in each forest varied: there were 18 in Boyne, and 18 in Enzie in 1327,[83] 2 in Drum in 1388,[84] and 4 in Menteith in 1503.[85] By 1305, as has been mentioned, a sub-forester in Ettrick was called a currour, a word which, in 1319, described a central royal official. Robert I, for instance, ordered that no currours other than justiciars be placed over the keeper of Kilgarie forest,[86] but in 1476 in Darnaway a currour was once again a forest official.[87] 'Cursor' usually meant a courier of some sort,[88] and while that meaning could be allied to the general use of currour it is obviously not appropriate for the specifically forest official. In Ettrick, currours had financial duties, presenting their accounts to the exchequer,[89] and acted as an executive of the forest court. The factor common to both types of currour may have been their financial responsibilities, but this is not certain since the evidence from the exchequer rolls is biased towards a financial interpretation. What one can say is that in the fifteenth century the general currour was a courier of the king sometimes stationed in a particular part of the country who may have had financial duties but acted mainly as a messenger.[90] When directly connected with a forest the currour had financial duties[91] and, in some cases, a judicial function. This dual function may be responsible for the confusion in Ormond of the 'currourcroft' and the 'crownarcroft'.[92] The *Dictionary of the Older Scottish Tongue* recognises both types of currour but does not explain why 'currour' has two meanings.[93]

Like head foresters, lesser officials might receive lands from the king: David I granted his foresters of Gala and Leader part of the lands of Blainslie;[94] and consequently they could as in the fifteenth century be paid by remission of ferme.[95] Sub-foresters might also receive a gift from the king if he was hunting in the area,[96] and often had special rights in the forest in which they worked. The foresters of Boyne and Enzie in 1327 and before were allowed to pasture 20 cows and 3 broken horses anywhere in the forest.[97]

In the fourteenth and fifteenth centuries the land which the forester held either inside or outside a forest was known as the forestercroft or forester-seat,[98] even after the forester ceased to stay there.[99] Currours and currour-crofts are similarly related. A sub-forester was not the only official who might hold lands within a forest, since from the fourteenth century onwards, if not before, there were forester-tenants. The distinction between the sub-forester who held a foresterseat in a forest[100] and the forester-tenant who held lands in a forest[101] was that the latter exercised the forester's duties only on his own holding, whereas the sub-forester's authority applied outside his holding as well. Although the inhabitants of Jedburgh and Ettrick forests were called foresters in the early fourteenth century, it is impossible to tell whether at that date they performed any duties or whether forester merely signified someone who lived in a forest. Nevertheless, there are some signs of the existence of forester-tenants in the fourteenth century, for the Boyne and Enzie charter of 1327 stated that Gilbert Hay *may have* eighteen foresters in each forest.[102] That the charter thus limits the number of foresters, that the number of eighteen is large when one considers that there were only four sub-foresters in Menteith in the late fifteenth century and that the foresters' pasture rights within the forest were closely regulated argues that the foresters held land within the forest and were, from their numbers, forester-tenants rather than sub-foresters. Since the names of none of these lesser foresters have survived other than in Mamlorne (see Table 10, p. 156), one can only assume that they varied in status from lairds to humble tentants. The foresters of Mamlorne, Darnaway and Glenfinglas must have been fairly important men while the thirty-six foresters of Boyne and Enzie were probably less important. Indeed the foresters of Mamlorne between 1457 and 1462, Patrick McGilcallum and subsequently Patrick Malcolmson,[103] were probably in charge of the forest, and after 1478[104] this responsibility was most likely shared by two foresters who received an allowance of 13s 4d each. There is no mention of one head forester, though the bailie of royal lands in that area may have fulfilled that function. A similar arrangement may also have operated in Darnaway in the middle of the fifteenth century.[105] Whether or not the local bailie of royal lands fulfilled the duties of head forester, the official on the spot was not a magnate likely to take over the forest as his own but a lesser man whom the king could more easily control. It is hard to tell what subordinate foresters thought of their offices but it is relevant that Forester, by 1300, was used as a surname and Currour by 1294.[106]

Before examining more fully how the general administration of royal lands applied to royal forests in the fifteenth century, it is necessary to consider the singular administration of Ettrick forest in more detail, for Ettrick, often known simply as 'the Forest',[107] was subject both to the forest administration in the thirteenth and early fourteenth centuries before it was granted to the Douglases in free regality and to the general administration of the crown lands after 1455.

It has already been argued that Ettrick by the early fourteenth century contained three internal divisions, each of which was controlled by a forester and possibly by a currour. (See pp. 30, 40.) In the early fourteenth century the Douglases were head foresters of Ettrick,[108] whose divisions were presumably under the control of currours and master currours, for in 1423/4 and 1425 two grants made by Archibald, Earl of Douglas, confirmed by James I, illustrate that the divisions or wards were run by a master currour and a currour who each had a specific 'stede' or *locus*, a holding within the forest, allocated to him and that the forest was largely, if not completely, let to foresters who held a 'stede' or some other holding such as the 'lesu' of Glengaber.[109]

The administration of Ettrick after 1455, when the forest returned to the crown and came under the general administration of royal lands, must be examined here in detail since previous examinations are incomplete.[110] Since the forest was a complete unit of crown lands, it was administered, not by a forester, but by a bailie, appointed presumably by the king, an office held by the Cranstons of Cranston from 1455 to 1488,[111] when Home, the chamberlain, took over. (See Table 11, p. 158.) In 1488 Home held the stead of Kirkhope,[112] remission from the fermes of which was allocated to all the bailies as their fee,[113] and in 1489/90 he and his son were appointed joint bailies of the forest for nineteen years.[114] In 1490 parliament approved Lord Home's appointment and arranged that he should hold the office for nineteen years and if he died within that time the office was to pass to his son.[115] When his son did take over as bailie in 1502, he was appointed by the Privy Seal but only for nine years.[116]

After 1455 each ward of the forest was administered by a currour and a master currour who were presumably appointed by the bailie since they no doubt were the deputies and servants whom the bailie was allowed to appoint.[117] There was a fair degree of continuity in the administration of Ettrick before and after 1455: in 1425 Archibald, Earl of Douglas, had granted the office of master currour of Yarrow ward to Sir William and George Middlemast for life and the Middlemasts held this office till they were replaced by Lord Home in 1488 (see Table 11, p. 158), and the Pringles who were currours and master currours of Tweed ward were closely associated with the Douglases and may have been first appointed by them.[118] In Ettrick ward the master currours were all members of the family of Scott of Branxholm, and in Tweed this office was usually held either by a Pringle or a Crichton. Three of the currours of Yarrow were Liddels, while in Ettrick ward all the currours were Scotts. Whether or not the offices were granted heritably, they were kept predominantly in the one family and in Ettrick, the richest ward, the Scotts had something of a stranglehold. The social standing of currours, master currours and bailies before 1488 was approximately uniform, since most could not be described as powerful barons but they were all fairly well-endowed lairds. Several of these officials did hold other offices: Robert Liddel, currour of Yarrow, was keeper of Dunbar Castle;[119] John Murray of Touchadam, currour of Yarrow between 1483 and 1488, was a lord of council in 1485 and a commissioner of crown lands in 1486.[120]

From 1455 to 1461 the bailie of Ettrick presented a single annual account for the forest to the exchequer, making no division between the wards, but the currours, who made payments to the comptroller from 1455 onwards and incurred other expenses,[121] probably gave returns to the bailie who then completed his account. Furthermore, when the currour's account for Tweed appeared in 1462, the arrears of Tweed ward were mentioned. Therefore the arrears of Tweed ward for 1459-1460 were known although they had not been listed in the account of the whole forest for 1460 to 1461.[122] From 1462 the currours presented their own accounts separately to the exchequer,[123] the only exception being the account presented by Patrick Crichton for the steads which he held in stelebow in 1491.[124] In James IV's reign several important changes occurred in Ettrick's administration. When Lord Home was appointed currour and master currour of Yarrow and bailie of the forest,[125] the accounts of Yarrow, although nominally presented by the currour, were in fact being presented by the bailie, and on 1 October 1498 Home became receiver of the whole forest[126] and was called either the bailie, chamberlain or receiver of the forest. The master of Home could have acted as his deputy till he received his separate appointment in 1502.[127] Lord Home from 1499 onwards returned one account for the whole forest, although the charge and discharge of this account did distinguish between the three wards and he sometimes returned an interim account.[128] The offices of currour and master currour were abolished by the Lammas term in 1499, since they received no remission of ferme for that or any subsequent term[129] and were replaced by two groups of officials appointed, by the comptroller,[130] one to collect the fermes and the courts' fines, and the other to bring cases to court and supervise the reservation of the wood and the deer in the forest.[131] The currours mentioned in 1509 may have been central officials or the name may simply have been transferred to the comptroller's officials.[132]

There could have been several reasons behind this reorganisation of Ettrick in the first half of James IV's reign. The first stage, when three offices were granted to one man, was a political move to reward Home since he had supported James IV against his father. The second stage, the 1499 reorganisation, was obviously carried out for administrative reasons since the new administration had distinct advantages over the old. Firstly, the financial and forest functions of the officials were clearly stated. Secondly, the comptroller had direct control over the money reaching him, whereas previously he had always received money from individual currours on several occasions per year, recorded in the discharge side of their accounts, from fermes, grassums, entries and escheats.[133] After 1499 these payments, which were still recorded by Home, were in the hands of officials appointed by the comptroller who consequently could have more control over the revenue reaching the central government. In Home's accounts the new officials were never named but the money discharged to the comptroller was regularly paid by the same people who may, therefore, have been the comptroller's financial officials: William Chisholm, Patrick Crichton,[134] John Murray of Falahill, James Stewart of Traquair and perhaps Adam and Walter Scott.[135] If this system worked properly, it may well have broken the hold of certain families on each ward.

Before 1499 the officials were all paid by the remission of the fermes of a stead which accompanied the office. The steads of Tinnis and Whitehope were allocated to the currour and master currour of Yarrow respectively, Redhead and Torwoodlee to the currour and master currour of Tweed, Cacrabank and Annelshope or Aldinshope to the currour and master currour of Ettrick, and Kirkhope to the bailie of the forest.[136] The ferme of each stead was £6, with a varying number of marts, lambs and bowcows. After 1499 all these steads except Kirkhope returned to the king's hands and the officials appointed by the comptroller were paid by him while the bailie received £50 *per annum* allowed to him from his account.[137]

These officials were assisted by forester-tenants. Each ward of the forest in 1455 was divided into a certain number of holdings (see App. B, p. 329), each of which was let to a tenant on condition that the tenant kept it 'forestlike',[138] a condition which probably existed under the Douglases and may have been initiated in the fourteenth century when the thirteenth-century wards were altered to their fifteenth-century pattern, although it is not till 1480 that there is any mention of the tenant being responsible for the vert and venison.[139] The duties of a forester-tenant, clarified by the statutes of 1499 which all tenants had to obey,[140] were summarised most concisely by ordering the tenant to keep the forest in 'wod, der and teling'.[141]

By way of payment the tenant after 1499 was allowed to take timber for his own needs from his own stead.[142] The tenants varied from important magnates such as Lord Hamilton or William Douglas to lairds such as the Kers[143] and to men who may have held no other land at all, such as Thomas Dickson and James Achilmere.[144] The largest number of tenants was composed of lairds designated by lands which they held in the form AB of X where AB is the person and X the lands with which he was associated.[145] Many of the tenants would not be resident and they would therefore appoint deputies or, if they had permission, sublet to a reliable tenant, but if they did so, the statutes of 1499 ordered that a tenant must either stay on his stead or appoint a sufficient keeper.[146]

In addition to these resident or supposedly resident forest officials, Ettrick was subject to the commissioners of crown lands, first mentioned in Ettrick in 1455, who let the lands of the forest and held courts. (See Table 12, p. 162.) Although the commissioners could, as in 1484, be appointed for Ettrick and Ettrick alone,[147] since Ettrick was one complete unit of crown lands, in 1488 and 1499 the commissioners in Ettrick were appointed not just for Ettrick but for all royal lands.[148] Frequently members of the Ettrick commission were commissioners for crown lands elsewhere but usually under a separate Privy Seal letter of commission.[149] By comparing the *sederunts* in the *Acts of the Parliaments of Scotland* and the *Acta Dominorum Concilii,* one can see that many commissioners were drawn from lords of council, and lords of the articles and members of parliament. The comptroller always and the treasurer and chancellor sometimes were members of the commission both in Ettrick and elsewhere. (See Table 11, p. 159.) There were usually between five and seven commissioners with a *quorum* of three of whom one had to be the comptroller, and from 1499 the treasurer also had to be one of the three.

Because Ettrick forest formed a unit of royal lands on its own, the general administration of royal lands in Ettrick was virtually a forest administration, an identification impossible in those forests which only formed part of a unit of royal lands. It is, therefore, important to consider the role of the general administration of crown lands in forests other than Ettrick.

In the fourteenth century sheriffs, who were responsible for the administration of royal lands, were charged with revenues from certain royal forests.[150] The writ 'Contra transgredientes forestam' could have been sent to a sheriff in the fourteenth century, since the mode of address does not mention either a forest or a forester and the 'ballia' of the recipient seems to cover a larger area than the forest. (See p. 92.)

It was not till the reign of James I that sheriffs started to be replaced by *ballivi ad extra* who were responsible for returning the revenue of their group of royal lands and presenting an account to the exchequer. In the fifteenth century every royal forest came under one or other of these *ballivi* and on one occasion the local *ballivus* was appointed forester of a forest within his jurisdiction.[151] Sheriffs did not account for lands taken over by *ballivi*,[152] and during the reigns of James I and II *ballivi* made allowances for the revenue which was still the sheriffs' responsibility.[153] Not surprisingly, disputes did arise between the various members of the royal administration, as at Torwood in 1498/9, where a dispute over the right to escheat goods and cattle trespassing in the forest occurred.[154] The bailie depute, acting on royal orders, had escheated 40 cattle which the forester then seized from him. The lords of council decided that the forester was right with regard to the escheat but was wrong to act on his own authority against a royal command. Generally, foresters, bailies and sheriffs managed to work in co-operation rather than in opposition to one another.

Commissioners of crown lands were concerned with the leasing of forests other than Ettrick, as in 1484 when they conducted an *assedacio,* the occasion on which royal lands were let, of various lands including Strathgartney and recorded the lands which had been laid waste for the forest and were not let,[155] or as in 1507 when they recorded that the forest of Drumine was waste[156] and that part of Darnaway called Sluipool was let.[157] Although commissioners are not recorded in the exchequer rolls till the reign of James II, their introduction could reasonably be associated with the administrative and financial measures of James I.

Throughout the Middle Ages there had been a constant interaction between the administration of royal lands and a forest administration. In the twelfth and thirteenth centuries sheriffs had played an important role in the administration of royal forests, until in the late thirteenth century and in the fourteenth century a separate forest administration had become predominant. A result perhaps of the tendency of foresters to take over for their own use the forests in their charge was that the role of the general administration of royal lands, in the guise of *ballivi ad extra,* had in the fifteenth century once more been strengthened. Apart from Ettrick, where the two aspects of royal administration merged, royal forests, in general, were administered as hunting reserves by foresters and as part of the royal lands by *ballivi ad extra* and commissioners, a distinction seen in the functions performed by the various officials connected with royal forests.

The duties of the forester, whether head or subordinate, which remained almost unchanged throughout the medieval period, are best summarised in the Glenfinglas letter of 1507/8 in which the forester had to prevent anyone poaching game, making common tracks and pasturing animals and had to escheat all cattle and goods found in the forest and to punish offenders. (See p. 92.) This letter, however, does not mention one very important duty fulfilled by the forester in the twelfth, thirteenth and fourteenth centuries, the protection of wood. The forester might receive a writ from the king which ordered him to permit a certain abbey to take timber,[158] frequently under view or supervision by the forester,[159] who would ensure that as little damage as possible was done to the forest in accordance no doubt with a writ recorded in the Ayr Ms. of the late thirteenth century.[160] This writ, which concerns the grant of a specific number of oaks, is more suited to the period of Edward I's influence after 1286 than before. The foresters' view also included the supervision of clearing[161] and, one can assume, the supervision of building and grazing and the detection of poaching. Evidence for the foresters' protection of game can be found in Alexander II's grant to Pluscarden.[162] Their supervision of grazing in general terms amounted to the discovery of illegal grazing, the imposition of a fine on offenders or the forfeiture of a fixed number of the offender's animals. The forest laws also illustrate that the foresters' duties comprised the apprehension of trespassers found in the forest.[163]

Since, in the fourteenth century, the foresters continued to supervise cultivation[164] and the cutting of timber, when the king granted timber rights to anyone he sent a writ to the foresters notifying them of this grant and instructing them not to interfere with the grantee.[165] Not till the fifteenth century, when parliamentary enactments extended the reservation of timber to the whole country, did the foresters lose their responsibility for timber protection.[166] Nor is it till the fifteenth century that a clear picture emerges of the forester's duties as they related to the royal use of these reserves: the forester supplied deer to the king, prepared for the king's hunting expeditions,[167] collected revenue from the forest in his charge which he then presumably submitted to the bailie or sent direct to the comptroller,[168] and kept any royal stock in the forest[169] although a keeper of sheep or horses might also be appointed.[170]

While the forester was concerned largely with the forest as a hunting reserve, the bailies of crown lands in the fifteenth century never dealt with such matters, although they might finance the cutting of wood in a forest[171] and make the necessary allowances in their accounts for payments or remissions of fermes to foresters and sub-foresters both for fulfilment of ordinary and extraordinary duties, usually on receipt of an order either from the king or the exchequer.[172] When there was no *assedacio* held by commissioners of crown lands, the bailie was responsible on receipt of an order for leasing lands in the forest.[173] The bailie accounted for any fermes due from a forest, although these may have been collected by the forester, and he also recorded the loss of fermes on lands declared waste for forest.

The commissioners of crown lands, on the other hand, by the later fifteenth century had a more comprehensive range of duties: in 1486 the commissioners of Menteith, Strathearn and Stirling had to hold a court to let those lands, summon the tenants, fine absentees, collect amercements and unlaws, make statutes for the good of the lands and the tenants, punish all officers negligent in their duties and any other trespassers and attend to all other matters connected with leasing the lands.[174] The twenty points of inquest for commissioners[175] covered crimes and offences of various sorts, encroachments on royal lands, matters concerning the leasing and tenants of the lands, extortions by officers, destruction of wood by any means, widows married without the king's licence, breakers of common, slayers of the king's deer, unlawful beasts in forests and the keeping of the forests 'forestlike'. In Menteith it is clear that their duties duplicated those of the forester, for although the forester's responsibility for the vert had probably terminated, the forester still supervised the detection of poaching, control of pasture, cultivation and the keeping of forests 'forestlike'. The reason for this apparently needless duplication may lie in the ultimate responsibility of the commissioners for the royal lands and their delegation of work to foresters or in the arrangement whereby the commissioners tried offenders after the forester had caught them, as seen in the Glenfinglas letter of 1507/8 and in Ettrick.

In Ettrick before 1499 the currours, the backbone of the administration, collected fermes, grassums and entries, made allowances for other officials, received orders from various quarters concerning the disposition of their revenue, and presented the accounts of their ward to the exchequer, usually in June or July for the terms of All Saints (1 November) and Lammas (1 August). They were also responsible for collecting and accounting for fines levied by the forest courts on persons who lived both inside and outside the forest.[176] While the sources make few direct references to the duties of the master currour — he is called 'magistratus warde' in 1486,[177] thus suggesting a judicial function — it is possible to deduce from the rearrangements made in Ettrick in 1499 what his functions must have been. The currour and master currour were replaced in that year by two officials appointed by the comptroller, one to collect fermes and court fines and the other to present forest cases to the court and to protect the wood and deer.

Since the former official was clearly replacing the currour, it seems reasonable to suppose that the latter replaced the master currour. Consequently, the master currour's main responsibility must have been to protect the timber and deer by bringing cases to court in much the same way, perhaps, as the sheriff and coroner in other areas would prepare for a justice ayre. In these functions the master currour would be assisted by the forester-tenants. The duties of the forester-tenant, who was responsible for maintaining the vert and venison on his stead, were clarified by the statutes of 1499.[178] When a calf, fawn, roe-kid or any other deer was killed on his stead, he had to find the slayer or else pay the penalty for the offence himself, and under pain of escheat of his goods he had to keep various users of wood as well as swine and goats out of his stead, nor was he allowed to sell wood or cut it other than for his own needs. The forester-tenant, who also had to ensure that there was no illegal cultivation of hay or grain crops on his stead, fulfilled duties essential to the maintenance of the forest.[179] His duties in respect of poachers resemble the second part of Forest Law 23, which may have been practised in Scotland in the fourteenth and fifteenth centuries, whereby anyone who saw an offence being committed in the forest had to raise the hue and cry in the nearest settlement and inform the forester subject to a heavy amercement. The forester-tenant in Ettrick would presumably have informed not a forester but the master currour of his ward. By comparison with the procedure used to prepare for a justice ayre it would, therefore, appear that after 1499 the forester-tenant had to report cases to one of the comptroller's officials who would then present the case to the appropriate court, but in 1506, perhaps because the comptroller's officials were not functioning satisfactorily, the tenants had to give entry of cases against the vert direct to the commissioners' court in Edinburgh.

The bailie of Ettrick could take part in an *assedacio* with the comptroller,[180] hold special forest courts, different presumably from those of the commissioners, punish offenders, collect amercements and apply distraint if necessary.[181] The bailie's courts dealt with non-forest matters such as neighbourhood and military equipment, as well as with forest offences.[182]

The commissioners in Ettrick probably had to deal with more forest offences than in any other group of royal lands. The letter of commission for Ettrick was slightly different from other such letters in that it specified that the commissioners were to hold forest courts and named foresters and currours instead of tenants and officials.[183] They held the bound courts, and as part of their duty of leasing they probably were concerned with raising the rents as in 1500 x 1501.[184]

The *raison d'être* of the forest administration was the enforcement of the king's rights, the efficiency of which depended not only on the administration of the royal forests but also on the judicial system which tried forest offenders.

While there is no dubiety about the existence of courts to try forest offenders, the nature of these courts, in the absence of references to forest courts in the twelfth and thirteenth centuries, is far from clear. The close link of sheriffs and foresters already examined favours the view that forest and sheriff courts may also have been closely connected, a view supported by two forest laws which probably belong to the twelfth and thirteenth centuries. If the forester apprehended animals grazing illegally in the forest for a third time or if he apprehended trespassers, he had to take them to the king's castle where, it can be inferred, some form of trial occurred, perhaps under the auspices of the sheriff in charge of the castle. (See p. 292, Laws 2, 11.) The association of a court of forestry with a court of sheriffdom can be seen in the judgement of a synod at Perth in 1206 referring to a case between the bishop of St Andrews and Duncan of Arbuthnott *c* 1165 x 1178.[185] In the evidence John de Hastings, sheriff and forester of the Mearns, stated,

quod si homines illius terre [Kirkton of Arbuthnott] in aliquo quod spectaret ad vicecomitatum vel forestariam vexarentur ballivi domini episcopi veniebant ad eum cum brevi domini regis et fidejusebant pro eis sicut pro hominibus episcopi et ad curiam episcopi.

While Hastings' evidence shows that a court of forestry did exist and that in this case forestry, though different from, is discussed in the same terms as sheriffdom, it does not reveal who held the court of forestry. While it is possible that the sheriff and, by analogy, the forester may have held their own courts in the late twelfth century, there is no proof that the sheriff dispensed royal justice at this time.[186] That function was left to the king and his justices, whether a *judex*[187] or a justiciar. While in the twelfth century the role of the forester in the forestry court may have been limited, that role could have developed in the thirteenth century along the same lines as that of the sheriff to the point where the forester could dispense justice. In the thirteenth century, forest cases may have come before royal justiciars as they did in Robert I's reign and as the adoption, probably in the early fourteenth century, of certain English forest laws which mention justiciars also suggests. (See p. 296, Laws 19-24.) That a justice ayre held in Tynedale for Alexander III in 1279 heard a case concerning the hay or park of William de Bellingham, the royal forester,[188] although not a forest case, tends to support this argument, but perhaps more convincing is the continued absence in the thirteenth century of any reference to forest courts, implying that other courts whether of forester-sheriffs or of justiciars tried forest cases.

In certain forest cases relating to illegal grazing and trespass, however, the forester was able to exact a fine or impose a forfeiture without the formality of a trial, or such is the impression conveyed by forest laws passed probably in the late twelfth century. (See p. 292, Laws 2-5, 6, 9 and 10.) On other occasions the calling of witnesses and hence a trial were necessary (see p. 292, Laws 1, 2, 4 and 11) and the provision that a forester should mark the spot where he found certain animals would serve as evidence at a future, though unstipulated trial. (See p. 292, Laws 2 and 5.) No further details of procedure can be gleaned from twelfth- and thirteenth-century sources and one is tantalised by the laconic 'et sic perduntur viii vacce' of the second forest law.

The evidence of the fourteenth century is more informative than that of previous centuries about the role played by both foresters and justiciars when trying forest cases.

Firstly, there is no doubt that a forester could hold a court in the forest of which he was the keeper, but it would be a forest court only if forest cases were heard. While James, Lord Douglas, held the forests of Selkirk, Ettrick and Traquair in free barony,[189] and while barony powers were sufficient to control a free forest, it seems improbable that he heard cases against the king's vert and venison in his baron court since he, as the forester, did not possess the forest rights. This does not, however, preclude the possibility of a separate forest court held by Douglas as forester, and when Douglas received Ettrick in regality from David II he would of course have been able to try forest cases.[190]

Secondly, there are two further relevant cases, in the first of which the forester could hear forest cases and in the second of which he could not. In 1313 Robert I granted Aberdeen the custody of Stocket forest, reserving his vert and venison and promising that no justiciar or any other royal official should intromit or have cognisance of forest cases except himself or his chamberlain.[191] In 1319, when this grant was repeated, the forest was granted to the burgh in free burgage and the king reserved large trees, any game which happened to be found, his vert and his venison.[192] The phraseology makes it clear that intromission by the chamberlain was the exception rather than the rule, since the grants do not say that the chamberlain had to intromit but only that no one was to intervene except the chamberlain. The burgh records show that the burgh court, the body which acted as forester, did hear forest cases, as in 1499.[193] The bailies, however, may no longer have considered themselves as acting on behalf of the king, for when a dispute arose over Stocket in 1494 it was decided that the forest belonged not to the king but to Aberdeen.[194] In the second grant in 1327, the king gave Gilbert Hay free forest rights in Boyne and Enzie with escheats and amercements but reserved 'quatuor articulis spectantibus ad coronam homicidio ac viridi et venatione'.[195] The forester, therefore, by virtue of his free forest grant could hunt in the forest but could not try offences against the vert and venison. Consequently, it appears that Robert I might grant or might withhold the right to try forest cases. There are suggestions in Edward's grant of 1335 to William Montague, the forester and sheriff of Selkirk, of the right to try all pleas, offences, disputes and felonies which arose in the forest, town or sheriffdom of Selkirk except the four pleas of the crown,[196] and also in the fourteenth century writ, 'Contra trans-gredientes forestam', which could conceivably have been sent to a forester, of the forester's right to try forest cases. (See p. 92.) On the other hand a forest law introduced from England and adapted to Scottish use forbade the forester to deliver an offender without the king's or the justiciar's permission (see p. 297, Law 23), and in Torwood in the 1370s there were foresters and a justiciar.[197]

The use of justiciars to hear forest cases would appear to have passed the formative stage by the second decade of the fourteenth century, for not only could the ordinary justiciar try forest offences,[198] but the more specialised forest justiciar had appeared in Stocket by the second decade of the fourteenth century.[199] It is, therefore, arguable that the forest justiciar may have appro-priated functions practised by the ordinary justiciars in the thirteenth century. That the forest justiciars operated in two ayres north and south of the Forth supports this argument. While no reference to a justiciar south of the Forth survives, Henry Sinclair is recorded as forest justiciar north of the Forth *c* 1320.[200] There is no indication during Robert I's reign of the frequency of their ayres. In 1327 they had to check that the sub-foresters in Boyne and Enzie did not abuse their pasture rights,[201] and Henry Sinclair was able to order the forester of Alyth to respect the bounds of Coupar's grange of Drimmie. In Robert II's reign the practice of appointing justiciars to individual forests — Robert Erskine to Torwood and Clackmannan in 1377[202] and John Ross to Clunie and Alyth in 1376/7[203] — seems more likely to have developed as a result of the loss of royal forests and the ensuing contraction of ayres rather than to have been the norm of the fourteenth century. These resident justiciars had to arrest, accuse and punish all offenders against the vert and venison or any other laws of the forest in accordance with the laws and customs of the kingdom. In Erskine's case arrangements were made to ensure that his jurisdiction did not clash with that of the sheriff and his bailies. The justiciar had complete control of the foresters and might receive the profits and amercements of his court. This type of resident justiciar was closer to a head forester than a justiciar on ayre. Those forest laws borrowed from England probably in the early fourteenth century and adapted for Scottish use clearly show that the justiciar was the main judicial officer in the forests, for in Law 24 the English verderer has been replaced by the justiciar on ayre, and Laws 21 and 23 show that the forester was subordinate to the justiciar, perhaps preparing for the justice ayre in much the same way as a coroner. (See p. 296, Laws 21, 23 and 24.)

Forests in the fourteenth century may have been affected by the judicial side of the administration of crown lands as well as by the national judicial system, for the fourteenth-century writ 'Contra transgredientes forestam' could have been sent not only to a resident justiciar but also to a sheriff. Moreover, when Robert Erskine was appointed justiciar in 1371, the sheriffs of Stirling and Clackmannan were ordered:

quod dicto Roberto sufficientem curiam habere faciant quociens ipsum contigerit cognoscere de premissis [forest cases]

— which certainly suggests that sheriffs were competent to try forest cases. There is, however, no extant example of a sheriff trying a case connected with an offence against the vert or the venison in a forest.

The impression gained from fourteenth-century sources is that while the justiciars were mainly responsible for trying forest offences, the whole judicial system in forests was continually changing. This variability is seen in two unique pieces of fourteenth-century evidence. Firstly, in the above-mentioned Stocket grants of 1313 and 1319 the chamberlain, as a result no doubt of his supervision of burghs, could try forest cases. Secondly, although the business of the lords, John Crawford, and Alexander Raath and a clerk, Robert Dumbarton, sent to Ettrick in 1343[204] probably concerned the English,[205] it could have been associated with the administration of Ettrick forest, in which case it would be an early example of a royal commission on crown lands, a common occurrence in the later fifteenth century.

In the fifteenth century the roles of foresters, justiciars and the administrators of crown lands when hearing forest cases emerge more clearly than in the fourteenth. Like Robert I, James IV could either grant to or withhold from the forester the right to try forest cases. In 1492 George Gordon, earl of Huntly, forester of Boyne and Enzie, appears to have had the right to try forest cases,[206] while Edmonstone in Glenfinglas in 1507/8 had to send the names of forest offenders to the king so that the king could try and punish them.

Forest justiciars, absent from fifteenth-century record, were probably replaced by the commissioners of crown lands, and when forest offences were heard by a justiciar, as at Peebles, it was by an ordinary and not a forest justiciar.[207] As a result of parliamentary enactments, justices on ayre were responsible for preventing the destruction of wood,[208] preventing rabbits or deer from being hunted in winter,[209] and preventing the theft of deer from parks, of rabbits from cunningars, of hounds and of hawks.[210] James I, as already discussed, may even have tried to enforce a general reservation of deer through the justice ayres. Consequently, when justice ayres heard offences against wood or game, it was usually as a result of these points of dittay rather than because they held a specific forest jurisdiction such as the justice ayre at Peebles possessed.

Most forest offences in the fifteenth century must have been tried before the commissioners of royal lands, who had a fairly comprehensive judicial competence over the royal lands including royal forests. Their letter of commission[211] authorised them to hold courts, punish trespassers, raise unlaws, amercements and escheats, and to resort to distraint if necessary. The points of inquest given in the crown rental book for 1499 to 1507, which presumably applied to commissioners and which have already been discussed,[212] instructed the commissioners to enquire into unlawful beasts such as goat and swine, ploughing and sowing in any of the king's woods or forests, slayers of the king's deer, users of wood, enclosures, shielings, and whether the forests were kept forestlike or were occupied by anyone, all of which were clearly forest matters. Procedure in their courts was no doubt by inquisition and assise and of course a *quorum* of the commissioners would have to be present. It was no doubt a commission court which in 1507/8 was to try offenders apprehended by Edmonstone and which enforced the reservation of greenwood in Strathdee forest.[213] Although the *ballivus ad extra* did not generally try forest cases, in the fifteenth century he could have been ordered to do so by the writ 'Contra transgredientes forestam'. Otherwise a *ballivus* may have tried forest cases, but only when he held both the office of *ballivus ad extra* and the office of forester; for example, in Strathearn in 1474 John Drummond of Cargill was steward, coroner and forester[214] and may well have heard forest cases in his steward's court[215] if there was no commission court. In 1483, however, when William Murray of Tullibardine became the steward, coroner and forester,[216] he received the power

dicta officia exercendi causas tenendi . . . forestas infra dictas bondas custodiendi,

which implies that hearing causes and keeping forests were separate activities in accordance with the usual role of the *ballivus*. In the fifteenth century, therefore, the main responsibility for hearing forest cases devolved on the commissioners, though the justiciars did not lose their competence in this field.

In Ettrick, which possessed its own unique judicial arrangements, well documented in the exchequer rolls, the commissioners also had an important part to play. The basis of Ettrick's judicial peculiarities, as of its administrative character, is the fact that the forest formed a complete unit of royal lands. As a result, when the bailie held a court it was not simply a bailie court for royal lands but a forest court, and when commissioners were appointed for Ettrick it was a forest court which they held.

The most important courts were held at Beltane (1 May) and All Saints (1 November) by the commissioners, who usually conducted their *assedaciones* at the same time. There were also bound courts and after 1499, if not before, bailie courts. (See Table 12, p. 164.)

The All Saints and Beltane courts first obtained their names from the day on which they commenced, although by the late fifteenth century there was a certain amount of flexibility in their dates. In 1494 the Beltane court was held on 3 May[217] and was not again called Beltane court till 1499.[218] The dates could vary further, since in 1490 the courts were held on 7 June[219] and in 1495/6 on 18 February[220] when both courts may have been held on the same occasion. Before 1461 there was probably one All Saints court and one Beltane court, both held at Newark, for the whole forest.[221] After 1461 there were nominally separate Beltane and All Saints courts for each ward, although all the courts were still held in the one place, usually Newark or Peebles, and at the one time.[222] After 1499 there are no references to Beltane and All Saints courts in the exchequer rolls, although these courts were still supposed to be held by the commissioners.

Before 1461 these courts were always held by commissioners or their equivalent, such as lords of council.[223] After 1461 commissioners continued to hold these courts and the first extant example of a Privy Seal letter of commission, dated 1484, makes it clear that they were appointed to hold these forest courts.[224] The commissioners as non-resident officials must have seemed like justiciars in many ways, and it is not surprising to find that these courts were sometimes called ayres.[225] They did not, however, hold every Beltane and All Saints court, since, even allowing for loss of evidence, there are not nearly enough references to commissioners in Ettrick. The implication is that the bailie held these courts when no commission was appointed. Although there is no reference in the exchequer rolls before 1499 to the bailie holding a forest court other than his presence at an *assedacio* in 1469 in the Beltane court,[226] the letter appointing the Homes, father and son, bailies of the forest in 1490 gave them full power to hold 'speciales curias dicte nostre foreste'.[227]

The procedure in the courts was by inquest and assise. The foresters and inhabitants were summoned and when absent were fined for non-compearance.[228] When information was required an inquest was held,[229] and when culprits were brought before the court and pleaded innocent they were tried by assise. In 1477 x 1478 four men were excused an amercement of £30 for killing four hinds because 'non erant convicti per assisam sed per secretam inquisicionem'.[230] Presumably the members of the assise had to be chosen fairly and the assise held before the assembled court, suitors and *quorum* of judges. The court had the right of continuation, at least when held by the commissioners,[231] and in the 1450s three days was its usual length.[232]

A full range of fines could be imposed (see Table 13, p. 165) and whenever the exchequer rolls record the returns of the courts separately, it is interesting to note that the proceeds of the All Saints court were in kind and those of the Beltane court in money,[233] which corresponds to a similar division in the returns from the fermes.[234] The All Saints court was perhaps concerned mainly with collecting fermes which had not been paid and seizing goods to that end, whereas the Beltane court may have dealt both with the collection of fermes and all other judicial business. Generally, the currours had to raise the fines, but when fines or amercements were imposed by these courts and the offender did not pay and had no distrainable goods in the forest, the justice ayre or the sheriff was asked to raise the fine from the offender's goods in their jurisdictions.[235]

The *assedacio* was part of the function of these courts. It was usually held in conjunction with the Beltane court,[236] but could also be conducted in the All Saints court, since the 1484 *assedacio* was held on 17 September.[237] In 1485, 1486 and 1490 the *assedacio* was held in June, which might suggest that on these occasions it was held out of court, but since the commissioners were authorised to hold the forest courts it is more likely that the Beltane court was postponed till their arrival.[238] Although leases were usually three to five years in length, the *assedaciones* were held more frequently.

The proceedings of these courts were recorded in court rolls,[239] and an extract of these proceedings detailing the fines and returns of the court was sent to the currour so that he could be charged to collect these fines.[240] From 1455 to 1459 there was a clerk of courts and offices.[241]

In 1499 the statutes of Ettrick give a clear picture of the new judicial system in the forest.[242] The courts of All Saints and Beltane ceased to be held every year, and when they were held they were to be held by commissioners. The bailie of the forest was to hold at least four courts to deal with all forest cases, good neighbourhood, and the military levy of the forest, on which matter he had to refer recalcitrants to the commissioners. There had been no mention of bailie courts on this pattern previously, which suggests they were first created in 1499. One can see here that the bailie courts, regardless of when they were held, replaced the Beltane and All Saints courts as the everyday court of the forest.[243] On the special occasion of the feuing of the forest in 1506, the commission court was held in Edinburgh and is referred to simply as the forest court.[244] There was no need to qualify it as the Beltane or All Saints court, since the court held by the commissioners was the chief forest court. Only in 1506 is there any evidence that the commissioners held more than one court per year, and then the feuing of the forest necessitated the above court in Edinburgh in April as well as an *assedacio* in February.[245] The court in April 1506 was described as 'plena curia foreste'. In February 1505/6 the tenants of the forest had been ordered to make entry of all offences against the greenwood at this court and to present their letters of tack there, and so one can see that 'full court' was used in the sense of an open court to which the forester-tenants could bring their cases.[246]

L

The statutes of the forest also mention bound courts.[247] All the courts so far discussed had competence only over the inhabitants of the forest and could not try offenders in the forest who came from outside its bounds. Bound courts had been established to try outsiders, or people who lived round the bounds of the forest, who committed offences in the forest. Professor Dickinson unfortunately confused the bound courts with the courts of Beltane and All Saints.[248] The Douglases had held bound courts in Ettrick and in 1446 exempted Melrose Abbey from 'curiis nostris de le boundis foreste nostre de Ettrike'.[249] Whether the Douglases had established these courts or whether they had been introduced before *c* 1320 when Ettrick was still in royal hands cannot now be determined, but what is clear is that in 1455 the crown continued to use them. The first extant reference to royal bound courts is in 1472.[250] Courts of Beltane and All Saints were also held that year, which proves that they were not the same as bound courts. There were separate bound courts for each ward and it is possible that they were all held together, although in 1478 the bound court of Tweed was held in Peebles.[251] The evidence does not reveal when bound courts were held, but it is clear that there was only one bound court per year in each ward. The statutes of 1499 state that the bound courts were to be held by the comptroller and commissioners, which probably confirmed existing practice.

Although the Beltane and All Saints courts had to resort to the justice ayres when collecting fines outside the forest, the bound courts of Tweed tried to raise an amercement of £62 on the burgh of Peebles.[252] This was never paid, since in 1480 Peebles was exempted from the bound courts and placed under the justice ayre for forest offences.[253] To a certain extent the jurisdiction of the bound courts and the justice ayre of Peebles overlapped, and in 1477 x 1478 three unfortunates were amerced twice for the one offence against the vert.[254] The extracts of the bound courts detailing the returns which were submitted to the currours show that the courts were finding plenty of work to do, and in 1499 it was the bound court and not the justice ayres which was exhorted to discipline offenders living round about the forest.[255]

In both the bound courts and the internal courts cases were probably raised by the master currour before 1499 and the comptroller's judicial officers after 1499, acting on information from the forester-tenants.[256] In addition inquests conducted by the commissioners could start cases.

The enforcement of the king's rights concerned not only the punishment of offenders within the forest but also the resistance of external claims to rights within or ownership of a royal forest or forestership. Such disputes did not go before the courts already examined which tried forest offenders, but went to the king's court, although in the late twelfth and early thirteenth centuries Melrose Abbey did try to have such cases tried in a church court.[257] In 1180 the king at Haddington settled a dispute between Melrose Abbey and Richard de Morville over pasture and hunting rights in Threepwood on the northern boundary of Gala and Leader forest. At this time Richard de Morville appears to have had temporary custody of this forest, since he had foresters there and was in receipt of the forfeitures of the forest.[258] By 1189 x 1190, however, William had resumed control of the forest,[259] perhaps on the occasion of Richard's death.[260] While this dispute was settled before the king, allowance was made for ecclesiastical privilege in that if Richard accused any monk or any of their servants of a forest offence, the monks were entitled to try the culprit 'ad portam de Melros'. If, however, the servant was caught in the act of poaching or if he failed in his defence, the monks had to pay Richard a half of the servant's annual salary and dismiss him unless Richard wished otherwise. If one of Richard's or one of the monks' foresters found anyone damaging the monks' wood, pasture or flocks in the forest, a similar compromise was arranged, for the monks were to receive the 'trigild', a compensatory payment rather than the £10 fine for damaging the vert of a royal forest, and Richard the forfeiture imposed for the offence.

In 1184 it was a perambulation in the king's presence which settled the dispute of Melrose Abbey and Stow over the extent of that abbey's pasture probably within the forest of Ettrick and not, as Lord Cooper suggested, within the forest of Gala and Leader.[261] The dispute of Melrose and Patrick, Earl of Dunbar, over pasture rights within the forest of Gala and Leader around Sorrowlessfield to the south-west of Earlston was not so easily settled.[262] In 1206 Melrose appealed to the pope, and judges delegate were appointed, but Patrick refused to compear. When he finally came before a diet after his lands had been placed under interdict, his defence was that the court was not competent: he was a layman, and the dispute concerned a lay holding; and the accuser ought to follow the accused's court. Patrick lost this plea for, as the pope agreed, the land was held in free alms and it was the custom for churchmen to convene a layman in an ecclesiastical court. After Patrick's objection to the bishop of St Andrews' presidency of the judges delegate, Innocent III issued a fresh mandate to judges delegate who remitted the case to Rome. Following Patrick's understandable absence from Rome, a third mandate was issued and each party had fifteen days to name one of the judges. Neither party did so and agreement was finally reached in the king's full court at Selkirk in 1208 and not in an ecclesiastical court. During the remainder of the medieval period there is no further example of the church challenging the jurisdiction of a royal court on a dispute in a royal forest. (See Table 14, p. 169.)

In the fourteenth century the king and council dealt with disputes over the possession of rights in royal forests,[263] but towards the end of the fifteenth century such disputes were heard by the lords of council,[264] and for the first time the lords auditors of parliament were involved. Since the dispute over the forestry, stewartry and coronership of Strathearn involved both the lords auditors and the lords of council, it is worth considering more closely. In 1473/4 the three offices were granted heritably to John Drummond of

Cargill,[265] but in 1482/3 James III proceeded to grant the offices to William Murray of Tullibardine not heritably but for life.[266] By 1490, the Murrays and the Drummonds were at each other's throats, since they had disputed the possession of various lands before the lords of council[267] and had argued over the teinds of Monzievaird, resulting in the Drummonds setting fire to the Murrays in Monzievaird church. That this wide-ranging antipathy of Murray and Drummond extended to the offices of Strathearn is not surprising. In 1491 the case came before the lords auditors, who desired both parties to present proof of their title. In the meantime a just man, 'unsuspect' to both parties, chosen by the king and lords, was to be given the offices.[268] The man may have been Lord Home, since in August 1495 Lord Drummond brought a case before the lords of council complaining that the king had given the offices to Lord Home. Murray was also present on this occasion, and after examining the evidence the lords decided that Drummond should retain the offices till a final decision was made.[269] Finally, in October 1495, the lords of council decided in favour of John, Lord Drummond. William Murray of Tullibardine did not compear.[270]

Except at the start of the thirteenth century, therefore, when a dispute occurred over rights in a forest or over possession of a forest, there was little doubt that, if the case went to court at all, it would go to the king's court. Thus the king's courts could control those who enjoyed the royal forests.

Table 9. GRANTS OF THE OFFICE OF FORESTER

Forest[1]	Date	Grantee	Lands accompanying grant	Rights accompanying grant[2]	Source
Lennox B	ante 1270 x 1303	Patrick de Lyndesay		'Toschederach'	Lenn. Cart., 49
Stocket	1313	Burgh of Aberdeen		j, easements	Abdn. Chrs., p. 10, 6
Stocket	1319	Burgh of Aberdeen	forest of Stocket	j, pa, p, building	RMS, i, app. 1, 4
Kilgarie	1319	Peter Spalding	'Ballourthy' 'Petmethy'	f	Fraser, Southesk, ii, 482
Killanel and Fromartein	1320s	Patrick 'de Monte Alto'			RMS, i, app. 2, 420
Drumine B	c 1341 x 1342	John Urwell	lands of forest		RMS, i, app. 2, 784
Glenken	c 1343 x 1344	John Crawford of Cumnock			RMS, i, app. 2, 910
Plater	c 1345	Restenneth Priory?		w	RMS, i, app. 2, 958
Alyth	c 1345	William Menzies			RMS, i, app. 2, 979
Darnaway B	1346	John Grant	Dowally		Fraser, Grant, iii, 8
Cardenden	c 1340 x 1350	William and/or Adam Spens			RMS, i, app. 2, 1120
Boyne and Enzie	1361	William Vaus		liberties of office	RMS, i, app. 2, 1364
Darnaway	1369	Richard Comyn	Dowally	justiciar, j	RMS, i, 285
Clackmannan and Torwood	1371	Robert Erskine			SRO, Mar and Kellie Papers, GD 124/6/1
Darnaway	1371	Thomas Grant	Dowally, 'Dollyndutf'	h in park	Moray Reg., 473, no. 22
Plater	1375	Alexander Lyndesay	Finavon	h, f	RMS, i, 618
Clunie and Alyth	1376/7	John Ross		justiciar, j	RMS, i, 595

1. B—Baronial forest and baronial grant. All other entries are royal grants.
2. pa—pasture, p—ploughing, j—judicial rights for forest cases, f—foggage, h—herbage, w—wood cutting, hu—hunting pertinents.

Table 9. Grants of the Office of Forester (continued)

Forest	Date	Grantee	Lands accompanying grant	Rights accompanying grant	Source
Clackmannan	1382	William Menteith	Wester 'Kers', Alva, Ochiltree, 'Perdovenyne'	hu, j, free forest and warren	APS, i, 564
Plater	1384 x 1385	David Lyndesay	Finavon		RMS, i, 762
Torwood	1398	William More to David Fleming	lands of forest	pa, f	SRO, Transcripts of Royal Charters, RH 1/1/2, 4 Aug. 1398 Stirlings of Keir, 201
Clackmannan	1411	William Menteith	Wester 'Kers', Alva, Ochiltree, 'Pordovyne'	free forest and warren	
Clunie	1430	John of Airth	lands in Carrick		RMS, ii, 172
Strathearn	1473/4	John Drummond of Cargill		steward and coroner	RMS, ii, 1160
Torwood	1476	David Forester		with the profits of the office	RMS, ii, 1249
Drumine	1478	James Urwell	lands of Sanquhar		RMS, ii, 1398
Drumine	1478	Thomas Comyn			RMS, ii, 1399
Glenfinglas	[c 1478/9]	William Edmonstone	lease of the forest by Privy Seal		ADA, 7lb (PS grant lost)
Strathearn	1482/3	William Murray of Tullibardine		steward and coroner	RMS, ii, 1540
Torwood	1488	Duncan Forester of Gunnarschaw	Torwood and Torwoodhead		RMS, ii, 1802
Torwood	1497	Walter Forester	Torwood, Torwoodhead, Garden, Skipinch etc.		RMS, ii, 2384
Rannoch	1502	Robert Menzies	lands of Rannoch 'Parcarhill' 'Folablakwatir', Blackhall	9 year lease	RMS, ii, 2664
Woodcockair	1502/3	Simon Carruthers			RSS, i, 912
Garioch	1503	William Blackhall			RMS, ii, 2755

Table 9. Grants of the Office of Forester (continued)

Forest	Date	Grantee	Lands accompanying grant	Rights accompanying grant	Source
Woodcockair	1503/4	John Murray of Falahill		f, pa, in ward	RSS, i, 1029
Darnaway	1507/8	Andrew, Bishop of Moray	mains of Darnaway		RSS, i, 1628
Woodcockair	1508/9	Robert Lauder of Bass		f	RSS, i, 1799
Strathdearn B	1509	Hugh Ross of Kilravock		j	Rose of Kilravock, 180
Cluanie	1509	John Grant of Freuchy	shieling of forest,		RMS, ii, 3390
Drimmie	1510/11	Robert Urwell of Sanquhar	lands of forest etc.		RMS, ii, 3552
Darnaway	1512/13	Andrew, Bishop of Moray, and William Ogilvy of Strathearn			RSS, i, 2482

Table 10. FORESTERS

Date[1]	Forest[2]	Name[3]	Source
a 1144	Lesmahagow B	Archebald forester	*Kelso Lib.*, 187
1151 x 1198	Coldingham C	Richard forester and William forester	Raine, *ND*, app., 46 no. 201
1182 x 1213	Stenton ? B	Edwin forester	*Melr. Lib.*, 54, 63
c 1190	Mow B	William forester	*Kelso. Lib.*, 147
1198	Coldingham C	Richard forester	Raine, *ND*, 42, no. 177
1219	Selkirk/Leithen?	Nigel de Heriz	*Newb. Lib.*, 121
a 1232	Duns ?	Hugh forester	*Cold. Cart.*, 30
1279	Tynedale	William de Bellingham	*CDS*, ii, 168
1289/90	Tynedale	Thomas le Forester	*CDS*, ii, 407
c 1306	Plater	Philip forester?	Barbour, *Bruce* (Skeat), bk 9, 1 312
c 1306	Selkirk	Walter de Burghdon	Stones, E.L.G., *Anglo-Scottish Relations* (Oxford, 1970), 265
1322	Plater	Finlay forester	*RMS*, i, app. 1, 29
a 1323	Drum	Alexander Burnett	*Burnett of Leys*, 154
1324	Ettrick	James Douglas	*RMS*, i, app. 1, 38
1326	Clunie	Hugh of Airth	*CA Chart.*, 108
1327	Boyne and Enzie	Gilbert Hay	*RMS*, i, app. 1, 65
a 1375	Plater	David 'de Anandia'	*RMS*, i, 618
a 1382	Clackmannan	Marjory Stirling and John Stirling?	*APS*, i, 564
1388	Drum	Alexander Irvine John Moigne	*A.B. Antiqs.*, iii, 294
1398	Stocket	Matthew Pynches	*Abdn. Counc.*, 3
1399	Stocket	Matthew Pynches William Spalding	*Abdn. Rec.* 167
1407	Burgh of Edinburgh[4]	William Currour forester	*RMS*, i, 913
c 1430	Trostach C	William Middleton	*Arb. Lib.*, 64
1448	Stocket	John Spens Alexander Anderson	*Abdn. Counc.*, 18
1449-1450	Burgh of Edinburgh[4]	William Currour forester	*RMS*, ii, 359 *ER*, v, 385
1452	Coldingham C	John Forester	*RMS*, ii, 560
1457-1458	Mamlorne	Patrick McGilcallum	*ER*, vi, 411
1461-1463	Mamlorne	Patrick Malcolmson	*ER*, vii, 111, 204
1462-*a* 1476	Torwood	Malcolm Forester	*ER*, vii, 275; *RMS*, ii, 1249
1470	Forter[5] C	'Makychol' Duncanson John Duncanson	*CA Rent*, i, 157

1. a — *ante* or before.
2. B — baronial, C — church.
3. This list is not exhaustive. It gives foresters not mentioned in Tables 1 and 9 and on pp.   and   above. w — concerned with preserving wood.
4. He presumably worked in woods belonging to the burgh.
5. Once part of Glenisla free forest.

Table 10. Foresters (continued)

Date	Forest	Names	Source
1472	Campsie C	Andrew Hughson, forester general Andrew Bell w Hugh of Campsie w David Anderson w Laurence Watson w	*CA Rent*, i, 220
1473	Drimmie C	Gilchrist of 'Mallas' w 'Tazour of Candow' w William Reid w	*CA Rent*, i, 197
1473	Strathardle C[1]	Neil McKeden w	*CA Rent*, i, 198
1473	Murthly C	Alexander Gibbunson w	*CA Rent*, i, 169
1473	Persie[2]	Alan 'Roeoch' w John 'Malyoch' w	*Arb. Lib.*, 245
a 1473/4	Strathearn	Maurice Drummond of Cargill	*RMS*, ii, 1160
1476	Innerwick C	Duncan Patrickson w	*CA Rent*, i, 225
1477	Torwood	Alexander Forester	*ER*, ix, 678
a 1478	Drumine	Andrew Urwell	*RMS*, ii, 1398
1479	Campsie C	Alexander Dawson w Patrick Bell w John Bell w Andrew Hughson w	*CA Rent*, i, 227
1483	Campsie C	John Cragow w Andrew Hughson w Patrick Bell w John Bell w	*CA Rent*, i, 237
1483	Easter Persie[2]	David Annand w	*Arb. Lib.*, 229
1484-1485	Darnaway.	Alexander Dunbar?	*ER*, ix, 310
1486-1487	Darnaway	James Douglas of Pittendriech	*ER*, ix, 500
a 1488	Torwood	Henry Forester	*RMS*, ii, 1802
1488	Drimmie C	Henry Neilson w	*CA Rent*, i, 246
1495	Strathearn	Lord Home	*ADC*, i, 385 a
1497	Culface	William Farny	*ER*, x, 764
1497/8	Boyne & Enzie	George Earl of Huntly	*RMS*, ii, 2389
1501-1502	Bute	William Reid John Reid	*ER*, xii, 65
1502	Glen Artney	John Murray of Strowan	*ER*, xii, 625
1506-1508	Bute	Alexander Reid	*ER*, xii, 511; xiii, 79
1508-1509	Bute	John Reid	*ER*, xiii, 138
1511	Birse C	Andrew Elphinstone of 'Selmys'	*Abdn. Reg.*, 371

1. Once part of Drimmie forest.
2. Once part of Kingoldrum forest.

Table 11. THE OFFICIALS OF ETTRICK FOREST

A *Bailies*

Date	Name	Source ER
1455-1471 x 2	Thomas Cranston of that ilk	vi, 225; viii, 43
1471 x 2-1488	John Cranston of that ilk	viii, 141
1488-1502	Alexander, 2nd Lord Home	x, 654 *sub* Kirkhope; *RMS*, ii, 1921 (1489/90)
1502-1513	Alexander, Lord Home, son of above and joint bailie since 1489/90	*RSS*, i, 839; *ER*, xiii, 524

B *Master Currours*

1 *Tweed Ward*

Date	Name	First Recorded	Last Recorded
1455-1460	George Pringle	vi, 225	
1460-1469 x 70	Robert Pringle	vii, 24	1469; vii, 623
1469 x 70-1474	William Douglas of Cluny	viii, 47	
1474-1484	David Crichton	viii, 269	
1484-1499	Patrick Crichton	ix, 318	xi, 201

2 *Ettrick Ward*

1455-1469	Walter Scott of Kirkurde	vi, 225	
1469-1475	Alexander Scott of Kirkurde	vii, 619	
1475-1482 x 84	David Scott of Kirkurde	viii, 356	1482; ix, 185
1482 x 84-1499	Walter Scott of Howpaslot	ix, 607 *sub* 'Aldishope'	xi, 98, 205

3 *Yarrow Ward*

1455-1460 x 67	William Middlemast	vi, 225	1460; vi, 620
1460 x 67-1488	Thomas Middlemast	vii, 530	1487; ix, 473
1488-1499	Alexander, Lord Home	x, 650, *sub* 'Whitehope'	xi, 202

C *Currours*

1 *Tweed Ward*

1455-1466	David Pringle	vi, 225	
1466-1492 x 93	James Pringle of Smailholm	vii, 475	x, 343
1492 x 93-1499	David Pringle of Smailholm	x, 429	xi, 201

2 *Ettrick Ward*

1455-1467	Aitken/Adam Scott	vi, 225	
1467-1478	David Scott	vii, 477	
1478-1487 x 88	William Scott	viii, 587	ix, 473
1488-1492 x 93	Adam Scott	x, 100	x, 347
1492 x 93-1499	Walter Scott	x, 431	xi, 205

3 *Yarrow Ward*

1455-1469 x 70	Robert Liddel of Balmure	vi, 225	vii, 620
1469 x 70-1482 x 83	James Liddel of Halkerston	viii, 100	ix, 187
1482 x 83-1488	John Murray of Touchadam	ix, 271	x, 95
1488-1499	Alexander, Lord Home	x, 97	xi, 203

Table 11. The Officials of Ettrick Forest (continued)

D *Visiting Commissioners for crown lands*

Date	Personnel	Source	Comment	Source
1455 All Saints	Lord of Hamilton	*ER*, vi, 227		
1455 Beltane?	Lord Ninian of Spot Abbot of Holyrood Treasurer Alexander Napier, comptroller	*ER*, vi, 227		
1456 All Saints	Lords of council	*ER*, vi, 372		
1457 Beltane	Chancellor	*ER*, vi, 372		
1458 All Saints	Chancellor Comptroller	*ER*, vi, 545		
1459 Beltane	Chancellor Comptroller	*ER*, vi, 545		
1466 All Saints	Commissioner	*ER*, vii, 478		
1467 Beltane	Lords of council	*ER*, vii, 478		
1468 Beltane	Comptroller Thomas Cranston of that ilk	*ER*, vii, 527		
	Master James Lyndesay	*ER*, viii, 45		
1470 x 1471	Lords of council Commissioners	*ER*, viii, 44, 48, 101		
1478 x 1479	Commissioners	*ER*, viii, 585		
1483 x 1484	Commissioners	*ER*, ix, 271		
17 Sept. 1484[1]	Archibald, Earl of Angus	*ER*, ix, 605	Lord of articles, 1481/2	*APS*, ii, 137
	Alex. Leslie of Wardis, comptroller			
	John Murray of Touchadam		Lord of council, 1485	*ADC*, i, 116[X] b
	Master Alexander Murray, parson of Forest			
	David Luthirdale, parson of Arbuthnott			
10 June 1485	Lord Hailes	*ER*, ix, 609	Lord of council, 1485	*ADC*, i,* 115
	Alexander Lumsden, parson of Flisk Comptroller		Lord of council, 1485	*ADC*, i,* 115
	John Ross of Montgrenan		Lord of council, 1484 and 1485?	*ADC*, i,* 87

1. Henceforth commissions only tabulated when details of personnel are recorded. Commissioners in 1490s also attended some courts listed in Table 8.

Table 11. The Officials of Ettrick Forest (continued)

D (continued)

Date	Personnel	Source	Comment	Source
12 June 1486	Colin, Earl of Argyll, chancellor	*ER*, ix, 614		
	George Robison, comptroller			
	John Murray of Touchadam		Lord of council, 1485	*ADC*, i, 116* b
	Sir Alexander Scott, parson of Wigton, clerk register			
	Sir James Allardice, provost of College Royal of St Andrews		MP, 1484	*APS*, ii, 167
	Master Richard Lawson, clerk of justiciary		Lord of council, 1485	*ADC*, i, *115
			Lord of articles, 1482, 1487	*APS*, ii, 142, 175
	Sir Henry Alan, director of chancery			
7 June 1490	Colin, Earl of Argyll, chancellor	*ER*, x, 675		
	Alex., Lord Home, chamberlain		Lord of council, 1490	*ADC*, i, 142
	William, Lord of St John of Jerusalem, master of household		Lord of council, and articles, 1490	*ADC*, i, 142
	Master Alex. Inglis, archdeacon of St Andrews		Lord of council, 1490	*ADC*, i, 141
	Thomas Forest, comptroller			
18 April 1499	William, Bishop of Aberdeen	*ER*, xi, 396	Lord of council, 1499	*ADC*, ii, 321
	George, Abbot of Dunfermline		Lord of council, 1499	*ADC*, ii, 320
	James, Abbot of Scone		Lord of council, 1499	*ADC*, ii, 346
	Patrick Home of Polworth, comptroller			
	Robert Lundy of Balgownie, treasurer			
	Sir Henry Alan, archdeacon of Dunblane			
3 Dec. 1503	Comptroller	*ER*, xii, 658		
	Henry Alan, archdeacon of Dunblane			
	David Beaton			

Table 11. The Officials of Ettrick Forest (continued)

Date	Personnel	Source	Comment	Source
22 Feb. 1505/6	William, Bishop of Aberdeen	*RSS*, i, 1228	MP 1505/6	*APS*, ii, 262
	James, Abbot of Dunfermline, treasurer		MP 1505/6	*APS*, ii, 262
	Henry, Abbot of Jedburgh		MP 1505/6	*APS*, ii, 262
	Archibald, Earl of Argyll		MP 1505/6	*APS*, ii, 262
	James 'Redeuch', comptroller			
	Master Gavin Dunbar, archdeacon of St Andrews			
	Master Richard Law-son of 'Hieriggis'			
2 May 1511	Bishop of Caithness, treasurer	*ER*, xiii, 651		
	Henry, Abbot of Jedburgh			
	Archibald, Earl of Argyll			
	Master James Henryson			

Table 12. COURTS AND *ASSEDACIONES* IN ETTRICK
(All references are to the *Exchequer Rolls*)

Date	Court[1]	Ettrick Forest
1455	AS	vi, 227
1456?	B and A?	vi, 227
1456	AS	vi, 372
1457	B	vi, 372
1458	AS	vi, 545
1459	B and A	vi, 545
1460		

Date	Court	Ettrick Ward	Tweed Ward	Yarrow Ward
1461				
1462				
1463				
1465				
1466	B			
	AS	vii, 478	vii, 476	
1467	B and A	vii, 478		
	AS	vii, 527	vii, 525	vii, 529
1468	B and A	vii, 527	vii, 525	and A, vii, 529
	AS	vii, 619	vii, 622	vii, 620
1469	B	vii, 619	vii, 622	vii, 620
	AS			
1470	B			
	AS	viii, 43	viii, 47	viii, 100
1471	B and A?	viii, 43, 44	and A? viii, 47, 48	and A, viii, 100, 101
	AS			
1472	B			
	AS	viii, 141	viii, 140	viii, 143
1473	B	viii, 141	viii, 140	viii, 143
	AS			
1474	B		?viii, 211	
	AS		viii, 268	viii, 267
1475	B		viii, 268	viii, 267
	AS	viii, 356 n	viii, 353 n	viii, 355 n
1476	B	viii, 356 n	viii, 353 n	viii, 355 n
	AS	viii, 437	viii, 432	viii, 435
1477	B	viii, 437	viii, 432	viii, 435
	AS	viii, 482	viii, 478	viii, 477
1478	B	viii, 482	viii, 478	viii, 477
	AS	viii, 588	viii, 586	viii, 584
1479	B	viii, 589	viii, 586	viii, 584
	AS	ix, 31	ix, 29	ix, 33
1480	B	ix, 31	ix, 29	ix, 33
	AS	ix, 138	ix, 134	ix, 136

1. B — Beltane court, AS — All saints' court. A — *assedacio*, n — no extract of courts
returned when account presented, therefore proceeds of court not collected till later
if at all.

Table 12. Courts and *Assedaciones* in Ettrick (continued)

Date	Court	Ettrick Ward	Tweed Ward	Yarrow Ward
1481	B	ix, 138	ix, 134	ix, 136
	AS			
1482	B			
	AS			
1483	B			
	AS			
1484	B			
	AS	ix, 421 n	ix, 318 n	ix, 321 n
	A[1]	ix, 605		
1485	B	ix, 421 n	ix, 318 n	ix, 321 n
	AS	ix, 421 n	ix, 414 n	ix, 418 n
	A	ix, 609		
1486	B	ix, 421 n	ix, 414 n	ix, 418 n
	AS	x, 169 n	x, 162 n	x, 165 n
	A	ix, 614		
1487	B	x, 169 n	ix, 467;[2] x, 162	ix, 467[2]; x, 165 n
	AS	x, 169 n	x, 12, 162 n	x, 165 n
1488	B	x, 169 n	x, 12, 162 n	x, 165 n
	AS	x, 169 n[3]	x, 162 n[4]	x, 165 n[4]
	A	x, 650		
1489	B			
	AS			
1490	B		x, 163, 291	
	AS			
	A	x, 675	x, 291	
1491	B		x, 291	
	AS			
1492	B			
	AS			
1493	B	x, 431[6]		
	AS[5]	x, 431	x, 430	x, 433
1492/3	A	x, 735		
1494	B		x, 430[6]	x, 433[6]
	AS			
1495	B			
	AS	x, 599	xi, 7[7]	x, 601[8]
1496	B	x, 599		
	AS			

1. Henceforth *assedaciones*, although placed in the first column, apply to all wards.
2. Several courts held for this ward on 19th July.
3. No returns from several courts.
4. Returns of several courts together.
5. The dates when the courts of 1493 and 1494 were held are uncertain.
6. The account states that two courts were held for All Saints and for 'Invencionis Sancte Crucis.'
7. The account merely states that certain courts were held in February 1495/6.
8. The courts of Yarrow for 1494 and 1495 appear to have been held on 18 February 1495/6.

Table 12. Courts and *Assedaciones* in Ettrick (continued)

Date	Court	Ettrick Ward	Tweed Ward	Yarrow Ward
1497	B			
	AS			
1498	B	xi, 100[1]		
	AS	xi, 207[2]		
1499	B	xi, 207[2]		
	AS	xi, 402 *sub* Torwoodlee		
	A	xi, 396		
1500[3]	A	xi, 403 2 leases		
1501	A	xi, 457		
1503	A	xii, 658, 2 leases		
1505/6		xii, 658-9 a full court		
1510	A	xiii, 649		
1511	A	xiii, 651		

Bound Courts

1472 x 1473		viii, 141	viii, 140	viii, 143
1477 x 1478		viii, 482	viii, ·478	viii, 477

---

1. Five courts, presumably those of 1496-1498 were held on 20 July.
2. This court may have concerned the whole forest.
3. After the 1499 reorganisation only *assedaciones* are recorded in the exchequer records.

Table 13. FINES IMPOSED IN ETTRICK (BUT NOT COLLECTED[1])

A Tweed Ward

Date	Offence	Fine	Offender	Source[2]
1464	1 stag etc.	£16	William Douglas, warden	viii, 476
c 1466 x 1467	4 oaks	£40	Abbot of Newbattle	vii, 476, 623
1467	wood-cutting?	50s	a smith in Galashiels	vii, 476
	shieling & sub-letting	£8	inhabitants of Galashiels, Mossilee and Blyndlee	vii, 476
		£6	5 men, named	vii, 477
		50s	2 men, named	vii, 477
1467 x 1468	3 oaks	£30	Abbot of Melrose	vii, 525
	20 oaks	£200	William Douglas, warden	vii, 525
		10s	William Hervy	vii, 526
1469	2 shielings	£6	William Douglas	viii, 479
1469 x 1470	2 shielings	£6	William Douglas	viii, 48
1470	2 stags, 3 hinds	£35	William Douglas	viii, 479
1473	1 stag, 4 stags?	£15	William Douglas	viii, 479
	1 stag	£10	David Pringle	viii, 479
	non-compearance	£10	Robert Rutherford	viii, 479-80
	non-compearance	£10	James, Lord Hamilton	viii, 211, 587
1473 x 1474	in bound court	£10	Lord of Horsbruk	viii, 211
1474 x 1475		£7 3s 4d	William Vaich	viii, 269
		10s	Andrew Hervy	viii, 269

1. Fines were usually mentioned in the discharge of the currours' accounts and, therefore, were not collected. This is not a complete list of fines imposed.
2. All references are to *Exchequer Rolls*.

M

Table 13. Fines Imposed in Ettrick (but not collected) (continued)

A Tweed Ward (continued)

Date	Offence	Fine	Offender	Source
1477 x 1478	2 shielings	£9	inhabitants of Caddonlee & Galashiels (Queen)	viii, 480
	sheep	20 lambs, 4s 5d	David Crichton	viii, 480
	sheep	20 lambs, 8s 10d	David Pringle, Sr.	viii, 480
	sheep	40 lambs, 20s	inhabitants of Mossilee and Galashiels	viii, 480
	vert in bound court	50s	3 men, named	viii, 480
		16s	4 men, named	viii, 480
	in bound court	50s	5 men	viii, 481
	in bound court	55s	6 men	viii, 481
	in bound court	31s	4 men	viii, 481
	stags	£20	3 Taits and Walter Kerr	viii, 481
	sheep	26s 8d	David Crichton	viii, 481
	sheep	31s	David Pringle Jr.	viii, 481
1478 x 1479	18 oaks	£180	Abbot of Melrose	viii, 587
	stags	£30	Earl of Buchan	viii, 587
	in bound court	£62	Peebles	viii, 587
1479 x 1480	sub-letting	20s	Tenant of Fairnilee	ix, 30
1480 x 1481	sub-letting	44s	Thomas Kerr	ix, 135
1496	sowing		Tenant of Galashiels	ix, 7
1495 x 1497	1 stag and vert	£22 6s 8d	George, Master of Angus	xi, 9
1499	ditching and sowing	20 sheep	in Holylee	xi, 401
	ditching and sowing	20 sheep	in West Windydoors	xi, 401
	ditching and sowing	20 sheep	in Thornylee	xi, 401
	ditching and sowing	20 sheep	in East Windydoors	xi, 401-2
	ditching and sowing	10 sheep	in Craiglatch	xi, 402
	plowing and sowing	20 sheep	in Crosslee	xi, 402
	plowing and sowing	forfeiture of stead composition, 20 sheep	Torwoodlee, 'Toftnese'	xi, 402
1501 x 1502	paying old rents?	forfeiture of stead	Mid Windydoors	xii, 37

Table 13. Fines Imposed in Ettrick (but not collected) (continued)

B Yarrow Ward

Date	Offence	Offender	Fine	Source
1470 x 1471	stag and hind	William Cockburn	£15	viii, 101
1473 x 1474	1 stag	John Govan of Cardronno	£10	viii, 210
		James Lord Hamilton	£10	viii, 210
1477 x 1478	sheep	Patrick Murray	£3 2s	viii, 477
	wooden fence	Patrick Murray	40s	viii, 477-8
1478 x 1479	in bound court	Thomas Dickson	£5	viii, 584-5
	1 stag, 6 hinds		£70	viii, 584
	sheep	Tenant of Lewenshope & Hangingshaw	17s 9d	viii, 585
	sheep	6 men, named	53s 4d	viii, 585
	2 ash trees	Earl of Buchan	13s 4d	viii, 585
1479 x 1480	sheep	Tenants of Lewenshope & Hangingshaw	13s 4d	ix, 34
1486 x 1487	8 beech/birch ('lentisci')	Rebels in Ashiestiel	53s '4d	ix, 471
	40 beech/birch	Abbot of Kelso	£13 6s 8d	ix, 472
1499	sowing	in Yair	£20	xi, 400
	ditching & sowing	in Ashiestiel	20 sheep	xi, 400-1
	ditching & sowing	in 'Glenpoit'	20 sheep	xi, 401
1501 x 1502	payment of old rents?	½ 'Glenpoit'	forfeiture of stead	xii, 37

C Ettrick Ward

Date	Offence	Offender	Fine	Source
1468 x 1469		George Cranston son of baillie	£3	vii, 620
1470 x 1471	enclosure		40s	vii, 44
	1 stag	Abbot of Kelso	£10	viii, 45
	1 stag and hind	Fergus Graham	£15	viii, 45
1473 x 1474	4 stags	James, Earl of Buchan	£40	viii, 208
		James, Lord Hamilton, John Ross of Hawkhead & James Rutherford of that ilk	£40	viii, 209

Table 13. Fines Imposed in Ettrick (but not collected) (continued)

C *Ettrick Ward* (continued)

Date	Offence	Fine	Offender	Source
1476 x 1477	sheep and shieling	£6	James Scott	viii, 439
1479 x 1480	sheep	8s 10d	Tenant of Harehead	ix, 32
1495 x 1496		10s	a 'colthird'	x, 599
	sowing		in Fauldshope	x, 599
	4 beech/birch	£26 0s 8d	in Broadmeadow	x, 600
	5 oaks	£50	Lord Bothwell, Lord Home	x, 600
1499	ploughing & sowing	10 sheep	in Harehead	xi, 397
	ploughing & sowing	12 sheep	in Mid Hartwood	xi, 397
	sowing	forfeiture of ½ stead	Sundhope	xi, 399
1501 x 1502	payment of old rents?	no forfeiture of ½ stead	Sundhope	xii, 37
	payment of old rents?	no forfeiture of ½ stead	Kershope	xii, 37
	payment of old rents?	no forfeiture of ½ stead	Fauldshope	xii, 37
	payment of old rents?	no forfeiture of ½ stead	Hartwood	xii, 37
1502 x 1503	payment of old rents?	no forfeiture	Mountcommon	xii, 113

D *Ettrick Forest*

Date	Offence	Fine	Offender	Source
1502 x 1503	2 hinds kids	£10	Alex Vauch of Dawick & Alex Horsbruck	xii, 115

Table 14. JUDICIAL ARRANGEMENTS FOR DISPUTES

A *Major disputes*

1. Settled in a royal court

Date	Disputants	Source
1180	Melrose Abbey v De Morville	*RRS*, ii, 236
1184	Melrose Abbey v Wedale	*Chron. Melrose*, 44
1208	Melrose Abbey v Earl Patrick	*Melr. Lib.*, 101
1219	Newbattle Abbey v Innerleithen	*Newb. Reg.*, 121
1235	Melrose Abbey v Avenel	*Melr. Lib.*, 198

2. Settled in a church court

1208	Steward v Melrose Abbey	*Concilia Scotiae*, 234

B *Minor matters*

Date	Forest	Offender	Competent Court	Source
1180	Gala and Leader	Monks' servants	Abbey court	*Melr. Lib.*, 111
		Other offenders	Baron court	
			Abbey & Morville share fine	
1182/1212 x 1232	Trolhope	Baron's men	Baron court	*Melr. Lib.*, 307
		Monk's men	Abbey court with baron's licence	
1165 x 1169	Eskdale	All offenders	Baron court	*Melr. Lib.*, 39
1206	Mearns	Bishop's men	Bishop of St. Andrews' court	*Spalding Misc.* v, 205
1235	Eskdale	Monks' servants	Abbey court	*Melr. Lib.*, 198
1266	Ayr	Monks' men on baron's land	Abbey court	*Melr. Lib.*, 325
		Baron's men on monks' land	Baron court	

8

The Scope and Efficiency of the
Administration of Royal Forests

THE extent to which economic activity could take place within a forest depended firstly on the policy adopted towards a particular reserve, whether it was to be maintained strictly as a hunting reserve with no other activities permitted within it or whether economic activity was to be permitted on payment of a toll or as a mark of favour, and secondly on the efficiency with which the administrative and judicial system operated when carrying out that policy.

The enforcement of royal rights in forests was an enormous task entailing complete control or supervision of all activity within a certain area. There is, however, evidence to suggest that within a royal forest some areas would be regarded as better hunting areas than others and that the administration concentrated on banning economic activity only within these better areas. It is inconceivable that a reserve the size of that round Elgin, Forres and Inverness could have been strictly supervised over its whole extent twenty-four hours a day in the reign of William I. Consequently the forests of Darnaway, Pluscarden and Auchtertyre recorded in the thirteenth century within that reserve (see p. 339) may represent the better hunting areas where in the twelfth century economic activity was strictly controlled while other parts of the reserve were gradually alienated or ignored. Before their alienation the same may well have been true of the forests of Invercullen and of Maryculter, which were subdivisions of the forests of Banff and the Mounth respectively. (See Table 25, p. 338.) The inadequacy of the administration to cope with the reservation of the whole area of a forest can be seen in Robert I's policy of reducing the size of several of his reserves, such as Stocket, Drum and Boyne and Enzie in the hope, one assumes, of better protecting the game within a smaller, more suitable area. This was likewise the case when Alexander alienated or deforested parts of his forests of Gala and Leader, Gladhouse and Moorfoot, South-West Ettrick, Dollar and Dundaff and Strathcarron. The twelfth and thirteenth centuries, therefore, witnessed a process whereby many reserves were reduced in size because the royal forest administration found itself unable to enforce the king's rights efficiently and to withstand or control the economic inroads of the abbeys over the whole area of a forest.

The efficiency of the administration depended not only on the area to be covered but also on the chief administrator's control of his subordinates and on the subordinates' execution of their duties. As early as 1189 x 1190 there are indications[1] that the king was experiencing difficulty in controlling foresters who were exploiting their position, perhaps through their ability on certain occasions to impose fines or forfeitures without trial, a difficulty which would not have been helped by the appearance of hereditary forester-sheriffs. To strengthen his control and to encourage the foresters to perform their duties, the king may have taken an oath from his foresters, as Alexander II did from the monks' foresters in the purlieu of Pluscarden where:

forestarii predictorum monachorum quas ipsi [monks] ad custodiendum dicta foresta posuerint nobis [king] vel ballivis nostris presentabuntur fidelitatem nobis de predictis feris facturi.[2]

All the evidence suggests that these problems were never solved in the twelfth and thirteenth centuries, but the approach to the problem was practical, for the forest laws recognised that a cart might enter a forest illegally without being apprehended and, probably in the fourteenth century, that game could be killed illegally without the arrest of the offender. (See pp. 293, 297, Laws 10 and 24.)

In the fourteenth century the officials fitted into a supervisory hierarchy; the justiciar and perhaps a general 'cursor'[3] supervised the head forester; and the head forester would be expected to control the sub-foresters. The efficiency of the administration, however, can not have been furthered by the forester's or a tenant's acquisition of rights in the forest equivalent to possession as a result of hereditary tenure of the office and the right to use the lands of the forest. (See Table 8 and 9, pp. 119, 153.) Some of these reserves eventually granted in free forest, such as Clackmannan, Plater, and Boyne and Enzie, were probably inefficiently run in the fourteenth century. The efficiency of the administration probably varied from forest to forest and reign to reign, depending on the forester, what rights he held, and whether the king frequented the forest in order to hunt. It is noticeable that the trial of forest cases was, at the start of the fourteenth century, the responsibility not of local magnates but of judges sent out by the central government, which would have occasioned an efficient judicial system until the latter part of the century, when the justiciars themselves appear to have become resident officials. Generally, the problems presented to the forest administration were not grasped firmly but were by-passed. Weak administrative solutions such as reducing the size of a forest or permitting the forester to abuse the forest were current.

In the fifteenth century, however, there are signs that positive administrative solutions were applied to the problems of running the royal lands and that the medieval administration's capacity for action increased. The advent of bailies and commissioners during the fifteenth century must have helped the administration, for the commissioners had to check all royal officials including bailies, foresters and sub-foresters, punish negligence and, if necessary, replace unsatisfactory officials. Combined with this there is the possibility in the reigns of James II and James III that men of non-magnate status became head foresters under the bailie, thus removing the risk, seen in the fourteenth century, of the forester taking over the forest. Such foresters could be more easily controlled and in the 1460s the exchequer could order that no more than a certain sum be paid to the foresters of Mamlorne by the bailie till a new order was issued[4] authorising further payment. In 1478-1479 the forester of Darnaway received his usual allowance of 53s 4d 'ita quod bene conservet forestam'.[5]

All did not run smoothly, however, even in those areas where the king hunted frequently. For example, the foresters of Darnaway had to be ordered to cut neither timber nor undergrowth,[6] and James IV's letter of 1507/8 had to remind Edmonstone, the forester of Glenfinglas, of his most basic duties. Although the exchequer's accounts for the latter area present a picture of lands lying waste and of foresters being able to supply deer to the king and provide for hunting expeditions, the preamble to this letter, admittedly somewhat rhetorical, suggests that the forest administration was extremely lax: animals were pastured daily in the forest, deer were hunted and killed illegally and other rules were broken. James, however, was trying to remedy the situation. The trial of forest offenders must also have suffered from the irregularity of justice ayres in the earlier part of the fifteenth century, while in the latter part of the century the commissioners of crown lands held their courts fairly frequently and were an experienced judicial body: the comptroller was always a member, while the chancellor and the treasurer were often members. The presence in their number of lords of council and lords of the articles argues that the king and parliament were informed of their actions and able to influence them. There is not evidence to evaluate their efficacy, but in 1492 and 1493 disputes over holdings in Ettrick which the commissioners should have determined came before the lords of council.[7] By the end of the fifteenth century and in the early sixteenth century, when justice ayres were held fairly regularly and when their concern with certain types of offences was based on parliamentary enactments and not on a specific forest jurisdiction, the ayres paid considerable attention to wood-cutting offences and in 1510 heard 138 cases of theft and destruction of wood in Ettrick.[8] Most offenders actually paid their fines but some arranged compositions with the treasurer. In the early sixteenth century also James tried to improve the performance of his Glenfinglas administration in bringing offenders before the court. The impression gained is that by the early sixteenth century an administrative structure had been developed which had the capacity to run hunting reserves efficiently but that the personnel of this administration were not sufficiently numerous to apprehend all offenders and did not fulfil their duties to the letter. The efforts made to make the administration work can be examined in detail in Ettrick after 1455.

In the supervisory hierarchy of Ettrick the forester-tenants were checked by the currour and the master currour. The currours were controlled by the bailie and all officials came under the commissioners. The lynch pins of this administration were the currours who, to judge by the frequency of their accounts to the exchequer, functioned adequately. Only exceptionally, however, did they collect all the revenue which they were supposed to collect. The full potential revenue which included the proceeds of courts and rents was given in the charge of their account with the arrears of the previous account. The discharge of the account listed not only money collected and disposed of but also made allowances for items charged which could not be or were not collected. The total of these discharges was then subtracted from the total of the charges. The resultant sum, the rests, was the amount of the charged revenue which was neither collected nor allowed for. If the currours were collecting all the revenue, the rests should never have exceeded the arrears from the previous account. This argument is based on the assumption that the discharge side of the account allowed for all charged items which, for one reason or another, could not be collected. Dr Madden has argued, however, that the arrears of the currour's account increased because allowances from the exchequer were slow in coming.[9] Nonetheless, allowances were granted frequently and regularly and the arrears of rents if they could not be paid seldom were kept on any account for more than ten years before allowance was made for them. If anything, allowances could be too readily granted to cover up for failure to collect rent or for waste, and some allowances were continued after the need for them had been removed.[10] When the accounts were still presented as a whole, there was between 1456 and 1457 a drop in the arrears from £318 3s 6d to £74, but from 1457 to 1461 they rose from £74 to £593 3s 4d. (See Table 15, p. 180.) Between 1461 and 1466 the arrears of Tweed rose from £89 0s 11d to £508 14s. By 1469 they were down to £130 15s 8d, but from then till 1477 they rose slowly to £293 0s 6d. Thereafter they fluctuated, with a significant increase in 1489. In Yarrow the arrears varied insignificantly but increased from £62 5s to £420 1s between 1483 and 1484. The arrears of Ettrick ward rose steadily from £78 11s 6½d in 1472 to £2114 11s 6d in 1487. As a general and approximate guide these figures show that the currours' efficiency varied from year to year and from ward to ward, but overall the situation worsened towards the end of James III's reign, especially between 1483 and 1487. None of the accounts balanced before 1488, mainly because of the non-collection of fermes and of fines imposed by the courts.[11] Obviously, if the currours could not collect all the fines imposed by the court, then the maintenance of the forest must have suffered. The fact that explanations of the arrears were entered in some accounts suggests that the currours were fully aware of their shortcomings. In 1485 John Murray of Touchadam laid his arrears squarely at the feet of the forester-tenants of Yarrow, and when he threatened distraint the tenants seemed to have pleaded waste as an excuse and so an inquisition was ordered for the following year.[12] Since in 1487 the tenants were again blamed for not paying their fermes,[13] it would appear that if they refused to pay their fermes little could be done and the arrears increased. In 1485 and 1486, when the forester-tenants were proving troublesome, the arrears of the previous currour of Yarrow, James Liddel, were allowed.[14] In Liddel's last account in 1483, the arrears amounted to £62 5s. In 1485 x 1486 the king seized Liddel's goods and punished him 'usque ad mortem' for an unknown reason. The succeeding accountant was not responsible for his predecessor's arrears unless specifically charged with them.[15] Consequently, if a retiring accountant or his heirs moved away from the forest it was possible not only for tenants to escape paying fermes but also for offenders to escape paying fines. Nevertheless fermes were collected and fines were raised: in 1477 the total revenue sent from Ettrick to the comptroller was £1328 3s 2d.[16]

The returns of the courts in Ettrick, which could vary enormously, also suggest that a fair number of offenders were apprehended and fined. While many offenders may have escaped, many were brought before the courts by the forester-tenants and master currours and fines imposed. (See Table 13, p. 165.) In 1478 £158 13s 8d was charged from the bound-court of Ettrick[17] and in 1480 £191 from the Beltane court of Tweed,[18] although in 1480 the returns of the Beltane and All Saints courts of Yarrow amounted only to £9 2s 2d and 11¼ marts.[19] Towards the end of James III's reign, however, the collection by the currours of fines imposed by the courts fell behind because the returns of the courts were not submitted on time. (See Table 12, p. 162.) In order to avoid paying fines, not all could try, as Peebles did, to be excused from the bound-court,[20] but many made compositions often by paying a smaller sum than the original fine. Compositions of fines imposed for game offences, which first appeared in 1471,[21] continued regularly thereafter. The king also granted remissions for various reasons including favour, but the most interesting is that of David Pringle who was amerced £10 for killing one stag in 1473 'ad nupcias suas', but he did not have to pay the fine 'ex eadem consideracione et curialitate dictarum nupciarum'![22] The lords of council or the commissioners might also arrange remissions,[23] and despite parliament's legislation to the contrary in 1478,[24] remissions continued to be granted.

In the 1490s, while courts were held extremely erratically (see Table 12, p. 163), the amount of the arrears decreased overall, most notably in Ettrick ward, perhaps because of Home's activities as bailie and allowances made to him. As currour of Yarrow he had made the accounts balance for the first time. At this point, with the administration seemingly improving, James IV and the commissioners completely re-organised the administration of Ettrick because the administration no longer held courts at the recognised times or intervals and had proved unable to cope with the severe problems imposed in a forest which contained around a hundred tenants. In 1499 James, attempting to learn from past deficiencies, re-organised it by abolishing the previous pattern of courts, substituting four new bailie courts, clearly splitting the financial and forest duties of his officials, thus recognising the need for specialisation, and by placing more stress on the financial returns of the forest by giving the comptroller responsibility for appointing subordinate personnel. Also, his regulations for forester-tenants placed direct responsibility on the lower echelons of the administration. Given this new start with all arrears wiped out, Lord Home and his son made the accounts for the whole forest balance in 1500, 1503, 1507 and 1509. The amount of money reaching the comptroller rose from £427 4s in 1498[25] to more than double that amount in 1499.[26] After rent increases which occurred on all royal lands, the crown's revenue from Ettrick rose to £2,271 in 1509.[27] The reorganisation of 1499 was, therefore, successful in a financial sense, but this stress on finance and the advent of feuing rendered the maintenance of Ettrick as a hunting reserve impossible. Ettrick, on which time and effort were spent in the fifteenth century, must have been a source of frustration to the king and his officials, for while the administration functioned adequately under James II and throughout most of James III's reign and improved under James IV after 1499, it never regulated the life of the forest in complete accord with the king's forest rights. While the administration of Ettrick may be considered to have provided a thorough coverage of the forest with a variety of officials and courts co-operating with each other, one feels that this was the thoroughness of desperation rather than of confidence and that despite it all, offenders slipped by unmolested. In 1499 the statutes of Ettrick complained of the offences committed by outsiders 'for the quhilkis thair has ben na remeid this langtyme to gret prejudice and hurt of the king and forrest and landis . . .'.[28] The extent of the control which the administration did exercise was nevertheless remarkable.

The problems facing the administration were aggravated by the rights which the king granted to certain people to live in a forest or to receive game or timber from a forest or to pursue otherwise restricted activities within a forest. While such exemptions permitted economic activity and so softened the effect of hunting reserves, a lot was expected of the forester, who had to distinguish those with a right to enter the forest and those without such a right.

That the king might alienate part or all of the lands of a forest has already been mentioned when discussing the separability of the lands and rights of the forest. In Scotland the area of land alienated would be a fairly large tract of land in the forest and, from the fourteenth century onwards, often extending to the whole forest. Only in the vast reserve round Elgin, Forres and Inverness in the twelth and thirteenth centuries is the English custom of granting out individual woods and small parcels of land recorded.[29] Theoretically, when the king granted a forest or its lands he retained control over the vert and venison, and the grantee, unless he received the lands in free forest, could only hunt if given permission to do so. Such alienations of lands, however, often led to the alienation of the forest rights. Alexander II's grants of forest lands to Newbattle, probably including the Leithen grant, and to Melrose, which gave these abbeys control of hunting in a royal forest, were only preparatory to free forest grants. (See Table 8, p. 119, *sub* Gala and Leader 1236, and Leithen 1241.) In the fourteenth and fifteenth centuries huntings were frequently included in the pertinents of grants of royal forest lands[30] and gave the grantee the right to hunt in, but not control of hunting within, the forest unless of course he was also the forester. (See Table 8, p. 119.) The loss of a royal forest which could result from the association of the lands or the herbage or the foggage of a forest with the forestership has already been discussed. By the later fifteenth century, when a grant was made of the lands of a forest or of lands accompanied by a forest or of lands with a forest in the pertinents, it is hard to know whether the forest was a hunting reserve or a wood or simply the name of an area which had at one time been a hunting reserve. In 1500 the grant of Lochaber to Alexander, Lord Gordon 'unacum forestis et silvis dictis terris spectantibus' could refer either to hunting reserves and woods or to woods alone,[31] and in 1496 the 'forestam de Boithvile' was simply the name applied to the lands of 'Coldoun' and 'Birnthous'.[32]

The leasing of forest lands, which also created difficulties for the forests' administration, was conducted in two ways: on the one hand the forest could be let to numerous tenants and on the other to one or two persons only. The earliest evidence that there were tenants in royal forests comes from Ettrick and Jedburgh in 1299 and 1301 respectively, although there had been inhabitants in these forests at an earlier date.[33] Whether they held their land for a rent or by some form of customary tenure is not certain. In addition, the whole of Jedburgh forest was let to the abbot of Jedburgh and Sir Ivo de Aldeburgh in *c* 1298, and Aymer de Valence held Ettrick from Edward I as a knight's fee for £130.[34] In the fourteenth century the sheriffs collected returns from forests, which in the cases of Killanel,[35] Darnaway[36] and Boyne and Enzie[37] were the fermes of a varying number of tenants. Leasing continued in the fifteenth century, and fermes of lands within forests were often mentioned in the accounts of the *ballivi ad extra*:

Fermes of Lands within Forests

Forest	Date[38]	Annual ferme	Source
Clunie	1451	£13 6s 8d	*ER*, vi, 480
Buchan (in Galloway)	1456	£10	*Ibid.*, vi, 193
Darnaway	1458	53s 4d	*Ibid.*, vi, 461
Rannoch	1479	4 bolls of barley	*Ibid.*, vii, 595 and
		4 bolls of oats	*Ibid.*, ix, 529
		2 marts	
Mamlorne	*ante* 1457	16s 8d	*Ibid.*, vi, 366.

Forests were still let to single tenants, e.g., Abernethy in 1498[39] and Buchan in the 1480s.[40] In the fourteenth and early fifteenth centuries forest rents formed a small but important part of the royal revenue, a part which dramatically increased when Ettrick was annexed to the crown in 1455.

Ettrick was let to more tenants than any other royal forest,[41] and many of them by 1500 had, after the removal of previous restrictions, special freedoms to cultivate, graze and build which will be discussed below. Following rent increases in 1501, the king between 1506 and 1510 started to set Ettrick in feu ferme. The relevance of feuing to this discussion lies in the rights which the feu-ferme tenants received, to build and maintain a farmhouse with out-buildings, orchards and gardens, to plant oak trees, to make fish ponds and to build bridges.[42] Whether or not tenants in Ettrick did develop their holdings in this way, feuing brought a great relaxation of forest restrictions, since previously such freedom had been only sparingly granted. This does not signify the end of the forest,[43] for the vert was still reserved and there is no evidence that in most steads the venison was not still reserved, the main exception being that when Lord Home feued Tinnis he was freed from the justice ayres and forest courts as far as offences against the vert were concerned.[44] When, however, hereditary feu-ferme is taken in conjunction with the generous leases of 1509 and 1510 which granted freedom from forest courts and freedom to plough, to sow and to sublet,[45] it is clear that restrictions on farming were considerably reduced on some steads as a result of these special leases and moderately reduced on others as a result of feu ferme charters.

Other forests such as Cluanie,[46] Corriemuckloch and Glen Shervie[47] were also let in feu ferme, and although such lands ceased to be waste for forest, the king still kept his forest rights, since only the lands of the forest were feued and only hunting pertinents included. While feu ferme tenure encouraged the development of forest lands and so reduced the value of the area as a hunting reserve, the king still maintained the forest rights and in theory no one could hunt on these lands without permission.

The tenure of forest lands was not, however, a prerequisite of exemption from forest rights which could also take the form of a direct grant of the produce of a forest or of a grant of freedom to perform certain activities within the forest. In the twelfth century the direct grant took the form of carefully dis-tributed grants of tithes of hunting. Only three such grants were made in the medieval period and they were obviously so arranged that they would not overlap and take too heavy a toll from the royal reserves: Jedburgh Abbey received a tithe of the hunting from Teviotdale;[48] Dunfermline from the lands between the Forth and the Tay;[49] and Scone from lands to the north of the Tay.[50] Similarly grants of tithes of hides, fat and grease were closely regulated.[51] This type of direct grant of produce was replaced in the fourteenth century by a grant of a fixed number of deer[52] on the pattern adopted by Edward I in Scotland,[53] and perhaps by grants of a certain number of trees as suggested by a late thirteenth-century writ.[54] No such grants survive from the fifteenth century.

Freedom to pursue either one or more activities in a forest was granted thoughout the medieval period. The earliest of these to appear was freedom from pasture restrictions, a freedom which included both the right to graze pigs and the right to be quit of pannage[55] in a forest. The freedom to graze animals in a forest would not necessarily be unlimited. A toll might have to be paid and the number of animals and the time and place of grazing might be controlled.[56] Such control is found in Ettrick in the fifteenth century, where tenants could graze animals but where fines were still imposed for grazing sheep illegally,[57] although in some steads the tenants did receive complete freedom to pasture sheep. (See Table 24, p. 267.) Common pasture was also, on occasion, permitted in royal forests.[58]

Wood-cutting was another essential activity which was permitted within forests from the reign of David I.[59] It appears that a tenant could hold a wood within a forest,[60] but this was a practice which never became common in Scotland. The use of estovers to describe the right to take wood, which was common in England, occurs seldom in Scottish sources.[61] Grants of the right to wood were continued in the fourteenth century,[62] but as a result no doubt of a growing shortage of timber, the freedom to cut wood was not granted in the fifteenth century except in the confirmation of charters.

Ploughing within a forest, permitted in the thirteenth century as freedom to assart,[63] was also the subject of grants throughout the fourteenth century, although in Ettrick it was only permitted in those places where there had been ploughing previously.[64] This limitation continued in Ettrick into the early sixteenth century,[65] although general freedom to plough and sow might, as already mentioned, be granted to tenants in that forest.

Building, which seldom meant permanent human habitation but more often shielings for herdsmen or shelters for animals, was also permitted by special grant in the fourteenth century and earlier.[66] In the fifteenth century shielings were allowed in Ettrick and Cluanie forests.[67]

These liberties, when they were not granted individually, could be summarised as 'aisiamenta', usually followed by a list of the freedoms[68] or as the 'totum usagium nemoris'[69] granted to Melrose Abbey in a large part of Gala and Leader forest. More general freedom of action must also have gone to the grantee of the lands of a forest and to the holders of herbage and foggage. In the early sixteenth century in Ettrick several steads including Blackhouse and Gartlacleuch were freed from the control of the forest court.[70] This virtually amounted to the removal of these steads from the forest.

Such exemptions from the forest rights of the king not only complicated the foresters' administrative tasks but also represent the means by which the royal monopoly of the royal forests could be relaxed to admit various economic activities.

The study of the enforcement of royal rights, of the efficiency of that enforcement and of the exemptions from the royal rights yields three main conclusions. Firstly, certain royal forests which must at one time have been valuable as royal hunting reserves had ceased to be so as a result of grants from the crown, inefficient administration and economic pressure, for example, Gala and Leader by 1236, and Boyne and Enzie, Drum, Plater,

Cowie and Stocket by the beginning of the fifteenth century. In the fifteenth and early sixteenth centuries Birnam, Corriemuckloch and Cluanie can be added to this list. Secondly, every effort was made to retain some forests, waste and intact. The most prominent example of this type of forest was Menteith in the fifteenth and early sixteenth centuries, although Ettrick in the twelfth and thirteenth centuries and Ben More, Balquhidder and Mamlorne in the fifteenth century can also be considered to be in this category. In some ways the forests which did not appear in this second category till the fifteenth century replaced those forests lost in the fourteenth century. Thirdly, there were those forests where an attempt was made to adapt the maintenance of a hunting reserve to the existence of tenants and grants of freedoms within that reserve. Boyne and Enzie in the mid-fourteenth century, Darnaway in the later fifteenth century, and most notably Ettrick after 1455, can be allocated to this group. It is striking that these three types of forest could exist concurrently.

While freedoms and leases were being granted, the forest rights still remaining to the crown were reserved. While the feuing of Ettrick was under consideration, every effort was made to reserve Glenfinglas. This dichotomy shows that, in general, the Stewart kings before 1513, perhaps as a result of their own inability to enforce a harsh and rigid forest system but perhaps also as a result of their own wishes, possessed a flexibility and maturity of attitude towards their reserves absent in many other European monarchs.

Table 15. ARREARS OF ETTRICK

Date[1]	Ettrick Forest	Source[2]
1456	£ 318 3s 6d	vi, 370
1457	£ 74 8s 6d	vi, 442
1458	£ 123 17s 5d	vi, 543
1459	£ 210 12s 9d	vi, 619
1460	£ 279 0s 2d	vii, 24
1461	£ 593 3s 4d	vii, 25

Date	Ettrick Ward	Source	Tweed Ward	Source	Yarrow Ward	Source
1460			(£ 89 0s 10d)[3]	vii, 135		
1461			N[4]			
1462			N[4]			
1463						
1464						
1465						
1466	(£ 126 17s 10½d)	vii, 477	(£507 14s)	vii, 475		
1467	£ 143 0s 10½d	vii, 478	£463 10s	vii, 477		
1468[5]	£ 328 8s 9½d	vii, 529	£305 9s 8d	vii, 526	£100 8s 2d	vii, 531
1469	£ 369 5s 1½d	vii, 620	£130 15s 8d	vii, 623	£ 52 13s	vii, 622
1470	(£ 249 15s 0½d)	viii, 42	(£197 17s 8d)	viii, 46	(£ 57 19s 7d)	viii, 100
1471	£ 131 13s 10½d	viii, 46	£210 0s 8d	viii, 49	£ 60 5s 11d	viii, 102
1472	(£ 78 11s 6½d)	viii, 141	(£184 12s 8d)	viii, 139	(£ 16 16s 2d)	viii, 142
1473	£ 264 15s 3½d	viii, 142	£260 16s 5d	viii, 141	£ 52 12s	viii, 143
1474	£ 231 8s 9d	viii, 209	£ 29 17s	viii, 210	£262 11s 5d	viii, 212
1475	£ 264 2s 9d	viii, 271	£263 17s 6d	viii, 270	£ 26 0s 1d	viii, 268

1. The date given is the end of the year of account.
2. All references are to the *Exchequer Rolls*.
3. Brackets signify that no account is extant for that year. The figures are taken from the following account's statement of arrears for the preceding year. Otherwise where no account is extant a blank is left in this list.
4. N — account returned but no arrears detailed.
5. Henceforth till 1471 rents in kind are realised at the following rate: bowcow — 22s, mart — 12s, lamb — 12d. [*ER.* vii, 622 (1489)]

Table 15. Arrears of Ettrick (continued)

Date	Ettrick Ward	Source	Tweed Ward	Source	Yarrow Ward	Source
1476	£ 331 15s 9d	viii, 357	£271 3s 10d	viii, 354	£ 26 19s 1d	viii, 356
1477	£ 519 6s 10d	viii, 439	£293 0s 6d	viii, 433	£ 27 10s 7d	viii, 436
1478	£ 561 15s 9d	viii, 483	£247 19s 9d	viii, 481	£ 52 7s 10d	viii, 478
1479	£ 598 3s 6d	viii, 590	£147 3s 11d	viii, 587	£ 42 10s 9d	viii, 585
1480	£ 567 16s 8d	ix, 33	£ 88 19s 6d	ix, 31	£ 42 10s 9d	ix, 35
1481	£ 742 0s 2d	ix, 139	£ 88 19s 6d	ix, 136	£ 51 15s	ix, 137
1482	£ 662 11s 2d	ix, 186	£102 17s 6d	ix, 187	£ 62 5s	ix, 188
1483	(£ 845 11s 2d)	ix, 421			(£ 62 5s)	ix, 271
1484[1]	N		£ 15 13s 8d	ix, 271	£420 1s	ix, 273
1485	N		23s 4d	ix, 320	£455 16s 8d	ix, 322
1486	£1812 11s 2d	ix, 422	£ 49 5s 8d	ix, 417	£317 4s 6d	ix, 421
1487	£2114 11s 6d	ix, 475	N		£116 12s 2d	ix, 473
1488	N		£ 62 5s 1d	x, 13	£ 68 15s 10d	x, 97
1489	N		£236 15s 5d	x, 100	£211 2s 8d	x, 99
1490	£3168 15s 6d	x, 173	£179 1s 3d	x, 164	£ 93 1s 5½d	x, 167
1491	N		N		£334 18s 9½d	x, 293
1492	£ 896 11s	x, 348	£406 2s 11d	x, 345	£432 7s 9½d	x, 347
1493	(£1143 4s 6d)	x, 431	(£108 13s 5d)	x, 429	(£602 3s)	x, 432
1494	£1248 10s 11d	x, 432	£232 0s 6d	x, 430	Equal	x, 435
1495	£ 111 3s 5d	x, 507	£ 65 3s 3d	x, 509	Equal	x, 505
1496	£ 424 6s 5d	x, 600	N		£ 33 15s 8d	x, 603
1497	£ 482 10s 3d	xi, 10	£205 12s 9d	xi, 9	N	
1498	N		£165 0s 9d	xi, 102	N	
1499	N		N		N	

1. Returns in kind from 1483 to 1500 are realised at the following rates: bowcow — 20s, mart — 12s, lamb — 12d,[ER. viii, 141, (1473) ER. x. 603, (1496)]. Returns of grain are excluded.

Table 15. Arrears of Ettrick (continued)

Date	Ettrick Forest	Source
1500	£ 3 12s	xi, 207
1501	£ 238 10s 5d	xi, 323
1502	£ 568 19s 11d	xii, 38
1503	Equal	xii, 116
1504	£ 736 7s 4d	xii, 205
1505	£ 545 13s 11d	xii, 318
1506	£ 584 10s 6d	xii, 392
1507	Equal	xii, 538
1508	Equal	xiii, 35
1509	Equal	xiii, 181
1510	Equal	xiii, 354
1511	(£1072 3s 9d)	xiii, 410
1512	£ 632 15s 8d	xiii, 415
1513	£ 108 16s 1d	xiii, 529

9

Non-Royal Forests

ROYAL control of non-royal forests was not only an integral part of a forest system but was essential for a king who was the fount of justice and the guardian of his subjects, since the existence of baronial reserves entailed the exercise of judicial rights by their owners and the limitation of the hunting rights of subjects other than their owners. In Scotland royal control was exercised by the establishment in David I's reign of the principle that baronial forests could be created only by a forest grant from the king. (See Table 28, p. 345, which lists all forest grants.)

The earliest extant Scottish forest grant is that of David I in 1147 x 1153, granting Annandale to Robert de Bruce:

in foresto . . . sicut aliud forestum suum tenetur . . . Quare defendo ne ullus venetur in predicto foresto nisi per ipsum super forisfactum decem librarum et ne ullus eat per praedictum forestum nisi recta via nominata. (See Fig. 19.)

This grant contains two features common in forest grants till the end of the fourteenth century, the grant of the lands in forest and the sanction clause which stated that there was a £10 penalty for anyone hunting in the forest without the grantee's permission. It seems likely that this form of grant was borrowed from England. David in 1103 had witnessed Henry I's grant of lands in Yorkshire to Robert de Bruce which, although it did not concede that the lands were held in forest, stated

Et volo ut habeat istam terram ita ne aliquis in ea fuget nisi licencia sua.[1]

It is conceivable that these lands were the 'aliud forestum' mentioned in the Annandale grant and that David remembered the form of Henry's grant when drawing up his grant to Bruce in 1147 x 1153. The form of David's grant, however, more closely resembled the form of the English warren grant —

Concedo . . . quod habeat warennam in terra sua . . . et prohibeo ne aliquis in ea fuget nisi per ipsum super decem librarum forisfacturam[2]

— which had been current in Henry I's reign,[3] and it is more likely that he adopted that form as the basis of his forest grant. Although only one other forest grant, made to Nicholas the clerk, which follows the variant form —

in firmam forestam et ideo prohibeo super forisfactum XL solidorum ut nullus omnino venetur in eo [Pettinain] aut aliquid molestiae ei vel successoribus eius faciat nisi per licenciam et benevolentiam eorum

— is extant from David's reign, other grants were probably made by David.[4]

While there are no definite examples of forest grants from Malcolm IV's reign, a charter of Alexander II records that Dunlappie was held 'in libero foresto. Sicut carta Regis Malcolmi'. It is doubtful if Malcolm would have used the form 'in free forest', since it was probably introduced in Alexander II's reign. The most interesting grant of Malcolm's is his confirmation of David's grants to Walter the first Steward including 'in foresto in tristris' in the pertinents. Although these pertinents, which differ from the usual hunting pertinents 'aucupationibus, venationibus', could represent either an initial forest grant or the recognition of reserves created by the Stewards without a royal grant they do, as has been explained, most probably represent a confirmation of a previous forest grant or grants.[5]

The first of William's extant grants is also the earliest surviving forest grant to an abbey: in 1171 x 1178 William granted his waste and his chase, the alternative English name for a forest,[6] to Coupar Abbey

in liberum forestum. Ita ut nullus infra eandem terram sine predictorum monachorum licencia secet aut venetur super nostram plenariam'forisfacturam decem librarum.

This grant, written in a hand of the early thirteenth century, is authentic,[7] but the form 'liberum forestum' would be more appropriate to the reigns of Alexander II and III. The scribe, copying a genuine grant, may have used the thirteenth-century form to which he was accustomed. The same may also be true of 'nostram', which explains that it was the royal forfeiture which was collected for an offence in a subject's forest.

The remaining grants of William were all made to lay grantees and five followed a common form. The forest grant was given in the *tenendas* section,

Concessi etiam Ricardo et heredibus suis ut habeant prefatam terram de Kergille in foresto, et prohibeo firmiter ne quis in ea venetur vel secet sine licencia eorum super meam forisfacturam decem librarum.[8]

Despite minor variations, the royal clerks appear to have followed a set formula for this type of grant, as was to be expected with the development of a full-time chancery.[9] Since four of William's grants are witnessed by the chancellor, Hugh de Roxburgh, and consequently dated to 1189 x 1199, the adoption of this form, which had been used in the warren grant by 1173 x 1178,[10] for the forest grant may be attributed to Hugh de Roxburgh.

Of the first five grants of Alexander II between 1214 and 1226, four followed the form of William's grants, the exception being the grant of Dunlappie in free forest, not simply in forest. The Dunlappie grant, which survives only in a fifteenth-century copy, may be the first example of a free forest grant, a style adopted from 1233 onwards in Alexander II's grants, of which only two out of twenty-one were not free forest grants. The style of the free forest grant became more formalised as a result of the use of the royal plural:

Concessimus etiam eisdem monachis ut predictam terram de Nigg habeant in liberam forestam. Quare firmiter prohibemus ne quis sine eorum licencia in eadem terra de Nigg secet aut venetur super nostram plenariam forisfacturam decem librarum.

The adoption of these alterations can probably be attributed to William de Bondington, who became chancellor in 1231 and witnessed the first four definite extant free forest grants in 1233 and 1234. Since 14 of Alexander's 19 free forest grants after 1233 were made to ecclesiastical grantees, it might at first sight appear that the free forest grant had peculiarly ecclesiastical connotations, perhaps linked with tenure in free alms, but this would not account for the five grants made to lay grantees. It is more likely that the 'free' was added as part of the increasing formality of the grant and its meaning, if it had one, may be reflected in Forest Law 14, which probably belongs to the thirteenth century and which discusses the rights in the forest of the man 'qui liberam habet potestatem venandi' in his land beside the forest. (See p. 294, Law 14.) The increasing formality of this grant is also seen in the generalisation given in Alexander's grants to Patrick, Earl of Dunbar, and to David de Graham of Dundaff and Strathcarron,

in libero foresto adeo libere et quiete sicut aliquis aliquam terram de nobis tenet liberius[11] in libero foresto in toto regno nostro.

Alexander III's few extant grants followed the form of his predecessor's, but he did combine free forest and free warren in a grant to Coldingham, a combination perhaps made by Alexander II in 1239. Alexander III's grant to the earl of Lennox is valuable not only for the light it throws on the attitude of the native aristocracy towards hunting reserves, already discussed, but also because it required that nothing be done 'in contradictione juris dicte libere foreste'. The existence of such a right suggests that free forests were governed by a set of rules or laws.

Despite these developments, variations in practice did occur, the most significant of which is John de Vesci's grant of lands in Mow to William de Sprouston in 1279,

in forestam. Quare firmiter prohibeo ne quis in eadem terra sine eorum licencia secet aut venetur super meam plenariam forisfacturam decem librarum.

This original grant, in the form current from 1189-1233, is one of only three forest grants made by barons to survive from the medieval period and contradicts the principle of royal control of non-royal forests. (See Table 28, p. 351.)

By the end of this reign formularies or registers of writs no doubt contained copies of the free forest grant, although it is the free warren grant, identical to the free forest grant apart from the use of warren, which is given in the register of writs contained in the late thirteenth-, early fourteenth-century Ayr Ms.[12] Not till the Bute Ms. of the middle or late fourteenth century is the form of the free forest grant given.[13] Both versions include a prohibition of fishing in the sanction clause, which seldom occurs in extant forest grants. Since the forest grant was more common in Scotland than the warren grant, the Bute Ms. is, in this context, more representative of Scottish practice. English practice which preferred the warren grant may be responsible for the absence of any forest grants between 1285 and 1315 x 1321, although few charters of any type have survived from this period.

In Robert I's reign the form of the forest grant underwent several important and unheralded developments. Of twelve grants extant, only four contained the sanction clause common to nearly all previous forest grants, and when that clause was included it varied from the thirteenth-century pattern. In 1236 fishings had been included in the sanction clause of one free forest grant (see Table, 28, p. 345, *sub* Gala and Leader), but in 1322 one of Robert's grants amplified that simple prohibition of fishing by forbidding fishing in lakes, rivers and pools. Another in 1322/3 forbade fishing in any form whatsoever without the permission of the grantees. The control of fishing as part of the game in a forest, at first sight incongruous, can be traced back to the origins of the forest system in the Carolingian Empire.[14] In most grants the forest grant was included in the *tenendas* section with an introductory phrase such as 'volumus eciam et concedimus'. If the charter also granted the lands in free barony, a practice first recorded in Robert's grants, the forest grant followed the barony grant either immediately — 'in libera baronia et libera foresta' — or later in the charter. Forest pertinents appear more regularly than in the thirteenth century: in 1319 Staplegordon was granted in free forest 'cum curiis et escaetis ad liberam forestam pertinentibus', as was Jedburgh in 1320. When Robert I, in 1321, confirmed the rights which Melrose held from Nicholas Graham in Westerker, his charter included huntings, hawkings, fishings and courts with escheats concerning trees, birds, birds' nests and game and their custody. Although similar pertinents were current in grants concerning this area in the twelfth and thirteenth centuries, Eskdale was never subject to a forest grant nor was it ever called a forest.[15] One can, therefore, infer that the Avenels and then the Grahams possessed game rights similar to the pertinents in the Melrose charter, but never forest rights. In 1327, when Alexander Fraser and his son John received Cowie in free forest, they held the forest with all just pertinents 'owing and accustomed to pertain' to the forest. There were, therefore, four trends in the reign of Robert I. Firstly, the sanction clause was only occasionally included and secondly, when it was included, it did not always follow a set wording, nor did it include a given set of rights. Thirdly, more pertinents relating specifically to the free forest appeared and fourthly, the forest grant could be combined with a barony grant. The formality of the thirteenth century which had tended towards rigidity was replaced after the upheavals of war by a more formative situation as in the twelfth century, where no one form of the forest grant predominated.

From David II's reign only six free forest grants are extant, presumably because of the lack of Great Seal records. They show that all four developments of Robert I's reign, including the more detailed prohibition of fishings in the sanction clause (see Table 28, p. 345, *sub* Leithen), were continued.

Of the four extant forest grants of Robert II's reign, only one included the sanction clause and none contained any specific forest pertinents. The Clackmannan grant of 1387 was distinctive in that it was the vert and venison of Clackmannan and not the forest or the lands which were granted in free forest.

Both the grants which survive from Robert III's reign were combined free forest and warren grants. The unique version of the sanction clause in the 1392 grant of Bolton, Carriden and Langton is the last extant example of the sanction clause which had become increasingly rare during this century.

In James I's reign only two grants survive and both are from the period of Albany's governorship. That the duke of Albany might make a grant at all was remarkable, since this broke the royal monopoly of the forest grant, although it could be argued that as governor he was entitled to do so. What is more remarkable is his confirmation in 1410 of a forest grant made by Henry Sinclair, earl of Orkney, since it recognised the right of barons to create reserves without a royal grant.

From James II's reign four forest grants are extant, and of these three were made in free forest and warren. The first extant examples of the combination of a forest grant with a regality grant were made in 1452: the bishop of Moray held his barony of Spynie in free regality 'cum libera foresta et varenna'; and when the Queen received the Garioch in free regality, 'libera foresta et warenna' were included in the pertinents. In conjunction with a regality grant, free forest rights were sometimes reduced to the status of a pertinent and did not form a separate part of the grant. For instance, in 1458 Callendar was granted to James, Lord Livingston 'cum libera foresta et warenna' and not 'in libera foresta et warenna'. Although several barons had held forest and regality rights over the one piece of land, these rights had not previously been combined in any one extant grant.

The rarity of forest grants, which hampers the analysis of the forest grant, began in David II's reign, and continued until James III's reign, from which only five grants remain, but these suggest that the period of neglect through which the forest grant had passed was ending. Grants in 1474 and 1483 combined free regality and free forest on equal terms: in 1483 Alexander, Duke of Albany, received Garioch and Mar 'in liberam regalitatem et forestam'. For the first time since David II's reign specifically forest pertinents were included in an extant grant: in 1488 Thomas Culface received half of Kilgarie forest in free forest with vert and venison 'ac cum onmibus privelegiis ac libertatibus libere foreste';[16] and when John, Earl of Atholl, received Clunie forest in Perthshire in free forest in 1481 he held it with

omnibus amerciamentis ad liberam forestam ex usu et consuetudine regni nostri pertinentibus, cum veridibus arboribus et venationibus, videlicet vert et venison, cum escaetis suis, ac cum omnibus bondis, commoditatibus, libertatibus et justis pertinentiis quibuscunque tam inhabitatis quam non inhabitatis ad forestam predictam spectantibus.

These pertinents, which are a more complex version of those included in Robert I's reign, suggest that developments had been taking place in non-royal forests which have not emerged in the surviving free forest grants and that the rights conveyed by a forest grant were once more, if they had not always been, of importance.

With James IV's reign there is for the first time since Robert I's reign a moderate number of extant forest grants, twenty-three in all. The forest grants are often combined on equal terms either with a barony or with a regality grant, although in 1489 free forest and warren were given as pertinents when Birse was granted in free regality to the bishop of Aberdeen, William Elphinstone. While several grants contained forest pertinents on the lines of those of James III's grants, the pertinents of three of James IV's grants show distinctive features. Firstly, in 1494 Master Andrew Lyall, prebendary and pensionary of Brechin, held Redgorton in free forest 'adeo libere sicut alique terre infra regnum Scotie in liberis forestis conceduntur aut eriguntur'. The last extant example of such a generalising phrase belonged to 1237.[17] Secondly, from 1509 onwards the pertinents say slightly more about forest courts: John Haldane held the barony of Haldane in free forest 'cum forestariis et forestariorum curiis et eschaetis earundem'.[18] Thirdly, the most interesting feature of the pertinents in James IV's reign is the mention of forest laws in two grants made in 1511. John, Earl of Crawford, and Adam, Earl of Bothwell, received Glenesk and Bothwell respectively in free forest 'cum eschaetis . . . amerciamentis . . . legibus foreste concordantibus'. Crawford's pertinents also included the only occurrence of the general phrase 'libera forestaria'.[19]

Undoubtedly the most important development in the forest grant in James IV's reign was its application only to woods on the lands in question. The first surviving example of this type of grant was made in 1488 when James granted Patrick, Lord Hailes, the lands and lordship of Bothwell in free barony with the woods in free forest. James made ten grants of this type mainly after 1496, but it was not always simply woods which were granted in free forest: in 1507 James granted the 'forestas, silvas, et lucos videlicet le schaws et glennys' of Invernochty in free forest to Andrew Elphinstone. In this grant the forests were those of Corgarf and Baddynyon, and 'foresta' was probably used in a vegetational sense. In 1511 the 'silve et arbores crescentes' of Glenesk were the subject of such a grant.

James IV's reign also throws some light on the process by which a free forest was formed. On 24 January 1505 James IV granted to John and his brother germane, William Forbes, the woods, bogs and shaws of Glencarvie and Glenconrie in free forest. On 3 February a Privy Seal letter 'ex deliberacione dominorum concillii' which publicised the creation of this free forest was sent to sheriffs in the north-east who were ordered to command all lieges in the area not to destroy or waste the forests or any part of them by hunting, hewing or cutting under pain of the fines contained in the free forest laws and statutes. A public proclamation, therefore, was associated with the creation of a free forest, as with the creation of a royal forest. The council were consulted on this matter and probably had to give their approval. Unfortunately the records of the lords of council which were completed for 2 and 4 February contain only a blank page for 3 February.[20]

The grantees of forest grants were usually the more important tenants of the crown. From the twelfth and thirteenth centuries there were almost as many grants made to ecclesiastical as to lay grantees, but from the fourteenth and fifteenth centuries only four grants to ecclesiastical grantees have survived. In most cases Cosmo Innes is correct in saying that a forest grant was an erection of an existing holding,[21] but lands could be granted for the first time by the charter which contained the forest grant.[22] When a forest grant was not combined with an original grant of lands, the complete holding was usually in the twelfth and thirteenth centuries the subject of a forest grant, but in the later Middle Ages it became more common to grant only part of a holding in free forest. Scattered groups of lands might also be the subject of a free forest grant.

Forests were held by the usual tenures: ecclesiastical reserves were held in free alms and lay reserves by knight service, more common in the twelfth and thirteenth centuries, or by blenche ferme or by some unstated accustomed service. The last two tenures were more common in the fourteenth and fifteenth centuries. Forests were held heritably, but if the owner of a non-royal forest granted the lands of the forest to another, the forest rights did not accompany the grant.[23]

The number of forest grants extant and their form argue that the forest grant was more highly valued in the twelfth and thirteenth centuries than thereafter. In the early Middle Ages the forest grant was valuable, not only because it conveyed a hunting monopoly but also because, in the absence of the barony grant, it was the only grant to convey a special set of rights. Like a barony, a free forest was a legal conception imposed on a geographical area but was not itself a recognisable geographical feature. Certain judicial rights accompanied both the forest grant and the barony grant, but while 'baronia' was applied to certain holdings as early as the thirteenth century, there are no extant copies of a formalised grant 'in baronia' or 'in libera baronia' till the fourteenth century.[24] In the twelfth and thirteenth centuries the forest grant alone could be granted as a mark of favour over and above a grant of lands, whereas in the fourteenth century barony and regality grants also adopted that role. Consequently, by the later Middle Ages the forest grant was less important than it had been.

When combined with a barony or a regality grant, the forest grant was always placed second. When no sanction clause was included, the phrase 'in libera foresta' was tacked on almost as an afterthought. In the later fifteenth century, when forest pertinents were more detailed, they were nevertheless relatively insignificant beside the fuller forms of the barony and regality grants. Specifically forest grants did survive throughout this period, which shows that although they may have taken second place to barony and regality grants, they were still important.

It might seem reasonable to suppose that the barony grant took precedence over the forest grant because it also comprised forest rights, but this was not the case. In 1315 x 1321, when Hartschaw was granted to Robert Boyd, Robert I conceded that the lands be held in free barony and moreover ('Praeterea concessimus') in free forest. That a barony could be granted in free forest and free warren also implies that a barony grant did not by itself convey forest or warren rights.[25] Although in the seventeenth century Stair considered that the recipient of a barony grant was entitled to hunt deer, this does not mean that the grantee could control the hunting of deer in his barony. The only forest grant to suggest that a barony did include forest rights was that of Callendar in 1458, when the lands were granted in barony 'cum libera foresta et warenna'.

The regality grant, however, most likely did convey forest rights. Firstly, a regality, although only a barony with increased powers, was a piece of land whose holder possessed certain royal rights. Secondly, when the holder of a regality was given the right to hold justice ayres and the four pleas of the crown, there was no way in which the king could prevent the grantee taking forest rights. Thirdly, on three occasions[26] the phrase 'libera foresta et warrena' was included in the pertinents of a regality grant. After a regality grant a forest grant was never preceded by the phrase 'insuper concessimus' and there is no extant example of a regality being granted in free forest. Obviously the regality grant would diminish the value of the forest grant.

Although the forest grant cannot be equated with the regality grant in the manner in which it can be with the barony grant when a free forest was created, it is possible to regard the king as creating a piece of royal forest specially for a subject. It has already been explained that the king who could claim forest rights over the whole country did so not by the reservation of game but by the creation of his own forests on his own land and by the control of his subjects' forests. Against this background it is not unnatural to regard subjects' forests as areas of royal forest.

When William in 1195 x 1210 granted Robert London, his illegitimate son, 'forestum meum de Outh', Robert was to hold it 'in forestum . . . sicut illud habui in forestum', and in 1320 James Douglas received Jedburgh forest in free forest,

adeo libere et quiete sicut nos [Robert I] aut predecessores nostri reges Scottorum dictam forestam liberius aut quietius tenuimus aut tenuerunt.

A royal forest was, therefore, conveyed to a baron by a free forest grant and, although it became that baron's forest, the king regarded the baron as holding it in the same way as he himself had held it. Consequently, to the king, it still resembled a piece of royal forest, an attitude which enabled David II in 1342 x 1343 to grant Kelso the right to cut timber in Jedburgh forest.[27]

When a free forest grant did not involve a royal forest, the evidence still supports the view that the king regarded the free forest as a piece of semi-royal forest. In 1505 the sheriffs, on the advice of the lords of council, were ordered to proclaim the creation of a free forest and there appears to have been only the one body of law for royal and non-royal forests, although part of the traditional body of forest law may have had special relevance for free forests.[28] (See p. 293, Laws 11-18.) Finally, the wording of the sanction clause whereby the king forbade anyone to hunt or cut in the forest without the grantee's permission under pain of the full royal forfeiture of £10 could be considered as instructions given to the forester of a royal forest. Such an implication may have been one reason for the discontinuation of that clause by the end of the fourteenth century. The similarity of the holder of a free forest with the forester of a royal forest is specified in Robert's charter to Gilbert Hay of 'Loucherwarde' granting him the lands of the royal forests of Boyne and Enzie in free forest 'ad faciendum omnia et singula que ad dictum officium juste debeant pertinere'.[29]

Although free forests can, therefore, be regarded as areas of royal forest specially created for the king's subjects, they were not in fact royal forests, for in royal forests the hunting was reserved for the king, while in free forests it was reserved for certain of the king's subjects.

The forest grant gave the grantee the same powers in his forest as the king had in a royal forest. (See Table 16, p. 204.) The right to control hunting, the *raison d'être* of the grant, which was stated in the sanction clause was, after the demise of that clause, presumably conveyed by the pertinent, venison. While in practice a baron hunted deer before he received a forest grant, it is possible that this grant not only empowered a baron to control hunting but also in theory conveyed to him for the first time the right to hunt greater game, since theoretically the king could claim the right to reserve deer over the whole country. This possibility suggests that the use of 'free' in the phrase 'in free forest' may have implied that the grantee had free power to hunt because he was free of the royal forest right to reserve game for the king. The penalty for illegal hunting, stated in the sanction clause, was £10, which was also the penalty for cutting wood illegally in a free forest.

The reservation of the vert, especially timber, became more important in the fifteenth century: not only did 'viridibus arboribus' appear in the pertinents, but in some instances only the woods on certain lands were granted in free forest. In the second half of the fifteenth century it was control of timber and not of game which Coupar Angus and Arbroath abbeys exercised in their forests of Drimmie, Campsie and Kingoldrum.[30] The penalty for wood-cutting probably entailed the amercement of goods found on the offender[31] as well as the £10 fine, the 'pena libere foreste'.[32]

The tolls associated with the control of pasture in a free forest, pannage, herbage and foggage followed a similar line of development to their counterparts in royal forests: pannage died out in the fourteenth century;[33] herbage and foggage could refer to a toll[34] or to grazing;[35] and foggage could be let to the keeper of a forest, for instance in Birse in 1511.[36] A toll called parcage was also levied on occasion[37] and may originally have been associated with parks or enclosed areas. In Renfrew in the thirteenth century the pasture fines were carefully organised. For example, in 1208 x 1214 Walter the third Steward imposed the following fines on animals found in his forest:[38]

Fines	Watch Set	Season
1d for 10 animals		open
5 cows amerced	with watch set	close
1d for 5 animals	without watch set	close

In 1294/5 the fines had been altered:[39]

Fines	Watch Set	Season
1d for 5 animals	without watch set	open
6d for 5 animals	with watch set	open
1 animal amerced	with watch set	close
12d for animals or animal*	without watch set	close

*'Et si animalia . . . perstransierunt, duodecim dabuntur denarii pro onmibus animalibus sive animali.' Although this phraseology suggests 12d was a flat rate regardless of the number of animals, it could have been the fine *per* individual animal.

In 1208 x 1214 the levy or fine was heavier in the close season and when watch was set, although no distinction was made in the open season between tended or untended animals. While these exactions could be regarded as charges for grazing in the forest, the basis on which they were collected was that the lord could ban or control pasture wherever he wanted within his forest. Walter in 1208 x 1214 permitted Paisley to graze animals freely on their lands between the Old Patrick Water and the Espedair Burn (see Map 7, p. 193), but these lands remained within his forest since he reserved his birds and beasts on them. If, however, the abbey's beasts grazed outside these bounds they would be fined. That they were fines rather than tolls can be seen if one considers that every time a forester came across beasts outside the permitted area in the open season he could collect 1d for every 10 animals. For a sizeable herd this was a fair sum to pay on a regular basis and the abbey cannot have considered grazing animals outside their lands on a daily basis. That they may, in certain circumstances, have considered so doing would explain why by 1294/5 the fines were known as parcage, a toll for pasture. By 1294/5 the exactions had assumed the character of fines to a larger extent, since they had to be paid by the abbey when their beasts were found in the unlet parts of the forest, which would presumably include the specially reserved 'foresta prohibita'. (See Map 7.) The levy of ½d which they had to pay in other parts of the forest which had been let and which the Steward's men had to pay if their beasts grazed on the abbey's lands, is more in character of a pasture toll than a fine.

It has been suggested by Professor Barrow that these exactions varied not in accord with the open and close seasons but with the time of fence.[40] Professor Barrow has argued that two old French words 'fermeson', the close season, and

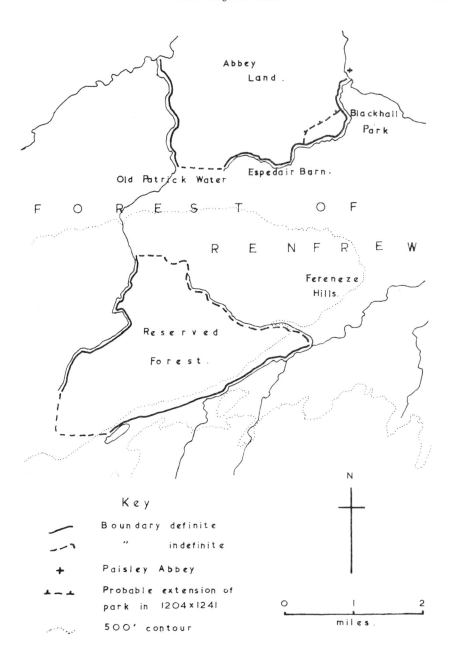

Abbey Land.

Blackhall Park

Espedair Barn.

Old Patrick Water

F O R E S T   O F

R E N F R E W

Fereneze Hills.

Reserved

Forest.

Key

Boundary definite

"   indefinite

Paisley Abbey

Probable extension of park in 1204 x 1241

500' contour

N

O   1   2

miles.

7. Renfrew Forest.

'fonneson', fence, have been mistranscribed in the sixteenth-century Paisley cartulary. Where the Stewards refer to the season in which they hunted the deer of whose hides Paisley abbey was to receive a tenth, the cartulary should read 'fermeson'[41] for close season, but in the above instances concerning pasture the correct reading should be 'fonneson'.

In the cartulary 'fermeson' has been mistranscribed as 'formeisun' and 'fermeisun'.[42] If the cartulary was copied from an accurate original, 'formeisim' of the 1208 x 1214 charter and 'formeson' of the 1294/5 charter could be derived from either 'fermeson' or 'fonneson', although the similarity of 'formeisun' and 'formeisim' does suggest 'fermeson' as the original. The main reason, however, for accepting that the pasture arrangements varied depending on the hunting season and not the time of fence lies in the practical application of these penalties. If the heavier fines applied only to the time of fence and not to the close season, then one has the unlikely situation in 1294/5 of grazing being fined at comparatively low levels for most of the year in the Steward's specially reserved forest where economic activity was banned. It is far more reasonable to suppose that the heavier fines applied to the close season when pasture, especially in the medieval period, was at a premium during the winter. During the remainder of the year, the long open season, the fines were less but still sufficient to deter grazing by the monks or their men. The fines could have been reduced in the open season because grazing in summer by cattle and sheep could improve the pasture for deer.[43]

The fines of 1294/5 were presumably increased because the Stewards wished to deter what grazing may have been occurring and to increase judicial profits and because the fines now applied not to the whole forest but only to the unlet lands including, one assumes, the specially reserved forest. The puzzling reduction of the fine on tended animals in the close season could represent generosity, but in view of the increased fine on untended animals it may well be a mistranscription.

There is a similarity between the 1294 and 1208 x 1214 levies in Renfrew and clauses 1, 4 and 16 of the forest laws (see pp. 291-2, 294) in the importance of the herdsman but the fines in the forest laws, especially in clause 1, were heavier. While the Renfrew charters were only concerned with the presence or absence of the herdsman, Forest Laws 1 and 16 were also concerned with his possession of a fire and a horn. Moreover, the forest laws do not distinguish between open and close seasons. For these reasons the fines in the Stewards' charters and in the forest laws cannot be accurately compared other than to say that the fine of 1 animal is common to clauses 4 and 6 of the forest laws and to animals in Renfrew in the close season. While the principle behind the charters and the laws take into account the role of the herdsman, the variation in the fines shows that there is no direct link between the extant version of clauses 1, 4 and 16 of the forest laws and the Stewards' charters. In this instance, therefore, the royal forest law did not apply to a baronial forest and the Stewards must have made their own regulations.

The administration of non-royal forests varied greatly throughout Scotland during the Middle Ages. Unlike the royal forest administration there was no central control, and in the early medieval period the administration of the Bruces in Annandale or of the Stewards in Renfrew or of Arbroath Abbey in its reserves may well have differed in constitution and efficiency from that of William Gifford in Strachan or Lindores Abbey in Fintray. Not only might the aims of magnates and abbots be dissimilar, but while some lords might possess only one forest others might possess several. In the latter case there would be some form of central direction.

By 1214 Walter Steward held three reserves, Renfrew, Ayr and Sanquhar, with foresters in Renfrew, and servants in Sanquhar and presumably in Ayr. (See Table 29, p. 352.) In Renfrew the Stewards faced the same problem as the king faced in royal forests, namely, the difficulty of maintaining a forest as a hunting reserve while at the same time permitting economic activity, whether grazing, wood-cutting or leasing within the forest. James Steward by 1294/5 had tackled this problem in much the same way as Robert I did after him. He created a 'foresta prohibita' within his reserve where no economic activity was permitted, but liberated such exploitation in the rest of his reserve.[44] Behind this there must have lain the hope that his foresters, with less ground to cover and no exceptions to make, could operate more consistently and efficiently than they had done in the past. A similar policy of reserving only part of a forest was followed in the fifteenth century by Coupar Angus Abbey in Campsie[45] and by the bishop of Aberdeen in Birse.[46] In the latter case the reserved forest probably corresponded with William I's forest of Birse and the leased lands to the additional royal lands of Birse which were included in the forest grant of 1242.

In many instances free forests may have been administered by the lord's barony or regality officials and not by a special forest administration, as would appear to have been the case in Ayr forest. It is possible that the difficulty in distinguishing head and subordinate foresters in the twelfth and thirteenth centuries may stem from the fact that bailies or stewards were the equivalent of head foresters and that barons only gradually developed a special forest administration from their barony officials, in much the same way as the royal forest administration appears to have developed from the general administration of the sheriffs.

Confusion also arises from the fact that it was possible for foresters to be employed in woods as well as forests: Kelso Abbey had a forester in its wood in Innerwick by permission of Alan Steward in 1190 x 1203;[47] and in 1282 Coupar Abbey had a forester in the wood of Kilbrothay.[48] In such cases the owner of the wood usually possessed a forest elsewhere, as in both of the above examples.

While the duplication of barony and forest administration probably meant that in many forests a steward or bailie would be the head forester, he might in turn appoint subordinate foresters, for example in Birnam in 1346, Campsie in

1472 and Strathdearn in 1509.[49] The head forester of Birnam was entitled the chief forester and that of Campsie the forester-general. Although John Grant, the head forester of the earl of Moray in Darnaway in 1346, held his office heritably,[50] not all baronial foresters did so. Most of these foresters would probably have the right to certain escheats from the forest, as did their royal counterparts. In 1452 the forester of Coldingham received a most extraordinary list of dues including horse fodder, 12d in the pound from 'wrac et waif', several mercantile levies, a levy on timber carriage, woodcocks and a robe.[51] In some cases lands and rights in the forest went with the office: Dowally went with the office in Darnaway in 1346; Alexander Stewart, earl of Buchan, who was probably the bishop of Moray's forester in Rothiemurchus in 1383,[52] held the lands of the forest and could probably hunt there; and Andrew Hughson in 1479 was a tenant of the unreserved forest of Campsie.

The status of head foresters varied enormously. If those foresters who witnessed charters in the twelfth century were head foresters, they were fairly humble men,[53] and in the late Middle Ages John Forester in Coldingham and Andrew Hughson in Campsie were probably humble tenants and not such influential persons as Hugh Rose of Kilravock in Strathdearn.

One of the most interesting appointments of a head forester to survive is that of Patrick de Lyndesay as forester of Lennox *ante* 1270 x 1303. (See Table 9, p. 153.) Patrick received the office heritably along with all the rights which went with the office. *Ante* 1270 x 1333 Patrick also received lands in Bonhill. He was, therefore, a fairly important tenant of the earl of Lennox.[54] The interest of this grant lies in the light which it throws not only on the adoption of Norman customs by a native but also on the emergence of a baronial forest administration in a native earldom. For Patrick also received in the same grant the office of 'toschederach', an officer who may have had responsibility for strangers in his jurisdiction.[55] Consequently, the earl of Lennox, when introducing the office of forester, perhaps after receipt of the forest grant in 1272, may have awarded it to the official who had previously performed all or some of the forester's functions, the 'toschederach'. In the forest of Lennox, therefore, as in other non-royal forests, a special forest administration may have developed from the previous administration of the lord's lands.

Subordinate foresters in the twelfth and thirteenth centuries pass unnamed but are referred to in the disputes of Melrose Abbey with Richard de Morville,[56] in Crawford forest in *c* 1242 x *c* 1249,[57] and in Renfrew in 1208 x 1214. The forester in Mow whose house was a boundary mark in *c* 1190 was perhaps a sub-forester.[58]

In the fourteenth and fifteenth centuries subordinate foresters were tenants of the land of the forest holding lands either inside or outside the forest. The forest of Stocket was kept by two foresters, who might also be serjeants of the burgh of Aberdeen,[59] to whom the forest was let by the burgh.[60] The length of their appointments varied and could be terminated by the bailies of the burgh.

In the fifteenth century Arbroath Abbey made similar arrangements with its tenants in Trostach *c* 1430 and Pearsie in Kingoldrum in 1483.[61] Coupar also used its tenants in the fifteenth century to keep the forest of Campsie and the woods of Forter in Glenisla.[62] The most interesting of these four examples is Campsie, which in *c* 1443 was let to three tenants for five years for teind sheaves. They had to pay 19 bolls, of which 4 were allotted to a forester and 9 to three fishers.[63] By 1472, Campsie was let to four tenants for five years for returns in money and kind. The wood of Campsie was divided into four equal parts and each of the tenants received with his part of the land a quarter of the wood which he had to keep, and certain lands with grain went to the forester-general. Each tenant was to be 'clientulus generalis' for his own quarter of the wood as well as for the others. This could mean that each tenant was held responsible for following up an offence no matter where it was committed or that one tenant could act for the others or that the tenants were responsible for each other's defaults. It was perhaps the responsibility of each tenant to discover offences in his own quarter and then to publicise them so that any or all of the keepers could take action. All five men had rights in common pasture. Similar arrangement continued till 1508,[64] but by 1494 and perhaps by 1474 one of the tenants had the right to graze cows in the forest and in 1479 the tenants were allowed to cultivate part of the forest.

The duties of head and subordinate foresters covered the essential functions of protecting game,[65] supervising wood-cutting, protecting wood[66] and apprehending trespassers.[67] In 1345/6 the head forester of Birnam was charged with the maintenance of the bounds of the barony of Murthly which contained the forest of Birnam.[68] There is no record, however, of non-royal foresters supervising grazing and collecting pasture tolls, functions which they must have performed.

How effectively the lord's rights were enforced in non-royal forests is not revealed by the evidence, but there are signs that efforts were made to prevent inefficiency. The bailies of Aberdeen kept a watchful eye on their forester: in 1398 they tried their foresters for not performing their duties adequately,[69] but their efforts cannot have met with much success, since in 1400 one of the foresters was amerced for failing to perform his duty[70] and similar proceedings are recorded in 1410 and 1448.[71] Nevertheless, offenders against the vert were brought to trial. [72] Arbroath and Coupar tried to ensure that their foresters performed their duties by stipulating that negligence would lead to the loss of their lease, and the forester of Trostach, if he was remiss in his duty, had to submit to the correction of the abbot.[73] In Pearsie the tenants were to collect the unlaws of the wood, but if they themselves were at fault the unlaws were to be given to the abbot.[74] There must always have been some difficulty in making efficient foresters out of tenants who lived beside or in the forest, since they had the right to use the forest for building wood and could easily take more than their allowance without anyone checking on them. Likewise when other tenants took wood illegally the forester, if he knew the offender, may

P

well have connived at the abuses. In these forests run by corporate bodies, burghs and abbeys, there must have been a constant struggle between the local interests of the tenant and the wishes of the owners similar to the influences operating on the forester-tenants of Ettrick in the later fifteenth century. In forests in the hands of individual lords the efficiency of baronial foresters most likely varied according to the power of the lord of the forest and the efficiency of his baronial administration. When the forest covered a scattered group of lands, its administration must have been more difficult than when the forest formed one compact area. In Renfrew before 1294/5 the foresters of James Steward appear to have abused their rights and exacted unjust amercements, perhaps both from a desire to seize on any marketable commodity and from inability to detect genuine offenders and prevent misuse of the forest.[75] There is no evidence, therefore, that lords of free forests were any closer to a permanent solution of the problems of running their reserves than was the crown.

A forest grant conveyed not only a monopoly of hunting and wood-cutting but also the judicial rights necessary to enforce that monopoly. This forest jurisdiction in the twelfth and thirteenth centuries was always combined with a previous or concurrent grant of ordinary jurisdiction, e.g., sac and soc. There was, therefore, in the fourteenth and fifteenth centuries a close link between forest courts and baron courts.

Forest cases in the twelfth and thirteenth centuries were frequently tried in the lord's ordinary court and not in a special forest court. (See Table 14, p. 169.) Allowance was usually made for benefit of clergy, for instance in Trolhope in 1182 x 1232, in Eskdale after 1235 and in Ayr in 1266. In the later Middle Ages in Stocket, where the burgh of Aberdeen was acting for the king in name only, cases from the forest were heard in the bailies' court.[76] In the fifteenth century cases from the forests of Coupar were heard in the abbey's barony or regality courts. In 1461 the court of Sir Thomas Livingston, bishop of Dunkeld and commendator of Coupar, held by Patrick Ogilvy, the bailie-depute, tried offenders against the wood of Campsie.[77] In the more outlying areas both Arbroath and Coupar probably had local courts held by a forester or keeper of the wood, so that cases may not always have been tried at the centre.[78]

The holder of a free forest was entitled to hold a special forest court since the pertinents of forest grants from 1320 onwards might include 'cum curiis et escaetis ad liberam forestam pertinentibus' or a similar phrase.[79] Not till the early sixteenth century, however, do definite examples survive of courts held by baronial foresters. Two grants in January and May 1509 were made, 'cum forestariis forestariorumque curiis'.[80] In August of that year Hugh Rose of Kilravock was appointed forester of Strathdearn by Alexander, Earl of Huntly, with the right to punish trespassers, and to collect unlaws and escheats in accordance with the laws of Scotland.[81]

In such cases the court of free forest would be a court not so much of a certain group of free forest rights as of a certain area of land called a free forest and might hear both forest and non-forest cases. The pertinents of forest grants often connected the normal returns of a barony with free forest courts. The heriots and bludwites of Clunie free forest were mentioned in 1481 and of Redgorton in 1500.[82] Consequently, it is not surprising to find that forest courts, while still separate from barony courts, were not always held by foresters. In Ettrick in the first half of the fifteenth century the bound courts of the Douglases were held by their 'officiales et ministros'.[83]

It is not always possible, however, to determine who held forest courts. In 1321, the pertinents of Melrose's free forest charter of Westerker repeated the former unique arrangements for Eskdale and granted Melrose not forest courts but courts for trees, birds and game, a clear guide to the work of a forest court but not to the man who held those courts.

Beside this picture of free forest offences being tried by the lord's court must be set the contradictory statements of the sanction clause and of Forest Law 18. (See p. 295.) In the twelfth, thirteenth and fourteenth centuries, according to the sanction clause of the free forest charter offenders were to be placed under the full royal forfeiture of £10, thus implying that the king received a £10 forfeiture and that the case could be tried in a royal court. Forest Law 18, which probably can be attributed to the thirteenth century, accepts that free forest cases could be heard in a royal court. (See p. 316.) If the baron, this law states, did not raise the case of a forest offence in the king's court or ignored the offence, the king could seek the forfeiture himself by raising the suit. If the lord accepted a bribe, tried to conceal the offence and did not prosecute, the king could fine the lord £10.

These arrangements, which contradict the picture already given, should be seen against the background of the view that free forests were portions of royal forest specially created for a baron. The king, by encouraging the prosecution of offences and by asking for the £10 forfeiture, would be ensuring the maintenance of what could be regarded as his forest. Moreover, the £10 penalty would be a welcome addition to the royal revenue. Barons did not, apparently, approve of this royal interest for, as already explained, it gave their reserves the character of royal reserves. To avoid royal interference they had, to judge by Forest Law 18, by the thirteenth century stopped raising forest offences in the king's court and taken steps to ensure that the king did not hear of such offences.

In the fourteenth century, although the crown maintained its claim to try free forest offences — no forest grant included both the sanction clause and pertinents which specified the courts of free forests — the sanction clause which embodied that claim did become less common. By the end of the century it was no longer included in forest grants in recognition, no doubt, of the king's inability to hear forest cases or to try them. In the free forest grant of Bolton, Carriden and Langton to Alexander Cockburn in 1391/2, the king still encouraged the prosecution of offenders not by the sanction clause but by stating that offenders be punished 'sub pena decam librarum sine misericordia domini'. The £10 penalty was no longer called the full royal forfeiture but in 1368 was entitled 'pena liberi foresti'.[84] One cannot, therefore, assume that the king always or even frequently received the £10 forfeiture as has been suggested,[85] and that this was the reason why the forest laws were not harshly enforced by barons in baronial forests. Inefficiency rather than lack of judicial profit seems a more likely explanation.

Nonetheless there had probably in the twelfth century and in the early thirteenth century been some substance in the sanction clause and the provisions of Law 18. By comparison with practice in English warrens which, as mentioned, were created by a similarly worded grant, one can surmise that the king might have collected the £10 forfeiture, but only when the trespass against the forest was unduly serious and the lord was taking no action, or when the sheriff or his servant was at the court.[86]

Despite the discontinuance of the sanction clause, Forest Law 18 continued to be copied into legal treatises of the fifteenth century. Vestiges of this law and of the sanction clause can be seen in one case before the justice ayre at Kirkcudbright in 1508.[87] Donald Red Makcolmin was amerced £10 for hunting the animals of Dundrennan with dogs in 1482 outside his own lands. That the amercement was £10 and that the animals belonged to Dundrennan argues that Dundrennan possessed either free forest or free warren rights. In fact Dundrennan had received warren rights from Edward I in 1305,[88] a grant which may have been confirmed by a Scots king or even extended to forest rights, perhaps with a regality grant. Even if it were not so extended, this example is still relevant for the purposes of this argument because of the institutional similarity of forests and warrens. Dundrennan had probably been attempting to bring Donald to trial since 1482 and, having met with no success, taken the case before the justice ayre in 1508. If this reconstruction is accurate, this case was tried, in the terms of Forest Law 18, at the suit of the grantee in the king's court.

In disputes involving forests, the role of the royal courts in relation to forests was more certain. Generally disputes over forest rights or ownership were decided in the king's court. In the early thirteenth century, while the dispute of the Avenels and Melrose Abbey over rights in the reserve of Eskdale was decided before a 'colloquium' at Listun in 1235, some cases might go before ecclesiastical courts. (See Table 14, p. 169.) When a dispute arose between Melrose Abbey and Alan the second Steward over Alan's right to hunt on certain lands of Mauchline which had at one time lain in the forest of Ayr, Melrose *ante* 1204 appealed to Innocent III, who appointed judges delegate. The case was remitted to Rome, where a diet was arranged to hear the case, but after the hardly surprising absence of the defender a second mandate was issued to judges delegate in 1203/4, who in accord with Innocent's opinion decided in favour of Melrose.[89] Disputes over the bounds of forests were in the thirteenth century decided by a perambulation ordered by the king and often carried out by the justiciar.[90]

In the fourteenth century the king could still hear major disputes between his tenants-in-chief, for example, the dispute between the bishop and the earl of Moray over the bishop's timber rights in the earl's forests,[91] but lesser disputes could be determined locally.[92] In the fifteenth century disputes came before the lords auditors[93] and the lords of council.[94] In 1500 when James IV, ignoring the free forest grant of 1481, tried to claim 20 merks due to him from Clunie forest by John, Earl of Atholl, the case came before the lords of council.[95] James may have lost the case, for in 1505 he granted Clunie forest to Atholl.[96] In these instances, therefore, the procedure followed was that normal in disputes between two subjects of the crown.

Throughout the medieval period exemptions from forest rights frequently accompanied the alienation of the lands of part of a free forest. (See Tables 17 and 18, pp. 205, 207.) In the twelfth and thirteenth centuries the lord might retain his hunting monopoly on the alienated lands, thus demonstrating the separability of the lands and the rights of the forest. The Stewards in their grants from the forest of Ayr to Melrose[97] and from the forest of Renfrew to Paisley[98] retained their game rights in 'feris et avibus' over part of the lands alienated. William Bruce placed a similar limitation on his grant of Kinmount in Annandale to Adam of Carlisle.[99] In part of their grants to Melrose and Paisley, however, the Stewards dropped their forest rights. Maich and Calder, held by Paisley, was said to be 'deforestatam'[100] and Mauchline, held by Melrose, was similarly liberated.[101] William de Morville also lifted his forest rights from the lands of Carfrae in Lauderdale and Loudon in Cunninghame.[102]

Whether or not the lord's hunting monopoly was raised, the tenants received considerable rights in the forest. North of the river Ayr Walter the third Steward allowed Melrose to plough and sow in the forest and to graze whatever size of herds they wished wherever they wished.[103] Only when the forest rights were abandoned, however, might the tenant hunt.

While a baron was entitled to include hunting pertinents, hawkings, huntings and fishings in a grant to a tenant, he was not in theory entitled to make a forest grant. If he wished to do so he could cease the enforcement of his own forest rights on the lands in question, then seek a forest grant from the king for his tenant. This procedure was followed by Alexander Steward in Ayr and Gerard de Lyndesay in Crawford.[104] Alternatively, Alan Durward made a grant of Trostach 'in forestum' without the sanction clause[105] which was confirmed by a royal forest grant in 1233. Similarly, the forest grant which included the sanction clause made by John de Vesci in Mow may, in fact, have been confirmed by Alexander III. This practice was also followed by the earl of Huntly in Boyne[106] in 1492, although the royal confirmation was not made until 1495.[107] Finally, in 1382 the bishop of Moray conveyed Rothiemurchus to the earl of Buchan as freely as he himself had held it in free forest.[108]

In the fourteenth and fifteenth centuries it is more common to find leases rather than alienations of forest lands. By *c* 1376 Liddesdale forest was let to several tenants,[109] and in the fifteenth century Archibald, Earl of Angus, continued to lease Jedburgh forest and let the lands of Glen Prosen forest to Robert Graham of Fintry.[110] It has already been mentioned that Coupar and the bishop of Aberdeen let part of their reserves, as did Kelso[111] and Arbroath.[112] Such leases were accompanied by the right to use the lands in question in the forest.

Following royal practice, barons also released their forest rights by making direct grants of produce from their forests[113] or by granting freedom to pursue certain activities in their forests.[114] Both types of grant belong to the twelfth and thirteenth centuries rather than to later centuries despite one or two rare examples from the early sixteenth century of gifts of deer to the king.[115]

The evidence examined in this study of non-royal forests has revealed that both the king and his subjects gave more attention to non-royal forests in the twelfth and thirteenth centuries than thereafter. While the decline in value of the forest grant can, in part, be attributed to the advent of the barony and regality grants and probably to the ability of barons to acquire hunting rights by other means,[116] it also raises the question of why the king's subjects wished to receive a free forest grant. There can be little doubt that at first the prime motive in seeking a forest grant was to acquire a monopoly of hunting,[117] but the motives of ecclesiastical magnates in acquiring forest grants are less clear. The prior allocation of the produce of hunting was taken into account when allocating forest grants to abbeys, for only those abbeys which had not received a tithe of hunting received forest grants. Without doubt the leather, tallow and venison obtained from game were valued by ecclesiastical bodies. It is striking that while most of our knowledge is derived from ecclesiastical sources, it relates predominantly to lay forests. Ecclesiastical cartularies provide no insight into the hunting arrangements or rights in ecclesiastical forests, even when grants from these forests are recorded,[118] such as would be expected if the produce of hunting were the prime motive for acquiring a free forest grant.

When Melrose Abbey received in free forest those lands which it held in the royal forest of Gala and Leader, the entry in the Melrose chronicle that Alexander II, 'abbaciam de Melros cum quatuor grangiis circumjacentibus a foresta sua liberam esse constituit',[119] argues that the importance of the grant was the freedom which the monks received from the royal forest rights. Since Melrose already had considerable freedom to pursue agricultural and pastoral activities on these lands, the value of this grant may not have lain in the additional economic freedom which the raising of the royal forest rights would convey but in the freedom from hunting by the king or those who hunted on his authority. Regular hunting parties would obviously have disrupted the agricultural and pastoral pursuits of the abbey. In baronial forests also the same factors would have operated. When Melrose received its lands in Ayr forest in free forest and Paisley its lands in Renfrew forest, they would be able to pursue their economic activities free of any hunting disruptions such as appear to have occurred in Eskdale before 1235[120] where Roger Avenel may have taken action against the granges of Melrose Abbey because they were hindering his hunting. Finally it must not be forgotten that the possession of forest rights presented numerous opportunities for gain. Not only could the lord of a forest try to obtain a wide range of penalties in his court, but he could also exact tolls for activities such as grazing. In the twelfth and thirteenth centuries, therefore, the control of hunting conveyed by the forest grant was desirable both to lay and ecclesiastical grantees.

Table 16. ACTIVITIES CONTROLLED IN NON-ROYAL FORESTS

A *Venison*

Hunting: *Melr. Lib.*, 39 (1165 x 1169); Fraser, *Johnstones*, i, 1, no. 2 (1194 x 1214); Raine, *N.D.* app., 586 (1332); Forest grants, Table 28

Hawking: *Newb. Lib.*, 135 (1185 x 1200); *Pais Reg.*, 92 (1294); *RMS*, i, app. 1, 14 (1321)

Fishing: Table 28 *sub* Gala and Leader (1236), Westerker (1321), Seton (1322), Drum (1322/3); *Pais. Reg.*, 92 (1294)

B *Vert*

Wood-cutting: *Pais. Reg.*, 17 (1208 x 1214); Raine, *N.D.*, 418 (*post* 1276 x 1282); *RMS*, ii, 1784, (1488); Forest grant, Table 28

Pasture: *Pais. Reg.*, 17 (1208 x 1214); *CA Rent.*, i, 220, no. 290; Pannage: See Table 7

     Parcage: *Pais. Reg.*, 92 (1294); *Newb. Lib.*, 275 (1368)

     Herbage/foggage: *Inchaff Chrs.*, 39 (1219); *Arb. Lib.*, 19, (1340); *Moray Reg.*, 151, (1369); *Abdn. Recs.*, 83; *Abdn. Reg.*, i, 371, *sub* 'Westirclune' etc., (1511)

Assart: See Table 7

Building/Ploughing: Fraser, *Johnstones*, i, 1, no. 2 (1194 x 1214); *Melr. Lib.*, 73, (1204 x 1214); Fraser, *Johnstones*, 7, no. 11 (*post* 1271); *Abdn. Reg.*, 371, *sub*, 'Quhitstane', (1511)

Industry: *Pais. Reg.*, 92, (1294)

Travel: *ESC*, 199, (1147 x 1153); Fraser, *Johnstones*, i, 1 no. 2, (1194 x 1214); *CA Chart.* 31, (c 1220); *Abdn. Reg.*, 371, *sub* 'Quhitstane', 'Mill of Clune', (1511).

Table 17. GRANTS OF LANDS OF NON-ROYAL FORESTS TO 1286

Name	Date	Grantor	Grantee	Source
Annandale	1194 x 1214	William Bruce	Adam of Carlisle	Fraser, Johnstones, i, 1 no. 2
	c 1218	Robert Bruce	Roger Crispin	Ibid., i, 5 no. 7
	post 1271	Robert Bruce, earl of Carrick	William, Lord of Carlisle	Ibid., i, 7 no. 11
Ayr	1165 x 1177	Walter Steward	Melrose Abbey	Melr. Lib., 66
	1177 x 1204	Alan Steward	Melrose Abbey	Ibid., 67
	1204 x 1214	Walter Steward	Melrose Abbey	Ibid., 72
	1204 x 1214	Walter Steward	Melrose Abbey	Ibid., 73
	1204 x 1214	Walter Steward	Melrose Abbey	Ibid., *72
	1204 x 1214	Walter Steward	Melrose Abbey	Ibid., *73
	1204 x 1214	Walter Steward	Melrose Abbey	Ibid., 74
	1241 x 1283	Alexander Steward	Melrose Abbey	Ibid., 322
	1266	Alexander Steward	Melrose Abbey	Ibid., 325
Cargill	c 1220	William de Montfiquet	Coupar Abbey	CA Chart., 30
Crawford	1165 x 1200 (c 1185 x 1200)	William de Lyndesay	Newbattle Abbey	Newb. Reg., 135
	1200 x 1214	David de Lyndesay	Newbattle Abbey	Newb. Reg., 136
	1214 x 1241	David de Lyndesay	Newbattle Abbey	Newb. Reg., 138
	1214 x 1222/41	David de Lyndesay	Newbattle Abbey	Newb. Reg., 139
	c 1215 x 1242	Gerard de Lyndesay	Newbattle Abbey	Newb. Reg., 143
	1242 x 1249	Gerard de Lyndesay	Newbattle Abbey	Newb. Reg., 144
Cunninghame	1190 x 1196	William de Morville	James Loudon	NMS, i, 2 no. 2
Dalbeattie	1161 x 1174	Uchtred of Galloway	Holm Cultram Abbey	Holm Cultram Chrs., 120
	1185 x 1186	Roland of Galloway	Holm Cultram Abbey	Holm Cultram Chrs., 121
Dalquhairn	ante 1250	Isabella de Valognes	Bishop of Glasgow	Glas. Reg., 199
Drumsled	1265	Arbroath Abbey	Alexander Comyn	Arb. Lib., 311
Dundaff & Strathcarron	1235 x 1237	Patrick, Earl of Dunbar	David de Graham	Anderson, Diplomata, 30

Table 17. Grants of Lands of Non-Royal Forests to 1286 (continued)

Name	Date	Grantor	Grantee	Source
Eskdale	1165 x 1169	Robert Avenel	Melrose Abbey	Melr. Lib., 39
	1178 x 1185	Robert Avenel	Melrose Abbey	Melr. Lib., 40
	1185 x 1192	Gervase Avenel	Melrose Abbey	Melr. Lib., 41
	1214 x 1218	Gervase Avenel	Melrose Abbey	Melr. Lib., 196
	1218 x 1221	Roger Avenel	Melrose Abbey	Melr. Lib., 197
Hownam	1195 x 1198	William, son of John	Melrose Abbey	RRS, ii, 382
	1185 x 1199	William, son of John	Melrose Abbey	Melr. Lib., 130
Kingoldrum	1226 x 1239	Arbroath Abbey	Walter, son of Turpin	Arb. Lib., 306
Kinkell	1199 x 1205	Humphrey de Berkley	Arbroath Abbey	Arb. Lib., 89 / RRS, ii, 413
Lauderdale	1189 x 1196	William de Morville	Henry St. Clair	Hay, Genealogical Collections, 245
Lennox[1]	1273	Malcolm, Earl of Lennox	Paisley Abbey	Pais. Reg., 215
	c 1270 x 1333	Malcolm, Earl of Lennox	Patrick de Graham	Lenn. Cart., 38
	c 1270 x 1333	Malcolm, Earl of Lennox	Arthur Galbraith	Lenn. Cart., 29
	c 1270 x 1333	Malcolm, Earl of Lennox	Patrick de Lyndesay	Lenn. Cart., 50
	c 1270 x 1333	Malcolm, Earl of Lennox	Patrick Galbraith	Lenn. Cart., 31
Outh	c 1211 (1208 x 11)	Robert de London	Dunfermline Abbey	Dunf. Reg., 167 / RRS, ii, 495
Renfrew	1165 x 1172	Walter Steward	Paisley Abbey	Pais. Reg., 5
	1202	Alan Steward	Paisley Abbey	Pais. Reg., 13
	1208 x 1214	Walter Steward	Paisley Abbey	Pais. Reg., 17
	1208 x 1214	Walter Steward	Paisley Abbey	Pais. Reg., 23
Strathearn	ante 1244 x 1258	Malise, Earl of Strathearn	Inchaffray Abbey	Inchaff. Chrs., 12
	c 1284	Muriel, daughter of Conewall	William de Moray	Inchaff. Chrs., 16

1. The following grants may be within the forest.

Table 18. GRANTS OF LANDS OF NON-ROYAL FORESTS AFTER 1286

Date	Forest	Source
1303 x 1328	Eskdale	*Melr. Lib.*, 377
1327	Crawford	*Newb. Reg.*, 149
1358	Bennachie	*APS*, i, 524
1358	Glenken	*SHS, Misc*, v, 23 no. 14
1375	'Coulpersauche'	*RMS*, i, 500
1383	Rothiemurchus[1]	*Moray Reg.*, 162
1398	Torwood	SRO, *Transcript of Royal Charters*, RH 1/1/2. 4 Aug. 1398
1406	Kintore	*RMS*, i, 884
1410	Pentland[1]	Ibid., 93
1426	Dalton	Ibid., ii, 71
1426	Buchan	Ibid.. 57 and SRO, C/2/3
1426	Ettrick	*RMS*, ii, 59
1438	Boyne and Enzie	SRO, *Gordon Castle Muniments*, GD 44, p. 102
1452	Dalton	*RMS*, ii, 546
1452	'Garnetulach'	Ibid., 590
1471	Plater	Ibid., 1028
1477	Glen Prosen	Ibid., 1559
1491	Glen Fiddich	Ibid., 1997
1492	Boyne and Enzie	SRO, *Gordon Castle Muniments*, GD 44, 106; *ER*, xii, 711
1495	Boyne and Enzie	*RMS*, ii, 2289
1496	Boyne and Enzie	SRO, *Gordon Castle Muniments*, GD 44, 104
1499	Alyth	*RSS*, i, 334
1505	Boyne and Enzie	SRO, *Gordon Castle Muniments*, GD 44, 93, 105
1510	Dye	*RMS*, ii, 3413

1. See Table 28 *sub* Baronial Grants.

10

Non-Royal Warrens and Rabbit Warrens

THE king could convey a hunting monopoly to his subjects not only by a forest grant but also by a warren grant. The recipient of a warren grant received the right, as will be shown, to control the hunting of lesser game. Unlike the forest grant, the warren grant did not give the grantee the right to create a replica of a royal institution, for the king did not possess large areas of land in which lesser game were reserved in the same manner as game in his forests. The king only possessed rabbit warrens which were recognisable features on the ground and the purpose of which was simply to raise and protect rabbits, a concept quite different from that of the abstract institution created by a warren grant. (See Table 30, p. 354, which lists all warren grants.)

The earliest recorded warren grant is that of Malcolm IV to Coldingham in 1153 x 1161-2, in which he confirmed to the prior

ut habeatis bosca vestra et garenniam vestram per terram vestram et ut de boscis vestris aut de garennia vestra nullus intromittere vel in illis quicquam capere presumat nisi per vos et siquis forte hanc vestram libertatem infringere presumpserit: super meam plenariam forisfacturam hoc faciet.

Although this grant does not copy the English form of this grant, as the forest grant may have done, it includes the full royal forfeiture and treats the 'garennia' as a geographical feature rather than a legal entity, thus corresponding to the English practice of granting a warren in certain lands rather than granting certain lands in warren. When William I repeated this grant in 1165 x 1171 he conceded that

omnia nemora et gwastina sua sint sub defensione prioris et custodia necnon et monachorum de Collingham ne aliquis super x libras forisfacture quicquam in predictis nemoribus vel gwastinis capiat nisi per ipsum priorem.

Having thus confirmed Malcolm's grant, William added,

Insuper addo et illis concedo quod predictus prior et monachi habeant gwarennam in predictis nemoribus et per totam terram suam . . . ita quod nullus ibi aliquid capiat nec ligna nec aliquam bestiam silvestrem nisi per ipsos. Quod si aliquis . . . capiatur venando vel ligna secando . . . habeant prior et monachi quod super illum et cum illo invenerit et ego forisfacturam prenominatam.

Still following the English form, this grant extended the warren rights to cover the whole of Coldingham's lands, and William made it quite clear that the £10 forfeiture mentioned in the sanction clause accrued to the king while the goods found on any offenders belonged to the priory. By 1173 x 1178 the warren grant had finally adopted the same phraseology as the forest grant, in that it became a grant of lands 'in warren' and no longer followed the English custom.

The wording of this warren grant was, as has been mentioned, adopted by the free forest grant and, whether the chancery clerks adopted the same style for both grants simultaneously or not, the development of the warren grant parallels that of the forest grant. The grant 'in free warren', using the royal plural, appeared in Alexander II's reign, though admittedly not till 1248/9. If these alterations were not made concurrently with the identical alterations in the forest grant, then they may be associated with Robert, Abbot of Dunfermline, who witnessed the last two warren grants of Alexander II. Robert was chancellor in the opening years of Alexander III's reign and may well have filled that office since 1246/7.[1] The institutional similarity of forests and warrens as well as their interrelation as reserves for greater and lesser game is also seen in Alexander III's grant of free forest and warren rights to Coldingham.

The free warren grant was, therefore, a grant with a set formula, and as such was included in the Ayr Ms. styles of the late thirteenth or early fourteenth century.[2] That this Ms. included this grant in its form 'in liberam warennam' and not 'in liberam forestam' may well represent English influence, since the forest grant was extremely rare in England. The omission of the full royal forfeiture in the version of the warren grant given in the Bute Ms.[3] of the later fourteenth century led Cosmo Innes to suggest that the omission of the royal forfeiture distinguished the warren grant from the forest grant.[4] No extant twelfth or thirteenth century grant, and only one in the fourteenth century, omits the sanction clause.

In the later Middle Ages two of Balliol's warren grants survive, five of Robert I's and four of David II's. Two grants of Edward I and one of Edward III were made in the standard English form, and as such are only of marginal relevance to this study.

In the fourteenth century a warren grant and a barony grant could be combined but, contrary to some statements, a grant in free barony did not convey warren rights. When Robert I in 1315 x 1321 granted the lands of Loudoun and Stevenston in free barony to Duncan Cambell, his grant included the following clause: 'Concessimus eciam . . . uti ipse . . . habeant dictas terras suas in liberam warennam', showing that the warren grant was additional to the barony grant. The sanction clause in Robert I's and David II's reign often contained a prohibition against fishing as well as against hawking, hunting and cutting. The prohibition against fishing was included proportionately more frequently in warren than in forest grants. The regular inclusion of the sanction clause in fourteenth-century warren grants represents the first major divergence in the development of the forest and warren grants. The reasons, however, for the regular inclusion of the sanction clause in the warren grant, while it was omitted in the forest grant, are obscure. The royal interest which the sanction clause implied may have been accepted by holders of free warrens, although in status and influence they were no different from the lords of free forests. Alternatively, the king in the fourteenth century may have made no attempt to realise his interest in practical terms. It is also possible that the magnates regarded the warren grant as of little value and did not consider it necessary to try to remove what royal interference there may have been.

The reign of David II saw the last of the extant free warren grants to be made separately from a free forest grant. Free forest and warren grants had been combined before the grant of 1366/7, but thereafter the free warren grant occurred only in conjunction with a free forest grant. In such a parternership, free warren rights definitely took second place and in 1507 warren rights were included in the pertinents of the forest grant of Cullerlie. The warren grant had become part of the forest grant.

The reasons why the separate warren grant was discontinued may never be fully understood, but several suggestions can be made. In the fourteenth century the warren grant appears to have suffered from a general lack of interest. Whereas the style of the forest grant incorporated new developments in response, one can assume, to the changing wishes of the grantees, the warren grant did not. For example, the sanction clause was retained and the pertinents of the grant were not amplified. Moreover, there is no evidence for the existence of a separate code of warren law, occasioned most likely by the absence of royal warrens. The primary reason for the neglect of the warren grant may be in its concern with lesser rather than greater game.

In England the animals reserved in a warren were hares, rabbits, foxes, wild cats, partridges, pheasants and other small game.[5] It is, therefore, probable that similar animals would have been reserved in Scottish free warrens. The *bestia silvestria* which Coldingham were entitled to reserve in their warren by William's grant of 1165 x 1171 resembles the phrase 'animalia silvestria' which occurs in the late thirteenth-century treatise *Quoniam Attachiamenta*.[6] In the latter context, 'ad lepores et ad alia animalia silvestria vel campestria', *animalis silvestris* appears to be associated with lesser game. Had this specification applied to greater game, the inclusion of 'lepores' at the outset would, to say the least, be illogical. The most reasonable interpretation is that the other animals of field and wood were on a par with hares, the most important animal of the lesser game. Furthermore, as the phrases, beasts of the warren and beasts of the forest, do not occur in Scottish sources, the author of this clause of *Quoniam Attachiamenta* has chosen a fairly obvious alternative for the phrase, the lesser game, by specifying hares, which would be known to his readers to be the most important of the lesser game, and other animals of wood and field. Taken in conjunction with English practice, it seems fairly certain that a warren grant conveyed a monopoly only of lesser game. The forest grant, on the other hand, conveyed a monopoly of all game, but primarily of greater game. A forest grant, consequently, would be a more valuable grant to receive than a warren grant, thus perhaps explaining the loss of interest in the warren grant.

The warren grant, in its legal position, may also have suffered from a contradiction not experienced by the forest grant. Chapter 31 of *Quoniam Attachiamenta* clearly stated that

non prohibebatur [tempore regis Alexandri] aliquis venari ubique ad lepores et ad alia animalia silvestria vel campestria extra forestas et warennas.

Taking this statement to apply only to lesser game, it can be inferred that the king did not, indeed could not, reserve lesser game throughout his kingdom to himself, and yet the fact that a free warren grant existed and included the full royal forfeiture in the sanction clause implied that the king could, if he wished, reserve lesser game throughout the country to himself. A realisation of this contradiction may have operated in the fourteenth century against the continuance of the separate free warren grant.

While the lack of interest in the warren grant and the contradiction implied in its existence may explain why the separate free warren grant became obsolete, they do not explain why its discontinuation occurred towards the end of the fourteenth century.

If barons, by the end of the fourteenth century, were able to control lesser game without a warren grant because of weak central control, they would have had no need for a warren grant and so that grant could have fallen into disuse. It is also possible that the disappearance of the separate warren grant may be connected with a probable growth in the number of rabbit warrens in the fourteenth century. While rabbit warrens could be constructed and protected within a free warren, their creation was not dependent on free warren rights. Of the lesser game, barons may have become most interested in rabbits as game to be coursed and as saleable commodities. Consequently, they may have been content with the creation of a rabbit warren without receiving free warren rights.

Rabbit warrens were areas set aside for the production of rabbits. They were usually situated on sandy or light gravelly soils covered with a dry heath association[7] and sometimes surrounded by a shallow ditch.[8] Since no royal grants conveying the right to construct a rabbit warren are extant, rabbit warrens were probably constructed on the basis of property rights. (See Table 19, p. 214.) A landholder, if he wished to construct a rabbit warren, could do so on his own land without seeking permission from the king. The king also might construct rabbit warrens.

The earliest rabbit warrens to be recorded were those at Crail in 1264-6. They may have been situated on the moor of Crail, since in 1358 Crail warrens were located there.[9] If these warrens were placed on the moor of Crail, it is possible that they were in existence in 1189 x 1195 when heath and whins could be found on the king's moor of Crail.[10] In the late thirteenth century the crown probably held warrens in or near Cramond and at Perth,[11] and in the fifteenth and early sixteenth centuries there were several royal warrens in East Lothian.

Rabbit warrens in the hands of lay or ecclesiastical landholders are first encountered in the fourteenth century. Although far from numerous, they may have been more common in the fourteenth than in the thirteenth century. By the late fifteenth and the early sixteenth centuries non-royal rabbit warrens most likely existed in East Lothian and Fife, and in 1503/4 parliament encouraged lords and lairds to construct rabbit warrens along with parks, dovecots, fish-ponds and orchards.[12]

The use of 'cunicularius' to denote a rabbit warren, first encountered in 1325,[13] is also found in 1398.[14] The Scots form, 'cuningar', occurs in 1473 as 'kunynzare'[15] and in 1491.[16] In the early sixteenth century rabbit warrens might simply be called 'links', the word which described the area in which they were situated.[17]

In the thirteenth and fourteenth centuries a rabbit warren would be specially protected if it lay within a free warren. After the disappearance of the free-warren grant, however, there was no means of providing special protection for a rabbit warren other than by a combined forest and warren grant. Consequently, in 1424/5 an act of parliament replaced the protection previously provided by the separate warren grant by requiring destroyers of cuningars and also of dovecots to appear before the justice ayre, give satisfaction to the injured party and pay a 40s fine.[18] The justice ayre, which previously might have heard offences against rabbit warrens on the basis of the sanction clause in a warren grant, could now do so on the basis of a parliamentary enactment. An act of 1457/8 confirmed the role of the justice ayre in this context,[19] and in 1474 another act required the justice ayre to punish anyone who stole rabbits from a warren.[20] In 1503/4 parliament drafted an act requiring justice ayres to impose an unlaw of £10 on those who stole rabbits from cuningars, but this part of the act relating to cuningars was deleted in the final version.[21] Rabbit warrens, therefore, were once again subject to special protection based on parliamentary enactment, not on the warren grant.

That the justice ayres did, in fact, try offenders against rabbit warrens can be seen in their journal books of the early sixteenth century. The Kirkcudbright ayre of 1511 heard cases from Kirkandrews warren,[22] and in 1510/11 the justiciary court in Edinburgh heard several cases concerning royal warrens which had been let, e.g., Dirleton, and non-royal warrens, e.g., Oldhamstocks.[23] If the offender pleaded guilty to the theft of rabbits, he was fined £5 and, if he pleaded innocent but was found guilty, he was banished, penalties which did not correspond to the draft act of 1503/4.

The protection of rabbit warrens was entrusted to warrenners. The royal warrenner of Crail in 1350 was allowed 40s by the sheriff and was supervised by the chamberlain.[24] In the early sixteenth century the commissioners from crown lands had assumed responsibility for warrens: in 1505 they enacted, presumably during an *assedacio*, that no one should enter the links of

PLATE
SECTION

Fig. 1. The Hilton of Cadboll Pictish Stone. A hunt is portrayed at the bottom left with two greyhounds attacking a deer.

Fig. 2. The Drostan Stone. At the foot a huntsman is shown in disguise stalking a boar. The huntsman is holding an early type of crossbow.

Fig. 3. A sixteenth-century wall painting from Kinneil House. A smooth-coated greyhound is shown hunting a stag.

Fig. 4. A drawing of the Burghead Pictish Stone. Two large greyhounds, one smooth-coated and the other rough-coated.

A

B

C

D

Fig. 5. The MacMillan Cross. From left to right: 5a shows the complete late fifteenth-century cross and 5b the hunting scene. 5c shows three mastiffs with collars attacking a stag and 5d the huntsman with his horn and axe.

Fig. 6. The early sixteenth-century tomb of Alexander MacLeod at Rodel in Harris. Two mastiffs, perhaps with studded collars, are held on a swivel leash. The huntsman on the left holds a crossbow and carries a quiver for crossbow bolts at his waist.

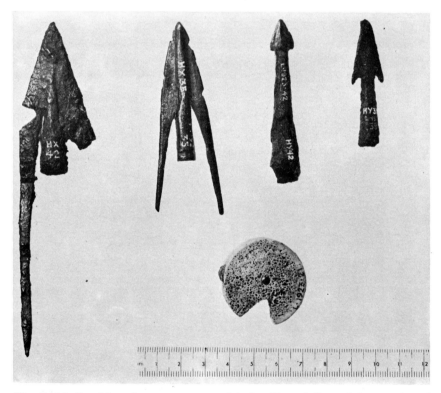

Fig. 7. Medieval broad arrows, nuts and bolts. From left to right: two broad arrows from Kindrochit and Urquhart Castles; two crossbow bolt heads from Urquhart Castle; one crossbow nut from Urquhart Castle (beneath). Scale in cms.

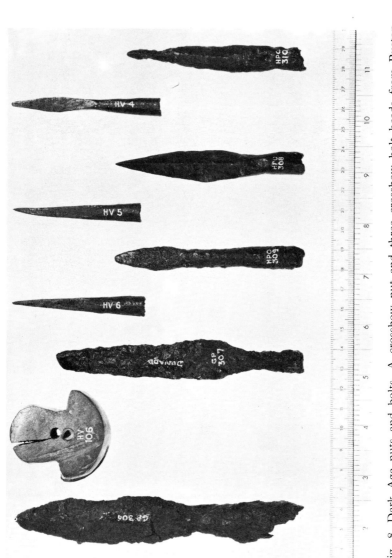

Fig. 8. Dark Age nuts and bolts. A crossbow nut and three crossbow bolt heads from Buston Crannog are set along the top. Along the bottom are five bolt heads from Dunadd Fort. Scale in cms. and inches.

Fig. 9. Print of a smooth-coated greyhound from Gesner, *Icones Animalium* (1560).

Fig. 10. Print of a rough-coated greyhound by Aldovrandus, 1637.

Fig. 11. Print of a rauch from Gesner, *Icones Animalium*.

Fig. 12. Print of a sleuthhound, also from Gesner.

Fig. 13. Contemporary portrait of James IV (1488–1513). He carries a peregrine falcon on his left hand and holds a bow perch in his right.

Fig. 14. A view of a possible site for the Hunthall of Glenfinglas. The tree on the right of the mound is approximately four metres high. The view is from the west.

Fig. 15. A view from the south of the possible site for the Hunthall of Glenfinglas. The flat-topped nature of the mound is clearly visible.

Fig. 16. The park pale of Kincardine park. The mound with the ditch on the right can be seen in the foreground and in the distance to the left of the track. The stick in the ditch is 1.2 metres long.

Fig. 17. The best preserved portion of the park pale of Kincardine park. The ditch is on the right. The stick on top of the bank is 0.4 metres long. This is the northerly stretch of the main park pale.

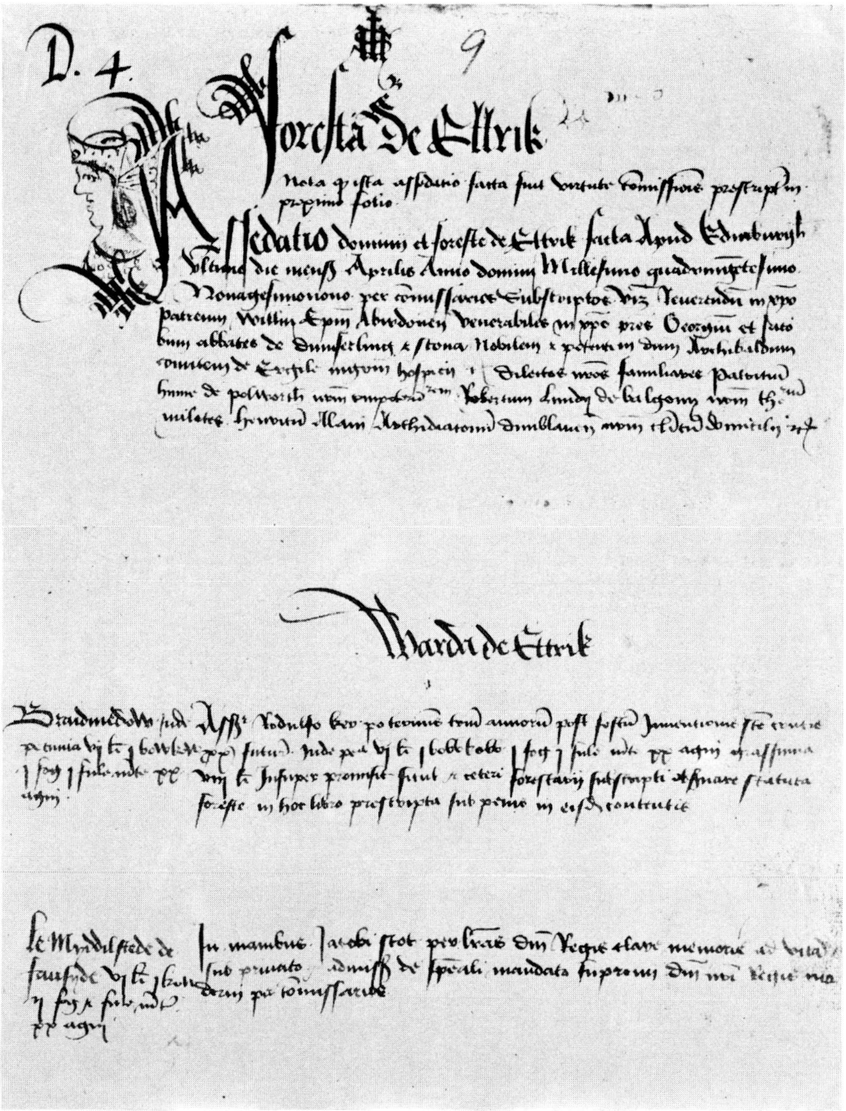
D. 4.

9

Foresta de Ettrik

Nota quod ista assedacio facta fuit virtute commissionis prescripte in primo folio

Assedatio dominii et foreste de Ettrik facta apud Edinburgh ultimo die mensis Aprilis Anno domini Millesimo quadringentesimo Nonagesimonono per commissarios subscriptos

Wardi de Ettrik

Fig. 18. The *Assedacio* of Ettrick Forest in 1499 from the royal rental book. The leases of Broadmeadow and the Midstead of Fauside in Ettrick ward are shown.

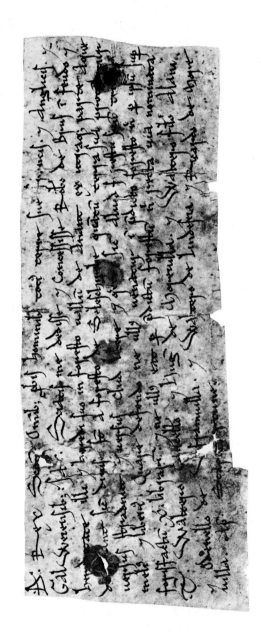

Fig. 19. David I's grant of Annandale in forest to Robert de Bruce in 1147 × 1153.

Dirleton, West Fenton, St. Patrick's Chapel and Gullane apart from their keepers, tacksmen and inhabitants under a fine of 40s.[25] The local people were to be charged 2s for every rabbit slain to ensure that they took action on this point.

Baronial warrens were administered along similar lines. The abbey of Coupar held a cuningar at Keithick in 1473 which was kept by a warrenner who held two acres of land in Keithick, presumably as his fee.[26] His duties entailed the protection of the warren, working it for the abbey's profit and the protection of broom parks beside the warren which would both shelter the warren and provide pasture for stock.[27]

The importance of a rabbit warren to its owner lay in the value of rabbit meat and skin. Warrens may have supplied some rabbits or hares for coursing, but their main purpose was economic and not recreational. The customs accounts show that in the early fifteenth century, if not before, there was a moderate trade in rabbit skins, which were usually handled in batches of a hundred and twenty, which was the long hundred.

Trade in Rabbit Skins in the Early Fifteenth Century

Date[1]	Port	No. of Skins	Custom	Source[2]
1425	North Berwick	720	6s 2d	386
1428	Haddington	wool and rabbit skins	34s	442
1428	Aberdeen	720	6s	442
1430	Aberdeen	wolf and rabbit skins	23½d	509
1431	Aberdeen		6s	535
1431	Inverness	30 from Wick, customed at Inverness and shipped from Aberdeen		536-7
1431	North Berwick	240	4s	525
1434	North Berwick	420	3s 6d	559
1435	Haddington	1692 and one pot	14s 1d	608
1428	Edinburgh	90	9d	435

In Robert I's reign the 'Assisa de Tolloneis' set the duty on 120 hare skins at 1d,[28] and in 1424 parliament set the duty on 'cunyng skynnis' at 12d.[29] The output of a rabbit warren could be considerable, as the lease of the Dirleton warrens to William Wawane in 1505 shows.[30] His rent was to be 160 rabbits by Lent in the first year and 720[31] between 1 August and Lent each year thereafter.

1. Date given is the date of the end of year of account.
2. All page references are to *ER*, iv.

Q

Table 19. RABBIT WARRENS[1]

Date	Name	Owner	Source
1264 x 1266	Crail	Royal	*ER*, i, 4
1288-1290	Cramond	Royal	*ER*, i, 43
1325	'Spedalfield'	Arbroath Abbey	*Arb. Lib.*, 352
1398	Leith	Robert Logan of Restalrig	*Edinb. Chrs.*, 48, no. 20
1431	Wick	Non-Royal	*ER*, i, 536-7
1455 x 1456	Dunbar	Royal	*ER*, vi, 257-8
1473	Keithick	Coupar Abbey	*CA Rent*, i, 187, no. 231
1503/4	Cockburnspath	Queen	*APS*, ii, 271
1505	Dirleton	Royal	*ER*, xii, 693
1511	'Balcomy'	John Lesley of Warderis/Royal	*RMS*, ii, 3556
1510 x 1511	East Lothian: Dirleton Skougall North Berwick Tantallon Oldhamstock West Craigs		SRO, *Justice Ayre Journal Books*, RH 2/1/6, 369
1511	Kirkandrews	John Ramsay	SRO, *ibid.*, RH 2/1/7, 251

1. This list is not exhaustive.

11

Parks

A PARK was an enclosed game reserve surrounded by a ditch and bank on the top of which was a palisade. The Latin words 'parca', 'indago' and 'clausura' were all used in this sense.[1] 'Park' might also signify an enclosed area where stock other than game was kept.[2] Finally, when a game park was no longer reserved, it might still be called a park; James III granted Alexander Gordon the lands of Lagan and 'Balmaklellan . . . vocatas le Park'.[3] Similarly, when a park was broken up, the woods and hills previously within the park might still retain such names as Parkshaws and Parkhill.[4]

The king created parks from lands in his own hands and often from forest lands. While Stirling old park, formed in 1165 x 1174, may not have enclosed forest lands, the park of Jedburgh and the new park of Stirling created by the late thirteenth century probably did. (See Table 31, p. 356.) When Robert I established parks in several of his forests, the baron who enclosed the park for him might also be appointed the keeper of the park or have to make a contribution towards its maintenance.[5] Although Falkland park probably replaced the fourteenth-century forest of Falkland, there was not always a connection of parks and forests. Kincardine park, created perhaps by William I, who issued several charters there, and extended by Alexander III in 1266,[6] was not created from forest lands, nor was Tarbert park, completed in 1330.[7] In the fifteenth century the exchequer rolls recorded the creation of parks by entering the resultant loss of fermes, as with creation of forests: between 1481 and 1513 the fermes of Lochside in Linlithgow were lost because they were 'deputatarum ad parcam palacii';[8] and fermes were lost when the old park of Stirling which had fallen into disrepair was revived in the early sixteenth century and entitled the new park.[9] The extension of Falkland park in 1505 to include the ward of Falkland was also recorded in the exchequer rolls[10] and the repetition in the exchequer rolls from 1508 to 1513 of an entry detailing to the tenants of Cash, compensation for crops destroyed by fallow deer and mares may represent either another extension of that park or the carelessness of the exchequer clerks. The former seems more likely, since in Glenfinglas in 1503 the destruction of crops by game was recorded shortly before the lands in question were declared waste.[11]

The king's subjects also created parks and needed no permission or grant from the king to enable them to do so. (See Table 32, p. 357.) One law copied into the late fourteenth-century Cromertie Ms.[12] stipulated that a deer as *fera natura* was free to move as it pleased, but as long as it stayed on or returned to one man's woods it was that man's property. If it left his lands it again became *res nullius*. By feeding deer or by constructing a park with deer leaps by which deer could enter the park but could not leave, a baron could obtain possession of deer. If they broke out of the park and left his lands he could not reclaim them.

Nonetheless, some control was exercised over the creation of parks by the king's subjects in or near forests. Before 1245 Robert Bruce in Annandale quit claimed all his 'communia' in his wood of Stapleton and allowed Robert de Crosby 'ad habendum liberum parcum de predicto basco'. (See Table 32, p. 357.) The Bruces, therefore, controlled the construction of parks in their forest, as did Thomas Randolph, earl of Moray, whose receipt of a regality grant would have given him forest rights.[13] Robert I in 1319 granted Arbroath Abbey permission to enclose parks and to construct deer leaps in Dumbarrow and Conan, which lay close to the forest of Plater. (See Table 32, p. 357.) In general, however, landholders were free to create parks where and when they wished.

Since parks were created on the basis of property rights, one would expect to find that they were protected in the same way as other property held by their owners and by no special code of law. In England, where most royal parks were created within forests, royal parks were subject to the forest law but baronial parks were not.[14]

In the fourteenth and fifteenth centuries several factors suggest that royal parks in Scotland may have been subject to forest law. Firstly, when a park was created in a forest it seems unlikely that the forest law would have been lifted from that particular area. Secondly, in 1452 James II granted Thomas Home and his heirs the 'forestaria et custodia' of Duns park.[15] Thirdly, when the old park of Stirling was renewed it was declared waste for forest.[16] None of these three points, however, can be taken as proof that the forest law applied to parks. In the first instance, when parks were created within a forest, the rest of the forest was usually granted to a baron. Although the king in the fifteenth century still regarded Boyne and Enzie as his own forest, usually when a park was created within a forest, the forest was alienated by the crown. Nevertheless, a park created in a forest may still have been subject to the forest law, but this type of park should probably be regarded as an enclosure of part of the forest rather than as a separate park, and it is probably for that reason that the park in Boyne and Enzie forest was called a 'clausura' and not a park. In the second case, since the king granted the 'forestaria' and 'custodia' of a royal park to a baron, one might conclude that the king had held forest rights over the park and that the park was, therefore, subject to the forest law. This need not have been so, since the king could grant forest rights over an area where he had not previously created a forest or enforced the forest law. The grant of forestry to Home may only have conveyed the right to hunt in the park. In addition, although Home received the forestry and keepership of the park and the animals in it, he had still to maintain the park for the king, which suggests that he did not have free forest rights over the park. It is still possible, however, that the king enforced the forest law in this park. The third example gives the least dubious statement of the application of forest law to a park. In 1501 x 1502 some of the lands of the old park of Stirling were deputed waste for forest and for feeding wild animals, and a pale was built round this reserve, which was known subsequently as the new park.[17] The reserve, therefore, was subject or intended to be subject to the forest law. 1502, however, was the only year in which the exchequer rolls recorded that these lands were waste for forest. From 1503 to 1508 the lands were stated to be waste for 'nova parca et feris pascendis' and not for forest.[18] That 'nova parca' was substituted for 'foresta' suggests that there was a distinction between a park and a forest and that a park was not subject to the forest law. In other words, the intention in 1501 may have been to create a forest and not a park, but when that intention was dropped the wording in the exchequer rolls had to be altered.

Most, probably all, royal parks were not subject to the forest law simply because they lay outwith royal forests. The forest laws support this argument, since nowhere do they mention parks, and when they discuss enclosures in the first clause they are all called 'coopertorium silvarum' and not parks. (See p. 291, Law 1.) Even in fifteenth-century copies which included alterations resulting from different practices there is still no reference to parks. Some royal parks, nonetheless, may have been subject to the forest law.

Since non-royal parks were not subject to the forest law, other measures were adopted to give them more protection than that afforded by property rights. In the early fourteenth century a park might be the subject of a free-warren grant: Arbroath held its park of Dumbarrow and Conan which had once been a free forest in free warren; and John Carlisle received Kinmount in free warren from Thomas Randolph, earl of Moray. (See Table 32, p. 357.) The sanction clause of the warren grant enabled the owners of these parks to impose a £10 penalty and to appeal to higher authority for assistance when enforcing their hunting and cutting monopoly. The free-warren grant was not a satisfactory form of protection, since it applied only to lesser game and not to greater game, which also could be reserved in a park.

David II was likewise concerned to afford extra protection for his subjects' parks and, when he granted his park of 'Galchill' to Aberdeen chapter and college of canons in 1361, he stipulated that, if anyone should hunt, cut wood, graze animals or leave the rights of way without the chapter's permission, they would be fined 6 cows, 'sine diminucione quacunque'.[19] David thus tried to ensure that offenders would be punished in this park. In 1367/8 he granted Newbattle Abbey the valley of Leithen in free forest 'cum modo parcandi et pena pargagii'. Consequently, these parks, which lay in a free forest, would be protected by the forest law and the £10 penalty. In the fourteenth century, however, such cases of special protection were exceptional.

In the fifteenth century special protection for parks, as for rabbit warrens, came not from the sanction clause of a royal grant but from parliament. In 1474 parliament legislated that anyone who hunted, shot or slew deer or roe deer in another man's enclosure or park should be tried by the justice ayre for theft.[20] In 1503/4 parliament went one stage further by enacting that justice ayres impose a penalty of £10 on offenders in parks.[21] A park now had the same degree of protection for the greater game as a forest. Only the justice ayre, however, could impose the £10 penalty on a park offender, whereas the owner of a forest could in practice impose the penalty himself. The baron who created his own park did not create the equivalent of a forest, since he was dependent on royal justice for the enforcement of the £10 penalty. The fundamental difference between a park and a forest was of course that a forest was created by a royal grant, while a baron could create a park for himself.

At a theoretical level baronial parks raised contradictions which were accepted but not removed. Firstly, the existence of parks contradicted the theory that game was *res nullius,* since game in a park was the property of the park's owner. Game in a park was still, however, *fera natura* and had to be free to come and go as the fourteenth-century law mentioned above implied. In fact, game was not free to leave, since deer leaps allowed only incoming animals to pass. Secondly, parks also infringed the king's theoretical right to reserve deer to himself. Robert I accepted this infringement when conceding in 1319 that no blame was to be attached to Arbroath Abbey 'pro feris et animalibus dictos parcos [*sic,* Dumbarrow and Conan] ingredi volentibus'. By ensuring that the animals acted of their own accord, allowance was being made for the nature of the game and for the king's theoretical right to that game. Barons were presumably not supposed to stock their parks by driving deer into them from the surrounding countryside. In practice, therefore, a realistic compromise was worked out, rejecting neither theory completely and yet allowing barons to create their parks.

Within a park the king reserved his vert and venison[22] but might also grant exemptions from these restrictions.[23] Only in David II's grant of 'Galchill' to Aberdeen chapter is there any reference to the penalty imposed in a park. The amercement of six cows which David wished the chapter to impose on offenders was described as the 'amerciamenta sive escaeta ejusdem parci ab antiquo consueta'. In this instance the previous royal penalty was to be collected by the new non-royal possessors. Throughout the medieval period the justice ayres were associated with the trial of park offenders. In 1279 in the honour of Tynedale negligence in the maintenance of non-royal parks came before a justice ayre of Alexander III at Wark.[24] In the fifteenth century also the justice ayres had jurisdiction over offenders in non-royal parks.

Royal parks were administered by keepers appointed by the king either heritably or for life. Hereditary appointments such as that of the Frasers in Cowie in 1327[25] or of Thomas Home in Duns Park in 1452[26] were usually made in Great Seal charters, but in 1498 the Privy Seal was also used when the abbot of Lindores was appointed keeper of Linlithgow palace, park and loch for five years.[27] Not all park keepers were prominent people: Gilfolan and Gilchrist were keepers of Cardross in 1329; William Bowman was keeper of Falkland in 1450 and George Parklee in Falkland in 1488. (See Table 20, p. 223.)

One of the main duties of park-keepers was to maintain the palisade round the park so that no deer escaped. The palisade with its associated bank and ditch was often described as the 'pale'[28] or the 'fovea' of the park.[29] A considerable amount of work went into the construction of a park pale because of the size of parks such as Stirling and Kincardine. Since no park pale has as yet been excavated, the nature of any fence placed on top of the bank cannot be determined from archaeological evidence. On the mid-fifteenth-century seal of George Douglas, fourth earl of Angus, however, the park pale is portrayed as a wattle fence with branches woven round uprights which are either posts or trees growing on the correct line.[30] There is no medieval record of the height of a park pale fence, but on the experimental deer farm at Glensaugh just to the east of Kincardine park 7' fences were found to be highly deer-proof and 6' fences were sufficient to contain partially domesticated deer, as deer in a park may have been.[31] In the twelfth and thirteenth centuries the construction of park pales was a duty which the king could exact from tenants in the same way as bridge-building.[32] The maintenance of these pales also cost substantial sums of money:

Date	Park	Work	Cost	Source
1264-1266	Kincardine	700 perticates	14d per perticate	ER, i, 21
1264-1266	Stirling parks	construction & repairs	£83 16s 3d	ER, i, 24
1329-1330	Tarbert		£7	ER, i, 239, 287
1331	Cardross	600 roods	£3	ER, i, 360
1491-1498	Linlithgow	repairs	£195 0s 8d	TA, i, 195, 380
1501-1503	Stirling old park	renewal	£51 5s.	TA, ii, 105, 146, 345, 355, 362, 372

By the late fifteenth century the park dyke of Linlithgow was probably made of stone and not of wood. When Stirling park was renewed, masons and pale men were employed to enclose it. Gates would of course be placed in the boundary fence or wall and would be lockable.[33] When park-keepers did not repair the pales, their allowances were withheld, as with Bannantyne, keeper of Falkland in 1468-1469.[34] Despite all efforts deer did escape, although in 1504 the king was favoured by good fortune since a 'wif' chased one of his deer back home to Stirling![35]

The game enclosed in parks included red deer and fallow deer, which first appear in 1288 x 1290.[36] Both fallow and red deer were kept in Stirling and in Falkland in the early sixteenth century.[37] This combination is interesting, since it was believed in some places in the sixteenth and seventeenth centuries that red and fallow deer should not be mixed.[38] Roe deer also were probably reserved in parks, but since 'buck' and 'doe' were used to describe both fallow and roe deer, one cannot be certain where roe deer were kept. Other animals also were protected: boars and swans in Falkland,[39] and white deer in Stirling.[40]

The greater game enclosed in parks had to be carefully tended. It had to be protected from natural predators such as wolves and foxes: wolf-hunters were appointed in Stirling in 1288 x 1290;[41] and in 1505 a trap was made to kill foxes in Falkland park.[42] Game also had to be fed: in 1288 x 1290 hay was given to fallow does in Stirling park during the winter;[43] and from 1504 to 1507 oats were given to the game in Falkland park.[44] The park-keepers were, no doubt, also responsible for stocking the parks by protecting young calves and by importing deer. In 1479 x 1480 two cows were bought to rear calves in Falkland park, presumably because the doe had rejected them or died.[45] Whether this was a common expedient or even a successful one is not stated.

The financial administration of royal parks was handled in the same way as royal lands, by sheriffs in the fourteenth century and by *ballivi ad extra* in the fifteenth century. The treasurer in the early sixteenth century administered a large part of the expenses involved in building park dykes and transporting deer, but he never took over the regular payment of park-keepers.

The extant evidence for Falkland park allows a fairly full picture of the running of a park in the late fifteenth and early sixteenth centuries to be drawn. Along with Stirling and Linlithgow, it was one of the most important royal parks at that time, since it adjoined a favourite royal residence. Perhaps the most frequently used method of stocking this park was that employed in 1505.[46] John Balfour went into the 'cuntre', in this case presumably the Lomond hills, with bloodhounds or rauchs to drive deer towards the park, where a 'hay yard' had been prepared for their capture. Someone had to 'wynd' the hay yard, which suggests that it resembled the entrance to the park shown on the mid-fifteenth-century Douglas seal, mentioned above, where the wattle fence was bent back at the entrance, thus providing a v-shaped aperture into which deer could be driven. The 'wynding' could refer to the weaving of a wattle fence. This hay yard was repaired in 1508 by Andrew Matheson.[47] In this context 'hay' may be used in the sense of a fence, as it had been at one time a synonym for park. This meaning of 'haia' and 'la haie' may not, however, have penetrated into the vernacular use of 'hay'.[48] The park bounds of Kincardine and Lintrathen, which may have belonged to the Durwards, appear to have been specially constructed to accommodate this method of stocking a park, even though barons may not have been entitled to employ this method.[49] Falkland park was also stocked by importing deer from elsewhere: deer were sent from Torwood to Falkland in 1504.[50] Similarly, Stirling was stocked with deer from Falkland and from Little Cumbrae in 1502.[51] There was a regular supply of venison and of live deer from Falkland to other parts of lowland Scotland. In 1502 and 1505 Master Levisay, an Englishman, was responsible for catching deer alive without harming them.[52] He used nets to 'draw' the deer,[53] presumably by encircling them before driving them into a fold or enclosure, a temporary structure rebuilt from year to year. Such a structure, which had its own special keeper,[54] was built in 1504 by one Andrew Matheson, who had completed several construction jobs in the park.[55] In 1503, when a stalker and two servants worked for twelve days in the park to take deer and wild animals for the king's wedding, similar methods were no doubt employed.[56]

The first reference to the transportation of live deer, which was a regular occurrence, may well be in 1461 when two 'ferae foreste' were taken from Ettrick to Stirling.[57] In the early sixteenth century Matheson and Sir Harry Wood,[58] who took charge of the re-building of Stirling park, organised the transportation of deer by carrying them in litters drawn by horses,[59] with four men in attendance.[60] It was a tricky business transporting live deer: the journey from Falkland to Stirling when there was no delay took three days.[61] It was also a costly one: in 1504 transportation, probably from Falkland to Stirling, cost 14s per litter.[62] One of the main recipients of deer thus transported was the renewed park of Stirling, which required regular stocking in the early sixteenth century. There was, in the late fifteenth and the early sixteenth centuries, a network set up throughout the country for the supply of game. There were primary sources of deer, at Little Cumbrae in the west, the Lomond hills, Torwood, and perhaps Ettrick, from which deer were moved to the main centres of Falkland or Stirling. At the same time deer were sent from Falkland to Stirling and from both to Edinburgh.[63]

Live deer were also transported for sport. In 1508 a tame hart taken from Stirling to Edinburgh was slain 'in the barres',[64] perhaps in some sort of animal contest, and in 1503 a deer was conveyed to outside Edinburgh to be coursed on Princess Margaret's arrival there.[65] In 1505 deer were taken to Inverness and in 1509 to Glenfinglas, presumably for coursing or perhaps to improve the supply of deer in that forest.[66] Parks might be used for various purposes but the primary use, for which there is little direct evidence, must have been hunting. The only recorded occasion when a king did hunt in a royal park was in Falkland in 1508, when a certain John Methven went with James IV 'to stalk ane deir with the culveryn'.[67] Parks also provided a convenient supply of fresh meat both from the game and from other animals grazed there.[68] They also had less serious uses: in 1505 there was an equestrian display in Stirling park by a Spanish horseman;[69] and there were white cattle in the same park in 1509.[70] The fourteenth century saw a marked decline in the number of royal parks, just as it saw a reduction of royal lands. (See Table 21, p. 224.)

By contrast, there would appear to have been a growing interest in baronial parks, presumably because they were more easily maintained than forests and a more certain source of game. (See Table 32, p. 357.) Firstly, while only six baronial parks are known from the thirteenth century, sixteen appear for the first time in the fourteenth century, and despite the greatly increased volume of evidence for the fifteenth century, only twenty-two new parks have been encountered in fifteenth-century sources. Secondly, the most informative evidence for the organisation and creation of baronial parks belongs to the fourteenth century. The neglect of the forest grant in the later fourteenth and early fifteenth centuries, therefore, may in part be attributed to this increasing interest in parks.

The examination of parks and rabbit warrens thus suggests that the fourteenth century witnessed a change of emphasis in the nature of hunting reserves. Specific reserves created by the owner, parks and rabbit warrens, may have replaced the more general and less manageable forests and warrens created by royal grant as the most desirable type of reserves from which all economic activity could easily be excluded.

Table 20. ROYAL PARK KEEPERS

Park	Name	Source
Wark		
1286-1287		Stevenson, *Documents*, 16
Stirling		
1288-1290[1]	Two Keepers	*ER*, i, 38
1288-1290	Richard Rasmer	*ER*, i, 38
1507/8	Alexander Elphinstone of Invernochty	*RSS*, i, 1590
Cardross		
ante 1328	William	*ER*, i, 130
1328-1329	Gilfolan	*ER*, i, 130
1328-1331	Gilchrist	*ER*, i, 130, 359
Plater		
1328-1328/9	John Lyall	*ER*, i, 147
Tarbert		
1329-1330	William Scot	*ER*, i, 239, 287
Darnaway		
1371	Thomas Grant	*Moray Reg.*, 22
Dundonald		
1425-1426	Fergus Kennedy?	*ER*, iv, 401
Collessie		
1450-1451	Bishop of St. Andrews	*ER*, v, 473; *RMS*, ii, 385 (See Table 32)
Duns		
1452	Thomas Hume	*RMS*, ii, 541
Falkland		
1450-1453	William Bowman	*ER*, v, 472, 538
1453-1480 x 1487/8	George Bannatyne	*ER*, v, 689; ix, 52; x, 209 (1489)
1487/8	Nicholas Ramsay	*RMS*, ii, 1721
Doune		
1459-60	One Keeper	*ER*, vi, 639
1491-1492	Archibald	*ER*, x, 312
Linlithgow		
1488	George Parklee	*RMS*, ii, 1735
1490/91	William, Lord St John	*RMS*, ii, 2003
1498	Abbot of Lindores	*RSS*, i, 296
1502/3	John Ramsay of 'Trarinzeane'	*RSS*, i, 909

1. The dates given are the dates of the source references and not necessarily the dates when appointments were made or ended.

Table 21. REDUCTION OF ROYAL PARKS IN THE FOURTEENTH CENTURY

Date	Name	Recipient	Source
1320	Jedburgh?	James Douglas	RMS, i, app. 1, 36
c 1326	Stirling old and new parks	Adam Barbetonsor	RMS. i, app. 2, 251
c 1341	'Galchill'	Adam Buttirgask	RMS, i, app. 2, 782
1345 x 1346	Kincardine	Earl of Sutherland	RMS, i, app. 1, 120
ante 1359	Maldisley		ER, i, 582
1359	Drum	Walter Moigne	A.B. Antiqs., 293
1361	'Galchill'	Aberdeen Chapter	RMS, i, 115
1368	Clackmannan (part)	Robert Erskine	APS, i, 531
1370	Stirling new park	Alexander Porter	RMS, i, 317

12

Vert and Venison Outwith Reserves

THE existence of forests and warrens would have been pointless had not the freedom to hunt prevailed outwith these reserves. In medieval Scotland the king and his subjects could hunt relatively freely outside forests, warrens and parks.

The king, who seldom if ever tried to enforce his right to reserve greater game over the whole country, could hunt wherever he wished. When Robert II hunted at Kindrochit, when James II hunted at Strathbraan and when James IV hunted in Strathfillan, they were hunting in areas in which there is no record of a royal forest. James IV also exercised the king's right to hunt where he wished during his pilgrimages to Whithorn and to Tain, during the 'raid' of Liddesdale in 1504 and on the occasion of Princess Margaret's arrival in Edinburgh.[1]

When examining the hunting rights of the king's subjects, both the possession of the right to hunt and the area over which those who possessed that right could hunt must be considered. The latter problem, which concerns the principle that game, as *res nullius,* did not belong to anyone, is succinctly considered in clause 31 of *Quoniam Attachiamenta*. This clause, which first appears in the mid-fourteenth century Bute Ms.,[2] was omitted by Cooper in his edition of *Quoniam Attachiamenta* on the grounds that it was unimportant and consequently, he may have assumed, not part of that treatise.[3] If this clause was not part of that late thirteenth-century work[4] — and the use of the past tense suggests that this clause was written in the reign of Alexander III or later — it must have been written in the early fourteenth century and may well relate to thirteenth-century practice. The content of the clause and of *Quoniam Attachiamenta* may never have been the subject of a royal assise or of enacted law, but it was the opinion and record of legal practitioners:

Tempore regis Alexandri nulle aque fuerunt prohibite de piscacione salmonum nisi aque currentes ad mare. Item non prohibentur aliquis venari ubique ad lepores et ad alia animalia silvestria vel campestria extra forestas et warennas.[5]

This clause clearly states that anyone could hunt anywhere outside forests and warrens, a statement which describes free hunting and not rights to common hunting of the same type as rights in common wood and pasture, which were in effect controlled by the lord. He granted the right of common pasture to certain people who could exercise that right on a certain area of land, and they

225

grazed on that land a fixed number and type of animal. The type of hunting described in *Quoniam Attachiamenta* does not correspond to this form of common right nor does it correspond to the only recorded mention of common hunting. Waldeus of Strichen in 1224 x 1240 granted 'Blarkerroch'[6] to St Andrews Priory with common pasture for 60 pigs, 60 cows, timber in his wood of Goauch[7] for the new hall and

communem venacionem in tota terra mea tam in plano quam in bosco per homines suos cum canibus vel quocunque alio modo.[8]

This grant raises several problems. Firstly, if game was regarded as *res nullius,* there would have been no need for Waldeus to grant St Andrews the right to hunt on his lands. If these lands had lain within the Giffords' forest of Strachan,[9] that would explain why Waldeus granted St Andrews common hunting. It is, however, equally possible that these lands lay outwith that forest or that the Giffords no longer held Strachan and consequently that the forest rights had lapsed. Secondly, this grant of common hunting applied to the whole of Waldeus' land and not only to a certain area within his lands set aside for rights such as common grazing. The practice of common hunting over a complete holding recalls the importance of the right to hunt on one's own land in pre-Norman Scotland, and it is possible that in some areas influenced by Irish practices the landholder could prevent other people hunting on his own land. It is conceivable that Waldeus practised such a custom and made a grant of common hunting to allow the men of St Andrews to hunt on his lands. In a similar grant in 1200 Gilbert, Earl of Strathearn, granted to Inchaffray

libertatem piscandi et aucupandi per omnes terras et aquas et lacus nostras ubi [et] quando voluerint . . .[10]

Although this grant mentions neither hunting nor common hunting, it shows a native landholder granting the right to hawk and fish anywhere on his lands. Such a grant would coincide exactly with Irish practices which may have been current in pre-Norman Scotland.

The clause from *Quoniam Attachiamenta,* therefore, recognised the right of free hunting outside reserves, the right of one man to hunt across another man's land and consequently that game was *res nullius* outside reserves. It is in the light of such rights that the hunting pertinents of feudal charters must be considered. Within a forest in the twelfth and thirteenth centuries the significance of the pertinents, 'feris et avibus', is fairly clear. If they were withheld, the grantor maintained his forest rights over the alienated land, but if they were included the grantor's forest rights lapsed and the grantee was able to hunt on the lands received. (See p. 201.) Outwith reserves the inclusion of hunting pertinents cannot have conveyed control over hunting to the same extent as the pertinents, wood, pasture and mills, conveyed control over wood, pasture and mills, since game was considered to be *res nullius.* If game belonged only to the person who killed it, then it could not be controlled in the same way as pasture and wood. Furthermore, if hunting pertinents had conveyed control over hunting in the same way as pasture pertinents gave control over grazing, then the forest grant would have been to all intents and purposes superfluous, since it existed primarily to give a landholder control over hunting. If in a forest hunting pertinents conveyed only the right to hunt and not the right to control game, which only belonged to the grantee of a forest charter, it seems likely that they would perform the same function outside a reserve. Outside forests, therefore, hunting in the pertinents probably confirmed the grantee's general right to hunt and did not convey any control of game. Since, as clause 31 of *Quoniam Attachiamenta* argues, the right to hunt freely was generally recognised, hunting pertinents were not included in every grant of land but presumably only in those where they were of some significance, where the grantor possessed forest rights or where the grantee wanted his hunting rights confirmed lest he find them for some reason taken away. In Lennox and Strathearn the earls frequently included hunting pertinents in their grants[11] and in that 'native' context hunting pertinents may have conveyed some control over hunting on the grantee's land on a parallel with Irish custom. In some cases hunting pertinents may have been included for no special reason.[12]

In Scotland before 1124, it has been argued, game was not universally regarded as *res nullius*. (See p. 10.) Although hunting was probably free on waste ground or ground belonging to the tribe or kin, the concept of game as *res nullius* could have been limited by a landholder's right to prevent other people hunting on his land or by his right to take part of a stranger's kill for himself. The extent to which such rights were enforced must have varied throughout Scotland from complete enforcement to virtually none, depending on the influences which had operated on the hunting custom of the area. The idea of game as *res nullius* was, therefore, current in Scotland before the Normans arrived and must have been more strongly established in some areas than others, depending on whether Irish, Welsh, Anglo-Saxon or Scandinavian custom predominated. It would appear that the idea of game as *res nullius* developed in the twelfth and thirteenth centuries to the stage recorded by *Quoniam Attachiamenta* where hunting was free outside forests and warrens. The Normans, who were acquainted with the concept of game as *res nullius* before their arrival in Scotland, may have regarded this concept as an ideal excuse for hunting across the lands of native landholders. They would, however, not only have gained from this concept but also suffered from it since others would be free to hunt on their lands. It seems more likely that interaction of Norman and native customs produced a clear statement that hunting outside reserves was free, although evidence of this process is lacking. In England, where the Anglo-Saxon concept of *res nullius* was most likely weaker than in Scotland, no clear statement was made of the common people's right to hunt freely outside reserves, although it is assumed that they could do so.[13] The existence in Scotland of a clear statement of the people's hunting rights outside reserves may, therefore, be attributed to the strength of the concept of game as *res nullius* in Scotland before the arrival of the Normans. By the end of the thirteenth century the position that 'native' and Norman landholders could not prevent other people hunting on their lands unless they received a forest or warren grant, must have raised practical problems.

The implementation of *res nullius* implied that a landowner would have to permit any number of people to hunt on his land as often as they wished. In practice this theoretical position was qualified, as in Roman and Carolingian times. The late fourteenth-century Cromertie Ms. contains a miscellaneous collection of laws and decisions, one of which, 'De feris bestiis',[14] is borrowed from Justinian,[15] and which fifteenth-century manuscripts included as one of the miscellaneous forest laws. (See p. 298.) While this clause, like that in *Quoniam Attachiamenta*, was not enacted law, it was no doubt included in legal collections by the end of the fourteenth century, if not before, because it was relevant and helpful. This argument is borne out by the fact that it is an explanatory version of Justinian's law, not simply a copy. The sections in brackets expand and alter Justinian's institute. The second section in brackets summarises Justinian, *Institutes*, Section II, part 1, chapt. 13:

Item fere bestie ut volucres et pisces et omnia animalia que in celo mari et terra nascuntur si ab aliquo capta fuerint jure gentium statim illius esse incipiunt quia quod ante nullius est illud naturali racione conceditur occupanti nec interest feras bestias nec refert et volucres utrum in suo fundo aliquis eas capiat aut alieno. Sed qui alienum fundum ingreditur venandi et aucupandi gratia potest a domino suo si providerit prohiberi ne ingrediatur (ad capiendum aliquam earum quamdiu fuerit in sua custodia. Qui autem aliquam earum capiat quamdiu fuerit in tua custodia contra legem facit quum tua esse intelligitur quamdiu fuerit in tua custodia sed cum tuam custodiam dimiserit et alibi transierit seu volaverit) naturalem libertatem recepit et definit esse tua et rursum occupanti conceditur. Naturalem libertatem recipere intelligitur cum oculorum tuorum visum effugerit et difficilis sit eius execucio. (Illud est quesitum insuper si fera bestia te sit ita vulnerata ut capi possit statim tua esse intelligitur et dicendum ipsam esse tuam quam diu eam prosequeris quod si desieris eam prosequi definit esse tua et rursum fieri occupantis.)

The original statement of the right to hunt game on another man's land contains the provision that a landowner can, if he wishes, keep outside hunters off his land. This provision, unqualified in Justinian's code, can only operate according to this clause when the outsider is chasing game which is in another landowner's custody, which meant in effect in another man's park, a qualification which in Scotland may stem from the strength of the idea of game as *res nullius*. It is also added that once game was seriously wounded it belonged to the hunter as long as he continued to chase it. A landowner would also, presumably, be able to prevent outsiders hunting on his land if they damaged his property in the process. Apart from these exceptions, a landowner who did not have forest or warren rights was not entitled to prevent outsiders hunting on his land.

Even the possession of forest and warren rights did not completely remove the operation of *res nullius*. Forest Law 14, which can be attributed to the thirteenth century, provided that a free man with free power to hunt on his land beside a forest, perhaps because he held a free forest charter, could follow game from his own land into the forest provided he kept his dogs under control. (See p. 294, Law 14.) This right, obviously based on the same principle as the possession of game by wounding it, was current in England not as enacted law but as a right which might be specially granted.[16] If a landholder beside a forest did not have forest rights himself, he might still follow game from his own land into the forest with a scenting hound, provided he left the capture of the animal entirely to the dog, provided he did not use his bow and provided the dog continued to chase the same animal. (See p. 294, Law 15.)

Not only did the conception of game as *res nullius* penetrate forests but rights to common wood and pasture also did: the priory of May in *c* 1143 received from David I 'communitatem nemoris de Clacmanec';[17] in Annandale the Bruces permitted and regulated common pasture and wood in the manner customary outwith forests;[18] in 1317 it was recognised that the inhabitants of Stirling, on the payment of a toll, had the right to common pasture and wood in the forests of Stirling and Torwood;[19] and in 1498 Alexander, Lord Gordon received the right to common pasture in the forest of Darnaway.[20]

In the twelfth and thirteenth centuries the creation of hunting reserves on the Norman-Carolingian pattern, while opposed to the principle that game was *res nullius*, did not obliterate that principle. Not only did the principle of *res nullius* as applied to game receive a firm restatement, but it was permitted to encroach on the recently established reserves. A compromise of extreme simplicity allowed the creation of reserves and the continuation of *res nullius* outside these reserves. Although the principle of *res nullius* had probably operated with varying degrees of freedom before the arrival of the Normans, the allowances made for its continuation in Scotland in the twelfth and thirteenth centuries illustrate the interaction of native and Norman custom.

In the later Middle Ages, however, the principle of *res nullius* became increasingly limited in its application to game. The theory that the king might reserve all greater game to himself since it had never been seriously enforced did not limit the operation of *res nullius*. It was the actions of the king's subjects which did so. It was always the case that any hunting reserve, whether forest or park or warren, limited the area on which people could hunt. While any baron could reserve game by creating a park, such reservation applied only to his park. It is conceivable that those who did not have forest or warren rights may have wished to control hunting not only in parks but over their lands as a whole. They would thus be able to prevent outsiders hunting across their lands. It is, therefore, assumed firstly, that in the twelfth and thirteenth centuries the king's subjects did hunt across other people's lands and secondly, that landowners eventually came to oppose this practice if they did not do so at first. There were several courses of action open to the landowner who wished to control hunting without a forest grant. He was entitled by Justinian's law to prevent anyone whom he saw from entering his land to hunt deer in his park, a right which could easily be stretched or abused, especially since the original clause had omitted any reference to parks. He might also prevent access to his lands except by certain routes[21] and so turn back any hunters not on these routes. The landholder, therefore, did not set about establishing that he had an absolute right of property over the game on his land, but simply that he had the right to prevent others hunting on his land.

This process is reflected in the inclusion of hunting pertinents in charters. That the pertinents, hawkings, huntings and fishings, were stated far more frequently in the fourteenth than in the thirteenth century may reflect not only the expanded form of many fourteenth-century grants but also the growing interest of landholders in having their hunting rights stated. Although these pertinents previously only confirmed the general right of the grantee to hunt, and although the pertinents included in grants had become formalised by the fourteenth century, it would be sensible for a landholder who hoped to control hunting on his land to ensure that these pertinents were specifically stated. They provided a basis from which he could work.

On two occasions, in fact, pertinents clearly implied that the grantee could control hunting even although forest rights were not involved. In 1278 x 1306, when Robert I confirmed Westerker to Melrose Abbey, the pertinents included

in venacionibus, piscacionibus, aucupacionibus . . . exchaetis omnimodis contingentibus arboribus avibus et nidis avium quam salvagina ac custodiis earundem.[22]

Melrose Abbey could obviously control the game and hunting. Eskdale, however, was in many ways an exceptional case since it was almost a forest. No special circumstances surrounded William, Earl of Douglas' grant of Ringwood to Melrose in 1357 x 1371, which included similar pertinents,

venationibus, aucupationibus, piscationibus . . . cum omnimodis feris et avibus ac nidis avium salvagina et custodiis earundem.[23]

Pertinents might thus convey not only a confirmation of a general right to hunt, but also by the fourteenth century custody of game. This stress on the rights conveyed by the pertinents is not unreasonable, since, after the demise of the sanction clause in a free forest grant, it would be the pertinents, vert and venison, which conveyed the judicial rights of the forest. Similarly claims may have been made that hunting pertinents also conveyed judicial rights. Such custody with associated judicial rights may have applied only to game in parks, but the Westerker grant suggests that the custody conveyed was more general. That pertinents were used as a basis on which to control game is borne out in the late seventeenth century in Stair's *Institutes*, where Stair has to explain that hunting pertinents do not convey property in game.[24] That Stair felt it necessary to explain that pertinents did not convey property in game argues that at some previous date this claim had been made. Moreover, Stair recognised that exclusion of outsiders was one way of acquiring control of game not conveyed by the pertinents.

That barons were establishing some sort of limitation of hunting on their own lands may explain the terms of Robert Scott of Rankilburn's grant to Melrose in 1415.[25] When he granted Melrose Abbey Glenkerry in exchange for Bellendean, both Robert Scott and Melrose had the right to hunt on the lands which they then held, but Scott retained 'licencia piscandi et venandi' in Glenkerry and Melrose retained the freedom 'piscandi et venandi' in Bellendean. If game had still been considered as *res nullius* or if landholders had not tried to prevent outsiders hunting on their lands, there would have been no need for Scott or Melrose Abbey to reserve the right to hunt on the lands which they had relinquished.

The application of *res nullius* to forests also showed signs of weakening when in 1294/5 in Renfrew forest the monks of Paisley, who held forest rights in the adjoining lands of Maich and Calder, were forbidden to harm birds and beasts in the whole of the Stewards' forest.[26] These arrangements suggest they they could not hunt from their own land into the Stewards' forest in accordance with Forest Laws 14 and 15. That the Douglases in the early fifteenth century, if not before, held bound-courts in Ettrick forest also argues that outsiders were prevented from hunting in the forest, and in the early sixteenth century the neighbours of Glenfinglas forest could not hunt in that forest. It is not surprising to find that in the fifteenth century the principles of *res nullius* did not allow men to hunt across the border into England.[27]

The principle of *res nullius*, therefore, from the fourteenth century and perhaps from the late thirteenth century was becoming limited in its application to game both inside and outside reserves.

The hunting rights of the common people were affected not only by the history of *res nullius* but also by customs concerning which animals could be hunted and who had the right to hunt them. In the Middle Ages all types of game were considered to be *res nullius* according to Justinian's institute, but clause 31 of *Quoniam Attachiamenta* does not support that interpretation. The animals which everyone could hunt everywhere were, according to that clause, 'lepores et alia animalia silvestria vel campestria' which, as has been explained, probably referred to lesser game. (See pp. 99, 210.) Consequently, the first clear Scottish statement embodying the principle of *res nullius* applied only to lesser and not to greater game. If this interpretation is correct, the author of this clause may have been taking into account the theoretical right of the king to reserve all greater game to himself. In practice, however, it would be hard to accept that greater game were not hunted as *res nullius*, especially since barons could create parks for greater game without the royal consent. By the sixteenth century barons could also keep roe deer in their own woods, presumably on the same basis as they kept deer in a park.[28] The gifts of deer which James IV received from his subjects imply that his subjects could hunt deer. Many of the gifts came from magnates who possessed forest rights,[29] but Sir John Wemyss, who in 1507 sent James one roe buck, three white deer, one hart and four roe deer,[30] did not have forest rights. Since 1468 the lairds of

Wemyss had held their lands only with hawkings, huntings and fishings,[31] and none of the extant Wemyss' charters mentions a park on Wemyss' lands, although there had been a park at Elcho in the early fourteenth century.[32] It is, therefore, possible that the deer gifted by Wemyss were hunted by him as part of his general right to hunt. In the west of Scotland Macgregor's gift of venison to James IV in 1503[33] and the later medieval sculptured stones which portray deer being hunted with two or three hounds[34] point to greater game being hunted as part of a subject's ordinary hunting rights. Hunting rights in the north and west of Scotland in the medieval period are, in fact, fairly obscure because of lack of evidence. An early fifteenth-century Gaelic poem makes frequent mention of hunting, but little can be deduced from it other than that the Clan Gregor did hunt freely in the hunting season and that Malcolm, son of John the Black, could hunt freely in Alba, whereas, so the poet says, Finn had to ask permission to hunt.[35] This seems to imply that, as one would expect from early Irish parallels, there was some kind of control of hunting in the west, but the nature of that control is not clear.

When the game was a pest, its pursuit by everyone everywhere was encouraged, the most notable example being wolf-hunting. Hunting the wolf was permitted when other forms of hunting were not, for example, in Eskdale in 1165 x 1169[36] and in Pluscarden in 1230.[37] In the fifteenth century wolves still posed a considerable problem and parliament had to pass several acts encouraging wolf-hunting. In 1427/8 every baron in his barony was to be responsible for summoning his tenants to at least four wolf-hunts in the spring of every year and for rewarding with 2s the man who killed a wolf.[38] In 1457/8 responsibility for raising the wolf-hunts was transferred to the sheriff or bailie and the number of hunts was reduced to three between 25 April and 1 August when the wolf cubs could be caught. Anyone who killed a wolf was to receive 1d from every householder in the parish where he killed it, and anyone who killed a fox was to be paid 6d.[39] In 1458 x 1459 the bailie of the earldom of March paid Gilbert Home 5s for killing ten wolves in Cockburnspath 'secundum actum parliamenti desuper confecti'.[40] In 1498, the lords of council at Inverness enacted that if anyone brought a wolf's head to the sheriff, the sheriff or bailie was to see that he received 1d from every five houses in the parish. They also enacted that when a wolf was located, the hue and cry was to be raised, and the penalties — to be collected by the lord or bailie — for not joining the chase were heavier on the second and third offences than for all such offences in the above acts of parliament. If the lord or bailie failed in this he could be fined £20 by the justice ayre. That wolves were treated in the same way as thieves and outlaws illustrates the danger which wolves still posed in fifteenth-century Scotland.[41]

Similarly, 'foulis of reif', namely rooks, crows, eagles, buzzards, kites and mittens (a type of hawk) could be killed by everyone because they ate corn and killed birds valued for sport such as partridges, plovers, blackcocks, greyhens and moorcocks.[42] Whether or not all men had the right to hunt all of the latter group of birds is obscure. When a case of theft of eggs of partridges or wild duck came before a justice ayre, it is not clear whether the ayre had to protect the eggs for the king or the landholder.[43] By 1474 a landholder did have the right at least to all hawks and their nests found on his land and their theft could lead to a £10 fine before the justice ayre.[44]

This right of free hunting outwith reserves, not seriously hampered in practice by limitations on the game which could be hunted, was not a right possessed by all the inhabitants of early medieval Scotland. Forest Laws 14 and 15 clearly imply that only free men can benefit from the principle of *res nullius* by hunting into a forest, and clause 13 of the forest laws states the fine for a free man found committing an offence against the venison. The forest laws which elsewhere mention *nativi* in connection with grazing do not mention *nativi* in connection with hunting. It would seem that *nativi* were not entitled to hunt. Whether in the twelfth and thirteenth centuries other ranks who, although enjoying more freedom than the *nativi,* were not completely free were entitled to hunt is not clear. The fifteenth-century Scots version of Forest Law 21 which was borrowed from English law probably during the early fourteenth century did state in a Scots insertion that different penalties were to be imposed on a freeman and a bondman whose dogs were found in the forest. A bondman may conceivably have been entitled to hunt. When *Quoniam Attachiamenta* stated that 'aliquis' could hunt freely, 'aliquis' probably referred to any free man and not literally to anyone. In the thirteenth and fourteenth centuries, as servility became increasingly rare,[45] a growing proportion of the population may have acquired the right to hunt. The impact of such an increase would have depended on the numbers involved, but it is significant that it is to the fourteenth century that the increased interest in parks and rabbit warrens and of landholders in controlling hunting on their lands can be attributed.

As the treatment of game as *res nullius* became less common, so the right to hunt would become limited because there would be fewer places in which to hunt. In some areas this may have reached the position where only landholders were able to hunt. Ultimately, in 1621 parliament enacted that

no man hunt nor haulk at anye tyme heirefter quha hes not a pleughe of land in heretage under the payne off ane hundrethe pundis.[46]

Not only were landowners the only ones who could hunt: they were, after 1621, the only ones with the right to hunt. This act, therefore, gave legal form to what has been suggested was the practical if not the theoretical position which resulted from the gradual limitation in the later Middle Ages of the concept of game as *res nullius*. By the seventeenth century the landowner, as Stair recognised, had established a right to prevent others hunting on his land. That Stair recorded that landowners seldom took such action[47] does not signify that *res nullius* was still unlimited but that no one at that time hunted outside his own land. While the act of 1621 had not in theory abolished the application of *res nullius* to game and while the landowner still had no absolute property in the game on his own land, the application of *res nullius* to game was in practice dubious.[48]

The principle of *res nullius* and the right of all free men to hunt had survived longer in Scotland than in England or in France. In a European context, therefore, the limitation of these rights in Scotland was unique only with regard to the date when it occurred.

To compare grazing rights and control of wood within and outwith forests in the early Middle Ages concerns the rights conveyed by the pertinents, 'boscis' and 'pascuis'. The pertinents of a charter specified the grantees' rights in accordance with the Norman feudal theory that everything on the land belonged to its holder. There is no doubt that a baron controlled the woods[49] and the pasture[50] on his lands. He could also have a forester or a serjeant to supervise wood-cutting[51] and could stipulate the number of animals which could graze on his pasture. A baron, however, only exercised such rights over unalienated land and could not, as the lord of a forest might do, alienate the lands yet retain control of the wood and pasture. Rights in common wood and pasture also came under the lord's control: in 1248 Freskin of Moray granted the bishop of Moray rights in the common pasture and wood of Findrassie.[52] As already stated, a lord could specify not only who used common pasture, but also he could limit the number of animals grazed on it.[53] Usually, there was a certain area set aside for common pasture, frequently a moor, and the animals utilising this right could not graze over the whole of a lord's holding.[54] In the early Middle Ages, therefore, the lord had control over pasture and wood on the lands which he held in demesne and could presumably punish in his court those who abused their rights in wood and grazing. He could not, however, expect to raise a forfeiture of £10 for such offences, nor could he control pasture and woods on lands alienated to tenants by charter, both of which the grantee of a forest might do.

In the fourteenth and fifteenth centuries barons continued to control wood-cutting on their lands, although they usually allowed their tenants timber for building.[55] Coupar Abbey in the fifteenth century reserved wood as carefully in Drimmie[56] and Atholl,[57] where it had no forest rights, as in Campsie and Glenisla where it had.[58] In 1488 the bailie of William, Earl Marischal in the barony court of Keith forfeited the lease of a tenant who had destroyed woods in the barony and ploughed and sowed a large part of the lands of the woods.[59] This corresponded with one of a group of laws given in the early fifteenth-century Harleian Ms. of Scots laws which stated that a lord may forfeit a tenant's lease for destroying wood by burning or selling it and for building on the lord's lands.[60] In the fifteenth century the control or rather the preservation of wood was encouraged by parliamentary legislation which made it possible for a baron to seek justice before the justice ayre. In 1424/5 parliament imposed a 40s fine on those who stole wood at night or peeled the bark off the trees, and gave the lord whose wood had been stolen the right to try the thief in his court.[61] In 1503/4 parliament raised to £5 the unlaw on felling or burning wood, regardless of whether it belonged to the king or to his subjects.[62]

Enclosure of woods first appeared in the fifteenth century. The king had reserved certain special woods, for example, at Collessie, Falkland, and Earnside, all in Fife,[63] but in 1458 x 1459 James II enclosed the wood of Falkland.[64] Coupar Abbey also ordered that several of its woods be 'hanyt', which may mean either enclosed or protected.[65]

In the later Middle Ages both the king and other landholders continued to limit the number of animals which grazed on common pasture and on other lands outwith hunting reserves.[66] Although herbage and foggage could be collected outside reserves,[67] a baron could not impose fines such as those imposed in Renfrew forest by the Stewards on lands which did not lie in forests, nor could he forbid pasture on his tenants' lands in June and July, the time of fence. When Anselm de Mow *ante* 1190 forbade Kelso Abbey to graze sheep between 9 June and 1 August, the prohibition applied to pasture on his own lands, extended beyond the time of fence, and was presumably intended to stop over-grazing.[68] While it was possible for a baron to control rights of way on his lands, whether or not he held forest rights,[69] he could not forbid economic activity such as ploughing and building on his tenants' lands *per se*, unless wood was destroyed in the process.

Although in the early Middle Ages a baron had considerable control of vert outside forests, it was not so intensive as the control inherent in forest rights. A forest grant was, therefore, significant in that respect and in the control of hunting which it also conveyed. As a result of the limitation of *res nullius* in the later Middle Ages and of the increasing protection afforded to timber by the early sixteenth century by acts of parliament, the owners of forest rights were no longer in so unique a position as they had been in the thirteenth century with regard to the control of hunting and wood-cutting.

The extent of woodland and its reduction in the medieval period must be considered, since the control of wood-cutting, both within and outwith hunting reserves, became more important in medieval Scotland as the supply of timber became increasingly scarce in certain areas. The natural vegetation of Scotland in prehistoric times has been described by V. Gordon Childe and by M. L. Anderson.[70] The valleys and sheltered slopes were forested and the uplands were usually covered with dense scrub, although between Clydesdale and Ayrshire and between Lothian and Clydesdale forest and swamp formed the moorland vegetation. The poorly drained lowland plains were heavily forested and dense oak woods grew on heavier lowland soils, as in the Merse, the Solway, central Ayrshire, Strathearn and Strathmore. In Galloway, the Southern Uplands and the midland valleys, oak woods gave way at higher altitudes to pine, ash and birch woods. In the Highlands the same pattern prevailed, with birch being quite common and native evergreens being slightly more widespread than oak. It should be remembered that on high ground dense forest did not occur and woodland was patchy and scattered.

This general pattern of vegetation must have survived more or less intact till the early Middle Ages, even although wood was cleared to make way for agriculture, to provide building material, fuel and implements, and was destroyed by grazing. Nonetheless, in areas where any or all of these activities were concentrated a shortage of timber could have developed. In the twelfth and thirteenth centuries the inclusion of woods in the pertinents of a charter already provided the landholder with the means to control the use of wood and to counteract any threatened shortage. That wood was becoming scarce in some areas in the thirteenth century is witnessed by the control which some landholders exercised over their tenants' use of wood on their lands.

Further evidence of a shortage of wood can be found in *Regiam Majestatem*, which stated that if someone forfeited his land or holding, he was allowed to take with him the timber of his buildings.[71] The creation of a timber shortage can be seeen in Mow, which was a highly developed area of land in the Cheviots.[72] There the pastoral pursuits of Melrose and Kelso Abbeys led Richard de Lincoln in 1250 to permit the monks of Kelso to take timber for building repairs from his wood in Mow only on condition that they gave that wood twenty to thirty years to recover.[73] Moreover, when Kelso took wood to make sheep shelters, Richard required that the wood be cut under view of his servants without causing unnecessary waste. The Southern Uplands also must have lost large areas, though by no means all, of their timber cover through the pastoral pursuits of Melrose, Dryburgh and Newbattle Abbeys.

Reduction of woodland also resulted from high timber demands occasioned by industrial uses such as charcoal-burning and iron-smelting — there were mines in Crawford forest and in Pluscarden[74] — but the most common industrial use for wood in the twelfth century was in salt pans as at Preston, Callendar, Turnberry and Lochkendelloch.[75] Where the demand for timber exceeded the local supply, as with the creation of burghs, a timber trade developed. In several cases timber for building could be obtained near at hand, as was the case in Ayr, Elgin, Forres, Inverness and Crawford,[76] but in other places it had to be transported to the burgh, as at Perth and Kelso.[77] The demands for timber, however, were not sufficient in the thirteenth century, so far as the Scottish evidence tells, to require the importation of timber from abroad.

By the end of the thirteenth century it would appear that there was a shortage of wood only in certain well developed areas or where there was an exceptionally high demand for timber. Timber, when required in large quantities, was transported, and even then it was probably not taken far. There must still have been a general abundance of wood in lowland and highland areas. Consequently, timber in hunting reserves, although it was exploited, can have been under no serious pressure, a situation reflected in the fact that those forest laws which belong to the twelfth and thirteenth centuries mention wood-cutting only briefly, and then in only two laws probably of thirteenth-century date. (See Laws 13 and 16, pp. 293, 294.)

Local shortages of wood continued in the fourteenth century and restrictions on timber-cutting within reserves were broken: the burgh of Aberdeen did not respect Robert I's reservation of the vert in Stocket forest in 1313, with the result that in 1319 Robert reserved his vert in the wood of Stocket only and not in the whole forest.[78] Nevertheless, in 1399 wood was still being cut illegally in Stocket.[79] Within Scotland shortages were alleviated by transporting timber from one place to another. One of the main highways for the domestic timber trade was the Forth, which flowed past Stirling, Torwood forest, Alloa wood, Clackmannan forest, Blackness for Linlithgow, and Leith.[80] In addition to the everyday uses of timber, the exchequer rolls throughout this period show a regular use of timber for royal residences and for repairing burgh trons in the 1370s.[81] That the shortage of timber was growing is suggested by the importation of timber from Norway or the Baltic and Prussia in 1329 and 1382.[82] An increasing shortage of timber may also be reflected in the English forest laws introduced to Scotland in the early fourteenth century, since two of them related specifically to wood-cutting. Although these two laws were not carefully adapted to Scottish use, their inclusion in Scots legal treatises may reflect increasing pressure on the woods within hunting reserves. (See Laws 19 and 20, p. 296.) The pressure on timber within reserves, however, was not yet severe, since the twelfth- and thirteenth-century practice of granting abbeys a general right to cut timber in royal forests was continued at least till 1364.

Only in the fifteenth century is there evidence for a serious shortage of timber in large areas of Scotland. That the availability of timber was causing some concern is witnessed by parliamentary interest in the subject, beginning with an act of 1424/5 instituting a 40s fine on stealers of green wood and bark peelers, to be imposed by the justice ayre.[83] In 1457/8 parliament advocated that all landlords should only grant leases on condition that the tenants planted trees, made hedges of live wood and saved broom.[84] In 1503/4 parliament not only encouraged lords and lairds to plant an acre of wood where there were not extensive woodlands, but also increased the penalty for destroying greenwood to £5.[85]

Similar concern can also be seen in the efforts which lords made to protect their own woods by taking court action when necessary.[86] The abbeys of Arbroath and Coupar both concentrated on the protection of timber in areas which had once been free forests and where their tenants might take wood for essential building but were not allowed to sell it or give it away. The seriousness of the situation is reflected in the appearance in the mid-fifteenth century of the practice of enclosing woods. In 1451 James II appointed a keeper for the royal wood of Earnside, and in 1458 x 1459 he enclosed his wood of Falkland.[87] In 1483 Coupar Abbey ordered a wall to be built around half of the forest of Campsie.[88] No longer did the king grant the right to cut timber freely in his forests as had been done in preceding centuries. Even the free forest grant in several instances from 1488 onwards was limited only to wooded areas, which obviously reflects the concern caused by the wood supply.

The reduction of woodland in Ettrick forest illustrated how the shortage of wood exerted pressure on those woodlands still protected within hunting reserves. Although in the twelfth century Melrose Abbey had received the right, subsequently confirmed by Robert II,[89] to take timber freely from the forest, the abbot of Melrose along with the abbot of Newbattle was fined for cutting wood in the forest in the second half of the fifteenth century.[90] Although their fines were remitted, that they were fined at all suggests that the forest officials were trying to curtail their rights. While the exchequer rolls record only those fines which were remitted, it is apparent that most wood-cutting offences occurred in Tweed ward. Since the eastern part of the forest was the most accessible area of the reserve, more offences against the venison[91] occurred in Tweed ward than in the other wards and more steads in the east of the forest had the right to keep sheep.[92] Over and above parliamentary legislation, the statutes of Ettrick in 1499 tried to control wood-cutting but with limited success, since in 1510 a justice ayre at Selkirk recorded 148 wood-cutting offences, nearly all committed by inhabitants of the forest.[93] The journal book does not say where the offences were committed within the forest and one cannot assume, as Professor Anderson did, that the offences were committed in the steads from which the offenders came.[94] Indeed the steads from which the offenders came were probably those steads where timber was most scarce. It must not be forgotten, however, that if 148 wood-cutting offences could be committed within the forest, there must still have been reasonable areas of woodland there.

In consequence of the growing shortage of wood, the timber trade became increasingly important. The timber trade with Prussia and the Baltic continued and expanded during the fifteenth century[95] and James IV wrote to the Baltic countries and to France to obtain wood especially for ship masts.[96] The area where there was the greatest demand for timber was probably east-central Scotland, and timber was obtained from there and from the rest of Scotland. Leith, Inverkeithing, Kirkcaldy, Dundee, Montrose and other east coast ports all handled timber.[97] As early as 1435 timber had to be transported to Leith from 'partes boreales',[98] and by the beginning of the sixteenth century there was a fairly steady flow of timber from the north of Scotland, Darnaway and Loch Ness.[99] The Forth continued to be an important highway for timber, since timber from Clackmannan was moved by ship to Leith,[100] while the Tay was also used to transport wood from Earnside.[101] The timber for royal ships and for military requirements was obtained in the late fifteenth and early sixteenth centuries from woods in the Loch Lomond area, Clydesdale, the Lothians, the Borders and Galloway.[102]

The existence of a domestic timber trade suggests that there was still plenty of wood available in the early sixteenth century, a view supported by the justice ayre journal books, which record wood-cutting offences in woods in

Ayrshire, Galloway, the Borders and the Lothians in 1510 and 1511. (See Table 22, p. 240.) Although this evidence seems to contradict the evidence which points to concern over the supply of wood, both sets of evidence are compatible.

Firstly, wood could become scarcer not because there was an overall shortage but simply because timber could no longer be obtained within a few miles of its point of use: it had to be sent to Edinburgh from Inverness or Galloway. Secondly, the woods which still grew in the Lothians and central Scotland such as Borthwick, Saltoun, Clackmannan and Torwood may not have contained timber of sufficiently good quality to provide for all the parts of a ship or for artillery works. Such timber would have to be obtained from sources such as Darnaway or the Baltic countries. As a result, measures were taken to preserve timber, not because the country was devoid of wood but because good timber had to be obtained from further and further afield from its point of use. Even although there were still woods throughout Scotland, they must have been gradually reduced in size, and action was taken because it was hoped, no doubt, that the rate of this reduction could be decelerated. It is now apparent that those travellers who described Scotland as destitute of wood were mistaken.[103] In their defence it may be said that if the Scots parliament could state in 1503/4 that the wood of Scotland was 'uterlie distroyit',[104] it is hardly surprising that foreign travellers believed Scotland to be totally denuded of wood!

Table 22. WOODS MENTIONED IN THE JUSTICE AYRE JOURNAL BOOKS

Date	Place of Ayre	Wood	Source
			RH 2/1/5[1]
1493	Lauder	Cranshaws	7
1493	Lauder	'Caudschele'	7
1493	Lauder	'Bowne' and 'Blith'	18
1502	Jedburgh	'Woddoun'	255
1502	Jedburgh	'Lymekilwood'	257
1504	Dumfries	Park and Lochmaben	317
			RH 2/1/6
1507	Kirkcudbright	Wood of forest of Buchan	29
1507	Kirkcudbright	'Garrolerg'	30
1507	Kirkcudbright	'Ard'	33
1507	Kirkcudbright	Wood of Newforest	34
1507	Kirkcudbright	'Holme'	36
1507	Kirkcudbright	'Toungland'	43
			RH 2/1/7
1508	Kirkcudbright	'Corsluth'	87
1508	Kirkcudbright	'Killogoune'	87
			RH 2/1/6
1508	Ayr	Cumnock	63
1508	Ayr	'Glendowische'	63
1508	Ayr	Craikston	109
1508	Ayr	'Aneane'	123
1508	Ayr	'Birbeth'	123
1508	Ayr	'Clongil' and 'Cragintalze'	123
1508	Ayr	'Cassilis'	123
1508	Ayr	'Makiliveynston'	123
1510	Jedburgh	'Gaitschaw'	224
1510	Jedburgh	'Woddone'	228
1510	Jedburgh	'New Park'	237
1510	Jedburgh	Caphope	239
1510	Jedburgh	Wood of Jedforest	257
1510	Jedburgh	Wood near Jedburgh	266
1510	Selkirk	Woods of Ettrick Forest	280 ff
1510	Peebles	'Kingildurris'	311
1510	Peebles	Kischawis	311
1510	Peebles	'Petcorso'	311
1510	Peebles	Kirkurd	311
1510	Peebles	'Wodhous'	311
1510	Peebles	Dawick	330
1510	Peebles	Hankschawis	330
1510	Peebles	'Hopraw'	332
1510/11	Edinburgh	'Barbachlo'	350
1510/11	Edinburgh	Roslin	360
1510/11	Edinburgh	Hawthornden	360
1510/11	Edinburgh	'Dridan'	360
1510/11	Edinburgh	'Yorton'	361
1510/11	Edinburgh	Clerkinton	361
1510/11	Edinburgh	Keith	379

1. Located in SRO.

Table 22. Woods Mentioned in the Justice Ayre Journal Books (continued)

Date	Place of Ayre	Wood	Source
			RH 2/1/7
1511	Ayr	Dalrymple	23
1511	Ayr	'Terrizearn'	28
1511	Ayr	'Blackcrag'	28
1511	Ayr	'Eklis.'	31
1511	Ayr	'Smethstoun'	31
1511	Ayr	Cumnock	56
1511	Ayr	'Dalquhatis'	56
1511	Ayr	Loudon	56
1511	Kirkcudbright	'Kinhilt'	122
1511	Kirkcudbright	'Garchlon'	122
1511	Kirkcudbright	'Knokglas'	122
1511	Kirkcudbright	Mochrum	124
1511	Kirkcudbright	'Pleuland'	124
1511	Kirkcudbright	'Logane'	131
1511	Kirkcudbright	'Etoun'	156
1511	Kirkcudbright	'Parton'	206
1511	Kirkcudbright	'Dowlark'	216
1511	Kirkcudbright	'Rowtanebroig' in Bishopforest	223
1511	Kirkcudbright	'Garmagacha'	224
1511	Kirkcudbright	'Ammernes'	226
1511	Kirkcudbright	'Kers'	230
1511	Kirkcudbright	'Clachan'	230
1511	Kirkcudbright	'Gileston'	237
1511	Kirkcudbright	'Monigaff'	237
1511	Kirkcudbright	'Southek'	241
1511	Kirkcudbright	'Geoken'	241
1511	Kirkcudbright	'Berclay'	250
1511	Kirkcudbright	Glenken	251
1511	Kirkcudbright	Wood of New Forest	252
1511	Kirkcudbright	'Drumbrek'	259
1511	Kirkcudbright	'Glaschilze'	259
1511	Kirkcudbright	'Garrulee'	262
1511	Kirkcudbright	'Camloden'	262
1511	Kirkcudbright	'Kirkennan'	264
1511	Kirkcudbright	'Cardines'	268
1511	Kirkcudbright	'Drumcali'	268
1511	Kirkcudbright	Tongland	271
1511	Kirkcudbright	'Langwood'	271
1511	Kirkcudbright	'Wodhed'	271
1511	Kirkcudbright	'Cowgarthschaw'	271
1511	Kirkcudbright	'Douchray'	274
1511	Kirkcudbright	'Kers of Clauchan'	274
1511	Kirkcudbright	Balmaclellan	275
1511	Kirkcudbright	'Drungech'	275
1511	Kirkcudbright	'Erleston'	275
1511	Wigtown	'Barrinrauer'	352
1511	Wigtown	'Glesich'	352
1511	Wigtown	'Garthlon'	352

Table 22. Woods Mentioned in the Justice Ayre Journal Books (continued)

Date	Place of Ayre	Wood	Source
1511	Wigtown	'Croschre'	353
1511	Wigtown	Mochrum	371
1511	Wigtown	'Glassach'	371
1511	Wigtown	'Bogessech'	371

13

The Forest Law

THE forest laws regulated the life of a large part of medieval Scottish society for the purpose of reserving and preserving game, a purpose revealed in their content which has already been examined. Some picture of the extent and efficiency of that regulation has already emerged from the study of the enforcement of forest rights, but more can be learned of the character of that regulation from the form and nature of the forest laws.

Of the extant manuscript volumes into which these forest laws were copied, the earliest belongs to the fourteenth century and the majority to the fifteenth century. (See App. A for full discussion of the editing and dating of the laws.) These legal collections contained not only enacted Scots law but also laws, references and practices which their compilers, legal practitioners, found useful in their work.[1] In the late fourteenth century the Cromertie Ms. probably belonged to the priory of Chartreux at Perth.[2] A mid-fifteenth century manuscript from Edinburgh University Library belonged to a certain R. Alexander, a law clerk, who made notes in the margins and on blank pages.[3] Another mid-fifteenth-century manuscript belonged to the family of Arbuthnott and was autographed by Alexander Arbuthnott, a member of the 'College of Advocates'.[4] The manuscript written by James Monynet in 1488 had various owners including Master David Dun of Edinburgh, W. Sinclair of Roslin, T. Nicholson, king's advocate in Charles II's reign, and Balfour Denmilne.[5]

In these manuscripts the forest laws, which vary in number from 10 to 90 or more, can be divided into four groups. The first group, clauses 1 to 11, is the earliest, probably dating from the twelfth century. The second group, clauses 12 to 18, may well belong to the thirteenth century. Together these two groups form a single series of laws best described as the original Scots forest law. The third group, clauses 19 to 24, comprises laws borrowed from England which were probably introduced to Scotland during Edward I's attempted settlement in the early fourteenth century, and the final group is a collection of miscellaneous laws. The earliest version of the first group of laws survives in the Bute Ms. of the mid-fourteenth century, of the second group in the late fourteenth-century Cromertie Ms., and of the third and fourth groups in the Harleian Ms. of the late fourteenth or early fifteenth century. These manuscripts of course need not be the earliest written versions of the forest laws.

In the twelfth century the enactment of rules or laws to be applied to forests must have been essential, since forests had not previously existed in Scotland. It is reasonable to assume that such rules or laws were enacted by royal assises given by the king and council. Since it could not possibly be claimed that forest regulations were the recognition or judgement of previous custom and since an assise could create legal innovations,[6] an assise would have been the most appropriate way of creating rules for forests. David, Malcolm and William all issued assises,[7] and it would be natural for them to issue forest regulations by assise. Such assises were presumably recorded by the royal clerks and so were copied into now lost collections and eventually into the extant manuscripts. Professor Duncan has suggested that it was in the reign of Alexander II that the value of such collections was first realised. The promulgation of such assises would presumably be the responsibility of the barons and of royal officers, especially the sheriffs, who could proclaim the assises in the courts and possibly also at parish kirks, since throughout the medieval period parish kirks seem to have been a focal point for announcements concerning forest regulations.[8]

The inclusion of English laws in the Scots forest laws during the fourteenth century reflects the borrowings made by Scots law at this time. There is, however, some dispute about the extent and sources of the borrowings made by Scots lawyers in the fourteenth and fifteenth centuries, but none deny that borrowings were made.[9] It has recently been argued that English material introduced to Scotland in the thirteenth and fourteenth centuries was examined and included in a fifteenth-century restatement of the law, the impetus for which led to the formation of legal treatises and to the legislation of James I and III encouraging the collection of Scots laws.[10] It was as part of this process of collection and examination of earlier material that the four groups of forest laws were combined into one body of law by the late fourteenth or early fifteenth century.

In this form the forest laws as they were known in the fifteenth century did not represent a single body of enacted law. Some laws compiled probably in the twelfth century to regulate pannage were long since out of date. Although the purpose and principles of the forest laws remained the same, their provisions and details did vary. Nevertheless, in the early sixteenth century clear references were made to the forest laws. In 1507/8 James IV ordered that offenders in Glenfinglas be punished according to the king's laws and statutes[11] and mentioned 'leges forestarum nostrarum' in a charter of 1508.[12] Since the traditional forest law belonged to the twelfth and thirteenth centuries, one might have expected parliament to have carried out the necessary revision. All parliamentary acts which concerned relevant topics applied either to the whole country or to parks and rabbit warrens but never to forests. It is unlikely that any acts relating to forests have been lost, since in the sixteenth century those manuscripts of the forest laws which appended a section of parliamentary enactments did not mention any acts not now extant.[13] The laws referred to by James IV were, therefore, the traditional forest laws. In fact these laws were subject to various interpretations and alterations which kept them up to date.

Even in the late twelfth century there is evidence that there were local as well as national laws applied to the forests. For example, any servant of Melrose Abbey who committed an offence in Gala and Leader or Trolhope forests had to pay half a year's wages to the lord of the forest according to the assise of the Abbey.[14]

When Robert II instructed Robert Erskine, justiciar of Clackmannan and Torwood, to try offenders 'sicut leges et consuetudines requirunt', the customs may have comprised practices and innovations made since the laws were first promulgated.[15] The fifteenth-century copies of the forest law included alterations which, since they cannot be attributed to copyists' errors, were made to keep the laws up to date. In a fifteenth-century manuscript in the National Library (N)[16] all reference to pannage, which died out in the fourteenth century, was omitted in clause 1, as were all the miscellaneous laws which do not directly concern forest matters. That variant editions of these laws did appear in the fifteenth century[17] suggests that they were still in use. There was nothing unusual in the fact that these laws were subject to various interpretations, since variations between the enacted law and practice have already been pointed out with regard to timber-cutting and rewards for wolf-hunting,[18] and the points of dittay listed in the justice ayre journal book in 1508 did not include the hunting of deer in winter, which parliament had made a point of dittay in 1474.[19] It is in this context that the statutes of Ettrick forest must be considered.

In 1484 James III instructed his commissioners for Ettrick forest to enforce the 'actis and statutis of our said forest maid of befor for the reuyle of the samyn', obviously referring to a series of local laws for Ettrick forest.[20] The 'statuta foreste' mentioned in 1471 which forbade the erection of gardens or enclosures in Ettrick may also have been of local provenance.[21] These statutes of Ettrick were probably enacted by the commissioners for crown lands, since their letter of commission authorised them to make such new statutes as were deemed necessary. The commissioners for Menteith, which included the forest of Glenfinglas, had the same power.[22] Indeed a baron court could enact laws on certain matters such as good neighbourhood which had to be obeyed by the local inhabitants. In 1499 twelve laws were published by the commissioners in the forest court of Ettrick in the Tolbooth of Edinburgh in the presence of the forester tenants.[23] Such action clearly illustrates that the existing forest law was found to be inadequate. These statutes of Ettrick were clearly geared to the existence of forest steads which were not common in other forests. In effect these statutes were an up-to-date version of the traditional laws adapted to the conditions of Ettrick forest. Despite these new statutes, it was still possible for the royal rental of Ettrick to record that 'thir thre statutis to be kepit in forest in wod, der and teling, that is to say the wod and der punist be auld statutis and the corn eschete'.[24] Old and new operated side by side, for there was no contradiction in purpose.

s

By leaving various courts to interpret the traditional forest law and bring the penalties and procedure up to date, a rather confused situation may have arisen. The traditional forest laws were still the basis of the law in forests, but they could be clarified and expanded by local statutes enacted by the commissioners for crown lands, and when James IV referred to the enforcement in Glenfinglas of his 'lawis and statutis maid thairapoun', he was possibly referring to statutes supplementing the traditional forest law and not simply to laws and statutes relating to forest matters.

The laws which applied to royal forests probably also applied to non-royal forests. Not only would such an arrangement make practical sense but non-royal forests, as explained, could be regarded as areas of royal forest specially created for a subject. In the traditional body of forest law two clauses, 15 and 18, specifically allow for non-royal forests, while clause 14 may indirectly refer to the holder of a free forest beside another forest. Since the second group of laws, 12-18, probably belong to the thirteenth century and since they alone refer to non-royal forests, it is possible that, if they were not actually enacted as a group of baronial forest laws, non-royal forests were given careful consideration when they were formed. The rules enforced in non-royal forests did not always correspond exactly to the regulations contained in the forest laws, as the fines imposed in Renfrew forest illustrated.[25] In baronial as in royal forests the law was subject to local variations. In 1508 non-royal forests were still subject to the royal forest law: witness the baronial forest of Cabrauch which had to be kept according to the laws of the king's forests.[26] That the additional statutes for royal forests were also applicable to free forests is suggested by the proclamation made by the lords of council in 1504/5 that the baronial forest of Glencarvie and Glenconri be kept 'undir all pane and charge contenit in the lawis of fre forest and statutis maid thairupoun'.[27]

Forests, although subject to a special code of law, were not removed from the jurisdiction of other laws. Non-forest offences in forests, although seldom recorded, were subject to the same law as elsewhere. In the twelfth and thirteenth centuries it can be assumed that the sheriffs and justices responsible for the trial of forest offences were also competent to try non-forest offences. In non-royal forests the lord of the forest and the royal courts must have divided non-forest jurisdiction in accordance with the customs common throughout the country, certain cases going to the baron, certain to the sheriff court and certain by the later thirteenth century to the justiciar on ayre.

In the fourteenth century the justiciars of the forest were presumably competent to hear non-forest offences, and the fact that the sheriff in 1371 had to ensure that the justiciar of Clackmannan and Torwood had a sufficient court argues that the sheriff within the forest had judicial competence which in this case was assumed by the justiciar.[28] When the lands of the forest were alienated in free barony, as those of Ettrick were to James Douglas,[29] the grantee would of course possess barony jurisdiction over the forest lands.

That non-forest cases were not neglected in the fourteenth century is supported by the inclusion in the forest laws of a large group of miscellaneous laws. Although one of these laws was usually the clause 'de feris animalibus' borrowed from Justinian, and although another 'de venientibus ad guerram' stated the armour to be kept by persons of poor means in forests,[30] most related to non-forest matters. They touched on heredity, marriage, oath-taking, exceptions to writs and other matters relevant to courts held in forests whose competence extended beyond forest matters.

In the later fifteenth century the commissioners for crown lands could try non-forest cases, as their points of inquest demonstrate,[31] and justices on ayre dealt with crimes committed in any royal forest: in 1495 and 1510 the ayre at Selkirk heard cases of theft of stock and of murder from Ettrick.[32] There appears to have been one coroner for each ward in Ettrick, since in 1495 David Pringle, the currour of Tweed ward, was the coroner of Tweed,[33] and in 1501 Walter Scott of Tushielaw was the chief coroner of Ettrick.[34] In Ettrick, therefore, forest and ordinary justice were closely linked. Lesser civil offences from forests, which may have gone before the bailie or the sheriffs, were in Ettrick after 1499 definitely the responsibility of the bailie, who had to determine matters of good neighbourhood.[35] Considering the arrangements for the trial of non-forest offences within forests gives an impression of the burden which the forest laws could have imposed. In a certain area of land the forest laws established a series of rules and regulations, and offences and trespasses, which the inhabitants had to obey and avoid over and above those of ordinary civil and criminal law.

The nature and form of the forest law has, therefore, revealed conclusions about the character of the forest system which are in accord with the picture obtained from other sources. The forest law was not static. After its initial statement in the twelfth and thirteenth centuries it was adapted and developed by the addition of English laws and by the enactment of additional statutes to emphasise and clarify points of local significance. Yet it was local courts and not parliament which had to modify and renovate the law which applied to royal and non-royal forests. Between 1424 and 1513 no act of parliament even mentioned forests as hunting reserves. From one point of view the history of the forest law reflects a flexible and adaptable institution, but from another it reflects the neglect which forests appear to have suffered in the fourteenth and earlier fifteenth centuries.

14

The Economic and Social Impact of Hunting Reserves

IT is important to decide to what extent the owner's wishes controlled the exploitation of the reserve and the concession of exemptions, and to what extent exemptions were made and the reserve exploited in response to demands from outsiders, in other words to determine whether the wishes of the owner overruled those of outside users or *vice versa.* The only means which the owner of the forest possessed with which to impose his wishes was his forest administration which, it has been explained, seldom functioned efficiently in medieval Scotland. It was, therefore, possible for the wishes of outside users to influence the exploitation of a forest or hunting reserve. In 1226, for instance, Andrew, Bishop of Moray sought certain lands in the forest round Elgin, Forres and Inverness.[1] In most instances, in fact, the lord of the forest would have been able to profit from the exploitation of the resources of his forest by charging tolls for their exploitation.

Consequently, the alienations and exemptions granted within a forest reflected the economic life of the country. When many such grants were made, the reserve in question was under considerable economic pressure arising most likely from economic expansion in its vicinity. When assessing economic expansion or contraction in this manner, certain qualifications must be borne in mind. Firstly, it is only the first alienation of a piece of forest land which is relevant to a study of economic pressure, since only the first such grant represents the change from a hunting reserve to a fully exploited area. Secondly, although the existence of such a grant with the right to cultivate an area of a forest does not prove that that area of forest was cultivated, it can generally be assumed that there was an intention to cultivate even if that intention was not in every case realised. Thirdly, the concession of alienations and exemptions need not always have been governed by the economic environment of a reserve. Political considerations could have an effect and forests were administered not as reserve supplies of natural resources to be released when the demand for them rose, but as areas for hunting. If the lord of the forest was sufficiently powerful and determined, then probably no amount of demand could make him grant economic concessions within his forest, for example, the case of James IV and Glenfinglas.

Generally, the initial exploitation of a reserve would be effected by the owner. Apart from the sport and the produce of game, the value of a hunting reserve to its owner lay in the revenue which he could raise from it and the economic activities which he could pursue in it. Tolls levied on animals grazing within the reserve provided revenue the amount of which can seldom be determined. In the later thirteenth century, however, the returns from pannage in Ettrick and in Tynedale have survived:

Forest	Date	Pannage	Source
Ettrick	1265	13 swine	*ER*, i, 30
Ettrick	1288 x 1290	20 pigs	*ER*, i, 35
Wark	1264-1266	£4 4s 11d for 2 years	*ER*, i, 23

In the fourteenth century the value of hunting reserves was sufficient for several forests and parks to be included in the revocations of David II's reign. Several royal forests were let in the fourteenth century either directly or by the collection of fermes of foggage or herbage,[2] and by the fifteenth century rent collected from forest tenants provided more revenue than tolls for pasture, penalties for offences and compositions of fines. Many of the royal forests let in the fifteenth century had probably been let by their previous owners before the forest entered or returned to royal hands:[3]

Date	Forest	Rents charged	Source
1451	Clunie	£ 13 6s 8d	*ER*, vi, 480
1456	Darnaway	53s 4d	*ER*, vi, 461
1461	Ettrick	£519 13s 4d	*ER*, vi, 371

The returns from Ettrick forest in the later fifteenth century were one of the largest sources of royal revenue and they could exceed £1,000. The king's subjects also let their reserves and received rent from them in the fourteenth and fifteenth centuries.[4]

The owner of a hunting reserve could, of course, graze his own animals within the reserve. The Avenels grazed animals in Eskdale in the early thirteenth century,[5] as did the Stewards in Renfrew.[6] The number of animals grazed in forests, as in common pastures, was carefully regulated. In Boyne and Enzie in 1327 Gilbert Hay, the forester, was permitted to graze in each forest 24 cows, one bull, 300 ewes, 300 two-year old sheep or 'hoggis', and six mares in Boyne. The sub-foresters were allowed to graze 20 cows and three broken-in horses.[7] The king also grazed animals within his forests: in 1330 the royal stud was removed from 'partibus ultramontanis', perhaps in Mar, to Ettrick;[8] in 1487 this stud was still maintained in Catcarmauch,[9] where it probably remained till 1501; James III and James IV both kept unbroken horses in the forests of Glen Artney, Glen Almond and Glen Shee;[10] and in the later fifteenth century royal cattle and horses were kept in Torwood,[11] Lochin-dorb[12] and Glenfinglas.[13]

In Ettrick forest, where the largest number of royal animals were grazed, flocks of sheep were first established by James I when Ettrick was still in the hands of the Douglases,[14] and they survived till 1455 when the forest lands returned to the crown.[15] At first only five steads were held by the crown, East and West Mountbenger, Catslack, Blakgrain and Catcarmauch,[16] but gradually the king put his flocks onto steads held in stelebow. In 1501, when there were 21 stelebow steads[17] in the forest, if James IV had kept a full quota of sheep on these steads he would have had 8,820 sheep in Ettrick. On certain of the stelebow steads 420 sheep formed a full quota,[18] but the number varied between 240 and 480.[19] In fact in 1501 only 15 stelebow steads had their full complement of sheep,[20] and so there would have been approximately 6,300 sheep there. With the advent of feuing, these steads were no longer let in stelebow and the king's sheep were supposed to be returned to him.[21]

The value of a hunting reserve to its owner also stemmed from the timber and on occasion from the arable land within the reserve.[22] Hunting reserves, in theory opposed to economic exploitation, were nonetheless exploited by their owners who would as a matter of policy try to determine the nature and the extent of the exploitation of their reserves.

Hunting reserves were not only exploited by their owners. In the twelfth and thirteenth centuries the recipients of grants of exemptions from forest rights were frequently abbeys, especially Cistercian abbeys. Melrose, Newbattle, Arbroath, Coupar Angus and Holm Cultram all received some rights of usage in Scottish forests. (See Tables 17 and 23, pp. 205, 266.) With their capital, organising ability and expertise the Cistercians could graze large flocks of sheep and embark on extensive projects to break in new land. On their estates where sheep were grazed there were granges run by lay brothers who were assisted by other labourers on the grange in tending the flocks. The provision of fuel, the grazing of the flocks, the construction of folds and shelters for the animals and of temporary shielings for the herdsman must have made considerable inroads into a forest's vegetation and put pressure on the maintenance of a hunting reserve.[23] Such pressure was exerted in the reserves of Gala and Leader, Ettrick, Ayr, and Eskdale by Melrose Abbey, in Pentland, Crawford and possibly Leithen by Newbattle Abbey, in Trostach, Ochtirlony and Kinkell by Arbroath Abbey, in Renfrew by Paisley Abbey, in Cargill by Coupar Angus Abbey and in Dalbeattie/Dumfries by Holm Cultram Abbey. A closer examination in certain reserves of the activities of the abbeys of Melrose and Paisley, so far examined only in a judicial or procedural context, reveals the process by which the maintenance of a hunting reserve could be placed under stress.

The royal forest of Gala and Leader, first recorded in 1150 x 1152,[24] must have been created shortly after 1136 when Melrose Abbey received pasture, pannage and the right to cut wood there.[25] From its creation this forest was subjected to the common activity of both laymen and ecclesiastics. The earliest recorded lay activity dates to the reign of David I when William Soroules held the lands of Sorrowlessfield,[26] when Alwin asserted part of the forest near

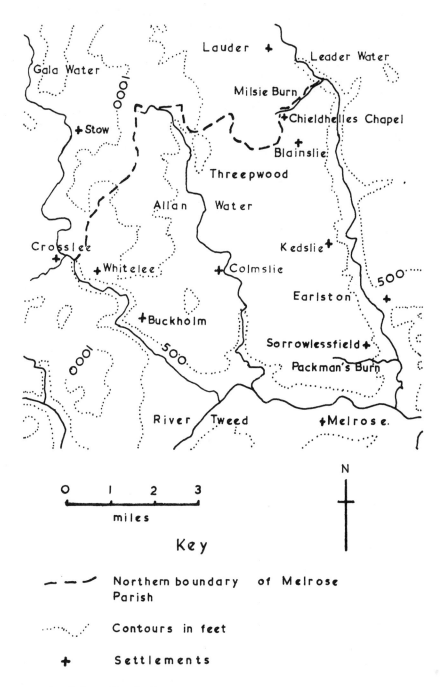

Key

— — — Northern boundary of Melrose
        Parish

··········· Contours in feet

+   Settlements

8. Gala and Leader Forest.

Kedslie,[27] and when the foresters held lands at Blainslie which William I later gave to William, son of Oein.[28] More powerful laymen also had an interest in this forest: the de Morvilles held their own reserve to the north of the royal forest;[29] William de Lyndesay held lands near Kedslie;[30] the Stewards had the right to pasture animals near Blainslie;[31] and the earls of Dunbar by and probably before the early thirteenth century held lands at Sorrowlessfield, Earlston and Lauder.[32] The activity of these barons and their men would have placed certain areas of the reserve under pressure, but their rights are less important in this respect than the rights granted to Dryburgh Abbey and especially to Melrose Abbey.

In 1162 x 1165 Malcolm IV confirmed that Melrose held pasture rights over the whole of the land between the Gala and Leader rivers and south of the lands of Richard de Morville and the men of Wedale and that they held the lands of Gattonside between the rivers 'Elwyn' or Allan and Leader and south of the 'Fauhope' or Packman burn. He also allowed them to build a cowshed for 100 cows and a sheep-fank at Colmslie.[33] The monks of Dryburgh, who held a grange at Kedslie with the right to pasture on the forest,[34] can have been none too happy with the pasture rights of Melrose, and *c* 1160 Melrose and Dryburgh defined the boundary between their granges of Kedslie and Colmslie and agreed that the animals of Melrose could only be pastured on Dryburgh's lands with Dryburgh's permission.[35] By Malcolm IV's reign, therefore, the resources of the forest were no longer sufficient to meet the demands being made of them without further regulation.

After settling their relations with Dryburgh, the monks of Melrose next had to turn their attention north to Richard de Morville. Richard, while in charge of this forest in the years before his death in 1189,[36] granted Melrose certain carefully regulated rights within the forest in charters which can only be dated to 1174 x 1189.[37] It is probable though not definite that they were issued in clarification of the settlement made in 1180 of the dispute between himself and Melrose.[38] The terms of the settlement suggest that the dispute arose because Richard tried to share in Melrose's pasture rights in the royal forest, especially in Threepwood, and because the monks objected to Richard's hunting throughout the forest, especially in Threepwood, and tried to increase their buildings in the forest.

By the terms of the 1180 settlement Richard's activity in the royal forest was limited to hunting, although Threepwood was to be held by him. The monks of Melrose were entitled to graze their flocks anywhere in the forest, including Threepwood, and to use the wood of the forest, although they could not grant or sell timber from the forest nor increase the number of buildings which they held in the forest without Richard's permission. The charters of 1174 x 1189 clearly defined the buildings and rights of the monks at their granges of Blainslie, Buckholm and Whitelee. The monks were free to plough and to sow in Blainslie but were to make no assart in one part of Blainslie.[39] In Buckholm they were entitled to have two buildings and no more,[40] and in Whitelee they could build a cowshed for 120 cows or a sheep fank, a hay barn and a dwelling house with a hearth. The only other buildings which the monks could erect were wattle bivouacs for their shepherds.[41] Finally, the 1180 settlement provided that the monks have a forester with responsibility for their pasture, that the de Morvilles have a forester to protect the game, and that the monks pay Richard de Morville 100 merks of silver as compensation.

This settlement, therefore, attempted to organise conflicting activities within the forest in such a way that they could co-exist. Without careful regulation the pastoral interests of the monks had conflicted with the hunting interests of the de Morvilles. The settlement was not wholly satisfactory, since the de Morvilles could still hunt in the monks' pasture lands and the monks, with certain limitations on building, still maintained their granges and flocks within the forest. Both sides now knew their rights but the problem had not been solved.

Melrose Abbey continued to further its interests in the forest by the receipt of additional arable lands at Blainslie, in 1180 x 1193, with freedom to build.[42] In 1189 x 1190 William's confirmation of Melrose's rights in the forest recorded two additional settlements at Milsieside and Chieldhelles Chapel and stipulated that royal foresters could not sell wood from the monks' lands and that the monks needed William I's permission before erecting any new buildings.[43] In 1189 x 1196 Melrose received from William de Morville additional lands at Milsieside.[44] The continuing expansion of the monks' pastoral farming may have occasioned Alan Steward's cession to Melrose Abbey of all his pasture rights on the west side of the Leader in 1189 x 1193[45] and Melrose Abbey's complaints before 1202 that Patrick, Earl of Dunbar, had tried to seize their pasture at Sorrowlessfield.[46] These complaints once again reflected the over-exploitation of the forest and the need for careful regulation. The dispute of Melrose Abbey and Patrick, Earl of Dunbar, was resolved in 1208 when it was settled that Melrose held the arable lands of Sorrowlessfield from him with the right to graze their animals on the land between Kedslie in the north, Gattonside in the south, Malcolm's road in the west and the river Leader in the east. On this land the monks could graze 500 sheep and 140 working oxen or cows and Patrick also had the right to graze animals there, although neither party could leave their herds there overnight. The monks were to erect no buildings on the pasture lands and the trees were to be in Patrick's hands.

The exploitation of this reserve by so many people and especially by Melrose Abbey not only led to disputes between the exploiters of the forest but must also have hindered the maintenance of the forest as a hunting reserve. An attempt to limit pastoral activity within the reserve in order to facilitate the maintenance of the forest proved unsuccessful in 1180 and grazing continued to thrive. Finally, in 1236 Alexander II gave up the struggle to maintain the lands between Gala and Leader as a hunting reserve, deforested the lands which Melrose held there and granted them to Melrose in free forest.[47]

The Stewards in their forests of Renfrew and Ayr had to cope with the activities of the monks of Paisley and Melrose respectively. In 1165 x 1172 Walter Steward granted Paisley Abbey easements in his forest of Paisley with pasture there for the beasts and pigs of the monks and their men in the same way as Walter and his men could pasture their herds in the forest. Walter stipulated that if he introduced his own flocks into the forest he would set aside one part of his forest specially for the monks' pasture.[48] Alan Steward confirmed these provisions in 1177 x 1199,[49] and in 1208 x 1214 Walter the third Steward granted Paisley lands between the Old Patrick and Espedair rivers and between the rivers Maich and Calder, as a result perhaps of the introduction of his own flocks into the forest.[50] The lands between Maich and Calder were deforested for the monks, but Alan reserved his game on the lands between the Old Patrick and Espedair. In the latter area he did, however, permit the monks to assart, plough and build as they wished and to collect wood and graze 100 pigs in the surrounding forest. Any other grazing was subject to certain fines.[51] The detailed nature of these provisions suggests that Alan was aware of the damage which unregulated grazing would cause in his reserve and may well have arisen from trouble resulting from the absence of such regulations in the grant of Walter the first Steward. Alan also ceded the lands and pasture of 'Drumley', Swynesholes', and 'Petihaucingavin' to Paisley with the right to assart and build, although he still reserved his game on these lands.[52] After the deforesting of the lands of Maich and Calder it is not surprising to find that they were granted to Paisley in 1219 x 1230 in free forest along with Monaibrock in Strathgryfe,[53] which Paisley had received in 1202.[54] The Stewards, therefore, divided their forest into those areas where the monks could operate and those where they could not. This policy seems to have operated tolerably well, but trouble must have arisen by the end of the thirteenth century, for in 1294, in order to preserve his game, James Steward had to create a specially reserved part of his forest where no economic activity could be pursued either by the monks or by his own tenants.[55] The creation of this 'foresta prohibita' was accompanied by a heightening of the fines for illegal grazing which by this time were called parcage. As a result of the activities of the monks of Paisley and no doubt of their own husbandmen who leased lands in the forest, the Stewards had been forced to concentrate their efforts on maintaining only a small part of their original reserve. In the forest of Ayr economic pressure on the reserve commenced with Walter Steward's grant of Mauchline, in 1165 x 1177, to the monks of Melrose, and of meadows north of the river Ayr where they could plough. Moreover he granted Melrose all the pasture of his forest as far as Douglas, Lesmahagow and Glengavel, with easements in the wood and one carrucate of land for cultivation, 'Salva tamen foresta mea tantum in bestiis et avibus'.[56] Although Alan Steward confirmed this grant,[57] as did William I,[58] Alan appears to have had second thoughts about his father's generosity, as a result no doubt of the economic activity of the monks. In the years before 1204 Alan claimed that the reservation of his forest rights applied not only to the pasture lands in the forest but also to the lands of Mauchline and the meadows north of the Ayr. Melrose appealed to the pope, and in 1203/4 Alan lost his case with the result that he could not reserve his game on the latter group of lands.[59] The monks of Melrose and their men were, therefore, able to pursue their economic activities without the interruption of the Stewards' hunting parties, and the administrators of the hunting reserve of Ayr had a serious obstacle to contend with. Walter the third Steward confirmed this decision when in 1204 x 1214 in confirmation of Melrose lands he permitted the monks 'totam forestam meam ad utendum secundum eis utilius visum fuerit' for ploughing.[60] He also let them graze in his forest flocks as large as the monks thought the pasture could support, but on this pasture neither the monks nor the *conversi* were to hunt because hunting 'illorum ordini non convenit nec illis credimus expedire'. Walter was here perhaps making a quiet thrust at monks who would not let him hunt. He also granted the monks the lands of Cairntable to the south of the river Ayr but, remembering his earlier experience, he specifically reserved his game on that land![61] Walter had thus surrendered a large part of his reserve to the monks' pastoral and agricultural activities, with the result that in 1264 after Alexander Steward had deforested his pasture of Mauchline and Cairntable on both sides of the Ayr,[62] Alexander III granted them to Melrose in free forest.[63] The king in the thirteenth century did not always yield to economic pressure. In 1189 x 95 William I permitted Richard, Bishop of Moray to pasture animals and have easements of wood from the bishop's wood in the royal forest round Elgin, Forres and Inverness.[64] The bishop did not have to pay pannage to the king but was permitted to collect pannage there from his own men. Bishop Andrew obviously hoped to extend these forest privileges by acquiring more land in the same forest at Pluscarden and Darnaway and also in the forest of Invercullen. Alexander II did not, however, yield these lands but instead, in 1226, granted the bishop Rothiemurchus in forest in exchange for these additional lands.

In these and similar instances certain common features can be detected.[65] The owners of the reserves, after their generous initial grants to the abbeys, must have experienced certain misgivings when they realised the threat which the economic and pastoral activities of the monks posed to the maintenance of their hunting reserve. In several cases during the reign of William I barons tried to amend the generous grants of their predecessors either by re-asserting their hunting rights on the monks' lands, as in Gala and Leader and Ayr, or by hindering the monks' activities, as in Eskdale. In 1166 x 1169 Robert Avenel had granted Melrose Abbey lands in Eskdale in which he exercised the equivalent of forest rights although it was never described as a forest. Robert reserved his greater game and undertook not to damage the abbey's fields, meadows, flocks and herds when hunting. His generosity went further, for he agreed to keep no forester on the monks' lands but only officials who would arrest thieves and trespassers and protect the nests of hawks and sparrow hawks. The monks, however, were not allowed to destroy the nests of hawks or to hunt with packs of hounds or with nets. This implies that they were permitted to stalk or course for lesser game, and they were specifically allowed to place traps for wolves.[66] In 1214 x 1218 Gervase Avenel further granted that the abbey could construct huts for their herdsmen wherever they wished.[67] Trouble ensued. The monks' men appear to have chased hawks away from their nesting areas so that they might cut the trees, and Roger Avenel started to graze his horses and beasts on the monks' land, to destroy the monks' houses, and to level their ditches and enclosures. Once more the interests of hunting and farming were in conflict. Although in 1236 it was agreed at a 'colloquium' that the monks could not fell trees till hawks had failed to nest in them for one year and that they could not hunt with nets or packs of hounds, Roger failed to limit their other economic activities, and when thereafter he hunted in this part of his reserve he had to avoid disturbing the monks' flocks or destroying their enclosures.[68] Elsewhere attempts to limit the monks' economic pursuits were equally ineffective. After these disputes further concessions followed, frequently resulting in free forest grants or the alienation of part of a forest. Alexander II's reign saw free forest grants to abbeys in Crawford, Renfrew, Gala and Leader, Pentland and Moorfoot, Pluscarden and Trostach. Also in this reign, the pastoral pursuits of abbeys were firmly established in the forests of Eskdale, and Ettrick.[69] Consequently, after a period in William's reign when attempts were made to curtail economic activity in several hunting reserves, the owners of these reserves yielded to the pressure being put on them.

The extent to which these events can be interpreted as the effect of an expanding economy depends on the extent to which the monks could force their wishes on the owners of reserves. In the cases of Eskdale, Gala and Leader, and Ayr there is little doubt that the abbeys exerted such pressure by means of judicial proceedings. Once confirmed in their rights they presumably proceeded to exploit the forest as they wished, taking advantage of any failings of the forest administration to stretch their rights to the limit and beyond until the owner of the forest saw little point in continuing to try, by means of his inadequate administration, to maintain that part of his reserve. Although forests were administered by their owners as hunting reserves, it is possible to regard forests as reserves of resources which could be released as the demand for them rose. In this context, the tolls charged for pasture within a forest represent the price charged for the use of these resources. The increase of the fines or levies in Renfrew by the Stewards between 1208 x 1214 and 1294 can, therefore, be interpreted as an increase in the price charged for the use of these resources. Such an interpretation can be supported by the introduction of the tolls of herbage and foggage, probably in the thirteenth century, which effectively relaxed the restrictions placed on pasture within forests, probably in William I's reign.[70]

In conclusion, in the earlier part of the twelfth century the resources of forests were not over-exploited, pasture was permitted relatively freely, grants were made to abbeys permitting their exploitation, and game would appear to have been successfully preserved. Towards the end of the century, when hunting and economic interests came into conflict, the economic advance was held in check if not reduced. In the thirteenth century, however, this economic pressure could no longer be held in check and the owners of reserves yielded to it. This picture of a healthy and expanding economy corresponds with what is already known of the Scottish economy in the twelfth and thirteenth centuries.[71]

In the fourteenth century it is the alienations of all or part of royal reserves which serve as a guide to the economic life of the community. When Robert I created internal reserves in several of his northern forests, he was probably responding not only to administrative inefficiency and poaching but also to the demand for land for pasture and agriculture, as the detailed pasture arrangements in Boyne and Enzie suggest. (See p. 249.) In David II's reign seven new alienations were made from royal forests, four of which occurred before 1350 and three thereafter.[72] One further grant of the lands of a forest, Cabrauch, was made in 1373/4. That lands in four forests were alienated after 1350 partially contradicts the picture given by Franklin and accepted in the *Cambridge Economic History*[73] that little new land was broken in after the Black Death. These grants show that areas previously reserved for game with limited pasture and agriculture were transformed to areas where grazing and ploughing could be pursued with complete freedom. While in these cases the agriculture and pasture restrictions may have been abused before these grants were made and while there is no evidence that agricultural and pastoral activities were pursued after these grants were made, they would have encouraged fresh economic activity. More definite evidence of the expansion of agriculture within a reserve can be found in Enzie, where in 1362 John Hay of 'Tolyboylle' received the right to 'redigere in culturam' certain lands in the forest,[74] and in Plater in 1375 where Alexander Lyndesay received the forestership with the herbage and forage and was forbidden to break in any new land, thus implying that he might otherwise have done so.[75]

This evidence, which relates mainly to Scotland north of the Forth, gives the impression that the economy of the country did not stagnate after the Black Death, a view which can be supported from the healthy state of the customs and of the royal finances at the end of David II's reign.[76] The degree of economic expansion in terms of agricultural activity, however, must not be exaggerated. The cultivation of new land in several forests after 1350 does not prove that land was being broken in elsewhere, because several of these forests such as Cabrauch, Glasgoforest, Enzie, Kintore and Glenken lay in the more remote parts of the kingdom where economic activity may only just have begun to reach the intensity attained in the south-east in the thirteenth century. Furthermore, forests by their nature would be some of the last areas to be given over to agriculture.

This picture of varying degrees of economic activity can be supplemented from the alienations and creations of parks in the fourteenth century. On the one hand several royal parks throughout the country were alienated during the fourteenth century,[77] thus suggesting increased economic activity on these lands. On the other hand sixteen baronial parks appeared for the first time in the fourteenth century,[78] which argues that there was land available to enclose and that the economic pressure on lands was not uniform throughout the country. It is not, however, certain that these parks were all created in the fourteenth century.

The history of hunting reserves in the fourteenth century thus offers a picture of limited economic expansion in some areas after 1350.

In the fifteenth century the alienations of forest lands are a less certain guide to the state of the country's economy because a conscious effort was made to preserve and increase the royal lands, which meant that economic pressure on forest lands would be less likely to result in alienations of forest lands, especially in the reigns of James I and James II, as the following table of alienations illustrates:

Alienations of forest lands

Reigns	Acts in *RMS*, ii	New Alienations
James I	200	0
James II	555	3
James III	974	1
James IV	2152	12

These figures perhaps underestimate the amount of economic pressure being placed on reserves, but they do suggest that the pressure was less than in the thirteenth and fourteenth centuries.

While it was possible for James II to maintain several reserves in the southern Central Highlands waste and to forgo rents when extending these reserves, opposition to such extension was raised by the exchequer during James III's minority.[79] The economic pressure thus came not from the farmers on the lands beside the forest but from the exchequer, presumably because it did not wish the king to alienate his rents. The economic pressure on reserves had thus adopted another form, that of the king's need for revenue as opposed to his need for hunting areas. It is important that on this occasion the interests of hunting predominated, since the needs both of the king's finances and of the people for agricultural and pastoral land could have been met by leasing the forest lands. Although in the Highlands the king's wish to maintain un-exploited reserves appears to have prevailed over economic pressure, else-where the leasing of forest lands which had begun in the fourteenth century was continued and probably expanded in certain forests in the fifteenth century. Leasing the lands of royal forests would, of course, lessen the demand for the alienation of forest lands by Great Seal charter.

The continuing demands being made on reserves can be seen in the leasing and exploitation of Campsie forest. By 1443 part of Campsie was let by

Coupar Abbey and an internal reserve created there.[80] Not even that reserve could be protected, since in 1474 tenants' cattle were allowed into it and in 1479 ploughing was permitted within part of the forest.[81] In the lands of Dumbarrow belonging to Arbroath Abbey similar encroachments may have taken place. Arbroath had held Dumbarrow in free forest but received it in 1319 as a park in free warren. The need for the perambulation of Dumbarrow conducted in 1434[82] may well have been the result of neighbouring landlords' encroachment on the park, for in 1483 it was let to one of those landlords, Alexander Garden.[83] While similar examples can be detected, they are not numerous, and so the history of hunting reserves in the earlier fifteenth century does not give the impression of an expanding economy. The encroachments already made in forests were most likely sufficient to meet the demands of agriculture and grazing being made at that time.

By James IV 's reign, however, economic pressure was once more making serious inroads into hunting reserves. Not only do more alienations of forest lands survive from James IV's reign than from those of his three immediate predecessors, but also in 1495 the forester of Boyne, the earl of Huntly, sold lands within the forest to Walter Ogilvie with the right to plough previously uncultivated land.[84] Moreover, at Redgorton between 1494 and 1500 purprestures were committed on the free forest of Andrew Lyall, prebendary of Brechin.[85] Various neighbours, the lairds of Essendy, Meikleour and Lethandy, had encroached and cultivated part of his forest with the result that in 1500 Lyall let the forest to Coupar with the right to cultivate the whole forest.[86] That a free forest might be cultivated and not be kept waste was recognised in 1508 when Cabrauch was granted to Alexander, Earl of Huntly, in free forest with the right either to cultivate the lands or to reserve them as a forest. The wish to cultivate land within free forests could have helped to occasion the free forest grant which applied only to woods,[87] thus permitting the protection of timber and game without restricting economic and pastoral activity on open land.

In Ettrick, where every attempt was made to accommodate economic activity, the effects of increased economic expansion are clearly visible towards the end of the fifteenth century. When Ettrick forest returned to the crown in 1455 it was already let to numerous tenants and consequently agriculture and pasture were fairly generally pursued, as the return of rents in kind, first recorded in 1468, shows.[88] Grazing was probably limited to certain recognised areas or by the number of animals allowed to graze, since sheep could still be fined for illegal grazing[89] and special permission to own sheep was still required. Sheep farming soon enjoyed a much greater degree of freedom, for in 1470 x 1473 sheep were entitled to graze on nine steads, five in Tweed, two at the east end of Ettrick and two in Yarrow. (See Table 24, p. 267.) Between 1476 and 1479 two more steads in Yarrow and one in Ettrick received this right as well as permission to erect 'casae' or shielings. With such freedoms the tenant could no doubt graze sheep anywhere on his holding, regardless of forest restrictions. Certain tenants also obtained the right to sub-let their lands, as in Galashiels in 1466 x 1467 and in Fairnilee in 1479 x 1480. Other steads obtained this right from 1498 onwards.[90] The total ban on agri-culture imposed by the 1499 statutes was something of a forlorn hope,[91] for although fines for ploughing, sowing and ditching were imposed in 1499, by 1509 freedom to plough in customary places had been granted to several tenants.[92] That certain places for ploughing were considered to be customary shows that ploughing had been common in the forest for some time. In Ettrick, therefore, it was sheep farming which first broke free from the restrictions imposed by the forest, and before the end of this period agriculture also was free on some steads. The fact that the crown did increase the length of leases to nine years and did set Ettrick in feu fermes argues that the economic development of the forest was being encouraged under increasingly lenient restrictions. The corollary is that there was a demand for facilities for economic activity

These indications of growing economic activity in the later fifteenth century and in James IV's reign are in accord with what is already known of the economy of Scotland at that time.[93] Consequently, reserves which lay in the lowlands or more developed parts of Scotland had to yield to and accommodate pastoral and agricultural activities, whereas in the southern central Highlands and in the north it was still possible for James II, James III and James IV to try to maintain reserves free of all economic exploitation. The policy of Scots kings in the fifteenth and early sixteenth centuries towards their hunting reserves was, therefore, influenced by the economic life of the areas in which their reserves were situated.

Hunting reserves by the nature of the rights which their owners enforced within them were bound to affect the lives of the people, as the study of the economic effects of reserves has revealed. The inhabitants of a forest were not entitled to hunt game as a sport or for food. What must be more closely examined is the extent to which these reserves caused economic hardship for the people. The effect of a reserve on the people would depend on the efficiency of the reserve's administration and the nature and number of the exemptions granted within the reserve — in short, on the owner's policy towards his reserve.

In the medieval period there were basically three different policies which lords of forests might adopt towards their reserves. Firstly, the holder of forest rights might decide to exclude completely all economic activity from the whole of his reserve. Into this category in the fifteenth and sixteenth centuries fall the royal reserves of Menteith, Ben More, Balquhidder and Mamlorne. No baronial example of a reserve of this type has been encountered. Secondly, the recipient of a forest grant or the king could decide to reserve only part of the area which he was entitled to reserve. This policy could take several forms. The lord of the forest might create an internal reserve or even a park in which all economic activity was forbidden and relax or abandon his forest rights on the rest of his lands, as happened in Renfrew in 1294/5 and as Robert I did in Drum, Kintore, Stocket, and Boyne and Enzie. In Gala and Leader, Ettrick, Renfrew, Ayr, Eskdale, and the Moray coast in the twelfth and thirteenth centuries, large areas of land within the forest were alienated to abbeys to exploit economically. Part of these forests was always retained by the lord. In other words the lord, whether a baron or the king, kept one part of his reserve as a strict hunting area with no economic activity but permitted grazing in certain areas of his reserve with varying degrees of freedom, depending on whether or not tolls were collected, how many huts could be built and whether or not the lord sent a forester on to the alienated lands. At a later date part of the forest might be rented rather than being alienated. .It was also possible that economic activity might be permitted within the specially reserved area on payment of heavier tolls, while agriculture and grazing could be pursued freely or under lighter tolls elsewhere. No example of this last variation of forest policy has been found, unless one considers the fines imposed in the reserved forest of Renfrew in 1294/5 to be tolls and not fines. Thirdly, an attempt could be made to accommodate economic activity within certain limitations throughout the forest without any specially reserved areas. In the mid and late fourteenth century, Boyne and Enzie, and Plater illustrate this type of reserve, as do Darnaway and most notably Ettrick in the fifteenth and sixteenth centuries. Here the reserve was run for profit and the hunting reserve had to co-exist with ploughing and grazing. Ultimately this policy could result in the collapse of the reserve and the removal of all restrictions of time, place and price from economic activity, as in Ettrick.

Obviously these policies would have different effects on the people who lived in and around the forests where they operated.

There can be no doubt that strict enforcement of the owner's rights, the prevention of grazing and wood-cutting, whether over all or part of a forest, would cause considerable hardship to tenants within or beside the reserve if they did not have the social standing to better their position. Even where the lord permitted economic activity on all or part of his forest, the effect could still be harsh if that activity was limited, carefully supervised and subject to tolls.

The inhabitants of Annandale, Ettrick and Stirling must have been adversely affected by the creation of these reserves. The tenants of Birse, who had originally lived outside·the royal forest of Birse in the twelfth century,[94] cannot have approved of the inclusion of their lands in Aberdeen's free forest of Birse in 1242.[95] Similarly, in the fifteenth century when James II expanded or declared waste his reserves as in the Menteith area, Ben More, Corriemuckloch and Glen Shervie in Strathearn, Mamlorne, Duchinloch, Cambuskist in Strathdee, Lochindorb and Darnaway, the tenants of these lands must have suffered considerable hardship.

Ultimately the hardship occasioned by any hunting reserve depended on its

T

administration, that is, on the foresters. There seems little doubt that, despite the inefficiency of medieval forest administration, foresters, paid from the proceeds of their exactions and able to impose fines without trial, could act harshly. While the harshness of foresters is never explicitly mentioned in the sources, it appears indirectly throughout the twelfth and thirteenth centuries. After the dispute of Melrose Abbey with Richard de Morville, the functions of their foresters were carefully defined, presumably to prevent any abuses arising.[96] In 1208 x 1214 Walter the third Steward clearly stipulated that Paisley Abbey was free to assart 'absque molestia et impedimento'.[97] In 1236, in the settlement of the dispute of Roger Avenel and Melrose Abbey, it had to be stated that the monks of Melrose and their men would not be adjudged trespassers when they went to graze their flocks.[98] In 1294/5, once again in Renfrew, James Steward provided that within the monks' lands in the forest of Renfrew none of his servants would seize any essential goods which were being taken to Paisley Abbey.[99] These provisions are most suitably interpreted as clauses inserted in charters or agreements to terminate abuses previously committed by foresters. The fourteenth-century forgery of a charter which granted the bishop of Aberdeen the right to choose one of the four foresters in the forest of Aberdeen may be interpreted in a similar manner.[100] The bishop may have felt that without his own forester his pasture rights within the forests would be abused or curtailed by the foresters of the king or of the burgh of Aberdeen. This problem must have continued into the fifteenth century, for in 1499 the commissioners of crown lands had to enquire into oppressors of the king's tenants and extortions made by officers upon the king's tenants,[101] and their letters of commission gave them the right to replace and appoint officials.[102] The harshness of officials would appear, however, to have been a more serious problem in the earlier medieval period.

The harshness of the forest system did penetrate the literature which was current in or related to medieval Scotland. Reginald of Durham tells the story of a miraculous stag hunted and killed by a certain Robert fitz Philip in 1165 in Lothian.[103] The dead stag had been left by the hunters and so when a comb-maker passed by he broke off the horns. When blood flowed on to him the craftsman was terrified because the blood would be taken as a sign that he had killed the stag and he would be punished. Although this story may be of English origin, it does suggest that the killing of a stag was not lightly under-taken without permission. In 'Johnnie Cock', a fifteenth-century Scottish ballad, the unpopularity of foresters is seen when they are portrayed as vindictively thirsting to capture the poacher:[104]

> There are seven forsters at Pickeram side
> At Pickeram where they dwell,
> And for a drop of thy heart's bluid
> They wad ride the fords of hell . . . .

It is thus apparent that while the leniency of the Scots as opposed to the English law[105] and the inefficiency of the forest administration might moderate the hardships occasioned by a strictly run hunting reserve, they did not remove these hardships.

In those forests where the lord created or retained an internal reserve while permitting his tenants' economic activity elsewhere, the restrictions imposed and, therefore, the inconvenience resulting cannot have been so severe. This type of partial reserve was probably the most common policy adopted in the medieval period. The lords of the forests, realising the severe limitations of their administration, the economic needs of their tenants, and the chance to profit from pasture tolls, must usually have permitted economic activity within a variety of limits. It is inconceivable that pasture was ever totally forbidden throughout the whole of such large forests as Renfrew, Annandale, Stirling, Ettrick and that round Elgin, Forres and Inverness. While the law may have permitted such restrictions and while in some areas they were applied, most landholders simply did not have the means or the wish to ban all economic activity. Thus the tenants of the external parts of Renfrew forest after 1294/5, of Plater in the fourteenth century[106] and of numerous other reserves of this type, while they could not pursue economic activity as readily as tenants who did not live in forests, cannot have been seriously troubled by the existence of a forest.

As the Middle Ages progressed, the difference in the control of game and wood within and outwith forests decreased, with the result that by the early sixteenth century it made little difference so far as these activities were concerned whether a tenant lived inside or outside a reserve.[107] That life within a forest where an attempt was made to accommodate economic activity was not unduly harsh explains why there was no shortage of tenants in Ettrick and why the same families continued to live within the forest.[108] In Ettrick in 1501 most tenants were willing to pay a substantial increase in their rent in order to have greater security of tenure. Admittedly inflation may have reduced the effect of the increases, but it is significant that the remaining forest restrictions in Ettrick, especially on wood and grazing, did not act as a disincentive to paying an increased rent. In Ettrick, while forest restrictions were enforced with varying degrees of efficiency, pasture and ploughing were permitted and adequate exemptions for expansion were granted so that there was no great inconvenience when leasing lands in the forest. This must also have been true of such forests as Clunie, Alyth, Killanel, and Boyne and Enzie in the fourteenth and fifteenth centuries. The increasing use of a free forest grant only in wooded areas would also have considerably reduced the inconvenience caused by the creation of a baronial reserve. In those reserves where economic activity was accommodated, the inefficiency of the administration would encourage people to continue living there and would enable them to abuse if not to ignore the regulations.

Furthermore, the king and his government showed concern for the well-being of the people in various ways. The king afforested only lands which were in his own hands, and fines for forest offences were not only remitted as a favour but also on account of the offender's poverty.[109] If the king damaged someone's corn or field while out hawking or hunting he would pay compensation to the farmer,[110] and where crops were lost to a forest extension he might occasionally grant compensation.[111]

In short, while hunting reserves could create genuine suffering in Scotland, in general they caused inconvenience rather than hardship. Although the attitude of the people towards hunting reserves is obscure, it may be most accurately reflected in the fourteenth- or early fifteenth-century poem entitled 'Rauf Coilzear'. Built on the familiar theme of a poor man giving shelter to the king *incognito* who had lost his way while out hunting, this poem includes a unique passage in which Rauf describes how he lived in dread of the foresters:[112]

> Schir the forestaris forsuith of this forest
> Thay have me all at invy for dreid of the deir
> Thay thriep that I thring doun the fattest
> Thay say I sall to Paris thair to compeir
> Befoir our cumlie king in dule to be drest
> Sic manassing thay me mak forsuith ilk zeir
> And zit aneuch sall I have for me and ane gest . . .
>
> Of caponnis and cunningis thay had plentie
> With wyne at thair will and eik vennysoun.

Looking at the medieval period as a whole, the twelfth century has emerged as the era of royal and baronial hunting reserves *par excellence*. By the thirteenth century economic activity had begun to make considerable inroads into many reserves and the holders of forests were forced to make concessions against their will. In the fourteenth and fifteenth centuries barons showed a distinct preference for specific reserves, rabbit warrens and parks, because they were more easily administered than free forests and warrens and because they would counteract any possible shortage of game. Consequently, the free forest and free warren grants were eclipsed by the barony and regality grants, the warren grant never to recover. It was also easier to control poaching in parks, an important consideration in the fourteenth century when an increasing number of people had the right to hunt because of the decline of servility. The free forest grant also was devalued in the fourteenth and early fifteenth centuries by the growing restrictions on timber-cutting outside reserves and by the developing ability of barons who held no forest rights to prevent other people hunting on their lands. Not till the later fifteenth century did the forest grant return to prominence on account of the protection not of game, but of timber, which it offered.

The Scottish forest system has also been seen to display certain characteristic features. Firstly, there are signs of a practical common sense. The forest system was marked by several theoretical contradictions. The right to the greater game to which the king was entitled through his control of the free forest grant contradicted the existence of parks where barons could enclose deer at will. The king's entitlement to lesser game, which was derived from his control of the free warren grant, contradicted the principle that the lesser game was *res nullius*. In both instances a practical compromise or solution was found and the theoretical position was placed second to practical considerations. In the first instance the king seldom if ever claimed his right to the greater game and deer were supposed to be free to leave and enter parks. In the second case, the separate free warren grant was discontinued in the fourteenth century, by which time rabbit warrens were probably becoming more popular.

Secondly, the Scots forest system is marked by a considerate attitude towards the people of the country. This characteristic is of importance, for hunting reserves, created at a time when hunting was no longer a necessity alone but also a sport, were the privilege of the 'worthy men' and of the king. Not only was the Scots forest law more considerate than the English, but the Scots system was less rigid: common pasture was permitted within reserves; the divisions of types of game were less precise than in England; and the king did on occasion compensate hardship.

Thirdly, the forest system in Scotland was flexible. Petit Dutaillis considered that the total area of the royal forests reflected the power of the central authority.[113] In this view he was considering primarily the ability of the central authority to withstand political pressure, but in Scotland it has been shown that economic pressure was equally important. Because hunting reserves withdrew certain economic resources from general use, the owner of a reserve had to possess a certain degree of authority or power if he was to preserve these resources against the economic pressure for extending their use. Consequently, economic pressure and the holder's power could be reflected not only in the size of a reserve but also in the nature of a reserve. It has been shown how some forests at one time maintained as hunting reserves ceased to be so because of economic activity and how different types of reserves were established in different areas. The owner's policy towards his reserve was influenced by the economic environment of his reserve. Consequently, the people were able to influence the development of this landholders' privilege. In this sense the Scottish forest system was flexible. The owners of hunting reserves, although they could prohibit or severely limit economic exploitation in an attempt to maintain their forests solely as hunting reserves, usually permitted such activities throughout all or part of their reserves. It thus follows that the overall effect of these reserves on the people was not harsh and that the history of hunting reserves was not marked by that acrimony, seen in Magna Carta and the Forest Charter, which characterised the English forest system.

As an institution, therefore, Scottish hunting reserves possessed that ability which may be considered the greatest strength of any institution which tries to control human relations and activities, the ability to adapt to varying circumstances.

Table 23. ECONOMIC CONCESSIONS AND DISPUTES

Owner of Reserve	Name of Reserve	Date of 1st Concessions	Evidence of Disputes	Further Concessions
King and de Morvilles	Gala and Leader	1161 x 1165 (RRS, i, 235)	1180 (RRS, ii, 236); 1184 (Chron. Melrose, 44); 1208 (Melr. Lib., 101)	1236 (Melr. Lib., 258)
King	Leithen[1]			
Stewards	Renfrew	1165 x 1173 (Pais Reg., 5)	1219 (Newb. Reg., 121); 1208 x 1214 (Pais. Reg., 17); Detailed pasture provisions perhaps resulting from dispute	1241 (Newb. Reg., 120); 1208 x 1214 (Pais. Reg., 17; RRS, ii, 518); 1219 x 1230 (Pais. Reg., 253)
	Ayr	1165 x 1174 (Melr. Lib., 66; RRS, ii, 78)	1204 (Concilia Scotiae, 234)	1204 x 1214 (NMS, 53; Melr. Lib., 73, *73); 1264 (Melr. Lib., 324); 1266 (Ibid., 325)
	Sanquhar	1208 x 1214 (Pais. Reg., 18)		
Muschamps	Trolhope (Northumberland)	1182/1214 x 1232 (Melr. Lib., 305)	1182/1214 x 1232 (Melr. Lib., 305, 307); Detailed arrangements perhaps settling a dispute	
Walter, son of Turpin	Ochtirlony		1226 x 1239 (Arb. Lib., 306, 232)	
Avenels	Eskdale	1165 x 1169 (Melr. Lib., 39)	1235 (Melr. Lib., 198)	
Lyndesays	Crawford	1185 x 1200 (Newb. Reg., 135)		c 1249 (Newb. Reg., 143-145)

1. Possibly a forest.

Table 24. ECONOMIC ACTIVITY IN ETTRICK

This table lists the steads in which certain economic activities were permitted. Only the earliest reference for each activity is given for any one stead. Where royal flocks or herds were kept on a stead, the word 'stelebow' is entered.

Ettrick Ward

Stead	Date[1]	Activity	Source[2]
Mid-Fauside	1477	sheep and shielings	viii, 439
Harehead	1473	sheep	viii, 142
	1502	stelebow	xii, 33
Haining	1473	sheep	viii, 142
East Gildhouse	1499	passage and pasture	xi, 398
Fawoodshiel	1502	stelebow	xii, 34
Catcarmauch	1468	royal stud	vii, 528
Eldinhope	1500	stelebow	xi, 206
Altrieve	1502	stelebow	xii, 34
Bowhill	1467	stelebow	vii, 478

Yarrow Ward

Fairmanhope	1502	stelebow	xii, 32
Gartlacheuch or	1502	stelebow	*Ibid.*
Blackhouse	1502	stelebow	*Ibid.*
Douglas Craig	1500	stelebow	xi, 204
East and West Mount- benger	1457	stelebow	vi, 373
Catslack	1468	stelebow	vii, 530
Blackgrain	1468	stelebow	*Ibid.*
Deuchar	1502	stelebow	xii, 34
Tinnis	1502	stelebow	xii, 32
Lewenshope	1471	sheep	viii, 101
Hangingshaw	1502	stelebow	xii, 32
Yair	1469	stelebow	vii, 621
Williamhope	1479	sheep	viii, 585
Glengaber	1502	stelebow	xii, 32

Tweed Ward

Gaithope	1502	stelebow	xii, 32
Gaithope/Seathope	1500	stelebow	xi, 206
Holylee and Thornylee	1471	shielings	viii, 48
	1473	sheep	viii, 140
Caddonlee	1478	shielings	viii, 480
Galashiels	1466 x 1467	shielings and subletting	vii, 476
Mossilee	1470	sheep	viii, 48
Blindlee	1502	stelebow	xii, 33
Galashiels	1478	shielings	viii, 480
Fairnilee	1480	subletting	ix, 30

1. Date given is the year of the end of the account.
2. All references are to the *Exchequer Rolls*.

APPENDICES

APPENDIX A
The Forest Laws

Previous Editions and Examinations

The forest laws have already been edited by C. Innes and T. Thomson[1] and by Professor M. L. Anderson.[2] In *The Acts of the Parliament of Scotland (APS)* Innes and Thomson provided a description of the manuscript volumes consulted and a comparative table of the clauses in those manuscripts.[3] Anderson used only those manuscripts mentioned in *APS* and carried out some very loose collation of them. Since the manuscript volumes which contain the forest laws also contain *Regiam Majestatem*, they have been examined as part of the study of *Regiam Majestatem* by J. Buchanan,[4] H. G. Richardson,[5] Professor A. A. M. Duncan,[6] and Lord Cooper.[7] Some of these manuscripts have been studied by J. J. Robertson in his edition of 'De Composicione Cartarum'.[8] It was necessary to compile a new edition of the forest laws because the previous editions were not based on a full collation nor on all the available manuscripts, and one lost manuscript was found.

The Manuscripts

In the preparation for this edition of the forest laws the following 24 manuscripts were consulted:

Name	Date/Century	Ref. Letters[1]		APS[2]	Location
Bute	mid 14th	(A)	B	X	EUL Microfilm no. 131
Cromertie	late 14th, early 15th	(B)	C	X	NLS Ms 25.5.10
Edinburgh University	late 14th, early 15th	(L)	E	X	EUL Ms 206
Harleian	early 15th	(L) [O]	H	X	BM Ms Harleian 4700
Edinburgh University	mid 15th	(M) [M]	Ed		EUL Ms 207

1. The reference letters in column (1) are those used by Buchanan. Robertson's reference letters are given in square brackets. The reference letters of the present edition are given in the third column.
2. Those mss. marked with an X were consulted by the editors of the first volume of the *APS*.

271

Name	Date/Century	Ref. Letters		APS	Location
St Andrews	mid 15th	(T) [T]	S		St Andrews University Library Ms K.F. 51-R4
Arbuthnott	mid 15th	[W]	A		NLS Ms Acc 2006
National Library	late 15th		N	X	NLS Ms 24.4.15
Drummond	late 15th	(K)	D	X	SRO Search Room, P A5/3
Monynet	1488	(D) [D]	M	X	NLS Ms 25.5.6
Colville	late 15th, c 1496	(N) [N]	Co	X	EUL Ms 208
Cambridge University	c 1541	(R) [R]	Ca	X	Cambridge University Library Ms Ee.4.21
Hailes	15th-16th		Ha	X	NLS Ms 25.4.11
John Bannatyne	1520	(F)	J	X	NLS 25.5.9
Lambeth Palace 1	early 16th	(P) [P]	L_1	X	Lambeth Palace Ms 167 f 212 r
Lambeth Palace 2	early 16th	(P) [P]	L_2	X	Lambeth Palace Ms 167 f 217 r
Yelverton 1	mid 16th		Y_1		BM Add Ms 48050
Yelverton 2	c 1570		Y_2		BM Add Ms 48032
Thomas Bannatyne	mid-late 16th	(H) [H]	T	X	NLS Ms 25.4.12
Malcolm	late 16th		Ma	X	NLS Ms 7.1.9
Edzell	1555-1601		Ez		NLS Ms 25.9.7
Balfour 1	1593		Bal_1		NLS Ms 24.2.4 b
Balfour 2	late 16th		Bal_2		NLS Ms 24.2.4
First Skene	1601-2		Es	X	NLS Ms 7.1.10

Of these 24 manuscripts, 16 are described in *APS*. Those three in Edinburgh University Library are described in C. R. Borland's *Catalogue of Western Manuscripts*.[9] The St Andrews manuscript has been discussed by Buchanan[10] and the Arbuthnott manuscript by Richardson,[11] Robertson[12] and Duncan.[13] The Balfour manuscripts are mentioned in the *Summary Catalogue of the Advocates' Manuscripts*,[14] while both are considered in the Stair Society's edition of *Balfour's Practicks*.[15]

The Edzell manuscript was previously known only from marginal notes in the First Skene manuscript of 1601-2 beside clauses 1 and 16, where a manuscript belonging to 'Domini Lindesay de Edzel militis Senatoris in supremo senatu' was recorded by Skene. This manuscript was discovered when following up information from Dr. J. Bannerman that there was a manuscript of the forest laws in the Riddel Papers in the National Library of Scotland (NLS). Originally catalogued as RC 19, this manuscript is now catalogued as MS 25.9.7. The forest laws are written on 6 folios now bound with other original papers. These 6 folios have at one time been folded with f1 as the covering page. On f1 r in the top right-hand corner is written 'Leges Forestarum' in a seventeenth-century hand. Below it is written in pencil 'Edzell Charter Chest'. The laws commence on f2 r and are written in a hand of the later sixteenth century. This manuscript must have been compiled before 1601-2 when it was consulted by Skene and after 1555 since a law of that date is given in c 21. It was probably written between 1555 and 1578 since c 22, the last clause, written in a hand different from that which wrote the other clauses, contains a law of 1578.

In future these manuscripts will be known by their reference letters listed above. Only those laws which related to forest matters were transcribed in full, since most manuscripts also included a larger number of miscellaneous laws in their collections of forest laws. These miscellaneous laws were noted only by their rubric.

Method of Collation

To determine which ms. or mss. represented the best tradition and so to provide an edition as close as possible to the original it was necessary to collate or compare the manuscripts. Collation of the manuscripts was facilitated by the content of the laws, since the correct version of a law could on many occasions be decided by the sense and by comparision with what is known of forests from other sources. Before starting the collation, certain principles were accepted:

(a) A ms. without rubrics, numbers or spaces between the clauses represents an older tradition than a ms. which includes any one or any combination of these features. This argument, first put forward by R. W. Southern,[16] is based on the view that a scribe would not purposely be less precise when copying a text, because this would hinder future reference or cross reference. A scribe confronted by a set of laws separated in some form would not choose to run them all together, unless compelled to do so by shortage of space. It follows, therefore, that a ms. with rubrics and spaces between the laws is of a later tradition than a ms. without these features.

(b) Error in transcription in one ms. indicates not only that it is a copy of another, but also that it is secondary to a manuscript which does not contain that error. Error in transcription is usually detected by an alteration to, or error in, the sense of a law such as would not be expected in an original ms. Such mistranscription might arise for three reasons: (i) carelessness, e.g., 'abductis testibus' for 'adductis testibus' in clause 1; (ii) the scribe's inability to decipher an abbreviation, e.g., 'vice' for 'veteri' in S in clause 8; and (iii) the scribe's ignorance of what the correct version should be, e.g., the errors which occur in fifteenth-century manuscripts in clause 8 which concerns pannage, a custom which had died out by the fourteenth century.

(c) Omissions and/or additions, again recognisable by alterations in the sense, have to be considered. It is only the sense which can tell whether the absence in one ms. of a line or two, given in other mss., represents the correct version or an omission by that scribe. For instance, in clause 21 Co omits from 'erit de illo facto quietus' to 'ipse cuius fuerit mastinus', with the result that this law reads as though a man was guilty of an offence if he had his dog chained or on a lead. This is obviously an omission, since every other ms. reads that a man was innocent when the dog was chained and guilty when it was not chained. In clause 8, E and B have 'meliorem', whereas all the other mss. have 'meliorem porcum'. Since 'porcum' clarifies the meaning, it must be considered as an addition in later mss. rather than an omission in B and E.

(d) It is possible for several changes to appear in a text in the course of one copying. Consequently, if there are two mss., A and a derivative B, and if B has three variations from A, this does not mean that there were two intervening mss., since all three variants might be the work of B's scribe.

(e) Although a ms. of late date may represent the earliest tradition, it is assumed that if two mss. were alike, one early and the other late, the later ms. was copied from the earlier either directly or indirectly unless there are strong reasons to the contrary.

(f) When it is stated that M was copied from H, it means that M or a ms. very like M was copied from H or a ms. very like H. There is, in fact, no way of proving that one manuscript was directly copied from another manuscript unless the manuscript actually states that it was copied from that other manuscript.

By collating these differences between manuscripts, it is possible to allocate the manuscripts to groups or families. Each group or family has a parent manuscript and several of these groups may form a tradition. Traditions are derived from varying redactions of the original or autograph. The parent manuscript of a tradition is known as an archetype. The differences between traditions are usually greater than the difference between families.

Before tackling the textual collation, the clauses included in the various manuscripts were collated and the results tabulated. In the following table the mss. consulted are listed along the top, including the edition in *APS*, and the numbers of the clauses in the present edition are listed down the lefthand side. The other columns contain the number given to these clauses in the various mss.

From this tabulation four groups of clauses emerged, clauses 1-11, clauses 12-18, clauses 19-23/24, and the 80 or more miscellaneous non-forest clauses, not tabulated, which occurred after clause 11 and after clause 24. Every ms. included clauses 1-11, whereas only six mss. included all or some of clauses 12-18. Most mss. included clauses 19-23 but only six included clause 24. Each group of clauses was collated in turn, since it seemed possible that the best

Comparative Table of Clauses

B	C	E	H	Ed	S	A	N	D	M	Co	Ca	Ha	J	L₁	L₂	Y₁	Y₂	T	Ma	Ez	BaL₁	BaL₂	Es	APS
1	1	X	1	1	1	1	X	1	1	1	1	2	1	1	2	2	1	1	1	1	1	1	1	1
2	2	X	2	2	2	2	X	2	2	2	2	3	2	2	2 3	3	2	2	2	2	2	2	2	2
3	3 4	X	3	3	3	3	X	3	3	3 4	3	4	3	3	3	4	3	3	3	in 3	in 3	in 3	3	3
4	5	X	4	in 4	4	4	X	4	4	5	4	5	4	4	4	5	4	4	4	4	4	5	4	4
5	6	X	5	5	5	5	X	5	5	6	5	6	5	5	4 5	6	5	5	5	5	5	5	5	5
6	7	X	6	6	6	6	X	6	6	7	6	7	6	5	6	7	6	6	6	6	6	6	6	6
7	7	X	7	7	7	7	X	7	7	8	7	8	7	6	6	7	7	7	7	7	7	7	7	6
8	8 9	X	8	8	8	8	X	8	8	9	8	9	8	7	7	8	8	8	8	8	8	8	8	6
9	10	X	9	9	9	9	X	9	9	10	9	10	9	8, 9	8 9	9	9	9	9	9	9	9	9	7
10	11	X	10	10	10	10	X	10	10	11	10	11	10	10	9	11	10	10	10	9	11	11	10	8
11	12	X	11	11	11	11	X	11	11	11	11	13	11	11	11	11	11	11	11	11	7	7	16	9
12	13											7								13, 14	in 13	in 13	17	15
13																				in 13	14	14	18	16
14	14						X													13	in 13	in 13	17	17
15	15						X													in 13	in 13	in 13	18	18
16	16						X																17	19
17	17						X																in 17	20
18	in 18						X																	21
19		X	89	89	88	89		89	89	14	88	1, 14	89		88	12 in 1	88	88	87	15	15	15	11	10
20		X	90	90	89	90	X	90	90	15	89	15	90		89	13	89	89	88	17	17	17	12	11
21		X	90	90	89	90		90	90	15	89	12	90		89	10	89	89	88		10	10	13	12
22		X	91	91	90	91		91	91	16	90	16	91		90	in 14	90	90	89		in 12	in 12	14	13
23		X	92	92	91	92	X	92	92	17	91	17	92		91	in 14	91	91	90		12	12	15	in 23
24		X					X													16	16	16	20	22

Note: 'In 4', as in column Ed, means that a part of clause 4 in the present edition is contained in Ed clause 4. The clauses in E and N were not originally numbered.

version of each group might be found in different mss. The rubrics of the miscellaneous clauses were collated last. From the table of clauses it became evident that certain mss., Co, Ha, Ez, Bal$_1$, Bal$_2$, Y$_1$, Y$_2$, and Es, had rearranged the clauses and that they were most likely edited mss. These mss. were collated separately and only the best, Ez, was used in the preparation of the present edition. The collation of these mss. and of L$_1$, which also proved to be edited, is given below after the examination of the miscellaneous clauses.

Although the collation is conducted by groups of clauses, the relations of mss. discovered when collating one group of clauses can be applied to the same mss. in a following group of clauses. To facilitate comprehension of the collation, a select transcription of the most important clauses referred to in the collation is given at the end of this Appendix. While nearly all the examples used in support of arguments given in the collation are presented in this select transcription, it is to be understood that other examples to support these arguments can be found in other clauses and that only the most important examples are given in the collation and the select transcription.

To assist the detection of the best version of each group of clauses, stemmata were constructed to show graphically the relation of the various mss. When a limited number of mss. are under consideration the primary mss., that is those at the head of the stemmata, could be expected to be the most accurate, though this was not always so. It cannot, moreover, be assumed that the earliest mss. chronologically are the most accurate.

There are, however, certain difficulties in producing a stemma. Firstly, edited mss. which draw on several sources cannot be placed on a stemma, and even non-edited mss. can be open to more than one tradition, with the result that one can only hope to represent the main line of influence. Where a scribe copies a few words or phrases from another tradition that manuscript is said to be polluted. Secondly, numerous mss. have been lost — two mss. referred to in Ez are no longer extant — which prevents the construction of direct links between mss. Thirdly, each ms. is the product of two influences, the ms. or mss. on which it was based and the scribe's alterations and/or mistakes, and if a scribe makes several alterations or mistakes it is difficult to decide which type of ms. he was copying. Finally, a stemma or genealogy has to be represented in two dimensions, and certain links, therefore, are impossible or clumsy to draw. A stemma can take various forms. It may be drawn like a family tree[17] or on a circular pattern with the autograph in the centre and the copies stretching out towards the circumference.[18] The former is by far the more common and has been adopted here. Where two manuscripts are connected by a solid line, the connection is very close and possibly direct. A broken line indicates that the link is less certain and indirect.

Nevertheless, as the collation proceeded it became evident that certain groups of mss. could be neatly drawn in stemmata but that a complete stemma representing all the mss. would be at best somewhat loose and arbitrary.

In view of the complex nature of the surviving mss. of the forest laws, it was impossible to determine editorial policy before completing the collation, but two possibilities were under consideration: firstly, to give an edition based on the single best ms. for each group of clauses; and secondly, to present a composite edition based on the best mss. for each group of laws. It was decided to adopt whichever practice would render the edition as close as possible to the original, which is not extant.

The Collation

Clauses 1-11

The format of the mss. suggests that B, E, C, N, and L₁ represent earlier copyings than all the other mss. None of these mss. has rubrics, while B and E have neither rubrics for nor spaces between the clauses, whereas all other mss. have both rubrics for and spaces between the clauses, B, E, C, and N are probably earlier than L₁ since in clause 8 they have simply 'pannagii', although in B 'ponagii' has been added later as a gloss, whereas L₁ and all other mss. add either 'oportet' or 'videlicet'. This addition is unlikely to have arisen from the 'ponagii' of B since, however else it might have been transcribed, it does not resemble 'oportet' or 'videlicet' which must, therefore, be later additions. That B, E, and C are primary mss. is borne out by the most complicated section in clause 8 and indeed in the first 11 clauses. Clause 8 proved most valuable when collating these mss. because the custom of pannage, which it describes, died out towards the end of the thirteenth century and consequently much more variation occurs in clause 8 than in the other clauses. B, E and C have 'rex nichil habebit set forestarius habebit unum hog', while N omits this sentence, and all the other mss., apart from A, Ed, D and Ez, contain 'rex non habebit nisi unum hoggastrum'. A, Ed, D and Ez can at present be discounted as secondary to B, E and C for reasons of format already given. In the first version of this sentence in clause 8 the hog goes to the forester and in the second to the king. The former represents the earlier version, since the simple and accidental omission of 'set forestarius habebit' would lead to the second reading and it is hard to imagine any reason why a conscious attempt would have been made to change the law by adding that phrase in the fourteenth or fifteenth century when the custom of collecting pannage had already died out. N's omission of this passage renders it unsuitable for the basis of an edition of the first 11 clauses, and since it is in Scots, it must be a later copy.

Of the three remaining mss., C may be set aside as the base for an edition since it includes many readings peculiar to itself and is in many ways an explanatory version of B and E: in clause 8, C alone omits 'si aliqui ibi fuerint'; in clause 1 it alone adds 'ad forisfactum' and 'vel berset'; and in clause 2 it alone adds 'vel cornizare menetum', all of which provide clarification of B and E. These readings are sufficiently numerous to suggest that manuscript C represents a different tradition from B and E, and they may well result from a separate redaction.

U

B and E represent the best version of their tradition. Neither has rubrics for nor spaces between the clauses, although in B the clauses are numbered in the left margin. Moreover, in clause 1 only B and E have 'meliorem', whereas all the other mss. have 'meliorem porcum' by way of explanation. It is impossible to separate B and E. B could be considered secondary on account of its inclusion of clause numbers, but it includes the break, omitted in E, after 'pannacionis' in clause 1 required by the sense. It has been suggested that the first part of this clause concerns the time of fence, reading 'fannacionis' for 'pannacionis', but all mss. give the latter reading. As will be explained (see p. 312) clause 1 is probably a condensed version of three laws and it is essential to have a break between the first section on pannage and the second section on the time of fence. In clause 1 also E concludes with 'producuntur' and B with 'perduntur', while in clause 2 these readings are reversed.

B is perhaps the slightly better ms. but it is impossible to print one ms. without including some mistakes as with 'producuntur' in clauses 1 or 2. A more accurate edition of clauses 1-11 can, therefore, be obtained by using B and E, and where they vary and neither is obviously correct, N can be used to decide which version to follow, since it is more accurate than C, or if the Scots of N renders this impossible, C can be used. Important variants from all four mss. are given in the footnotes.

At this point B, C and E can be fitted into a stemma by using the content of their versions of the forest laws and the fact that none of them represents the original version of the law. It should be noted that although E includes clauses 19-23 and the miscellaneous clauses in its *tabula*, it does not give the text of these clauses. The relationship of B, E and C can be summarised as follows:

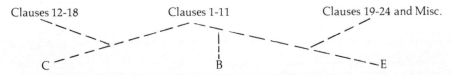

Clauses 12-18   Clauses 1-11   Clauses 19-24 and Misc.

C   B   E

Previous editions of the forest laws have included certain inaccuracies in their versions of clauses 1-11. In the first volume of *APS*, the editors have correctly based their edition on B and E: in clause 1 'warseth' is from E; in clause 4, 'ld capiat tantum de grege' is from B; and in clause 8 'et hic enim' is from E. They have also used readings from C: in clause 5 'inveniebantur'; and from H: in clause 2 'menetum' as in the present edition. The *APS* edition does, however, combine clauses 6, 7 and 8, even although they are numbered separately in B and arranged separately in N. In clause 9 the preference of 'pullum' from C rather than 'pullanum' from B and E is puzzling, and in clause 11 'non agnoverit' has been printed instead of 'non noverit' or 'agnoverit', and the final phrase in that clause is taken from C, 'suam de eo fecerit voluntatem' when the reading of the better tradition of B and E is quite satisfactory. The editors of *APS* have also printed the Scots of N.

Professor M. L. Anderson, by printing the Scots of N, has preferred a later version, since the earliest version must have been in Latin. Otherwise N contains a fairly reliable version except on three important occasions: in clause 1, N so condenses the original as to omit any reference to pannage; and in clause 8, N omits from 'rex nichil habebit' to 'unum hog' and gives 'the best swyn', both of which readings are secondary.

Clauses 12-18

Of the three mss. collated, Ez is an edited ms., and certain features in C and N suggest that their scribes, if not actually editing the forest laws, were doing more than simply copying their exemplars. It has already been explained that C contains additional explanatory phrases, and N's treatment of clause 1 to exclude pannage and its exclusion of the miscellaneous laws argues that the author of N altered his exemplars as he thought fit.

C cannot form the basis of an edition since it contains serious omissions. In clause 14 it omits 'leash' and 'lets', both essential to the sense and included in N and Ez. It would appear that C is a poor copy of its Latin exemplar, since the scribe could not decipher some words and so left them blank and also in clause 14 probably copied 'liber' instead of 'libere'. It does, however, contain the correct version of clause 8, as does Ez which, as an edited ms., cannot be taken as the basis of an edition. N is, therefore, the best ms., although it includes a serious omission in clause 8, and in clause 14 gives 'with chalance of any man' instead of 'without' as in Ez and C.

The edition should, therefore, use C and N, giving preference to N, and where C and N disagree and neither version seems appropriate, Ez can be used to decide which reading is the more accurate. Although N and Ez are both in Scots, the present edition has been given in Latin since the models of C, which is in Latin, and of N were in Latin. An example of the Scots of N shows that it is a literal translation of a Latin ms: in clause 17, 'apper and pruf that befor lauchfully to perten till him'. The Scots of Ez has been rearranged to 'compeiris and offeris him to preif lauchfullie that the same pertenis to him'. Since Ez copied these clauses from the lost ms. Car, one can only assume that Car had a similarly rearranged wording in Scots. It could quite easily, however, have been a Latin manuscript.

Clause 18, of which the major part survives only in Scots, is given in Scots. A translation into Latin from the Latin-style Scots of N is given in brackets alongside. A full discussion of this translation is given in the section on principles of translation.

In view of the necessity of providing a Latin text, the editorial policy for these clauses was revised. While an edition based on C alone would be inaccurate for the reasons already given, it was felt that a Latin version based only on the Scots of N would be wrong when a Latin ms., C, is extant. The edition is, therefore, based on C corrected by N. Such corrections are annotated and important variants of all three mss. are given in the footnotes.

It is possible to construct a stemma for these three mss. Since C is in Latin, it must be earlier, though not necessarily more accurate, than N and Ez. N and Ez, though similar, have enough differences to make it clear that neither was copied from the other. The most striking example of the similarity of N and Ez is that they both finish clause 18, which C terminates after the first few lines. Since Ez includes the correct version of clause 8, it cannot be copied from N, and N, since it is a translation of a Latin ms. and since it gives 'with' instead of 'without' in clause 14, as mentioned above, cannot be copied from Ez. They may both, nonetheless, have had a common parent ms. N and Ez cannot be derived from C, since they both include a selection of clauses 19-24 omitted in C and since they include readings not found in C, as in clause 18 and in clause 14: N 'that man sal frely tak'; Ez 'that man incontinent sal tak'; and C 'idem liber reportabit'. It is possible, however, that the parent ms. of C could also be the parent ms. of N and Ez. It is unlikely that Car was the parent manuscript of N, since N includes clause 16, but Ez, which states that it copies the second group of clauses from Car, excluded clause 16, thus suggesting that Car did not include clause 16. Since these manuscripts are the only ones to include clauses 12-18, they form a distinct tradition. This information can be summarised graphically as follows:

Clauses 12-18   Clauses 1-11

C   Clauses 19-24

[Car]   N

Ez

Ez, an edited manuscript, also used a source other than Car, but that source cannot be represented on this stemma.

The edition of these clauses in *APS* gives both the Latin of C and the Scots of N but does not correct C with N, with the result that in clause 14 'reportavit' is given rather than 'libere reportabit'. In clause 18, of which C includes only the first few lines, the editors of *APS* continued with a Latin translation of a Scots ms. but unfortunately translated Es and not N. After preferring N for their Scots edition, the reasons for translating Es are somewhat obscure, but perhaps they wished to reserve N solely for their Scots version. The result is that the *APS* edition of clause 18 contains secondary readings: *APS*, 'iste malefactor convictus de tali transgressione ad instantiam baronis in curia regis'; and the present parallel text based on N, 'aliquis liber delinquans ad sectam baronis in curia regis de sic transgressione legittime convictus'. In addition, when translating from Scots into Latin, the editors did not give sufficient attention to the Latin style of other clauses in the forest laws: clause

14 'permittet' is probably better than 'patitur', which occurs nowhere else in the forest laws.

Once again Professor M. L. Anderson prints the Scots of N, even although these laws were originally written in Latin. N also contains a few inferior readings: in clause 12 it gives '8d', as a result of confusion with '8 Ky', instead of 'unum d'; at the end of clause 17 Ez may well contain a better reading than N and C; and in clause 18, N gives simply 'forest' instead of 'foresta libera'.

Clauses 19-24

Although all of these clauses were borrowed from English sources, clause 24 must be considered separately, since it occurs only in N and Ez. The edition of the other English clauses cannot be based on those mss. which have already been shown to be primary, since E only gives the rubric of these clauses and N, to avoid duplication with clauses 12-18, omits some clauses and alters others to fit Scottish circumstances. The edition of clauses 19-23 must, therefore, be based on secondary mss.

Of these mss., Ed, A and D represent the best family. In clause 21 they conclude 'qualis fuerit canis', whereas H, S, M, Ca, J, L_2, T and Ma conclude 'qualis fuerit casus'. 'Canis', which makes more sense than 'casus', is also the reading given in N. Ed, A and D are also the only mss. in this group to contain the correct reading of clause 8.

Of these three mss., A emerges as marginally the best copy. Ed in clause 4 omits the second part which begins 'de ovibus . . .', and in clause 21 it omits 'Et ipse cuius mastivus fuerit'. A also contains a better version of clauses 19-23 than D: in clause 19, A 'memoria', D 'memoriam'; A 'inveniet', D 'invenit'; and A 'attachiare', D 'attachiari'. In clause 19 also, by comparison with English mss., A's inclusion of 'et retineri' is more accurate than D's omission of that phrase.

Before determining the editorial policy for these clauses, the other mss. must be examined more carefully with a view to providing the more important of the variant readings. H, S, M, Ca, J, L_2, T and Ma can be separated by collating their versions of clauses 1-11. H, M, and J form one group, since they alone add 'illa animalia' in clause 1 and give 'porcis' instead of 'porcorum' in clause 8. These three mss. are virtually identical, with only minor variations: in clause 1, H 'warsatte', M 'warsaite' and J 'warsett'; and in clause 8, H, M 'iste est modus', J 'Item est modus'. The earliest ms. chronologically, H, can, therefore, be taken as the best representative of this group.

S and L_2 also form a separate group, since they contain several unique readings: in clause 8 both give 'vice' in mistranscription of 'veteri'; in clause 1, S presents 'varset' and L_2 'versate'; and in clause 11 both mss. contain 'per forestam'. S is the best ms. of this family, since L_2 omits part of clause 8 and confuses clauses 4 and 5.

The remaining mss. Ca, T and Ma also form a group which can be detected by their omissions in clause 21; Ca and T omit from 'quietus erit' to 'mastivus fuerit'; and Ma omits from 'et ipse cuius mastivus' to 'mastivus fuerit'. Of these three mss. T is the most accurate: in clause 1, T 'post idem festum', Ca 'post dictum festum' and Ma 'post festum diem'; and in clause 11, T 'quod forestario pertinet', Ma 'ad forestrium pertinet' and Ca 'id forestario pertinet'. In view of their omissions in clause 21, however, this group of mss. must be secondary to the previous two groups and so, as far as the edition of the English clauses is concerned, it is necessary only to give variant readings from S and H.

The edition of the English clauses is based on A, but since A was only marginally preferable to Ed and D, A, when inaccurate, has been corrected by Ed and D. The readings peculiar to N have been placed alongside the text based on A, since they represent adaptations of the English clauses to fit the Scottish forest system. Significant variants from S and H are given in the footnotes of the present edition.

Since clause 24 has survived only in N, Ez and other edited mss, no real collation could be carried out. Since Ez is an edited manuscript, the Scots of N has been chosen for the edition with a Latin translation in brackets alongside. There are no significant variants of this clause in Ez.

While it is not possible to provide a single stemma for all these mss., a stemma can be constructed for three groups of these mss. In the first and best group, A, Ed and D, A and D are closer to each other than to Ed: in clause 1, A, D 'abductis', Ed 'adductis'; A, D 'perduntur', Ed 'perdantur'; A, D 'forestariis', Ed 'forestariie'; and in clause 21, A, D 'natet', Ed 'mittet'. As already mentioned, A and D give a better version of clause 4 than Ed. These three mss. may at one stage have had a common parent ms., but the similarities of A and D suggest that they also had a common model. There are sufficient variations between A and D to ensure that the one was not copied from the other: in clause 1, A 'dampnantur', D 'damnantur'; A 'warsett', D 'warsete'; in clause 2, A 'eoroae jumentum', D 'cornuare menetum'; and in clause 8, A 'Rex', D 'Lex'. The relations of these three mss. can be summarised as follows:

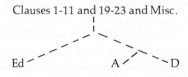

Clauses 1-11 and 19-23 and Misc.

Ed   A   D

The family H, M and J were so similar that only the date of each manuscript could be used to place them in any sort of order. It would have been possible to construct a stemma for these manuscripts, giving H as the exemplar of M, and M as the exemplar of J, but for the fact that M and J include one miscellaneous clause excluded by M. Their stemma may, therefore, be constructed as follows:

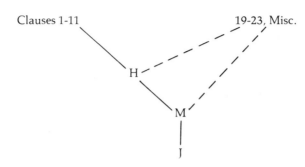

Ma, T and Ca, which must at one time have had a common parent ms., can also be drawn on a stemma. Ca and T are closer to each other than to Ma and may have had their own model: in clause 21, as already mentioned; in clause 4, T, Ca 'Id tantum', Ma 'I denarium'; in clause 8, Ca, T 'nisi obolum', Ma 'unum obolum'; and in clause 11, Ca, T 'forestam', Ma 'in forestam'. They do, however, all vary from each other as has been mentioned in clause 1 and also in clause 8: T 'etest decem', Ca 'Et in decem' and Ma 'id est decem'. The similarity of Ca and T shows that they could not have been copied from Ma and *vice versa*, and the above variations suggest that Ca and T are not copies of each other. This argument can be more neatly presented in graphic form:

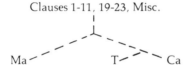

S and L_2, which formed a distinct pair, must at one stage have had a common parent manuscript but L_2, in view of its careless mistakes, is too loosely linked to S for this connection to be shown graphically.

English Originals of Clauses 19-24

It is possible to determine the English sources of clauses 19-24. Clause 22 is taken from c 11 of the Charter of the Forest as re-issued either by Henry III in 1225 or by Edward I in 1297.[19] Both re-issues differ from the 1217 original[20] by the addition of 'et sic redeundo domum . . .', which is given in the Scottish version. The other clauses were all borrowed from the English *Consuetudines et Assisae Foreste*, (referred to in E's *tabula*), and issued in the earlier part of Edward I's reign:[21]

Comparative Table of Clause Nos.

This Edition	Customs and Assise
19	1 + 2
20	3
21	7 + 8
23	9 + 10
24	6

These laws could have been borrowed by Scots lawyers from the late thirteenth century onwards. The following English mss. were consulted briefly:

Manuscript Reference	Century		Type	f. no.[1]	Ref. Letters
BM Stowe Ms. 937/Add. Ms. 37022	late	13th	2	139	ES
Cambridge Ms. Dd vii 6(AA)	late	13th	1	5	ECD
	early	14th			
Lambeth Palace Ms. 429	late	13th	1	12	ELP_1
	early	14th			
BM Harleian Ms. 858	late	13th	1	69	EH_1
	early	14th			
BM Harleian Ms. 1259	late	13th	1	6	
	early	14th			
Lambeth Palace Ms. 166	early	14th	1	54	ELP_2
BM Harleian Ms. 489	early	14th	2		EH_2
BM Harleian Ms. 1120	early	14th	1	82	EH_3
BM Harleian Ms. 1690	early	14th	1	41 (pencil)	EH_4
BM Royal and Kings Ms. 10 A V	early	14th	1	146	ER
Cambridge Ms. L1 iv 17 (E)	early	14th	1	74	ECL
Cambridge Ms. Dd 9 38		14th	1	206	
Cambridge Ms. Hh iv 1(E)		14th	2	135	ECH
BM Harleian Ms. 1807		14th	1	221	
Cambridge Ms. Ee 1. 5		14th	1	89	
BM Harleian Ms. 1011	late	14th	1	39	
	early	15th			
BM Landsdowne Ms. 464[2]	mid	15th	2	195 (ink)	EL
Cambridge Ms. Ii vi 53(G)	late	16th	2	14	
BM Cottonian Ms. Vespasian IV	16th-17th		2	177	

1. This colum gives the folio numbers on which the Customs and Assise of the Forest begin.
2. Printed in the *Statutes of the Realm,* where it is called Landsdowne Ms. 480.

The relevant clauses of the Customs and Assise of the Forest in those manuscripts which have been given reference letters were transcribed in full. These manuscripts were of two types: the first gave the first 11 clauses; and the second presented 18 clauses. The second type had several distinctive as well as inferior readings: in clause 19,[22] type 1 'extra dominicum', type 2 'fraxinus'; type 1 'seisitus', type 2 'in seysina'; at the end of clause 20 type 2 omits from 'si alias inveniatur' to 'eius corpus'. Since A and S, which represent the best Scots version of these clauses, have type 1 readings in all the above examples, the Scots version of these laws must have been taken from a manuscript or manuscripts of type 1. Where some but not all of the type 2 manuscripts differ from type 1 manuscripts, the Scots manuscripts invariably follow the type 1 readings: clause 19, type 1 and EH_2 'primam villam', the rest of type 2 'proximam villam', Scots manuscripts 'primam villam'; and clause 23 type 1, ES and ECH 'non liceat forestario deliberare', EL and EH_2 'non deliberetur',

Scots manuscripts 'non liceat forestario diliberare'. Nonetheless the Scots versions of these laws do contain some type 2 readings: clause 20 'prosternentem', not 'prostrantem'; clause 23 'mandato', not 'precepto'; and in clause 19 the Scots manuscripts all omit the phrase 'iuratus cuilibet facere attachiamentum' between 'forestarius' and 'invenerit', which in the English manuscripts is omitted only by EL and EH$_2$. Clause 24 also comes from English manuscripts of the first type: N 'the flesh forsuth aw to be sent', type 1 'caro autem debet mitti', type 2 'caro mittatur'; and N 'thar be ony sic ner by in the cuntre', type 1 'prope fuerit in partibus illis', type 2 'prope fuerit'. It thus appears either that these laws in Scotland were copied from an English manu-script of type 1 which had been polluted with some type 2 variants or that the Scottish scribe or scribes, while depending largely on a type 1 manuscript, introduced some readings from a type 2 manuscript which was also available to them. Since E lists these laws in its *tabula*, they must have been copied in the mid-fourteenth century or earlier. They may have been copied in the early fourteenth century, since type 1 manuscripts proliferated at that time. Such dating is only approximate, but it is possible that these English laws were first introduced to Scotland by Edward I in the early fourteenth century, since he had issued the *Consuetudines et Assisae Foreste* and re-issued the Forest Charter.

Since Professor M. L. Anderson presented no edition of these laws, the only previous edition of clauses 19-24 is that given in *APS*. Innes and Thomson have based their edition on Co and H: in Clause 23 'debet teneri et forestario seu viridario presentari' occurs only in Co; 'casus' most probably is taken from H; and in clause 19 'sunt regis' is taken from H. Consequently, and especially where Co has been followed, inferior readings are included. This is not surprising, since the editors did not consult A and S. Their examination of Ed and D, however, should have led them to suspect the reliability of Co and H.

The more important differences between the edition in *APS* and the present edition are as follows:

1. In clause 19 *APS* reads 'coram viridario id est capitali custode foreste', and this edition, 'coram viridario capitali custode foreste'. The reading in *APS* occurs only in Co and is extremely dubious, since in England the verderer and the keeper of the forest were separate officials and there is no evidence that verderers or their equivalents ever existed in Scotland.
2. The addition of 'non' in the same clause in line 151 is unnecessary. 'Non' is not given in any English ms.
3. Clause 23 is split into two parts in *APS* and given in clauses 14 and 23, but while this clause does fall neatly into two parts, there is no need to separate them. Only the edited mss. separate them.
4. The Latin translations of Scots mss. are inconsistent. While the editors have correctly recognised the significance of the alternative readings of N —they represent adaptation of English law to Scots practice — and have placed a

Latin translation of N in brackets in the second part of clause 23 and in clause 24, this practice was not followed in clause 18 where Es was translated, nor in clause 21 where a Latin translation of N's variant readings would be equally appropriate. Once again the Latin translation is inadequate, because in clause 24 the translation of N takes no cognisance of the original English version and so presents 'in parte sive provincia' instead of 'in partibus illis'.

5. Perhaps the major criticism of the edition of these clauses, and indeed of all the forest laws in *APS*, is that it follows the re-arrangement of the clauses carried out in Es by Skene, whose reasons for re-arranging the clauses are obscure. The result is that in *APS* the English clauses are scattered throughout the forest laws in clauses 10, 11, 12, 13, 14, 22 and 23, thus giving the whole body of laws an English character which it did not originally possess. This, more than anything else, has led to the Scots forests laws being regarded as English borrowings.

It is now possible to consider the results obtained by Buchanan in his collation of short passages from *Regiam Majestatem*. He suggested that H and M belonged together, but he did not add J to that group and he also considered that Ed, D and L_1 formed a group. While it has been shown in the above collation that L_1 contained some readings in common with Ed and D, L_1 did not belong to the group A, D, Ed. Buchanan also considered that Ca and T belonged together and that C and Co were single mss. While the above-mentioned variations may occur because Buchanan collated only a few short passages and because different treatises in the ms. volumes may behave in different ways, there is a broad similarity between Buchanan's and the present collation.

Miscellaneous Clauses

Although these clauses were not transcribed in full, it was possible to detect two basic traditions from the lists of rubrics. While E provides only a list of rubrics for these clauses in its *tabula* on f 7, comments on this list have been made in a sixteenth-century hand. In those miscellaneous clauses given before the English forest clauses, a bracket or, as the commentator has called it, a 'tik', has been placed around all of them excluding 'Gylda continens xxij statuta'. What clearly emerges is that there is an earlier tradition of these miscellaneous clauses containing this 'Gilda Scocie', as it is later entitled, and a later tradition excluding it. A, D and Ed include the 'Gilda Scocie', while all the other mss. exclude it. Since the latter group of mss. do not all contain the same miscellaneous clauses, it is possible to describe H, M and J as a group. M and J, however, appear to have been influenced by the earlier tradition, since they include 'De raptu monialium' excluded by H. S is exactly like A, except that it excludes the 'Gilda Scocie'.

The number of miscellaneous clauses added after the English forest clauses varies, although all mss. agree on those rubrics which they do provide. A adds 14 more clauses than E, and H adds one more than A. The list of rubrics before the English forest clauses is, therefore, based on E, and after the English forest clauses on E, A and H. Significant variants from A, H and S are given in the footnotes. Since the text of these clauses has not been edited here, the edition used when discussing their content is that of *APS*.[23]

Edited Mss.

In this collation an edited ms. is understood to be a ms. whose author did not set out simply to copy a previous ms. or mss. but was prepared to considerably rearrange material as he saw fit and to gather together all available material on certain topics. It is evident that in normal circumstances an edited ms. cannot be used in the formulation of an edition of the forest laws, but since certain clauses occurred in only a few mss., most of which were edited mss., it was felt that the best of the edited mss. could be used in the preparation of an edition of the forest laws.

Several edited versions of the forest laws were encountered, of which the best known is that given in Balfour's *Practicks*. In the Stair Society edition of Balfour's *Practicks* it is stated that the sources of Balfour's work could not be accurately defined, although there were similar mss. current in the sixteenth century.[24] From the table of clauses it appeared that edited mss. of this type were Ma, Ez, Bal_1, Bal_2, Y_1, Y_2 and Es, the last of which may not have been used by Balfour. Co and L_1, which differ from the other mss. in that they were not definitely known to be edited until the collation was completed, will be discussed last.

One feature of the edited mss. apart from Y_2 was that they usually gave the source of their version of the laws either as 'Leg Forestae' or 'Lib Carbraith'. These references can be tabulated:

Clause nos. in this edition	Ha	Y_1	Bal_1	Bal_2	Ez
1	$LF^1$1	LF 1	LF 1	LF 1	LF 1
2	LF 2	LF 2	LF 2	LF 2	LF 2
3	LF 3	LF 3	LF 3	LF 3	LF 3
4	LF 4	LF 4	LF 4	LF 4	LF 4
5	LF 5	LF 5	LF 5	LF 5	LF 5
6	LF 6	LF 6	LF 6	LF 6	LF 6
7	LF 7	LF 7	LF 7	LF 7	LF 7
8	LF 8	LF 8	LF 8	LF 8	LF 8
9	LF 9	LF 9	LF 9	LF 9	LF 9
10	LF 10	LF 10	LF 10	LF 10	LF 10
11	LF 11	LF 11	LF 11	LF 11	LF 11
12			LFiij LC^2	LF 7	LF in LC
13			LFiiLC	LFC	LF in LC
14					

1. LF — Leg. Forestae.
2. LC — Lib. Carbraith.

Clause nos. in this edition	Ha	Y₁	Bal₁	Bal₂	Ez
15			LFLC	LFC	LF in LC
16					
17			LF ex LC	LFC	LF ex LC
18			LF ex LC	LFC	LF ex LC
19	LF 89	LF 89			
20	LF 90	LF 90			
21	LF 90	LF 90	LF 90	LF 90	LF 90
22	LF 91	LF 91	LF 9[1]	LF 9[1]	LF 9[1]
23	LF 92	LF 92	LF 92	LF 92	LF 92
24			LF ex LC	LF	LF ex LC

From the numbers given to the clauses in source LF, it is obvious that clauses 1-11 and 19-23 were borrowed from a ms. similar to A or H, and most probably a ms. similar to A, since all the edited mss., apart from Y_2, give the correct version of clause 8, part of which is omitted in H. The source 'Lib Carbraith' has not, however, been identified. In the Stair Society edition of Balfour's *Practicks* several of the laws are said to come from 'Leg. forest . . . ex libro Galbraith' and it has been suggested that this was a ms. in the hands of Robert Galbraith who made a note on ms. Ca.[25] Unfortunately, the forest laws stated to be 'ex libro Galbraith' are not given in Ca, so another ms. must have been concerned. It seems likely, however, that both the book of Carbraith and the book of Galbraith are one and the same on account of the similarity of the name. The location of this ms. would be of great value, since it includes a copy of clauses 12-18 and of clause 24. It may itself be an edited ms., since Bal_1 states that it borrowed clause 13 from the 2nd law in the Carbraith ms. and clause 12 from the 3rd clause. Since both N and C did not arrange these clauses in that order, the author of the Carbraith ms. may have rearranged and perhaps edited them.

Balfour's *Practicks* may be discounted as the best of these edited versions, since its sources are available. Although it is difficult to be certain which mss. were used in Balfour's edition of the forest laws, the arrangement of the clauses and the use of the Carbraith/Galbraith ms. point to Ez and Bal_1 as the most likely sources, while Y_1, Y_2 and Bal_2 are less likely.

Y_2, Y_1, and Ha can be discounted as reliable edited mss. because they include no version of clauses 12-18 or of clause 24, and Es may be discounted because Skene's source for these clauses, Ez, is available.

Of the three remaining mss., Bal_1, Bal_2 and Ez, Bal_1 and Bal_2 are closely related. Not only is their numbering of clauses 6, 7 and 8 unique (see Table, p. 275), but both contain readings unique to themselves. In clause 8, for instance, they both misplace 'auld' in line 45 and so present 'and gif thai be auld hoglingis'. Bal_2 is secondary to Bal_1, since in clause 12, numbered 7 in Bal_1, Bal_1 gives the source as 'Leg. forest. iij Lib Carbraith', whereas Bal_2 gives the source as 'leg. forest c 7'. Bal_2 is, therefore, a copy of Bal_1 and may be discounted.

Bal$_1$ and Ez are in many respects identical. They both refer to the Carbraith ms. They give acts of parliament at the end of the forest laws, and in their 18th clause both give an act of 1557 which has been subsequently altered to 1457. The numbering of their clauses is identical and both contain the unique reading in clause 6, lines 34 and 35, 'forbidden be fund'. There are, nonetheless, sufficient differences between them to prove that the one was not copied from the other, and it is these differences which show that Ez is a slightly more accurate ms. than Bal$_1$: as already mentioned, Bal$_1$ in clause 8 misplaced 'auld' and so contains an inferior version of that clause; and in clause 1, Bal$_1$ omits 'feist' in line 5, included by Ez. Ez is, therefore, taken to be the best of the edited mss.

Co and L$_1$, which include neither clauses 12-18 nor clause 24, were found to contain readings from a variety of different mss. In clause 3, Co and L$_1$ include 'personaliter', as do B, C and E alone. In clause 8 they contain 'si pauciores sint hoggastri', a form which occurs only in B and E, yet both contain 'Rex non habebit nisi unum hoggastrum', as in S and H. In clause 21, Co omits from 'quietus erit' to 'mastivus fuerit', as in Ca. Co and L$_1$, therefore, contain borrowings from the B, H and T groups of mss. at least.

General Genealogy

While no accurate genealogy can be constructed showing the inter-relations of all the manuscripts, it is possible to illustrate roughly the position of the

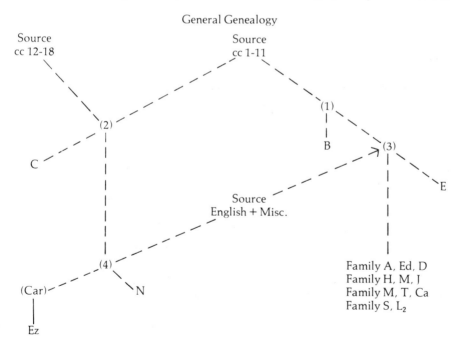

General Genealogy

different manuscripts on one diagram. The stemmata already provided for manuscripts B, C and E and for manuscripts C, N and Ez can be neatly fitted together. The English clauses must reach both point 3 and point 4. The other four groups of manuscripts which have been recognised, A Ed D, H M J, M T Ca, and S L₂, must derive from point 3, since they include clauses 1-11 and the English and miscellaneous clauses, but not clauses 12-18. This stemma as it stands illustrates only the main line of influence. N, for instance, contains some readings in common with B and E which are not found in C: c8 'the forester a hog'; and 'gif ony be thar'; while A and S contain some readings found in C: c1 'Inhibitum est'; and c3 'animalia burgensium'.

Presenting the inter-relations of manuscripts in this generalised form reveals that the compilers of manuscripts often used more than one source. It also shows how the forest laws were built up from three separate sources: cc1-11 of the twelfth century, cc12-18 of the 13th century, and the English and miscellaneous clauses added in the fourteenth century. Using the clause content of the manuscripts as well as the variations in the text of the laws, it can be seen that four major redactions of the forest laws must have been made. Firstly, to form the earliest tradition, clauses 1-11 were copied. Another copyist then combined clauses 1-11 and clauses 12-18, which gave rise to the second tradition represented by C and then by N and Ez. A third redaction was made when the English and miscellaneous clauses were added to clauses 1-11, and a fourth when the English and miscellaneous clauses were added to the second tradition.

Editorial Policy

The edition of the forest laws presented in this Appendix is a composite edition. This policy has been used frequently in recent years to provide a text as close as possible to the original.[26] This edition, therefore, does not present a copy of the laws as contained in any one ms., since to do so would have necessitated the printing of inaccurate and secondary readings. It is composite in the sense that the edition of each group of clauses is based on one or two almost identical mss., which have been corrected if necessary by the other best available mss. No correction has been made without ms. authority. On two occasions, however, in clauses 18 and 24, a Latin translation of the Scots of N has been provided, bracketed as a parallel text even although no Latin version of these clauses has survived. Such insertions are clearly marked, and the need for them has been explained in the collation. Full details of the principles of translation from Scots into Latin are given in the Principles of Translation following the edition.

In this edition the following conventions have been adopted:
(a) Modern capitalisation has been adopted in the use of capitals at the beginning of a sentence.
(b) Modern punctuation has been inserted where essential for the sense. All

the original punctuation has not been given, since this would be impossible in a composite edition. Where essential, for instance, in clause 1, the punctuation has been annotated. The most frequent alteration in punctuation has been the insertion of a full stop at the end of a sentence.

(c) Modern orthography has been used: i and j have been distinguished; i has not been substituted for y; where necessary þ and ȝ, thorn, have been rendered as th; u as v and v as u; and z, yogh, has not been changed to y.

(d) The method employed for the insertion of footnotes is:

  (i) The number of the footnote is inserted in the text immediately after the word or words annotated. Where a longer passage is concerned, two numbers are used, one at the beginning and one at the end of the passage.

  (ii) An alternative reading which does not challenge the reading of the edition, either because it is unique or is of a later tradition or because of sense or grammar, is given as 2. X 'et caetera' where 2 is the number of the footnote and X the reference of the ms. The implication is that the edition bears the reading of the other ms. or mss. on which it is based.

  (iii) If there is a disputed reading and one reading has been preferred, the supporting mss. and the alternative readings are given as 2. From X, Y and Z: W 'et caetera', where 2 is the number of the footnote and W the reference of the ms. which contains the alternative reading.

  (iv) The abbreviation 'om' has been used for 'omitted'.

(e) No rubrics have been given, since a table of rubrics is given afterwards.

(f) Clause numbers are placed on the left-hand side and line numbers on the right-hand side.

(g) Abbreviations and contractions are written in full and are not marked in any way, since that is impossible in a composite edition.

LEGES FORESTARUM

1. [1]Inhibita est silva tam cohabitantibus eam quam aliis ne in aliquod coopertorium silvarum intrent cum animalibus suis tempore pannacionis;[2] nisi libertatem habeant vel licenciati fuerint a forestariis per xv dies ante festum beati Johannis baptiste et per alios xv dies post idem festum qui amittent viij vaccas. Post 5 lapsum vero temporis vel mensis ipsius non perdentur viij[3] vacce nisi animalia inveniantur per forestarium dispersa cum custode eorum ignem cornu vel[4] canem habente qui warset[5] appellatur vel inveniantur in foresta nocte cubancia et tunc adductis testibus legalibus[6] perduntur[7] viij vacce. 10

1: 1— Clause nos from B. 2— ';' from B, om. in E. 3— E 'octo'. 4— B 'seu'. 5— From B & N; E 'warseth'. 6— E 'fidelibus'. 7— E 'producuntur'.

2. Item si aliquis iuxta forestam manens ex consuetudine animalia
sua per forestam intrare ter permiserit pro qualibet vice dabit
forestario iij d. Et si quarta vice inveniantur ibidem quamvis
nullo custode presente tunc adductis testibus legalibus[1] perduntur[2]
viij vacce. Si autem solus fuerit forestarius debet facere crucem   15
in terra vel arbore ubi animalia inveniuntur et ter cornuare menetum[3]
et postea adducere animalia ad castrum domini regis et sic
perduntur viij vacce.

3. Item[1] de animalibus burgensium[2] ter inventis in foresta qualibet
vice iiij d[3] et quarta vice adductis legalibus testibus perduntur   20
viij vacce. Item de animalibus nativorum domini regis inventis
in foresta ter[4] qualibet vice detur forestario j d. et quarta vice
debent illi nativi personaliter incarcerari in carcere domini regis
per xl dies.

4. Item[1] de ovibus in foresta inventis adductis testibus fidelibus   25
sive pastor fuerit presens sive non forestarius potest capere ad
opus suum unam ovem de grege. De ovibus vero bondorum[2] domini
regis j d. tantum[3] capiat de grege.

5. Item de capris inventis in foresta licitum est forestario[1] per
tres vices qualibet vice unam ex eis per cornua pendere in arbori-   30
bus et quarta vice unum ex eis debet occidere et[2] ibidem eius
viscera relinquere ad signum quod ibi inveniebantur.[3]

6. Item de porcis consuetudo est quod publice in ecclesiis paroch-
ialibus defendantur ne forestam intrent et si post dictam defensionem
inveniantur licitum est forestario per tres vices qualibet vice   35
unum ex eis capere[1] ad opus suum et si quarta vice forestam
intraverint omnes capiantur ad opus domini regis.

7. Item si de copia glandium in foresta domini regis contigerit[1]
forestarius debet citare tam burgenses quam ruremanentes quod
ibi porcos suos adducant ut dominus rex ab eis pannagium habeat.   40

8. Et hic est[1] modus pannagii de qualibet sundra[2] videlicet de decem
porcis rex habebit meliorem et forestarius j hog[3] et si pauciores

2: 1— E 'fidelibus'. 2— B 'producuntur'. 3— From H; B 'minatim', E 'minutim';
'menetum' is the most accurate form, *Revised Medieval Latin Word List*, ed. Latham,
R.E., (London, 1965), *sub* 'menetum'.
3: 1— B 'Et si'. 2— From E, C & Co; B 'burgensis'. 3— B 'iiij ᵒʳ d'. 4— From B & N; E
'inventis ter in foresta'.
4: 1— B 'et'. 2— B (interlinear and in a later hand) & A 'husbandorum'. 3— From E &
N; B 'capiat tantum'.
5: 1— B adds 'facere'. 2— E 'ac'. 3— From C, Co & N; B & E 'inveniuntur'.
6: 1— From E, C & A; B 'accipere'.
7: 1— From B, N & Co; E 'in foresta contigerit domini regis'.
8: 1— From C & N; B & E 'enim'. 2— From B, C, A & S; E 'synidra', N 'sundir', H
'cindra'. 3— E adds 'habebit', A & S 'hoggastrum' throughout. 4— S 'non habebit
nisi unum hoggastrum. Et pro . . .', N om. 'et si' to 'tantum'. 5— B 'capiet'.

sint quam decem rex nichil[4] habebit set forestarius habebit j hog
tantum et pro quolibet veteri porco j d. si aliqui ibi fuerint.
Et si omnes fuerint hoggis non habebit forestarius nisi unum hog   45
de decem. Et si fuerint pauciores quam x forestarius accipiet[5]
pro quolibet hog j obolum.

9. Item de equicio[1] si post defensionem inveniantur in foresta licitum
   est forestario capere prima vice pullanum unius anni, secunda
   vice pullanum duorum annorum, tercia vice equum[2] trium annorum et 50
   si quarta vice[3] inveniantur in foresta capiatur totum equicium
   ad opus domini regis. Item de quolibet equo domito et equitato
   in foresta invento capiat forestarius iiij d.

10. [1]Item[2] de carris et bigis sine licencia in foresta inventis de
    qualibet carra et biga xxx d. Set si aliam[3] viam extra forestam   55
    intraverint antequam a forestario deprehendantur quieti erunt.

11. Item si aliquis extraneus infra forestam in aliqua via inusitata[1]
    inveniatur si iurare voluerit super crucem[2] quod illam viam
    nescivit esse defensam vel quod rectam viam[3] agnoverit forestarius
    deducet[4] eum ad communem viam et ibi permittet[5] eum transire   60
    sine aliquo gravamine. Si autem homo notus fuerit debet capi
    et adduci ad castrum domini regis et ibi extra portam adductis
    testibus forestarius capiet[6] pannum eius superiorem et si
    quid in bursa sua fuerit quod ad opus eius sit[7] et tradat corpus
    suum[8] ianitori castri ut servetur quousque dominus rex de eo   65
    facere voluerit suam voluntatem.

12. [1]Item si dominus rex voluerit herbagium locare per tempus fogagii
    quid est a festo omnium sanctorum usque ad festum sancti patricii[2]
    in quadragesima quodlibet animal solvet unum[3] denarium pro fogagio
    et iumentum duos denarios.   70

13. Item si liber homo capiatur pro viridi[1] in foresta dabit octo
    vaccas ad forisfactum si pro venacione solvet[2] decem libras.
    Si vero liber homo consuetus fuerit amputare vel scindere in foresta
    per tres vices[3] dabit qualibet vice octo vaccas et[4] quarta vice
    decem libras.   75

9: 1— E adds 'quod'. 2— H, C & A 'pullum'. 3— From E, N, C & Co; B 'inveniantur quarta vice'.

10: 1— B includes this clause in clause 9. 2— From E, C and N; B 'et'. 3— E 'altam'.

11: 1— H 'inhabita', S 'inchibita', N 'forbodyn'. 2— N 'wapin', C & H 'arma'. 3— B (interlinear and in a later hand) adds 'non'. 4— The future tense seems more appropriate than the present 'deducat' of B & E; A & H 'conducet', N 'sal lede'. 5— E 'permittat'. 6— From E & N; B, C & Co 'capiat'. 7— S 'ad forestarium pertinet', A 'ad forestam pertinet'. 8— S & A add 'ad constabulario'.

12: 1— Clause nos from C. 2— From 1st November to 17th March. 3— N 'viii d' in confusion for 8 cows.

13: 1— C 'v' only, N 'grene wod'. 2— Om. in C, N 'he sal pay'. 3— From N; C 'per tres vices in foresta dabit'. 4— Om. in C.

v

14. Item si aliquis libere tenens per cartam qui liberam habet potest-
    atem venandi in terra sua marchie iuxta forestam permittet[1]
    leporarium[2] suum in propria terra[3] currere et ille[4] leporarius
    sequatur bestiam in foresta ille liber potest sequi leporarium suum
    in foresta regis adeo longe sicut potest proicere cornu suum vel   80
    ligaturam[5] suam. Et si forsan leporarius suus ceperit bestiam quam
    insecutus fuerit infra predictum spacium ille libere[6] reportabit
    illam[7] bestiam et leporarium suum sine calumpnia alicuius et sic[8]
    ille liber infra forestam predictum spacium egrediatur solvet[9]
    octo vaccas et amittet[10] leporarium suum et bestiam.   85

15. Item si canis[1] currens in propria terra alicuius liberi[2] et forsan[3]
    currat cum bestia in foresta regis a propria terra eius[4] ille liber
    vel ille[5] venator potest sequi canem suum currentem removendo[6]
    arcum suum et sagittas suas vel potest[7] ligare sagittas et arcum
    cum corda et si dictus canis ceperit bestiam[8] venator cum cane[9]   90
    et bestia quiete et libere[10] redibit[11] sine aliqua calumpnia regis
    vel domini illius foreste.[12]

16. Item si animalia[1] bondi[2] alicuius inveniantur in foresta de
    nocte cubancia vel de die pascencia cum pastore ignem et cornu
    habente ille bondus dabit unam vaccam vel quinque solidos[3] vel   95
    quadraginta dies incarcerabitur.[4] Et si bondus ille inveniatur
    scindens vel amputans in foresta simuli modo dabit unam vaccam
    vel quinque solidos vel incarcerabitur per quadraginta dies[5]
    ut predictum est.[6]

17. Item si animal vagrans reperiatur in foresta[1] debet custodiri per   100
    tres curias et in quarta curia domino regi adiudicabitur pro
    eschaeta nisi[2] dominus illius apparuerit et[3] illam ad se prius

14: 1— N 'lattis' translated as 'permittet', om. in C, *APS*, i, 691 'patitur'. 2— N 'rych'.
3— From N 'in his awin land', C 'propere'. 4— From N 'that fre man'; C 'ipse'. 5— N
'lesch' translated as 'ligaturam' as in *Pais. Reg.*, 92, (1294/5); om. in C. 6— From N
'that man sal frely tak'; C 'idem liber reportabit'. 7— From N 'that'. 8— N 'and that'.
9— From N 'he sal pay'; C 'dabit'. 10. N 'sal tyn'.
15: 1— N 'hund'. 2— N 'of ony fre manis propir land' combined with C 'alicuius liberi
chaciantis in propere'. 3— From N 'and happyn to ryn'; om. in C. 4— From N 'fra
his propir land'; om. in C. 5— From N 'that'; om. in C. 6— N 'remofand'. 7— From
N 'he may bind'; om. in C. 8— C adds 'suam'. 9— C adds 'suo'. 10— From N 'quyt
and fre'; om. in C. 11-12— From N 'but ony chalangis of the king or of the lord of
that forest'; C 'dummodo idem canis bestiam quam primo insecutus fuerat non
mutaverit. Et si mutaverit venatore sequente perdet canem nichilominus et octo
vaccas'.
16: 1— N 'the best'. 2— From N 'of ony bonde'; om. in C. 3— C adds 'ad forisfactum'.
4— C adds 'pro forisfacto'. 4-5— Om. in C. 5-6— N includes this final phrase
showing that its tradition at one time included 4-5.
17: 1— C adds 'vel habitu derelicto'. 2— N 'but if'. 3-4— From N 'and pruff that befor
lauchfully to perten till him'. The Latin translation of this reading had been
rearranged to what appears to be a more sensible form. C 'et illud ad se pertinere

pertinere legittime probaverit.[4] Inventor vero[5] animalis illius
debet illud publicare ad capitale manerium et in locis circum
vicinis ut constare poterit cuicunque[6] violenti prosequi animalem   105
sic inventum.[7]

18. Item si liber homo forsan[1] delinquat in foresta libera[2] alicuius
baronis cui dominus rex per cartam[3] forestam liberam concesserit
inhibens ne quis sub forisfactura decem librarum delictum faciat
in eadem[4]   110

ilk fre man trespassand	[5][aliquis liber delinquans
at the soyt of the baroun	ad sectam baronis
in the kingis court	in curia regis
apon sic transgressioun	de sic transgressione
lauchfully convickyt	legittime convictus 115
x lib. sal pay to the king	decem libras solvet regi
for the forfalt and the hors	ad forisfactum, et equum
and all that is fundin with him	et omnia inventa cum eo
trespassand in the forest	delinquente in foresta
the lord of the forest	dominus foreste 120
or his forster	vel forestarius
till him for that transgressioun	suus sibi pro illa transgressione
for evermar sal halde.	semper retinebit.
And gif the lord of the forest	Et si dominus foreste
sic soyt wil nocht mak	talem sectam non voluerit facere 125
or for thank disimilis him	vel pro gratia dissimulaverit se
sic transgressioun to misknaw	talem transgressionem agnoscere
the king sal haf his soyt	rex habebit sectam suam
til ask x lib. for the forfalt	petendi decem libras ad forisfactum
again his inhibicioun maid.	contra suam inhibitionem factam. 130
Gif forsuth that lord resavis	Si vero dominus ille acceperit
mone or ony other thing	pecuniam vel aliquod aliud
fra that trespassour	ab illo delinquente
and helis the forfalt	et forisfactum concelaverit
or will nocht folow therfor	et non voluerit prosequi igitur 135
the king sal haf his soyt	rex habebit sectam eius
for x lib. anent the samyn	pro decem libris contra eundem

legittime probaverit'. 5— From N 'forsuth'; C 'autem'. N 'on ilka syde about'. 6-7—
From N 'to quhamsoever will folow that sic a best is fundyn'; C 'vendicare violenti
ad prosequendum si voluerit', Bal₁ 'that will challenge and follow the beist that is sa
found', Ez 'that will challenge and will follow the beist that is sa fundyn'. The Latin
'animalem sic inventum' could easily have given rise to N's translation.

18: 1— From N 'happyn to'; om. in C. 2— Om. in N. 3— N adds 'fre' to charter and
not to forest. 4— C ends here. The following Latin text is a translation of N which is
printed on the left in Scots. 5— For detailed comment on translation see Principles of
Translation, p. 301.

lord sa desistand	dominum sic desistentem
the quhilk is haldyn till	qui ad satisdationem
assith to the king x lib	regi decem libras tenetur.] 140

19. Si quis forestarius inveniet[1] aliquem attachiabilem pro viridi in
foresta primo debet eum attachiare per duos plegios si inventi
fuerint in loco. Sinautem debet eum ducere ad primam villam
et ibi ponere ipsum per plegios. Et si idem alias inventus fuerit
cum viridi debet ipsum attachiare per quatuor plegios. Et si tercio   145
in viride coram veredario[2,3] capitali custode foreste debet presentari et poni per octo plegios et post tertium attachiamentum
tunc debet corpus attachiari et retineri.[4] Ut in memoria habeatur
quod viridum[5] sit;[6] sciendum est quod omnes arbores fructum
non portantes et eciam hee que fructum portant per totum annum   150
extra dominicum si antiquitus fuerit in foresta et arabiles[7]
quia dominus rex est saisitus.

20. Si quis forestarius invenerit aliquem extra dominicum boscum[1]
infra rewardam prosternentem quercum sine visu vel deliberacione
forestarii vel veredarii[2] debet per quatuor plegios ipsum attachi-   155
are per visum forestarii debet quercus ille appreciari et in
rotulo forestarii vel veredarii inbreviari et debet poni per
sex salvos plegios et si alias inveniatur debet duplicari eius
plegius et si tercio detineatur eius corpus.

21. [1]Si autem leporarius inventus fuerit currens ad nocumentum foreste   160
debet[2] retineri et presentari forestario seu veredario qui mittet[3]
eum domino regi seu capitali justiciario foreste. Si aliquis
mastinus[4] inventus fuerit in aliqua foresta et ipse mastinus
vinculatus fuerit et ipse cuius mastinus fuerit quietus erit de
illo facto. Sed si non fuerit vinculatus ipse cuius mastinus   165
fuerit[5] erit culpabilis tamquam de manupasto et[6]

debet poni per sex plegios	(fully in the forfalt to the king
quorum nomina debent inbreviari	sal pay after as he is
vel qualis fuerit canis.[7]	free man or bonde.)

22. Quicunque comes episcopus vel baro veniens ad mandatum domini   170
regis transierit per forestam domini regis liceat ei capere unam

---

19: 1— S & H 'invenerit'. 2— S & H 'viridario'. 3— M & Ed 'Et', H & S add 'in'. 4— M
is the only ms. to provide the break required by the sense. 5— H & S 'viride'. 6— A
break is provided here in all mss. as in the English mss. 7— From S; A 'arabilis', H
'arabiles sunt dominus Rex est saistur de illis'.

20: 1— H adds 'vel'. 2— S & H 'viridarii'.

21: 1— In A this clause is included in the previous clause. 2— N 'the forster aw till hald
him'. 3— From Ed and S; A 'natet'. 4— From the mss. this word could be either
'mastinus' or 'mastivus'. Y_1 and Es clearly read 'mastinus'. 'Mastinus' is given here
since it is the better form. *Revised Medieval Latin Word List*, ed. Latham, R.E.,
(London, 1965) *sub* 'mastinus'. 5— From Ed, D, H and S; om. in A. 6-7— The Latin
text is taken from A and the Scots from N. 7— H 'eciam qualis fuerit casus'.

vel duas bestias per visum forestarii si presens fuerit. Sinautem faciat cornare[1] ne videatur hee[2] furtive facere. Et sic
redeundo domum liceat ei facere sicut predictum est.

23. Si quis ceperit aliquam feram sine warranto in foresta corpus   175
suum arrestandum est[1] ubicunque inveniatur intra metas foreste.
Et quando captus fuerit non liceat forestario deliberare ipsum
sine speciali mandato domini regis vel iusticiariorum suorum.
Si quis viderit aliquos malefactores infra metas foreste capere
aliquam feram[2] vel asportare debet illos capere secundum posse   180
suum et si non possit debet levare hw et cry.[3]

Et si non fecerit remanebit	(to the nerrest tounys beside the	
in misericordia domini regis.[4]	forest and to pas and manifest	
	to the kingis forster and gif he	
	dois nocht he sal remayn in the	185
	kingis hewy mercy.)[4]	

24. [1]Item gif ony wylde best   [Item si aliqua fera
   be fundyn dede or wondyt   inveniatur mortua vel vulnerata
   and the trespassour be nocht fundyn   delinquente non invento
   at the next mut thar aw to be   ad prima placita debet fieri   190
   inquisicioun made and the findar   inquisicio et inventor
   in the mene tym aw to be attachit   interea debet attachiari
   with siker borowis quhill   per salvos plegios donec
   it be knawyn of the transgressioun   transgressio cognoscatur.
   the flesch forsuth aw to be send   Caro autem debet mitti   195
   to the hous of the lepir men   ad domum leprosum
   gif thar be ony sic ner by   si qua prope fuerit
   in the cuntre   in partibus illis.
   gif forsuth nane sic hous   Si autem nulla talis domus
   be ner by the flesch aw to be   prope fuerit caro debet   200
   gevin to pur folk and to sek   dari pauperibus et infirmis
   and the hed and the skyn   et caput et pellis
   and the arow gif ony be fundyn   et sagitta si qua inveniatur
   salbe presentit to the iustice   presentabuntur justiciario
   quhen he cumis in his iustice ayr.   quando in itinere venerit.]   205

22: 1— H 'commode', S 'quo more'. 2— S 'hoc'.
23: 1— S and H 'arrestetur'. 2— N 'der'. 3-4— The Latin text is from A and the Scots is
   from N.
24: 1— The Scots text is from N and the Latin text is a translation of the Scots of N.
   See Principles of Translation, p. 301.

Table of Rubrics

De Animalibus
Juxta forestam manentes[1]
De animalibus burgensium et nativorum
De ovibus husbandorum
De capris
De porcis
De copia glandis
De pannagio porcorum
De equis
De carris vel bigis
De homine qui intrat in forestam
De nauta et navi
De quietis a toloneo et custuma
De conquerente super aliquo
De divisione etatis ad iudicatum
De occultatione thesauri inventi
De pisce invento qui dicitur cetus
De namis redigiandis[2,3]
De warantia terre per cartam
Qualiter felo restituetur ad sua
Exceptiones ad breve
Exceptiones ad actionem
Exceptiones contra brevem de recto de dote
Forma citacionis in burgo
De modo vendendi terram et de saisina terre vendite
Distinctio inter heredes diversarum uxorum
De firmario dando vel accipiendo
De manaleta
De bastardo
De falsa carta
Leges de dampno animalium
De feris animalibus
Iudex non debet iudicare antequam recognoscatur per testes

Gylda continens xxij statuta[4]

1. In E an introductory note states that 17 rubrics are omitted: in fact clause 1, 'De Animalibus', and 16 clauses at the end.
2. 'Capiendis' in other mss.
3. S and A add 'Distinctio inter firmarium et feodifirmarium'.
4. This clause is not enclosed in brackets in E. It is called 'Gilda Scocie' in Ed and om. in H and S. The bracket includes all previous and subsequent clauses. A 16th century marginal note states that the clauses within 'this tik' are in the statutes of Alexander in this book.

De aracione terre

De constitutione de indictamentorum

De iniuria et non racione

De non habente plegium ad prosequendum

De vita et membro[1]

De convicto per duellum

Distinctio mobilium domesticorum inter heredem et alios liberos

De terris non alienandis in lecto egritudinis

Quod infra etatem existens iurare non debet

De intestato damnato

De porcis in burgo

De purgacione burgensis contra regem

De satisfactione dampni facti per animalia

De aucis gallinis et capris

De privelegio terre et capris

De rebus emendis sagaciter in burgo

De plegiagio burgensis pro burgense

De pena uxoris burgensis delinquentis

De probacione et acquietacione simul et semel

De attachiamento vel summonicione

Casus pro quibus uxor subibit iudicium[2]

Quot testes sufficiunt ad probandum debitum

De eschaeta maris que dicitur Wrekis

De debitis regis levandis

De libero homine intestato discendente[3]

De debitoribus intestatis

De modo faciendi homagium et fidelitatem

De puero infra etatem vocato ad warantum

Quod puer non vocabitur ad warantum sine carta

De maritagio

De maritati in disparagio

De hiis qui nolunt maritari per dominis suis

De venientibus ad guerram

Quod nullus distringat nisi pro secta contenta in carta

De secta inter plures

De hiis qui subtrahunt a dominis suis sectas suas

Qualiter herj s recuperabit hereditatem

De debitoribus et eorum plegiis

De proprietate releviorum

De dissaisina cum roboria

Ad quem de duobus dominis pertineat maritagium duplicis heredis

1. Om. in H. In S and A this clause is given as part of the previous clause.
2. H adds 'De serviente vulnerato per magistrum suum'.
3. 'Decedente' in later mss.

De raptu mulierum maritarum
De raptu monialium[1]
De raptu puerorum
De non pertinentibus se distringi
De hiis qui deforciant officiarios
De replegiacione terre
Casus de duabus sororibus
De dono facto domui religiose
Expressum auxilium dominis per homines suos
De defenso aquarum et de punicione transgressorum
De debitis mercatorum
Breve formatum super eiusdem
Consuetudo et assisa de foresta
De quercu
De licencia capiendi feram
De fera capta sine waranto
Tractatus de bastardia
Tractatus corone
De dampnis viduarm super dotibus et quarantenis suis recuperandis
Quod vidue possunt legare blada de dotibus suis
De usuris non currentibus contra minorem
Quot modis dicitur exceptio
Exceptiones generales contra brevia[2]
(Exceptiones contra accionem)[3]
Exceptiones contra iudicem
Exceptiones contra assessores
Exceptiones contra locum
Exceptio contra citationem
Exceptio contra actorem
Exceptio contra testes
Exceptio contra advocatum
Exceptio contra sententiam diffinitivam
De elemosina non alienanda
Quibus modis sit dissaisina
Casus de diversis sororibus
Quibus casibus potest permitti duellum
In casu sanguinis
Iudicium de pillory
Quoddam statutum notabile editum per burgenses de Perth
Forme brevium diversorum[4]

1. Om. in H.
2. The following 16 clauses om. in E are taken from A, S and H.
3. An alternative for the preceding rubric in H or an additional rubric in S.
4. Om. in A, S & E; from H.

Principles of Translation

Latin to English:

The English translation of these laws is not literal, since it is essential in the interests of clarity to re-arrange the word order and to alter the idiom. The readings of ms. N, which is itself a literal Scots translation of a Latin ms., have proved useful when translating this edition. Where a considerable change has been made to the Latin order, the literal translation is given in the footnotes, and where an insertion has been made for the sense it is placed in square brackets. As a point of style, 'et' and 'item' at the start of a clause or sentence have not been translated and long sentences have on occasion been subdivided for clarity and are so annotated. The following matters of vocabulary and construction must be discussed in more detail:

1. Constructions:
    (a) Conditional sentences are treated in these laws in a variety of different ways, and in a sentence including two conditional clauses both clauses may have verbs of different tense and mood. An attempt has been made to reflect these different usages by allowing for the hypothetical sense implied by the use of the subjunctive and for the more factual sense conveyed by the indicative. The following table gives examples of the translation of conditional sentences:

	Protasis (Conditional Clause)	Apodosis (Principle Clause)	Example	Frequency in Laws
(1)	Future Perfect Indicative permiserit / if he allows	Future Indicative dabit / he will give	c 2	Common
(2)	Future Perfect Indicative fuerit / if he is	Present Indicative debet / he ought to	c 11	Occurs only with debet
(3)	Present Subjunctive (a) sint / if they be, should they be (b) egrediatur / if he exceed	Future Indicative habebit / he will have solvet / he will pay	c 8 c 14	Common
(4)	Present Subjunctive inveniantur / if/should they be found	Present Subjunctive capiatur / let it be taken	c 9	Fairly common
(5)	Present Subjunctive sequatur / if he follow	Present Indicative potest / he can	c 14	Rare
(6)	Present Subjunctive inveniantur / if/should they be found	Present Indicative perduntur / will be lost	c 1	Rare
(7)	Future Indicative inveniet / if he finds	Present Indicative debet / he ought to	c 19	Rare

In these cases the form 'inventi fuerint' or 'concelaverit' is taken to be the future perfect indicative unless difficulties arise, as in clause 13 where N appears to translate 'consuetus fuerit' as a perfect subjunctive 'be wont'.

(b) The present participle used in an adjectival sense is usually translated by an adjectival clause, e.g., c 22.

(c) The one gerundive, encountered in c 19, has been translated by 'it is to be known'. Two gerunds, found in clauses 15 and 22, have been preceded by 'after' and 'when' according to the sense.

(d) In two cases, in clauses 14 and 18, a future perfect indicative verb in an adjectival clause is translated by a simple past tense.

(e) The subjunctive after 'antequam' in c 10 where no sense of purpose is conveyed is translated in the indicative.

(f) The subjunctive after 'ubicunque' in c 23 is translated in the indicative.

(g) Miscellaneous: (i) 'Ad signum quod' is translated by 'as a sign that' in c 5.

(ii) The construction 'iurare quod nescivit vel agnoverit' is found in c 11.

2. Vocabulary:

(a) Expression of penalties: 'Perdo', 'amitto', 'dabo' and 'solvo' are all used when stating penalties. 'Perduntur viij vacce' is translated not as 8 cows are lost but as 8 cows are forfeit. While escheat could be implied by 'perduntur', forfeiture is more general and in a forest context more appropriate. 'Amittent', 'dabit' and 'solvet' are all literally translated.

(b) Since these laws are stating orders or rules, the third person future tense is always given as 'he shall', not 'he will'.

(c) 'Ille' usually translated as 'that' is sometimes translated as 'the', e.g., c 11.

(d) The phrase 'liceat forestario', which can be translated as 'the forestar may', is sometimes translated as 'it is lawful for the forester' in accordance with the style of ms. N as in c 9.

(e) 'Debet' is translated by 'he ought' and not by 'he should' or 'he must'.

(f) 'Eius' and 'suus' are not separated in the Latin mss. 'Suus' usually only refers to the subject of the principal clause, but in c 11 when the forester is the subject of the principal clause 'bursa sua' obviously refers to the offender's purse. Consequently, in the clause 'si quid in bursa sua fuerit quod ad opus eius sit', 'eius' could refer to the forester or to the offender. Since 'sua' was used in the same clause to denote the offender, it seems likely that 'eius' denotes the other participant, the forester.

Explanation of terms is not given in the footnotes of the English translation but in the Commentary which follows.

Scots-Latin

Only two clauses, 18 and 24, were translated into Latin from the Scots of N.

1. Clause 18. Constructions
   (a) By comparing N's Scots with the Latin edition in other clauses, it is possible to determine the Latin original of the conditional clauses in c 18. N only uses 'will' as in 'wil nocht mak' in a conditional clause when 'volo' is used in the Latin, e.g., cc 12, 16. N always translates the future perfect indicative in a conditional clause by the present indicative. Therefore 'wil nocht mak' and 'disimilis' can be translated into Latin as 'non voluerit facere' and 'dissimulaverit'. The other conditional clauses in c 18 are similarly translated.
   (b) The genitive gerund after 'sectam' is used to convey purpose. 'Ad petendum' would be equally suitable.
   Vocabulary:
   (a) 'Disimilis' is most likely N's literal translation of 'dissimulo'.
   (b) 'Misknaw' is translated by one word 'agnoscere' rather than two 'non noscere'.
   (c) 'Ask' in the sense of seek or pursue is best translated by 'petere'.
   (d) 'Helis' in the sense of hides can be translated by 'concelo'.
   (e) 'Anent', taken in the sense of against, is translated by 'contra'.
   (f) 'Desistand' sounds as though it comes straight from the Latin 'desistere'.
   (g) 'Haldyn til assyth' in the sense of compensation is translated by 'ad satisdationem' which occurs in medieval Scots documents including the *Justice Ayre Journal Books* (SRO, RH 2/1/5, 83, 109, 114).

2. Clause 24. Constructions
   (a) N always translates the present subjunctive in a conditional clause in the form 'gif it be fundyn' and 'debet' in the principal clause by 'aw to be'; therefore 'inveniatur' can be given in line 188 and 'debet' in line 190. By this practice 'gif thar be ony sic' sounds as though it should be translated by 'si. . .sit. . .' but 'fuerit' is given, as in the English mss., for N could have read 'fuerit' as a perfect subjuctive.
   (b) Temporal clauses using 'donec' and 'quando' are followed by classical constructions which could give rise to N's version.
   Vocabulary
   (a) 'Wylde best' is adequately translated by 'fera'. 'Bestia' does not convey wildness.
   (b) 'Trespassour' is translated by 'delinquans' because in c 18, N translated 'delinquat' as 'trespass'.
   (c) 'Next mut' could be translated by 'proxima curia' but 'prima placita' of the English mss. is adequate.
   (d) 'Til it be knawyn', in the sense of taking cognizance, is translated by 'cognoscatur'.
   (e) 'Flesch' is given as 'caro' in the English mss.
   (f) 'In the cuntre' must be given as 'partibus illis' as in the English mss. and not as 'regno' or 'patria' which are precluded by the sense.

Translation of the Forest Laws

1. [1]Both inhabitants of the wood and others are forbidden to[2] enter any enclosure of the woods with their animals in time of pannage; unless they have freedom from or are permitted by the foresters [to enter] they[3] shall lose 8 cows [if they enter] 15 days before the feast of St John the Baptist and for another 15 days after the said feast. After this[4] time [of pannage] and[5] month [of fence] 8 cows shall be forfeit only if the beasts be found by the forester scattered with a keeper who has a fire or a horn or a dog which is called 'warset' or if they are found sleeping at night and then, when lawful witnesses have been brought, 8 cows shall be forfeit.

2. If anyone customarily living beside a forest allows his animals to enter the forest thrice, each time he shall give the forester 4d. And if they be found there on a fourth occasion even although no keeper is present then when lawful witnesses have been brought 8 cows shall be forfeit. If the forester is alone he ought to make a cross in the ground or on a tree where the animals are found and thrice blow the *menée* and afterwards lead the animals to the king's castle and so 8 cows shall be forfeit.

3. Concerning the animals of burgesses which were found in the forest on three occasions, on each occasion 4d is forfeit and on the fourth occasion when lawful witnesses have been brought 8 cows are forfeit. Concerning the animals of the king's *nativi* which were found in the forest on each of three occasions let [the *nativus*] give the forester 1d and on the fourth occasion the *nativi* ought to be imprisoned for forty days in the king's prison.

4. Concerning sheep found in the forest the forester can take one sheep from the flock for his own use when trusty witnesses have been brought as to whether or not a herdsman was present. Concerning the sheep of the king's bondmen he may only take 1d from the flock.

5. Concerning goats found in the forest it is lawful for the forester on each of three occasions to hang one of them by the horns in the trees and on the fourth occasion he ought to kill one of them and leave its entrails there as a sign that they were found there.

6. Concerning pigs the custom is that in parish churches they should be publicly prohibited from entering the forest and should they be found [there] after this prohibition it is lawful for the forester on each of three occasions to take one of them for his own use and if they enter the forest a fourth time let them all be taken for the king's use.

7. If there is an abundance of acorns in the king's forest the forester ought to summon both town and country dwellers to bring their pigs there so that the king may have pannage from them.

1: 1-2— Lit(eral) trans(lation) is 'The wood is forbidden both to inhabitants and others lest they . . .' 3— Lit. trans. 'who will lose . . .' 4— 'Vero' trans(lated) by 'this'. 5— 'Vel' trans. by 'and' according to *Medieval Latin Word List*, ed. Latham.

8. This is the method of pannage. From each sounder, namely 10 pigs, the king shall have the best and the forester one hog and if there be fewer than 10 the king shall have nothing but the forester shall have only one hog and 1d for each old pig if there are any. If they are all hogs the forester shall have only one hog for [every] ten. If there are fewer than ten the forester shall receive ½d for each hog.

9. Concerning a stud [of horses] if they should be found in the forest after prohibition it is lawful for the forester to take a one-year-old foal the first time, a two-year-old the second time and a three-year-old horse the third time and if they be found in the forest a fourth time let the whole stud be taken for the king's use. The forester may take 4d for each tame or broken horse found in the forest.

10. Concerning carts and wagons found without permission in the forest [the forester may take] 30d. But if they reach another road outside the forest before they are apprehended by the forester they shall be quit.

11. If any stranger be found in the forest on any forbidden route [and] if he swears on a cross that he did not know that the road was forbidden nor that he knew the right road the forester shall lead him to [continue to] traverse [the forest] without harm. But if the man is not ignorant[1] he ought to be taken and led to the king's castle and there, outside the gate, when witnesses have been brought, the forester shall take his outermost garment and whatever is in his purse which he[2] needed and let him hand over his person to the porter of the castle to be kept during the king's pleasure.[3]

12. If the king wishes to set herbage in time of foggage which is from the feast of All Saints to the feast of St Patrick in Lent [the owner of] each beast shall pay 1d for foggage and a mare 2d.

13. Should a free man be taken for [an offence against the] vert in the forest he shall forfeit 8 cows [and] if for venison he shall pay £10. If a free man is accustomed to cut off and fell [wood] in the forest for each of three times he will give 8 cows and the fourth £10.

14. If anyone who freely holds [land] by charter and who has free power to hunt on his land which adjoins the forest allows his greyhound to run on his own land and that greyhound follow a beast in the forest that free man can follow his greyhound in the king's forest as far as he can cast his horn or his leash. If, perchance, the greyhound takes the beast which it followed[1] within the foresaid distance[2] that free man shall freely take away that beast and his greyhound without any blame and if that free man exceed the foresaid distance[2] in the forest he will pay 8 cows and will lose his greyhound and the beast.

11: 1— Lit. trans. 'is known', i.e. 'is notorious' or 'is knowledgeable'. 2— Probably referring to the forester, but 'eius' could apply to the offender. 3— Lit. trans. 'as long as the king wishes to have his will of him'.
14: 1— Best translation of future perfect tense. 2— Lit. trans. 'space'.

15. Should a dog running on any freeman's land run from his own land after a beast into[1] the king's forest that free man or that hunter can follow his running dog after[2] removing his bow and arrows or he can bind the bow and arrows with the bow-string[3] and if the said dog takes the beast the hunter shall return quit and free with the dog and beast without any blame from the king or lord of that forest.

16. If any bondman's beasts be found sleeping in the forest at night or pasturing by day with a herdsman who has a fire and a horn that bondman shall give one cow or 5s or be imprisoned for 40 days. If that bondman be found felling or cutting off [wood] in the forest he shall likewise give 1 cow or 5s or be imprisoned for 40 days as said above.

17. Should a beast be found wandering in the forest it ought to be kept for three courts and in the fourth court it will be adjudged escheat to the lord king unless its lord appear and lawfully prove that it formerly belonged to him. The beast's finder ought to publicise it at the head manor and in the neighbourhood[1] so that anyone wishing to claim or pursue an animal so found can learn of it.[2]

18. Should a freeman commit an offence in the free forest of any baron to whom the lord king has granted[1] a free forest by a charter which forbids anyone to commit an offence in the same under forfeiture of £10 any free man committing [such] an offence [and] lawfully convicted of such an offence in the king's court at the suit of the baron shall forfeit £10 to the king.[2] For that offence the lord of the forest or his forester shall always keep for himself the horse and everything found with the offender. If the lord of the forest does not make such a suit or for a favour pretends that he does not know of such an offence the king shall have the lord's suit to seek £10 as forfeiture against the prohibition which he made. If that lord receives money or anything else from that offender and conceals the [offence[3] for which a] forfeit [is due] and does not, therefore, prosecute the king shall have his suit for £10 against the same lord who thus refrains and who will be held to make satisfaction to the king of £10.

19. If any forester finds anyone attachable for vert in the forest he firstly ought to attach him by 2 pledges if they are to be found in the place. But if not, he ought to take him to the first town and there put him under pledges. If he is found there again with vert he ought to attach him by 4 pledges. If [he is found] a third time in vert he ought to be presented to the verderer [or] head keeper of the forest and be placed under 8 pledges and

---

15: 1— 'in' and dative trans. as 'into'. 2— Best trans. of ablative gerund. 3— Lit. trans. 'cord'.

17: 1— Lit. trans. in 'places' or 'steads'. 2— Lit. trans. 'so that it can be known by anyone wishing to claim . . .'

18: 1— Best translation of future perfect tense. 2— New sentence begun for clarity. 3— Since no prosecution has been made it must be the offence and not the forfeiture which is concealed.

after the third attachment his person ought then to be attached and retained. So that it is remembered what vert is it is to be known as all trees not carrying fruit and those which carry fruit throughout the year, outside the demesne if formerly in the forest and maple trees because the lord king is seised [of them].

20. If any forester finds anyone cutting oak outside demesne wood in the regard without view or delivery of the forester or verderer he ought to attach him with 4 pledges.[1] The oak ought to be evaluated by view of the forester and recorded in the roll of the forester or verderer and it ought to be placed under 6 sure pledges. If he is found again his pledge ought to be doubled and if a third time let his person be detained.

21. If a greyhound is found damaging[1] the forest it ought to be retained and presented to the forester or verderer who will send it to the lord king or chief justiciar of the forest. If any mastiff is found in any forest and the mastiff is chained the mastiff's owner will be quit of that deed. But if it is not chained the mastiff's owner will be culpable as for mainpast and[2] ought to be placed under 6 pledges whose names ought to be recorded and [he should record] what the dog was like.[3]

22. If any[1] earl, bishop or baron who comes at the lord king's command passes through the lord king's forest he may take one or two beasts by view of the forester if he is present. But if not let him blow his horn lest he seem to do these things secretly. He may do as aforesaid when returning home.

23. If anyone takes any beast in the forest without warrant he must be arrested wherever he is found within the bounds of the forest. When he is taken the forester may not deliver him without the lord king's or the justiciar's special order. If anyone sees any evil-doers within the bounds of the forest taking or carrying off any wild animal he ought to [try to] take them to the best of his ability and should he be unable [to do so] he ought to raise the hue and cry.[1] If he does not do this he will be amerced.[2]

24. Should any wild beast be found dead or wounded and the offender be not found, at the next court an inquisition ought to be made and the finder, meanwhile, ought to be attached by sure pledges until cognizance has been taken of the offence. The flesh ought to be sent to the lepers' house if there is any nearby in the district. But if there is no such house nearby the flesh ought to be given to the poor and infirm and the head, skin and arrow if any be found shall be presented to the justiciar when he comes on ayre.

20: 1— New sentence begun for clarity.
21: 1— Lit. trans. 'running to the damage of'. 2-3— N's version of this passage is not translated.
22: 1— Lit. trans. 'whichever'.
23: 1-2— N's version of this passage is not translated. 2— Lit. trans. 'will remain in the king's heavy mercy'.

Commentary

Clause 1

Line 2: For discussion of enclosure of woods see pp. 234-235 and the discussion of the date of the laws below. 'Animalia' or animals is used throughout these laws for beasts or cattle. The distinction between 'animalia' and 'oves' can be seen in *Kelso Lib.*, 152 (*ante* 1190) and in *Pais. Reg.*, 5 and 17 when compared with *Pais. Reg.*, 92. (See p. 108.)

Lines 4-5: '15 days before the feast of John the Baptist to 15 days after the said feast' is from 9th June to 9th July. See p. 105.

Line 8: Fire-horn and dog called warset are discussed on pp. 105-106. The full etymology of 'warset' suggested to me by Dr Aitken is:

'*Warset* (h n. ?watchdog, one who sits on guard. O Anglian **weardsēta* (ONhb. probably **ward—*) (*sēta* from ē ǣ grade of *sittan* to sit, cf. pret. pl. nWS *sēton*, WS. *sǣton*). Cf. *burhseta* oppidanus, town-dweller (Wright-Wülcker 110/40). *Werdsetl*, place where guard is kept, those who keep guard.' Should the 's' of 'warset' be a mistranscription of 'f', this word may be derived from 'cum warda facta' or 'wardefet', meaning with watch set. See p. 105.

Clause 2

Lines 11-15: This specification of penalties for four offences also occurs in English forest laws, e.g., *Statutes of Realm*, i, 243-5.

Line 14: Witnesses in the forest laws are described either as lawful or trusty and see p. 144.

Line 15: A cross would have no special significance but would simply be a convenient mark. See p. 144.

Line 16: 'Menetum' or 'menée' is a blast on the horn. Originally from the Latin 'minare', 'minatum' was corrupted by the French 'menée' to 'menetum'. See Tilander, *Cynegetica*, i, 69. See Chapter 4 for use of the menée, p. 63.

Line 17: 'Castrum' implies the proximity of a royal castle.

Clause 3

Line 21: 'Nativi' or neyfs were unfree in the sense that they were bound to their lords by reason of their place of birth; Duncan, *The Making of the Kingdom*, 329.

Line 23: The king's prison would presumably be in a royal castle or perhaps a burgh tolbooth.

Clause 4

Line 26: The importance of the herdsman's presence or absence is again stressed. See p. 106.

Line 27: A bondman was a peasant who had to perform seasonal labour services for his lord; Duncan, *The Making of the Kingdom*, 326.

Clause 5

Line 30: Hanging up a goat by the horns would in effect kill it unless its owner

reclaimed it. The forester, however, must have had some fun getting the goat up there! (It is assumed there will be trees in the forest.)
Line 32: In this case the goat's entrails, not a cross, mark the spot.

Clause 6
Lines 33-4: Parish churches were used to publicise royal orders. See p. 92.

Clause 7
Line 38: According to M. L. Anderson, years when there is an abundance of acorns are rare in Scotland. See Anderson, *History of Scottish Forestry*, i, 133.

Clause 8
Line 41: Pannage is discussed above, pp. 107-108. A sounder applied to a group of 10 pigs and in the Scots of N is given as 'sundir'. It could also apply to a herd of pigs.
Line 42: A hog was a two- or three-year old pig. See York, *Master of Game*, (Grohman), 205-6. Two-year old sheep were also called 'hoggis'. See above, p. 249.
Line 44: An old pig is presumably 4 years or over in age. These terms for animals of different ages are essential for stock farming.

Clause 9
Lines 49-50: These reveal that foals were aged 1 and 2 years and became horses when 3 years old. Information concerning royal studs is given in Chapter 4 and above, p. 249.

Clause 10
Line 54: 'Carris et bigis' is translated by N as 'wanys and cartis'.
Line 56: Quit is used in a technical sense meaning free of blame and accusation.

Clause 11
Line 57: 'Inusitata' must be translated by forbidden, i.e., 'unused' in the sense of 'not to be used'. Right of way is discussed above, p. 112
Line 58: Swearing on a cross would give added conviction to the oath. A cross could easily mean a sword, as N's translation of cross by 'wapin' implies.
Line 59: 'Defensam' is used in the technical sense of forbidden.
Line 60: The common road would be the highway or right of way through the forest. Named roads in the forests of Ettrick and Gala and Leader probably represent these rights of way as Professor Barrow has suggested, e.g., Minchmoor Road, Girthgait and Malcolm's Road.
Line 61: However 'notus' is translated, it implies that the subject knew the correct routes and was, therefore, more culpable than if he were ignorant of them.
Line 62: Offenders in the forest of Gala and Leader were to be tried at the gate of Melrose in 1180. See above, p. 151 and Dickinson, *Sheriff Ct Book*, xi-xii.

w

Line 63: The offender's outermost layer of clothing can be variously interpreted! Presumably it was his cloak or jacket and hose if not his trousers.

Line 64: The offender's purse would no doubt be interpreted as his belongings generally.

Line 65: The porter would take custody of the offender since the trial took place at the gate of the castle.

Clause 12
Line 67: Herbage and foggage have been fully discussed above, pp. 107-110.

Clause 13
Lines 71-2: Vert and venison are discussed above, pp. 98-103; 103-112.

Clause 14
Lines 76-7: Hunting rights of those living beside the forest are discussed above, p. 229.
Free power to hunt may imply a free forest charter (see above, p. 231) or hunting pertinents (see above p. 185 and 226).

Line 78: This concerns a greyhound which hunted by sight and not by scent.

Lines 80-1: 'To cast his horn and leash' must presumably be interpreted in terms of controlling the greyhound. He could hunt in the forest as long as his hound was on a leash or could be controlled by his hunting horn. For use of horns see Chapter 4.

Clause 15
Lines 86-88: 'Canis currens' could imply a running or scenting hound.

Line 89: The bow and arrows were removed so that they could not be used. Although the use of 'corda' for the bow-string suggests a crossbow, the use of 'sagittas' definitely implies a short bow or long bow.

Clause 16
Line 94: This gives the conditions of c 1 apart from 'warset' and the mention of animals being scattered.

Line 98: 40 days' imprisonment is specified in this clause and in c 3.

Clause 17
Line 101: The passing of 4 courts may cover one year (Dickinson, *Sheriff Ct Book*, xiv).

Line 104: 'Ad capitale manerium', translated in N as 'cheff maner place', means the 'caput' of the holding where the head courts were held.
'Locis' could be translated as steads but would apply to holdings other than in Ettrick forest.

Clause 18
Lines 124-8: It is calmly assumed that the king will hear of the offence which, if the baron did not report it, would be unlikely. The provisions of this clause are discussed above, p. 200.

Lines 124-130: This sentence concentrates more on the suit prosecuting the offender while the following sentence concentrates on the forfeiture which the king should collect.

Clause 19

Line 142: To attach by pledges means that the pledges will swear to produce the offender when the trial is held.

Line 146: The verderer was an English forest official, usually a knight or landowner with property in the forest. He was elected in the county court and had to attend the forest courts which examined various matters including vert. See Petit Dutaillis, *Stubbs,* 160. There was no Scots equivalent.

Lines 148-152: Vert is defined as all trees. For the translation of 'arabiles' as maple trees see Turner, *Select Pleas of the Forest,* 133 and L. Dudley Stamp, *Man and the Land,* (London, 1955), 175. Even trees no longer within the forest were still part of the vert and so reserved and in the king's 'seisin' or possession.

Clause 20

Line 154: The 'regard' was the name given to the visit or court held by the English itinerant justices once every three years in English forests. Regarders presented cases to the court. The offender in this clause would presumably be tried in the 'regard'. See Petit Dutaillis, *Stubbs,* 161.

Line 156: The view of the forester, a phrase used in Scotland, is described above, p. 140.

Lines 156-7: Recording the value of the oak and having it confirmed would be important when the question of compensation arose.

Clause 21

Line 161: The verb 'to present' occurs frequently in those English clauses and is related to the jury of presentment which would bring cases before a court. In a forest regarders presented cases to the itinerant justices.

Line 163: A mastiff was a large dog capable of defending its master and his goods and powerful enough to attack a predatory wolf or boar. See Chapter 4.

Line 164: If the mastiff was chained it would be muzzled or on a lead. English mss. give 'mutulatus', not 'vinculatus'.

Line 166: 'Manupasto' is literally translated in N by 'hand fed'. It is translated as 'household' in the *Medieval Latin Word List*. See F. Pollock, F. W. Maitland, *The History of English Law,* (Cambridge 1898), 419, 568.

Line 169: The mastiff was a mongrel and therefore it was sensible to record the size and appearance of the dog.

Clause 22

Line 173: If a hunter was blowing his horn he was obviously operating openly, whereas stalking silently he might be suspected of poaching. See Chapter 4.

Clause 23

Line 177: to deliver the offender would be to try him or to fine him and release him.

Line 181: Raising the hue and cry was the traditional way of catching a thief and failure to take part was always punished.

Line 183: To be in the king's mercy is perhaps best understood as being at his mercy with regard to the amount of fine to be paid.

Lines 182-3: It is of note that N considers all towns to be around the forest and not within it, a stipulation not made in the English mss. in this clause or in clause 19.

Clause 24.

Line 191: The inquest would record the crime to be presented to the court held later, and it may have tried to determine who the culprit was.

Line 196: While Friars might administer to lepers in Scotland, some leper-houses had been founded before 1296. See Nicholson, *The Later Middle Ages*, 13, and *An Historical Atlas of Scotland, c400-c1600*, ed. P. McNeill, R. Nicholson (St Andrews, 1975), 47.

The Date of the Laws and Analysis

It is possible to date the laws by studying their content, by noting contradictions within them and by comparing the laws with external evidence of the forest system. It has been assumed that where one law contradicts another law the laws are probably of differing date. Similarly if a charter reference exactly matches one of the laws then it is assumed that the law was current when the charter was issued although the law need not have been issued at the same time. It has already been explained that a written set of rules was essential for the establishment of a forest system in Scotland and so the forest laws can be expected to belong to the 1130s and later. It is, nonetheless, conceivable that some earlier customs may have been embodied in the forest law and it is also conceivable that the first laws issued on forest matters would have subsequently to be altered to fit changing circumstances.

Evidence of such adaptation is seen in the fact that several forest laws are contradictory and that the laws are not one homogeneous body of law as the table of clauses showed. The laws will, therefore, be examined in the same groups as in the collation, clauses 1-11, clauses 12-18 and the English clauses 19-24. The dates to which these laws may be allocated are often broad and uncertain and never precise and definite.

1. Clauses 1-11.
    (a) Clause 1:
        Clause 1 comprises 3 parts which deal in turn with pannage, time of fence and pasture generally. It has been suggested by Professor

Barrow[27] that the first section dealt not with pannage but with time of fence, since 'pannacio' could easily be a mistranscription of 'fannacio'. This would seem reasonable since the first clause does read as though pannage occurred between 9 June and 9 July which was the time of fence. Moreover, there is no other example in medieval Latin of 'pannacio' and even Forest Laws 7 and 8 use 'pannagium'. There are, however, several objections to this interpretation. Pannage as a custom died out in the late thirteenth or early fourteenth century and, therefore, it is most unlikely that 'fannacionis' would be replaced by 'pannacionis'. In the twelfth and thirteenth centuries no-one would have made this substitution since pannage was still being collected in the autumn and it would be clearly seen that this substitution would imply the collection of pannage in June and July. In the fourteenth century, when pannage was no longer collected or mentioned, it would be unlikely for a scribe or lawyer to insert 'pannacionis', a dead custom mentioned only in confirmations of charters, for 'fannacionis', a live one. Since pannage as a custom did die out, the laws on pannage did suffer from alterations and copyists' errors and it is not surprising that problems arise with 'pannacionis' in this clause. One manuscript, N, obviously saw this difficulty in clause 1 with pannage occurring at the time of fence and simply omitted all reference to pannage rather than inserting 'fannacionis'. No manuscripts give the reading 'fannacionis', but what is more interesting is that no Scottish manuscript or charter so far encountered actually uses 'fannacio'. The only contemporary reference to fence is by date and not by name.[28] It is not till 1499 that 'fense' is recorded in Scottish sources.[29] There is some other evidence that the law should be considered as three sections. Manuscript B does provide a break between the section on pannage and that on fence and the third part of this clause begins with the phrase 'post lapsum vero temporis vel mensis', which seems to refer to the two preceding sections about a time and a month, i.e., time of pannage and month of fence. The compiler of clause 1, therefore, considered that it was divided into three parts.

The first part of this clause states that no beasts may enter any enclosure of woods in time of pannage. In other words only pigs could enter the woods at that time.[30] This part of clause 1 applies not to forests, as do clauses 6, 7 and 8 which concern pigs and pannage, but to woods and enclosures of woods. While enclosures of woods and 'hanyt' woods are recorded both within and outwith forests in the fifteenth century,[31] there is no earlier reference to enclosures of woods or covert of woods within forests in Scottish sources. Pannage, however, was probably collected in Scotland before David I established forests,[32] as the existence of the name 'Swinewood' suggests.

This law may, therefore, reflect Anglo-Saxon influence, although it is not couched in the same terms as any Anglo-Saxon pannage law, or it may reflect Norman influence in that Robert I, Duke of Normandy, had collected pannage 'in omnibus silvis' in 1032[33] and Normans in Scotland before the 1130s would have been aware of this custom. Whether this law reflected Norman custom and was enacted by David I or Alexander I before forests were established or whether it embodied earlier custom, it appears to have preceded the arrival of forests in Scotland or to have applied to woods where pannage was collected outside forests.

The second part of clause 1, which states the time of fence and the penalty for entering the forest at that time without permission, does apply to forests and was a ruling essential to any hunting reserve, and so the law may have been compiled in the 1130s. Since fence was only enforceable in a forest it follows that the first part of this law which applied to woods cannot refer to fence.

The third section of clause 1 states that beasts could be grazed freely in a forest provided they were not left in the forest at night and that the custom of 'wardefet' was observed.

Clause 1, therefore, represents three laws probably dating from the reign of David I and earlier. If they were issued or re-issued together and not combined at a later date by the compiler of a legal treatise, they may well have been the subject of a forest assise of David I. The text of clause 1 as it survives today may not be the original text. It seems likely that after the end of pannage collection the compilers of legal treatises did not fully understand the law and so condensed it till it read as though pannage occurred in time of fence.

(b) Clauses 2-9:

These clauses must all be of a different and probably later date or dates than clause 1 since, apart from clauses 7 and 8, they assume that pasture in forests is forbidden under pain of fine, whereas in the third part of clause 1 pasture was free. Clauses 6, 7 and 8 amplify the first part of clause 1 and provide more complex pannage arrangements. That clauses 2 to 9 are later and more complex than clause 1 can be clearly seen from the fact that in clause 1 the regulation of pasture took 10 lines, whereas in clauses 2 to 9 the same regulation takes 43 lines. In clauses 2, 3, 5, 6, and 9 the imposition of penalties is more refined than in clause 1, since the maximum penalty is not reached till the fourth offence.

While it is possible to distinguish clauses 2 and 3 which concern beasts in general from clauses 4 to 9 which deal with specific animals, this distinction does not facilitate dating. Clauses 2 to 3, on account of their more general nature, may be prior to clauses 4 to 9 but all are subsequent to clause 1. The departure from the free pasture situation of clause 1's third part and the initiation of year-round pasture restrictions may well reflect the clash of hunting and pastoral interests towards the end of the twelfth century. Clauses 2 to 9 may have been issued by

William I to contend with the growing difficulty of maintaining hunting reserves in the face of economic exploitation.[34] If they were issued as one group they may have been the subject of an assise in the early thirteenth century. Clauses 7 and 8 on pannage, which are obviously linked to clause 6 on pigs, are primarily concerned with pannage as a toll and with collecting as much pannage as possible. This attitude towards pannage appears to have developed in the late twelfth or early thirteenth century and so clauses 6, 7, and 8 may belong to that time.[35]

(c) Clauses 10 and 11:

These clauses both concern the imposition of rights of way through forests, a practice essential in any reserve and first recorded in 1147 x 1153 in the baronial reserve of Annandale.[36] Clause 10 could be considered to be a specific application of clause 11, although neither gives the impression of being the original prohibition of travel through forests which must have been issued by David I.

2. Clauses 12-18.

Clause 12, which discusses herbage and foggage, probably belongs to the thirteenth century. Herbage and foggage are first recorded in the later thirteenth century and provided a system of tolls whereby animals could be grazed in the forests. Clause 12 could, therefore, be later than the total ban on pasture of clauses 2 to 9 and may be associated with the relaxation of forest rights to permit economic activity in the mid-thirteenth century.[37]

Clause 13 deals with the basic reservation of vert and venison within reserves and in substance must belong to David I's reign. The second sentence, which grades the penalties for vert over four offences, is a development of the first section which states that the penalty for an offence against the vert is 8 cows and against the venison £10. This first sentence may represent a law of David I. Only clauses 1, 2 and 3 mention the penalty of 8 cows, which has an early ring to it since the laws of Malcolm MacKenneth stipulate that the penalty of 8 cows north of the Forth equalled the fine of £10 south of the Forth.[38] The second part of clause 13 may be later in origin because, like clauses 2 to 9, it does not impose the maximum penalty till the fourth offence.

Clauses 14 and 15 both concern the rights of people living around a forest to hunt in that forest and as such are associated with the *purlieu* and with the concept of *res nullius*.[39] These clauses are complementary. Clause 14 states that a man with free power to hunt, presumably as a result of a free forest charter or hunting pertinents, may follow his greyhound into a forest provided he can control it by horn or leash. In clause 15 a man who holds lands with or without hunting pertinents can follow his scenting hound into a forest. Since this hound would probably be kept on a leash, the law only stipulated that the hunter remove his bow and arrows. Both laws most likely belong to the thirteenth century, for it is then that the *purlieu* first appears, it is then that *res nullius* receives a clear Scottish statement, and in 1294/5 a charter of James Steward requires the removal of bow and arrows in a reserved forest.[40] This same charter, however, also prevented the monks of Paisley who held forest rights in the lands of Maich and Calder from hunting in the whole of the Steward's adjacent forest. In other words, Laws 14 and 15 did not operate in Renfrew in 1294/5. While the application and enforcement of the forest law was by no means uniform, this does suggest that these clauses do not belong to the last quarter of the thirteenth century or thereafter.[41]

Clause 16 is probably later than clause 1 because it is a specific application of the third part of clause 1 omitting any reference to 'warset'. The second part of clause 16 applies the regulations of clause 13 on vert solely to a bondman. In both parts of clause 16 the bondman receives reduced penalties and it is the penalty of 1 cow or 5s or 40 days in prison which gives some guide as to the date, since the price of a cow is given as 6s in *Regiam Majestatem* bk 4, c 54. The later thirteenth century and early fourteenth century are therefore possible dates for this law. The use of bondman, however, would argue for an earlier date and would tend to exclude the fourteenth century.

Clause 17, which concerns an animal lost in the forest, resembles *Quoniam Attachiamenta*, c 32, which states that a stray animal found in a lord's lands must be publicised in markets, churches and in the neighbourhood. It cannot be escheated by the lord for a year and a day which may, in effect, be the same length as the four courts of clause 17.[42] Clause 17 is, therefore, a more detailed application of *Quoniam's* clause and as such can be ascribed to the later thirteenth century.

Clause 18, which discusses the trial of offences in baronial forests, mentions the free forest grant, a form which was not introduced till the 1230s,[43] and must belong to the mid-thirteenth century or thereafter.

While clauses 12 to 18 have been attributed to varying dates, there is an essential unity to them since they occur in only a few mss., a fact presumably occasioned by some circumstance in the origin of these laws. The most appropriate circumstance would be if all the laws had been promulgated at one time, perhaps the later thirteenth century, and if only a few copies had survived. It is also possible that these laws were of special relevance to baronial forests: clauses 15, 18, and possibly clause 14 mention baronial forests or free forest charters; in clause 16 'bondi regis' of clause 4 has been altered to 'bondi alicuius'; and the forester is mentioned only in clause 18, which would be in accord with the barons' use of other servants to administer their reserves.[44] If these laws were a code of baronial law, clause 13 may have been repeated because of its important content and clause 12 included out of interest. Whether or not clauses 12 to 18 do form a group of laws for baronial forests, they could have been issued at one time in the later thirteenth century.

3. Clauses 19-24.

The collation of these laws and the examination of English mss. has already suggested that these laws were introduced to Scotland by Edward I. Clause 22 supports this view, since outside the period of Edward I's influence there is no external evidence to suggest that clause 22 was enforced or even of practical value. Edward, however, granted numerous Scottish barons the right to take deer in Scottish forests,[45] and clause 22 which permits bishops, earls and barons — archbishops have been excluded — to hunt when passing through a royal forest whilst obeying a royal command is consistent with such a practice.

When these clauses were adopted by Scots lawyers they were altered to fit Scottish conditions: the introduction of 'capitali custode foreste' in clause 19; 'per visum forestarii' and not 'viridarii' in clause 20; and the insertion of 'forestarii seu' in clause 21. The greatest alterations are those made in the clauses included in N. N did not include clauses 19, 20 and 22 because they were presumably inapplicable to Scotland and because the procedural or administrative arrangements, to a certain extent, duplicate and contradict clauses 13 and 16, both included by N.

It is in clauses 21, 23 and 24 that the alterations made by N's tradition, probably in the fourteenth century, can be seen. Clause 21, which was in many ways complementary to clauses 14 and 15 since it concerned a mastiff in the forest which belonged to anyone and not just a neighbour of the forest, would be of value to lawyers. N, considering that clauses 14 and 15 applied to landholders, added to clause 21 that the penalty should vary depending on whether the culprit was a freeman or a bondman, which suggests the early fourteenth century. To clause 23 detailing procedure when poachers were seen and could or could not be caught, N adds that it was to the nearest towns that the hue and cry had to be taken and that the forester must be informed. Such a law would be of value in Ettrick in the fifteenth century and in other forests where forester-tenants had to preserve the vert and venison.[46] It would be after the execution of these regulations that the writ 'Contra transgredientes forestam' might be required.[47] Clause 24 requires the holding of an inquest when a dead beast was found in the forest and the culprit was unknown, a procedure closely related to the inquest ordered by the above-mentioned writ. N, by substituting 'justice on ayre' for 'verderer', has adapted this clause to Scottish circumstances.[48]

While these clauses were never enacted by a Scots parliament, they all contained administrative provisions which would be of use to Scots lawyers and forest officials. The alterations made in them most likely belong to the early fourteenth century, but the laws so altered would have continued to be of value in the fifteenth century when N was compiled.

Select collation

Clause 1

Lines[1]	B	C	E	H
1	Inhibita	Inhibitum	Inhibita	Inhibitum
3	licenciati fuerint	licenciam habuerint	licenciati fuerint	licenciati fuerint
4	forestariis	forestariis	forestariis	forestariis
5	idem festum	idem festum	idem festum	idem festum
5	ammitent	perdent ad foris- factum	amittent	damnantur
7				illa animalia
8	warset	warset vel berset	warseth	warsatte
9	nocte cubancia	nocte cubancia	nocte cubancia	
9	adductis	adductis	adductis	adductis
10	perduntur	perduntur	producuntur	perduntur

	Ed	S	A	N
1	Inhibitum	Inhibitum	Inhibitum	forbodyn
3	licenciati fuerint	licenciati fuerint	licenciati fuerint	
4	forestariie	forestariis	forestariis	the forstar
5	idem festum	idem festum	idem festum	the said fest
5	dampnantur	damnantur	dampnantur	**aw to the forfalt**
7				
8	warseate	varset	warsete	warset
9				be nycht lyand
9	adductis	adductis	abductis	to brocht
10	perdantur	perdantur	perduntur	thar sal be tynt

	D	M	Co	Ca
1	Inhibitum	Inhibitum	Inhibendum	Inhibitum
3	licenciati fuerint	licenciati fuerint	licenciati fuerit	licenciati fuerint
4	forestariis	forestariis	forestario	forestariis
5	idem festum	idem festum		dictum festum

1. Line nos. in the present edition.

Lines

Line				
5	damnantur	damnantur	perdunt	damnantur
7		illa animalia		
8	warsete	warsaite	warset	warseate
9		nocte in foresta cubancia		
9	abductis	adductis	adductis	adductis
10	perduntur	perduntur	perdent	perdent

Line	J	L₁	L₂	T	Ma
1	Inhibitum	Inhibitum	Inhibitum	Inhibitum	Inhibitum
3	licenciati fuerint	licenciati fuerint	licenciati fuerint	licenciati fuerint	licenciati fuerint
4	forestariis	forestariis	forestariis	forestariis	forestarius
5	idem festum	idem festum	idem festum	idem festum	festum diem
5	damnantur	perduntur	dampnantur	dampnantur	damnantur
7	illa animalia				
8	warsett	warset	versate	warsette	varsette
9					
9	abductis	adductis	adductis	adductis	abductis
10	perdantur	perduntur	perduntur	perdantur	perdantur

Line	Ez
1	forbiddin
3	they . . . have licence
4	the forrester
5	same feist
5	under the pain of tinsale
7	
8	warsett
9	lyand all the nycht
9	in presens of
10	may be escheitit

Clause 2

Line	B	C	E	A	Ed
16	cornuare minatim	cornare vel cornizare menetum	cornuare minutim	eoroae jumentum	coronare in muentum

Line	D	H	S
16	cornuare menetum	cornare menetum	cornare menetum

Clause 3

Lines	B	C	E	S	A
19	animalibus burgensis	animalia burgen- sium	animalibus burgen- sium	animalia burgen- sium	animalia burgen- sium
23	personaliter	personaliter	personaliter		

	Co	L₁	N	H	Ed
19	animalibus burgen- sium	animalia burgen- sium	of the bestis of burges	animalia burgen- sium	animalis burgen- sium
23	personaliter	personaliter	bodilik		

	Ez
19	cattel perteining to burgessis
23	

Clause 4

	E	H	Ed	S
25	adductis	adductis	abductis	adductis
26	forestarius	forestarius	forestarius	forestarius
27	vero bon- dorum . .	vero husband- orum . .		vero husband- orum . .
28	1 denarium tantum	1 d. tantum		1 d.
28	capiat de grege	de grege		

	A	D	M
25	abductis	abductis	adductis
26	forestarius	forestarius	forestarius
27	vero husband- orum . .	vero husband- orum . .	vero husband- orum . .
28	1 d tantum	1 d tantum	1 d tantum
28			de grege

	Co	Ca	L₁
25	adductis	adductis	adductis
26		forestarius	
27	non husband- orum . .	vero husband- orum . .	vero husband- orum . .
28	unum denarium tantum	1 d tantum	de grege
28	capiet de tota grege		1 d.

Lines	L₂	T	Ma
25	adductis	adductis	adductis
26	forestarius	forestarius	forestarius
27	husband- orum . .	vero husband- orum . .	vero husband- orum . .
28	denarium tantum	1 d tantum	1 denarium
28			

Clause 5

	B	C	E	H	Ed	S	A	N	Co
30	arboribus	arbore	arboribus	arbore	arbore	arbore	arbore	treis	arbore

	Ez
30	one trie

Clause 8

	B	C	E
41	Et hic est	Et iste est	Et hic enim
41	pannagii (ponagii)	pannagii	pannagii
41	videlicet de decem	videlicet de decem	videlicet de decem
42	porcis	porcis	porcis
42	Rex	Rex	Rex
42	meliorem	meliorem porcum	meliorem
42	forestarius	forestarius habebit	forestarius
42	unum hog	unum hog	unum hog
43	set forestarius habebit	set forestarius habebit	set forestarius habebit
44	veteri	veteri	veteri
44	Si aliqui ibi fuerint		Si aliqui ibi fuerint
45	unum hog de decem	unum hog de sundra	unum hog de decem
46	Et si fuerint pauciores	Et si pauciores fuerint	Et si fuerint pauciores
47	j obolum	obolum	j obolum

	H	Ed	S
41	Iste est modus	Iste est modus	Iste est modus
41	pannagii videlicet	pannagium oporet	pannagii oportet
41	id est decem	videlicet decem	id est decem
42	porcis	porcorum	porcorum
42	Rex	Rex	Rex
42	meliorem porcum	meliorem porcum	meliorem porcum

Lines

Lines			
42	forestarium	forestarius	forestarius
42		habebit	habebit
42	unum hoggastrum	unum hoggastrum	unum hoggastrum
43	nisi	set forestarius habebit (twice)	nisi
44	veteri	veteri	vice
44	si aliqui ibidem fuerint	si aliqui ibidem fuerint	si aliqui ibidem fuerint
45	unum hoggastrum	unum hoggastrum	unum hoggastrum
46	si pauciores fuerint hoggastri	si pauciores sint hoggastri	si pauciores fuerint hoggastri
47	nisi obolum	nisi obolum	nisi obolum

Lines	A	N	D
41	Iste est modus	this is the maner	Iste est modus
41	pannagii oportet	pannage	pannagii
41	id est decem	that is to say of x	id est decem
42	porcorum	swyn	porcorum
42	Rex	king	lex
42	meliorem porcum	the best swyn	meliorem porcum
42	forestarius habebit	the forster	forestarius habebit
42	unum hoggastrum	a hog	unum hoggastrum
43	set forestarius habebit		set forestarius habebit
44	veteri	ald	veteri
44	si aliqui ibidem fuerint	gif ony be thar	si aliqui ibidem fuerint
45	unum hoggastrum	j hog	unum hoggastrum
46	si pauciores sint hoggastri	and thar be fewer	si pauciores sint hoggastri
47	nisi obolum	j obol	nisi obolum

Lines	M	Co	Ca
41	Iste est modus	Iste est modus	Iste est modus
41	pannagii videlicet	pannagii videlicet	pannagii oporte
41	id est decem	id est de decem	Et in decem
42	porcis	porcis	porcorum
42	Rex	rex	rex
42	meliorem porcum	meliorem porcum	meliorem porcum
42	forestarius	forestarius	forestarius habebit
42	unum hoggastrum	unum hoggastrum	unum hoggastrum
43	nisi		nisi
44	veteri	veteri	veteri

Lines

44	si aliqui ibidem fuerint	si aliqui ibidem fuerint	si aliqui ibidem fuerint
45	unum hoggastrum	nisi (from above)	unum hoggastrum
46	si pauciores fuerint hoggastri	unum hoggastrum si pauciores fuerint	si pauciores sint nisi obolum
47	nisi obolum	hoggastri nisi unum obolum	

	J	L₁	L₂
41	Item est modus	item est modus	Iste est modus
41	pannagii videlicet	pannagii videlicet	pannagii oportet
41	id est decem	x	id est x
42	porcis	porcorum	porcorum
42	Rex	Rex	Rex
42	meliorem porcum	meliorem porcum	meliorem porcum
42	forestarius	forestarius	forestarius habebit
42	unum hoggastrum	unum hoggastrum	hoggastrum
43	nisi	nisi	
44	veteri	veteri	vice
44	si aliqui ibidem fuerint	si aliqui ibidem fuerint	si aliqui ibidem fuerint
45	unum hoggastrum	unum hoggastrum	unum hoggastrum
46	si pauciores fuerint hoggastri	si pauciores fuerint hoggastri	si pauciores fuerint
47	nisi obolum	nisi obolum	nisi obolum

	T	Ma	Ez
41	Iste est modus	Item iste est modus	This is the manor
41	pannagii oportet	pannagii oportet	of pannage viz
41	etest decem	id est decem	that is ten
42	porcorum	porcis	swyn
42	Rex	rex	king
42	meliorem porcum	meliorem porcum	best swyn
42	forestarius habebit	forestarius habebit	the forester
42	unum hoggastrum	unum hoggastrum	ane hogling
43	nisi	nisi	but the forester shall have
44	veteri	veteri	ald
44	et aliqui ibi fuerint	si aliqui ibidem fuerint	that sal happin to be thair
45	unum hoggastrum	unum hoggastrum	ane hogling of ten
46	si pauciores sint	si pauciores sint	gif thay be fewar
47	nisi obolum	unum obolum	no thing bot ane half pennie

Clause 11

Lines	B	C	E	H
57	aliquis extraneus	aliquis extraneus	aliquis extraneus	aliquis extraneus
57	infra forestam	infra forestam	infra forestam	intraverit in forestam
57	inusitata	inusitata	inusitata	inhabita
58	crucem	arma	crucem	arma
60	ad communem viam	ad communem viam	ad communem viam	in rectam viam et communem
64	quod ad opus eius sit	quod ad opus eorum sit	quod ad opus eius sit	quod ad forest- arium per- tinent

Lines	N	D	M
57	ony stranger	aliquis	
57		intraverit per forestam	
57	habitabile	inchibita	habitabile
58	arma	arma	arma
60	in viam rectam et communem	in rectam viam et communem	in viam rectam communem
64	quod ad forest- am pertinet	quod ad forest- arium per- tinent	quod ad forest- pertinet

Lines	Co	Ca	MA
57	ony stranger		aliquis extraneus
57	within the forest		intraverit in forestam
57	forbidden	habitabile	inhibita
58	wapin	arma	arma
60	to the common way	in viam rectam et communem	in viam rectam et communem
64	that is for his behuf	quod ad forest- am pertinet	quod ad forest- am pertinet

Lines	T	Ez
57	aliquis	ony unknawin personis
57	intraverit forestam	enter within the forest
57	inhabitata	forbiddin
58	arma	solemnitlie

Lines

60	in rectam viam · et communem	to the ryt and common passage	
64	qd. forestario pertinet		

Lines	Co	Ca	Ma
57	si quis	aliquis	aliquis
57	intraverit in foresta	intraverit forestam	intraverit in forestam
57	inhibita	inhabitata	inhibita
58	crucem	arma	arma
60	in viam communem	inrectam viam et communem	in rectam viam et communem
64	quod ad eum pertinet	id forestario pertinet	ad forestarium pertinet

Clause 14

Lines	N	C	Ez
77	and lattis		lettis
79	that free man may	Ille liber potest	It is lesume to him to follow his hundis
79	folow the rach in the kingis forest	sequi leporarium suum in foresta regis	within the kingis forest
80			
81	his lesch		his doggis lesch
82	that man sal frely tak	idem liber reportavit	that man incontinent sal tak
83	with chalance	sine calumpnia	without challenge

Clause 17

Lines	N	C	Ez
105	to quhamsoever	cuicunque	to all and sundrie
105		vendicare volenti ad prosequendum si voluerit	that will challenge and follow
105	that sic a best		the beist that
106	is fundin		is sa fundin

x

Clause 19

Lines	H	Ed	S	A	D
141	invenerit	invenerit	invenerit	inveniet	invenit
142	attachiare	attachiare	attachiare	attachiare	attachiari
148	retineri	retineri	retineri	retineri	
148	in memoria	in memoria	in memoria	in memoria	in memoriam
151	extra dom- inicum	extra dom- inicum	extra dom- inicum	extra dom- inicum	extra dom- inicum

	EL	ELP₁
141	invenerit	invenerit
142	attachiare	attachiare
148	redineri	retineri
148	memoria	in memoria
151	fraxinus	extra dominicum

Clause 21

	H	Ed	S
161	mittet	mittet	mittet
164	ipse cuius mastinus fuerit		ipse cuius mastinus fuerit
164	erit quietus de	quietus erit de	quietus erit de
165	illo facto to	illo facto to	illo facto to
165	ipse cuius mastinus fuerit	ipse cuius mastinus fuerit	ipse cuius mastinus fuerit
169	casus	canis	casus

	A	N	D
161	natet	send	natet
164	ipse cuius mastinus fuerit	he that aucht that mastice	ipse cuius mastinus fuerit
164	quietus erit de	sal be of the	quietus erit de
165	illo facto to	deed quyt to	illo facto to
165	ipse cuius mastinus	he that aw that mastice	ipse cuius mastinus fuerit
169	canis		canis

	Co	Ca	L₂
161	nocet	mittet	mittet
164	ipse coastinus fuerit	ipse cuius mastinus fuerit	ipse cuius mastinus fuerit
164			quietus est de
165			illo facto
165			
169	canis	casus	casus

Lines	T	Ma	Ez	EL
161	mittet	mittet	sent	mittere
164	ipse cuius masti-nus fuerit		the owner of the said dog	ipse cuius erat
164			sal be quit and free	quietus de illo
165			thairanent to	facto to
165			his maister or awnier	ipse cuius fuerit mastinus
169	casus	casus	dog	canis

ELP₁

161	mittere
164	ille cuius mastinus fuerit
164	erit de illo facto quietus to
165	ipse cuius fuerit mastinus
169	canis

Clause 23

	H	Ed	S
175	corpus suum	corpus suum	corpus suum
176	arestetur	arrestandum est	arrestandum est
177	non liceat forest-ario deliberare	non liceat forest-ario deliberare	non liceat forest-ario deliberare
181	levare hii et cry	levare hii et cry	levare hy et cry

	A	N	Co
175	corpus suum	his body is to	corpus suum
176	arrestandum est	be arestyt	arrestandum est
177	non liceat forestario deliberare	it is nocht lefull to the forester to deliver	non liceat et forestario deliberans
181	levare hw et cry	to rays hoy and cry to the nerrest tounys	levare how et cry

	Ez	EL	ELP₁
175	his body may be	corpus suum	corpus suum
176	arestit	arestetur	resistendum est
179	it is nocht lesum to the forester to relief him	non deliberetur	non liceat forestario ipsum deliberare
181	raise ane hoy and cry to the narrest tounis	levare hutes et crie	levare hu et cri

Clause 24

Lines	N	Ez	EL
195	the flesh forsuth	the flesch of that beist fundin	caro mittatur
195	aw to be sent	sal be sent	
197	gif thar be ony sic ner by	if thair be ony thair about	si quis prope fuerit
198	in the cuntre	in the cuntrey	

ELP$_1$

195	Caro autem
195	debet mitti
197	si qua prope fuerit
198	in partibus illis

APPENDIX B

The Tenants and Tenancy of Ettrick Forest

WHEN Ettrick forest returned to the crown in 1455, it was divided into a series of ideal or theoretical units called *loci*. The holding which a tenant rented might comprise either a whole *locus*, a half *locus* or a quarter *locus*, which last could also be a hamlet or a 'lesu' which meant pasture.[1] Obviously the number of *loci* differed from the number of individual holdings. A tenant's holding, whether a complete or part *locus*, could be called a 'stede' or a 'forester-stede',[2] while a locus might also be called a 'forester-stede'.[3]

Holdings and *Loci* in Ettrick in 1455

	Ettrick	Tweed	Yarrow
Holdings	47	19	26
Loci	45½	17	23¾

Each *locus* paid a rent of £6 and most also paid 1 bowcow, 1 fogmart, 1 fulemart and 10 or 20 lambs.[4] Marts, lambs and half the money rent were paid at All Saints and bowcows and the other half of the money rent at Lammas.[5] The leases lasted from three to five years but were renewable, and grassums and entries were charged as usual. Tenants could hold more than one stead and when a stead was held jointly the tenants were usually related.

Several steads in Ettrick were held in stelebow, which was in many ways a substitute for specific royal demesne. Whereas previously the king's *nativi* would have kept his flocks on his demesne, as may have been the case in Philiphaugh before 1288,[6] the flocks were later kept by tenants on land which was let to them. In 1455 several steads were held by the king and queen, but since the king had sheep in Ettrick in 1434[7] it is possible that he had held these steads before 1455. In 1466 x 1467 Bowhill, one of these holdings which were still held by the king and queen in 1460-1461,[8] was probably held in stelebow since it was stated to be occupied by the king's goods and the usual fermes were lost.[9] In 1468 the first definite example of stelebow tenure in Ettrick was recorded, when East and West Mountbenger, Catslack and Blackgrain were held by David Crichton with the king's goods for which he paid 40 merks (perhaps a mistake for 400 merks, see below), and the usual fermes were discharged.[10] These steads had been in Queen Mary's hands in 1460-1461 and were probably let in stelebow on her death in 1463, and similarly in 1486 x 1487 Caddonlee was placed in stelebow on the death of Queen Margaret who had held it previously.[11] Patrick Crichton, son of David Crichton, received a

Privy Seal letter authorising him to hold the same four steads in stelebow for five years at 400 merks *per annum* on condition that he kept them forestlike.[12] In 1499 John Murray of Falahill and David Pringle of Tinnis received four steads in stelebow for nine years for £300 *per annum*.[13] By 1501, twenty-one steads were let in stelebow, probably for nine years at 100 merks each.[14] When Ettrick was set in feu ferme these steads were no longer let in stelebow but for a feu which was usually higher than the feu for other steads.

In 1501, in an *assedacio* held by the king and lords of council, the rents of all steads except those held in stelebow were increased, the length of tenure was extended to nine years, all tenants were required to keep the statutes of 1499[15] and revenues in kind were no longer paid or charged. The rent of five steads was increased from £6 to £30 or over, of twenty-four steads to anything between £20 and £25 and the majority of the remaining rents were increased to anything between £12 and £20. Tenants were allowed to complete the terms of their previous lease before transferring to the new rental.[16] In 1504-1505, however, certain steads were still not paying the new rental[17] and although it stated that leases were to be for nine years, when a commission was appointed to hold an *assedacio* in 1506 it was instructed as previously to make leases of three to five years.[18] Nevertheless, from 1500 onwards several Privy Seal letters of tack provided for leases of nine years.[19]

Subletting, which was permitted by a special grant, first appeared in 1479 x 1480,[20] and from 1498 onwards several Privy Seal letters permitted subletting as part of the lease.[21]

The process of feuing Ettrick forest commenced in the *assedacio* of February 1505/6 when the tenants of Ettrick were ordered to present their letters of tack to an open court of the forest in Edinburgh on 17 April 1506.[22] On 18 April in the court the tenants were ordered to go before the treasurer, comptroller and commissioners between 18 April and Whitsunday in order to have their steads set in feu ferme. This was to be done according to the 'bill'[23] produced by the treasurer in this court or as the tenants could agree with the lords. After Whitsunday the king was to set any remaining steads in feu to whomsoever he wished. This was to be done despite the conjoint infeftment of Ettrick to the queen, and previous leases were to be unaffected. This last point is important since many leases from 1501 onwards were for nine years and in 1509 and 1510 leases on the old pattern were still being granted for nine years.[24]

The first extant feu charters for Ettrick date from 5 December 1507 when three were issued. Twelve survive from 1510, three from 1511 and three from 1512.[25] In 1510 the feus of all the steads were listed in the royal rental book and probably most of the steads entered into feu ferme tenure in that year. At the 1510 *assedacio* in Edinburgh the commissioners ordered the tenants and foresters to come and raise their 'signatouris', pay their grassums and show their 'certificatioun' or title to their stead within the next twenty days.[26] The feuing of Ettrick was considered by the commissioners in May, June, July and August 1510 at Stirling, Peebles and Edinburgh. Since fermes of Ettrick up to and including 1509-1510 had been charged at the same rate as in 1502,[27] it appears the exchequer did not consider Ettrick to be set in feu ferme till 1510, although in fact some feu ferme charters were granted earlier and some steads were not held in feu ferme till later.

The amount of the feu ferme appears to have been settled individually with each tenant. While the feu was always more than the 1501 rent, the increases which varied from £2 to £16 were not proportionately so large as in 1501. Such matters as the quality and size of the stead and the ability of the tenant to pay as well as his power to arrange a good rent for himself probably influenced the amount of the feu. Those steads which were let in stelebow received more standardised feus, for all but four were feued for £50. The two Mountbengers were feued for £70 10s and Catslack and Blakgrain for £70 3s 4d. In other words, on all but four of the stelebow steads the return was reduced by £16 13s 4d. The feuing of Ettrick does not appear to have produced any lasting increase in crown revenue, although Dr Madden has recently argued to the contrary.[28] The form of the exchequer accounts renders the calculation of revenue somewhat difficult but it can be done in two ways, by using the gross theoretical revenue in the charge side of the account or the actual revenue collected and accounted for in the discharge side of the account. In 1501 the gross revenue from rents alone rose from £700 approximately to £2,670. The sum of £700 is obtained by adding the money rents to the money value of the rents in kind at 1473 prices, which were current in 1495-1496.[29] The gross rent of the forest had remained unchanged between 1455 and 1501. The rent increases of 1501 could, therefore, have produced a sizeable rise in the royal revenue. In 1512, however, the gross revenue charged was only £2,672 approximately. The feuing of Ettrick forest brought no increase in gross crown revenue. The comparison of actual revenue before and after feuing is more difficult. The following figures have been obtained by adding together from the discharge side of the account all rents in kind and sums of money which were collected and sent to the king, the comptroller or others, or spent. Sums which were never collected but simply allowed, e.g., the rents of the forest officials, have been excluded. The real revenue before 1501 varied considerably: £904 8s in 1490;[30] £282 19s 4½d on average in 1491 and 1492;[31] and £862 10s in 1494.[32] Not all of this revenue ended up in the hands of the comptroller. In 1494 only £477 13s was recorded in the discharge side of the account as being sent to the comptroller. In 1502 the real revenue rose dramatically to £1,779,[33] in 1506 to £2,098 13s 2d,[34] and after the start of feuing to £2,174 13s 1d in 1512,[35] but it fell in 1513 to £1,867 14s 9d.[36] The sums received by the comptroller rose to £718 14s 10d in 1502, £1550 12s 2d in 1503,[37] and £1,721 15s 2d in 1506, but fell to £1,484 3s 9d in 1512 and to £1,470 2s 11d in 1513. In terms of real revenue, therefore, it was not feuing but the rent increases of 1501 which enlarged the royal revenue. In other words the feuing of Ettrick forest brought no lasting increase of crown revenue. In 1510, when most of the steads appear to have been let, the entry fee which equalled the feu would of course have brought a large increase in the revenue. Unfortunately the account of 1510-1511 which should have shown this increase is not extant and in the account of 1511-1512 one finds that £500 worth of entries had been remitted by the king under the Signet.[38] The financial benefit therefore even of the entries was diminished.

In view of the conditions under which Ettrick's tenants lived, subject to forest restrictions, changes in rent and administrative changes, the frequency with which the steads changed hands is important. Although the rentals of Ettrick provide considerable information, one can never make a complete comparison of the tenants of all steads in two different years since the rentals do not mention the tenants of every stead, and even where a comparison of tenants is possible the composition of the holding may have altered. Before the rentals begin in 1484, the accounts of Ettrick furnish some information. In the ensuing table a holding is any unit whether a group of *loci*, a single *locus* or any part of a *locus* held by an individual tenant or by joint tenants.

Years	ER	No. of comparable holdings	No. which change tenant	Comment
1456-1468	vi, 223 ff vii, 521 ff	19	8	Of these 8, 4 were transferred from the king to a tenant who held in stelebow.
1468-1479	viii, 583 ff	8	1	
1479-1485 and 1486	ix, 609 ff, 614 ff	20	5	The rentals of 1485 and 1486 are examined together. The rental of 1484 differs only slightly from those of 1485 and 1486.
1486-1488	x, 650 ff	62	44	
1486-1490	x, 675 ff	82	42	
1488-1490		57	25	Of these 25, 7 returned to tenants, removed in 1488 but who held steads in 1486.
1490-1499	xi, 396 ff	74	36	18 of these steads returned to tenants, removed in 1488 and 1490 who held steads in 1486.
1499-1501	xi, 457 ff	59	18	
1501-1510	xiii, 649 ff	73	23	12 steads returned to tenants, removed in 1501 who held steads in 1499.

The most striking fact to emerge from this table is the very high turnover of tenants between 1486 and 1490, when a total of 56 steads changed hands. This may be connected with the change of government in 1488, and if so it suggests that most of the tenants in Ettrick forest had sided with James III despite the fact that the Merse and Teviotdale sided with the future James IV.[39] There could be several reasons for this. It is possible that the tenants would side with their landlord since they did after all lease their lands from the king, and if they had no strong feelings for one side or the other it would be better to side with James III rather than against him. On the same argument the officials of the forest may have been more inclined to support James III. John Murray of Touchadam, the currour of Yarrow, had been a commissioner for crown lands till 1486 and lost his office in 1488. As currour he probably could secure the following of his ward for James III, with the result that of 19 comparable holdings in Yarrow 19 changed hands between 1486 and 1490. The bailie of the forest, John Cranston of that ilk, was replaced in 1488 by Lord Home, a supporter of James IV, which again suggests that Cranston had favoured James III. Some tenants may have supported James III as a result of local rivalries. In the sixteenth century after Flodden there was a traditional rivalry between the men of the Forest and the men of the Merse, as a popular ballad bears witness.[40] This rivalry may date from the fifteenth century. The tenants of the Forest may have sided with James III in opposition to Lord Home and perhaps to other Homes who dwelt nearer to the Forest. There may of course have been other family rivalries. Thirdly the king may well have been more able to raise military support from his own lands. In the rental of 1490 the tenant of Mid-Fauside had to provide one lance and two archers for the king in time of war.[41] In 1499 the ninth statute of Ettrick required that each stead be able to provide two bows and a spear with horse and gear. Both these examples suggest that there was provision for a customary levy of soldiers in Ettrick in the fifteenth century, and James III may have tried to raise that levy in 1488. The fact remains that the changeover of tenants in 1488 and 1490, for whatever reason it occurred, was exceptionally high.

There was, however, a tendency despite the changes between 1488 and 1490, in 1501 when the rents increased and in 1510 when feuing was officially established, for holdings to revert to families who had held the same or other holdings and thus for steads to stay in the hands of certain families and their branches.

When one looks at the period 1486-1510, one can see the effect of this gradual change of tenants. Of 80 comparable holdings, 44 were held by different families in 1510 from those who held in 1486. Therefore, probably half of the holdings in the forest changed hands in 24 years: averaged out over the approximate total of 96 holdings, that is two per year. At first sight one might suspect that tenants were leaving the forest as a result of forest restrictions and increased rents, but this was not the case. Firstly, the restrictions were being reduced and secondly, although half the holdings had new owners, this does not mean that the tenant families had altered drastically. Disregarding for the present the total number of steads held by each family, the families who were best represented in 1486 were still top of the list in 1510: in 1486 ten Kerrs, nine Scotts, nine Murrays and six Pringles held lands in the forest, while in 1510 the families with most tenants in the forest were the Kerrs with eight, the Murrays with seven, the Scotts with five, the Crichtons with five, the Pringles with three or five and the Homes with three. (See table below.) Other families such as the Turnbulls, Elphinstones, Liddels and Taits who held steads in 1486 still held lands in 1510. Although the same families still held steads, the balance of the number of steads held by each family had altered. In 1510 Lord Home held ten steads and the other Homes four steads, whereas in 1486 they had held none.

The tenancy of the forest was not static and despite the constant changing of steads, the reasons for which remain obscure, there was an overall continuity, since the tenants were still largely members of the same families. The position regarding the tenancy of the forest is, therefore, best described as one of changing continuity rather than one of continuous change.

When examining the tenants in Ettrick, it is noticeable that certain families predominated in certain wards and also that the currour was usually of the same family as several of the tenants in his ward. Of 17 holdings in Yarrow in 1485 and 1486 when the currour was a Murray, four were held by Kerrs and three by Murrays. Of 43 holdings in Ettrick when the currour was a Scott, nine were held by Scotts and in Tweed six out of seventeen tenants were Pringles including the currour. Moreover, when tenants required pledges they usually found them within the forest and the master currour might stand as a pledge.[42] To a certain extent, therefore, the residents of the forest formed a community with tighter social groupings in each ward.

The Tenants of Ettrick Forest

I 1485-6 (*ER*, ix, 609, 614)

If the tenant changed between 1485 and 1486, the 1485 tenant has been placed in brackets.

Ettrick Ward

John Ross of Hawkhead	George Robison, comptroller
James Scott	John Cranston of that ilk
Patrick Murray	Ralph Kerr
Robert Scott	David Scott-Edschaw
Archibald, Earl of Angus	David Scott of Buccleuch
James Rutherford	William Scott
William Turnbull-Gargunnock	Walter Scott
Robert Rutherford	Joan Douglas, mother of Walter Scott
Ninian Rutherford, nephew of above	James Achilmere
John Turnbull-Fauldshope	Roger Achilmere, son of above
Alexander Murray	Stephen Lockhart
John Scott of Todshawhauch	Walter Turnbull of Gargunnock

Peter Murray
James Kerr
Thomas Kerr, son of above
Ninian Murray
Thomas Murray
William Murray
Archibald Scott-Branxholm

Alexander Dalmahoy
John Achilmere, son of James
Walter Kerr of Cessford
Robert Kerr, son of above
Patrick Cockburn (William Cockburn
    of Henryland)
Patrick Crichton

Yarrow Ward

William Cockburn of Henryland
George Robison, comptroller
James Achilmere
Alexander Dalmahoy
Alexander Dalmahoy, son of above
Lord Borthwick
John Murray of Touchadam
Patrick Murray
John Murray, son of above
William Kerr

Sir James Chisholm
Andrew Ormiston
Margaret Kerr
Andrew Kerr, son of above
Walter Kerr (John Liddel)
Thomas Middlemast
Thomas Lawis of Memar
Thomas Dickson of Ormiston
William Inglis of Murthawston
Patrick Elphinstone

Tweed Ward

David Tait-Pyrne
George Tait-Pyrne
Margaret Schaw
Patrick Crichton-Cranston
Lord Borthwick
Alexander Pringle
Roger Pringle, son of above
Roger Rutherford of Chatto
George Rutherford, son of above
Walter Kerr of Cessford
Roger Kerr, son of above
William Pringle
Alexander Pringle, son of above

William Vaich of Davick
John Vaich, son of above
David Pringle-Smailholm
James Pringle
George Kerr

II 1510 (*ER*, xiii, 649)

Ettrick Ward

Patrick Murray
Margaret Scott
John Murray
Alexander, Lord Home
Thomas Kerr
Elizabeth Stewart
John Home, son of above
John Murray
Walter Scott
William Cranston
Thomas Cranston
Peter Turnbull
Elizabeth Kerr
Walter Scott of Buccleuch, son of above

Adam Scott of Tushielaw
Stephen Scott
James Stewart
Patrick Cranston
Andrew Kerr
Gavin Murray
James Murray-Falahill
Andrew Kerr of Cessford
Andrew Home, brother of Alexander
Peter Murray
Thomas Murray
Robert Turnbull

Yarrow Ward

George Hepburn-Bothwell
James Stewart of Traquair
David Pringle of Tinnis
John Murray of Falahill
Robert Crichton of Cranston-Riddel
James Crichton
William Crichton } sons of above
David Crichton
Alexander, Lord Home

Nichola Kerr
William Kerr
Christian Kerr, mother of above
Andrew Kerr of Mersington
John Liddel
Andrew Kerr of Fernihurst
John Elphinstone
David Elphinstone

Tweed Ward

Alexander Tait of Pyrne
Andrew Stewart, bishop of Caithness
Patrick Crichton of Cranston-Riddel
David Home-Wedderburn
Andrew Kerr of Cessford
William Pringle
Robert Pringle
John Wauche
David Pringle

APPENDIX C
MAPS AND TABLES

Table 25. ROYAL FORESTS

Name	Date[1]	Source	Later history[2]
Ettrick (Selkirk, Traquair, Tima)[3]	1136	ESC, 141	Tima lost 1236 (Melr. Lib., 264); lands lost 1320 (RMS, i, app. 2, 232); annexed 1455 (APS, ii, 42, c1)
Pentland (Gladhouse, Moorfoot)	c 1142	ESC, 146	Gladhouse lost 1236 (Newb. Reg., 23); Moorfoot lost 1239 (Newb. Reg., 22); Moor lost 1315 x 21 (RMS, i, 67)
Stirling (Torwood, Dundaff and Strathcarron)	c 1143	ESC, 153	Dundaff and Strathcarron lost 1235 (Mort. Reg., i, app. 3)
Clackmannan (Dollar, Tillicoultry)	c 1143	ESC, 153	Dollar lost 1237 (Dunf. Reg., 75, 76); Tillicoultry lost 1262, (SRO, Mar and Kellie Papers, GD 124/1/513.) Lost 1359 x 1398 (ER, i, 573; SRO, Mar and Kellie Papers, GD 124/1/525); status still confused 1411 (Stirlings of Keir, 201)
Gala and Leader	1150 x 52	ESC, 193	Lost 1236 (Melr. Lib., i, 258)
Clunie (Perthshire)	1161	RRS, i, 226	Part of earldom of Fife in 14th century (SP., iv, 14); forfeited 1425 (ER, vi, lxxvii) and let by 1450 (ER, v, 480)
Aberdeen	c 1163	RRS, i, 238, p.83	Lost 1313 (Abdn. Chrs., p. 10, no. 6)
Birse	1180 x 1184	RRS, ii, 251	Lost 1180 x 1184 (RRS, ii, 251)
Drimmie	1161	RRS, i, 226	Probably granted to Coupar before 1224. (CA Chart., 31)
Banchory	1171 x 1174	RRS, ii, 128	Perhaps in earldom of Mar by 1362 (RMS, i, 124)

1. Date when first recorded or when first in royal hands.
2. Only the loss of the forest from or the return of the forest to royal hands is given here. This coverage, therefore, is not exhaustive.
3. Part of or later names of forests are placed in brackets.

Table 25. Royal Forests (continued)

Name	Date	Source	Later history
Elgin, Forres and Inverness[1]	c 1150	*Kinloss Recs.,* 1 Anderson, *Early Sources,* ii, 210; *RRS,* ii, 362.	b and c lost in 1230. The forest would be in earldom of Moray in 1312 (*Moray Reg.* 264, Barrow, *Bruce,* 381). Parts returned to crown in 1368 (*SP,* vi, 298) and in 15th century (*ER,* iv, 109, *RMS,* ii, 2319) and were alienated thereafter (*ER,* vi, 376, *RMS,* ii, 2586)
(a) Darnaway	1226	*Moray Reg.,* 29	
(b) Pluscarden }	1230	*Pluscarden,* 69, 199.	
(c) Auchtertyre }			
(d) Drumine	1236	*Moray Reg.* 31.	
(e) Sanquhar }	c 1341 x 1342	*RMS,* i, app. 2, 784	
(f) Tulloch }			
(g) Sluipool	1507	*ER,* xiii, 590	
Mauldslie	1214	*Dryb. Lib.,* 218 *ER,* i, 39.	Lost 1288 x 1321 (*ER,* i, 39; *RMS,* i, 76)
Invercullen	1226	*Moray Reg.,* 29	Lost by 1382? (*RMS,* i, 698)
Maryculter	1235 x 1236	*Abdn. Reg.,* 269	
Lennoch	1236	*Pluscarden,* 204	In earldom of Moray in 1312 (*Moray Reg.,* Barrow, *Bruce,* 381)
Leitiien?	1241	*Newb. Reg.,* 120	Lost 1241 (*Newb. Reg.,* 120)
Banff	1242	*A.B. Antiqs.,* ii, 109	
Drum	1247 (1203 x 1214)	*A.B. Antiqs.,* ii, 298; *Arb. Lib.,* i, 65	Lost 1323 (*A.B. Antiqs.,* 292; *Burnett of Leys,* 154)
Jedburgh	1258	*Chron. Melrose,* 183-4	Lost 1320 (*RMS,* i, app. 1, no. 36)
Cluny (Fife)	1266	*ER,* i, 19	Lost c 1315 (*RMS,* i, app. 2, 635) in earldom of Fife

1. A list of later sub-divisions follows.

Table 25. Royal Forests (continued)

Name	Date	Source	Later history
Cowie	1266	ER, i, 21	Lost 1327; (RMS, i, app. 1, 73)
(a) Mounth	1375	RMS, i, 499	Lost 1375
Spey	1291	Rot. Scot., i, 5a	In earldom of Moray (see Elgin above)
Enzie	1292	Rot. Scot., i, 9a	Lost 1327 (RMS, i, app. 1, 65)
Buchan	1292	Rot. Scot., i, 9a	Lost 1324 x 1346 (APS, i, 482; RMS, i, app. 2, 1020)
Durris	1292	Rot. Scot., i, 10a	
Plater	1292	APS, i, 115	Lost 1474 (RMS, ii, 1191)
Coulter	1296	Stevenson, Documents, no. 386	
Langmorn	1303	Stevenson, Documents, no. 625	In earldom of Moray (see Elgin above)
Kintore (Glasgoforest)	1304 / c 1345	CDS, ii, 1506 / RMS, i, app. 2, 960	Lost c 1316 x 1321 (RMS, i, app. 2, 46)
Carluke	1304	CDS, ii, 1626	
Cordyce	1316	Abdn. Reg., i, 43	Lands lost 1316 (Abdn. Reg., i, 43)
Kilgarie	1319	Fraser, Southesk, ii, 482, no. 31	Lost 1500 (RMS, ii, 2529, 2530)
'Glenabeukan'	c 1319 x 1321	RMS, i, app. 2, 299	
Killanel	c 1320	RMS, i, app. 2, 420	
Kinross	c 1323	RMS, i, app. 2, 697	
Kelwood	c 1323 x 1324	RMS, i, app. 2, 307	Let by 1348 (ER, i, 542)

Table 25. Royal Forests (continued)

Name	Date	Source	Later history
Glenken	1306 x 1329	*SHS, Misc.*, v, 23 no. 14	Lost by 1358 (*SHS Misc.*, v, 23 no. 14)
Boyne and Enzie	1327	*RMS*, i, app. 1, 65	Lands lost by 1327 (*RMS*, i, app. i, 65)
Mar			
(a) Kildrummy	1342	*ER*, i, 499	1. Mar in dower grant 1452 (*RMS*, ii, 592)
(b) Garioch	1452	*RMS*, ii, 592	2. In countess' hands in 1476 (*RMS*, ii, 1239)
(c) Strathdee	1454	*ER*, vi, 70; v, 657	3. In free forest grant 1482/3 (*RMS*, ii, 1541)
(d) Cambuskist	1461	*ER*, vii, 86	4. Royal again by 1503 (*RMS*, ii, 2755)
Cardenden	c mid- 14th century	*RMS*, i, app. 2, 1120	
'Cardenauche'	c 1346	*RMS*, i, app. 2, 1020	Lands lost c 1346 (*RMS*, i, app. 2, 1020)
Lochindorb	c 1312 [1368]¹	*RMS*, i, 279; *SP*, i, 510	Lost 1368 (*RMS*, i, 279)
Cabrauch	1374	*RMS*, i, 474	Lost 1374
Bothwell	1425	*RMS*, ii, 19	Let by 1479 (*ER*, ix, 6). In free forest grant 1488 (*RMS*, ii, 1784)
Dalton	1440 [1426]	*ER*, vi, p. cvii *RMS*, ii, 71]¹	Lost 1452 (*RMS*, ii, 546: *ER*, v, 669)
Dye	1434 [1451]	*ER*, vi, p. cv *ER*, v, 487]	Lost 1450 x 1510 (*ER*, v, 487; *RMS*, ii, 2106, 3413)
Menteith	1426 [1454]	*ER*, vi, lxxx *ER*, v, 676]	
Garvock	1451	*ER*, ix, 661	

1. Date when first recorded. The preceding date is when the lands entered royal hands and when the forest may have been in existence.

Y

Table 25. Royal Forests (continued)

Name	Date	Source	Later history
Glen Shervie Corriemuckloch	1437	SP, i, 488; ER, vi, p. xxxiii	Lost 1510 (ER, xiii, 647)
	[1454]	ER, vi, 282]¹	
Glen Artney	1437	SP, i, 488; ER, vi, p. lxxxiii; ER, vi, 282]	
	[1454]	ER, vi, p. cxxxiv; ER, vi, 655]	
Cluanie	1372?	ER, vi, 213	
	[1454]		
Strathdearn	1455	ER, vi, 213	Let 1455 (ER, vi, 213)
Duchinloch	1437	SP, i, 438; ER, vi, 366; ER, vi, 242]¹	
	[1456]		
Buchan (Galloway)	1456	ER, vi, 193	Let by 1456 (ER, vi, 192)
Mamlorne	1456	ER, vi, 366	
Ormond	1455	ER, vi, cxl; ER, vi, 468]¹	Lost 1481 (SP, i, 245). Forest had died out in 1470s (ER, viii, 563)
	[1457]		
Ben More	1437	SP, i, 438; ER, viii, 60]¹	
	[1470]		
Corscarie	1437	SP, i, 438; ER, vi, p. xc; ER, viii, 441]¹	Lost 1481 (ER, xii, p. xxxii; SP, i, 245)
	[1476]		
Rannoch (Ross)	1475	SP, v, 46, 47. ER, viii, 595]¹	Temporary resignation to crown
	[1476]		
Cumbernauld	1480	RMS, ii, 1453	
Arran and Cumbrae	1487	ER, x, 5	Lands let by 1487 (ER, x, 5)

1. Date when first recorded. The preceding date is when the lands entered royal hands and when the forest may have been in existence.

Table 25. Royal Forests (continued)

Name	Date	Source	Later history
Culface	1425, [1492	*ER,* vi, p lxxvii *ER,* x, 764][1]	Lands lost by 1492 (*ER,* x, 764)
Glenalmond	1437 [1496	*SP,* i, 438 *ER,* x, 566][1]	
Glen Shee	1495	*ER,* x, 566	Let by 1492 (*ER,* 729)
Bute	1498	*ER,* xii, 65 *ER,* xi, 392	
Abernethy	1498	*RSS,* i, 268	Let by 1498 (*RSS,* i, 268)
Strathbraan and Birnam	1389 [1499	*ER,* vi, p lxxxvii] *Fraser, Grandtully,* i, p li; *RMS,* ii 2502][1]	Lost 1499 (Fraser, *Grandtully,* i, p li)
Lochaber	1372? [1500	*ER,* vi, cxxiv *RMS,* ii, 2559]	Lost 1500 (*RMS,* ii, 2559)
Woodcockair	1503	*RSS,* i, 912	Lands let since 1452 (*ER,* v, 669)
Rannoch	1502	*RMS,* ii, 2664	Lost 1502 (*RMS,* ii, 2664)
Corgarf and Baddynyon	1507	*RMS,* ii, 3159	Lost 1507 (*RMS,* ii, 3159)
Drumselch/ancient forest	1507/8	*RMS,* ii, 3173	Perhaps a forest in 12th century (Barrow, G.W.S. 'Treverlen, Duddingston and Arthur's Seat', *Old Edinburgh Club,* xxx, (1959); *Holyrood Ordinale,* 64)

1. Date when first recorded. The preceding date is when the lands entered royal hands and when the forest may have been in existence.

Table 26. ROYAL HUNTING AREAS

Name	Date	Source
Gairloch	1330	*ER*, i, 250
Kindrochit	1371-1388	*ER*, ii, 364; *ER*, iii, 177
Glenfinglas	1382-1454	*Abdn. Reg.*, pp. 155-6; table 1 *sub* Menteith
Cockburnspath	1454	*ER*, v, 646
Strathbraan	1456	*ER*, vi, 242, 243, 637, 679
Duchray[1]	1469	*ER*, vii, 614
Balquhidder	1467	*ER*, vii, 488
Strathfillan	1502	*TA*, ii, 119

1. Perhaps in Menteith Forest.

Table 27. FORESTS OF UNCERTAIN OWNERSHIP

Name	Date	Comment	Source
Culblane	1334	Vegetational?	*Chron. Fordun*, i, 349
Dalswinton	1334	Royal?	*CDS*, iii, 1166
Strone	1511	Vegetational?	SRO, *Justice Ayre Journal Book*, RH, 2/1/7, 237
'Glenaan'	1511	Royal?	*Abdn. Reg.*, 371

Table 28. FOREST GRANTS

Name	Date	Details of Grant¹	Grantee	Tenure	Source
Annandale	1147 x 1153	F.S.	Robert de Bruce	as freely as his other forest	ESC, 199
Pettinain	1147 x 1153	'firmam forestam' S of 40s	Nicholas, royal clerk		ESC, 205
Renfrew (?)	1161 (or 1162)	'in forestis et tristriis'	Walter Steward	5 kts.²	RRS, i, 184
Dunlappie	1153 x 1165				See Dunlappie 1223
Annandale (?)	1165 x 1173 possibly 1172	'in forestis et'	Robert de Bruce	10 kts.	RRS, ii, 80
Strathearn (?)	1172 x 1173	'in forestis et tristriis'	Malise, son of Ferteth, Earl of Strathearn	1 kt.	RRS, ii, 136
Campsie	1173 x 1178	FF, S	Coupar Angus Abbey	free alms	RRS, ii, 154
Hownam	1189 x 1195	F, S	William, son of John		RRS, ii, 314
Cargill	1189 x 1195	F, S	Richard Montifiquet		RRS, ii, 334
Strachan	1189 x 1195	F, S	William Giffard		RRS, ii, 340
Kinkell	1189 x 1195	F, S	Humphrey [de Berkeley]		RRS, ii, 346
Outh	1195 x 1210	F, S	Robert de London		RRS, ii, 463
Dunlappie	1165 x 1214				See Dunlappie 1223
Kingoldrum	1214 x 1225	F, S	Arbroath Abbey		Arb. Lib., 105
Maich, Calder & Monaibrock	1219 x 1230	F, S	Paisley Abbey		Pais. Reg., 253

1. F — in forest. FF — in free forest. S — sanction clause. FW — free warren. FB — free barony. FR — free regality. w — grant applied to woods. FL — free lordship.
2. Kt. — Knight.

Table 28. Forest Grants (continued)

Name	Date	Details of Grant	Grantee	Tenure	Source
Dunlappie	1223	FF	Laurence, son of Orm		NLS, Collections of Walter Mcfarlane, Adv. Ms. 35.4.12a, 3
Dumbarrow & Conan	1223	F, S	Arbroath Abbey		Arb. Lib., 103
Rothiemurchus	1226	F, S	Andrew, Bishop of Moray	free alms	Moray Reg., 29
Nigg	1233	FF, S	Arbroath Abbey	free alms	Arb. Lib., 101
Glenisla	1233 (1451)	FF, S	Coupar Angus Abbey		C.A. Chrs. 41
Trostach	1233	FF, S, w	Arbroath Abbey		Arb. Lib. 129
Balmerino & Barry	1234	F, S	Balmerino Abbey		Balm. Lib., 8
Tarves	1234	FF, S	Arbroath Abbey	free alms	Arb. Lib., 102
Lesmahagow	1235	FF, S	Kelso Abbey		Kelso Lib., 10
Dundaff & Strathcarron	1235	FF, S	Patrick, Earl of Dunbar	1/3 kt.	Mort. Reg., i, app. 3
	1237	FF, S	David de Graham	1/3 kt.	Anderson, Diplomata, facsimile no. 30
Drumsled	1236	FF, S	Arbroath Abbey		Arb. Lib., 312
Gala & Leader	1236	FF, S	Melrose Abbey	free alms	Melr. Lib., 258
Mow	1236	FF, S	Melrose Abbey		Melr. Lib. 299
Dollar	1237	FF, S	Dunfermline Abbey		Dunf. Reg., 75
Kilsyth etc.	1239	FF, FW (?)	Malcolm, son of Duncan		Nisbet, Ragman Roll. p. 19
Moorfoot	1239	FF, S	Newbattle Abbey		Newb. Reg., 22

Table 28. Forest Grants (continued)

Name	Date	Details of Grant	Grantee	Tenure	Source
'Kelcamsy'	1240 x 1242[1] (x 1249)	F, S, w	Scone Priory		*Scone Lib.*, 76
Newbattle Drumpellier	1240/41	FF, S	Newbattle Abbey		*Newb. Reg.*, 157
'Glengeyth' etc.	1241	FF, S	Patrick, son of W—son of Orm		HMC, Report 7, *The Athole Charters*, 704, no. 6
Birse & Fetternear	1242	FF, S	Ralph, Bishop of Aberdeen		*Abdn. Reg.*, p. 15
Glasgow	1242	FF, S	William, Bishop of Glasgow		*Glas. Reg.*, 180
Leslie	1248	FF, S	Alformo, son of Norman		*A.B. Coll.*, p. 548
Crawford	c 1249	FF, S	Newbattle Abbey		*Newb. Reg.*, 145
Fintray	1251	FF, S, w	Lindores Abbey		*Lind. Cart.*, 289, no. 6
Tillicoultry	1262	FF, S	William, Earl of Mar	1 kt.	SRO, *Mar & Kellie Papers*, GD 124/1/513
Lindores	1264/65	FF, S	Lindores Abbey		*Lind. Cart.*, 291 no. 15
Mauchline	1264	FF, S	Melrose Abbey		*Melr. Lib.*, 324
Lennox	1272	FF, S	Malcom, Earl of Lennox		*Lenn. Cart.*, p. 2
Coldingham	1276	FF, FW	Coldingham Priory		Raine, *ND*, App. 16 no. lxxvi
Kinmuck Kilravock }	*ante* 1282				*APS*, i, 110; Lost charters
Staplegordon & Wauchope	1285	FF or FW	John de Lyndesay		*Mort. Reg.*, ii, 12
Hartschaw	1315 x 1321	FF, S, FB	Robert Boyd	1 kt's. service	*RMS*, i, 46

1. Walter Bisset a witness, exiled 1242 (*Coupar Chrs.*, p. 111).

Table 28. Forest Grants (continued)

Name	Date	Details of Grant	Grantee	Tenure	Source
Liddesdale	1315 x 1321	FF, FB	Robert Bruce	accustomed service	*RMS*, i, 53
Ross	c 1315 x 1321	FF	Hugh, Earl of Ross		*RMS*, app. 2, 383 no. 12
Staplegordon	c 1319	FF, FB	James, Lord of Douglas	suit of court	Fraser, *Douglas*, iii, 10
Jedburgh	1320	FF, FB	James Douglas	1 kt. ser. 100s	*RMS*, i, app. 1, 36
Westerker	1321	FF, S	Melrose Abbey	free alms	*RMS*, i, app. 1, 14
Lennox	1321	'cum libera foresta'	Malcolm, Earl of Lennox		Fraser, *Lennox*, ii, 19 no. 18
Seton	1322	FF, FW, S	Alexander Seton		*Seton*, ii, 118
Drum	1322/3	FF, S	William Irvine	blenche ferme	*A.B. Antiqs.* iii, 292
Drum	1323	FF	Alexander Burnett	blenche ferme	*Burnett of Leys*, 154
Boyne & Enzie	1327	FF	Gilbert Hay of Locherworth		*RMS*, i, app. 1, 65
Cowie	1327	FF	Alexander and John Fraser		*RMS*, i, app. 1, 73
Polbuthy	1306 x 1329[1]	FF	James, Lord of Douglas	blenche ferme	*RMS*, i, app. 2, 526
Drum	1359	FF	Walter Moigne	blenche ferme	*A. B. Antiqs.*. iii, 293
Leithen	1367	FF, S	Newbattle Abbey		*RMS*, i, 269
Leithen	1367/8	FF, S	Newbattle Abbey		*RMS*, i, 275
Lochindorb	1368	FF	Simon Reed, constable of Edinburgh Castle	3 broad arrows	*RMS*, i, 279
Dalkeith	1369	FF, FB	James Douglas		*RMS*, i, 335
Boyne & Enzie	1329 x 1371[2]	FF			*RMS*, ii, 2958
Tillicoultry	1372	FF, S	William, Earl of Douglas		*RMS*, i, 504

1. 1318 x 1329 on basis of *RMS*, i, app. 2, no 226.
2. c 1362 on basis of *RMS*, i, 118.

Table 28. Forest Grants (continued)

Name	Date	Details of Grant	Grantee	Tenure	Source
Cowie & Mounth	1375	FF	Robert Keith	acc. service	*RMS*, i, 499
Wester Kers & Alva	1382	FF, FW, FB	William of Menteith	acc. service	*APS*, i, 564
Clackmannan	1386/7	FF	Thomas Erskine	acc. service	SRO, *Mar & Kellie Papers*, GD 124/1/524
Bolton, Carriden & Langton	1391/2	FF, FW, S	Alexander Cockburn	military service, doorwards & blenche ferme	*APS*, i, 580
Manor	1395	FF, FW, FB	William Inglis		*Peebles, Recs.*, 206, no. 3
Spynie	1452	'cum libera foresta et varenna', FR	Bishop of Moray	blenche ferme	*Moray Reg.*, 194
Garioch	1452	FF, FW, FR	Queen Mary	for life	*RMS*, ii, 592
Callendar	1458	'cum libera foresta et warenna', FB	James, Lord Livingstone		*RMS*, ii, 606
'Glen M'kern'	1458/9	FF	John of Colquhoun		*RMS*, ii, 679
Plater	1474	FF, FR	Alexander Lyndesay		*RMS*, ii, 1191
Clunie (Perth)	1480/1	FF	John, Earl of Atholl	blenche ferme	*ER*, xii, 42
Garioch & Mar	1482/3	FF, FR	Alexander, Duke of Albany	blenche ferme	*RMS*, ii, 1541
Kilgarie	1488	FF	Thomas Culface		*RMS*, ii, 2529
Kilgarie	1488	FF	Thomas 'Somyr' of 'Balzardy'		*RMS*, ii, 2530
Bothwell	1488	FF, FB	Patrick, Lord Hailes	blenche ferme	*RMS*, ii, 1784
Birse	1489	FR 'cum libera foresta'	William Elphinstone, bishop of Aberdeen	prayers	*RMS*, ii, 1911
Liddesdale	1491/2	FF, FR	Patrick, Earl of Bothwell, Lord Hailes		Fraser, *Douglas*, iii, 130 no. 127

Table 28. Forest Grants (continued)

Name	Date	Details of Grant	Grantee	Tenure	Source
Redgorton	1494	FF	Master Andrew 'Liell', prebendary and pensionary of Brechin	prayers	RMS, ii, 2206
Drummond	1495/6	FF, FB	John, Lord Drummond	feu ferme	RMS, ii, 2299
Bothwell	1498	FF, FL, FB	Patrick, Lord Hailes	blenche ferme	RMS, ii, 2452
Darnaway	1501	FF, FW, FC	James Stewart		RMS, ii, 2586
Milton of Earlsruthven	1504	FF, FW, FB	Adam Crichton of Ruthven-davy	blenche ferme	RMS, ii, 2802
Glencarvie & Glenconrie	1504/5	w, FF	John & William Forbes		RMS, ii, 2812
Clunie	1505	FF	Andrew Stewart, son of Earl of Atholl	blenche ferme	RMS, ii, 2853
Cullerlie	1506/7	FF, FB	Alexander, Earl of Huntly	blenche ferme	RMS, ii, 3071
Drum park	1506/7	FF	Alexander Irvine of Drum	blenche ferme	RMS, ii, 3070
Invernochty	1507	w, FF, FB	Andrew Elphinstone and spouse		RMS, ii, 3159; ER, xiii, 70
Cabrauch	1508	FF, FB	Alexander, Earl of Huntly		RMS, ii, 3218
Haldane	1508/9	w, FF, FB	John Haldane of 'Glennegas'		RMS, ii, 3288
'Corylundy & Mewy'	1508/9	FF, FW	John, Lord Drummond		RMS, ii, 3306
Glenturret	1509	FF, FB	Andrew Toschach of Monzievaird		RMS, ii, 3343
Gartness	1509	FF	Archibald Napier of Merchiston		RMS, ii, 3347
'Herys'	1510	w, FF, FB	Andrew, Lord Herys		RMS, ii, 3446
Garioch	1511	FF, FB	John Lesley of Warderis	feu ferme	RMS, ii, 3556

Table 28. Forest Grants (continued)

Name	Date	Details of Grant	Grantee	Tenure	Source
'Aldnakist & Lechory'	1511	w, FF	William Strathachin		*RMS*, ii, 3589
Glenesk	1511	w, FF, FB	John, Earl of Crawford		*RMS*, ii, 3627
Bothwell	1511	w, FF, FB	Adam Hepburn, earl of Bothwell		*RMS*, ii, 3635
Strathglass	1513	FF	William Chisholm of 'Comyr'		*RMS*, ii, 3831

Baronial Grants

Name	Date	Details	Grantee	Grantor	Tenure	Source
Mow	1279	F, S	William de Sprouston, chaplain	John de Vesci		*Melr. Lib.*, 346
Pentland Moor	1410	FF	John Sinclair	Henry Sinclair, earl of Orkney		*RMS*, i, 931
Wester Kers & Alva	1411	FF, FW, FB	William of Menteith	Robert, Duke of Albany	acc. service	*Stirlings of Keir*, 201

Approximate forest grants by barons

Strathearn (?)	1172 x 1173	'forestis et tristriis'	Malise, son of Ferteth	Earl Gilbert		*RRS*, ii, 136
Trostach	1232 x 1233	F	Arbroath Abbey	Alan Durward		*Arb. Lib.*, 128
Rothiemurchus	1383	as freely as bishop held in FF	Earl of Buchan	Bishop of Moray		*Moray Reg.*, 162
Boyne	1492	with power of FF	Walter Ogilvy	Earl of Huntly		SRO, *Gordon Castle Muniments*, GD 44, 106
	1495	royal confirmation				*RMS*, ii, 2289

Table 29. BARONIAL FORESTS — NO GRANT EXTANT

Name	Date	Holder	Source
Renfrew	1161 (or 1162)	Walter Steward	RRS, i, 184
Eskdale (?)	1165 x 1169 (1124 x 1153)	Robert Avenel	RRS, i, 60; Melr. Lib., 39
Ayr	1165 x 1173 (1174)	Walter Steward	RRS, ii, 78; Melr. Lib., 66
Strathearn	1172 x 1173	Malise, son of Ferteth, Earl of Strathearn	RRS, ii, 136
Lauderdale	1189 x 1196	William de Morville	Hay, Genealogical Collections, 245
Crawford	1185 x 1200	William de Lyndesay	Newb. Reg., 135
Dalbeattie	1214 x 1249 (1153 x 1165)	Roland, son of Uchtred of Galloway	Holy Lib., 73, 23
Cunninghame	1190 x 1196	William de Morville	NMS, ii, 2
Sanquhar	1208 x 1214	Walter Steward	Pais. Reg., 18
Renfrew (?)	1123 x 1233	Paisley Abbey[1]	Pais. Reg., 19
Ochtirlony	ante 1226 x 1239 (?)	Walter, son of Turpin	Arb. Lib., 232, 306
Outh	1231	Dunfermline Abbey	Dunf. Reg., 192
'Lyffedin'	1272	Gilbert de Umfraville, earl of Angus	Fraser, Southesk, ii, 479 no. 28
Inverpeffer	1324	Robert Keith	APS, i, 482
Birnam	1345/6	Earl of Fife	Fraser, Grandtully, i, 2
Bennachie	1358	Thomas, Earl of Mar	APS, i, 524
Ryeland	1359	Thomas, Earl of Mar	SRO, Mar and Kellie Papers, GD 124/1/112
Falkland	1371	Countess of Fife (?)	Fraser, Menteith, ii, 251
'Coulpersauche'	ante 1375	William Keith	RMS, i, 500
Dalton	1419	Archibald, Earl of Angus	RMS, ii, 71

1. Roger, prior of Paisley, retained from Walter Steward 'totum ius quod habuimus in foresta *mea* de Renfru de dono Walteri avi sui' [i.e., Walter 1st Steward.] The only recorded gifts of the 1st Steward are of rights to use Steward's forest. (*Pais. Reg.*, 5.) 'Mea' although written clearly may be a mistranscription in the cartulary.

Table 29. Baronial Forests — No Grant Extant (continued)

Name	Date	Holder	Source
'Garnetuloch'	1452	William of Moray/Simon 'Waldein'	*RMS*, ii, 590
Tomaknock	1462	Queen	*ER*, vii, 62
'Craggilee'	1466	William Murray	*ER*, ix, 671
Glen Prosen	1482/3	Archibald, Earl of Angus, to Robert Graham of Fintry	*RMS*, ii, 1559, 1560
Culface[1]	1492	William of Farny	*ER*, x, 764
Lauder	1493		SRO, *Justice Ayre Journal Book*, RH 2/1/5, 58
Glenrinnes	1511	Bishop of Aberdeen	*Abdn. Reg.*, 369
Irongray	1511	Bishop	SRO, *Justice Ayre Journal Book*, RH 2/1/7, 271

1. Perhaps previously royal or connected to Falkland.

Table 30. WARREN GRANTS

Date	Name	Detail[1]	Tenure	Grantee	Source
1153 x 1162	Coldingham	garennia, S		Coldingham Priory	RRS. i, 189
1165 x 1171	Coldingham	garennia, S		Coldingham Priory	RRS. ii, 46
1173 x 1178	Bolton, Carriden & Langton	W, S		William de Vipont	RRS. ii, 182
1214 x 1224	Coldingham	garennia, S		Coldingham Priory	Raine, ND. Appendix p. 13 no. LX
1230	'Clein'	W, S		Scone Priory	Scone Lib., 69
1214 x 1249 (probably 1222 x 1249)	Blair	W, S		Scone Priory	Scone Lib., 64
1248/9	Musselburgh	FW, S		Dunfermline Abbey	Dunf. Reg., 77
1248/9	Moncrieffe	FW, S		Mathew de Moncrieffe	Moncrieffs., ii, 635
1249	Crail	FW, S		Galfridus de Ferseley	BM. Add. Chart, 66570
ante 1282	'Caldouircler'	F(?)W		Robert de Bruce (?)	APS. i, 110
1294	Keith	FW, S (?)		Robert of Keith Marischall	Dalrymple, Collections, 86
1295	Errol	FW, S		Nicholas Hay	Spalding, Misc. ii, 313
1305	Sweetheart	Warren grant of Edward I		Sweetheart Abbey	CDS. ii, 1703
1305	Dundrennan	Warren grant of Edward I		Dundrennan Abbey	CDS. ii, 1702
1319	Dumbarrow & Conan	FW, S		Arbroath Abbey	Arb. Lib. 286
1315 x 1321	Loudon	FW, FB, S	1 kt.[2]	Duncan Campbell and wife	RMS. i, 38
1315 x 1321	Pentland moor	FW, S	1/10 kt.	Henry Sinclair	RMS. i, 67

1. W — in warennam, S — Sanction clause included, FW — Free warren, FF — free forest, FB — free barony, FR — free regality.
2. Kt. — Knight.

Table 30. Warren Grants (continued)

Date	Name	Detail	Grantee	Tenure	Source
1321	Torthorwald	FW, S	Humphrey Kirkpatrick		Fraser, *Johnstones*, i, p. 8 no. 13
1322	Barlanark	FW, S	John Wishart, canon		*Glas. Reg.*, i, 272
1335	'Dachete'	Warren grant of Edward III	John de Molyns		*CDS*, iii, 1178
1345	Rothiemay	FW, S	William Abernethy	blenche ferme	*Frasers of Philorth*, ii, 54
1353/4	Ettrick/Douglas lands	FW, FR	William Douglas		*RMS*, i, app. i, 123
1366/7	Kinnoul	FW, FB, S	Nicholas Erskine	accustomed service	*RMS*, i, 246
1357	'Wamphray and Drumcreth'	FW	Roger of Kirkpatrick by Robert, Steward of Scotland		Fraser, *Johnstones*, i, 11 no. 17

Table 31. ROYAL PARKS

Date	Name	Source
1165 x 1174	Stirling old park	*RRS*, ii, 130
1266	Kincardine	*ER*, i, 21
1264	Stirling new park	*ER*, i, 24
1288	Jedburgh	*ER*, i, 43
1315	Duns	*RMS*, i, 5; *CDS*, iii, 440
1316 x 1321	Kintore	*RMS*, i, app. 2, 46
1323	Drum	*Burnett of Leys*, 154
1325	Fyvie	*Arb. Lib.*, 353
1326	Cardross	*ER*, i, 56
1327	Boyne	*RMS*, i, app. 1, 65
1327	Cowie	*RMS*, i, app. 1, 73
1329	Plater[1]	*ER*, i, 147
1329	Tarbert	*ER*, i, 239
1359	Mauldslie	*ER*, i, 582
1359	Clackmannan	*ER*, i, 572
1371	Darnaway	*Moray, Reg.*, p. 473
1426	Dundonald	*ER*, iv, 401
1426/1433 x 1434	Linlithgow	*ER*, iv, 415, 556 (1433-4)
1434	Tranent[2]	*ER*, iv, 598
1439	Kelly	*ER*, v, 69
1451	Falkland	*RMS*, ii, 462
1456	Doune	*ER*, vi, 285
1456	Park[2]	*ER*, vi, 192
1473	Bothwell[3]	*ER*, viii, 175
1496	Methven	*ER*, x, 556

---

1. Reference to a park keeper.
2. Perhaps not a hunting park.
3. No longer a hunting park by 1473.

Table 32. BARONIAL PARKS[1]

Date[2]	Name	Details[3]	Holder	Source
ante 1189	Milsieside or Leuedeparc		Morville	RRS, ii, 301; Melr. Lib., 79, 96, 108
ante 1245	Stapleton	permission to empark	Robert de Crosby	Fraser, Johnstones, i, 5, no. 8
post 1246	Blackhall		Alexander Steward	Pais. Reg., 88, 92
1250 x 1267	Yester		Hugh Giffard	Yester Writs, 16
1262/3	'Irschyn'		Walter Steward, Earl of Menteith	Fraser, Menteith, ii, 216, no. 9
1287	'Kelling'		Alexander Comyn, Earl of Buchan	Arb. Lib., 319
c 1253 x 1291	Newbattle			Newb. Reg., 6
1292/3	Inverarity		Alexander Abernethy	APS, i, 447 CA Chrs., i, no. lxv
1319	Dumbarrow & Conan		Arbroath Abbey	Arb. Lib., 286
1315 x 1321	Baliferne	KG	John, son of Lochlan	RMS, i, 31
1324	'Kindoles'	KG	Archibald Douglas	RMS, i, app. 1, 66
ante 1329	Newlands	BG permission to empark	William Carlisle	Fraser, Johnstones, p. 9 no. 14
1329/30	Kinmount	BG permission to empark	John Carlisle	Ibid., p. 10 no. 15
1335 x 1336	Stanton		Elizabeth Lauder	CDS, iii, 338
c 1341	'Galchill'	KL	Adam Buttergask	RMS, i, app. 2, 782
1335	Ditton & 'Dachete'	permission to empark from Edward III	John de Molyns	CDS, iii, 1179

1. This Table is compiled from the written and not from the archaeological evidence.
2. Date when first recorded.
3. This column shows which parks were the subject of a grant or a lease by the king or a baron. R — royal, B — baronial, G — grant, L — lease, FF — free forest, C — confirmation.

Table 32. Baronial Parks (continued)

Date	Name	Details	Holder	Source
1361	'Rossemorys'	Royal confirmation of BG	Walter Fosselane	Fraser, *Lennox*, p. 29, no. 25
1362	'Dursclune'	KG	David Fleming	*RMS*. i, 175
1367/8	Leithen	Licence to empark in FF grant	Newbattle Abbey	*RMS*. i, 275
1373 x 1374	'Clounqwarn'	RC of BG	John Sympill	*RMS*. i, 490
c 1376	Morton	BL	Gilbert, son of Duncan	*Mort. Reg.*. i, p. lvi
c 1376	Castleton[1]	BL		*Mort. Reg.*. i, p. lxxiii
c 1376	Hermitage	BL		*Mort. Reg.*. i, p. lxxiii
1380	Drimie (Ross)		Walter Lesley	SRO, *Munro of Foulis Papers*, GD 93, no. 12 box 1
1381 x 1384	'Invermorsyn'	RG	Alexander, Earl of Buchan	*RMS*. i, 789
1405	Carmyle	BG	John Strachan	*RMS*. i, app. 2, 1941
1426	Blantyre[1]	RC of BG	Patrick of Dunbar	*RMS*; ii, 66
1428	Tarbolton	RG	John Stewart of 'Dernle'	*RMS*. ii, 108
1431	Lochloy	RC of BG	William Hay	*RMS*. ii, 193
1444	Boardland[1]	RC of BG	John Scrimgeour	*RMS*. ii, 281
1451	Collessie		Bishop of St Andrews	*ER*. v, 473
1462	Parkhill[2]		Abbot of Lindores	*ER*, vii, 73
1468	Houston	RG	John Houston of that ilk	*RMS*. ii, 969
1473	Newbigging[1]		Coupar Angus Abbey	*CA Rent.*, nos. 222, 230
1474	Kinneil	RG	James, Lord Hamilton and wife	*RMS*. ii, 1178
1476	Roslin	RG	Oliver Sinclair	*RMS*. ii, 1270
1475/6	Rossie[2]	RG	Elizabeth, Countess of Ross	*RMS*. ii, 1227

1. Possibly not a hunting park.
2. Possibly no longer a hunting park.

Table 32. Baronial Parks (continued)

Date	Name	Details	Holder	Source
1480	'Largewey'	RL		ER, ix, 18, 585
				RMS, ii, 1833 (1488)
1483/4	Crichton²		William, Lord Crichton³	RMS, ii, 1575
1484	Park²		Parks of that ilk (?)	RMS, ii, 1574, 1848
1488	Balmaclellan¹	KG	Alexander Gordon	RMS, ii, 1722
1488	Carruthers	KG	Patrick, Earl of Bothwell	RMS, ii, 2452
1494	Presmennan		Robert Lauder of the Bass	ADA, 196 a
1498	Longcastle	RC of BG	Patrick Vaus and Margaret Kennedy	RMS, ii, 2464
1505	Applegarth²	RG	Alexander Jardine	RMS, ii, 2844
1510	Corrie²	RG	Robert Maxwell	RMS, ii, 3522
1511	Parton²			SRO, *Justice Ayre Journal Books*, RH 2/1/7, p. 197
1511	Balhelvy²	RG	James Kincragie, dean of Aberdeen	RMS, ii, 3672
1512	Little Park²	RG	Duncan Mackee of 'Camlodane'	RMS, ii, 3801
1512	Sundrum	RG	John, Lord Cathcart	RMS, ii, 3720

1. Possibly not a hunting park.
2. Possibly no longer a hunting park.
3. Pending regress of 540 merks.

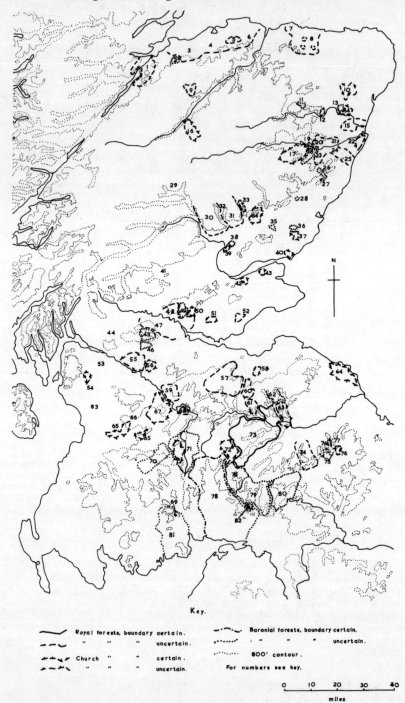

9. Scottish Hunting Reserves in the Thirteenth Century.

Two keys are provided for this map of Scots hunting reserves. The first gives the forests in numerical order and the second gives them in alphabetical order. The forests are numbered from 1 in the north to 82 in the south with certain late additions.

The boundaries of these forest are based on the sources given in Tables 25 and 28 and on sketch maps of land-holdings in thirteenth-century Scotland prepared by D. W. Hunter Marshall, now in Glasgow University Library, *Hunter Marshall Papers*, MS. General 1052. Where no information is available, no boundary is given. Although this map is based on sources for the period 1124-1286, it is called Scottish Hunting Reserves in the Thirteenth Century because it shows forests as they would have been towards the end of that century.

KEY 1

No.	Forest	Type[1]	No.	Forest	Type
1	Inverness	R	34	Kingoldrum	C
2	Kilravock	B	35	'Lyffedin'	B
3	Darnaway	R	36	Ochtirlony	B
4	Darnaway/Drumine	R	37	Dumbarrow and Conan	C
5	Pluscarden/Auchtertyre	C	38	Cargill	B
6	Elgin and Forres	R	39	Campsie	C
7	Invercullen	R	40	Balmerino and Barry	C
8	Banff	R	41	Strathearn	B
9	Lennoch	R	42	Lindores	B
10	Tarves	C	43	Balmerino and Barry	C
11	Leslie	B	44	Lennox	B
12	Fetternear	C	45	Dundaff and Strathcarron	R to B
13	Kinmuck	B	46	Kilsyth	B
14	Fintray	R to C	47	Stirling	R
15	Aberdeen	R	48	Clackmannan	R
16	Rothiemurchus	C	49	Tillicoultry	B
17	Birse	R to C	50	Dollar	R to C
18	Strachan	B	51	Outh	R to B
19	Trostach	C	52	Cluny	R
20	Banchory	R	53	Renfrew	B
21	Drum	R	54	Maich and Calder (Monaibrock)	B to C
22	Nigg	C	55	Glasgow	C
23	Durris	R	56	Drumpellier	C
24	Maryculter	R	57	Pentland and Moorfoot	R
25	Cowie	R	58	Newbattle	C
26	Kinkell	B	59	Mauldslie	R
27	Drumsled	C	60	Gladhouse	R to C
28	Dunlappie	B	61	Leithen	C
29	Atholl	B	62	Gala and Leader (Lauderdale)	R to B
30	Clunie	B	63	Gala and Leader	R to C
31	Alyth	R	64	Coldingham	C
32	Drimmie	R	65	Mauchline	C
33	Glenisla	R			

1. R — royal, B — baronial, C — church

Key 1 (continued)

No.	Forest	Type	No.	Forest	Type
66	Ayr	B	78	Annandale	B
67	Lesmahagow	C	79	Eskdale	B
68	Pettinain	B	80	Liddesdale	B
69	Dalquhairn	B	81	Dalbeattie	B
70	Sanquhar	B	82	Staplegordon and	B
71	Crawford	B		Wauchope	
72	Ettrick/Tima	B	83	Cunninghame	B
73	Ettrick	R to C			
74	Jedburgh	R	*Unlocated*		
75	Hownam	B		*Name*	*Type*
76	Mow	C		'Glengeyth'	B
77	Mow	B		'Kelcamsy'	C

KEY 2

No. on Map[1]	Forest	No. on Map	Forest
15	Aberdeen	79	Eskdale
31	Alyth	73	Ettrick
78	Annandale	72	Ettrick/Tima
39	Atholl	12	Fetternear
66	Ayr	14	Fintray
40 & 43	Balmerino and Barry	62	Gala and Leader R-B (Lauderdale)
20	Banchory	63	Gala and Leader R-C
8	Banff	60	Gladhouse
17	Birse	55	Glasgow
38	Cargill	33	Glenisla
39	Campsie	75	Hownam
48	Clackmannan	7	Invercullen
52	Cluny (Fife)	1	Inverness
30	Clunie (Perthsire)	74	Jedburgh
64	Coldingham	46	Kilsyth
25	Cowie	34	Kingoldrum
83	Cunninghame	26	Kinkell
81	Dalbeattie/Dumfries	13	Kinmuck
69	Dalquhairn	2	Kilravock
3	Darnaway	61	Leithen
4	Darnaway/Drumine	44	Lennox
50	Dollar	9	Lennoch
32	Drimmie (Perthshire)	11	Leslie
21	Drum	67	Lesmahagow
27	Drumsled	80	Liddesdale
37	Dumbarrow and Conan	42	Lindores
45	Dundaff and Strathcarron	35	'Lyffedin'
28	Dunlappie	24	Maryculter
20	Durris	54	Maich and Calder
6	Elgin and Forres	65	Mauchline

1. No. 1 is in the north and no. 82 in the south.

Key 2 (continued)

No. on Map	Forest	No. on Map	Forest
77	Mow B	16	Rothiemurchus
76	Mow C	70	Sanquhar
58	Newbattle	82	Staplegordon and Wauchope
22	Nigg	47	Stirling
36	Ochtirlony	18	Strachan
51	Outh	41	Strathearn
57	Pentland and Moorfoot	10	Tarves
68	Pettinain	49	Tillicoultry
5	Pluscarden/Auchtertyre	19	Trostach
53	Renfrew		

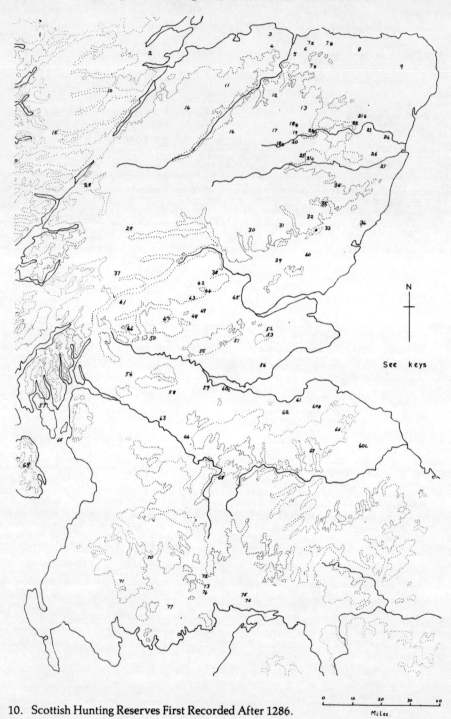

10.   Scottish Hunting Reserves First Recorded After 1286.

KEY 1

Two keys have been provided for this map. One gives the forests in numerical order and the second gives them in alphabetical order. The forests are numbered from 1 in the north to 77 in the south. No distinction is made between royal, baronial and ecclesiastical forests, but that information can be obtained from Tables 25, 26, 27, 28 and 29, pp. 338-353.

No.	Forest	No.	Forest
1	Ross	40	Plater
2	Ormond	41	Ben More
3	Spynie	42	Glen Shervie and Corriemuckloch
4	Langmorn	43	Glenturret
5	Spey	44	Glenalmond
6	Enzie	45	Redgorton
7	Boyne and Enzie	46	Menteith
8	Ryeland	47	Glen Artney
9	Buchan	48	Drummond
10	Strathglass	49	Tomaknock
11	Lochindorb	50	Haldane
12	Glenrinnes	51	Kinross
13	Cabrauch	52	Culface
14	Strathdearn	53	Falkland
15	Cluanie	54	Gartness
16	Abernethy	55	Wester Kers and Alva
17	'Aldnakist and Lechory'	56	Cardenden
18	Corgarf and Baddynyon	57	Bute
19	Invernochty	58	Cumbernauld
20	Glencarvie and Glenconrie	59	Callendar
21	Mar (K=Kildrummy, G=Garioch, C=Cambuskist)	60	B=Bolton, C=Carriden, L=Langton
22	Bennachie	61	Seton
23	Kintore	62	Dalkeith
24	Cordyce	63	Bothwell
25	Culblane	64	Carluke
26	Cullerlie	65	Cumbrae
27	Durris	66	Dye
28	Lochaber	67	Lauder
29	Rannoch	68	Coulter
30	Glen Shee	69	Arran
31	Glen Prosen	70	Glenken
32	Corscarie	71	Buchan
33	Kilgarie	72	Dalswinton
34	Garvock	73	Irongray
35	Glenesk	74	'Herys'
36	'Glenaan'	75	Dalton
37	Mamlorne	76	Woodcockair
38	Strathbraan and Birnam	77	Strone
39	Milton of Earlsruthven		

Key 1 (continued)

Unlocated	Possible Location	Unlocated	Possible Location
'Corylundy' and 'Mewy'	Strathearn	Hartschaw	
		Killanel	North-west of Fyvie
'Coulpersauche'		Kelwood	Dumfriesshire
'Craggilee'		'Polbuthy'	
'Duchinloch'		Rannoch	Near Strathconon
'Garnetulach'	Corntulloch south of Dunnet on R. Dee		(not Perthshire)
		Strathdee	Somewhere on R. Dee
'Glenabeukan'	Glenbuck in Ayrshire		
'Glen M'kern'			

KEY 2

No.[1] Forest		No. Forest	
16	Abernethy	36	'Glenaan'
17	'Aldnakist' and 'Lechory'	44	Glenalmond
69	Arran	47	Glen Artney
41	Ben More	20	Glencarvie and Glenconrie
22	Bennachie	35	Glenesk
60	Bolton, Carriden and Langton	70	Glenken
63	Bothwell	31	Glen Prosen
7	Boyne and Enzie	12	Glenrinnes
9	Buchan	30	Glen Shee
71	Buchan (Galloway)	42	Glen Shervie and Corriemuckloch
57	Bute	43	Glenturret
13	Cabrauch	50	Haldane
59	Callendar	74	'Herys'
56	Cardenden	19	Invernochty
64	Carluke	73	Irongray
15	Cluanie	33	Kilgarie
24	Cordyce	51	Kinross
18	Corgarf and Baddynyon	23	Kintore
32	Corscarie	4	Langmorn
68	Coulter	67	Lauder
25	Culblane	28	Lochaber
52	Culface	11	Lochindorb
26	Cullerlie	37	Mamlorne
58	Cumbernauld	21	Mar
65	Cumbrae	46	Menteith
62	Dalkeith	39	Milton of Earlsruthven
72	Dalswinton	2	Ormond
75	Dalton	40	Plater
48	Drummond	29	Rannoch
27	Durris	45	Redgorton
66	Dye	1	Ross
6	Enzie	8	Ryeland
63	Falkland	61	Seton
54	Gartness	5	Spey
34	Garvock	3	Spynie

1. No. 1 is in the north and No. 77 in the south.

Key 2 (continued)

No.	Forest	No.	Forest
38	Strathbraan and Birnam	49	Tomaknock
14	Strathdearn	55	Wester Kers and Alva
10	Strathglass	76	Woodcockair
77	Strone		

Notes

Chapter 1

1. Lindner, K., *Die Jagd Der Vorzeit*, 265; Clark G., *Archaeology and Society*, (London, 1957), 185, 220, 221.
2. Justinian, *Institutes*, section II, part 1, chapter 12; see below, ch. 9.
3. *Orkneyinga Saga*, part 3, 214.
4. Aelred, *Genealogia*, 735.
5. See p. 52.
6. *RRS*, i, 184; *RRS*, ii, 80, 136; see below, p. 25.
7. Wartburg, *Französische Etymologische Wörterbuch*, (Bonn, 1928), xvii, 369; Tilander, *Cynegetica*, i, 81 ff. I am indebted to Dr. Murison of the School of Scottish Studies of Edinburgh University and to Bror Danielson of Stockholm University for assistance with the etymology of this word. They did not think the word could have passed direct from Scandinavia to Scotland.
8. *Gula Ting Law*, cc 93, 95.
9. *Gula Ting Law*, c 91; *Frosta Ting Law*, cc 10, 11, 14.
10. *Frosta Ting Law*, cc 8, 9.
11. Lindner, *Die Jagd im Frühen Mittelalter*, 142, 147; *Scanian Law*, XI, c 5.
12. *ESC*, 5.
13. *ESC*, 178.
14. Gresswell, Rev. W. H. P., *The Forests and Deer Parks of the County of Somerset*, (Taunton, 1905), 24; Barrow, *Kingdom of the Scots*, 21; Thorpe, *Diplomatarium*, 114.
15. Barrow, *op. cit.*, 21, 27.
16. Barrow, *op. cit.*, 35 ff., 64.
17. Barrow, *op. cit.*, 64.
18. *ESC*, 15; Duncan, A. A. M., 'The Earliest Scottish Charters', *SHR*, xxxvii, (1958), 103-5; and *The Making of the Kingdom*, 364.
19. *EHD*, i, 369, cc 49; 49 part 3.
20. Robertson, *Laws of Kings of England*, 178, c 80.
21. Whitelocke, *The Beginnings of English Society*, 103; Thorpe, *Diplomatarium*, 65.
22. *EHD*, i, 369, cc 43, 44.
23. Jackson, *Deer*, 31, 34, 52, 93. Old Irish 'erelc' was metathesised to 'elerc'.
24. Watson, *Celtic Place Names*, 489.
25. See pp. 52, 55.
26. *ALI*, iii, 449; Binchy, D. A., 'The Linguistic and Historical Value of the Irish Law Tracts', *PBA*, xxix, (1943), 195.
27. Binchy, D. A., 'Irish History and Irish Law', *Studia Hibernica*, (1975), no. 15, 9; Kelly, F., 'The Old Irish Tree List', *Celtica*, (1976), xi, 108.
28. Binchy, D. A., 'An Archaic Legal Poem', *Celtica*, ix, (1971), 151-168.
29. Binchy, *op. cit.*, 167-168.
30. Cross and Slover, *Ancient Irish Tales*, 355, 397.
31. *ALI*, iv, cxxiii, 101.
32. *ALI*, iv, 147; Binchy, *op. cit.*, 157-159, 165.
33. Ellis, *Welsh Tribal Law and Custom*, i, 33.
34. *Ancient Laws and Institutes of Wales*, 799, Leges Wallicae, 2, XXVI, c i; p. viii.
35. *Ibid.*, 243, Dimetian Code, 2, XIII, c 16; 359, Gwentian Code, 2, XXV, c 5.

36. Lloyd, J., *A History of Wales* (London, 1911), i, 339.
37. Lloyd, *op. cit.*, i, 339; Lewis, T., *Black Book of Chirk*, ZCP, xx, (1933-6), 30-96; Lewis, T., *Glossary of Early Medieval Welsh Law*, (Manchester, 1913), 149; *Ancient Laws and Institutes of Wales*, Leges Wallicae, Venedotian Code.
38. *Ancient Laws and Institutes of Wales*, 799, Leges Wallicae, 2, XXV, c 6; 800, Leges Wallicae, 2, XXVI, c 1; Ellis, *op. cit.*, i, 33.
39. Ellis, *op. cit.*, ii, 52 ff.
40. *Ancient Laws and Institutes of Wales*, 800, Leges Wallicae, 2, XXVIII, c 1.
41. Ellis, *op. cit.*, ii, 52 ff.
42. *Chron. Picts-Scots*, 190; Barrow, *Kingdom of the Scots*, 172.
43. See p. 56.
44. Prou, M., 'La Forêt en Angleterre et en France', *Journal des Savants*, (1915), 241 ff; De Coulanges, F., *Histoire des Institutions Politiques de L'Ancienne France*, 425.
45. Latouche, *The Birth of the Western Economy*, 188; for a variant view see *Cambridge Economic History*, (Cambridge, 1941), i, ed. Koebner, R., 42 ff.
46. Petit Dutaillis, C., 'De La Signification du mot forêt à l'Epoque Franque', *Bibliothèque de l'Ecole des Chartes*, lxxvi, (1915), 97 ff; Prou, M., *op. cit.*
47. MGH, *Legum Nationum Germanicorum*, ii, 107.
48. Petit Dutaillis, *op. cit.*, 142; Latouche, *op. cit.*, 188; Lindner, *Die Jagd im Frühen Mittelalter*, 156.
49. Ganshof, F. L., *La Belgique Carolingienne*, (Brussels, 1958), 162.
50. MGH, *Capitularia*, i, 86, *Capitulare de Villis*, c 36.
51. MGH, *op. cit.*, 91, *Capitulare Missorum Generale*, (802), c 39.
52. Petit Dutaillis, *op. cit.*, 127.
53. MGH, *op. cit.*, 288, *Capitulare per se Scribenda*, (818 x 819), c 7.
54. Lindner, *Die Jagd im Frühen Mittelalter*, 164; Prou, *op. cit.*, 241-243.
55. Prou, *op. cit.*, 241 ff.
56. Latouche, *op. cit.*, 188.
57. Petit Dutaillis, *op. cit.*, 120-1.
58. Petit Dutaillis, *op. cit.*, 147.
59. *Actes des Ducs de Normandie*, 30, 35, 224.
60. *Ibid.*, 64, 99.
61. *Ibid.*, 140.
62. *Ibid.*, 208, 214.
63. The following information about Norman families comes from Barrow, G. W. S., 'Les Familles Normandes d'Ecosse', *Annales de Normandie*, (1965), 493 ff, and *The Kingdom of the Scots*, 315-336; Barrow, G. W. S., 'The Beginnings of Feudalism in Scotland', *BIHR*, (1956), and *The Kingdom of Scots*, 279-314; Ritchie, *Normans in Scotland*; see Map 1, p. 14.
64. Complete information on the English forest system can be found in Petit Dutaillis, C., *Stubbs*, ii, 149 ff; Petit Dutaillis, C., 'Franco Norman Origins of the English Forest', *Essays offered to C. H. Bémont*, 59 ff; Cronne, H. A., 'Forest under Henry I', *Essays to J. E. Todd*, 1 ff; *RRAN*, ii, p. xx, nos 629, 631, 696, 709, 799.
65. Petit Dutaillis, *Stubbs*, 173; Cronne, *ibid.*, 1 ff; Stubbs, *Select Charters*, 185, The Assize of the Forest, cc 1-6, 10-11, 14; Richardson, H. G. and Sayles, G. O., *The Governance of Medieval England*, (Edinburgh, 1963), 444 ff.
66. Information about English forests in the earldom of Huntingdon is taken from VCH, *Rutland*, ii, p. xxviii; *Northampton*, ii, 341; *Huntingdon*, ii, 73, 338; Bazely, M. L., 'English Royal Forests in the Thirteenth Century'. *TRHS*, (1921), 140-172.
67. For information about the earldom of Huntingdon and its tenants see Moore, *Lands of the Scottish Kings in England*, 13 ff; Farrer, *Honors and Knights' Fees*, ii, *passim*; VCH, *Rutland*, *Northampton* and *Huntingdon* under the appropriate manors.
68. Moore, *op. cit.*, 55.
69. Duncan, *The Making of the Kingdom*, 125.

70. ESC, 50.
71. *ESC*, 35; Barrow, *The Kingdom of the Scots*, 205.
72. Ritchie, *The Normans in Scotland*, 168.
73. *ESC*, 36; *RRS*, i, p. 36.
74. *RRS*, i, 118; *ESC*, 74.
75. *ESC*, 83.
76. *Ibid.*, 74.
77. *Ibid.*, 141, p. 376.
78. *Ibid.*, 146.
79. *Ibid.*, 153.
80. *Ibid.*, 193.

Chapter 2

1. Barbour, *Bruce*, (Skeat), bk 8, 1 424; see p. 176.
2. *Ibid.*, *Bruce*, bk 9, 1 672.
3. See *DOST sub* 'forest'.
4. Hay, *Book of Alexander*, ed. Ritchie, ii, 1 2835, 4042.
5. Petit Dutaillis, 'De La Signification du Mot Forêt à l'Epoque Franque', *Bibliothèque de l'Ecole des Chartes*, lxxvi, (1915), 144.
6. See *DOST sub* 'forest'.
7. SRO, *Mar and Kellie Papers*, GD 124/6/1.
8. *Arb. Lib.*, 232.
9. *Glas. Reg.*, 199.
10. *Chron. Fordun*, Annals, c 176.
11. *ER*, viii, 567.
12. *RMS*, ii, 3288; SRO, *Great Seal Register*, C/2/15.
13. *RMS*, ii, 3438.
14. Skene, J., *De Verborum Significatione*, (London, 1641), 67, *sub* 'forestarius'.
15. Stair, *Institutes*, bk 2, tit. 3, c 67.
16. Aelred, *Genealogia*, 714; Aelred, *De Bello Standardo*, 195; *ESC*, 414.
17. *Kinloss Recs.*, 105.
18. Easson, *Religious Houses*, 65.
19. See p. 98.
20. *ESC*, 74, 116.
21. *Ibid.*, 141.
22. *Ibid.*, 116, 188.
23. *Ibid.*, 116.
24. *Ibid.*, 156, 163, 188, 249; *CDS*, ii, 519.
25. See p. 183.
26. See p. 95.
27. See Table 28, p. 345.
28. Hay, *Genealogical Collections*, 245, (1189 x 1196).
29. *Melr. Lib.*, 39, (1165 x 1169).
30. *RRS*, i, 44; *Mort. Reg.*, i, p. lxxiii.
31. *RMS*, i, 53.
32. See p. 177.
33. *RRS*, ii, p. 19.
34. *Ibid.*, i, 118, 174, 243.
35. *ESC*, 136.
36. *RRS*, i, p. 42, no. 226.
37. *Dryb. Lib.*, 218; *CDS*, ii, 1626.
38. Barrow, *The Kingdom of the Scots*, 290-1.

39. *RRS*, ii, p. 81. The nos. of charters issued at each place respectively were 27, 17, 14, 3, 5, 8, 5, 10.
40. *Ibid.*, ii, 75.
41. *Ibid.*, ii, 128.
42. *Ibid.*, ii, 362.
43. *Ibid.*, ii, pp. 11-13.
44. *Ibid.*, ii, 463.
45. *Ibid.*, ii, 251.
46. *Ibid.*, i, pp. 31, ff.
47. See p. 184.
48. See p. 209.
49. *Pais. Reg.*, p. 5; *Melr. Lib.*, 66, 39, 94.
50. See p. 250.
51. Duncan, *The Making of the Kingdom*, 420-423, 365.
52. *RRS*, iii, (Handlist), *passim*. The nos. of charters issued at each place respectively were 8, 4, 7, 8.
53. *A. B. Antiqs.*, ii, p. 109; Dickinson, *Sheriff Court Bk.*, 351.
54. See p. 144.
55. See p. 185.
56. See Table 23, p. 266.
57. Watt, D. E. R., 'The Minority of Alexander III', *TRHS*, (1971), 1-24.
58. *CDS*, i, 1503, 1518, 1565, 1743.
59. Paris, *Chronica Majora*, v, 340; Paris, *Historia Anglorum*, iii, 322; *Patent Rolls*, (1247-1258), 162.
60. *Patent Rolls*, (1247-1258), 61.
61. Paris, *op. cit.*
62. Paris, *ibid.*
63. *Patent Rolls*, (1247-1258), 204, 234, 236, 237.
64. Rymer, *Foedera*, i, 566.
65. *RRS*, iv, (Handlist), *passim*. The nos. of charters issued at each place respectively were 4, 3, 10.
66. *RMS*, i, 67.
67. See p. 209.
68. See Table 23, p. 266.
69. *Holy. Lib.*, 23.
70. *Holm Cultram Chrs.*, 120.
71. *Holy. Lib.*, 73.
72. *St A. Lib.*, 246.
73. *Lind. Lib.*, 1, 2; *RRS*, i, 44.
74. Barrow, *The Kingdom of the Scots*, 36, 37.
75. *RRS*, i, 184.
76. *Ibid.*, ii, 80.
77. *Ibid.*, ii, 136.
78. *Inchaff. Chrs.*, 9, 17.
79. *Ibid.*, 12.
80. Fraser, *Lennox*, ii, 401.
81. *Lenn. Cart.*, p. 1.
82. *Lenn. Cart.*, pp. 25, 91, 35, 19; Fraser, *Colquhoun*, ii, 272; Fraser, *Lennox*, ii, 403.
83. See p. 196 and Table 9, p. 153.
84. Dickinson, W. C., 'The Toschederach', *Juridical Review*, (1941), 85-111.
85. See p. 226.
86. *Inchaff. Chrs.*, 17.
87. See p. 225.
88. See p. 294.
89. *RRS*, i, 11.

90. *Ibid.*, i, 7, 206; ii, 49, 56.
91. Bazely, M. L., 'English Royal Forests in the Thirteenth Century', *TRHS*, (1921), 140-172.
92. Moore, *Lands of the Scottish Kings in England*, 3.
93. *Ibid.*, 7; CDS, i, 1358.
94. *CDS*, i, 1895, 1845, 2221, 2266, 2291.
95. Petit Dutaillis, *Stubbs*, 200, 203.
96. *Ibid.*, 149 ff; see p. 312.
97. Stubbs, *Select Charters*, 186, Assize of Woodstock, c 16.
98. Hoveden, *Chronica*, iv, 63, c 1.
99. *Ibid.*, c 14.
100. Stubbs, *op. cit.*, 186, Assize of Woodstock, cc 3, 4, 7; cc 3 and 4 date from Henry I's reign and c 7 from Henry II's.
101. See p. 294.
102. Stubbs, *op cit.*, 186, Assize of Woodstock, c 2 which dates from Henry I's reign.
103. *Ibid.*, 346, Charter of the Forest, c 10.
104. *Ibid.*, 346, Charter of the Forest, c 14.
105. Petit Dutaillis, *Stubbs*, 117.
106. Jullien, *La Chasse*, 98.
107. Reed, *Forests of France*, 39.
108. Jullien, *op. cit.*, 96.
109. Petit Dutaillis, *op. cit.*, 177.
110. Jullien, *op. cit.*, 103.
111. *Ibid.*, 103.
112. Richebourg, *Nouveau Coutumier Général*, ii, part 2, 1202, c 18, art. 15; Petit Dutaillis, *op. cit.*, 195, 208.
113. Petit Dutaillis, *op. cit.*, 195, 200, 203, 208.
114. See p. 225.

Chapter 3

1. *Rot. Scot.*, i, 4a, 5a.
2. *Ibid.*, i, 8a-9a.
3. *Ibid.*, *op. cit.*, 7a.
4. *CDS*, ii, 1880.
5. Nicholson, *The Later Middle Ages*, 38, 41, 46.
6. *Rot. Scot.*, i, 31b.
7. *CDS*, ii, 1428, 1496, 1704, 1982.
8. Barrow, *Bruce*, 171 n., 215; *CDS*, ii, 1165.
9. *CDS*, ii, 1839.
10. See p. 129; *CDS*, ii, 1646.
11. *CDS*, ii, 1229, 1978; see p. 138.
12. *CDS*, ii, 853, (1296).
13. *Ibid.*, 1317.
14. Stevenson, *Documents*, 268, 296.
15. *CDS*, ii, 1978.
16. *Ibid.*, 1230, 1287, 1317, 1321.
17. *Ibid.*, 1226, 1229, 1782.
18. *Ibid.*, ii, 1646.
19. *Ibid.*, ii, 1839.
20. *Rot. Scot.*, i, 10a.
21. *CDS*, ii, 1708.
22. *Ibid.*, 1736.
23. *Ibid.*, 1736.

24. *Ibid.*, 1708.
25. *Rot. Scot.*, i, 36a; *CDS*, ii, 1868.
26. Stevenson, *Documents*, 265.
27. *CDS*, ii, 1229, (1301).
28. *Rot. Scot.*, i, 19a, (1292); *CDS*, ii, 1736.
29. *CDS*, ii, 1736.
30. Stevenson, *Documents*, 265.
31. See p. 177.
32. See p. 296.
33. *CDS*, ii, 1123, 1702, 1703, 1650, 1651.
34. *Pais. Reg.*, p. 92.
35. Barbour, *Bruce*, (Skeat), bk 17, line 64.
36. Barrow, *Bruce*, 300 ff; Barbour, *Bruce*, (Skeat), bk 11, lines 284, 357.
37. Barbour, *Bruce*, (Skeat), bk 19, line 490.
38. *Abdn. Reg.*, i, pp. 136-138, (1370 x 1390).
39. *SRO, Justice Ayre Journal Books*, RH 2/1/5.
40. See p. 69.
41. See Table 3, p. 77.
42. Duncan, A. A. M., 'Acta of Robert I', *SHR*, xxxii, (1953), 1-39, nos. 290-293.
43. *ER*, i, 250.
44. Nicholson, *The Later Middle Ages*, 92.
45. *APS*, i, 682; Barrow, *Bruce*, 381.
46. Barrow, *Bruce*, 390.
47. See p. 130.
48. See pp. 129, 153, 156.
49. *Rot. Scot.*, i, 276a.
50. *Ibid.*, 275a, 276a, (1334).
51. *CDS*, iii, pp. 329, 378.
52. *Rot. Scot.*, i, 380a.
53. *Ibid.*, 793b; *CDS*, iii, 1377 (1341/2).
54. *Ibid.*, 380a.
55. *Ibid.*, 278b, 380a, (1334).
56. *RMS*, i, app. 1, 36, 38; app. 2, 232, 729.
57. *Ibid.*, app. 2, 845, 856; Raine, *ND.*, app. p. 18, no. 84.
58. *Rot. Scot.*, i, 965a.
59. *Ibid.*, ii, 163b.
60. *RMS*, i, 227; app. 1, 123, 154; *ER*, i, 519, 522.
61. *CDS*, iii, 1178, (1335).
62. Balfour-Melville, E. W. M., 'Papers relating to the captivity and release of David II', *SHS, Misc IX*, (1958), 21.
63. See Table 3, p. 77.
64. *RRS*, vi, (Handlist), 39, 281, 401, 453.
65. *APS*, i, 491, c 7; Nicholson, *The Later Middle Ages*, 164.
66. *APS*, i, 491, c 7.
67. *ER*, i, 572. The following details of the history of the crown lands are taken from *ER*, vi, p. lxiv ff, and *The Scots Peerage* under the family who received or lost the lands. See Tables, 8, 9, 25 on pp. 119, 153, 338.
68. *ER*, i, 586.
69. *A. B. Antiqs.*, iii, 293; *Burnett of Leys*, 154.
70. *ER*, i, 586, 549.
71. *Ibid.*, 586.
72. *SRO, Mar and Kellie Muniments*, GD 124/1/518.
73. *RMS*, i, 175.
74. *Ibid.*, i, 258.
75. *APS*, i, 501-2; Nicholson, *The Later Middle Ages*, 177.

A

76. *APS*, i, 529.
77. *Ibid.*, 528.
78. *Ibid.*, 531.
79. *A. B. Antiqs.*, iii, 294.
80. *RMS*, i, 279.
81. See p. 92.
82. *Moray Reg.*, i, p. 473, no. 22.
83. *RMS*, i, 285.
84. Nicholson, *The Later Middle Ages*, 177.
85. *Chron. Pluscarden*, bk 10, c 1.
86. *RMS*, i, 400, 411, 515, 596-602, 653, 675, 697, 718, 757; *ER*, iii, 109, *Abdn. Reg.*, i, 155-6.
87. *ER*, iii, 25, 45, 51, 69, 90, 113, 117, 147; *RMS*, i, 653, 658.
88. See Table 3, p. 77.
89. See p. 225.
90. *Moray Reg.*, i, 473 no. 22.
91. *APS*, i, 564; *RMS*, i, 618.
92. SRO, *Mar and Kellie Muniments*, GD 124/1/524.
93. *RMS*, i, 757, 802, 803, 836.
94. *Pais. Reg.*, 96.
95. SRO, *Transcripts of Royal Charters*, RH 1/1/2/14 August 1398.
96. *APS*, i, 580.
97. *Peebles Recs*, 206 no. 3.
98. *APS*, i, 576.
99. *Stirlings of Keir*, 201.
100. See Table 28, p. 351.
101. See p. 271.
102. Petit Dutaillis, *Stubbs*, 243.
103. *Ibid.*, 249.
104. Jullien, *La Chasse*, 104-113.
105. Decq, E., 'L'Administration des Eaux et Forêts', *Bibliothèque de l'Ecole des Chartes*, lxxxiii, (1922), 67 ff.
106. Jullien, *La Chasse*, 104-113.
107. *Ibid.*, 114-121.
108. Petit Dutaillis, *Stubbs*, 154.
109. *Ibid.*, 277; *Statutes of the Realm*, ii, 65, c 13.
110. See p. 233.
111. See p. 231.
112. See p. 227.
113. York, *Master of Game*, (Grohman), pp. xlvi-xlviii.
114. Balfour-Melville, E. W. M., *James I, King of Scots*, (Edinburgh, 1936), 285.
115. *APS*, ii, 20, c 4; Nicholson, *The Later Middle Ages*, 284, 285.
116. See p. 141.
117. *RMS*, ii, 172.
118. *APS*, ii, 7, c 13; see p. 100.
119. *RMS*, ii, 59; see chapter 4, part 3, 137, 158.
120. Pitscottie, *Historie*, i, 31, c 5; Nicholson, *The Later Middle Ages*, 329-330.
121. *RMS*, ii, 383-392, 493, 496 etc.
122. *ER*, v, 595 (1451 x 1453).
123. *Ibid.*, 686, (1453 x 1454); vi, 639 (1459 x 1460).
124. *ER*, vi, 227, 371.
125. *Ibid.*, 656.
126. *Ibid.*, 325.
127. See pp. 80-82.
128. *ER*, viii, 441.

129. *Ibid.*
130. *APS*, ii, 61a.
131. *Ibid.*, 33.
132. *RMS*, ii, 491.
133. *Ibid.*, 546.
134. *ER*, v, 581.
135. *APS*, ii, 42.
136. *ER*, vi, 561.
137. *Ibid.*, 51, 366.
138. *Ibid.*, 269; vii, 86.
139. See p. 199.
140. See p. 136.
141. *ER*, vi, 411.
142. *Ibid.*, 70, 282.
143. *APS*, ii, 51, c 31; 15, c 12.
144. *Ibid.*, 51, cc 32, 35.
145. *Ibid.*, ii, 52, c 36.
146. *ER*, vii, 68.
147. Nicholson, *The Later Middle Ages*, 411.
148. *ER*, vii, 488.
149. *Ibid.*, 533.
150. *Ibid.*, 472.
151. *Ibid.*, 614.
152. See pp. 66, 67.
153. *ER*, viii, 143; x, 98, 166.
154. Murray, A., 'The Procedure of the Scottish Exchequer in the Early Sixteenth Century', *SHR*, xl, (1961), 103-104; 'The Crown Lands in Galloway 1455-1513', *DGT*, xxxvii, (1958-9), 9-25, at 16.
155. *ER*, vii, 3, 113.
156. *Ibid.*, 62.
157. *Ibid.*, 4.
158. *Ibid.*, 353.
159. Nicholson, *The Later Middle Ages*, 404, 412-414.
160. *ER*, vii, 252, 326.
161. *Ibid.*, 574.
162. See Table 5, p. 115.
163. *ER*, vii, 358.
164. See Table 6, p. 117.
165. *ER*, viii, 60.
166. *Ibid.*, 441.
167. Nicholson, *The Later Middle Ages*, 407, 454, 455.
168. *APS*, ii, 113; *RMS*, ii, 1191.
169. *ER*, xii, p. xxxii.
170. *Ibid.*, 42.
171. *RMS*, ii, 769.
172. *APS*, ii, 117, 188.
173. See p. 349.
174. See p. 139.
175. See p. 147.
176. *APS*, ii, 118; 165, c 2; 170, c 4; 176, c 1.
177. See p. 333.
178. *ADA*, 71b.
179. See Table 9, p. 153.
180. *APS*, ii, 107.
181. *Ibid.*, c 16.

182. See Table 4, p. 79.
183. *TA*, ii, p. xcvii.
184. Brown, P. Hume, *Early Travellers in Scotland*, (Edinburgh, 1891), 41.
185. *TA*, i, 92, 200.
186. *TA*, iii, 334-355.
187. Nicholson, *The Later Middle Ages*, 546.
188. Auchinnis Chalain is the modern form of 'Inchcailloch' NN 325, 355. Gillies, W. A., *In Famed Breadalbane*, (Perth, 1938), 63-64.
189. *APS*, ii, 211; Nicholson, *The Later Middle Ages*, 533.
190. *RMS*, ii, 2529, 2530.
191. *APS*, ii, 219.
192. *RMS*, ii, 1784.
193. *Ibid.*, 1492, 2106.
194. *RSS*, i, 268.
195. *ER*, vi, 193.
196. *RMS*, ii, 2586.
197. *Ibid.*, 2585.
198. *ER*, xii, 394, 671; xiii, 11.
199. *APS*, ii, 244, c 26.
200. *RMS*, ii, 2502, 3102.
201. *Ibid.*, 2464.
202. *ER*, xi, 417.
203. *Ibid.*, xii, 144, 214, etc.
204. See p. 97.
205. See p. 97.
206. *APS*, ii, 271.
207. See p. 188.
208. See p. 235.
209. *ER*, xi, 393.
210. *Ibid.*, 394.
211. See p. 137.
212. *APS*, i, 752, c 24; see p. 243.
213. *APS*, i, 473, c 27; Barrow, *Bruce*, 416.
214. *RMS*, ii, 3473, (1510).
215. *Ibid.*, 3390.
216. See p. 92.
217. See pp. 212, 218.
218. See p. 100.
219. Dalby, 'Lexicon of the Medieval German Hunt', Introduction, p. v.
220. York, *Master of Game*, (Grohman), 199 ff.
221. See p. 55.
222. See pp. 104, 110, 112.
223. Petit Dutaillis, *Stubbs*, 244.
224. Jullien, *La Chasse*, 125.
225. *Ibid.*, 130.
226. *Ibid.*, 130 ff.
227. *APS*, ii, 343.
228. *Ibid.*, 483; c 3.
229. See pp. 230-233.

Chapter 4

1. *Dunnaire Finn*, ii, 185, no. 54.
2. *Ibid.*, i, 130.
3. See p. 8.
4. Watson, W. J., 'Aoibhinn an Obair on t-sealg', *Celtic Review*, IX, (1913-1914), 156-168.
5. *Ibid*; Pitscottie, *Historie*, i, 56.
6. Aelred, *Genealogia*, 735.
7. See p. 7.
8. *The Holyrood Ordinale*, ed. F. C. Eeles, in *The Book of the Old Edinburgh Club*, vii, (1914), 64-66.
9. Bellenden, *Chronicles*, bk 12, c 6.
10. Wyntoun, *Chronicle*, bk 7, c 1, Wemyss Ms.
11. See p. 53.
12. Wyntoun, *Chronicle*, bk 6, 1 1038, Cott Ms.
13. Tilander, G., *Cynegetica*, i, 81.
14. Twici, *La Venerie*, (Tilander), 36.
15. York, *Master of Game*, (Grohman), 108, c 36.
16. Wyntoun, *Chronicle*, bk 6, 1038, Cott Ms.
17. *Ibid.*, bk 7, c 1, Cott Ms.
18. *RRS*, ii, 215.
19. York, *Master of Game*, (Grohman), 204.
20. See p. 220; Whitelocke, D., *Anglo-Saxon Wills*, (Cambridge, 1930), 79, 195.
21. York, *Master of Game*, (Grohman), 192, *sub* snares.
22. *ER*, xii, 205; see p. 221.
23. Fraser, *Douglas*, iii, 556.
24. See p. 85.
25. *TA*, ii, 119.
26. *Ibid.*, iii, 336.
27. Pitscottie, *Historie*, ii, 335, bk 21, chapts. 20, 21.
28. *TA*, iv, 137.
29. *Ibid.*, iii, 338, 339.
30. *Ibid.*, ii, 444.
31. Hay, *Book of Alexander*, 176, bk 2, 1 2709.
32. *Dunnaire Finn*, 218.
33. Lismore, Dean of, *Heroic Poetry*, (Ross), 13, no. 5.
34. Lesley, *History*, i, 19 ff.
35. Grant, I. F., *The Macleods, The History of a Clan 1200-1956*, (London 1959), 65.
36. Tilander, *Cynegetica*, i, 81 ff; York, *Master of Game*, (Grohman), 201.
37. Lesley, *History*, i, 19; Pitscottie, *Historie*, bk 21, cc 20, 21; Hume Brown, P., *Early Travellers in Scotland*, (Edinburgh, 1891), 12 ff; Barclay, W., *Contra Monarchomachos*, in Fittis, *Sports and Pastimes of Scotland*, 54, 55.
38. *CDS*, i, 2291.
39. York, *Master of Game*, (Grohman), xlvii.
40. Cross and Slover, *Ancient Irish Tales*, 242, 440.
41. Romilly Allen, *Early Christian Monuments*, 61, 135, 155, 201, 214, 237, 255, 347; Steer and Bannerman, *Monumental Sculpture*, 186.
42. Drummond, *Sculptured Monuments*, plates 25, 51, 56, 78, 80, 84; Loder, *Colonsay*, plate xxiv.
43. York, *Master of Game*, (Grohman), 142.
44. *Ibid.*, 63.
45. Scrope, *Deer Stalking*, 356-9.
46. Leland, *Collecteana*, iv, 286.
47. *TA*, ii, 154, 427.

48. Boece, *Historiae*, lxxxv, bk 5, c 11, 1 23; Bellenden *Chronicles*, i, 205, bk 5, c 10.
49. Romilly Allen, *Early Christian Monuments*, 68, 115; Cruden, *Early Christian and Pictish Monuments*, plate 47.
50. See p. 294.
51. Barbour, *Bruce* (Skeat), bk 7, 1 405.
52. See p. 100.
53. *RMS*, ii, 3193; *RSS*, i, 1637.
54. *ER*, vi, 639; vii, 60, 172, 614; viii, 56.
55. *TA*, iv, 115.
56. Bellenden, *Chronicles*, 229, bk 6, c 5.
57. York, *Master of Game*, 194.
58. Boece, *Historiae*, f 96, bk 6, c 6, 1 59; Bellenden, *Chronicles*, 229, bk 6, c 5.
59. Boece, *Historiae*, f 35, bk 5, c 11, 1 23; Bellenden, *Chronicles*, 205, bk 5, c 10.
60. Arrian, *Kunegetikos*, c 24, 129-30.
61. See p. 220.
62. Henryson, *Fables*, 54, 'The Lion and the Mouse', 1 1514.
63. *Melr. Lib.*, 198.
64. York, *Master of Game* (Grohman), p. 94, c 34.
65. *Ibid.*, xlvi.
66. Brander, *Hunting and Shooting*, 66; Jullien, *La Chasse*, 199; York, *Master of Game*, (Grohman), xlvi ff.
67. Henri IV, *Lettres*, vi, 160.
68. Jullien, *La Chasse*, 199.
69. *Ibid.*
70. James VI, *Basilikon Doron*, 48, part iii.
71. York, *Master of Game*, (Grohman), 185; see below, p. 64.
72. Xenophon, *Kunegetikos*, cc 5-9.
73. York, *Master of Game*, (Grohman), 97, 98.
74. Pitcairn, *Criminal Trials*, ii, 211, 212.
75. *Ibid.*, ii, 210.
76. *ER*, x, 505.
77. York, *Master of Game*, (Grohman), 172.
78. *Ibid.*, 107, 197; Tilander, *Cynegetica*, i, 90, 92.
79. *ER*, vi, 656.
80. *Ibid.*, 243.
81. *Ibid.*, xii, 27.
82. *Ibid.*, ii, 364.
83. *Ibid.*, 543.
84. *Ibid.*, iii, 68.
85. Fraser, *Menteith*, ii, 297 no. 59.
86. *ER*, iii, 45, 69, 90, 113, 147, 177.
87. *Ibid.*, vi, 243, vii, 181.
88. *Ibid.*, x, 187, 429; xiii, 192.
89. *Ibid.*, vi, 243; x, 429.
90. *Ibid.*, vi, 242.
91. *TA*, i, 274.
92. *Ibid.*, iv, 137.
93. See p. 81.
94. *ER*, vii, 614.
95. *TA*, ii, 119.
96. *Ibid.*, iii, 338.
97. *ER*, vii, 502; *TA*, iv, 530.
98. *TA*, iii, 156, 334.
99. *Ibid.*, i, 227.
100. *Ibid.*, i, clxxi.

101. Steer and Bannerman, *Monumental Sculpture*, 186.
102. Blackmore, *Hunting Weapons*, 2-14, 52-64.
103. York, *Master of Game*, (Grohman), 120, 122.
104. *ER*, xi, 333; *RMS*, i, 279.
105. Blackmore, *op. cit.*, 148.
106. Romilly Allen, *Early Christian Monuments*, 68, 115, figs. 69, 120; Cruden, *Early Christian and Pictish Monuments*, plate 47; Anderson, J., *Scotland in Early Christian Times*, 123.
107. Stuart, *op. cit.*, i, plate 76.
108. Romilly Allen, *op. cit.*, 150; Stuart, *op. cit.*, i, plates xix, xx; ii, plates xviii, xix.
109. Heath, E. G., *The Grey Goose Wing*, (Oxford, 1971), 285, 286.
110. Blackmore, *op. cit.*, 173-177.
111. *Ibid.*, 174, 175.
112. *Ibid.*, 178.
113. *Ibid*; MacGregor, A., 'Two Antler Crossbow Nuts and some notes on the development of the Crossbow', *PSAS*, 107, (1975-1976),317-21.
114. I am grateful to Mr J. Scott, Keeper of the Department of Archaeology, Ethnography and History in Glasgow Kelvingrove Museum, to Mr A. G. Credland, Keeper of Exhibitions in Hull Museum and especially to Mr D. Caldwell, Research Assistant in the National Museum of Antiquities of Scotland, for assistance with my enquiries into the crossbow.
115. *TA*, i, 45, 48; iii, 337.
116. Lesley, *History*, i, 19; Boece, *Historiae*, f 35, bk 5, c 11, 1 23.
117. York, *Master of Game*, (Grohman), 123.
118. See p. 221.
119. *APS*, ii, 483, c 3.
120. York, *Master of Game*, (Grohman), 123.
121. Barbour, *Bruce*, (Skeat), bk 7, 1 400 ff.
122. Froissart, *Chronicles*, (Joliffe), bk 3, c 130.
123. *RMS*, ii, 3173, 3568; *TA*, ii, 454.
124. York, *Master of Game*, (Grohman), 176, 177; Tilander, *Cynegetica*, i, 69; see p. 292, Law 2.
125. Laing, *Scottish Seals*, 127, 342, 678, 697.
126. The Savernake Horn: Article by Camber R. and Cherry, J. in *British Museum Yearbook*, vol. ii, (London, 1978). The Douglas Clephane Horn: *Scottish National Memorials*, (Glasgow, 1890), 26, plate 1. Horn of Burnetts of Ley: *Burnetts of Ley*, app. 292.
127. York, *op. cit.*, 185.
128. *RSS*, i, 1637.
129. Lesley, *History*, i, 119.
130. Boece, *Historiae*, f 7r.
131. Gesner, *Icones Animalium*, part 2, 25.
132. Barbour, *Bruce*, (Skeat), bk 7, 1 400ff.
133. Caius, *English Dogges*, 9.
134. Cash, *Dogs*, 71, plate 35; York, *Master of Game*, (Grohman), plate xvii.
135. Hartley, *The Deerhound*, 18.
136. *TA*, vii, 472.
137. Arrian, *Kunegetikos*, c 6, p. 87.
138. Richardson, J., 'Mural Decorations at the House of Kinneil, Bo'ness', *PSAS*, 75, (1940-1941), 199.
139. Jesse, *The British Dog*, i, 347.
140. York, *The Master of Game*, (Grohman), 143.
141. James IV, *Letters*, no. 228; Brodie, *Letters and Papers of Henry VIII*, 98 no. 54.
142. *RMS*, ii, 1645.
143. *ADC*, 36a, 342b.

144. York, *Master of Game*, (Grohman), 142.
145. *TA*, ii, 475.
146. Gesner, *Icones Animalium*, part 2, 26.
147. CDS, i, 348, 400.
148. *RCAM, Peebles*, ii, 320, plates 102, 103.
149. York, *op. cit.*, 172.
150. *RSS*, i, 1637.
151. Barbour, *Bruce*, (Skeat), bk 6, 1 468ff.
152. Blind Harry, *Wallace*, (MacDiarmid), bk 5, 1 25.
153. Henryson, *Fables*, 'The Lion and the Mouse', 1 1517.
154. *TA*, iii, 156.
155. York, *op. cit.*, 64, 68, plates xviii, xx.
156. *ER*, vii, 69, 76.
157. *Ibid.*, viii, 56, 425.
158. *Ibid.*, x, 638, 642.
159. *TA*, iii, 157.
160. *ER*, xi, 164; xii, 323, xiii, 59.
161. *TA*, ii, 117, 119; iv, 123.
162. *ER*, ii, 448; iii, 139.
163. *Ibid.*, iii, 2.
164. *Ibid.*, 109.
165. *TA*, iii, 164, 344.
166. *Ibid.*, ii, 97, 110, 127, 168, 311.
167. *Ibid.*, ii, 419, 449, 475.
168. *Ibid.*, ii, 32; iii, 355.
169. York, *op. cit.*, 172.
170. Steer and Bannerman, *Monumental Sculpture*, 186-187.
171. *ER*, vii, 459; *TA*, ii, 372.
172. James IV, *Letters*, 135, no. 219.
173. *Ibid.*, nos. 124, 219, 338, 340, 398.
174. *ER*, v, *passim*, see index.
175. *Ibid.*, xii, 73.
176. *Ibid*; York, *Master of Game*, (Grohman), 138.
177. *ER*, i, 130, 250, 359, 405; Black, *Surnames, sub* 'Stalker'.
178. See p. 57.
179. *ER*, x, 185.
180. *TA*, iii, 209.
181. *Ibid.*, 338, 339.
182. Boece, *Historiae*, f 16, bk 2, c 4, 1 35; Bellenden, *Chronicles*, 58, bk 1.
183. Child, *Scottish Ballads*, iii, 1, no. 114.
184. *Pais. Reg.*, 5; Barrow, *The Kingdom of the Scots*, 340.
185. Cooper, *Register of Brieves*, 52, c 81.
186. *RMS*, ii, 1939; *ER*, vi, 243.
187. *TA*, iv, 136 etc; iii, 156 etc; ii, 119 etc. See Table 4, p. 79.
188. Lismore, *Heroic Poetry*, 27, stanza 11.
189. *RMS*, ii, 2185; *ER*, x, 429.
190. *APS*, ii, 107, c 16.
191. *Ibid.*, 51, c 16.
192. Boece, *Historiae*, bk 5, c 11; Bellenden, *Chronicles*, 205, bk 5.
193. *APS*, i, 576; ii, 52, c 36; SRO, *Justice Ayre Journal Books*, RH 2/1/5, 7.
194. York, *Master of Game*, (Grohman), 188 ff; Turner, *Select Pleas of the Forest*, 142, 146.
195. Woodford, *Manual of Falconry*, 33. All general information on falconry is taken from this work.
196. Stevenson, *Documents*, ii, 137; *TA*, i, 304, 320, see index.

197. *RMS*, i, 172.
198. *ER*, i, 499.
199. *TA*, iii, 167.
200. *Ibid.*, 333.
201. *Ibid.*, iv, lxxxvi.
202. *Melr. Lib.*, 39, 198.
203. *ER*, i, 7, 8.
204. *Ibid.*, 15; *APS*, i, 100.
205. *ER*, i, 591.
206. *Ibid.*, viii, 276, 364, 483; x, 90, 262, 329, 510.
207. *Ibid.*, i, 499.
208. *TA*, i, 184; ii, 155, 368, 435, 464; iii, *passim*, see index.
209. *Ibid.*, iv, 78, 79, 81, 126, 135, 322, etc.
210. *Ibid.*, i, 95.
211. *Ibid.*, i, 332; iii, 131.
212. *Ibid.*, ii, 465.
213. *Ibid.*, i, 126, 175.
214. *Ibid.*, ii, 118.
215. *Ibid.*, 445.
216. *ER*, i, 123.
217. *TA*, iii, 384.
218. *ER*, xi, 142; *TA*, i, 280.
219. *TA*, iii, 202.
220. *Ibid.*, ii, 151.
221. *Ibid.*, iii, 147.
222. *Ibid.*, 120; ii, 368, 384.
223. *Ibid.*, i, 182, 365.
224. *Ibid.*, 366.
225. *ER*, iii, 269; *TA*, i, 304.
226. *TA*, ii, 153, 156; i, 360.
227. *Ibid.*, 446.
228. *Ibid.*, iii, 79.
229. *Ibid.*, 361.
230. *Ibid.*, i, 287.
231. *Ibid.*, 360.
232. *Ibid.*, ii, 348.
233. *Ibid.*, iii, 146.
234. *Ibid.*, 157.
235. *ER*, i, 542, 546, 551.
236. *APS*, ii, 107, c 15.
237. *TA*, ii, 445.
238. *Ibid.*, i, 304.
239. *Ibid.*, iv, 35, 78-80.
240. *Ibid.*, ii, 158, 159.
241. *Ibid.*, i, 93.
242. *Ibid.*, 127.
243. *Ibid.*, iv, 184; iii, 72, 413; ii, 466.
244. *Ibid.*, i, 304.
245. *Ibid.*, ii, 475.
246. *Ibid.*, i, 305.
247. *Ibid.*, iii, 72.
248. *Ibid.*, ii, 376; iii, 333.
249. *Ibid.*, i, 98.
250. *ER*, i, 216.
251. *TA*, i, 194.

252. *ER*, i, 210; *TA*, i-iv, *passim*.
253. *TA*, i, 367.
254. *ER*, x, 203, 257, 316, 449.
255. *Ibid.*, xi, 78, 155.
256. *TA*, iii, 118, 69; iv, 441.
257. See Table 3, p. 77.
258. *TA*, iii, 68.
259. *Ibid.*, iv, 267.
260. *Ibid.*, ii, 125, 127, 133, 135, 137, 342, 381.
261. *Ibid.*, iii, 131, 159, 161, 180, 186.
262. *Dunk. Rent.*, 65.
263. *RSS*, i, 28.
264. *Ibid.*, 1248.
265. Henryson, *Poems and Fables*, lines 1741, 1843.
266. *TA*, i, 45, 48, 92, ccliv.
267. *Ibid.*, iii, 161.
268. *Ibid.*, 180, 404.
269. *Ibid.*, 164, 307, 326.
270. *Ibid.*, iii, 168.
271. *APS*, ii, 15, c 12.
272. *Ibid.*, 51, c 31.
273. See p. 232.
274. *APS*, ii, 107, c 15.
275. See p. 100.
276. Stevenson, *Documents*, ii, 137.
277. Pitscottie, *Historie*, i, 163.
278. Hume Brown, P., *Early Travellers in Scotland*, (Edinburgh 1891), 52.
279. James IV, *Basilikon Doron*, part iii, 48-49.
280. Hay, *Book of Knighthood*, ii, 23.
281. *Dryb. Lib.*, 94.
282. Pitscottie, *Historie*, i, 56.
283. *Book of Alexander*, i, 13 1 366; 20 1 627.
284. Aelred, *Genealogia*, bk 5, c 9.
285. See pp. 40, 42.
286. Jesse, *The British Dog*, ii, 52; *Chron. Fordun*, Annals LX, 299; *TA*, ii, 444.
287. See p. 255.
288. *CDS*, i, 2267.
289. Gregory IX, *Decretals*, bk 5, tit. 24, cc 1, 2.
290. *Dunf. Reg.*, 312.
291. Cross and Slover, *Ancient Irish Tales*, i, 242, 408; *Dunnaire Finn*, i, 195.
292. See p. 56.
293. Boece, *Historiae*, bk 2, c 4; bk 5, c 11; bk 6, c 6.
294. Dalby, *Lexicon of Medieval German Hunt*, xl ff.
295. Dunlop, *Bishop Kennedy*, 364.
296. Dalby, *op. cit.*, xl ff.
297. Berners, *The Book of St. Albans*, f 26 v.
298. *The Bannatyne Ms.*, IV, (STS), 138.
299. Dalby, *op. cit*, xxvii.
300. Child, *Scottish Ballads*, i, 390, no. 43; ii, 355, no. 96.
301. Douglas, *Shorter Poems; The Poems of William Dunbar*, ed. W. Mackay Mackenzie, (London, 1932).
302. Douglas, *Poems*, 90, 1 129; 93, 1 21.
303. Caldwell, *Sir Eger*, 1 2469 HL.
304. *TA*, ii, 119; ii, 339.
305. Lismore, *Heroic Poetry*, 16, 18.

306. Lindner, *Die Jagd Der Vorzeit*, fig. 143; Arrian, *Kunegetikos*, 64, 178; Henderson, *The Picts*, 155.
307. Cruden, *Early Christian and Pictish Monuments*, 13-16.
308. Steer and Bannerman, *Monumental Sculpture*, 186.
309. See p. 65.
310. Henry, F., *La Sculpture Irlandaise*, (Paris, 1933), i, 117ff.
311. Réau, *Iconographie de l'Art Chrétien*, iii, 468, 659.
312. *RCAM, Edinburgh*, 143.
313. Réau, *op. cit.*, iii, 593.

Chapter 5

1. Duncan, A. A. M., Dunbar, J. G., 'Tarbert Castle', *SHR*, 50, (1971), 7-11.
2. Simpson, W. Douglas, 'The Excavation of Kindrochit Castle', *Antiquaries Journal*, vii, (1928), 69-75; see above, Ch. 3, p. 6.
3. *RCAM Selkirk*, 61-4.
4. *Abdn. Reg.*, i, 155-6.
5. *ER*, vi, 576.
6. *Ibid.*, 543.
7. *Ibid.*, 579.
8. *Ibid.*, vi, 637; *TA*, i, 93.
9. See Map 6, p. 123.
10. Colvin, *History of the King's Works*, i, 81-87; Rahtz, *Excavations at King John's Hunting Lodge*, 21, 25.
11. *ER*, vi, 243.
12. Roy, *Map of Scotland*, Sheet 17/3.
13. *RMS*, vi, 1778.
14. OS 6" Map, 1st. Edition, NN 80; OS 1" map, Sheet 52, NN 822403.
15. OS Map, Sheet 52, NN 864373.
16. Roy, *Map of Scotland*, Sheet 17/3.
17. OS Map, Sheet 52, NN 842400.
18. Stobie, *Map of Perthshire*.
19. *OS Name Book*, 35, no. 23.
20. See Map 6 and Key, p. 123.
21. *Air Photograph* RS CPE SCOT: UK: 194: 11 OCT 46/4316-7.
22. OS Map, Sheet 57, NN 523088.
23. Crawford, O.G.S., *Archaeology in the Field*, (London, 1953), 188-191.
24. See p. 215.
25. *ER*, xiii, 73.
26. *Ibid.*, vi, 65.
27. *RCAM, Stirling*, i, 192, 220.
28. *ER*, i, 24.
29. *Ibid.*, 38.
30. Miller, T., 'The Site of the New Park in the Relation to the Battle of Bannockburn', *Transactions of the Stirling Natural History and Archaeological Society*, (1921-22), 92-137.
31. See p. 215.
32. OS Map, Sheet 45, NJ 663780.
33. *Ibid.*, NJ 658783.
34. *Ibid.*, NJ 643784.
35. *Ibid.*, NJ 633781.
36. *Ibid.*, NJ 634770.
37. *Ibid.*, NJ 670753.
38. *Ibid.*, NJ 643485, see p. 215.

39. *Ibid.*, NJ 654788.
40. *ER*, i, 585; *RMS*, i, app. 1, 120.
41. *ER*, i, 585; *RMS*, i, 175; ii, 620, 1712.
42. OS Map, Sheet 54, NO 268540; my knowledge of this park comes from the Archaeological Division of the Ordnance Survey, Rose Street, Edinburgh.
43. See p. 220.
44. See p. 216.

Chapter 6

1. *ER*, vi, 355.
2. Edinburgh University Library MS Dept., *Regiam Majestatem*, MS 207, f 146 v, no. 76; printed in *Formulary E*, ed. A. A. M. Duncan (University of Glasgow, Scottish History Department Occasional Papers, 1976), 36.
3. Cooper, *Register of Brieves*, 4.
4. *RSS*, i, 1637.
5. See Table 5, p. 113, *sub* Darnaway, Glenfinglas.
6. *ER*, vi, 338.
7. *Ibid.*, 432.
8. *Ibid.*, 261.
9. See p. 43.
10. *ER*, vii, 252, 'nec aliqua inde poterat percipere'.
11. *Ibid.*, xii, 144.
12. *Ibid.*
13. *RRS*, ii, 397.
14. *ESC*, 33, (1107 x 1117).
15. *RRS*, ii, 367.
16. *Melr. Lib.*, 264.
17. *Holy Lib.*, 57.
18. Anderson, *Diplomata*, no. 30.
19. *A. B. Antiqs.*, ii, 109.
20. *RRS*, ii, 362.
21. See p. 36.
22. See p. 19.
23. *RRS*, ii, 362.
24. Hoyt, R. S., *The Royal Demesne in English Constitutional History 1066-1272*, (New York, 1950), 2.
25. *ER*, v, 474.
26. *Ibid.*, 459, (1451).
27. *APS*, i, 492.
28. *ESC*, 72, 83.
29. *RRS*, ii, 39.
30. *Ibid.*, i, 224.
31. *Ibid.*, ii, 163.
32. *ER*, i, 39, (1288 x 1290).
33. *APS*, ii, 42, cl.
34. *ER*, v, 480.
35. *APS*, ii, 42.
36. *RMS*, i, app. 2, 232.
37. Raine, *N.D.*, app., 17, no. LXXIX.
38. *RMS*, ii, 1976.
39. *Ibid.*, 2389.
40. *Ibid.*, ii, 3390.
41. *Ibid.*, i, app. 1, 4.

42. *Ibid.*, ii, 2185.
43. *ADC*, i, 331b.
44. *Ibid.*, ii, 293.
45. *Ibid.*, 315.
46. *Ibid.*, lix.
47. *ER*, xi, 393, c 14.
48. *RMS*, i, app. 1, 36, 73; ii, 2958.
49. *ER*, vii, 417; viii, 214.
50. *RMS*, i, app. 1, 65.
51. *ER*, xi, 417.
52. *Ibid.*, xii, 42.
53. *Ibid.*, xiii, 563.
54. Expressed in Anderson, *Scottish Forestry*, i, 90.
55. *Pais. Reg.*, 17; Fraser, *Lennox*, ii, p. 401.
56. *Abdn. Chrs.*, 10, no. 6; *RMS*, i, app. 2, 307, n. 7; app. 1, 73; ii, 2529.
57. Stubbs, *Select Charters*, 346, Charter of the Forest, cc 8, 16.
58. See p. 271.
59. Turner, *Select Pleas of the Forest*, cxiv, xccviii, x.
60. Macphail, *Pluscarden*, 69, 199; male and female red deer, roe deer and boar.
61. Fraser, *Johnstones*, i, 1 no. 2; red deer and hind, boar and roe deer.
62. *APS*, i, 7, 13.
63. *ER* xii, *passim*, see index.
64. See p. 232.
65. Lesley, *History*, i, 19.
66. *Scone Lib.*, 67.
67. *APS*, i, 652, c 31.
68. See p. 211.
69. *RSS*, ii, 253.
70. *RMS*, i, app. 1, 4.
71. *ER*, viii, 45.
72. *Ibid.*, viii, 45, 584.
73. *Ibid.*, xii, 115.
74. *APS*, ii, 235, c 19.
75. SRO, *Justice Ayre Journal Books*, RH 2/1/5, 60.
76. Petit Dutaillis, *Stubbs*, 153.
77. See p. 231.
78. *APS*, ii, 7, c 13.
79. *Ibid.*, 107, c 16; 251, c 13.
80. SRO, *Justice Ayre Journal Books*, RH 2/1/6, 144.
81. *ER*, xi, 393.
82. SRO, *Crown Rental*, 1499-1507.
83. *APS*, ii, 51, c 30.
84. SRO, *Justice Ayre Journal Books*, RH 2/1/5 and 6.
85. Stair, *Institutes*, i, 279, bk 2, tit. 3, c 68.
86. Petit Dutaillis, *Stubbs*, 154, n. 1.
87. *Ibid.*, 233.
88. *RRS*, ii, 335.
89. Macphail, *Pluscarden*, 69, 199.
90. *Scone Lib.*, 67.
91. *Ibid.*, 64.
92. *Arb. Lib.*, 286.
93. *RMS*, ii, 3193 and SRO, *Great Seal Register*, C/2/14; see Map 6 and Key.
94. *ESC*, 141, 153, 208.
95. See p. 177.
96. *RMS*, i, app. 1, 4.

97. *Ibid.*, i, app. 1, 30; *ER*, vii, 446.
98. *RRS*, i, 226.
99. *Pais. Reg.*, 23.
100. *ER*, xi, 394, c 7.
101. *APS*, i, 711, c 8.
102. *RMS*, i, app. 1, 4.
103. *ER*, viii, 585.
104. *Ibid.*, ix, 471.
105. *Ibid.*, x, 600.
106. See pp. 234-235.
107. *APS*, ii, 7, c 10.
108. *Ibid.*, ii, 242, c 15; 251, c 16.
109. SRO, *Justice Ayre Journal Books*, RH 2/1/5, 7.
110. *Ibid.*, RH 2/1/6, 27.
111. *Ibid.*, RH 2/1/6, 239, 282.
112. See p. 177; *RRS*, ii, 362; *ESC*, 146; *RMS*, i, app. 1, 65; *Moray Reg.*, 37.
113. See p. 291, Law 1.
114. See p. 312.
115. *Pais. Reg.*, 17.
116. *Holm Cultram Chrs.*, 121.
117. *Moray Reg.*, 37.
118. Turner, *Select Pleas of the Forest*, 162-3.
119. I am indebted to Dr Aitken of *DOST* for this suggested etymology, See p. 308.
120. Barrow, G. W. S., 'Hunting and the Forest in Medieval Scotland', Presidential Address to the Scottish History Society, 1975.
121. Turner, *op. cit.*, 162-3.
122. *Pais. Reg.*, 92.
123. *Inchaff. Chrs.*, CVIII.
124. See p. 192, Laws 2 and 4.
125. *Melr. Lib.*, 305.
126. *Melr. Lib.*, 307.
127. See p. 65.
128. *Melr. Lib.*, 101; *Holm Cultram Chrs.*, 133; Symon, *Scottish Farming*, 26.
129. *RRS*, i, 226.
130. See pp. 292-293, Laws 2-9.
131. *ESC*, 141.
132. *ESC*, 153.
133. *RRS*, ii, 362.
134. *ER*, i, 30.
135. See p. 293, Law 8.
136. *ER*, i, 29.
137. *Ibid.*, 35.
138. *Ibid.*
139. *Ibid.*, 35, 39.
140. *RMS*, ii, 337, 338.
141. See pp. 291, 292, Laws 1 and 8.
142. *Pais. Reg.*, 17, 92.
143. O.S., Sheet 75, NY 144 661; Fraser, *Johnstones*, i, p. v.
144. Fraser, *Johnstones*, i, 5, no. 7.
145. O.S., Sheet 85, NY 119 689, NY 170 723, NY 137 718; *ER*, v, 669.
146. *RMS*, ii, 546.
147. *DOST*, *sub* foggage.
148. *ER*, i, 29, 31.
149. *Moray Reg.*, 151.
150. *RMS*, i, 618; *Arb. Lib.*, ii, 19.

151. *CDS*, iii, 329.
152. *ADC*, i, 199 b (1491).
153. *ER*, vi, 273 (1455 x 1456); *ER*, xi, 341.
154. *Ibid.*, i, 40.
155. *APS*, i, 531, (1368); SRO, *Mar and Kellie Papers*, GD 124/1/518.
156. *Moray Reg.*, 473, no. 22.
157. *ER*, v, 579.
158. *Ibid.*, 581.
159. *Ibid.*, i, 35; *RMS*, i, 23.
160. *ER*, viii, 334.
161. *Ibid.*, xii, 334.
162. *ADC*, ii, 113, 496; *ER*, i, 573.
163. *ADA*, 15 a.
164. *Burnett of Leys*, 154.
165. *ER*, i, 576; SRO, *Transcripts of Royal Charters*, RH 1/1/2, 4 Aug, 1398.
166. *ER*, vii, 272.
167. *Ibid.*, viii, 527.
168. *Ibid.*, xi, 392.
169. *Ibid.*, xii, 511.
170. *Ibid.*, 66.
171. *RMS*, i, 618.
172. *Ibid.*, ii, 1191.
173. *APS*, i, 531; SRO, *Mar and Kellie Papers*, GD 124/1/518.
174. SRO, *Mar and Kellie Papers*, GD 124/6/1.
175. *Ibid.*, GD 124/1/524.
176. See p. 131.
177. See p. 97.
178. *ER*, xi, 393, c 9.
179. *Ibid.*, 394, c 11.
180. *Ibid.*, viii, 585.
181. *RSS*, i, 1637.
182. *RSS*, ii, 301.
183. *Abdn. Reg.*, 269.
184. *ER*, i, 21.
185. *Newb. Reg.*, 223.
186. *Regiam Majestatem*, bk 2, c 68.
187. Petit Dutaillis, *Stubbs*, 157.
188. *APS*, i, 113.
189. *Scone Lib.*, 131.
190. *Cambridge Economic History*, i, ed. R. Koebner, (Cambridge 1941), 666; Bath, *Agrarian History*, 142.
191. See p. 257.
192. *ER*, xi, 393, c 4.
193. *Ibid.*, 393, c 20.
194. *Ibid.*, xi, 397, 400.
195. *RRS*, ii, 215, 301.
196. *RMS*, i, app. 1, 4.
197. *ER*, viii, 44.
198. *Ibid.*
199. *Ibid.*, vii, 476; ix, 30.
200. Macphail, *Pluscarden*, 201-3; *C. A. Chrs.*, 25.
201. *ER*, xi, 401.
202. *APS*, i, 115; *C. A. Chrs.*, 108.
203. *RMS*, i, app. 1, 4.
204. *ER*, xi, 394, c 4.

205. *C. A. Rent.*, 327, no. 19.
206. *A. B. Antiqs.*, i, 298.
207. *ER*, i, 571.
208. *RSS*, i, 1637.

Chapter 7

1. Dickinson, *Sheriff Ct. Bk.*, xlix; Duncan, *The Making of the Kingdom*, 161.
2. *ESC*, 188.
3. *Ibid.*, 153.
4. *Spalding Misc.*, v, 209.
5. *ER*, i, 29.
6. *Ibid.*, 30.
7. *Ibid.*, 35.
8. *Rot. Scot.*, 271 b.
9. *APS*, i, 564; *Stirlings of Keir*, 201.
10. *ER*, ix, 661; *RMS*, ii, 2586.
11. From Dickinson, *Sheriff Ct. Bk.*, 349-367.
12. See Table 25, p. 338.
13. *RRS*, i, 43, 44; *RRS*, ii, 213.
14. Duncan, *The Making of the Kingdom*, 161.
15. *ESC*, 141.
16. *Melr. Lib.*, 39.
17. *Ibid.*, 264.
18. *ER*, i, 29, 30, 35.
19. *RRS*, ii, 582, p. 40; Dickinson, *Sheriff Ct. Bk.*, 357-8.
20. *CDS*, ii, 1317, 1321.
21. *Ibid.*, 1646.
22. *RMS*, i, app. 2, 232.
23. *CDS*, iii, 1123.
24. *RMS*, i, app. 1, 123.
25. *ER*, vi, 223-225; *RCAM, Selkirk*, 6.
26. *RMS*, ii, 59.
27. *ER*, vii, 521.
28. *RSS*, i, 334.
29. *ER*, viii, 336.
30. *RMS*, i, app. 1, 4.
31. *Ibid.*, 46.
32. *A.B. Antiqs.*, iii, 292, (1322/3); *Burnett of Leys*, 154 (1323).
33. *RMS*, i, app. 1, 65; *SP*, vii, 32, 424.
34. *Ibid.*, i, app. 1, 73.
35. *Moray Reg.*, 29; Macphail, *Pluscarden*, 69, 199.
36. *RMS*, i, 119 (1362); *ER*, x, 590 (1507).
37. See Table 10, p. 156.
38. *RMS*, i, app. 2, 389 (1327).
39. *ER*, vi, 282, (1454-1456).
40. SRO, *Mar and Kellie Papers*, GD 124/6/1, (1371).
41. *RMS*, i, 595, (1377).
42. *RRS*, ii, 265; 301; *ESC*, 153.
43. *Newb. Reg.*, 121.
44. *Melr. Lib.*, 264; *Newb. Reg.*, 120.
45. *RRS*, ii, 215; Duncan, *The Making of the Kingdom*, 161.
46. *ADA*, 71 b.
47. *RSS*, i, 1029.

48. *RMS*, i, app. 1, 65.
49. Raine, *ND*, app., 17, nos 79, 84.
50. SRO, *Mar and Kellie Papers*, GD 124/6/1.
51. See p. 132.
52. Dickinson, *Sheriff Ct. Bk.*, 357.
53. *ER*, i, 23.
54. *RRS*, ii, 145.
55. *RMS*, i, 618, 762.
56. *RSS*, i, 1637.
57. *RMS*, i, 697.
58. *ER*, i, 576; SRO, *Transcripts of Royal Charters*, RH 1/1/2, 4 Aug. 1398; *RMS*, i, 785.
59. *ER*, viii, 219 (1473-1474).
60. *Ibid.*, 578, (1478-1479).
61. *Ibid.*, xi, 159.
62. *Ibid.*, xii, 635, (1502).
63. *Ibid.*, 359; *TA*, iii, 412.
64. *RMS*, i, app. 1, 389.
65. Stair, *Institutes*, bk 2, tit. 3, c 67.
66. *RRS*, ii, 301, 362.
67. *Moray Reg.*, 473, no. 22, (1371); *ADA*, 150 b, (1491); *ADC*, ii, 315, (1498/9).
68. Rymer, *Foedera*, i, 566.
69. *ADC*, i, 385, 150 b.
70. *ER*, xiii, clx.
71. *RMS*, ii, 2389.
72. *Ibid.*, 1160 (1473/4); 2755, (1503).
73. *ER*, xii, 66, (1501-1502).
74. Edmonstone, A., *Edmonstones of Duntreith*, (Edinburgh 1875), 33, 35.
75. *ESC*, 153.
76. *Melr. Lib.*, 266.
77. Macphail, *Pluscarden*, 69, 199; *Scone Lib.*, 67.
78. *RMS*, i, app. 1, 41; *C.A. Chrs.*, i, 108.
79. *C.A. Chrs.*, 108, (1326).
80. *RMS*, i, app. 1, 65.
81. *Ibid.*, ii, 1540; SRO, *Great Seal Register*, C/2/10.
82. *RSS*, i, 912.
83. *RMS*, i, app. 1, 65.
84. *A.B. Antiqs.*, iii, 294.
85. *ER*, xii, 144.
86. Fraser, *Southesk*, ii, 482, no. 31.
87. *ER*, viii, 408.
88. *Ibid.*, x, 137, 364, (1492).
89. See p. 137.
90. *ER*, v, 208, 607.
91. *CDS*, ii, 1646.
92. *ER*, vi, 217, 459.
93. *DOST*, *sub* 'currour'.
94. *RRS*, ii, 301.
95. *ER*, vi, 461, 472, and possibly *ibid.*, viii, 608; ix, 8, 11.
96. *TA*, iii, 338.
97. *RMS*, i, app. 1, 65.
98. *ER*, vi, 217; *A.B. Antiqs.*, iii, 294.
99. *RMS*, ii, 3024.
100. *ER*, xiii, 53.
101. See p. 138.

B

102. *RMS*, i, app. 1, 65.
103. *ER*, vi, 411; vii, 111.
104. *Ibid.*, viii, 608.
105. *Ibid.*, vi, 461; viii, 219.
106. *CDS*, ii, 209; *Rot. Scot.*, ii, 123 b.
107. Barbour, *Bruce*, (Skeat), bk 9, line 673; *TA*, i, 195.
108. Raine, *ND*, app., nos. 79, 84; *RMS*, i, app. 1, 38.
109. *RMS*, ii, 58, 59; *DOST*, *sub* 'lesu', 'lesu' = pasture.
110. *RCAM*, Selkirk, 4-11; Anderson, *Scottish Forestry*, i, 164-181.
111. The greater part of the information in this examination is taken from the accounts of Ettrick forest in the *Exchequer Rolls* between 1455 and 1513. Where the information given is of special importance or where it can be deduced from one account, a specific reference is given. Otherwise when, for instance, the information is deduced from a series of accounts the source of all such information will be found in the accounts of the appropriate date or dates.
112. *ER*, x, 654.
113. *Ibid.*, viii, 43.
114. *Ibid.*, x, 173-4.
115. *APS*, ii, 219.
116. *RSS*, i, 838.
117. *APS*, ii, 219; *ER*, x, 161.
118. Pringle, A., *Records of the Pringles*, (Edinburgh 1933), 89.
119. *ER*, vii, 400.
120. *Ibid.*, ix, 620; *ADC*, i, 116* b.
121. *ER*, vii, 24.
122. *Ibid.*, vii, 135.
123. *Ibid.*, vi, 225.
124. *Ibid.*, x, 293.
125. *Ibid.*, 97, 651.
126. *Ibid.*, xi, 199.
127. *RSS*, i, 839; *RMS*, ii, 1921.
128. *ER*, xii, 35.
129. *Ibid.*, xi, 199 ff.
130. *Ibid.*, 394, c 1.
131. *Ibid.*
132. *RSS*, i, 1858.
133. *ER*, vi, 443; viii, 48; ix, 271, 319.
134. *Ibid.*, xii, 35, 36.
135. *Ibid.*, xiii, 526, 528.
136. *Ibid.*, viii, 101, 140, 141.
137. *Ibid.*, xii, 115.
138. *Ibid.*, ix, 606.
139. *Ibid.*, 30.
140. *Ibid.*, xi, 397.
141. *Ibid.*, 460.
142. *Ibid.*, 394, c 4.
143. *Ibid.*, vi, 226; vii, 621.
144. *Ibid.*, viii, 583.
145. C. Madden, 'The Feuing of Ettrick Forest', *Innes Review*, xxvii, (1976), 79-80.
146. *ER*, xi, 394, c 8.
147. *Ibid.*, ix, 604.
148. *Ibid.*, 629; xi, 395.
149. *Ibid.*, ix, 620; xi, 614.
150. *Ibid.*, i, 39 (1288-1290), 542; *APS*, i, 528.
151. *ADC*, ii, 315, 320.

152. *ER*, vi, 158.
153. *Ibid.*, v, 643.
154. *ADC*, ii, 320.
155. *ER*, ix, 595.
156. *Ibid.*, xiii, 592.
157. *Ibid.*, 590.
158. *ESC*, 153; *RRS*, ii, 128; *Arb. Lib.*, 15.
159. *Melr. Lib.*, 266.
160. Cooper, *Register of Brieves*, 52. c 81.
161. *Abdn. Reg.*, 269.
162. Macphail, *Pluscarden*, 69, 199.
163. See pp. 291-293, Laws 1-11.
164. *RMS*, i, 618.
165. *Ibid.*, i, app. 1, 30; *Scone Lib.*, 152; Raine, *ND*, app., 84.
166. See p. 237.
167. *ER*, x, 187; xi, 159.
168. *Ibid.*, xii, 625.
169. *Ibid.*, vii, 246.
170. *Ibid.*, xi, 313.
171. *Ibid.*, xii, 334 (1504 x 1505).
172. *Ibid.*, vii, 204 (1462 x 1463).
173. *Ibid.*, vii, 3 (1460 x 1461).
174. *Ibid.*, ix, 620.
175. See p. 100.
176. *ER*, viii, 43-46, (1470 x 1471).
177. *Ibid.*, ix, 616, *sub* 'Aldishope'.
178. *Ibid.*, xi, 394, cc 2, 3, 4, 5, 6. There is a mistake in the Ms. version and the printed version of c 5. The scribe, copying a Ms. of the statutes, should probably have written 'within the bondis of the forrest, the forrester of the said steid . . .', and not 'within the bondis of the forrest of the said steid', scoring out 'the forrest'.
179. *ER*, xii, 658-659.
180. *Ibid.*, vii, 527.
181. *RMS*, ii, 1921; SRO, *Great Seal Register*, C/2/12.
182. *ER*, xi, 394, c 9.
183. *Ibid.*, 605.
184. *Ibid.*, xi, 320, 394 c 10, 457.
185. *Spalding Misc.*, v, 209.
186. *RRS*, ii, p. 42; Duncan, *The Making of the Kingdom*, 597.
187. Barrow, *Kingdom of the Scots*, 70.
188. *CDS*, ii, 168.
189. *RMS*, i, app. 2, 1817.
190. *RMS*, i, app. 1, 123.
191. *Abdn. Chrs.*, 10, no. 6.
192. *RMS*, i, app. 1, 4.
193. *Abdn. Recs.*, 113.
194. *ADC*, i, 331 b.
195. *RMS*, i, 389.
196. *Rot. Scot.*, i, 380a.
197. SRO, *Mar and Kellie Papers*, GD 124/6/1.
198. Fraser, *Southesk*, ii, 482, (1319).
199. *Abdn. Chrs.*, 10; *RMS*, i, App. 1, 4.
200. *Inventory of the Writs of the lands of Wester Drimmie etc.* compiled in 1760, no. 5, at present in the hands of Brig. H. N. Crawford at Naughton House, Fife. I am indebted to Professor Barrow for informing me of this document and to Professor Duncan for supplying me with a photocopy of it.

201. *RMS*, i, app. 1, 65.
202. SRO, *Mar and Kellie Papers*, GD, 124/6/1.
203. *RMS*, i, 595.
204. *ER*, i, 519, 522.
205. Nicholson, *The Later Middle Ages*, 144.
206. *RMS*, ii, 2389.
207. *ER*, vii, 480, 585; *RMS*, ii, 1450.
208. *APS*, ii, 7, c 10; *APS*, 242, c 15.
209. *Ibid.*, i, 576; ii, 107, c 16; 242, c 15; SRO, *Justice Ayre Journal Books*, RH 2/1/5, 7.
210. *APS*, ii, 107, cc 16, 15; 242, c 12; SRO, *Justice Ayre Journal Books*, RH 2/1/6, 144.
211. *ER*, ix, 614; xi, 395.
212. *Ibid.*, xi, 393.
213. *Ibid.*, vi, 269, (1455 x 1456); *RSS*, i, 1026, (1505).
214. *RMS*, ii, 1160.
215. SRO, *Abercairney Muniments*, GD 24/5/1.
216. *RMS*, ii, 1540; SRO, *Great Seal Register*, C/2/10.
217. *ER*, x, 430.
218. *Ibid.*, xi, 207.
219. *Ibid.*, x, 163.
220. *Ibid.*, 601.
221. *Ibid.*, vi, 345, 372.
222. *Ibid.*, ix, 415, 418, 421.
223. See Table 11, p. 158.
224. *ER*, ix, 605.
225. *Ibid.*, viii, 432, 435, 437.
226. *Ibid.*, vii, 527.
227. *Ibid.*, x, 173.
228. *Ibid.*, viii, 210.
229. *Ibid.*, 45.
230. *Ibid.*, 481.
231. *Ibid.*, ix, 605; Rait, *Parliaments*, 327 ff.
232. *ER*, vi, 545.
233. *Ibid.*, viii, 437, 482, 586, 588.
234. See p. 329.
235. *ER*, viii, 45, 584.
236. *Ibid.*, vi, 478, 545.
237. *Ibid.*, ix, 605.
238. *Ibid.*, 605, 614; x, 675.
239. *Ibid.*, ix, 471.
240. *Ibid.*, vii, 525, 527, 530.
241. *Ibid.*, vi, 226, 544.
242. *Ibid.*, xi, 394, c 9.
243. *Ibid.*, 403.
244. *Ibid.*, xii, 658.
245. *Ibid.*, xiii, 658, 659.
246. Rait, *Parliaments*, 240-1.
247. *ER*, xi, 394, c 10.
248. Dickinson, 'Forest Courts', *Stair Society*, xx, (1958), 403.
249. *Melr. Lib.*, 564.
250. *ER*, viii, 141, 211.
251. *Ibid.*, 478.
252. *Ibid.*, 587.
253. *RMS*, ii, 1450.

254. *ER*, viii, 480.
255. *Ibid.*, xi, c 10.
256. See p. 142.
257. See Table 14, p. 169.
258. *RRS*, ii, 236.
259. *Ibid.*, 301.
260. *Ibid.*, 113.
261. Cooper, T, 'Melrose v the Earl of Dunbar', *Juridical Review*, (1943), lv, 1-9.
262. Cooper, *Select Cases*, 9 ff.
263. *RMS*, i, app. 1, 41; *Moray Reg.*, 473.
264. *ADC*, ii, 315, 320.
265. *RMS*, ii, 1160.
266. *Ibid.*, 1540.
267. *SP*, i, 476; *SP*, vii, 35, 40.
268. *ADA*, 150 b.
269. *Ibid.*, i, 385 a.
270. *ADC*, i, 309.

Chapter 8

1. *RRS*, ii, 301.
2. Macphail, *Pluscarden*, 69, 199.
3. *RMS*, i, 389; Fraser, *Southesk*, ii, 482, no. 31.
4. *ER*, vii, 3, 204.
5. *Ibid.*, viii, 578.
6. *Ibid.*, vii, 446.
7. *ADC*, i, 208 b, 293 b.
8. SRO, *Justice Ayre Journal Books*, RH 2/1/6, 280 ff.
9. Madden, C., 'The Feuing of Ettrick Forest', *Innes Review*, xxvii, (1976), 72.
10. Murray, A., 'The Procedure of the Scottish Exchequer in the Sixteenth Century', SHR, xl, (1961), 89-117.
11. *ER*, viii, 587; x, 603.
12. *Ibid.*, ix, 322.
13. *Ibid.*, 473.
14. *Ibid.*, 420.
15. Murray, A., 'The Procedure of the Scottish Exchequer in the early Sixteenth Century', *SHR*, xl, (1961), 89-117.
16. *ER*, viii, 476 ff.
17. *Ibid.*, 482.
18. *Ibid.*, 586.
19. *Ibid.*, ix, 33.
20. *Ibid.*, viii, 587.
21. *Ibid.*, 101.
22. *Ibid.*, 479.
23. *Ibid.*, 44.
24. *APS*, ii, 118, c 2.
25. *ER*, xi, 99-102.
26. *Ibid.*, 243, 245.
27. *Ibid.*, xii, 252.
28. *Ibid.*, xi, 199, c 10.
29. *Moray Reg.*, 29; *RRS*, ii, 362.
30. *APS*, ii, 61a; ii, 188b; *RMS*, i, 258; *Moray Reg.*, 264.
31. *RMS*, ii, 2559; SRO, *Great Seal Register*, C/2/13.
32. *RMS*, ii, 1784, 2311.

33. *CDS*, ii, 1229, 1978.
34. Stevenson, *Documents*, 265.
35. *ER*, i, 542, 546.
36. *Ibid.*, ii, 352.
37. *Ibid.*, i, 549.
38. The date given is the date of the end of the year of account.
39. *RSS*, i, 268.
40. *ER*, ix, 586; x, 659.
41. See App. B which discusses fully all matters relating to tenancy in Ettrick.
42. *RMS*, ii, 3473.
43. *RCAM*, Peebles, i, 6.
44. *RMS*, ii, 3775.
45. *RSS*, i, 1858, 1859, 1867, 1872.
46. *RMS*, ii, 3390.
47. *Ibid.*, 3464; SRO, *Great Seal Register*, C/2/15.
48. *ESC*, 189.
49. *Ibid.*, 209.
50. *RRS*, i, 215.
51. *Ibid.*, 36.
52. Raine, *ND*, app. 17, no. lxxix; app. 18, no. lxxxiv.
53. See p. 29.
54. See p. 140.
55. *ESC*, 141, 153.
56. *RMS*, i, 257, app. i, 65.
57. *ER*, viii, 585.
58. *RSS*, i, 246; *RMS*, i, app. 1, 41.
59. *ESC*, 141; *RRS*, i, 226; *Kinloss Recs.*, 1.
60. *RRS*, ii, 362; *Abdn. Reg.*, 269.
61. Raine, *ND*, 418.
62. *RMS*, i, app. 1, 30; i, app. 2, 856; *Scone Lib.*, 152.
63. *Abdn. Reg.*, 269.
64. *RMS*, i, 22, 118, and SRO *Great Seal Register*, C/2/14.
65. *RSS*, i, 1872.
66. *RMS*, i, 22; i, app. 1, 4; *RRS*, i, 235.
67. *RMS*, ii, 3390; see Table 24, p. 267.
68. *RRS*, i, 226; *RRS*, ii, 175.
69. *Ibid.*, i, 235.
70. *RSS*, i, 1858, 1872.

Chapter 9

1. *RRAN*, ii, 648.
2. *Ibid.*, iii, 27, (1136 x 1139).
3. *Ibid.*, ii, 629, (1103).
4. *RRS*, i, 184; see p. 21.
5. See p. 25.
6. Petit Dutaillis, *Stubbs*, 151.
7. *RRS*, ii, 224.
8. *Ibid.*, 334.
9. *Ibid.*, pp. 31-33.
10. See p. 209.
11. 'Liberius' only in 1237 grant to de Graham.
12. Cooper, *Register of Brieves*, 36, c 7.
13. *Ibid.*, 61, c 87.
14. MGH, *Capitularia*, i, 170, *Capitulare Aquisgranense*, (802/3), c 18.
15. See p. 21.

16. *RMS*, ii, 2529 and SRO, *Great Seal Register*, C/2/13.
17. See Table 28, *sub* Dundaff and Strathcarron 1237, p. 346.
18. *RMS*, ii, 3288 and SRO, *Great Seal Register*, C/2/15.
19. *RMS*, ii, 3627, 3635 and SRO, *Great Seal Register*, C/2/17.
20. SRO, *Acts of the Lords of Council*, 3 February 1505.
21. Innes, *Scotch Legal Antiquities*, 41.
22. Table 28, *sub* Pettinain *c* 1150, p. 345.
23. *Arb. Lib.*, 232, 306; *Newb. Reg.*, 135.
24. Dickinson, *Barony Ct. Bk.*, xviii, xix.
25. See Table 28, *sub* Bolton, p. 349.
26. See p. 187.
27. *RMS*, i, app. 2, 856.
28. See p. 316.
29. *RMS*, i, app. 1, 65.
30. *C.A. Rent.*, i, 130, 197, 198, 220, 222, 246; *Arb. Lib.*, ii, 229.
31. *APS*, i, 625, c 32; *Arb. Lib.*, ii, 229; see App. A, law 18.
32. *C.A. Rent.*, i, 130, no. 72.
33. See Table 7, p. 118.
34. *Moray Reg.*, 151.
35. *Arb. Lib.*, ii, 19.
36. *Abdn. Recs.*, 83; *Abdn. Reg.*, i, 377.
37. See Table 16, p. 204.
38. *Pais. Reg.*, 17.
39. *Pais. Reg.*, 92.
40. Barrow, G. W. S., 'Hunting and the Forest in Medieval Scotland', Presidential Address to the Scottish History Society (1975).
41. *Pais. Reg.*, 5, 12, 409.
42. NLS, *Cartulary of Paisley Abbey*, Adv. Ms. 34/4/14, in the charters printed in *Pais. Reg.*, 5, 12.
43. Shirley, *Deer Parks*, 240.
44. See Map 7, p. 128; *Pais. Reg.*, 92.
45. *C.A. Rent.*, i, 121, no. 20; 220, no. 293.
46. *Abdn., Reg.*, i, 371-381.
47. *Kelso Lib.*, 248.
48. *Fraser Papers*, 217-9.
49. Fraser, *Grandtully*, i, 3; see Tables 9 and 10.
50. See Table 9, p. 153.
51. *RMS*, ii, 560.
52. *Moray Reg.*, 162.
53. See Table 10, p. 156.
54. *Lenn. Cart.*, 50.
55. See p. 26.
56. *RRS*, ii, 236.
57. *Newb. Reg.*, 144.
58. *Kelso Lib.*, 147.
59. *Abdn. Recs.*, 192, (1400).
60. *Abdn. Ct. Bk.*, 3, (1398); *Abdn. Recs.*, 167, (1399).
61. *Arb. Lib.*, ii, 64, 299.
62. *C.A. Rent.*, i, 157, no. 177.
63. *Ibid.*, 121.
64. *C.A. Rent.*, i, 222 no. 299, 227 no. 319, 237 no. 361, 242 nos. 382 and 385, 274 nos. 548 and 549.
65. *RRS*, ii, 236; *RMS*, i, app. 1, 14.
66. *Newb. Reg.*, 144; *Pais. Reg.*, 18; *Rose of Kilravock*, 117, 180; *Arb. Lib.*, 229, (1483).

67. *Pais. Reg.*, 92; *Rose of Kilravock*, 78, 180; Fraser, *Grandtully*, i, 3.
68. Fraser, *Grandtully*, i, 3.
69. *Abdn. Ct. Bk.*, 3.
70. *Abdn. Recs.*, 129.
71. *Abdn. Ct. Bk.*, 4, 18.
72. *Ibid.*, 4; *Abdn. Recs.*, 113.
73. *Arb. Lib.*, 64 (c 1430).
74. *C.A. Rent.*, 201, no. 245, (1473).
75. *Pais. Reg.*, 92.
76. *Abdn. Recs.*, 114, (1399).
77. *C.A. Rent.*, i, 130 no. 72.
78. *Arb. Lib.*, 229, (1483); 64, (c 1430).
79. Fraser, *Douglas*, iii, 10 no. 12; *Mort. Reg.* ii, 25.
80. *RMS*, ii, 3288, 3347; SRO, *Great Seal Register*, C/2/15.
81. *Rose of Kilravock*, 180.
82. *Brechin Reg.*, i, 110.
83. *Melr. Lib.*, 564.
84. *RMS*, i, 275.
85. Duncan, *The Making of the Kingdom*, 421.
86. Turner, *Select Pleas of the Forest*, p. cxxvi.
87. SRO, *Justice Ayre Journal Books*, RH 2/1/7, 87.
88. *CDS*, ii, 1702.
89. Cooper, *Select Cases*, 4 ff; *Cal. Papal Letters*, i, 16.
90. *Dunf. Lib.*, 192; Barrow, *The Kingdom of the Scots*, 81; *Arb. Lib.*, 230, 294, 336.
91. *Moray Reg.*, 140, 141.
92. *Rose of Kilravock*, 117.
93. *ADA*, 13 a.
94. *ADC*, ii, 375.
95. *Ibid.*, 447.
96. *RMS*, ii, 2853; SRO, *Great Seal Register*, C/2/14.
97. *Melr. Lib.*, 66.
98. *Pais. Reg.*, 17.
99. Fraser, *Johnstones*, i, 1, no. 2.
100. *RRS*, ii, 518.
101. *Melr. Lib.*, 66; Cooper, *Select Cases*, 4 ff; *Melr. Lib.*, *73.
102. See Table 17, *sub* Cunninghame, Gala and Leader.
103. *Melr. Lib.*, 73.
104. *Newb. Reg.*, 144; *Melr. Lib.*, 322.
105. *Arb. Lib.*, 128.
106. SRO, *Gordon Castle Muniments*, GD 44, 106.
107. *RMS*, ii, 2289.
108. *Moray Reg.*, 162.
109. *Morton Reg.*, i, lxviii.
110. Fraser, *Douglas*, iii, 106 no. 107; *ADA*, 13 b.
111. *Kelso Lib.*, 533, (1495), 534 (1497).
112. *Arb. Lib.*, ii, 219.
113. *Pais. Reg.*, 5; *Holy. Lib.*, 23.
114. *Arb. Lib.*, 89 a, 89 b, (1189 x 1199); *Pais. Reg.*, 5; Fraser, *Johnstones*, i, 7, no. 11.
115. *TA*, iii, 189, 191, *sub* Earl of Huntly, Lord Drummond.
116. See p. 229.
117. See pp. 20-21.
118. *Arb. Lib.*, 306, 311.
119. *Chron. Melrose*, 85.
120. *Melr. Lib.*, 198.

Chapter 10

1. *HBC*, 174.
2. Cooper, *Register of Brieves*, 4, 36 c 7.
3. Cooper, *op. cit.*, 61 c 86.
4. Innes, *Scotch Legal Antiquities*, 41.
5. Petit Dutaillis, *Stubbs*, 155; Turner, *Select Pleas of the Forest*, ccxviii.
6. *APS*, i, 652, c 31.
7. *C.A. Rent*, i, 202, no. 248.
8. Wood, E. S., *Field Guide to Archaeology*, (London 1963), 236.
9. *ER*, i, 562.
10. *RRS*, ii, 370.
11. *ER*, i, 2, 17.
12. *APS*, ii, 251, c 19.
13. See Table 19, *sub* 'Spedalfield', p. 214.
14. See Table 19, *sub* Leith, p. 214.
15. See Table 19, *sub* Keithick, p. 214.
16. *DOST*, *sub* cuningar; *ADA*, 164 b.
17. *DOST*, *sub* linkis: open fairly level sandy ground used for . . . rabbit warrens; SRO, *Justice Ayre Journal Books*, RH 2/1/7, 369.
18. *APS*, ii, 7, c 10.
19. *Ibid.*, 52, c 36.
20. *Ibid.*, 107, c 16.
21. *Ibid.*, 242, c 12; 251, c 13.
22. SRO, *Justice Ayre Journal Books*, RH 2/1/7, 251, 268.
23. *Ibid.*, RH 2/1/6, 369 ff.
24. *ER*, i, 562.
25. *Ibid.*, i, xii, 693.
26. *C.A. Rent*, i, 187 no. 231, 194 no. 238.
27. *C.A. Rent*, i, 202, no. 248.
28. *APS*, i, 668, c 5.
29. *Ibid.*, ii, 6, c 23.
30. *ER*, xii, 693.
31. *Ibid.*, xiii, 76, 421, 544.

Chapter 11

1. *RMS*, ii, 1327, 1784.
2. *Ibid.*, 1178; *C.A. Rent*, i, 185 no. 226.
3. *Ibid.*, 1722.
4. *Ibid.*, 1784. This charter does not appear in some copies of *RMS*, ii, but it is given in the copy of *RMS*, ii, in the NLS reading room.
5. See Table 31, *sub* Cowie, Drum, Boyne, p. 356.
6. *ER*, i, 21; see p. 82.
7. *Ibid.*, 287.
8. *Ibid.*, ix, 105; xiii, 538.
9. *Ibid.*, xii, 73.
10. *Ibid.*, 277.
11. *Ibid.*, 144, 214.
12. *APS*, i, 748, c 8, 'de cervis domesticis'.
13. See Table 32, *sub* Newlands, Kinmount; *RMS*, i, app. 1, 34.
14. Petit Dutaillis, *Stubbs*, 151, 155.
15. *RMS*, ii, 541.
16. *ER*, xii, 73.

17. *TA*, ii, 105, 146.
18. *ER*, xii, 141; xiii, 23.
19. *RMS*, i, 115.
20. *APS*, ii, 107, c 16.
21. *Ibid.*, 251, c 13.
22. *RMS*, i, 317; *Arb. Lib.*, i, 284.
23. *RMS*, i, app. 1, 65.
24. *CDS*, ii, pp. 51, 53.
25. *RMS*, i, app. 1, 73.
26. *Ibid.*, ii, 541.
27. *RSS*, i, 296.
28. *ER*, v, 539, 'Lez palez'.
29. *Ibid.*, x, 121.
30. Fraser, *Douglas*, iii, 556 no. 3.
31. *Farming the Red Deer*, 25, 28.
32. *Abdn. Reg.*, ii, 269, (1235/6)
33. *TA*, iv, 524; *Arb. Lib.*, 284.
34. *ER*, vii, 653.
35. *TA*, ii, 433.
36. *ER*, i, 38.
37. *TA*, ii, 342, 424; iii, 348, 356, 362; iv, 128.
38. Shirley, *Deer Parks*, 240.
39. *ER*, xii, 189; and possibly *ER*, i, 7.
40. *TA*, iv, 76.
41. *ER*, i, 38.
42. *TA*, iii, 171.
43. *ER*, i, 38.
44. *Ibid.*, xii, 277, 441, 521.
45. *Ibid.*, ix, 54.
46. *TA*, iii, 172.
47. *Ibid.*, iv, 134.
48. Fauroux, *Actes des Ducs de Normandie*, 84, 90; Ritchie, *Normans in Scotland*, 371; *DOST, sub* 'hay'.
49. See pp. 85, 87.
50. *TA*, ii, 474.
51. *Ibid.*, 348, 349.
52. *Ibid.*, 408, 409; iii, 171.
53. *Ibid.*, ii, 407, 475.
54. *Ibid.*, 424.
55. *Ibid.*, 425.
56. *ER*, xii, 205.
57. *Ibid.*, vii, 25.
58. *TA*, ii, 151.
59. *Ibid.*, 425.
60. *Ibid.*, iii, 171.
61. *Ibid.*, 180.
62. *Ibid.*, ii, 419.
63. *Ibid.*, i, ii, iii, iv, *passim*, see indices.
64. *Ibid.*, iv, 128.
65. Leland, *Collecteana*, iv, 286.
66. *TA*, iii, 170; *ER*, xiii, 192.
67. *TA*, iv, 115.
68. *ER*, xii, 503, 540.
69. *TA*, iii, 157.
70. *ER*, xiii, 60.

Chapter 12

1. *TA*, ii, 118, 170, 400, 401, 454; Leland, *Collecteana*, iv, 286.
2. *APS*, i, 242.
3. Cooper, *Quoniam Attachiamenta*, 48.
4. *Ibid.*
5. *APS*, i, 652, c 31.
6. 'Blarkerroch' is unlocated.
7. OS Sheet 40, NO 666 952.
8. *St. A. Lib.*, 276.
9. *RRS*, ii, 340.
10. *Inchaff. Chrs.*, 17.
11. *Lenn. Cart.*, 19, 25, 29, 31, 38, 50, 91; Fraser, *Lennox*, ii, 403 no. 205, 401 no. 202; *Inchaff. Chrs.*, 12, 16; *Moray Reg.*, 469, no. 16, 465, no. 13.
12. *Moray Reg.*, 76; *Abdn. Reg.*, ii, 268; Fraser, *Lennox*, ii, 2, no. 2; Fraser, *Grant*, iii, 5 no. 7, 7 no. 11.
13. Petit Dutaillis, *Stubbs*, 154.
14. *APS*, i, 748, c 5; 262.
15. Justinian, *Institutes*, Section II, part 1, chapt. 12.
16. *Charter Rolls*, i, 140, (1231).
17. *ESC*, 156.
18. Fraser, *Johnstones*, i, 1 no. 2; 5 nos. 7 and 8.
19. *RMS*, i, app. 1, 41.
20. *RSS*, i, 246.
21. Stair, *Institutes*, Book 2, Titula 3, c 76.
22. *Melr. Lib.*, 376, 377.
23. *Ibid.*, ii, 461.
24. Stair, *Institutes*, Book 2, Titula 3, c 76.
25. *Melr. Lib.*, ii, 548.
26. *Pais. Reg.*, 92.
27. Rymer, *Foedora*, x, 688; xi, 213, 297, 431.
28. *APS*, ii, 251, c 13; 242, c 12.
29. *TA*, ii, 110, 366; iii, 163, 189.
30. *Ibid.*, iv, 76, 85, 362.
31. *Wemyss of Wemyss*, ii, 91 no. 61.
32. Blind Harry, *Wallace*, bk 10, 1 119.
33. *TA*, ii, 396.
34. Drummond, *Sculptured Monuments*, plates 25, 51, 56, 78, 80, 84.
35. Lismore, *Scottish Verse*, 262.
36. *Melr. Lib.*, 39.
37. Macphail, *Pluscarden*, 69, 199.
38. *APS*, ii, 15, c 5.
39. *Ibid.*, 51, c 35.
40. *ER*, vi, 540.
41. *ADC*, i, 101.
42. *APS*, ii, 51, c 32; 15, c 12.
43. *Ibid.*, 107, c 15 (1474).
44. *Ibid.*
45. Nicholson, *The Later Middle Ages*, 5, 6, 109.
46. *APS*, iv, 629, c 31.
47. Stair, *Institutes*, Book 2, Titula 3, chapt. 76.
48. *Encylopaedia of the Laws of Scotland*, eds. Black, A.C. and Work, J.L., vii, para 1046, notes 2, 3; Stair, *Institutes*, Book 2, Titula 3, chapt. 76, note.

49. *RRS*, ii, 487, (1209 or 1210); *Glas. Reg.*, 85, (c 1208); Fraser, *Carlaverock*, ii, 406.
50. *Dryb. Lib.*, 132, (1300); *Holm Cultram Chrs.*, 149, (c 1230 x 1240).
51. See p. 195; *Pais. Reg.*, 157, (1250); *Dryb. Lib.*, 132 (1300).
52. *Moray Reg.*, 99.
53. *Balm. Lib.*, 50; *Camb. Reg.*, 36, (c 1178); *RRS*, ii, 386, (1195 or 1196).
54. *Melr. Lib.*, 76, (1165 x 1182).
55. SRO, *Munro of Foulis Papers*, GD 93, box 1, no. 5, (1350 x 1371).
56. *C.A. Rent*, 197 no. 240, 198 no. 241, 246 no. 372.
57. *Ibid.*, i, 242, nos. 383 and 387, 225 no. 308, 169 no. 210.
58. See p. 197.
59. *Prot. Bk. Young*, 29 no. 135.
60. BM Ms Harleian 4700, (*Old Scots Laws*), f 282 r.
61. *APS*, ii, 7, cc 10, 11.
62. *Ibid.*, 251, c 16.
63. *RMS*, ii, 385; *ER*, vi, 419; *RMS*, ii, 145.
64. *ER*, vi, 566.
65. *C.A. Rent*, i, 169 no. 210; 225 no. 308; *DOST*, sub 'Hain, haining, hainit'.
66. *C.A. Rent*, i, 202 no. 248; 222 no. 299; *RMS*, i, 352; *ER*, xii, 189.
67. *Laing Chrs.*, no. 21; *ADC*, ii, 496; *ER*, v, 669; vii, 272; viii, 332, 334; xii, 73.
68. *Kelso Lib.*, 152.
69. *Lind. Cart.*, 135 (1259 x 1264); *C.A. Chart.*, i, 181 no. 83; *ADCP*, no. 61.
70. Childe, V. G., *Prehistory of Scotland* (London, 1935), 3-4; Anderson, *Scottish Forestry*, 20-23.
71. Cooper, *Regiam Majestatem*, bk 4, c 47.
72. *RRS*, ii, p. 283.
73. *Kelso Lib.*, 149.
74. *Newb. Reg.*, 140; Macphail, *Pluscarden*, 202-3.
75. Adams, I. H, 'The Salt Industry of the Forth Basin', *Scottish Geographical Magazine*, 81, (1965), 153-162.
76. *RRS*, ii, 362, 462; *Newb. Reg.*, 144.
77. *RRS*, ii, 64, 467.
78. *Abdn. Chrs.*, 10 no. 6; *RMS*, i, app. 1. 4.
79. *Abdn. Recs.*, 114.
80. *ER*, i, 574.
81. *Ibid.*, i, ii, iii; see indices, *sub* timber, boards, trons.
82. *Ibid.*, i, 215; iii, 659.
83. *APS*, ii, 7, c 10.
84. *Ibid.*, 51, cc 27, 30.
85. *Ibid.*, 251, cc 16, 19.
86. *Prot. Bk., Young*, 29, no. 135; *ADC*, ii, 375.
87. *RMS*, ii, 445; *ER*, vi, 566.
88. *C.A. Rent*, i, 237 no. 361.
89. *ESC*, 141; *Melr. Lib.*, ii, 478.
90. See Table 13, p. 165.
91. See Table 13, p. 165.
92. See Table 24, p. 267.
93. SRO, *Justice Ayre Journal Book*, RH, 2/1/6, 280 ff.
94. Anderson, *Scottish Forestry*, i, 176 and plate 5 after p. 386.
95. *ER*, iv, 580; *TA*, i, *passim* — see index, *sub* 'eastland boards'.
96. James IV, *Letters*, 141-4.
97. *ER*, iv, 482, 619; *TA*, ii, 83, and see index.
98. *ER*, iv, 626.

99. *TA*, iv, 45, 296; *ER*, xiii, 11, 209.
100. *TA*, ii, 435.
101. *Ibid.*, 425.
102. *Ibid.*, i, 274, 319; ii, 279, 281, 426; iv, see index; *ER*, iv, 579; viii, 268, 354.
103. Hume Brown, P., *Early Travellers in Scotland* (Edinburgh, 1891), 26.
104. *APS*, ii, 251, c 16.

Chapter 13

1. Robertson, J. J., 'De Composicione Cartarum', *Stair Society Misc.*, xxvi, (1972), 84.
2. *APS*, i, 183.
3. Borland, C., *Catalogue of Western Medieval Manuscripts in Edinburgh University Library*, (Edinburgh, 1916), 298.
4. NLS, *Arbuthnott Ms. of Scots Laws*, Acc 2006; see printed note included with this Ms, f 3 r 'in Collegio Advocatorum'.
5. *APS*, i, 196.
6. Jolliffe, J. E. A., *The Constitutional History of Medieval England*, (London, 1967), 239; Duncan, *The Making of the Kingdom*, 539.
7. *RRS*, i, p. 35; ii, pp. 42, 45, 69.
8. See p. 292, Law 6; *RRS*, i, 1637.
9. Duncan, A. A. M., 'Regiam Majestatem, a Reconsideration', *Juridical Review*, (1961), 199; Cooper, T. M. and Paton, G. C. H, 'The Dark Age, 1329-1532', *Stair Society*, (1958), xx, 18, 19.
10. Robertson, J. J., *op. cit.* and 'The Development of the Law' in *Scottish Society in the Fifteenth Century*, ed. Brown, J. M., (London, 1977), 143.
11. *RSS*, i, 1637.
12. *RMS*, ii, 3218 and SRO, *Great Seal Register*, C/2/14.
13. See App. A; such edited Mss. are NLS, Adv. Ms. 24.2.4 b (*Bal*), 128 c 18; NLS, Ms. R.C. 19 (*Ez*) fos. 4 b, 5 b.
14. *Melr. Lib.*, 307; *RRS*, ii, 111.
15. SRO, *Mar and Kellie Papers*, GD 124/6/1.
16. All Mss. are referred to by abbreviations listed in the table of Mss. in App. A, p. 271.
17. See App. A, Ms. *Co*. p. 289.
18. See pp. 104, 109, 194, 232.
19. SRO, *Justice Ayre Journal Books*, RH 2/1/6, 144; *APS*, ii, 107, c 16.
20. *ER*, ix, 605.
21. *Ibid.*, viii, 44.
22. *Ibid.*, ix, 620.
23. *Ibid.*, xi, 394.
24. *Ibid.*, x, 460.
25. See pp. 192-194.
26. *RMS*, ii, 3218; SRO, *Great Seal Register*, C/2/14, 'legum nostrarum forestarum'.
27. *RSS*, i, 1505.
28. SRO, *Mar and Kellie Papers*, GD 124/6/1.
29. *RMS*, i, app. 2, 232.
30. See pp. 46, 47 and Table of Rubrics, p. 299.
31. *ER*, xi, 393.
32. SRO, *Justice Ayre Journal Books*, RH 2/1/5, 109, 116; RH 2/1/6, 281, 286.
33. *Ibid.*, RH 2/1/5, 124.
34. *ER*, xi, 320*.
35. *Ibid.*, 394, c 9.

Chapter 14

1. *Moray Reg.*, 29.
2. See pp. 109, 110.
3. See pp. 135, 136.
4. See p. 202.
5. *Melr. Lib.*, 195.
6. *Pais. Reg.*, 5, 17.
7. *RMS*, i, app. 1, 65. Allowance has not been made for the long hundred in these figures, since they are not from the *Exchequer Rolls*.
8. *ER*, i, 340.
9. *Ibid.*, ix, 475.
10. *Ibid.*, ix, 329, 119; x, 566.
11. *Ibid.*, vii, 246; xiii, 121; *TA*, ii, 394.
12. *Ibid.*, vi, 518.
13. *Ibid.*, xii, 186.
14. *Ibid.*, iv, 576.
15. *Ibid.*, vi, 225.
16. See p. 329.
17. *Ibid.*
18. *ER*, xii, 34.
19. *Ibid.*, ix, 470; *RSS*, i, 435.
20. *ER*, xii, 34.
21. SRO, *ADC*, xxi, f 194; and see p. 331.
22. *RMS*, ii, 3218; SRO, *Great Seal Register*, C/2/14.
23. Symon, *Scottish Farming*, 51, 56; *Melr. Lib.*, 76; *Kelso Lib.*, 455.
24. *ESC*, 193.
25. *Ibid.*, 141; see Map 8.
26. *RRS*, ii, 441.
27. *Dryb. Lib.*, 110.
28. *RRS*, ii, 265.
29. Hay, *Genealogical Collections*, 245.
30. *Dryb. Lib.*, 110.
31. *Ibid.*, 112.
32. *Melr. Lib.*, 101; *Dryb. Lib.*, 114.
33. *RRS*, i, 235.
34. *ESC*, 193.
35. *Dryb. Lib.*, 113.
36. See p. 151.
37. *Melr. Lib.*, 94, 106, 107.
38. *RRS*, ii, 236; see p. 150.
39. *Melr. Lib.*, 94.
40. *Ibid.*, 107.
41. *Ibid.*, 106.
42. *RRS*, 265.
43. *Ibid.*, ii, 301; *Melr. Lib.*, 96, 108; *RCAM*, Roxburgh, ii, 291.
44. *Melr. Lib.*, 99; *RRS*, ii, 307.
45. *Melr. Lib.*, 97; *RRS*, ii, 364.
46. *Melr. Lib.*, 101; *RRS*, ii, 483.
47. *Melr. Lib.*, 257, 258.
48. *Pais. Reg.*, 5.
49. *Ibid.*, 11.
50. *Ibid.*, 17.
51. See p. 192.
52. *Pais. Reg.*, 23.

53. *Ibid.*, 253.
54. *Ibid.*, 13.
55. *Ibid.*, 92; see p. 195.
56. *Melr. Lib.*, 66.
57. *Ibid.*, 67.
58. *RRS*, ii, 78.
59. See p. 200.
60. *Melr. Lib.*, 73.
61. *Ibid.*, 74.
62. *Ibid.*, 323.
63. *Ibid.*, 324.
64. *RRS*, ii, 362.
65. See Table 23, p. 266.
66. *Melr. Lib.*, 39.
67. *Ibid.*, 196.
68. *Ibid.*, 198.
69. *Ibid.*, 264.
70. See p. 107.
71. Duncan, *The Making of the Kingdom*, 366, 425.
72. See Table 8, p. 120.
73. Franklin, *History of Scots Farming*, 17, 28; *Cambridge Economic History,* (Cambridge, 1941), i, ed. R. Koebner, 666.
74. *RMS*, i, 118.
75. *Ibid.*, 618.
76. Nicholson, *The Later Middle Ages*, 165, 176-8.
77. See Table 21, p. 224.
78. See Table 32, p. 357.
79. See p. 42.
80. *C.A. Rent*, i, 121.
81. *Ibid.*, 222, 227.
82. *Arb. Lib.*, 73.
83. *Ibid.*, 219.
84. *RMS*, ii, 2289.
85. *Ibid.*, 2203.
86. *Brechin Reg.*, i, 110.
87. See p. 188.
88. *ER*, vii, 524.
89. See p. 110.
90. *RSS*, i, 219, 435, 515.
91. *ER*, xi, 394, c 6.
92. See pp. 176-178.
93. Nicholson, *The Later Middle Ages*, 389, 440, 454, 565-7.
94. *RRS*, ii, 251.
95. *Abdn. Reg.*, 15.
96. *RRS*, ii, 111.
97. *Pais. Reg.*, 23.
98. *Melr. Lib.*, 198.
99. *Pais. Reg.*, 92.
100. *RRS*, i, 238.
101. *ER*, xi, 393, pts. 3, 8.
102. *ER*, ix, 605.
103. *Reginald of Durham*, ed. J. Raine (Surtees Society, London 1835), i, 186.
104. Child, *English and Scottish Ballads*, iii, 108, no. 114, a.
105. See p. 27.
106. *RMS*, i, 257, 618; i, app. 1, 30; app. 2, 958.

107. See p. 235.
108. See p. 334.
109. *ER*, xi, 401.
110. *Ibid.*, vi, 578; vii, 68; *TA*, ii, 119; iii, 153.
111. *ER*, xii, 144; xiii, 3; see above, pp. 94, 215.
112. Laing, D., *Early Popular Poetry of Scotland*, (London 1895), i, 222, 1 179 ff.
113. Petit Dutaillis, C., 'De La Signification du Mot Forêt à l'Epoque Franque', *Bibliothèque de l'Ecole des Chartes*, lxxvi, (1915), 143.

Appendix A

1. *APS*, i, 687.
2. Anderson, *History of Scottish Forestry*, 149-154, 265-267.
3. *APS*, i, 177-210, 248-249.
4. Buchanan, J., 'The Manuscripts of *Regiam Majestatem*', *Juridical Review*, (1937), 217-231.
5. Richardson, H. G., 'Roman Law in the *Regiam Majestatem*', *Juridical Review*, (1955), 155-187.
6. Duncan, A. A. M., '*Regiam Majestatem*, a Reconsideration', (1961), 199-217.
7. *Regiam Majestatem*, ed. Cooper, T. M., (Stair Society, 1947).
8. Robertson, J. J., 'De Composicione Cartarum', *Stair Society, Misc. I*, (Edinburgh, 1971).
9. Borland, C. R., *Catalogue of Western Manuscripts* (Edinburgh, 1916), MSS 206, 207, 208.
10. Buchanan, *op. cit.*
11. Richardson, *op. cit.*
12. Robertson, *op. cit.*
13. Duncan, A. A. M., 'Councils General', *SHR*, xxxv, (1956), 132-143.
14. *Summary Catalogue of the Advocates' Manuscripts* (HMSO, Edinburgh, 1971), 77 no. 917.
15. Balfour, *Practicks*, ed. P. McNeill, (Stair Society, 1963), xxiv, lviii.
16. Southern, R. W., 'Note on text of Glanville', *EHR*, lxv, (1950), 81; *Glanville*, ed. Hall, xl-xli.
17. *Leges Henrici Primi*, 68; *Walter of Henley*, 114.
18. Bracton, *De Legibus et Consuetudinibus Angliae*, i, 286.
19. *Statutes of the Realm*, i, 26, 27, 120.
20. Stubbs, *Constitutional Documents*, 347.
21. *Statutes of the Realm*, i, 243; Turner, *Select Pleas of the Forest*, 37ff. and n. 4. The first 11 clauses may date to Henry III's or even to John's reign.
22. The numbers refer to clauses in the present edition and not to numbers in the English mss.
23. *APS*, i, 'Fragmenta Collecta', 719-754.
24. Balfour, *Practicks*, lviii.
25. Balfour, *Practicks*, lx; *APS*, i, 193.
26. *Walter of Henley*, xvi; Bracton, *De Legibus et Consuetudinibus Angliae*, i, 287; *Leges Henrici Primi*, 46.
27. In his 1975 Presidential Address to the Scottish History Society entitled 'Hunting and the Forest in Medieval Scotland'.
28. See p. 105.
29. *ER*, xi, 394, c 11.
30. See p. 107.
31. See pp. 234, 235.
32. See p. 7.
33. Fauroux, *Actes des Ducs de Normandie*, 64.

34. See p. 22.
35. See p. 107.
36. See p.. 183 and Table 16, p. 204.
37. See pp. 256-257.
38. See p. 104.
39. See pp. 102-103; 225.
40. *Pais. Reg.*, 92.
41. See pp. 228, 229.
42. See Commentary, p. 310, c 17, line 101.
43. See pp. 184-185.
44. See p. 195.
45. See pp. 29-30.
46. See p. 142.
47. See p. 92.
48. See p. 146.

Appendix B

1. *DOST, sub* 'Iesu'.
2. *RMS*, ii, 3439.
3. *Ibid.*, 59.
4. *ER*, vii, 521 ff.
5. *Ibid.*, xi, 99-100, 200.
6. *Ibid.*, i, 35.
7. *Ibid.*, vi, 576.
8. *Ibid.*, vii, 24.
9. *Ibid.*, 478.
10. *Ibid.*, 530.
11. *Ibid.*, ix, 468.
12. *Ibid.*, 470.
13. *RSS*, i, 435.
14. *ER*, xi, 457; xii, 31 ff.
15. *Ibid.*, xi, 320, 460.
16. *Ibid.*, xii, 36 ff.
17. *Ibid.*, 316 ff.
18. *RSS*, i, 1228.
19. *Ibid.*, 468, 469, 671, 688, 809, 838, 839.
20. *ER*, ix, 30.
21. *RSS*, i, 219, 235, 1858.
22. *ER*, xii, 658.
23. *DOST, sub* 'bill', a formal or written document.
24. *RSS*, i, 1859, 1872, 2037.
25. *RMS*, ii, 3154-3156; 3438, 3439, 3441-3443, 3473, 3475-3477, 3502, 3505, 3507; 3591, 3596, 3617; 3737, 3758, 3775.
26. *ER*, xiii, 649.
27. *Ibid.*, 351.
28. C. Madden, 'The Feuing of Ettrick Forest', *The Innes Review*, xxvii, (Spring 1976), 73.
29. *ER*, viii, 141; x, 603.
30. *Ibid.*, x, 161-173.
31. *Ibid.*, 293-4, 344-8.
32. *Ibid.*, 430-5.
33. *Ibid.*, xii, 34-8.
34. **Ibid.**, 390-392.

c •

35. *Ibid.,* xiii, 411-5.
36. *Ibid.,* 524-9.
37. *Ibid.,* xii, 177.
38. *Ibid.,* xii, 412ff.
39. Nicholson, *The Later Middle Ages,* 529.
40. W. Scott, *Minstrelsy of the Scottish Border,* ed. T. Henderson, (London, 1931), 491-2.
41. *ER,* x, 675; see p. 47.
42. *ER,* xi, 606, 608; SRO, *Justice Ayre Journal books,* RH 2/1/5, 109.

Glossary

agister
: an English forest official who supervised the agistment or grazing of cattle and swine and collected rents for pasturage.

archetype
: the parent manuscript of a tradition of manuscripts.

Articles
: the Articles or the Lords of the Articles were those members of parliament who drew up the legislation to present to parliament for its approval. The Articles were the king's proposals for legislation.

assise
: literally a sitting or session but used to mean a court where the king drew up new legislation. The legislation itself might also be called an assise.

autograph
: the original manuscript.

ayre
: the route or *iter* which a justiciar had to follow when travelling round the country, the justiciar's circuit.

ballivus ad extra
: a bailie or official appointed by the king to manage the royal lands. They accounted to the exchequer for the fermes of the royal lands.

bludwite
: a penalty or payment imposed by the lord on those involved in a brawl in which blood was spilt.

boll
: a measure of grain. It could be 164 lbs or 12 gallons but did vary.

chalder
: a measure of grain. It could be 16 bolls but did vary.

charge
: the maximum theoretical amount which the exchequer expected from those who were accountable to it.

commissioners of crown lands
: a group of men, often lords of council or members of parliament, who received a letter of commission from the king under the Privy Seal authorising them to let royal lands and hold a court.

compear
: it was the duty of certain people in a locality to appear or compear at the local court, whether a sheriff, baron, burgh or regality court. These suitors would be fined for non-attendance or non-compearance.

demesne | the lands which were neither let nor alienated by a lord but which were retained in his own hands.

discharge | that part of an exchequer account which explained why the sums given in the charge side of the account could not be collected or what had happened to them once they had been collected.

distraint | if a tenant failed to perform the customary feudal services for his lord, the lord could proceed against him by distraint or by distress, seizing his chattels until the services were performed.

dittay | before a justiciar started his ayre he would issue to the sheriff of the shire in which the court was to be held, what was known as a brief of dittay or indictment ordering the sheriff to summon those fitted to give information about the crimes listed on the dittay. A point of dittay was one of the crimes listed on the indictment.

entry | a sum of money paid to the lord by the tenant when the tenant received a lease for the first time.

escheat | when a tenant died without heirs his land would escheat or return to his lord. It is also used in the sense of forfeiture.

extent | a valuation of land preparatory for taxation.

ferme | rent.

foggage | a pasture toll, winter grass.

forfeiture | a payment to the lord, taken by force if not paid voluntarily, for offences which were less serious than brawling and bloodshed.

formulary | a collection of the correct form of words for various types of charters, writs and orders.

free barony | if lands were granted to an individual in free barony by the king, the grantee was entitled to hold a court with jurisdiction roughly equivalent to that of the sheriff. The court of a barony could hang and drown those who were found guilty.

free regality | a grant of lands in free regality from the king enabled the grantee in most instances to try the four pleas of the crown, murder, robbery with violence, rape and arson.

governor | regent.

grassum | the sum of money paid by a tenant to a lord when a lease was renewed.

Great Seal | the main seal of the realm under which charters were issued. It was kept by the chancellor.

guardian	regent.
herbage	a pasture toll, summer grass.
heriot	a payment, usually the best animal, to the lord to permit the heirs of a dead man to succeed to the deceased's land and chattels.
Interregnum	the first Interregnum occurred between the death of Margaret, Maid of Norway in 1290 and the election of John Balliol in 1292 and the second between the deposition of John Balliol in 1296 and the coronation of Robert Bruce in 1306.
justiciar	a royal justice who travelled round the country on an ayre trying the four pleas of the crown, rape, arson, robbery with violence and murder, and any other causes which were points of dittay at the time.
journal books	the record kept of the courts held by a justiciar.
pannage	a toll collected for the grazing of pigs on the mast in autumn.
patrimony	a group of lands and possessions traditionally belonging to a king or a baron which had been passed on heritably.
pertinents	those rights which pertained to lands, e.g., the right to wood, pasture, peat, and which were listed in a charter.
prebendary	a canon of a cathedral who received a share of the revenues of a cathedral.
Privy Seal	no charter could be issued under the Great Seal till authenticated by the Privy Seal which was the second seal of state. Grants of offices and leases might be made under the Privy Seal.
purpresture	encroaching on the royal demesne in England. When applied to forests it meant assarting in the forest or limiting the movements of deer.
redaction	the process by which an archetype is formed, a copy from the original rather than a copy from a copy, the copying of a manuscript which starts a new tradition.
rests	the sum left in the exchequer accounts after the discharge had been subtracted from the charge, the arrears.
stemma	a table or diagram showing the relationship of several manuscripts.
tenendas section	that part of a charter which described in detail how lands were to be held, i.e., the manner of tenure.

venison	the greater game reserved in a forest, in Scotland the male and female red deer, roe deer and boar.
vert	the vegetation reserved in a forest, the green wood.
'waif'	the right to have stray and unclaimed animals.
'wrac'	the right to goods from wrecks washed ashore.
writ	a document written in Latin and sealed. The document might contain instructions to royal officials, a record of judicial proceedings or a grant of lands.

Bibliography

Abbreviations used in Bibliography

CDI   Collection des Documents Inédits sur L'Histoire de France
DGT   Dumfries and Galloway Transactions
EHR   English Historical Review
HMC   Reports of the Royal Commission on Historical Manuscripts (London 1870-)
MGH   Monumenta Germaniae Historica
PBA   Proceedings of the British Academy
RCAM   Royal Commission on Ancient Monuments
SBRS   Scottish Burgh Record Society
SGM   Scottish Geographical Magazine
SHR   Scottish Historical Review
SHS   Scottish History Society
SRS   Scottish Record Society
STS   Scottish Text Society
TRHS   Transactions of the Royal Historical Society
ZCP   Zeitschrift für Celtische Philologie

1 Primary Sources

(a) Unprinted

Edinburgh:

(i) National Library of Scotland (NLS)
The Collections of Walter Macfarlane, MS Adv 35, 4, 12a
Hay, *Genealogical Collections.*
    Father R. A. Hay, *Memoirs or Collections of several things relating to the history of the most famous families of Scotland*, (c 1700), Ms Adv. 34. 1.9
Stobie, *Map of Perthshire.*
    J. Stobie, *Map of Perthshire*, (1783)

(ii) Scottish Record Office (SRO)

Abercairney Muniments, GD 25
Acta Dominorum Concilii
Crown Rentals, 1499-1507, E 40
Gordon Castle Muniments, GD 44
Justice Ayre Journal Books, RH 2
Mar and Kellie Muniments, GD 124
Munro of Foulis Papers, GD 93
Registrum Magni Sigilli, C/2/3-5, 7, 9-10, 12-15, 17, 19
Transcripts of Royal Charters, RH 1

(iii) Edinburgh University Library (EUL)

Roy, *Map of Scotland.*
>   General William Roy, *Map of Scotland,* (c 1750), Phot. 1139

Glasgow:

(i) Glasgow University Library

Hunter Marshall Papers, Ms General 1052

London:

(i) British Museum (BM)

Additional Charter 66570

Forest Law Manuscripts: manuscript volumes consulted in the British Museum, Lambeth Palace, Cambridge University, the National Library of Scotland and the Scottish Record Office are listed in Appendix A on pp. 271 and 272.

(b) Printed

A.B. Antiqs.
>   *Illustrations of the Topography and Antiquities of the Shires of Aberdeen and Banff,* (Spalding Club, 1847-69)

A. B. Coll.
>   *Collections for a History of the Shires of Aberdeen and Banff,* (Spalding Club, 1843)

Abdn. Chrs.
>   *Charters and other writs illustrating the History of the Royal Burgh of Aberdeen,* (Aberdeen, 1890)

Abdn. Counc.
>   *Extracts from the Council Register of the Burgh of Aberdeen,* (Spalding Club, 1844-8)

Abdn. Recs.
>   *Early Records of the Burgh of Aberdeen 1317, 1398-1407,* ed. W. C. Dickinson, (SHS, 1957)

Abdn. Reg.
>   *Registrum Episcopatus Aberdonensis,* (Spalding and Maitland Clubs, 1845)

Actes des Ducs de Normandie
>   *Recueil des Actes des Ducs de Normandie,* ed M. Fauroux, (Caen, 1961)

ADA
>   *The Acts of the Lords Auditors of Causes and Complaints,* ed. J. Thomson, (Edinburgh, 1839)

ADC, i, ii
  The Acts of the Lords of Council in Civil Causes, ed. T. Thomson and
  others (Edinburgh, 1839 and 1918)
ADC, iii
  Acta Dominorum Concilii 1501-3, ed. J. A. Clyde, (Stair Society, 1943)
ADCP
  *Acts of the Lords of Council in Public Affairs 1501-1554; Selections from
  Acta Dominorum Concilii,* ed. R. K. Hannay, (Edinburgh, 1932)
Aelred, *De Bello Standardo*
  Chronicles of reigns of Stephen, Henry II and Richard I, ed. R. Howlett,
  (Rolls Series, 1886), iii, 181-199
Aelred, *Genealogia*
  Aelred, *Omnia Opera:* in *Patrologia Cursus Completus,* ed. J. P. Migne,
  cxcv, (Paris, 1855)
ALI
  The Ancient Laws of Ireland, ed. W. N. Hancock and others, (Dublin,
  1865-1901)
Ancient Laws and Institutes of Wales
  The Ancient Laws and Institutes of Wales, ed. A. Owen (London, 1841)
Anderson, *Diplomata*
  Selectus Diplomatum et Numismatum Scotiae Thesaurus, ed. J. Anderson,
  (Edinburgh, 1739)
APS
  The Acts of the Parliament of Scotland, ed. T. Thomson and C. Innes,
  (Edinburgh, 1814-75)
Arb. Lib.
  Liber S. Thome de Aberbrothoc, (Bannatyne Club, 1848-1856)
Arrian, *Kunegetikos. Arrian on Coursing,* (London, 1831)
  Arrianus F., *Scripta Minora et Fragmenta,* ed. A. G. Roos, (Leipzig, 1967)
Balfour, *Practicks*
  The Practicks of Sir James Balfour of Pittendriech, ed. P. McNeill, (Stair
  Society, 1963)
Balm. Lib.
  Liber Sancte Marie de Balmorinach, (Abbotsford Club, 1841)
Barbour, *Bruce,* (Skeat)
  J. Barbour, *The Bruce,* ed. W. W. Skeat, (STS, 1894)
Bellenden, *Chronicles*
  The Chronicles of Scotland compiled by Hector Boece, translated into Scots
  by John Bellenden 1531, (STS, 1938-41)
Berners, *Book of St. Albans*
  Dame Juliana Berners, *The Book of St. Albans,* facsimile edition,
  (Amsterdam, 1969)
Black Book of Chirk
  The Black Book of Chirk, ed. T. Lewis, in *ZCP,* xx, 30-96

Blind Harry, *Wallace*
  Blind Harry, *William Wallace*, ed. M. Macdiarmid, (STS, 1968-9)
Boece, *Historiae*
  Hector Boethius, *Scotorum Historiae*, (Paris, 1574)
Book of Alexander
  See Hay, *Book of Alexander*
Bracton, *De Legibus et Consuetudinibus Angliae*, ed. Woodbine, trans. with
  notes and revisions by S. E. Thorne, (Cambridge, Mass., 1968)
Brechin Reg.
  Registrum Episcopatus Brechinensis, (Bannatyne Club, 1856)
Brodie, *Letters and Papers of Henry VIII*, see Henry VIII, *Letters*
Burnett of Leys
  George Burnett, *The Family of Burnett of Leys*, ed. Col. J. Allardyce (New
  Spalding Club, 1901)
CA Chrs.
  Charters of the Abbey of Coupar Angus, ed. D. E. Easson, (SHS, 1947)
CA Rent.
  Rental Book of the Cistercian Abbey of Coupar Angus, ed. C. Rogers,
  (Grampian Club, 1879-80)
Caius, *English Dogges.*
  Caius J., *English Dogges*, (London, 1576; Amsterdam reprint, 1969)
Cal. Papal Letters
  *Calendar of Entries in the Papal Registers relating to Great Britain and
  Ireland: Papal Letters*, ed. W. H. Bliss and others, (London, 1893-)
Camb. Reg.
  Registrum Monasterii S Marie de Cambuskenneth, (Grampian Club, 1872)
Carnwath, The Barony Court Book of, ed. W. C. Dickinson (SHS, 1937)
CDS
  Calendar of Documents Relating to Scotland, ed. J. Bain, (Edinburgh, 1881-
  8)
Charter Rolls
  Calendar of Charter Rolls, (London, 1903-)
Chron. Fordun
  Johannis de Fordun, *Chronica Gentis Scotorum*, ed. W. F. Skene,
  (Edinburgh, 1871-2)
Chron. Melrose
  The Chronicle of Melrose, facsimile edition, ed. A. O. Anderson and
  others, (London, 1936)
Chron. Picts-Scots
  Chronicles of the Picts: Chronicles of the Scots, ed. W. F. Skene,
  (Edinburgh, 1867)
Chron. Pluscarden
  Liber Pluscardenensis, ed. F. J. H. Skene, (Edinburgh, 1877-80)

Chron. Wyntoun
  The Original Chronicle of Andrew Wyntoun, (STS, 1903-14)
Concilia Scotiae
  Concilia Scotiae: Ecclesiae Scoticanae, Statuta tam Provincialia quam Synodalia, ed. J. Robertson, (Edinburgh, 1866)
Cooper, T. M.
  See *Quoniam Attachiamenta*,
  Regiam Majestatem,
  Register of Brieves
Cross and Slover, *Ancient Irish Tales*
  Ancient Irish Tales, ed. T. P. Cross, C. H. Slover, (London 1936)
Dalrymple, *Collections*
  Collections Concerning the Scottish History, Sir James Dalrymple, (Edinburgh, 1705)
De Composicione Cartarum
  De Composicione Cartarum, ed. J. J. Robertson, in *Stair Society Misc.*, i (Stair Society, 1972), 84
Deer, Jackson
  The Gaelic Notitiae of the Book of Deer, ed. K. Jackson, (Cambridge, 1972)
Dickinson, W. C.
  See *Fife, Sheriff Court Book; Carnwath, Barony Court Book; Abdn. Recs.*
Douglas, *Shorter Poems*
  G. Douglas, *Shorter Poems*, ed. P. J. Bawcutt, (STS, 1967)
Dunf. Reg.
  Registrum de Dunfermelyn, (Bannatyne Club, 1842)
Dunnaire Finn
  Dunnaire Finn, ed. Eoin Macneil and Gerard Murphy, (Irish Text Society, 1908-1953)
EHD, i
  English Historical Documents, i, ed. D. Whitelocke, (London, 1955)
ER
  The Exchequer Rolls of Scotland, ed. J. Stuart and others, (Edinburgh, 1878-1908)
ESC
  Early Scottish Charters, ed. A. Lawrie, (Glasgow, 1905)
Fife, Sheriff Court Book of, ed. W. C. Dickinson, (SHS, 1928)
Formulary E, ed. A. A. M. Duncan (Glasgow University, Department of Scottish History, Occasional Papers, 1976)
Fraser, *Carlaverock*
  The Book of Carlaverock, ed. W. Fraser, (Edinburgh, 1873)
Fraser, *Douglas*
  The Douglas Book, ed. W. Fraser, (Edinburgh, 1885)
Fraser, *Grandtully*
  The Red Book of Grandtully, ed. W. Fraser, (Edinburgh, 1868)

Fraser, *Grant*
    The Chiefs of Grant, ed. W. Fraser, (Edinburgh, 1883)

Fraser, *Johnstones*
    The Annandale Family Book, ed. W. Fraser, (Edinburgh, 1894)

Fraser, *Lennox*
    The Lennox, ed. W. Fraser, (Edinburgh, 1874)

Fraser, *Menteith*
    The Red Book of Menteith, ed. W. Fraser (Edinburgh, 1880)
See *Stirlings of Keir*

Fraser, *Southesk*
    History of the Carnegies, Earls of Southesk, and of their kindred, ed. W.
    Fraser, (Edinburgh, 1867)
See *Wemyss*

Fraser Papers
    Papers from the Collection of Sir William Fraser, ed. J. R. N. Macphail,
    (SHS, 1924)

Frasers of Philorth
    The Frasers of Philorth, ed. A. Fraser, Lord Saltoun, (Edinburgh, 1888)

Froissart, *Chronicles*, (Jolliffe)
    Froissart's Chronicles, ed. and trans. J. Jolliffe, (London, 1967)

Frosta Ting Law and Gula Ting Law
    The Earliest Norwegian Laws, ed. and translated by L. M. Larson, *(Records
    of Civilisation*, xx, 1935)

Gesner, *Icones Animalium*
    Gesner, C., *Icones Animalium*, (Zürich, 1560)

Glanville
    *Treatise on the Laws and Customs of the Realm of England commonly
    called Glanvill*, ed. G. D. G. Hall, (London, 1965)

Glas. Reg.
    Registrum Episcopatus Glasguensis, (Bannatyne and Maitland Clubs, 1843)

Gregory IX, *Decretals*
    Decretals of Gregory IX, Corpus Iuris Canonici, (Augustae Taurinorum,
    1774), ii, 674

Gula Ting Law
    See *Frosta Ting Law*

Hay, *Book of Alexander*
    Gilbert of the Hay, *The Buik of Alexander*, (STS, 1921-29)

Hay, *Book of Knighthood*
    Gilbert of the Hay, *Book of Knighthood*, (STS, 1901-14)

Henry IV, *Letters*
    Recueil des Lettres Missives de Henri IV, ed. M. Berger de Xivrey, (CDI,
    1843-1876)

Henry VIII, *Letters*
   Calendar of Letters and Papers of Henry VIII, ed. R. H. Brodie, (London, 1920)
Henryson, *Poems and Fables*
   The Poems and Fables of Robert Henryson, ed. H. Harvey Wood, (Edinburgh, 1965)
HMC, *The Athole Charters*
   The Athole Charters in HMC Report 7 (London, 1879)
HMC, *Mar and Kellie Supp. Report*
   Mar and Kellie Supplementary Report, (HMC, London, 1930)
Holm Cultram Chrs.
   The Registers of Holm Cultram, ed. Rev. F. B. Swift, (Penrith, 1948)
Holy Lib.
   Liber Cartarum Sancte Crucis, (Bannatyne Club, 1840)
Holyrood Ordinale
   The Holyrood Ordinale, ed. F. C. Eeles, (Book of the Old Edinburgh Club, 1914)
Hoveden, *Chronica*
   Chronica of Roger of Hoveden, ed. W. Stubbs (Rolls Series, 1868-71)
Inchaf. Chrs.
   Liber Insule Missarum, (Bannatyne Club, 1847)
James IV, *Letters*
   The Letters of James the Fourth, 1505-13, ed. R. K. Hannay and R. L. Mackie, (SHS, 1953)
James VI, *Basilikon Doron* in *The Political Works of James I reprinted from the edition of 1616*, intro. by C. H. McIlwain, (Cambridge, Mass., 1918)
Justinian, *Institutes*
   The Institutes of Justinian, ed. J. T. Abdy and B. Walker, (Cambridge, 1876)
Kelso Lib.
   Liber S. Marie de Calchou (Bannatyne Club, 1846)
Kinloss Recs.
   Records of the Monastery of Kinloss, ed. J. Stuart, (Edinburgh, 1872)
Laing, *Charters*
   Calendar of the Laing Charters 854-1837, ed. J. Anderson, (Edinburgh, 1899)
Leges Henrici Primi
   Leges Henrici Primi, ed. L. J. Downer, (Oxford, 1972)
Leland, *Collecteana*
   De Rebus Britannicis Collecteana, ed. J. Leland, (London, 1770)
Lenn. Cart.
   Cartularium Comitatus de Levenax, (Maitland Club, 1833)
Lesley, *History*
   De Origine, Moribus et Rebus Gestis Scotorum Libri Decem and *The*

*History of Scotland from the Death of King James I in the year 1436 to the
year 1561,* (STS, 1888-95)
Lind. Lib.
    Liber Sancte Marie de Lundoris, (Abbotsford Club, 1841)
Lismore, *Heroic Poetry*
    Heroic Poetry from the Book of the Dean of Lismore, ed. N. Ross, (Scottish
    Gaelic Text Society, 1939)
Lismore, *Scottish Verse*
    Scottish Verse from the Book of the Dean of Lismore, ed. W. J. Watson,
    (Scottish Gaelic Text Society, 1937)
Macphail, *Pluscarden*
    See *Pluscarden*
Melr. Lib.
    Liber Sancte Marie de Melros, (Bannatyne Club, 1837)
Moncrieffs
    The Moncrieffs and the Moncrieffes, ed. F. Moncrieff and W. Moncrieffe,
    (Edinburgh, 1929)
MGH *Capitularia,* i
    Legum Sectio II, Capitularia Regum Francorum, part 1, ed. A. Boretuis,
    (MGH, 1883)
MGH *Legum Nationum Germanicorum*
    Legum Sectio I, Legum Germanicorum vol. iii, part 2, (MGH, 1954)
Moray Reg.
    Registrum Episcopatus Moraviensis, (Bannatyne Club, 1837)
Mort. Reg.
    Registrum Honoris de Morton, (Bannatyne Club, 1853)
NMS
    Facsimiles of the National Manuscripts of Scotland, (London, 1867-71)
Newb. Reg.
    Registrum S. Marie de Neubottle, (Bannatyne Club, 1849)
Nisbet, *Ragman Roll*
    Historical and Critical Remarks on Prynne's History so far as concerns . . .
    the Ragman Roll, in A. Nisbet, *A System of Heraldry,* (Edinburgh, 1816),
    vol. ii
Orkneyinga Saga
    Orkneyinga Saga, trans. G. W. Dasent (Rolls Series, 1887)
Pais. Reg.
    Registrum Monasterii de Passelet, (Maitland Club, 1832)
Paris, *Chronica Majora*
    Chronica Majora of Matthew Paris, ed. H. R. Luard, (Rolls Series, 1872-83)
Patent Rolls
    Calendar of Patent Rolls, (London, 1901-)
Peebles Chrs.
    Charters and Documents relating to the Burgh of Peebles, (SBRS, 1872)

Pitcairn, *Criminal Trials*
R. Pitcairn, *Criminal Trials in Scotland*, (Edinburgh, 1833)
Pitscottie, *Historie*
R. Lindesay of Pitscottie, *The Historie and Chronicles of Scotland*, (STS, 1899-1911)
Pluscarden
A History of the Religious House of Pluscardyn, ed. S. R. Macphail, (Edinburgh, 1881)
Prot. Bk. Young
Protocol Book of James Young 1485-1515, ed. G. Donaldson, (SRS, 1952)
Quoniam Attachiamenta
Quoniam Attachiamenta, ed. T. M. Cooper, in Stair Society vol. xi, (Stair Society, 1947)
Raine, *ND*
Appendix to J. Raine, *The History and Antiquities of North Durham*, (London, 1852)
Regiam Majestatem
Regiam Majestatem, ed. T. M. Cooper, (Stair Society, 1947)
Reginald of Durham
Reginald of Durham, ed. J. Raine, (Surtees Society, 1835)
Register of Brieves
Register of Brieves, ed. T. M. Cooper, (Stair Society, 1946)
Rymer, *Foedera*
T. Rymer, *Foedera*, (London, 1816-69)
Richebourg, *Nouveau Coutumier Général*
Nouveau Coutumier Général, ed. M. C. A. Bourdot de Richebourg, (Paris, 1724)
RMS
Registrum Magni Sigilli Regum Scottorum, ed. J. M. Thomson and others, (Edinburgh, 1882-1914)
Robertson, *Laws of Kings of England*
Laws of the Kings of England from Edward to Henry I, ed. A. J. Robertson, (Cambridge, 1925)
Rose of Kilravock
A Genealogical Deduction of the Family of Rose of Kilravock, H. Rose and L. Shaw, (Spalding Club, 1848)
Rot. Scot.
Rotuli Scotiae in Turri Londinense et in Domo Capitulari Westmonasteriense Asservati, ed. D. Macpherson and others, (1814-1819)
RRAN, i
Regesta Regum Anglo-Normannorum, i, ed. H. W. C. Davis, (Oxford, 1913)
RRAN, ii
Regesta Regum Anglo-Normannorum ii, ed. C. Johnson and H. A. Cronne,

(Oxford, 1956)

RRAN, iii

    Recueil des Actes de Henry II, ed. M. R. Delisle and M. E. Berger, (Paris, 1909-1927)

RRS, i

    The Acts of Malcolm IV, ed. G. W. S. Barrow, (Edinburgh, 1960)

RRS, ii

    The Acts of William I, ed. G. W. S. Barrow and W. W. Scott, (Edinburgh, 1971)

RRS, iii, (Handlist)

    The Acts of Alexander II, ed. J. M. Scoular (Edinburgh, 1959)

RRS, iv (Handlist)

    The Acts of Alexander III, The Guardians and John, ed. G. G. Simpson, (Edinburgh, 1960)

RRS, vi (Handlist)

    The Acts of David II, ed. B. Webster, (Edinburgh, 1962)

RSS

    Registrum Secreti Sigilli Regum Scottorum, ed. M. Livingstone and others, (Edinburgh 1908-)

Scanian Law

    Monumenta inedita rerum Germanicarum, ed. Ernestus Joachimus de Westphalen, (Lipsiae, 1739-1745), iv

Scone Lib.

    Liber Ecclesie de Scon, (Bannatyne and Maitland Clubs, 1843)

SP

    The Scots Peerage, ed. Sir J. Balfour Paul, (Edinburgh, 1904-14)

Seton

    A History of the Family of Seton, G. Seton, (Edinburgh, 1896)

Spalding Misc.

    Miscellany of the Spalding Club, (Spalding Club, 1841-52)

Stair, *Institutes*

    Sir James Dalrymple, Viscount Stair, *The Institutions of the Law of Scotland,* ed. G. Brodie, (Edinburgh, 1826-31)

St. A. Lib.

    Liber Cartarum Prioratus Sancti Andree in Scotia, (Bannatyne Club, 1841)

Statutes of the Realm

    The Statutes of the Realm (London, 1810-28)

Stevenson, *Documents*

    Documents Illustrative of the History of Scotland 1286-1306, ed. J. Stevenson, (Edinburgh, 1870)

Stirlings of Keir

    The Stirlings of Keir, ed. W. Fraser, (Edinburgh, 1858)

Stubbs, *Select Charters*

    Select Charters and other illustrations of English Constitutional History, W.

Stubbs, ed. H. W. C. Davis, (Oxford, 1962)

TA

Accounts of the Lord High Treasurer of Scotland, ed. T. Dickson and Sir J. Balfour Paul, (Edinburgh, 1877-1916)

The Bannatyne Ms.

The Bannatyne Ms., ed. W. Tod Ritchie, (STS, 1928-30)

Thorpe, *Diplomatarium*

Diplomatarium Anglicum Aevi Saxonici, ed. B. Thorpe, (London, 1865)

Twici, *La Venerie*, (Tilander)

La Venerie of Twici, ed. G. Tilander in *Cynegetica ii*, (Uppsala, 1956)

Walter of Henley

Walter of Henley and other Treatises on Estate Management and Accounting, ed. D. Oschinsky, (Oxford, 1971)

Wemyss of Wemyss

Memorials of the Family of Wemyss of Wemyss, ed. W. Fraser, (Edinburgh, 1888)

Xenophon, *Kunegetikos*

Xenophon, *Kunegetikos*, ed. E. C. Marchant, (New York 1925)

Yester Writs

Calendar of Writs preserved at Yester House 1166-1503, ed. C. C. H. Harvey and J. Macleod, (SRS, 1930)

York, *Master of Game*, (Grohman)

Edward, Second Duke of York, *The Master of Game*, ed. W. F. Baillie Grohman, (London, 1904)

2 Secondary Works

Adams, I. H

'The Salt Industry of the Forth Basin', *SGM* 1965, 153-162

Anderson, *Early Sources*

Anderson, A. O., *Early Sources of Scottish History*, (Edinburgh, 1922)

Anderson, *Scotland in Early Christian Times*

Anderson, J., *Scotland in Early Christian Times*, (Edinburgh, 1881)

Anderson, *Scottish Forestry*

Anderson, M. L., *A History of Scottish Forestry*, (London, 1967)

Barrow, *Bruce*

Barrow, G. W. S., *Robert the Bruce*, (Edinburgh, 1976)

Barrow, *Kingdom of the Scots*

Barrow, G. W. S., *The Kingdom of the Scots*, (London, 1973)

Bath, *Agrarian History*

Bath, G. M. Slicher van, *The Agrarian History of Western Europe, AD 500-1500*, (London, 1963)

D

Bazely, M. L.
'The Extent of the English Forest in the Thirteenth Century', *TRHS*, iv, (1921), 140-172
Binchy, D. A.
'The Linguistic and Historical value of the Irish Law Tracts', *PBA*, xxix, (1943), 195-227
Binchy, D. A.
'An Early Irish Legal Poem', *Celtica*, ix, (1971), 152-168
Binchy, D. A.
'Irish History and Irish Law', *Studia Hibernica*, (1975) no. 15, 7-36
Black, *Surnames*
Black, G. F, *The Surnames of Scotland*, (New York, 1946)
Blackmore, *Hunting Weapons*
Blackmore, H. L., *Hunting Weapons*, (London, 1971)
Browne, G. F.
Records of the Forest of Birse, (Edinburgh, 1923)
Buchanan, J.
'The Manuscripts of Regiam Majestatem', *Juridical Review*, xlix, (1937), 217-231
Brander, *Hunting and Shooting*
Brander, M., *Hunting and Shooting from the Earliest Times to the Present Day*, (London, 1971)
Caldwell, *Sir Eger, Sir Grym and Sir Gray Steel*
Caldwell, J. R., *Sir Eger, Sir Grym and Sir Gray Steel*, (Harvard, 1933)
Cash, *Dogs*
Cash, E. C., *Dogs, Their History and Development*, (London, 1927)
Child, *Scottish Ballads*
Child, F. J., *Scottish Ballads*, (Boston, 1898; New York reprint, 1965)
Colvin, *History of the King's Works*
Colvin, H. M., *History of the King's Works: The Middle Ages*, (London 1963)
Cooper, T. M.
'Melrose v Earl of Dunbar', *Juridical Review*, lv, (1943), 1-8
Cooper, *Select Cases*
Cooper, T. M., *Select Cases of the Thirteenth Century*, (London, 1944)
Cooper, *Regiam Majestatem, Register of Brieves, Quoniam Attachiamenta:* see above, 1(b).
Cooper, T. M., and Paton, G. C. H., 'The Dark Age 1329-1532', *Stair Society*, xx, (1958), 18-24
Cox, J. C.
The Royal Forests of England, (London, 1905)
Crawford, *Archaeology in the Field*
Crawford, O. G. S., *Archaeology in the Field*, (London, 1953)

Cronne, H. A.
'The Forest under Henry I', in *Essays to J. E. Todd*, (London, 1949)
Cruden, *Early Christian and Pictish Monuments*
Cruden, S., *Early Christian and Pictish Monuments of Scotland*, (Edinburgh, 1964)
Cupples, G.
Scotch Deer Hounds and Their Masters, (Edinburgh, 1894)
Dalby, *Lexicon of the Medieval German Hunt*
Dalby, D., *Lexicon of the Medieval German Hunt — Middle High German Terms (1050-1500)*, (Berlin, 1965)
Decq, E.,
'L'Administration des Eaux et Forêts; *Bibliothèque de l'École des Chartes*, lxxxiii, (1922), 67-110, 331-361, lxxxiv, (1923), 92-115
Delisle, *La Classe Agricole en Normandie*
Delisle, L., *Études sur la Condition de la Classe Agricole et l'État de l'Agriculture en Normandie en Moyen Age*, (New York reprint, 1964)
Dickinson, *Scotland from the Earliest Times*
Dickinson, W. C., *Scotland from the Earliest Times to 1603*, (Edinburgh, 1961)
Dickinson, W. C.
'Forest Courts', *Stair Society*, xx, (1958), 402-3
Dickinson, *Sheriff Ct. Bk.*, *Barony Ct. Bk*; see above, 1(b).
DOST
Dictionary of the Older Scottish Tongue, ed. W. A. Craigie and A. J. Aitken, (London 1937-   )
Drummond, *Ancient Scots Weapons*
Drummond J., *Ancient Scots Weapons*, (Edinburgh, 1881)
Drummond, *Sculptured Monuments*
Drummond, J., *Sculptured Monuments in Iona and the West Highlands*, (Edinburgh, 1881)
Dunbar, A.
Scottish Kings, 1005-1625, (Edinburgh, 1899)
Dunbar, J. G. and Duncan, A. A. M.
'Tarbert Castle', *SHR*, 1, (1971), (1-17)
Duncan, *The Making of the Kingdom*
Duncan, A. A. M., *Scotland: The Making of the Kingdom*, (Edinburgh, 1975)
Duncan, A. A. M.
'Acta of Robert I', *SHR*, xxxii, (1953), 1-39
Duncan, A. A. M.
'Councils General', *SHR*, xxxv, (1956), 132-143
Duncan, A. A. M.
'The Earliest Scottish Charters', *SHR*, xxxvii, (1958), 103-5
Duncan, A. A. M.

'Regiam Majestatem, a Reconsideration', *Juridical Review*, lxxii, 199-217
Dunlop, *Bishop Kennedy*
  Dunlop, A. I., *The Life and Times of James Kennedy, Bishop of St. Andrews*, (Edinburgh, 1950)
Easson, *Religious Houses*
  Medieval Religious Houses: Scotland, ed I. B. Cowan and D. E. Easson, (London, 1976)
Ellis, *Welsh Tribal Law and Custom*
  Ellis, T. P., *Welsh Tribal Law and Custom in the Middle Ages*, (Oxford, 1926)
Farming the Red Deer
  Baxter, K. L., Kay, R. N. B., *et al.*, *Farming the Red Deer, The First Report of an Investigation by the Rowett Research Institute and the Hill Farming Research Organisation*, (H.M.S.O., Edinburgh, 1976)
Farrer, *Honors and Knights' Fees*
  Farrer, W., *Honors and Knights' Fees*, (London, 1923-4)
Fasti Ecclesiae Scoticanae Medii Aevi, ed. D. E. R. Watt, (St Andrews, 1969)
Fittis, R. S.
  The Sports and Pastimes of Scotland, (London, 1891)
Franklin, *History of Scots Farming*
  Franklin, T. B., *A History of Scots Farming*, (London, 1952)
Hartley, *The Deerhound*
  Hartley, A. N., *The Deerhound*, (Peterborough, 1955)
Haskins, C. H.
  Norman Institutions, (Cambridge, Mass., 1918)
Haskins, C. H.
  The Normans in European History, (London, 1916)
HBC
  Handbook of British Chronology, ed. F. M. Powicke and E. B. Fryde, (London, 1961)
Heath, E. G.
  The Grey Goose Wing, (Oxford, 1971)
Henderson, *The Picts*
  Henderson, I., *The Picts*, (London, 1967)
Huizinga, J.
  Homo Ludens, (London, 1949)
Innes, *Scotch Legal Antiquities*
  Innes, C., *Scotch Legal Antiquities*, (Edinburgh, 1872)
Jesse, *The British Dog*
  Jesse, G. R., *Researches into the History of the British Dog*, (London, 1866)
Jullien, *La Chasse*
  Jullien, E., *La Chasse*, (Paris, 1868)
Kelly, F.
  'The Old Irish Tree List', *Celtica*, (1976), xi, 107-124

Latouche, *The Birth of the Western Economy*
   Latouche, R., *The Birth of the Western Economy*, (London, 1961)
Lewis, T.
   Glossary of Early Medieval Welsh Law, (Manchester, 1913)
Lindner, *Die Jagd der Vorzeit*
   Lindner, K., *Die Jagd der Vorzeit*, trans. C. Montandon, (Paris, 1941)
Lindner, *Die Jagd im Frühen Mittelalter*
   Lindner, K., *Die Jagd im Frühen Mittelalter*, (Berlin, 1937), trans. C.
   Montandon, (Paris, 1950)
Loder, *Colonsay and Oronsay*
   Loder, J. de Vere, *Colonsay and Oronsay in the Isles of Argyll*, (Edinburgh,
   1935)
MacVean, D. N. and Lockie, J. D.
   Ecology and Land Use of Upland Scotland, (Edinburgh, 1969)
Madden, C.
   'The Feuing of Ettrick Forest', *Innes Review*, xxvii, (1976), 70-84.
Medieval Latin Word List, ed. R. E. Latham, (London, 1965)
Moore, *Land of the Scots Kings in England*
   Moore, M. F., *The Lands of the Scottish Kings in England* (London, 1896)
Murray, A.
   'The Crown Lands in Galloway 1455-1543', *DGT*, xxxvii, (1958-1959), 9-25
Murray, A.
   'The Procedure of the Scottish Exchequer in the early Sixteenth Century',
   SHR, xl, (1961), 89-117
Murray, A.
   'The Exchequer and Crown Revenue of Scotland 1437-1542 (Edinburgh
   Ph.D. Thesis, 1961)
Nicholson, *The Later Middle Ages*
   Nicholson, R., *Scotland: The Later Middle Ages*, (Edinburgh, 1974)
OS Map
   Ordnance Survey 1¼" Maps (1:50,000 Second Series)
OS Name Book
   Ordnance Survey Name Book, located in OS Archaeological Division, Rose
   Street, Edinburgh (January 1978)
Payne-Gallwey, R.
   The Crossbow, (London, 1903)
Petit Dutaillis, Ch.
   'De La Signification du Môt Forêt à l'Époque Franque, *Bibliothèque de
   l'École des Chartes*, lxxvi, (1915), 97-152
Petit Dutaillis, *Stubbs*
   Petit Dutaillis, Ch., *Studies Supplementary to Stubbs' Constitutional
   History*, (Manchester, 1908-29)
Petit Dutaillis, Ch.
   'The Franco-Norman Origins of the English Forest' in *Essays offered to C.*

H. Bémont, (Paris, 1913)

Prou, M.
'La Forêt en Angleterre et en France', *Journal des Savants*, (1915), 241-253, 310-320, 345-354

Rahtz, *Excavations at King John's Hunting Lodge*
Rahtz, P. A., *Excavations at King John's Hunting Lodge*, (Bristol, 1969)

Rait, *Parliament*
Rait, R. S., *Parliaments of Scotland*, (Glasgow, 1924)

RCAM Peebles
An Inventory of the Ancient and Historical Monuments of Peeblesshire, (Edinburgh, 1967)

RCAM Roxburgh
An Inventory of the Ancient and Historical Monuments of Roxburghshire (Edinburgh, 1956)

RCAM Selkirk
An Inventory of the Ancient and Historical Monuments of Selkirkshire, (Edinburgh, 1957)

RCAM Stirling
Stirlingshire, An Inventory of the Ancient and Historical Monuments, (Edinburgh, 1963)

Réau, *Iconographie de l'Art Chrétien*
Réau, L., *Iconographie de l'Art Chrétien*, (Paris, 1955-59)

Reed, *Forests of France*
Reed, J. L., *The Forests of France*, (London, 1954)

Richardson, J.
'Roman Law in the Regiam Majestatem', *Juridical Review*, lxvii, (1959), 155-187

Richardson, J. S.
'Mural Decoration at the House of Kinneil, Bo'ness', *PSAS*, 75, (1940-1941), 184-204

Ritchie, J.
The Influence of Man on Animal Life in Scotland, (Cambridge, 1920)

Ritchie, *The Normans in Scotland*
Ritchie, R. L. G., *The Normans in Scotland*, (Edinburgh, 1954)

Robertson, *De Composicione Cartarum*. See above, 1(b) — *De Composicione Cartarum*

Romilly Allen, *Early Christian Monuments*
Romilly Allen, J., *The Early Christian Monuments of Scotland*, (London, 1904)

Savage, H. L.
'Hunting in the Middle Ages', *Speculum*, viii (1933) 30-41

Scrope, *Deer Stalking*
Scrope, W., *The Art of Deer Stalking*, (London, 1839)

Shirley, *Deer Parks*

Shirley, E., *Some Account of English Deer Parks*, (London, 1867)

Simpson, W. D.
'The Excavations of Kindrochit Castle', *Antiquaries Journal*, vii, (1928), 69-75

SP
See above, 1(b), *SP*

Steer and Bannerman, *Monumental Sculpture*
Steer, K. A. and Bannerman, J. W. M., *Late Medieval Sculpture in the West Highlands*, (RCAM, Edinburgh, 1977)

Stuart, J.
Sculptured Monuments, (Spalding Club, 1867)

Symon, *Scottish Farming*
Symon, J. A., *Scottish Farming Past and Present* (Edinburgh, 1959)

Thomas, Ch.
'The Animal Art of the Scottish Iron Age and its Origins', *Archaeological Journal*, cxviii, (1961), 14-64

Thomas, Ch.
'Interpretation of the Pictish Symbols', *Archaeological Journal*, cxx, (1963), 31-97

Tilander, *Cynegetica*, i
Tilander, G., 'Essais d'Etymologie Cynégêtique', *Cynegetica*, i, (Lund, 1953)

Turner, *Select Pleas of the Forest*
Turner, G. J., *Select Pleas of the Forest*, (Selden Society, 1901)

VCH
Huntingdon/Northampton/Rutland The Victoria County Histories of England, (1902-)

Watson, W. J.
'Aobhinn an Obair an t-sealg', *Celtic Review*, ix (1913-1914), 156-168

Watson, *Celtic Place Names*
Watson, W. J., *History of the Celtic Place Names of Scotland*, (Edinburgh, 1926)

White, T. P.
Archaeological Sketches of Kintyre and Knapdale, (Edinburgh, 1873-75)

Whitelocke, *The Beginnings of English Society*
Whitelocke, D., *The Beginnings of English Society* (Harmondsworth, 1952)

Woodford, *A Manual of Falconry*
Woodford, M. H., *A Manual of Falconry*, (London, 1966)

Index

The tables have not been indexed

E*